THE MAN WHO DARED THE LIGHTNING

Also by Thomas Fleming

HISTORY

The Man From Monticello
AN INTIMATE LIFE OF THOMAS JEFFERSON

West Point
THE MEN AND TIMES OF THE
UNITED STATES MILITARY ACADEMY

Affectionately Yours, George Washington
A SELF-PORTRAIT IN LETTERS OF FRIENDSHIP

One Small Candle
THE PILGRIMS' FIRST YEAR IN AMERICA

Beat the Last Drum

Now We Are Enemies

FICTION

The Sandbox Tree

Romans Countrymen Lovers

A Cry of Whiteness

King of the Hill

The God of Love

All Good Men

The Man
WHO DARED
THE
Lightning

A New Look at Benjamin Franklin

BY

THOMAS FLEMING

WM

WILLIAM MORROW AND COMPANY, INC.

New York

1971

ACKNOWLEDGMENTS

No book of this size and scope can be written without the help of many people. Librarians from the Huntington Library in California to the Massachusetts Historical Society in Boston have been extremely helpful. I would like to express my special appreciation to the staff of the Yale University Library, the New York Public Library, the American Philosophical Society Library and the New York Society Library, where I did most of my research. In particular I would like to thank Gertrude D. Hess of the APS and Dorothy W. Bridgwater of Yale for their prompt assistance in my numerous calls for help. I would also like to thank Lilla Lyon for assisting me with skill and fidelity in the final checking of the manuscript and preparation of my notes. Kay Daffron's help in seeing the manuscript through innumerable stages on her typewriter was equally invaluable.

THOMAS FLEMING

CONTENTS

ILLUSTRATIONS

A Franklin Family Gallery
between pages 180 and 181
Places and People
between pages 340 and 341

I don't think that Franklin has found his real place in American history yet—he was one of the great ones of his time and of all American history.

—*Harry S Truman*

Book One

FROM

Philadelphia in America

From bright June sunshine, the sky above hot, muggy Philadelphia began changing to a sour gloomy gray. Soon there came glowering down
upon the neat red-brick colonial metropolis a succession of huge black
clouds. Windows slammed, tradesmen shut doors left open to relieve the
stifling heat, mothers hastily called children indoors, and idlers vanished
from street corners into the nearest tavern. The city was obviously about
to endure that natural phenomenon known as a thunderstorm. People
hoped it would bring some relief from the humid heat, which often made
June in Philadelphia as unpleasant as equatorial Africa. But they also
shivered with involuntary apprehension, as the first rumble of thunder
surged over the city. Those black clouds carried in them deadly bolts of
lightning.

Only one man in Philadelphia greeted the oncoming storm with wholehearted delight. Benjamin Franklin had been waiting impatiently for
weather like this for days. In his comfortable house on the southeast
corner of Race and Second Streets, he called excitedly to his twenty-one-
year-old son William. In a moment, Billy, as he was known in the family,
appeared. He was a husky young man, over six feet tall, which gave him
a two or three inch advantage over his father. He lacked the muscular,
almost bear-like bulk of his father's chest and shoulders. But he carried
himself with the confident, martial erectness of a soldier. Handsome was
the only word to describe his rather narrow but fine-featured face. He
shared his father's high forehead, and solid chin, but his mouth was not
so relaxed or pleasant when it was in repose. Now it was pleasant enough,
because William Franklin's face was aglow with excitement.

Franklin asked if everything was ready. William nodded. Quickly they
slipped into loose cloth coats and hurried into the next room, where on
a long table stood a variety of strange machines and apparatus. There
were glass tubes and jars bound with strips of tin, glass globes on
spindles, silk strings dangling from the ceiling. To anyone acquainted
with eighteenth-century science, this apparatus, especially the tubes, and

the peculiar tin encased jars with corks in their tops, through which a wire protruded, meant that this was the laboratory of a man interested in exploring the mysteries of electricity. For the last four years, this exploration had occupied almost all of Benjamin Franklin's days and nights. To find extra hours he had even resigned from his printing business, sacrificing half his income, and moved to this house on the outskirts of Philadelphia where he was less accessible to his numerous friends.

When Franklin began his experiments electricity was a curiosity in the world of science. Experimenters created "electrical fire" by rubbing glass tubes with silk. They then stored the accumulated charges in the tin-lined bottles, called Leyden jars, in honor of the university where they were first invented. But beyond the fact that electricity created magical effects—it could, for instance, animate a piece of twisted wire so that it looked like a living spider, or in a darkened room cause the gold border on an expensive book to glow—no one knew very much about it. In a series of classic experiments, Franklin had transformed electricity from a curiosity to a full-fledged branch of science. He had discovered the existence of plus and minus charges, and invented such terms as battery, conductor, and condenser. Now he was about to test his most daring hypothesis: that electricity and lightning were identical.[1]

As the first pattering of rain pelted the windows, William Franklin took from a dark corner of the laboratory a strange looking kite. It was made of a large thin silk kerchief. To the top of the vertical stick was fastened a pointed wire about fifteen or sixteen inches long.[2] Benjamin Franklin took a Leyden jar and concealed it under his loose-fitting coat. Down the stairs and out the door went father and son. They hurried through the scattering raindrops to an open field not far from their house, part of the "commons" or grazing grounds of Philadelphia. On one side of the field was a shed, where citizens who grazed their cattle could take shelter from the rain or hot sun. While Franklin stood unobtrusively—he hoped—inside the shed, William raced across the empty pasture, and got the kite aloft in the tricky, gusty wind of the gathering storm. Then he too retreated under the shed.

William Franklin must have felt a little foolish, flying a kite in the rain. But he did not look nearly as ridiculous as his father would have looked, if someone had seen one of the leading citizens of Pennsylvania prancing across the commons on the same errand. There was the very large possibility that the hypothesis was wrong. If so, Benjamin Franklin did not want people guffawing at him in the streets, and maliciously asking him where he got his ridiculous idea about lightning. If his experiment turned out to be a dud, only William would know, and he could depend on his son to keep his mouth shut.

There was another reason why William was along. The experiment was dangerous. Franklin knew electricity could kill. He had killed animals with it, in his laboratory. Twice, by accident, he had knocked himself unconscious with it and, in another experiment, had prostrated six grown men with a single charge. He also knew that lightning was far more powerful electricity than anything he had created in his laboratory. He had seen it reduce the metallic part of a roof, such as a drainspout, to molten jelly. This was not an experiment you could ask a friend to share. Only a son, who had already shared many lesser risks in the laboratory, could join Benjamin Franklin at this climactic moment.

In a few minutes, the kite was only a small dancing dot in the gloomy sky. William handed the kite string to his father. To the end of the twine was tied a strip of silk ribbon. Silk did not conduct electricity; it was an insulator. This was the only safeguard Franklin used against the deadly amount of electricity in the clouds above him. Contrary to the traditional Currier and Ives print, which shows Franklin and his son (pictured as a small boy) gleefully rejoicing when a bolt of lightning hit the kite, this was the last thing Franklin wanted to happen. The pointed wire at the top of his kite was designed to silently draw off some of the cloud's electric charge, just as a pointed conductor attracted electricity from a charged body in the laboratory. There was no need, much less a desire, for the massive and dangerous discharge of a lightning bolt. Where the twine and the silk joined, a small house key was fastened. This was where Franklin hoped the electricity would appear. Again and again, he touched the key with his knuckle. Nothing happened.

Over the city, the storm increased in fury. Thunder rumbled and lightning glinted. Then, William pointed excitedly toward a massive cloud moving downwind toward them. On it came, booming thunder while it passed right over their heads. The little kite danced and dived in the gusts of turbulence. Again, Benjamin Franklin touched the key with his knuckle. Surely now—

His face fell. The key was as cold and inert as it had been the day it was cast.

Now the sky was so black it was impossible to tell one cloud from another. More rain began to fall. The kite whirled and twisted and dived. Close to despair, Franklin gave up touching the key and stared disconsolately up at the murky sky. His mind raced back across the hundreds of experiments he had conducted, the studies he had made of the effects of lightning on houses and trees, trying to see where he had gone wrong. Then his eyes drifted toward the string in his hand. With an exclamation of triumph, he clapped his son on the back and pointed excitedly at the twine.

The loose threads were standing erect, separate from each other, just as if they had been electrified when suspended on a laboratory conductor. Cautiously Benjamin Franklin moved his knuckle toward the key. Through his hand and up his arm rushed that familiar tingling, shocking sensation which experimenters called an electric spark. Again and again he touched it and then let William touch it.[3]

Now the rain began in earnest. As sheets of it swept across the field and thoroughly wet the string, Benjamin Franklin picked up the Leyden jar and touched its wire to the key. Electricity from the charged air within the cloud poured into it.

This was the moment of maximum danger. If the kite had been struck by a lightning bolt at this point, most scientists agree that the charge would have leaped the strip of silk and both Franklins would have become charred corpses there on the Philadelphia common. But father and son were too enraptured by their discovery to worry about danger now. It was true! Electricity and lightning were one and the same. It meant that if men could control this no longer so mysterious fire in the laboratory, they could also tame its brother from the heavens.

A few minutes later, the storm had passed. An exultant Franklin reeled in his kite and warned William to tell no one about their triumph. First he must communicate it to the scientific world. For the better part of the summer, father and son shared the momentous secret that was to catapult Benjamin Franklin into world fame.

II

It is difficult for the contemporary American to grasp why and how Benjamin Franklin's electrical achievements transformed an obscure Pennsylvania printer into the best-known American of his time. Today,

most scientists are faceless figures, toiling anonymously in esoteric labo-
ratories, their lives and works known only to fellow scientists. In the
eighteenth century, scientists were celebrities whose writings were read
by every educated man. When Franklin made his historic experiment
with the kite in June of 1752, he had already written his masterwork,
*Experiments and Observations on Electricity, Made at Philadelphia in
America*. It was soon translated into Latin, French, German, and Italian.
Scientists all over Europe attempted to prove or disprove his discoveries.

There is another reason why modern Americans find it hard to grasp
this world-famous Franklin. It is not the man who appears in the pages
of his *Autobiography*.

Phillips Brooks, the famed nineteenth-century preacher, wrote that
anyone who read Franklin's *Autobiography* had "always afterward the
boy-man who wrote it clear and distinct among the men he knows." This
observation pays tribute to the enduring power of the *Autobiography,* a
book so enormously popular throughout Brooks' era that it inspired an
inevitable reaction. When essayist and lecturer Theodore Parker complained that "Franklin thinks, investigates, theorizes, invents, but never
does he dream," when Herman Melville sneered that Franklin had "a
bookkeeper's mind," they were talking about the man portrayed in
the *Autobiography*. Even Mark Twain wrote that Franklin had "brought
affliction to millions of boys . . . whose fathers had read (the) per-
nicious biography." Perhaps the most total rejection of Franklin came
from D. H. Lawrence, who accused the American of fencing off the
human soul for the sake of profit. "He tries to take away my wholeness
and my dark forest, my freedom," Lawrence wailed.[4] Again, it is not the
mature Franklin about whom they are talking, but the struggling, self-
made man of the *Autobiography*. Nor has this prejudice subsided.
William Carlos Williams, in his *In the American Grain,* made a very
influential literary attack on Franklin. The American critic, John Sisk,
writing recently in the *Atlantic Monthly,* remarked that for most Americans the Franklin of the *Autobiography* "is likely to come through as
a smug, hypocritically venal and meanly rational person." [5]

This and previous harsh judgments could, of course, be contested. But
there may well be some grounds for accepting them as an indication that
the young Franklin, living his success story, is no longer as relevant for
an America grappling with the complexities of affluence and world
power as he was to an America facing the challenges of a raw, untamed
continent. Beyond the *Autobiography* there is another Franklin—the

mature man who, more than any other single person, presided over the birth of the American republic. That is why this book, with the exception of a few overlapping years, takes up Franklin's story where the best known part of the autobiography ends. Where the poor boy, the penny-pinching young tradesman, has been absorbed by an immensely more complex and significant man.

III

In Franklin's report of his laboratory experiments, he had suggested another way to prove the identity of lightning and electricity. Erect a sentry box on a mountaintop or inside a church steeple, he said. The box should have a pointed iron rod in the roof, which would be connected to a Leyden jar inside. Because there was neither a church steeple nor a high mountain in the vicinity of Philadelphia, Franklin had not tried the experiment himself, and only later had the idea of a kite occurred to him. Now, before he had time to make his report to the world, letters from Europe informed him that a half dozen French and English scientists had successfully performed the "Philadelphia experiment," as it was soon called, using sentry boxes. Later, from Russia, came news that emphasized the danger of Franklin's experimental approach. A scientist in St. Petersburg had tried a variation on Franklin's sentry box idea, and put a rod on top of his house. He had failed to ground it properly and had been killed by a direct hit from a lightning bolt.[6]

But the risk only made Franklin's triumph greater, in the eyes of an admiring world. The King of France sent his personal congratulations across the ocean. The Royal Society, the elite of the English scientific world, elected Franklin a member by unanimous vote and bestowed upon him its highest accolade, the Copley Medal. Yale, then Harvard, gave him honorary degrees of Master of Arts and Immanuel Kant, the greatest philosopher of his time, called him the modern Prometheus, who had brought down the fire from Heaven.

Kant's words underscore the emotional explanation of Franklin's fame. In 1752, most men still believed that there was something divine about lightning. Emanating from the heavens, striking with such arbitrary yet devastating force, it was easily associated with the vengeance of an angry God. The man who tamed it readily acquired an awesome, almost superhuman image.

But instead of capitalizing on such a potentiality, Franklin avoided it. He announced the practical application of his discovery in an offhand, matter-of-fact way in a publication that had already gained him some modest fame in America—*Poor Richard's Almanack.*

It has pleased God in his goodness to mankind at length to discover to them the means of securing their habitations and other buildings from mischief from thunder and lightning. The method is this: provide a small iron rod (it may be made of the rod-iron used by the nailers) but of such a length that one end being three or four feet in the moist ground, the other may be six or eight feet above the highest part of the building. To the upper end of the rod fasten about a foot of brass wire the size of a common knitting needle, sharpened to a fine point; the rod may be secured to the house by a few small staples. If the house or barn be long, there may be a rod and point at each end, and a middling wire along the ridge from one to the other. A house thus furnished will not be damaged by lightning, it being attracted by the points and passing through the metal into the ground without hurting anything. Vessels, also, having a sharp pointed rod fixed on the top of their masts, with a wire from the foot of the rod reaching down, round one of the shrouds, to the water, will not be hurt by lightning.[7]

Although it would be difficult to patent an invention as simple as a lightning rod, it was typical of Franklin to give his idea away. When he invented a stove in 1742 which heated a room instead of allowing most of the warm air to go up the chimney, the Governor of Pennsylvania proposed to give him a monopoly patent. Franklin not only refused the favor, he published a pamphlet in which he completely described the construction and operation of the stove, so that any good blacksmith could make one. He redesigned the street lights of his time, discarding the globe shape and substituting "four flat panes with a funnel above to draw up the smoke." This meant that the lamp did not grow dark in a few hours, but remained bright until morning. When one of his older brothers became afflicted with a bladder disorder, Franklin invented the rubber catheter which is still in use today. When his eyes began troubling him, he invented bifocals, which enabled him to get along with only a single set of glasses. All of these ideas he donated to the world, free of charge. "As we enjoy great advantages from the inventions of others," he said, "we should be glad of an opportunity to serve others by any inventions of ours."

Gradually, cities around the world—Philadelphia, Boston, London, Paris—began to sprout these small sharp pointed spires, called lightning rods. Inevitably, there was some opposition from those who made it a business to superintend the relationship between men and God. When an earthquake struck Boston in 1755, one preacher assured his congregation that it was a warning from on high, because so many in the city were defying the divine will by resorting to those works of the devil, lightning rods.

In Europe, what made Franklin's name even more famous was the last part of the title of his historic essay on electricity. That such discoveries could be made by a man from "Philadelphia in America" was doubly amazing to Europeans who had become accustomed to thinking of the New World as a region inhabited largely by savages and frontiersmen with little more brains than it took to swing an ax, plow a furrow, and fire a gun. To his fellow Americans, who knew him better, Franklin was amazing in still another way. Here was a man who had astonished the civilized world, yet his formal education had ended in the second grade. He had arrived in Philadelphia at the age of sixteen, with a Dutch dollar and a few pennies in his pocket, a dirty, hungry, runaway printer's apprentice from his native Boston. At the age of 42, he had made enough money from his newspaper, *The Pennsylvania Gazette,* and from *Poor Richard's Almanack,* to retire from business and devote himself to science.

Yet with all his fame, Benjamin Franklin remained the same charming, genial man his friends had always known. Commenting on the congratulations from the King of France, he told one of his New England correspondents that his feelings reminded him of the story of a young girl who suddenly began prancing about in a proud and haughty manner. No one could figure out why "till it came to be known she had got on a pair of silk garters." Although his honors were not covered by petticoats, Franklin decided he had "not so much reason to be proud as the girl had; for a feather in the cap is not so useful a thing, or so serviceable to the wearer, as a pair of good silk garters." [8]

At home, Franklin delighted in entertaining his friends and acquaintances with electrical showmanship. He placed a lightning rod on his chimney and connected it to two bells on his staircase. Between the bells was a little brass ball suspended by a silk thread. When the wire was charged, the ball would dance back and forth, striking the bells and announcing that the house was electrified. Often the bells rang when there was neither lightning nor thunder, making visiting ladies squeal with alarm. One night so much electricity rushed down the rod that Franklin was able to see it "in a continued dense white stream seemingly as large as my finger" between the bells. The whole staircase was "inlightened as with sunshine," he said, "so that one might see to pick up a pen." [9]

In his laboratory, Franklin let the ladies feel the tingle of gentle shocks, he created miniature bolts of lightning, he made metals glow and wires dance. Once, on the banks of the Schuylkill, he ignited some rum by sending an electric charge from one side of the river to the other. It was during one of these laboratory demonstrations that Franklin almost killed himself. He was showing how electricity could kill a turkey, using a charge from two specially constructed Leyden jars which contained as much power as forty of the ordinary size. The spectators were talking to Franklin and to one another. The conversation distracted him, and he accidentally touched the top wires of the jars while his other hand held the chain which was connected to the outside of both jars. There was an enormous flash and a crack as loud as a pistol. Franklin's body vibrated like a man in an epileptic convulsion. He described the impact as "an universal blow from head to foot throughout the body." Although he did not fall, for a few moments he blacked out completely. Lucky as usual, he escaped with nothing more serious than a soreness in his chest, "as if it had been bruised." [10]

One day a crowd of gawkers gathered in front of Franklin's house, hoping to catch a glimpse of an electrical miracle, or of the electrician himself. Franklin got rid of them with a humorous demonstration of his powers. He sent a healthy charge surging through the iron fence around the front of his house. The galvanized curiosity seekers vanished in a cloud of dust, convinced that the Devil himself was inside them.

This was the Franklin that Philadelphia loved—a man who somehow managed to combine laughter with everything, even the pursuit of scientific truth. Already his close friends in Philadelphia treasured gems of his wry humor. Once a neighbor came to him and asked how he could stop thieves from tapping a keg of beer he had in his backyard.

"Put a cask of Madeira beside it," was Franklin's answer.

This inexhaustible wit, which bubbled to the surface at the most unexpected moments, was one of the secrets of Benjamin Franklin's success. His profitable paper was always full of letters to the editor, some of which the editor wrote himself.

Pray let the prettiest creature in this place know (by publishing this) that if it was not for her affectation, she would be absolutely irresistible.

The following week the ladies of Philadelphia replied:

Mr. Franklin, I cannot conceive who your correspondent means by the prettiest creature in this place; but I can assure either him or her, that she who is truly so, has no affectation at all.

Sir, Since your last week's paper I have look'd in my glass a thousand times, I believe, in one day; and if it was not for the charge of affectation I might, without partiality, believe myself the person meant.

Mr. Franklin, They that call me affected are greatly mistaken; for I don't know that I ever refus'd a kiss to any body but a fool.[11]

Among other enjoyable *Gazette* correspondence were the laments of Anthony Afterwit, whose wife spent him into bankruptcy, and the harangues of Celia Single, a born shrew who lectured the editor in scorching terms because of his partiality to men. Even better was Alice Addertongue, who announced that she was organizing a kind of stock exchange for the sale and transfer of calumnies, slanders, and other reputation-wrecking pastimes of the gentler sex.

Then there was the worried reader who asked editor Franklin the following question: "If A found out that his neighbor B was sleeping with his wife, was he justified in telling B's wife and persuading her to seek a little revenge with A?"

The editor's reply: "If an ass kicks me, should I kick him again?"[12]

Even his news stories had the ring and sometimes the sting of wit in them.

An unhappy man; one Sturgis, upon some difference with his wife, determined to drown himself in the river and she (kind wife) went with him, it seems to see it faithfully performed, and accordingly stood by silent and unconcerned during the whole transaction: he jumped near Carpenter's Wharff but was timely taken out again before what he came about was thoroughly effected, so that they

*were both obliged to return home as they came and put up for that
time with the disappointment.*[13]

Franklin carried on a long, lively war with his chief newspaper opposition, the *Mercury,* winning round after round by making his readers laugh at his rival. He printed a letter pointing out that the *Mercury* had reported two prominent European soldiers had been killed by a single cannon ball—a remarkable achievement when one of them was fighting in the Rhineland, and the other in Italy.[14] Another letter called attention to the *Mercury's* claim that a prominent English admiral had died in the previous May, which was impossible "unless he has made a resurrection" since his death five years earlier. Moreover, said this same indignant reader, "a long story of murder and robbery" printed in the *Mercury* as fresh news was actually four years old.[15]

In tandem with Franklin's newspaper success was the triumph of *Poor Richard's Almanack.* Every newspaper publisher in the colonies tried to produce an almanac. It was an ideal way to use up "dead time" when the presses were standing idle, and if the book caught on, it could also be profitable. Everything depended upon the appeal of the "philomath" —or resident astrologer—who did the writing and predicting. The printer had to share not a little of the profits with him. The going rate was thirty to fifty pounds a year (perhaps 2500 dollars in today's money), but it was worth it if the seer was popular.

Some of the more simple-minded purchasers of almanacs actually believed in their predictions. One day an outraged farmer rode up to the office of one Philadelphia philomath determined to beat out his brains because he had promised sunny weather, and the farmer had brought his crops to market, only to see them ruined by a rainstorm. But Franklin knew that most people read an almanac for amusement. It was cheap, and the wise publisher filled it with poetry, wry observations, and miscellaneous information aimed more to amuse than inform. Franklin forthwith decided to be his own philomath and created out of his fertile imagination a character named Richard Saunders who introduced himself to the world with the ingenuous candor:

COURTEOUS READER,

I might in this place attempt to gain thy favor by declaring that I write almanacs with no other view than that of the public good, but in this I should not be sincere; and men are now-a-days too wise to be deceived by pretences, how specious soever. The plain truth of the matter is, I am excessive poor, and my wife, good woman, is I tell her excessive proud; she cannot bear, she says, to sit spinning in her shift of tow, while I do nothing but gaze at the stars; and has threatened more than once to burn all my books and rattlingtraps (as she calls my instruments) if I do not make some profitable use of them for the good of my family. The printer has offered me some considerable share of the profits, and I have thus begun to comply with my dame's desire.[16]

Franklin's predictions were a delightful burlesque of other almanacs. Some samples:

OF THE ECLIPSES THIS YEAR

During the first visible eclipse Saturn is retrograde: For which reason the crabs will go sidelong and the rope makers backward. The belly will wag before and the A——— shall sit down first. . . . When a New Yorker thinks to say THIS he shall say DISS and the people in New England and Cape May will not be able to say COW for their lives, but will be forc'd to say KEOW by a certain involuntary twist in the root of their tongues. . . .

OF THE DISEASES THIS YEAR

This year the stone blind shall see but very little; the deaf shall hear but poorly; and the dumb shan't speak very plain. And it's much, if my dame Bridget talks at all this year. Whole flocks, herds, and droves of sheep, swine and oxen, cocks and hens, ducks and drakes, geese and ganders, shall go to pot; but the mortality will not be altogether so great among cats, dogs, and horses.

OF THE FRUITS OF THE EARTH

I find that this will be a plentiful year of all manner of good things to those who have enough; but the orange trees in Greenland will go near to fare the worse for the cold. As for oats, they'll be a great help to horses. . . .[17]

Even wryer was Franklin's treatment of his chief rival, philomath Titan Leeds. After professing great friendship for him (he said he would have written almanacs long ago but he hated to cut into Titan's profits), he dolefully predicted his death. "He dies by my calculation made at his request, on October 17th, 1733, 3 Ho. 29 M., P.M. . . . By his own calculation he will survive until the 26th of the same month. This small difference between us we have disputed whenever we have met these nine years past; but at length he is inclinable to agree with my judgment. Which of us is most exact, a little time will now determine."

In the following year's edition, Poor Richard reported to his readers that his almanac had shown a whacking profit. His wife had stopped berating him, had bought a new dress, and no longer had to borrow her cooking utensils from the neighbors. Then he went to work on Titan Leeds. Was Titan dead? Poor Richard wasn't quite sure. He had been so busy at home, he had not been able to make the trip to the funeral. Also, he was aware that Providence sometimes interfered with the mathematical workings of astrology. The best evidence he had that Titan was dead was the almanac that appeared under his name for the year 1734 "in which," said Richard, "I am treated in a very gross and un-handsome manner; in which I am called a false predicter, an ignorant, a conceited scribler, a fool, and a lyar." His good friend Titan would never have treated him that way.

The following year, Poor Richard complained that he was still receiving "much abuse from the ghost of Titan Leeds, who pretends to be still living, and to write almanacks inspight of me and my predictions." But Richard assured his readers that whatever Titan's ghost might pretend, " 'tis undoubtedly true that he is really defunct and dead. First because the stars are seldom disappointed. . . . Secondly, 'twas requisite and necessary he should die punctually at that time for the honor of astrology, the art professed both by him and his father before him. Thirdly, 'tis plain to everyone that reads his last two almanacks [for 1734 and '35] that they are not written with that life his performances used to be written with; the wit is low and flat; the little hints dull and spirit-less. . . ." [18]

When Titan Leeds tried to deflate Franklin by proclaiming that there never was such a person as Richard Saunders, Franklin published a preface written by Saunders' wife Bridget, who shrewishly assured the world that Richard did indeed exist, much to her distress. The following year Poor Richard published a long letter from the departed spirit of Titan Leeds, admitting that he did die at the predicted time, and apologizing for the outrageous behavior of his ghost.

Along with this ingenious fooling, Franklin larded his pages with dozens of glittering proverbs. He took them from all sorts of sources—La Rochefoucauld, Rabelais, the Bible, often improving them by sharpening their wit or their point. More than a few of them had the tough, salty wisdom of a man of the world.

"He's a fool that makes his doctor his heir."

"Neither a fortress nor a maid will hold out long after they begin to parley."

"Fish and visitors smell in three days."

"Three may keep a secret, if two of them are dead."

"The worst wheel of a cart makes the most noise."

"Sal laughs at everything you say; why? because she has fine teeth."

"Let thy maidservant be faithful, strong, and homely."

"Keep your eyes wide open before marriage; half shut afterwards."

"To bear other people's affliction, everyone has courage enough and to spare."

"He that can have patience can have what he will."

"When the well is dry we know the worth of water."

"In the affairs of this world, men are saved not by faith but by the want of it."

"Experience keeps a dear school, yet fools will learn at no other."

"It is hard for an empty sack to stand upright."

Within a few years, Poor Richard's twenty-four-page almanac was selling 10,000 copies annually. In 1748, Franklin expanded it to thirty-six pages, and along with history and humorous prophecy, added literary and scientific essays, creating a miniature general magazine. But Poor Richard's goofy personality and pithy epigrams were still the main sources of reader appeal. The imaginary philomath became so famous throughout America that many people confused him with Franklin, considering them almost interchangeable.

IV

But Franklin was not all fun. His humor was only one side of a remarkable personality that swiftly made him Philadelphia's foremost citizen. He had scarcely arrived in the city when he organized the Junto, an informal discussion group aimed at stimulating intellectual and social growth. As the members of the Junto rose to prominence in various walks of Philadelphia life, the club became a political powerhouse. This was almost inevitable, with the rules Franklin had written for the club. He composed a set of twenty-four questions to be read at every meeting. Among them were: "Have you lately observed any defect in the laws of your country of which it would be proper to move the Legislature for an amendment?" and "Have you lately observed any encroachment on the just liberties of the people?" [19]

With the help of the Junto and the *Gazette,* Franklin founded Philadelphia's first volunteer fire department and America's first subscription library, and was the guiding spirit behind the creation of the Pennsylvania Hospital and The Philadelphia Academy, which eventually became the University of Pennsylvania. He helped to organize the colony's first militia, the Philadelphia Associaters, to provide a defense against a threatened French and Spanish invasion. For almost a decade he had served as clerk of the Pennsylvania Assembly and played a leading role in the creation of a paper currency in the colony. In all of these projects he practiced a strategy of leadership which he learned, as he did so many things, from pondering his experience.

When he first began soliciting subscriptions for the library, he met with "objections and reluctances" and swiftly saw that the trouble was the envy which others felt, when a man presented himself as "the proposer of any useful project that might be suppos'd to raise one's reputation in the smallest degree above that of one's neighbors." From that moment, Franklin put himself "as much as I could out of sight," and described the project as "a scheme of a number of friends" who had requested him to gather the support of "lovers of reading." The library was soon thriving, and Franklin applied this strategy with equal success in all the other public projects with which he became involved.[20] This "little sacrifice of . . . vanity" went back to a knock on the head he had received as a boy in Boston. The noted preacher, Cotton Mather, was following him down a narrow passage from the parsonage study, when he suddenly cried out, "Stoop, stoop." Before Franklin could understand him, his head had thumped a low-hanging beam. Mather was a man who never missed an opportunity to give advice, and as Franklin tried to reassemble his battered brains, the clergyman said, "You are young, and have the world before you. Stoop as you go through it and you will miss many hard thumps." Years later, in a letter to Mather's son, Franklin said, "This advice, thus beat into my head, has frequently been of use to me." [21]

Franklin's engaging personality, and his preference for this style of leadership made him look like "an easy man" to casual observers. But there was an underlying toughness in him that more than a few Philadelphians discovered the hard way. Once, early in his newspapering career, when he was dueling with his rival, Andrew Bradford's *Mercury,* several of his friends came in a delegation, to warn him to moderate his views. Bradford was siding with the so-called Proprietary Party, those who supported the rule of William Penn's sons, who ran Pennsylvania as their semi-public inheritance. Franklin sided with the people against the self-interested politics of the Proprietors. As soon as Franklin saw what the delegation had in mind, he said he was too busy to listen to them at the moment, but would be happy to hear their dire predictions if they would join him for dinner at his house.

That night, the doomsters showed up at Franklin's table. They were baffled when his wife Deborah served them nothing but a bowl of strange looking mush and a pitcher of cold water. Franklin spooned the mush into his dish, poured himself a glass of water, and began to eat. The doomsters tried to follow his example, but again and again they found themselves gagging in the midst of their cautionary speeches. Franklin, meanwhile, spooned down the mush without so much as a grimace. Finally, they could stand it no longer and asked him what in the world they were eating.

"Sawdust-meal and water," Franklin snapped. "Now go tell the rest of Philadelphia that a man who can eat that for supper doesn't need to be beholden to anyone." [22]

Franklin spoke out of an inner assurance that was rooted in the same experimental approach that had led him to his epochal discoveries in electricity. He had paid the same painstaking attention to human nature and had drawn certain conclusions about life. After a youthful flirtation with atheism, he had become convinced of the existence of a God whom "all nature cries aloud thro all her works." Although he could not accept the involved theology of any sect, he concluded that the creator of the physical universe had laid down certain moral laws for man, his most intelligent creature and the only one capable of freedom of choice, to follow. Interestingly, Franklin saw these moral laws as gateways *to* freedom, not barriers which deprived a person of this unique human experience.

At first, he thought it was simply a question of distinguishing right from wrong, and then following the lead of his moral intelligence. But he soon found that it was necessary to approach the goal more experimentally. So he drew up a list of thirteen virtues. Among them were silence, order, resolution, sincerity, justice, moderation, and humility. He practiced each virtue for a week at a time, enabling himself to go through an entire course four times in a single year. Like a good scientist, he kept a record of his progress in a small ruled book, carefully placing a dot before each of the virtues which, on reflection at the end of the day, he realized he had violated. In the beginning, he had seen himself moving relentlessly toward moral perfection, which he fully expected to achieve.

But once more, he let experience be his teacher. He made substantial progress in all the virtues except order. But he soon realized that his dream of moral perfection was illusory, and probably unwise. He saw that it might end in "a kind of foppery in morals, which if it were known would make me ridiculous." He also realized that "a perfect character might be attended with the inconvenience of being envied and hated." Above all he saw that "a benevolent man should allow a few faults in himself, to keep his friends in countenance."

He summed up this wisdom in a homely story about a man who bought an ax from a Franklin neighbor. The purchaser decided that he wanted the entire surface as bright as the edge. The neighbor, who was a blacksmith, said he would be glad to brighten it for him, if he would turn the grinding stone wheel. "He turn'd while the smith pressed the broad face of the ax hard and heavily on the stone, which made the turning of it very fatiguing." Finally, the weary purchaser said he would take his ax as it was and go home.

"No," said the smith, "turn on, turn on. We shall have it bright by and by. As yet 'tis only speckled."

"Yes," said the purchaser, wiping the sweat from his forehead and examining his purchase with a more experienced eye, "but I think I like a speckled ax best." [23]

Another favorite Franklin story, which he told and retold all his life, was the memory of a bitter boyhood experience. When he was seven years old, visitors to his father's house had given him some small change. A few hours later, he saw another boy playing with a whistle. Charmed with the sound, he gave the boy all his money for it. He loved the toy and went tooting all around the house with it. But he made the mistake of boasting to his older brothers and sisters about the purchase.

They told him that he had given four times as much for it as the whistle was worth. Instantly the whistle lost all its charm. When Franklin thought of what he could have bought with the rest of the money and heard the horse laughs of the rest of the family, he "cry'd with vexation."

He never forgot the experience. As he grew older, whenever he was tempted to buy some unnecessary thing, he would tell himself, "Do not give too much for the whistle." Gradually the memory generalized to an even larger principle. When he saw a man too fond of political popularity, neglecting his own affairs and ruining himself, Franklin would say, "He pays too much for his whistle." If he saw a miser who gave up all of life's comforts, "all the pleasure of doing good to others, all the esteem of his fellow citizens, and the joys of benevolent friendship for the sake of accumulating wealth," he drew the same conclusion. "Poor man, you pay too much for your whistle." When he met a man of pleasure who ignored all opportunities to improve his mind or his fortune, abandoning himself to sensuality, again the childhood voice spoke in Franklin's mind, "You pay too much for your whistle." He drew the same conclusion when he saw "a beautiful, sweet-temper'd girl, marry'd to an ill-natur'd brute of a husband."

"In short, I conceiv'd that the great part of the miseries of mankind," Franklin said, "were brought upon them by the false estimates they had made of the value of things, and by their giving too much for the whistle." [24]

At the heart of this judgment was the same insight that had inspired Franklin to experiment with the art of virtue. By giving too much for the whistle, he saw that people deprived themselves of a wider freedom—the freedom of the balanced, self-disciplined man. The person who surrendered himself to any extreme—whether it was political passion, or physical vice—was, in Franklin's view, sinning against this greatest of all human values—freedom.

In the Philadelphia of his time, one of the greatest vices, in Franklin's opinion, was what he called "the pursuit of wealth to no purpose." He was convinced that once a man had accumulated enough money to assure himself and his family of independence and moderate comfort, the good citizen should turn his hand to public service. Again, there is a vivid story that illustrates Franklin's point. He liked to tell of the time that a friend showed him through his magnificent new mansion. He took him into a living room large enough to quarter a congress. Franklin asked him why in the world he wanted a room this size. "Because I can afford it," said the man. Next came a dining room big enough to seat fifty people. Again Franklin wondered at the size and the man reiterated, "I can afford it." Finally, Franklin turned to him and said, "Why are you wearing such a small hat, why not get one ten times the size of your head? You can afford that too." [25]

Much as he loved science, Franklin was even more devoted to the ideal of public service. He once remarked, "Had Newton been pilot but of a single common ship, the finest of his discoveries would scarce have excus'd or aton'd for his abandoning the helm one hour in time of danger; how much less if she had carried the fate of the Commonwealth." As a newspaperman and keen observer of human nature, he was also deeply committed to improving the lot of the common man. He once remarked to a minister whom he respected that the person who discovered how to persuade men to practice virtue would "deserve more, ten thousand times, than the inventor of the longitude." [26]

Thus, when his fellow citizens elected him to the Pennsylvania Assembly in October, 1752, Franklin accepted the call and more or less abandoned his laboratory. It was not a step taken with total reluctance, out of some purely abstract sense of duty. This man who displayed to observers the cool, sunny serenity of a philosopher was by no means incapable of strong emotion. He had a really deep affection for his adopted "country," as he called Pennsylvania. He summed it up one day in a letter to a friend in England, who had asked his advice on buying land in Connecticut. Franklin assured him that land there was a good buy, and that the citizens of Connecticut were fine people. He had often thought of settling there himself. "But Pennsilvania is my darling," he said, and he had decided to stay where he was happiest.[27]

V

When Franklin took his seat in the Assembly, he resigned his clerkship. The Assembly promptly appointed William Franklin as his replacement. Here was someone else about whom Benjamin Franklin cared deeply.

If a single word had to be chosen to describe Benjamin Franklin, paternal would come close to saying it all. This burly, broad-shouldered man seemed to fulfill himself most when he was in a fathering role, sharing his strength, his wisdom, his generosity, and his humor with other people. Inevitably, this brought a special intensity to his relationship with his only son.

Another factor added extra urgency to Franklin's concern for William. He was illegitimate, the product of a liaison with a working-class woman, into which Franklin had stumbled during his first unmarried years in Philadelphia. William had apparently been born six months before Franklin married Deborah Read. As soon as he could possibly do so— when William was about six months old—Franklin had acknowledged the boy and taken him into his house, and raised him as his son. Franklin gave William's mother a modest sum of money each year, and she had accepted the arrangement amicably. But Deborah Read, a woman with a violent temper and a shrew's tongue, had much more difficulty reconciling herself to William's existence. She became even more antagonistic to the boy, when her own son, handsome little Francis Folger Franklin, died of smallpox at the age of four.

A young clerk named Daniel Fisher, who lived in Franklin's house for a time, left a vivid picture of Deborah Franklin's feelings toward William. In his diary Fisher wrote of seeing young Franklin pass through the house ";without the least compliment between Mrs. Franklin and him or any sort of notice taken of each other." Then one day, as Deborah was chatting with Fisher, and William Franklin passed them in silence as usual, Deborah Franklin exclaimed, "Mr. Fisher, there goes the greatest villain upon earth." While Fisher stared in bewilderment, Deborah proceeded to denounce William Franklin "in the foulest terms I ever heard from a gentlewoman." Young Fisher eventually quit his job and moved out of the Franklin household. He simply could not stand Deborah Franklin's "turbulent temper." [28]

Deborah seemed at first glance an unlikely wife for Benjamin Franklin. She was practically illiterate. She would sign her letters to him "Your afeckthone wife." He always began his letters to her: "My dear child." She was childishly jealous of the time he gave to public affairs. She told Daniel Fisher, "All the world claimed a privilege of troubling her Pappy," which was her family name for Franklin. Deborah was a living witness of the distance Franklin had traveled since his birth to a

Boston candlemaker. She was a shopkeeper's daughter with whom Franklin had flirted when he first arrived in Philadelphia. He thought of marrying her, but went to England instead. When he returned, Deborah was a grass widow, the victim of a ne'er-do-well who had married her, then skipped town leaving behind nothing but bills, and reportedly died in the West Indies. Franklin was perhaps attracted by the fact that Deborah had the liability of this fiasco, while he had the problem of his illegitimate son. A woman with a failed marriage and a not certifiably dead husband was less likely to reproach him. As usual, his judgment of human nature proved sound. Deborah was clearly grateful for being rescued from a lifetime of moral limbo, even if she never controlled her animosity toward William.

A big husky bustling woman, with some training as a bookkeeper, Deborah proved herself an invaluable helpmate. With obvious affection, Franklin later recalled how she "assisted me cheerfully in my business, folding and stitching pamphlets, tending shop, purchasing old linen rags for the papermakers, etc., etc." He also proudly recalled that in those days he had been "clothed from head to foot in woolen and linen of my wife's manufacture." Deborah kept the books, and maintained an impeccable order in the shop, a task which Franklin freely admitted was beyond him. Thanks to her unflagging help, Franklin had found the time to launch a program of self-education, which had swiftly carried him into a world of ideas and achievements infinitely beyond Deborah's intellectual horizon. But he never forgot the solid, middle-class virtues, and above all the loyalty and hearty affection with which his wife had worked beside him in those often precarious early years. He even wrote a song in tribute to her. It inadvertently also summed up their relationship.

MY PLAIN COUNTRY JOAN

Of their Chloes and Phillises poets may prate
I sing my plain country Joan.
Now twelve years my wife, still the joy of my life
Blest day that I made her my own,

My dear friends
Blest day that I made her my own.

Not a word of her face, of her shape, or her eyes
Or of flames or of darts you shall hear;

Tho' I beauty admire, 'tis virtue I prize,
That fades not in seventy year.
                    My dear friends . . .

Some faults have we all, and so may my Joan,
But then they're exceedingly small,
And now I'm us'd to 'em, they're just like my own
I scarcely can see 'em at all.
                    My dear friends

Were the finest young princess, with million in purse,
To be had in exchange for my Joan
She could not be a better wife, mought be a worse,
So I'd stick to my Joggy alone
                    My dear friends
I'd cling to my lovely ould Joan.[29]

Along with her ill-fated son, Francis, Deborah bore Franklin a daughter, Sarah, who was intellectually and physically an exact image of her mother. Inevitably, this meant still more tension in the family, since William Franklin had inherited his father's brains, was an ardent collaborator in his electrical experiments, and a ready companion in all of Franklin's intellectual pursuits. Much of the antagonism Deborah felt for William may well have been jealousy caused by the feeling that Franklin paid him far more attention than his less brilliant daughter.

The moment William obtained his first salary as clerk of the Assembly, he moved out of the Franklin house to escape Deborah's waspish tongue. He was already cutting a romantic swath through Philadelphia society, thanks to his good looks and engaging personality. But because the fact of his birth was well-known, he inevitably met with some cruel slights and backhand remarks. In his teens he had toyed with escaping this narrow world and had tried to run away as a sailor aboard a privateer. Returning home, he had badgered his father into getting him an army commission, and had marched off to fight the French in Canada. The war ended before he heard a shot fired in anger, but he came home with a military touch to his bearing, and an aura of adventure which did him no harm in his pursuit of the girls.

Almost immediately, William embarked on another, far more significant adventure. With fur trader George Croghan, he traveled west to an

Indian conference on the Ohio. Like many other Americans of his generation, young Franklin was struck by the fabulous richness of the land beyond the Alleghenies, and the almost boundless abundance of it. He poured out his story about "the country back of us," to his father who listened with keen interest, and was so impressed that he sent copies of William's journal to friends in England. William was convinced that a fortune was waiting for the men who first possessed these lands, so haphazardly "owned" by small bands of Indians, who regarded them only as hunting preserves. In fact, when he returned home, he talked of nothing but ways of organizing trading companies and colonizing expeditions which would establish England's grip on the territory. For a while, Ohio seemed to be the only thing that interested him, aside from the pursuit of Philadelphia's belles at the Assembly Balls.[30]

Finally, Franklin took William aside and quietly informed him that Ohio, fascinating and important as it might some day become, was about as substantial as a castle in the clouds at the moment. What Franklin feared was the possibility that William was assuming he could invest his time in cloud castles and Assembly Balls because he was eventually coming into a handsome inheritance. Bluntly, Franklin told his son that he planned to spend the modest estate he had accumulated on himself. William had better start thinking about choosing a profession. Shortly after the kite experiment, William too abandoned electricity and began studying law in the office of Franklin's good friend and political lieutenant, stocky, erudite Joseph Galloway. At the same time, Franklin wrote to England and asked friends there to register William in the Inns of Court where the elite of the British legal profession studied the common law. Hopefully, he said, he would make the trip to England with William when the time came for him to go.

Franklin was scarcely seated in the Assembly when another kind of public service called for his aid. As a man with a half ownership in a newspaper with the largest circulation on the American continent, Franklin had long been interested in the postal service. For sixteen years he had served as postmaster of Philadelphia, a job which he had taken to protect his newspaper. It was the habit of postmasters to permit the mailing of no newspapers except those they owned. This was one among the many defects of the American postal system. Letter delivery was haphazard and slow—it took six weeks for a letter to get from Boston to Philadelphia. When the Deputy Postmaster General for North America died, Franklin applied for his job. Peter Collinson, the London

Quaker merchant who had arranged for the publication of Franklin's experiments in electricity, used his influence, and early in 1753 royal approval came through.

The job opened a new era in Franklin's life. Although Pennsylvania remained his "darling" and he maintained an intense interest in its politics, his Deputy Postmaster General's responsibilities drew his eyes beyond the boundaries of the Quaker colony. He turned his zeal for improvement and his highly original mind toward thinking about all of British North America. The slow transformation of Benjamin Franklin from Pennsylvanian to American had begun.

V I

In Pennsylvania politics, Franklin tried to play a peacemaker's role. The governor, Robert Hunter Morris, was an American, formerly Chief Justice of New Jersey, and a man Franklin had known for years. He was, of course, the spokesman for the Proprietary Party. The Proprietors' main object was to prevent taxation on the millions of acres which they owned throughout the colony. For years they had taken the offensive against the Assembly, which was dominated by Quakers who found it difficult to vote appropriations for arming the colony or raising a militia, even when the purpose was strictly defensive. Franklin liked and admired the Quakers for their virtues, and he did his best to help them around the absurdities in which their strict pacifism often involved them.

For instance, when he first organized the Philadelphia Associaters in 1747, the Union Fire Company proposed to raise sixty pounds in a lottery to buy cannon. There were twenty-two Quakers in the Fire Company, and eight from other religions. The proposal looked doomed until Franklin suggested that the twenty-two Quakers quietly stay away from the meeting at which the cannon-buying proposition came to a vote. The motion was carried, and the Quakers' consciences were simultaneously protected.[31]

On large and small issues, Franklin soon proved himself an astute politician. More than once he demonstrated that the creator of Poor Richard had read his own maxims. In later years he told how he had converted one recalcitrant assemblyman. He wrote the man a note, asking if he could borrow "a certain very scarce and very curious book" which was in his library. A week later, Franklin returned it with an effusive note of gratitude. "When we next met in the House, he spoke to me (which he had never done before) and with great civility; and he ever after manifested a readiness to serve me on all occasions, so that we became great friends and our friendship continued to his death," Franklin said. "This is another instance of the truth of an old maxim I learned, which says, 'He that has once done you a kindness will be more ready to do you another, than he whom you yourself have obliged.' " [32]

But Franklin found peacemaking a difficult and frequently thankless role. He was soon writing his friend Collinson in England that "both sides expect more from me than they ought." Except for the fact that he was "able now and then to influence a good measure," he said, "I should be ready to swear never to serve again as an Assembly man." [33]

He found the challenge of reorganizing the post office a welcome excuse to escape from Pennsylvania's political feuding. Like the scientist that he was, Franklin preferred to learn from firsthand observation, and within a few months after his appointment, he set out on a ten-week journey "to the East," as he called it, in the language of the born Bostonian. He traveled across New Jersey, through New York, and up into Connecticut, Rhode Island, and Massachusetts.

The improvements he achieved in the postal service were nothing less than spectacular. He reduced the traveling time of a Boston-Philadelphia letter from six weeks to three. He abolished the old monopolistic system by which each postmaster sent the newspaper of his choice through the mail free and opened the service to all papers, for a small charge. He insisted on postmasters keeping precise accounts of their revenues and ordered them to print in the newspapers the names of persons who had letters waiting for them—a practice he had long followed in Philadelphia. People who did not call for their letters on the day they arrived had them delivered the following day and were charged an extra penny. Again, this was an innovation Franklin had tried first in Philadelphia, and it made the post office much more popular. Too often in many cities, letters were allowed to lie around for weeks, and were liable to be lost, or read by idlers. After three months, unclaimed letters were forwarded to the central post office in Philadelphia—thus creating the first dead-letter office.

On the post roads, Franklin had milestones erected, so that post riders could pace themselves better. By talking with riders and postmasters face to face, Franklin established an esprit de corps which also had much to do with getting a new vitality into the service. He consulted them on new roads, fords, and ferries. In three years, the service was completely overhauled, and its new speed and reliability won it a popularity it had never known before. In the fourth year of Franklin's administration, it paid a profit for the first time in its history, collecting more revenue in twelve months than it had in the previous thirty-six.

Traveling was a rugged business in the 1750s, and only someone with Franklin's tough constitution could have endured the bad weather, the rutted roads, too often either quagmires of mud or suffocating dust storms, the innumerable rivers which the traveler had to ford or ferry. Taverns and inns were few and often overcrowded. To get a place by the fire, after hours on the road in rain or cold, was often difficult.

Once Franklin used his wit to overcome this particular challenge. He stopped in a Rhode Island tavern on a raw, blustery rainy day and found two dozen locals and travelers crowded around the room's only fire.

"Boy," said Franklin in stentorian tones to the tavernkeeper's son, "get my horse a quart of oysters."

"A quart of oysters?" gasped the boy.

"You heard me, a quart of oysters," Franklin boomed.

The boy obeyed, and there was a general stampede out the door to see this incredible phenomenon, a horse who ate oysters.

The horse snorted and snuffled in indignation and refused to have anything to do with the oysters. Baffled, the curiosity-seekers trooped back into the tavern, to find Deputy Postmaster General Franklin sitting serenely in the chair closest to the fire.[34]

Franklin had always been an enthusiastic traveler. He had made three previous return visits to New England, and these, combined with his newspaper, his almanac, and his fame as a scientist, had woven a web of friendship and acquaintances in every colony along his route. In New Jersey was James Alexander, a Scottish nobleman who had fled to the New World after the collapse of the 1745 rebellion. As a lawyer, he had helped to defend the New York printer, Peter Zenger, in a trial that established the first rudiments of a free press in America. In New York,

Archibald Kennedy was a wealthy merchant who wanted to see the colonies united for mutual defense. Cadwallader Colden was a Crown official, as well as an expert on American botany and Indian history.

In Connecticut, Franklin had long corresponded with Jared Eliot, an expert on scientific agriculture, who doubled as pastor of the Congregational Church in Killingworth. He and Franklin discussed many things besides farming. Among the cleverest letters Franklin ever wrote was one in which he tried to convince Eliot that the world would take a step forward if it allowed people to heap praise on themselves instead of pretending they were indifferent to it. He pointed out that children regularly praised themselves, declaring, "I am a good boy; am I not a good girl?" But they soon gave it up when adults corrected them. The result, Franklin argued, was "being forbid to praise themselves, they learn instead of it to censure others; which is only a roundabout way of praising themselves; for condemning the conduct of another, in any particular, amounts to as much as saying, *I am so honest or wise or good or prudent that I could not do or approve of such an action.* This fondness for ourselves, rather than malevolence to others, I take to be the general source of censure and backbiting; and I wish men had not been taught to damn up natural currents, to the overflowing and damage of their neighbor's grounds." [35]

Dr. Samuel Johnson, an Episcopal clergyman and educator, whom one man called "the apostle of sound learning and elegant literature in New England," was another Connecticut friend. Franklin did his utmost to lure him to Philadelphia to take over the academy he had helped to found. He apologized for an outline of the academy's program which he sent Johnson, explaining that he had no education of his own (except as a tradesman) nor had ever been concerned in educating others. Nonetheless, he was brilliantly original in his sketch of an educational program designed for the emerging modern world. He boldly discarded Latin and Greek as useless, and urged the study of modern languages and science instead. "Nobody would imagine that the draught you have made for an English education was done by a tradesman," Dr. Johnson told him. "But so it sometimes is, a true genius will not content itself without entering more or less into almost everything, and of mastering many things more in spite of fate it self." [36]

Ezra Stiles, another clergyman who combined an intense interest in science with a subtle theological mind, was always ready to greet Franklin whenever he visited his parsonage in Newport, Rhode Island.

Boston fairly abounded in Franklin friends. Among the more prominent were John Winthrop, professor of mathematics and natural philosophy at Harvard College; Josiah Quincy, one of America's richest merchants; Dr. Samuel Cooper, pastor of Boston's Brattle Square Church; and James Bowdoin, wealthy businessman and pioneer astronomer. Another friend was Mather Byles, minister of the Hollis Street Church and one of the earliest American poets.

Many of these men were members of the American Philosophical Society, which Franklin had founded in 1743. It was barely breathing, largely because so many of its members were, in Franklin's words, "very idle gentlemen." It would take another decade and a half before it merged with another scientific group, the American Society, which had grown out of Franklin's old Junto, and began dispensing the "useful knowledge" which Franklin hoped to create by pooling the best brains in America.

In Boston, blood was at least as important as science, however. Benjamin's favorite among the Boston Franklins was his sister, Jane Mecom, younger than Franklin, a vivacious, high-spirited woman who already doted on her famous brother. She had married a nobody. Edward Mecom was a saddler who did not make enough money to support the eleven children Jane bore him, and the family was forced to take in roomers. Franklin's elder brother, John, on the other hand, had married a wealthy widow, Elizabeth Hubbard. Franklin made him Postmaster of Boston. He never had the slightest qualm about appointing relatives to posts in his power. He had already appointed William Franklin Postmaster of Philadelphia, before he departed. In this, Franklin was a man of his generation. British politics was organized around families and factions, and jobs were invariably handed out to family retainers and loyal followers on this rather crude basis. The concept of appointing the best qualified person, regardless of his political affiliation, had not yet occurred to anyone.

More important, to Franklin it was vital to have in these jobs persons he could trust, and who he knew would follow his reformist leadership. Earlier Postmasters had had a bad habit of keeping sloppy accounts and pocketing a lot of loose change for themselves. In Newport, Franklin appointed another man he knew well, Thomas Vernon. It was also a sentimental gesture. When Franklin was a young man, Thomas's father, Samuel Vernon, had asked him to collect a debt for him in Pennsylvania. Franklin had collected the money, but never forwarded it to Vernon.

Instead he frittered it away on trifles and loans to out-of-work friends. Only years later, when he was prosperous, did he repay it. Now he did his best to correct this youthful "erratum."

While Franklin traveled and hobnobbed, he did not stop thinking. In fact, moving from colony to colony inspired him to set down on paper one of his most important scientific insights. He waited a few years to publish it, under the title "Observations Concerning the Increase of Mankind, Peopling of Countries &c." With a brilliant combination of mathematics and social observation, Franklin noted that there were now well over 1,000,000 Englishmen in North America. Yet little more than 80,000 had emigrated from England. This fact alone showed a radical difference between the New World and the Old World, where population was relatively stable. America, with its almost unlimited land and productive capacity, placed no barrier to marriage and the raising of families, as the economically cramped Old World did. For this reason, the population of America would double every twenty or twenty-five years— a prediction which was fulfilled with scientific exactitude until 1860, when massive immigration created even more rapid growth. For Franklin, contemplating this increase in the early 1750s, it meant one significant thing. America will "in another century be more than the people of England, and the greatest number of Englishmen will be on this side of the water."

Franklin did not see this as a threat to the mother country. He boldly spoke and wrote as an Anglo-American and loyal member of the Empire. "What an accession of power to the British Empire by sea as well as land! What increase of trade and navigation! What numbers of ships and seamen!" Underlying this emotion, however, was a more uniquely American sentiment. In 1750, Parliament had restricted the manufacture of iron in Pennsylvania, because British ironmasters had complained that American-made iron was competing with their products. This made no sense to Franklin, because the population of the colonies was increasing so fast, there was sure to be an ever-growing market for manufactures, whether British or American. "A wise and good mother," Franklin said, placed no distressing restraints on her children. "To distress is to weaken, and weakening the children weakens the whole family." [38]

Franklin circulated this essay among the members of the American Philosophical Society, and then printed it, in 1755. Although it is relatively forgotten now, compared to his achievements in electricity, in his time it was almost as important in creating his international reputation.

The essay was reprinted widely throughout the British Isles, and more than one member of Parliament realized for the first time that America was no longer a vague entity on the other side of the world, which could be treated with what one Prime Minister called a policy of "salutary neglect."

Unfortunately, where power is concerned, men's first impulse is not to share but to grip more tightly what appears to be threatened. This was the British Establishment's reaction to Franklin's essay. Instead of creating a climate of freedom, it inspired even more restrictive legislation on American manufacturing and commerce by narrow-minded men, who were determined to maintain their traditional, if seldom exercised authority.

VII

Franklin returned to Philadelphia from his first postal journey to discover the colony in a swirl of excitement over two issues, one old and one new. The Proprietary Party and the Assembly were locked in the usual wrangle over taxation. But this time it had an urgency which made earlier quarrels seem academic. The French and a host of Indian allies were moving down the Ohio River valley, showing ominous signs of planning to stay in this territory, where both they and the English had shadowy claims. This meant that the Pennsylvania frontier was in danger of attack. The Indians who lived along it had long been allied to England, but this new French pressure on one side, coupled with little sign of adequate support from Pennsylvania, made them extremely restless. Like all small nations, they inevitably gravitated in the direction of the large nation that exhibited the most strength. Most ominous of all was news the Indians brought of a French fort on the southern shores of Lake Erie. A fort was expensive. It was also permanent. It meant the French were moving south to stay.

On May 9, 1754, Franklin printed in his newspaper a report from an obscure officer of the Virginia Militia, named George Washington. The report told of a French army of more than a thousand men appearing at the forks of the Monongahela (present-day Pittsburgh) where Virginians were building a small fort. With less than fifty men on duty, the fort's commander was forced to surrender to this overwhelming force. Franklin instantly grasped the nature of the crisis, and he summed it up in a unique way. Underneath the news story which told in blunt terms what was happening on the frontier he published America's first political cartoon. It was a snake broken into eight parts looking very dead. Under it was the motto: JOIN, OR DIE. In the news story he made the same point.

> The confidence of the French in this undertaking seems well grounded on the present disunited state of the British colonies, and the extreme difficulty of bringing so many different governments and Assemblies to agree in any speedy and effectual measures for our common defense and security; while our enemies have the very great advantage of being under one direction, with one council, and one purse. Hence, and from the great distance of Britain, they presume that they may with impunity violate the most solemn treaties subsisting between the two crowns, kill, seize and imprison our traders, and confiscate their effects at pleasure (as they have done for several years past), murder and scalp our farmers, with their wives and children, and take an easy possession of such parts of the British territory as they find most convenient for them; which if they are permitted to do, must end in the destruction of the British interest, trade and plantations in America.[39]

Franklin sent the cartoon and the story to Richard Partridge, Pennsylvania's agent in London. Coincidentally, the Board of Trade in London took a step which seemed at first to be in harmony with Franklin's thinking. As the officials in London saw it, the problem was the casual way in which the various colonies handled their Indian affairs, sometimes giving, then refusing to give presents, haphazardly letting settlers wander into tribal lands in violation of treaties. Moreover, no single colony was able to match the lavish scale of French present giving. All this was causing the Indians to become more and more restless, especially the vital Iroquois, who were the nucleus of a kind of buffer state between the French and the English. Accordingly, the Board of Trade ordered the governors of Virginia, Pennsylvania, Maryland, New Hampshire, Massachusetts Bay, and New Jersey to join the governor of New

York in appointing commissioners for an intercolonial conference with
the Iroquois and other tribes to be held at Albany in the middle of June,
1754. It was almost inevitable that Franklin was named one of the commissioners. But he went to Albany with far larger ideas in his mind than
Indian pacification.

It was obvious that England and France were headed for another war,
a final death-grapple that would decide who was to rule in North
America, in the West Indies, and even in distant India. In New York,
Franklin met his good friend James Alexander and the conversation
turned to the Albany Conference. Uniting the colonies was something
Franklin had already discussed with Alexander, and their mutual friend,
Archibald Kennedy, and Franklin now remarked that he thought he had
a plan that was workable. Alexander urged him to put it down on paper,
and three days later, shortly before he left New York for Albany,
Franklin delivered a note with an enclosure which began:

Short Hints Towards a Scheme for Uniting the Northern Colonies

A Governeur General
To be appointed by the King.
To be a military man.
To have a salary from the Crown.
*To have a negation on all acts of the Grand Council, and carry
into execution whatever is agreed by him and that Council.*

Grand Council
*One member to be chosen by the Assembly of each of the smaller
colonies and two or more by each of the larger, in proportion to the
sums they pay yearly into the general treasury.*

The rest of the paper went into the details of how the governor and
the Grand Council would be paid, where they would meet and when, and
what their powers would be.

Off to Albany Franklin went, where, at the city's courthouse, he
joined twenty-five commissioners from the four New England colonies,
from Maryland, from New York, as well as his own Pennsylvania. The
Virginia and New Jersey assemblies had declined to send anyone, in
itself a comment on colonial disunity. Franklin promptly proposed his
plan of union and to his delight, his fellow commissioners thought well
enough of it to appoint a committee consisting of one man from each
delegation "to prepare and receive plans or schemes for the union of the

colonies and to digest them into one general plan." [40] In the next two weeks of conferences and debates, Franklin's Short Hints were amplified and modified in minor ways—the Governor General became a "President General," and instead of the "Northern Colonies," the plan specified a "general union of the British colonies on the continent." On the floor of the Congress, more changes were made, largely in the powers of the Grand Council to buy Indian lands. But the plan remained essentially the one Franklin had jotted down for his friend Alexander in New York. [41]

Every delegation except Connecticut voted enthusiastic approval of Franklin's plan. For a few hours, there in Albany, the philosopher of electricity lived in the dazzling world of the political visionary. How easy it was for an ingenious man with a talent for words to solve the problems of his country! In his exultation, Franklin suggested to the Albany delegates still another idea, a plan to create two new colonies in the Ohio Valley to serve as buffers between the older colonies and the French. The idea called for a bold adaptation of the original English approach to colonization. Instead of moving the frontier westward "inch by inch," Franklin proposed sending an expedition, composed of a hundred families, supported by a well-armed body of young single men. They would thus be strong enough to resist Indian attacks, and could immediately get down to the business of laying out farms and organizing a government. Within the solid framework they created, more settlers would inevitably be attracted.

But even as Franklin spun out these pregnant ideas, other men were acting out one of history's harsher themes on the western frontier. Young Lieutenant Colonel Washington had returned to the frontier leading a regiment of Virginia militia. After winning an initial skirmish, he had retreated to an improvised stockade called Fort Necessity, where he made a stand against overwhelming French and Indian forces. On July fourth, a date which meant nothing to the mortified young Virginian nor to Benjamin Franklin, he had been forced to surrender Fort Necessity and lead his beaten men in a humiliating retreat, abandoning to the victorious French everything but what they could carry on their backs.

Obviously, war was imminent, and Franklin's politics of vision went glimmering. In colony after colony, Assemblies rejected the Albany Plan of Union, or ignored it completely. Not even Franklin's personal prestige could persuade the Pennsylvania legislature to look favorably upon it. The Massachusetts legislature rejected it without even taking a roll-call vote, inspiring one of his Boston friends to write Franklin sarcastically, "I thought you a wise man but . . . it has been proved by some of our own wise men and boys . . . that you and the rest of the Commissioners at Albany have shown yourselves by the projected plan for an *Union* to be arrant blockheads; and, at the same time, to have set up a scheme for destroying the liberties and privileges of every British subject upon the continent; but this, so thinly disguised and covered, that the meanest creature in the world could see through it in an instant." [42]

This was the reaction of most colonial legislatures, when they considered the plan at all. They felt it encroached upon their traditional rights and privileges. With not a little bitterness, Franklin wrote to his friend Peter Collinson in England, "Every body cries, a union is absolutely necessary; but when they come to the manner and form of the union, their weak noodles are presently distracted." [43]

In London, the plan was practically ignored. The King's ministers and the gentlemen in Parliament were too absorbed by the plunge toward war with France to pay attention to bright ideas from a colonial congress. Years later, Franklin summed up the harsh lesson he learned at Albany. "Those who govern, having much business on their hands, do not generally like to take the trouble of considering and carrying into execution new projects. The best public measures are therefore seldom adopted from previous wisdom, but are forc'd by the occasion." [44]

VIII

At home Franklin found the Assembly locked in familiar combat with Governor Robert Hunter Morris. The governor loved an argument almost as much as Franklin disliked one, and he was wholeheartedly committed to the Penns' favorite idea, getting money out of the rest of the colony without shaking a cent loose from their own pockets. This feckless, seemingly perpetual quarrel soured everyone's disposition and may well have had something to do with the fact that Franklin had barely come home from Albany when he about-faced and departed on another long tour of New England on behalf of the post office. In Boston he made the acquaintance of one of the most talented English officials ever to serve in America—William Shirley, the governor of Massachusetts.

An astute politician with a keen interest in the people he governed, Shirley had been a wholehearted supporter of the Albany Congress and the idea of uniting the colonies. He obtained a draft of Franklin's plan and it immediately suggested to him a number of alternatives which seemed logical to a man who saw the colonies through the eyes of the Crown. Let the governors and one or two members of their councils assemble annually, he said, work out plans for common defense, and pay for them from taxes laid on the Americans by an act of Parliament. Franklin met with Shirley several times and discussed these ideas at length. With obvious pride he wrote to his son William that Shirley was "particularly civil to me." [45] But no amount of civility could make Shirley's ideas attractive to Franklin. In three masterful letters, he demolished Shirley's plan by pointing out realities which were to have enormous significance in the later decades of the century.

The opening sentence of Franklin's first letter summed up the essence of his argument. "Excluding the people of the colonies from all share in the choice of the Grand Council would probably give extreme dissatisfaction, as well as the taxing them by act of Parliament where they have no representative." Franklin pointed out that it was important to consider what people "will *be apt* to think and say," as well as what they "ought to think." He insisted that the colonies were "as loyal, and as firmly attach'd to the present Constitution and reigning family, as any subjects in the King's dominions," but they frankly did not trust the royal governors, who often came to the colonies "meerly to make fortunes . . . are not always men of the best abilities and integrity, have no estates here, nor any natural connections with us, that should make them heartily concern'd for our welfare. . . ."

Franklin went on to point out why the colonists were touchy about taxes. They already paid "yearly great sums to the mother country unnotic'd." Americans were forced to carry most of their produce directly to Britain, pay duties there and sell it for less than it would bring in foreign markets. They were forbidden to manufacture many things, which they must therefore buy from British merchants whose prices had risen steadily in recent years, thanks to the fact that Parliament maintained for them a monopoly on the American trade, and forbade foreigners to sell any of their manufactures in America. The colonies made no complaints about these "secondary taxes," as Franklin called them.

But they were keenly aware of them, and to lay on top of them "Immediate heavy taxes" would be almost certain to arouse "animosities and dangerous feuds." [46]

The answer to the dilemma, Shirley replied in an ensuing conversation with Franklin, was clear: the colonies should have representatives at Parliament. It would be an ideal way of uniting both the colonies in America and America to the Crown. After thinking it over, Franklin agreed. "Such an union would be very acceptable to the colonies," he told Shirley, "provided they had a reasonable number of representatives allowed them; and that all the old acts of Parliament restraining the trade or cramping the manufactures of the colonies, be at the same time repealed, and that British subjects this side the water put, in those respects, on the same footing with those in Great Britain." Warming to the idea, Franklin unfolded the dream that was to dominate his life for the next decade. "I should hope too that by such an union, the people of Great Britain and the people of the colonies would learn to consider themselves, not as belonging to different communities with different interests, but to one community with one interest, which I imagine would contribute to strengthen the whole, and greatly lessen the danger of future separations." [47]

More than two decades later, James Madison, reading these letters, declared that Franklin had summed up the entire argument of the American Revolution "within the compass of a nutshell," twenty years before it occurred to anyone else. But to Franklin, the positive side of the argument was far more important. Always ready to accommodate differences reasonably, Franklin remained essentially confident that Great Britain's shortsighted colonial policies could be modified by vigorous debate. But there were times when his underlying toughness broke through this reasonable persona. Once, in the *Gazette,* he modestly proposed that since England was so fond of exporting her felons and murderers from her jails to America, the colonies should return the compliment by shipping to England all their rattlesnakes. Occasionally, this toughness could veer close to cynicism. In *Poor Richard* for 1755, the wisdom for the month of July was a good example of this side of Franklin's mind.

Who is wise? *He that learns from every one.*
Who is powerful? *He that governs his passions.*
Who is rich? *He that is content.*
Who is that? *Nobody.* [48]

IX

Part of this sentiment may have been inspired by a remarkable young woman Franklin met in Boston that year. While visiting the city of his birth, Franklin stayed at his brother John's house. Another guest was a very pretty twenty-three-year-old brunette, named Catherine Ray, a relative of John's wife. At forty-nine, Franklin was at that peculiar point in a man's middle age when he knows he is no longer a youth and yet feels himself very much in possession of his vital powers. It is a combination that can create a plaintive May-December romance. Catherine did everything in her power to encourage it. All she talked about was love. Hour after hour she regaled Franklin with stories of advances she had resisted from suitors young and old. There was a Spaniard who had wooed her with Latin passion and gone home to Spain in despair. There were a half dozen younger Americans who made pilgrimages to Block Island, off the Rhode Island coast, where she lived in almost monastery-like isolation with her parents. Katy, as Franklin called her, was a first-class flirt. She obviously took delicious pleasure in tormenting the opposite sex, luring them on with her eyes and with low-cut gowns, and simultaneously proclaiming her pride in her virginity, on which she set a very exorbitant price.

In Franklin she found a perfect foil, so it seemed at first. He loved witty conversation and the game of love always fascinated him. Svelte Katy awakened in him a long suppressed yearning for such a woman, so different from his rough, plain, indelicate Deborah. He plunged into a half-real, half make-believe romance that was all words and no action, at first. They talked about everything, from the value of virginity to the meaning of love and the problem of choosing a marriage partner for life. Franklin dazzled her with his casual wisdom and his effortless fun. One of their favorite games was forcing her to tell the whole truth when she began discussing her earlier loves, because he solemnly assured her, he was a conjuror who would find out everything anyway. Franklin was ideally equipped to play this role, because in the eighteenth century there was still an aura of the magician around the scientist, and it was especially applicable to the electrician, who was able to achieve so many strange and dazzling effects with his mysterious invisible fire. The game obviously made pretty Katy shiver with delight, and she poured out her romantic heart to Franklin, never realizing that she was stirring depths in her older friend.

One night he made it clear that this was more than a game to him. Katy instantly recoiled. Flirting was one thing, but serious love was something else for which she was simply not prepared—especially with a married man.

Franklin accepted defeat gracefully. It is hard to believe that he ever expected to triumph. With consummate tact, he let the friendship become a bittersweet romance in which the words were ardent and the actions more than proper. How much Katy trusted him was evident, on December 30, 1754, when she left Boston for Newport beside Franklin in his chaise. The seventy-mile journey almost certainly meant they stopped overnight at a tavern—a rather daring act for an unmarried girl. The weather was terrible. They drove all day in driving, soaking rain and compounded their misery by taking a wrong road. But Franklin later vowed he treasured the memory of those "hours and miles that we talked away so agreeably."

They continued to enjoy each other's company immensely at Westerly, Rhode Island, where they visited with Catherine's sister, Anna, wife of Samuel Ward. Then came an anxious message from Block Island— Katy's father was seriously ill. Although the day was raw and stormy, Katy insisted on making the eleven-mile crossing in a tiny skiff. Franklin stood on the rocky shore, sick with anxiety and sudden wrenching loss, watching the little boat plunging up and down on the heaving sea. Ignoring the weather, he held it in the round eye of his telescope, until it vanished into the threatening haze.

Soon after he arrived in Philadelphia, he wrote Katy a letter about how slowly he had journeyed home. Because of her he had hated to leave New England, he said. "I almost forgot I had a home," so slow and lingering was his journey, full of "loitering visits on the road, for three or four weeks."

On paper, he continued to play the ironic game of love for which he had settled. "Persons subject to the hyp [hypochondria] complain of the north east wind as increasing their malady. But since you promis'd to send me kisses in that wind, and I find you as good as your word, 'tis to me the gayest wind that blows, and gives me the best spirits. I write this during an N. east storm of snow, the greatest we have had this winter: Your favours come mixed with the snowy fleeces which are as pure as your virgin innocence, white as your lovely bosom—and as cold—" [49]

Katy replied with three long letters, begging his advice on new affairs of the heart. The correspondence continued on this plane, full of ribald good spirits which make it clear that a puritanical attitude toward sex was not one of the problems of eighteenth-century Americans. "I long to hear," Franklin wrote in another letter, "whether you have continued ever since in that monastery [Block Island]; or have broke into the world again, doing pretty mischief . . . what [is] the state of your heart at this instant? But that, perhaps, I ought not to know; and, therefore, I will not conjure as you sometimes say I do. . . . I commend your prudent resolutions in the article of granting favors to lovers. But if I were courting you, I could not heartily approve such conduct. I should even be malicious enough to say you were too *knowing*." [50]

Franklin often urged Katy to marry as soon as possible. As a man of the world, he knew what a dangerous game she was playing. He gave her the advice in his own inimitable fashion. Once wed, he told her, "you must practice *addition* to your husband's estate, by industry and frugality; *subtraction* of all unnecessary expenses; *multiplication* (I would gladly have taught you that myself, but you thought it was time enough, & wou'dn't learn) he will soon make you a mistress of it." [51]

When she sent him sugar plums made sweet by her kisses, Franklin told her they were so "sweet from the cause you mention, that I could scarce taste the sugar." But when she seemed reticent, in another letter, he warned her not to "hide your heart from me. You know that I can conjure." If the rest of her family failed to treat her with the utmost kindness, he would "send a young gentleman to steal & run away with you, who shall bring you to a country from whence they shall never hear a word of you, without paying postage." [52]

Franklin made no secret of his flirtation. He ended several of his letters by sending Katy Mrs. Franklin's regards, and at one point reported that Deborah was considering leaving him to Katy in her will. But Franklin added, "I ought to wish you a better [legacy] and hope she [Deborah] will live these one hundred years; for we are grown old together, and if she has any faults, I am so us'd to 'em that I don't perceive 'em . . . and since she is willing I should love you as much as you are willing to be lov'd by me; let us join in wishing the old lady a long life and a happy." [53]

X

Katy may have helped take Franklin's mind off the disastrous fate of his Plan of Union. When his fellow Americans either ignored or condemned his brainchild, he relapsed into a rather embittered colonial attitude. "If ever there be an Union, it must be form'd at home by the ministry and Parliament," he told his influential English friend, Peter Collinson. "I doubt not but they will make a good one, and I wish it may be done this winter." [54]

But the British reaction to the precarious situation in the colonies revealed their basic lack of confidence in the Americans. Franklin himself in his letter to Shirley had mentioned the possibility of an eventual separation. The King's ministers in Whitehall were intelligent men, perfectly capable of thinking the same thoughts. They saw no wisdom in a union that might make these distant children strong enough to defy the absent parent. Far better to send them proof of the parent's panoply and power. So in the spring of 1755, Sir John St. Clair, baronet of Scotland, arrived in Williamsburg, Virginia, as Deputy Quartermaster General of British forces in America. A few weeks later, Major General Edward Braddock, with a commission as Commander-in-Chief of His Majesty's Army in North America, followed him. In his wake came two British regiments in their brilliant red coats.

Governor Robert Hunter Morris immediately called on the Pennsylvania Assembly to vote a substantial sum in support of the war effort. The usual wrangle about taxing the Proprietors' estates ensued. Franklin, scarcely back from his lengthy tour of New England, was put on almost every committee by his fellow assemblymen and spent half his waking hours drafting replies to the governor's disputatious messages.

"Our answers as well as his messages were often tart and sometimes indecently abusive," he recalled later.

The net result was a standoff; General Braddock got no money from Pennsylvania. Although he conferred with as many as five governors at one time, Braddock did not have much better luck with other colonial Assemblies. Soon the choleric sixty-year-old soldier exploded into picturesque barracks-room oaths every time he heard the word American. Pennsylvanians were a special target for his wrath, because he heard that they were doing a brisk business selling supplies, and possibly even guns, to the French Canadians and their Indian allies. They were also supposed to be hard at work opening a road over the mountains to the French fort at the forks of the Monongahela, but thus far no one had swung an ax or turned a shovelful of dirt on it.

Braddock swore that in his march through Pennsylvania, he would treat the province as a conquered country, and for good measure quarter his troops there next year, at the colony's expense. Echoes of these threats came drifting into the Quaker colony's Assembly and the members decided it was vital to have someone explain to Braddock why they were refusing to support the King's arms. Franklin was selected as the diplomatic messenger. Thanks to his job as Deputy Postmaster General, he had a way of imparting this information to Braddock casually. He could approach the General wearing his Postmaster's hat, carrying with him a message from the Assembly. They were graciously offering to pay the expenses for a special postal service which would enable him to communicate with colonial governors and commanders on the northern front, where an offensive was also being planned.

As his chief adviser on this delicate diplomatic mission, as well as companion for the 120-mile ride to Frederick, Maryland, where Braddock was camped, Franklin chose his son, William. The Franklins arrived to discover Braddock on the point of apoplexy. The supplies sold to the Army by colonial contractors were rotten. There were only twenty-five wagons collected to transport tents and supplies for 2250 men. Braddock stamped up and down eloquently damning everyone involved, from the ministers in England who had thought up the expedition to the haggling farmers who would not risk a wagon in the service of their country. Franklin watched tall, earnest young George Washington, who was serving as Braddock's aide, expostulate with the general in vain attempts to defend America's reputation from wholesale slander.

Franklin's approach was less argumentative. Eager to convince the general of Pennsylvania's loyalty, Franklin sympathized with his critical shortage of transport, and remarked that there were plenty of wagons available in the Quaker colony. The desperate Braddock seized on this remark: "Then you, sir, who are a man of interest there, can probably procure them for us, and I beg you will undertake it." [55]

Franklin's expression remained serene, but inwardly he must have experienced a sinking sensation. He knew as well as anyone else that farmers in Pennsylvania were no more inclined to part with their wagons than farmers in Maryland and Virginia. But he gamely agreed to do the job for the distraught general if he would agree to paying some extra expenses. Pennsylvanians would probably want to drive their teams in person or send one of their servants as a wagoner. That would make the cost of the wagon, four horses, and a driver fifteen shillings a day. Perhaps Franklin hoped Braddock would find this prohibitive. Instead, the general took 100 pounds in hard cash from his money box and told Franklin to get to work.

The philosopher immediately conferred with Sir John St. Clair, who had just returned from a foray into western Pennsylvania to discuss the failure to build the road which was vital to keep the army supplied from Philadelphia. St. Clair was a thorough disciple of the Braddock style of command, and he gave Franklin a vivid report of what he had said to the lackadaisical westerners. If they did not get moving on the road, he warned them that he would march troops into Cumberland County, drive every able-bodied man into road gangs at the point of a gun, slaughter their cattle at his pleasure to feed his men, and if necessary confiscate their horses, burn their houses, and in general treat them as a "parcel of traitors."

Most of the inhabitants of Cumberland County were German immigrants. Franklin, studying St. Clair, noticed that his uniform resembled that of a Hussar, the fearsome light cavalry of the Austrian and German armies, famous for their disregard of all civilized niceties and their love of plunder and rapine.

Quickly Franklin dashed off a handbill, and had several thousand copies printed for distribution throughout Lancaster, York, and Cumberland Counties. He came down hard on the price—fifteen shillings a day was perhaps twenty-five dollars in modern money values. It was a good price for a wagon, four horses, and a driver. But the heart of Franklin's message was his warning that if the immigrants did not accept "such good pay and reasonable terms" their loyalty would be "strongly suspected." This would put the King's "brave troops" in an exceedingly bad mood and their progress through the counties would almost certainly be "attended with many and great inconveniences"—a remark which needed no amplification for anyone who understood the plundering inclinations of European armies. If he did not get the necessary number of wagons in fourteen days, he would be forced to notify General Braddock of his failure. "And I suppose Sir John St. Clair, *the Hussar,* with a body of soldiers, will immediately enter the province for the purpose aforesaid, of which I shall be sorry to hear, because I am very sincerely and truthfully your friend and well-wisher." [56]

Well within the deadline, over 150 four-horsed wagons, plus 259 pack horses streamed into Braddock's camp.

Everyone in the British Army was vastly amused by Franklin's Hussar ploy. "I cannot but honor Franklin," wrote William Shirley, Jr., son of the Massachusetts governor, "for the last clause of his advertisement." [57] General Braddock was ecstatic and he wrote to his superiors in London declaring that Franklin's achievement was "the only evidence of ability and honesty I have known in these provinces."

William Franklin played a key role in this operation, securing dozens of horses and wagons in Cumberland County, while his father was at work in York and Lancaster Counties. Also helpful was a singularly patriotic gesture on Benjamin's part. When he saw some farmers were still skittish, in spite of the appeal of hard money and the threat of Hussar St. Clair, he guaranteed the value of all the wagons by posting his personal bond for 20,000 pounds.

Back in camp, meanwhile, Franklin became General Braddock's favorite dinner companion. Before the fire in the tavern where they boarded, Braddock spread his maps and traced his line of march over the Alleghenies for Franklin's interested eye. The plan called for the speedy capture of Fort Duquesne at the forks of the Monongahela, and then a swing north to reduce the French fort at Niagara. Franklin listened politely. He was no soldier, but his omnivorous mind could easily grasp the basic essentials of Braddock's strategy. He also had an acute awareness that America was not Europe. Braddock was talking as if the rugged mountains, the impassable forests, and the rushing streams of western Pennsylvania did not exist. He was also assuming that the Indians were no threat whatsoever. In his mind's eye Franklin saw the army, strung out in a long narrow line along the road they would have to cut for their advance. Something shuddered inside him, imagining what might happen

if the Indians launched a surprise attack. Although he knew he was in
the ludicrous position of an amateur advising a professional, he felt compelled to warn Braddock: "The only danger to your march is an Indian
ambush," he said. "Your army will be near four miles long. Could not
an attack on its flanks cut it like a thread into several pieces?"

General Braddock took a swig of his apple toddy, pulled on his long
clay pipe and smiled benevolently at Franklin. "The savages may indeed
be a formidable enemy to your raw American militia," said the commander-in-chief, "but upon the King's regular and disciplined troops,
sir, it is impossible that they should make any impression." [58]

Franklin went home to Philadelphia, his mind still troubled by doubts.
A few days later, two old friends, Doctors Phineas and Thomas Bond,
came to Franklin asking him for a donation to buy several hundred
pounds of fireworks to celebrate the capture of Fort Duquesne. Franklin
let his glasses slip down a little on his nose and said: "I think it will be
time enough to prepare the rejoicing when we know we have a reason
to rejoice."

The doctors looked amazed. Like General Braddock, they assumed
that British regulars were invincible. "Why the devil," said one of them.
"You surely don't suppose that the fort will not be taken?"

"I don't know that it will not be taken," Franklin said, "but I know
that war is a very uncertain business."

The Doctors Bond abandoned their fund raising.[59]

A few days later, a messenger rushed into Philadelphia carrying the
stunning, unbelievable news that Braddock had been ambushed only a
few miles from Fort Duquesne, and two-thirds of his army killed or
wounded. Braddock himself, and young William Shirley, Jr., were among
the dead. The survivors, under the command of Colonel Thomas Dunbar, were in panicky retreat. What must have struck Franklin like a
blow in the solar plexus was the news that the wagoners, the moment
they saw the first frantic refugees from the front streaming past them,
cut loose the fastest horse in their teams and abandoned the other animals and their wagons to the enemy. He had pledged 20,000 pounds of
his own money for those horses and wagons. If the British government
decided, on some political quirk, not to pay those tight-fisted Germans,
they would descend on Benjamin Franklin like a swarm of locusts, and
devour him down to his shoe buckles.

Meanwhile, in a council of war held at Fort Cumberland on the Mary-

land-Pennsylvania border on August 1, Colonel Dunbar decided to retreat all the way to Philadelphia, taking with him every fighting man he
had. When Franklin, as head of the Pennsylvania Assembly's Committee
of Defense, asked him for a chance to discuss this insane move, Dunbar
suggested Trenton, New Jersey, as a likely place to meet. The governor
of Virginia, Robert Dinwiddie, called Dunbar's headlong flight "mon-
strous." Franklin made no comment on it, but it was obvious to him
that Pennsylvania would have to defend its own frontiers. The net effect
of Braddock's expedition had been to provide a handsome road down
which the French and Indians could now pour, unrestrained, to slaughter
hapless farmers and their families in their lonely cabins.

Not even desperate necessity, however, could reconcile Governor Morris and the Assembly. It had, in Franklin's words, "no more effect upon
[him] than the miracles of Moses had on the heart of Pharaoh." The
argument boiled down to a single word. Each time the Assembly sent a
money bill to the governor, there was a clause calling for a tax on all
estates real and personal "those of the Proprietaries not excepted." The
governor invariably tried to get the word "not" changed into "only." [60]

Although Franklin followed his usual strategy of keeping his head
down, the governor was a shrewd politician, and he had no trouble dis-
cerning who was the leading spirit of the opposition. In his wrath, he
wrote to his master, Thomas Penn, meanly pointing out that Franklin
held "an office of profit as Deputy Postmaster General." The Proprietor
promptly paid a visit to the Secretary of State for the Colonies and tried
to get Franklin fired. The minister showed Penn General Braddock's
letter of grateful praise for Franklin's services, and that was the end of
that bit of backstabbing.

Throughout the summer and into the fall the debate raged in the
Pennsylvania Assembly, while the Indians on the frontier picked off isolated farms and single travelers in small probing raids. When not even a
sign of resistance appeared, the savages grew bolder and struck with
more ferocious force. Full-scale raiding parties poured into Berks and
Northampton Counties and people died under the hatchet and scalping
knife less than eighty miles from Philadelphia.

Most of the victims were Germans, who had settled the rich country
that stretched from York to the Quaker enclave around Philadelphia.
Deeply religious to the point of pacifism, they had no enthusiasm for
taking on the best of the Shawnee and Delaware warriors. Frantically

they begged Governor Morris for help, and when that harried official failed to give them a satisfactory answer, more than a thousand of them marched on Philadelphia, carrying a wagonful of scalped corpses which they parked before the governor's mansion. Fortunately, Thomas Penn had only a few days earlier offered to donate 5000 pounds to the defense of the colony if the Assembly would agree to a money bill that did not tax his estates. The governor was able to mollify these enraged provincials with this proof of the Proprietors' concern, and the desperate Germans dragged their wagonload of corpses over to the Assembly, where Benjamin Franklin assured them that action was forthcoming.

Under Franklin's leadership, the Assembly immediately voted 60,000 pounds to raise and equip troops in accordance with a militia bill which the ubiquitous Mr. Franklin had likewise drawn up. But this did not prove to be an instant solution to the colony's woes. Volunteers came forward very slowly to form the military companies, because Franklin's bill expressly exempted Quakers from serving. This caused intense resentment among those who were being asked to risk their lives to defend the apostles of nonviolence.

Franklin attacked the problem in the Pennsylvania *Gazette* by publishing a dialogue between Citizens X, Y, and Z.

"For my part," says Z, "I am no coward, but hang me if I fight to save the Quakers."

X replies, "That is to say, you will not pump ship, because it will save the rats as well as yourself." [61]

Then late in November came the worst news yet from the still defenseless frontier. The Moravian village of Gnadenhutten had been surprised by a Shawnee war party, and every living soul slaughtered except a handful who escaped to the woods. The village had been burned to the ground. Mass terror swept Pennsylvania. Farmers and their families abandoned their homesteads and crowded into the towns. Governor Morris, shuddering at the possibility of another and larger German descent on Philadelphia, succumbed to the prevailing panic and fled to the aid of the man whom he had been denouncing in his letters to Thomas Penn for the better part of a year. Morris begged Franklin to raise and organize a force of 300 rangers immediately and lead them to the frontier, where he would have full authority to organize the region for defense. Franklin accepted, thus adding one more title to his already multiple career: General.

X I

On December 18, 1755, Franklin, former Governor James Hamilton, and Joseph Fox, who had been designated "Commissioners of Defense" by the governor, rode up Philadelphia's High Street and then north on Front Street to the Bethlehem Road with fifty troopers and three canvas-topped Conestoga wagons behind them. Beside Franklin rode his son, William, gorgeous in the uniform of a British grenadier, which he was entitled to wear, thanks to a half-year's service as an ensign during the conflict known as King George's War, a decade earlier. Although he technically served as his father's aide-de-camp, William soon took charge of the military details of the expedition while Benjamin handled the political diplomacy.

Down the road to Bethlehem, described by other travelers as little more than a cow path, the tiny army proceeded, the officers stopping at primitive inns along the way. In a letter to Deborah, Franklin told how the chambermaid almost froze him to death on the first night of the journey. He noticed the sheets she was putting on the bed were damp and asked her to air them first. An hour later, she announced the bed was ready, and Franklin slipped under the covers. A moment later he was on his feet again, shaking like a man who had just plunged into an icy pond. The chambermaid had aired the sheets on a hedge outside the inn and they were literally frozen. Franklin was forced to wrap himself in his greatcoat and woolen trousers to endure them.[62]

At Bethlehem the Defense Commissioners found a worried population, entertaining perhaps a thousand refugees. But they were in good spirits, thanks to the well-organized Moravian Brotherhood, who controlled the town. Under their vigorous leadership, the settlers had erected a stock-ade, were well-armed with guns they had purchased in New York, and had a regular system of sentries posted. They even had gathered paving stones near the upper story windows of their houses, for the women to drop on the heads of any Indians who attempted to break in. Franklin, as a man who had been repeatedly forced to deal with Quaker pacifists

49

in the Pennsylvania Assembly, was wryly amused by the way the Moravians had abandoned their professed pacifism when they heard of the catastrophe that had befallen Gnadenhutten. He could not resist needling the Moravian bishop, Augustus G. Spangenberg, about his "suprize." Hadn't they obtained an act of Parliament exempting them from military duties in the colonies, he asked the bishop. Didn't this mean "they were conscientiously scrupulous of bearing arms?" The bishop, no doubt squirming a little, replied that pacifism was not one of the "established principles" of the sect. But at the time that they obtained the act of Parliament, "it was thought to be a principle with many of their people." However, in the present emergency they found that very few adhered to it. Commenting later, Franklin said dryly, "It seems they were either deceiv'd in themselves, or deceiv'd the Parliament. But common sense aided by present danger, will sometimes be too strong for whimsicall opinions." [63]

At Easton, the next village on their route, Franklin and his companions found a far different situation. The town was equally jammed with refugees from outlying farms, including not a few friendly Indians converted to Christianity. Although many of the refugees were Moravian, the Brotherhood did not rule Easton, and the situation was chaotic. Food was disappearing at an alarming rate, and the disheartened refugees consoled themselves with whiskey. Neither of his fellow commissioners seemed inclined to do anything about the situation but write despairing letters back to Governor Morris. "The terror that has seized them is so great, or their spirits so small," lamented ex-Governor Hamilton, "unless men come from other parts of the province I despair of getting such a number here as will be sufficient to garrison the blockhouses we propose to build."

The two Franklins, father and son, had a private conference and decided the situation called for a drastic, military solution. With Benjamin signing the orders, William swiftly organized a town guard of twenty-four men. Sentries were placed at the ends of the four principal streets and rangers were ordered out to scour the area for Indian tracks. Communications were established with outlying farmhouses and the land around the town was cleared of bushes and trees for 200 yards—the range of an ordinary musket.[64]

Until Franklin went into action, James Hamilton had been smugly telling Governor Morris that the Militia Bill which he had already denounced as "the quintessence of absurdity" was proving itself to be a failure. The general terror created by the Indians' hit and run tactics made many slow to volunteer. But once these same frightened men saw genuine leadership, a story as old as human history was repeated. They volunteered by the dozen, and within ten days Franklin had 200 men under arms, and the Germans were calling him "General" and sometimes "Lieutenant General."

Pondering the problem of a guerrilla war against a foe trained from birth to live and fight in the wilderness, Franklin came up with an idea that was some 200 years ahead of his time. He suggested ranger companies with dogs, "large, strong, and fierce." Whenever a patrol came near "thick woods and suspicious places," they could "turn out a dog or two to search them."

With Easton secured, the Franklins jogged through rain and mud to Reading to confer with Governor Morris and friendly Indians. They found the governor in a swivet. Franklin's Militia Bill had provided that the enlisted men could choose their officers, with the approval of the governor and his council. The Philadelphia regiment, one of the first formed, had, not too surprisingly, elected Benjamin Franklin as its colonel. This put the governor in an excruciating bind. He knew that his employer, Thomas Penn, would foam at the mouth if he saw Franklin's name on the regimental list. Other members of the Proprietary Party were already warning Penn that Franklin was plotting a coup d'état, and his Militia Bill, as well as his march to the frontier, was part of this fiendish plan. With Franklin obviously the only man who could hold the frontier together, Morris was in no position to object to his colonelcy. In fact, just as he arrived at Reading, he got more bad news, which made the crisis all the starker. A small body of troops, sent to guard the Lehigh Gap near the ruins of Gnadenhutten, had been surprised and driven into chaotic retreat. This reduced the governor to complete collapse. He signed a "dedimus" which made Franklin in effect the military dictator of Northampton County, and rode off with the other two commissioners to sign a treaty with friendly Indians.

On January fifteenth, in weather that was unbelievably wretched, the two Franklins led 130 men out of Bethlehem for the twenty-mile march to Gnadenhutten. Rain came down in icy sheets, but the little expedition plodded grimly forward. Not till nightfall did they seek shelter in a German farmer's barn where, Franklin wrote, "We were huddled together as wet as water could make us." They stayed there the next day, trying to dry out their soaked clothes. In this damp and dreary atmosphere, with the icy rain still pouring down outside, Franklin celebrated his fiftieth birthday. That he survived this repeated exposure to a winter wilderness is the best possible proof of his remarkable physical vitality.

When the rain slackened, the little army moved out again and now, as they neared Gnadenhutten, William Franklin took over and organized the march with "great order and regularity," in the words of one eye-witness. William rode at the head of the column, with scouts probing the forest on each side of the trail. The troops on horseback followed him, and behind them were the jittery remnants of the companies that had survived the Indians' surprise attack on January third. In the center of the column William placed his father with the five wagons of baggage, tools, and stores. Two companies of foot soldiers composed the rear guard. More scouts swept the forest on the flanks and the rear of the column, reducing the possibility of a surprise attack to a minimum.

They were grimly aware that the enemy was all around them. Shortly before they left Bethlehem, thirteen farmers came to Franklin and asked him for guns and ammunition, so they could go back to their homesteads and rescue their cattle. Straggling along in the rain, they neglected to keep the priming pans of their muskets dry, and an Indian war party killed eleven of them. One of the weeping, hysterical survivors staggered into the Franklin camp with the harrowing story. Grimly Franklin issued orders to his men that made it clear he was ready to wage war with equal ferocity. He told them "forty dollars will be allow'd and paid by the government for each scalp of an Indian enemy so killed, the same being produced with proper attestations." [65]

Through the narrow Lehigh Gap the little army trudged, while every man struggled to obey Franklin's order to keep his musket dry and glanced jumpily up at the steep-sided "hills like Alps," as one young officer called them. It did not require a military genius to see that this narrow pass was their only line of retreat, and a handful of Indians could block it. A few hours later they emerged at the western end of the pass, to stand on the plateau before the ruins of Gnadenhutten. A young ensign with the expedition described the grisly scene. "All silent and desolate, the houses burnt, the inhabitants butchered in most shocking manner, their mangled bodies for want of funerals exposed to birds and beasts of prey—" [66] The soldiers needed no urging from the two Franklins to go to work. They knew that a stockade was far more reliable protection than any hope of retreat through the narrow pass at their backs. Quickly they buried the dead, threw up crude huts for living quarters, and began hacking at the plentiful timber around the ruined village. In seven days they had completed a fort, 455 feet in circumference, in spite of the fact that every other day it rained so hard they had to take shelter in their huts.

Ever the experimental observer, Franklin noticed that on the days that the men worked hard they were "good natured and cheerful." On the idle days they were mutinous and quarrelsome, "finding fault with their pork, the bread and &c, and in continual ill-humor." Franklin did his best to bolster their morale. As usual, his approach was original. The little army had a chaplain, a zealous Presbyterian named Charles Beatty. He came to Franklin complaining that the men "did not generally attend his prayers and exhortations." As a stern soldier of the Lord, he was probably hoping that Franklin would issue an order forcing the men to worship under threat of punishment. Franklin mused for a moment, stared out at the bleak Pennsylvania hills, and then with a small, shrewd smile noted that, along with pay and provisions, the men were guaranteed a gill of rum a day, half in the morning and half in the evening. He hoped the chaplain would not think it beneath the dignity of his profession, Franklin said, but if he would "act as steward of the rum . . . if you were to deal it out, only just after prayers. . . ."

This struck Mr. Beatty as a very good idea. He recruited a few chaplain's assistants to measure out the rum.

"Never were prayers more generally and more punctually attended," said Franklin.[67]

Deborah Franklin, worried about her husband, sent him a steady stream of food and wine, including roast beef, roast veal, minced pies and apples. Although he was actually sleeping on a pine-board floor, Franklin cheerfully told her that he was spending his nights in "feather beds, in warm blankets." With more truth he assured her that all the members of his staff drank a health to her at every meal, because there was "always something on the table to put them in mind of you." [68]

The moment the fort was completed, William Franklin ordered their lone cannon, a swivel gun, mounted in one of the angles and fired as an act of defiance to the Indians, who they knew were watching them from the surrounding forest. With the fort as a ready refuge, strong patrols were ordered out to "scour the adjacent country." On the neighboring hills they found proof that the Indians were watching them closely. Interested in everything, Franklin trudged up the slopes to inspect the savages' hiding place, and made careful notes on how they kept themselves warm, almost within sight and sound of the white men's fort. "A common fire on the surface of the ground would by its light have discover'd their position. . . . They had therefore dug holes in the ground about three feet in diameter, and somewhat deeper. We saw where they had with their hatchets cut off the charcoal from the sides of burnt logs lying in the woods. With these coals they had made small fires in the bottom of the holes, and we observed among the weeds and grass the prints of their bodies made by their laying all round with their legs hanging down in the holes to keep their feet warm." [69]

Franklin always maintained a lively interest in Indians and Indian affairs. He had seen too much of their cruelty and caprice to maintain any idealistic notions about the noble Redman. But he was always in favor of treating them fairly and honestly and later he was to prove himself ready to defend them at the risk of his life, against the cruelty of aroused whites.

Franklin named the stockade at Gnadenhutten Fort Allen, after the Chief Justice of Pennsylvania, and sent out working parties to construct two smaller stockades, fifteen miles to the east and west. With these crude bastions completed and manned, there was a string of forts along the mountain wall strong enough to repel the ordinary Indian war party of perhaps a dozen or two dozen warriors. On February first came a letter from Governor Morris urging Franklin to return to Philadelphia for an early meeting of the Assembly, which he had just called. Coincidentally, into Fort Allen strolled Colonel William Clapham, a professional Indian-fighter from New England. Franklin promptly appointed him commander, paraded the garrison, and turned over the fort to him. In a few days he was back in Philadelphia, General no more. [70]

XII

Franklin's military career was not quite over. The governor had finally signed his colonel's commission, and the Philadelphia regiment was proudly drilling on High Street each evening, under their officers', and

occasionally their colonel's, approving eyes. Franklin's political opponents decided to form a rival military organization and solicited recruits
for something called "the Regiment of Philadelphia County," headed by
one Jacob Duché. A brisk competition ensued, which soon led to sniping
in the newspapers. A Duché partisan sneeringly demanded whether "six
and seven hundred men and boys, a greater part of whom had never
appeared at a formal muster, can be called a 'well-trained regiment of a
thousand men.' "

William Franklin, intensely proud of his military reputation, undoubtedly spurred his father to retaliate. There were also sound political
reasons for a show of strength. Thus, on March 11, *The Pennsylvania
Gazette* carried an announcement in the largest, blackest type available
in the print shop of Franklin and Hall.

> *The Regiment of Philadelphia is to be reviewed on Tuesday next,
> the 16th inst., at 2 o'clock in the afternoon on Society Hill. By order
> of the Colonel.*

Swallowing hard, the Proprietary Party, including Governor Morris,
former Governor Hamilton, and other dedicated enemies of the philosopher of electricity took their place on a reviewing stand at the present
junction of Front and Pine Streets in Philadelphia. Around them
thronged a "vast concourse of people," according to the reporter in *The
Pennsylvania Gazette,* who may well have been Franklin himself.

Companies wheeled by the right flank and the left flank on Society Hill
and fired by platoons, while the spectators oohed and aahed with delight.
The artillerymen then demonstrated their dexterity with their brass cannon, firing a thunderous twelve-round salute in a single minute. The
soldiers were so delighted with themselves they escorted their colonel
back to his house and fired a farewell salute which shattered several
glasses in his electrical laboratory and terrified Deborah and Sarah
Franklin.[71]

The sight of Franklin at the center of this martial column inspired vast
alarm in the Proprietary Party. They rushed home to their desks and
fired off warnings to Thomas Penn. They found still more ammunition,
a few weeks later, when Franklin departed on another post office
tour, this one south to Virginia. William Franklin was determined to
miss no opportunity to heighten the colonel's reputation, and he persuaded some thirty grenadiers and twenty young officers in the regiment
to accompany Franklin to the ferry, about three miles from town. To

complete the dramatic effect, someone barked an order and out of their scabbards slid the grenadiers' long, gleaming swords. This display made Franklin look like Genghis Khan en route to a massacre, and when Thomas Penn heard about it, he exploded. No one had ever paid *him* such an honor, when *he* visited Pennsylvania. It was, he fulminated, reserved for princes of the blood royal. Now he was sure that Franklin was plotting to make himself the Cromwell, or possibly the King, of Pennsylvania.

Once more Penn renewed his intrigues against Franklin in London, this time going directly to Sir Everard Fawkener, the Postmaster General, asking him to write a letter all but ordering Franklin to become a Proprietary yes-man or lose his job. Fawkener, more impressed by Franklin's reputation than by Penn's whining, wrote what his American deputy called "a gentle admonition" and no more. Not a line did Penn write to Franklin, thanking him for the fifty days he had spent on the frontier in the worst of winter. Penn's petty meanness caused Franklin to regard him with almost total contempt. When his London friend, Peter Collinson, warned Franklin that Penn and his relations were "greatly incensed" at his military flourishes, Franklin tartly replied, "I am not much concerned at that because if I have offended them by acting right, I can, whenever I please, reverse their displeasure by acting wrong." [72]

XIII

Meanwhile, Franklin luxuriated in Virginia's early spring, "gay as a bird," as he wrote Deborah. He again met George Washington, en route home from a fruitless journey to Boston, where he had attempted to get the new British commander-in-chief, William Shirley, to back him in his claim that his provincial commission as a colonel of the Virginia militia was superior to the commission of a captain in the regular British Army. He was disgusted by his failure to get a clear statement of support from Shirley, who ruled instead that the Maryland officer with whom Washington was contending was not acting in the capacity of a regular, and therefore had to take orders from the Virginia colonel. Washington wanted himself and his men to be incorporated into the regular military establishment. But Shirley could only shrug his shoulders and say that would depend on orders from London. Although Franklin hardly needed the lesson, it was one more example of how disunited the colonies were and how inchoate was the British system of trying to govern them down to the most minute details from Whitehall Palace.

From Virginia, Franklin sailed to New York, where, to his relief, he learned that the British treasury would make good on the farmers' wagons and horses, lost in Braddock's disaster. He met and was unimpressed by Braddock's haughty slow-thinking replacement, Lord Loudon, who was planning an attack on the French fortress of Louisburg, on Cape Breton island. He was far more taken with one of Loudon's subordinates, Lieutenant Colonel Henry Bouquet, a Swiss-born officer, who had organized the Royal Americans, one of the first regiments recruited in America to win official recognition from London as equal in rank and prestige to British regular outfits. Bouquet was a thoughtful soldier, who made a point of seeking out the best American advice he could find. He and Franklin had several long discussions about how best to quiet the frontier. Between them, they conceived the idea of a military colony, which would be a buffer state between the settled colonies and the Indian nations.

Franklin had already suggested a similar idea to the Albany Congress. Now, stimulated by Bouquet, he wrote a letter to a man in England who could play a powerful role in making the idea a reality. His name was George Whitefield, and he was one of the greatest preachers of his time. He had been one of the prime movers of the "great awakening"—a religious revival which had swept the American colonies in 1735. Franklin and he became great friends when Whitefield preached in Philadelphia, and the minister and the philosopher had long earnest discussions of theology which deepened their friendship, but did not change either man's mind.

Franklin loved to tell the story of the time he had gone to see Whitefield preach, determined not to be impressed, and especially not to contribute to the inevitable collection at the close. "I had in my pocket," he said, "a handful of copper money, three or four silver dollars, and five pistoles in gold. As he [Whitefield] proceeded, I began to soften and concluded to give him the copper. Another stroke of his oratory made me ashamed of that, and determined me to give the silver; and he finished so admirably, that I emptied my pocket wholly into the collector's dish, gold and all."

Once, when Whitefield was in Philadelphia, Franklin invited him to stay at his house. Whitefield answered, "If you make that offer for Christ's sake, you will not miss of the reward."

Franklin, disliking such clerical one-upmanship, bluntly replied, "Don't let me be mistaken. It was not for Christ's sake, but for your sake." [73]

In spite of this and no doubt other rebuffs, Whitefield's friendship with Franklin remained warm. Franklin regularly published all his journals and sermons on his press. No matter what he thought of his theology, Franklin regarded him as an enormously powerful leader of men.

It was from this viewpoint that the philosopher wrote to the preacher, suggesting that they join forces to found a colony in the Ohio Valley. Sitting on the edge of the wilderness at Gnadenhutten the previous winter, Franklin had listened with freshly opened ears to his son William expounding the wealth and beauties of the Ohio country. The visit to the wilderness had awakened memories of William's trip west with George Croghan in 1748. Then, Franklin had been inclined to ignore his enthusiasm as the effusion of a seventeen-year-old. Besides, Franklin considered himself pre-eminently a city man; he had little or no appetite for roughing it on the frontier, which he had never visited. But his foray through the Lehigh Gap had awakened a hitherto slumbering strain of adventure in his nature. It was hardly surprising; there is always much of the explorer in the scientist, and much of the scientist in the explorer. Franklin was also pleasantly surprised by how well his rugged frame had withstood the hardships of the wilderness. "There are a great number of things besides what we have, that used to seem necessary to comfortable living, yet we have learned to do without them," he had written to Deborah.[74]

But Franklin's overriding motive was his concern for William. For all his warnings that he had no intention of leaving his son a handsome patrimony, Franklin was much too paternal a man to avoid this strongest of fatherly desires. At Albany he had proposed an Ohio colony as an abstract proposition, in the hope that the Crown might undertake it. But now, to his old friend Whitefield, he revealed a larger ambition. Together, they might found it, organize it, govern it. More and more, the idea became to Franklin the perfect project with which to close his career.

"What a glorious thing it would be," he told Whitefield, "to settle in that fine country a large, strong body of religious and industrious peoples! What a security to the other colonies; an advantage to Britain, by increasing her people, territory, strength, and commerce. . . . Life, like a dramatic piece, should not only be conducted with regularity, but methinks it should finish handsomely. Being now in the last act, I begin to cast about for something fit to end with. Or if mine be more properly compar'd to an epigram, as some of its lines are but barely tolerable, I am very desirous of concluding with a bright point." [75]

X I V

Back in Philadelphia, Franklin was engulfed once more in the old controversy between the Assembly and the Proprietors. A new governor, William Denny, arrived and at a public dinner presented Franklin with the Gold Medal of the Royal Society. After dinner, over several decanters of Madeira, the governor tried to lure Franklin into the Proprietary camp, promising him "every service" in his power, plus "acknowledgements and recompences" from Thomas Penn. Franklin coolly replied that he bore no personal enmity against the Penns but he intensely disliked seeing a man push his own interests at the expense of the people. He was ready to cooperate in every way to restore harmony in the province. He only hoped, he added, that the governor's freedom of action was not bound by "the same unfortunate instructions" that had hamstrung his predecessors.

Denny's eyes fell, he drank his Madeira, and said nothing.[76]

No sooner was the Assembly convened than the familiar battle began again. Franklin and his followers were outraged to discover that the 5000 pounds generously donated by Penn to the war effort consisted of back rents in Pennsylvania which they would have to collect. Then came a new disaster. The fort at Gnadenhutten was stormed by the Indians, while half of the garrison was skating on the Lehigh River. Colonel Clapham, the professional soldier Franklin had put in charge, had been too much of a disciplinarian for the militiamen, and they had connived to get him fired. Without him, the garrison's organization had evaporated and now the fort, constructed at the expense of so much time, money, and effort, was a pile of charred logs and the frontier was exposed to war parties again.

Worse, the Indians were now bolstered by French troops; a French officer had even been captured not far from Easton. From New York, Lord Loudon was demanding cash from Pennsylvania to support his northern offensive. Reluctantly the Assembly decided to raise 100,000 pounds for the King's use by taxing "all estates, real and personal." This included the Proprietors' estates, but when they submitted the bill to the governor and his council, these worthies proceeded to demand so many exceptions in the Penns' favor that the Assembly exploded in fury. Marching en masse through the streets, they delivered a scorching "remonstrance" to the governor, which said in part: ". . . . The Proprietaries professed willingness to be taxed . . . can be intended only to amuse and deceive their superiors; since they have in their instructions excepted . . . so much of their vast estate, as to reduce their tax as far as it appears to us, below that of a common farmer or tradesman." When the governor querulously insisted on following his instructions, the Assembly ripped off another resolution: "That a commissioner or commissioners, be appointed to go home to England, in behalf of the people of this province, to solicit a removal of the grievances we labour under by reason of proprietary instructions, &c." The Assembly then named the Speaker of the House, Isaac Norris, and his good friend, Benjamin Franklin, as these emissaries to London. Norris declined. He was old and ill. But Franklin quietly accepted, calling the nomination "a high honour." [77]

It was the first gleam of that bright point with which Benjamin Franklin dreamt of ending his life. But he, of course, did not see it that way. It was something else—a chance to enjoy a world even more fascinating than the wilderness beyond the mountains—the great metropolis of London, summit of imperial power. Best of all, he would take William with him. Together, they would "go home" and cement the already strong bond between father and son, beyond the range of Deborah Franklin's jealous tongue.

The timing was especially propitious as far as William was concerned. He had lately contracted a violent passion for poetess Elizabeth Graeme, daughter of one of the first families of Philadelphia. Elizabeth's father was Dr. Thomas Graeme, owner of Graeme Park, a sumptuous country estate twenty miles outside Philadelphia which his wife had inherited from her father, former Governor Sir William Keith. The house and grounds, complete with gardens, lakes and a 300-acre deer park, were the showplace of the colony. Obviously, William thought big. But Elizabeth's parents took an exceedingly dim view of an alliance with the Franklins. They were among the premier members of the Proprietary Establishment, and could not think of Benjamin Franklin without visualizing a pair of horns sprouting from his head. It was obvious to Franklin that William was heading for nothing but humiliation at the hands of these snobs. So the father was doubly pleased to dangle before his son an invitation that was superior to Elizabeth's poetic charms.[78]

It is easy to imagine the two Franklins walking home that evening through the winter twilight, the father holding back the invitation until they reached the door of William's lodging. Then with a sly smile, Benjamin wondered aloud if William could separate himself from Philadelphia's belles for a few years in London.

Almost certainly there was no argument, once the word London was spoken. No matter how sophisticated Philadelphia might see itself, with its talk of being the second city of the empire, London was still a magic name, evoking dreams of power and pleasure that no young man could resist. William rushed upstairs and began packing.

Deborah Franklin was hardly as enthusiastic. Although Franklin urged her to come with them, he knew in advance that she had an obsessive dread of sea voyages, and nothing in the world, not even his powers of persuasion, could get her aboard a ship. But her husband had long since become expert at wearing out her temper tantrums with a smile. Poor Richard for the year 1757 may have reflected, in two of his epigrams for January, thoughts which were very much on their author's mind.

> *Nothing dries sooner than a tear.*
> *He that would rise at court, must begin by creeping.*[79]

Book Two

Irresistible England

I

The *General Wall,* one of a half-dozen small, swift packet ships that carried mail, newspapers, dispatches, and other official matters between the British Isles and the American dominions of his Majesty, George II, bounded across the placid waters of the Atlantic at an astonishing thirteen knots. The ship was named for an Irishman, Richard Wall, who had entered the diplomatic service of Spain and played a peacemaker's role as his adopted country's ambassador to London.[1] In one of the trim ship's comfortable cabins, with a generous supply of good books and good wine, sat a man who was on his way to London to become an equally unlikely ambassador. Benjamin Franklin, of course, did not think of himself as wearing that august title, in the summer of 1757. He was simply the agent of the Pennsylvania Assembly, en route to London to do legal battle with the descendants of William Penn, the "Proprietors," as they were known in Pennsylvania. But if the almost 2,000,000 citizens of the thirteen American colonies on the continent of North America had by some miracle become united enough to send a single man to represent them in the capital of the British Empire, this fifty-one-year-old retired printer from Philadelphia would have been the logical candidate.

In the summer of 1757, the idea of an ambassador from America to England would have struck Benjamin Franklin as ridiculous. In his mind, England and America were one country—the mighty British Empire in which he gloried to be a moderately distinguished citizen. He was, in fact, sailing to England on a flood tide of patriotism, hoping to persuade Parliament to replace the venal government of the Penns with a royal charter, putting the province directly under the government of the King and Parliament.

The other passengers aboard the packet added substance to this sense of Anglo-American unity. Captain Archibald Kennedy, Jr., of the Royal Navy, was the son of Franklin's good friend, the wealthy Collector of Customs of the Port of New York. Boston-born John Temple was on

his way to England to seek a government job with the help of his powerful relatives, Lord Temple and George Grenville. William Franklin found
Temple's ability to drop the names of England's great and near-great
totally fascinating, and the two quickly developed a warm friendship.[2]

But the favorite topic of conversation aboard the *General Wall* was
not the intricacies of English high society. Every time a lookout bawled,
"Sail ho," a shiver of apprehension ran through the ship. The chances
were all too good that the sail was a French privateer, roaming the seas
in search of British ships as part of the global war that was now raging
between France and England in India, North America, Europe, and
on all the seas and oceans. Every time the warning was bawled, Walter
Lutwidge, the profane, salty skipper of the *General Wall,* piled on every
piece of canvas aboard, and left his pursuers lagging far behind. The
captain liked to boast that his little packet was the fastest thing under
sail on the Atlantic, and he had won money from Captain Kennedy
earlier in the voyage when the naval officer had refused to believe they
could hit thirteen knots.

In spite of this continuous tension, Ben Franklin spent much of the
voyage in his cabin, hard at work on a new edition of *Poor Richard's
Almanack*. With more time than he usually had at his disposal, he
paged through earlier editions—now numbering a full twenty-five—and
decided to make this one special. Beginning with his usual salute to the
courteous reader, Poor Richard observed that "nothing gives an author
so great pleasure as to find his works respectfully quoted by other
learned authors." Alas, this was a pleasure which Poor Richard had
"seldom enjoyed." Just a little peevishly, he pointed out that he was
"an eminent *Author* of almanacks" now for a full quarter of a century,
but his brother "authors" for some reason had been "very sparing in
their applauses." If his writings hadn't produced some "solid pudding,"
their small return in the way of praise would have discouraged him.
His only satisfaction had been, in his "rambles," to hear people repeating
one of his adages with "as Poor Richard says" at the end of it. "I own,"
he added, "that to encourage the practice of remembering and repeating
those wise sentences, I have sometimes quoted *myself* with great
gravity."

But now Richard had something truly joyous to report. He had
stopped his horse to watch a crowd milling impatiently around a
marketplace, waiting for merchants to open their shops for a special
sale. Everyone was conversing on the "badness of the times," and

finally someone called to "a plain, clean old man with white locks."

"Pray, Father Abraham, what think you of the times? Won't these heavy taxes quite ruin the country? How shall we ever be able to pay them? What would you advise us to?"

Father Abraham proceeded to preach a sermon on making and saving money, quoting Poor Richard every second line. It wasn't just the government that was taxing them, he told his listeners. Even if the government taxed the people one-tenth of their earnings, "Idleness taxes many of us much more and . . . sloth like rust consumes faster than labor wears, while the used key is always bright, as Poor Richard says. But doth thou love life then do not squander time, for that's the stuff life is made of, as Poor Richard says. How much more than is necessary do we spend in sleep! Forgetting that the sleeping fox catches no poultry, and that there will be sleeping enough in the grave, as Poor Richard says. If time be of all things the most precious, wasting time must be, as Poor Richard says, the greatest prodigality, since, as he elsewhere tells us, lost time is never found again; and what we call time enough always proves little enough: let us then be up and be doing, and doing to the purpose; so by diligence shall we do more with less perplexity. Sloth makes all things difficult but industry all easy, as Poor Richard says; and he that rises late, must trot all day, and shall scarce overtake his business at night. While laziness travels so slowly that poverty soon overtakes him, as we read Poor Richard, who adds, drive thy business, let not that drive thee . . ."

Before Father Abraham was through, Richard was the most thoroughly quoted author in history. How seriously Franklin took the whole idea is evident from the words Poor Richard added to the old gentleman's harangue. "People heard it and approved the doctrine, and immediately practiced the contrary, just as if it had been a common sermon; for the vendue [sale] opened and they began to buy extravagantly, notwithstanding all his cautions and their own fear of taxes." Richard admitted "that the frequent mention he made of me must have tired anyone else, but my vanity was wonderfully delighted with it, though I was conscious that not a tenth part of the wisdom was my own which he ascribed to me, but rather the gleanings I had made of the sense of all ages and nations." But Father Abraham made one convert, at least. "Though I had at first determined to buy stuff for a new coat," Richard said, "I went away resolved to wear my old one a little longer. Reader, if thy will do the same, thy profit will be as great as mine." [3]

To Franklin this was one more piece of Poor Richard's ironic fooling, and a pleasant literary exercise to while away the days at sea. But others, with more literal minds, for whom the name Franklin was already synonymous with wisdom and science, seized on this collection of adages as a master plan by which every man could become rich. One of the first was Franklin's nephew, Benjamin Mecom, son of his sister Jane, who was working as a printer in Boston. He published Father Abraham's "speech" on March 30, 1758, and a miscellany of other writings, including Franklin's song, "I Sing My Plain Country Joan." Before the end of the eighteenth century, the discourse was reprinted 145 times, and for millions of people, Benjamin Franklin became synonymous with industry and thrift, a thoroughly erroneous image which soon degenerated into the pursuit of money above all other values.

Meanwhile, the *General Wall* continued her cat and mouse game with French privateers. Finally, came that happiest of calls from a seaman in the bow of the packet: "And bottom at seventy fathoms, sir." The news, gained from the ship's 240-foot deep-sea lead line, told Captain Ludwidge he was about sixty miles west of the Scilly Islands, twenty-five miles off the southwest tip of England. A strong fresh wind was blowing, and the *General Wall* was fairly leaping from swell to swell. Captain Ludwidge made a dubious, daring decision. Night was falling, but instead of beating back and forth in deep water until dawn, he decided to pile on canvas and run hard for their destination, the port of Falmouth, in spite of the risks of the rocks and shoals of the Scilly Islands. Fifty years before, an entire British squadron, commanded by an admiral with a remarkable name, Sir Cloudsley Shovel, had blundered to disaster on those night-shrouded rocks, and more than one lone sailor had done likewise, in more recent years. But there was a lighthouse on the rocks now. That considerably lowered the risk and made the nighttime dash a better bet than a daytime run through the Channel, which was thick with French privateers.

Everyone went to bed. But no one, except Captain Ludwidge, seems to have gone to sleep. With all its canvas spread, the *General Wall*'s studding sails, set outboard of the regular square sails to add speed, obscured the vision of the helmsman and the rest of the watch. They depended for their safety on a lookout in the bow. Again and again the passengers heard the helmsman call, "Look well out before, there."

"Aye, aye," answered the watchman.

But after five or six hours the call and the response became mechanical. The rise and fall of the ship in the heaving sea, the hiss of the water past the prow became a lullaby for the lookout. Meanwhile, the tricky currents at the mouth of the Channel pushed the ship closer and closer to the Scilly rocks. About midnight, a heavy swell hit the *General Wall* at a slight angle, causing her to yaw. A moment later, as she crested the surging hump of sea, a cry of terror burst from the lips of the crew. There, almost dead ahead, was the Scilly lighthouse, blazing at them like a demon's eye. The two Franklins and the other passengers rushed onto the deck to stare at what looked like certain doom. They were so close, to Franklin the light looked "as big as a cart wheel." [4]

Frantic shouts. Where was Captain Ludwidge? Still snoring below. It was a crisis that demanded a man of action, and Archibald Kennedy, Jr., proved that he was not wearing the epaulets of a Royal Navy captain by chance. "Wear ship," he roared to the helmsman. The heart of every sailor skipped a beat. In the brisk night wind, this maneuver, turning the ship to leeward, where she would get the full impact of the gale, could easily send the masts overboard like broken toothpicks. Then it would be the rocks for sure. But there was neither room nor time for the much safer maneuver of coming about into the wind. With a gulp, the helmsman threw the wheel over.

The rigging whined and the masts groaned like living things, but they survived, and in a moment the *General Wall* was racing away from destruction, into the deep waters of the Channel once more. Morning found them shrouded in a thick fog. But the leadsman, at work in the bow, reported soundings that convinced Captain Ludwidge he was very close to Falmouth. The passengers paced the deck impatiently until about nine o'clock. Then "like the curtain at a playhouse," Franklin wrote, the fog magically lifted, and there was Falmouth, "the vessels in its harbor and the fields that surrounded it."

It was Sunday, July 17, 1757, and as they went ashore, they heard church bells ringing. "We went thither immediately," Franklin told his wife in the letter he wrote later that day, "and with hearts full of gratitude, returned sincere thanks to God for the mercies we had received." Anyone who had had such a narrow escape from death might have written those words. But the next sentence was pure Franklin. "Were I a Roman Catholic, perhaps I should on this occasion vow to build a chapel to some saint; but as I am not, if I were to vow at all, it should be to build a lighthouse." [5]

I I

William Franklin was much more literal and earnest in his report of their narrow escape. He had, it was true, an excuse. Behind him in Philadelphia he had left Elizabeth Graeme, sighing soulfully over his departure. Her parents still grumpily refused William's offer of marriage. Nevertheless, the young couple had parted with pledges of undying love, and William hastened to assure his "dearest Betsy" that he had survived the risky passage. "Let the pleasures of this country be ever so great, they are dearly earn'd by a voyage across the Atlantick. Few are the inducements that will tempt me to pass the ocean again, if ever I am so happy as to return to my native country." [6]

Nevertheless, at twenty-six, William was looking forward with considerable eagerness to a sojourn in the mother country. Not a little of this anticipation could be traced to his father, who had visited England himself as a young man of eighteen. But what a difference between young Benjamin's first visit, and this comfortable, carefree journey. Benjamin had arrived with scarcely a penny in his pockets, a victim of an older man's cruel deception. William Keith, the bombastic, debt-ridden governor of Pennsylvania, had conned young Franklin into going to England to buy equipment for a printshop, on Keith's nonexistent credit, and a flatulent promise of his support in Philadelphia. The stranded youngster had fortunately been able to make a living as a journeyman printer. He stayed in London for eighteen months, reading everything he could lay his hands on, during a decade when Jonathan Swift, Alexander Pope, and Daniel Defoe were writing some of their best books. The experience became a major influence in expanding Franklin's mind, and especially in refining his literary style.

With Benjamin's reminiscences to whet their appetites for London, the two Franklins were in an entirely agreeable harmony as they rode through the beautiful southwest countryside at the height of summer. They stopped on Salisbury Plain to view the looming massive monuments of Stonehenge and ponder for a moment the mystery of these relics of a forgotten era, when men worshipped strange, unknown gods. At the village of Wilton, they paused again to view the ruins of still another age, the crumbling monastery and chapel which had once dominated the little village, when England paid allegiance to the Pope of Rome. Nearby was Wilton House, the seat of the Herbert family, the Earls of Pembroke, one of those who had risen high on the wreckage of medieval England. The Franklins paid a visit to their magnificent mansion and gardens, crowded with paintings and Roman statuary.

As they drew nearer to London, the great city seemed to act as a sort of magnet on the philosopher of electricity and his son. They covered no less than seventy miles in a single day of furious riding, and "only a little fatigued," clattered into London town on the night of July 26, 1757.[7] At the Bear Inn, on the Southwark side of old London Bridge, they found dinner and rooms.

Even in this first evening's glimpse, Franklin must have been staggered by the immense growth London had experienced since his visit in 1725. For more than three miles the city spread along the north bank of the Thames, wrapped in clouds of sooty smoke that gave it, on gloomy days, an almost infernal appearance. On the south side of the river, the town of Southwark, eventually incorporated into Greater London, was rapidly matching its parent.

The next day, the two Franklins went to the offices of the textile merchant, Peter Collinson "in Grace Church Street at the Red Lyon." It was through his Quaker friend, John Bartram, the leading botanist of Philadelphia, that Franklin had been prompted to send to Collinson reports of his historic experiments with electricity. Collinson combined his Quaker faith with a keen interest in science, and his many contacts with members of the Royal Society had been instrumental in awakening this select body to Franklin's electrical achievements.

Collinson's political connections were equally powerful. He was a close friend of Lord Bute, the Scottish peer who was tutoring young Prince George, the future King. Another friend was the enormously wealthy Henry Fox, better known as Lord Holland. But for the moment at least, politics was not on Peter Collinson's mind. His pleasure at meeting Benjamin Franklin in person was immense. He sent messengers scurrying across London to other friends Franklin had made with his busy pen. Soon there was a veritable congregation of Franklinophiles embracing Benjamin and William in Collinson's offices.

One of the first to arrive was William Strahan, a fellow printer who published, among others, Dr. Samuel Johnson. For over a decade Strahan had been selling books through Franklin's Philadelphia shop. The two shared many things besides their trade. They were about the same age, both bulky, hearty types, who loved good jokes, good food, and good wine. They had long been kidding each other about the size of their waistlines. Informing Strahan that he was coming to England, Franklin had written, "If a fat old fellow should come to your printing house and request a little smouting [part-time work], depend upon it, 'tis your affectionate friend and humble servant." [8]

It is a tribute to Franklin's remarkable gift for friendship that he could make admirers out of men before they even met him personally. From America, his friend John Bartram was writing him another testimonial of this gift. "Pray, my dear friend, bestow a few lines upon thy ould friend. . . . They have a magical power of dispeling melancholy fumes and chearing up my spirits, they are so like thy facetious discource in thy southern chamber when we used to be together." [9]

But not everyone in England was in love with Benjamin Franklin. Robert Hunter Morris, ex-governor of Pennsylvania, had sent a letter to Ferdinand John Paris, the Penns' attorney, shortly after Franklin sailed, in which he called him "a sensible, artful man, very knowing in American affairs, and was his heart as sound as his head, few men would be fitter for publick trust; but that is far from being the case, he has nothing in view but to serve himself, and however he may give another turn to what he says and does; yet you may be assured that is at the bottom and in the end will shew itself." [10]

If Franklin had any illusions about solving the problems of Pennsylvania quickly, he soon lost them when he conferred with still another friend of Peter Collinson, Dr. John Fothergill. One of the most gifted physicians in England, he was intimately acquainted with the great and near-great and he made it clear to Franklin that there was no hope of altering the constitution of Pennsylvania at this time. England was fighting for her life and the men in charge of the government simply had no interest in the relatively trivial quarrel between a single colony and its proprietors. Moreover, Ferdinand John Paris' long years of experience in dealing with American affairs had given him a web of connections on the various boards and councils that governed the empire. Until Franklin acquired some contacts of his own, it would be madness to fight Paris on terrain that favored him so heavily. Far better, Fothergill advised Franklin, to approach the Proprietors directly and see if they would agree to negotiate the differences between them and the province on a personal basis.

Meanwhile, there was the more immediate business of getting Franklin and his son settled in London. No one stayed permanently at inns like the Bear. His friends found four rooms for him at No. 7 Craven Street, the home of an agreeable, well-to-do widow named Mrs. Margaret Stevenson. The house was only a few steps from the Thames, and near the government buildings in Whitehall Palace, and the Houses of Parliament, places the Franklins would be visiting frequently. Outgoing and cheerful, Mrs. Stevenson hit it off with the Franklins instantly, and so did her pretty teenage daughter, Mary, known as "Polly." Franklin was soon a contented member of the Stevenson household, a second father to Polly, and almost a husband to Mrs. Stevenson.

He set up his electrical apparatus in one of his rooms, and friends and acquaintances flocked to see his performances. Another Franklin diversion was the musical evening at which he and some chosen friends played (Franklin could perform on both the harp and the violin) their favorite songs. The Stevensons quickly got used to running a semi-public house. They also cheerfully adjusted to other Franklin idiosyncrasies, such as swimming in the Thames, and his daily air baths. From his boyhood, Franklin had been an enthusiastic swimmer. On his first visit to England, he had, on a bet, leaped into the Thames and swum over three miles. He attracted so much attention, he considered setting up a swimming school, and making it his career. His air baths were part of his belief that fresh air was good for the health. Each morning he invariably arose, opened all the windows in his room and sat around for an hour or so in the altogether. Not even winter weather discouraged him. He frequently recommended the practice to other people, but almost everyone who tried it received "such a shock to their constitutions," in the words of one man, that they rarely continued it. Apparently only a man of Franklin's rugged physique could tolerate frigid temperatures in the buff.

One unexpected visitor who showed up on Franklin's doorstep was James Ralph. The sight of him transported the American philosopher back once more to his first visit to London, almost four decades earlier. Ralph had come with him from Pennsylvania, dreaming of finding recognition, and perhaps greatness, as a poet. Alexander Pope had extinguished this hope by skewering him in the second edition of *The Dunciad*. Ralph had turned to writing plays and had been successful in a modest way, producing *The Fashionable Lady,* the first play by a born American to reach the boards in London. Later, he displayed a wicked pen in the political wars of the 1740s and early '50s, so wicked, in fact, that he was given a pension by the ministers in power at the time on the promise that he would abandon all political writing.[11] Eleven years older than Franklin, Ralph had left behind him a wife and daughter in Pennsylvania and had acquired another family in London. He was near the end of a somewhat feckless life, and he was pathetically swept by nostalgia for America and the family he had abandoned so long ago. Franklin brought him news of them, largely the uncertain consolation that they had gotten on pretty well without him. He also promised that he would say not a word about them to Ralph's English wife.

Perhaps it was the sight of Ralph that inspired Franklin to journey down to the old printing house in Wild Court, Lincoln's Inn Fields, where he had worked as a boy, and lent the penniless poet Ralph unwise amounts of his earnings. There was the same press he had sweated into so long ago. Franklin introduced himself to the two men who were working it, and sent out for a gallon of beer. "Come, my friends," he said, "we will drink together; it is now forty years since I worked like you at this press as a journeyman printer." The printers eagerly joined in his toast, "Success to printing." [12]

I I I

In spite of his friends' advice to negotiate directly with the Penns, Franklin decided it would do him no harm to try a little politicking with men of influence. When he heard that John Hanbury, a wealthy Virginia tobacco merchant, was anxious to meet him so that he could introduce him to Lord Granville, the president of the Privy Council and one of the most powerful men in England, Franklin arranged to make the visit the very next morning. Naturally he charmed Hanbury, and soon he was riding through London's odoriferous streets to Lord Granville's house. If he had stopped to think about Lord Granville, Franklin might not have rushed so eagerly to meet him. He was married to the sister of Lady Juliana, wife of Thomas Penn, and this inclined him to take a very jaundiced view of Franklin's role in Pennsylvania and the whole argument between the Assembly and the Proprietors.

After a few polite questions concerning politics and the war effort in the colonies, Granville suddenly tore into Franklin with pretentious arrogance. "You Americans have wrong ideas of the nature of your constitution," he intoned. "You contend that the King's instructions to his governors are not laws, and think yourselves at liberty to disregard them at your own discretion." He proceeded to lecture Franklin on how instructions to the governors were drawn up, first by judges, then the Privy Council, and finally signed by the King. "They are then so far as relates to you, the law of the land, for the King is the legislator of the colonies."

Franklin instantly saw it would be a waste of time to attempt to ingratiate himself with Lord Granville. His mind was already made up. So Franklin coolly and politely read him a lecture in return. "This is new doctrine to me," he said. "I always understood from our charters that our laws were to be made by our assemblies, to be presented indeed to the King for his royal assent. But that being once given, the King could not repeal or alter them. And as the assemblies cannot make permanent laws without his assent, so neither can he make a law for them without theirs."

Granville told him he was totally mistaken. With a polite bow Franklin took the mortified Hanbury by the arm and departed. Although he chatted cheerfully with the Virginia merchant on the way back to Craven Street, and showed not the least sign that he was ruffled by the encounter, Franklin found it deeply disturbing. If the rest of the English nobility thought this way about the colonies, the future of freedom for Pennsylvanians—or any other Americans—was grim. As soon as he could find pen and paper in his rooms, Franklin wrote down the conversation so that he could be sure to remember it accurately.[13]

Not a little chastened, Franklin now made an appointment with Thomas Penn. That acerbic gentleman must have been more than a little annoyed to see the Pennsylvania agent debarking in front of his house at Spring Garden from a carriage that would be the envy of a London nabob. Franklin was spending twelve guineas a month on it, partly for the convenience, but also because he wanted Penn and the rest of London to know that Americans were not penniless parvenus, crawling to beg favors from their masters.

Franklin did his best to negotiate amicably with Thomas Penn. "I am ready to do everything in my power to settle the differences between us," he told him. But Penn declined to discuss anything. His brother John was vacationing in the country and he stalled until he returned a week later. The Penns then said that they wanted to see something in writing, and Franklin prepared a brief memorandum which he entitled "Heads of Complaint." The Penns turned this over to Ferdinand John Paris, who tried to blitz Franklin with a hundred legal quibbles and objections. Franklin refused even to talk with him, insisting that face-to-face negotiation with the Penns was essential. They then went into a near frenzy of pretended rage because he had neglected to address them by their proper titles, "True and Absolute Proprietories of the Province of Pennsylvania."

Whether it was the Penns or London's traditionally miserable fall weather that sapped Franklin's vitality, he suddenly came down with one of the most serious illnesses of his life. For two months he was a feverish, coughing, wheezing captive of Dr. John Fothergill, who pumped him full of the atrocious remedies of the day. That Franklin survived is one more tribute to his rugged physique. While he was suffering, the Penns gave him no rest. They launched a propaganda attack in the newspapers, slandering the Pennsylvania Assembly and the Quakers as the cause of all the colony's woes. William Franklin replied with a vigorous rebuttal which was printed three times in the London papers, as well as in the prestigious *Gentleman's Magazine,* thanks largely to the influence of William Strahan. It was also reprinted in *The Pennsylvania Gazette,* and William made the mistake of writing to his beloved, Elizabeth Graeme, asking her opinion of it.

Elizabeth replied waspishly that she considered the letter—and Benjamin Franklin himself—"a collection of party malice," and deplored William's "attachment to a party." This was the end of the romance. A few months later, William wrote to a mutual friend explaining that he had broken off all contact with Betsy. She had changed, he said. Otherwise, how could she have called the man "whom she knew to be next to her in my heart" such nasty names? William then lashed into the Penns. He had written his public letter to rebut their "little dirty aspersions [which] they were continually publishing." He hoped, he said, that once the Proprietors were publicly refuted, and they saw they could not win a propaganda war, they might listen to "proposals for a friendly adjustment" of the argument. But for now, his father had laid aside "all thoughts of an amicable accommodation." [14]

The reason for this harsh decision was a face-to-face confrontation Franklin finally had with the Penns early in 1758. He pointed out to Thomas Penn that his father William's charter expressly guaranteed the Assembly of Pennsylvania all the powers and privileges of freeborn subjects of England.

"My father granted privileges he was not by royal charter empowered to grant," Penn coolly replied.

"Does this mean," Franklin asked, "that your father was a liar when he published this statement all over England and Europe to attract settlers? Are you saying that those original settlers were deceived and betrayed by William Penn?"

Penn burst into a shrill, triumphant laugh. The expression on his face reminded Franklin of a swindler who had just successfully cheated someone in a horse trade. "If they were deceived it was their own fault," Penn said. "The royal charter was no secret."

Franklin found it hard to believe his ears, or restrain his temper. This man was prepared to sacrifice his father's character for the sake of a few hundred pounds a year from his precious rents. Remembering the incident later, Franklin said he felt at that moment "a more cordial and thorough contempt" for Thomas Penn than he ever felt for any other living man.

But, as usual, Franklin controlled his temper. "The poor people who took your father at his word trusted him," he said. "They didn't think they had to consult lawyers to deal with William Penn."

With an expression on his face that made his contempt all too visible, Franklin walked out. [15]

By this time, William had enrolled as a student at the Middle Temple and was combining the law with his work as his father's right-hand man. In a letter William Strahan wrote to Deborah Franklin, William was described as his father's "friend, his brother, his intimate and easy companion." The letter was part of a campaign which Strahan launched to entice Deborah to London. He unleashed all his considerable verbal powers on Mrs. Franklin, pointing out that no one had been lost on a voyage from Philadelphia in recent memory, annotating the pleasures of London and hinting that he would like very much to meet her daughter Sally, and perhaps marry her to one of his sons. He also did not hesitate to point out a less obvious reason for her to risk the voyage. The ladies of London liked her "amiable" husband every bit as much as his men friends and if Deborah was wise, she would come over "with all convenient speed" to look after her interests. "Not but that I think him as faithful to his Joan as any man breathing," Strahan hastily assured her. "But who knows what repeated and strong temptation, may in time, and while he is at so great a distance from you, accomplish." [16]

The hearty Scotsman was wasting his time. Deborah's aversion to long sea voyages remained intense. Franklin tried to bridge the distance between them with presents. Even during his two months of illness, he managed to buy a "crimson satin cloak" for Deborah, and William sent Sally "a scarlet feather muff, and tippet" and a box of fashionable linen to make her a dress. Deborah responded with a blizzard of advice on taking better care of himself. Was he airing his shirts? If he burned wood instead of coal, the air in his house would be purer. Did he have warm night clothes? Was Peter, his Negro slave, misbehaving as usual? Wasn't he any help in running errands? Why didn't he get a carriage?

Franklin did his best to reassure her, and inadvertently gives us some interesting glimpses of life in London at the time. Burning wood was a waste of time, unless you could persuade everyone in the city to do it. "The whole town is one great smoky house, and every street a chimney, the air full of floating sea coal soot." Peter was behaving quite well and now knew London well enough to "go anywhere" on errands. Mrs. Stevenson took good care of his shirts. As for his night clothes, he was sleeping in a "short callico bed gown with close sleeves, and flannel close footed trousers; for without them I get no warmth all night." Franklin blamed this new susceptibility to cold not on his illness, but on growing older "apace." [17]

I V

Franklin was soon moving around London once more, acquiring new friends. One of these was Richard Jackson, a lawyer with whom he had corresponded when in America. Something of an amateur scientist, like so many other eighteenth-century intellectuals, Jackson was an immensely successful attorney, with a keen interest in American affairs. He served as agent for the colony of Connecticut and knew everyone worth knowing in London, as well as everything in the arcane reaches of the common law. Friends dubbed him "Omniscient Jackson" because of his encyclopedic knowledge of government, science, and literature. Through him, Franklin met an extremely influential nobleman, Lord Shelburne, not yet at the very summit of power, but close enough to it through his blood relationship to William Pitt, "the Great Commoner," and leading figure in Parliament, who was rapidly emerging as the most important man in the British government.

Around the world, the British war effort against France was going badly. Disaster after disaster engulfed British Armies in America and on the continent, largely because the British system was government by clique and men in power selected generals and admirals on the basis of family connection and influence rather than talent. Pitt was a ferocious opponent of this approach and more and more Englishmen were beginning to see the wisdom of his denunciations.

Meanwhile, Jackson and the two Franklins put their heads together and decided that the only answer to the Penns' intransigence was an all-out assault. With William Franklin doing most of the research, and Jackson most of the writing, they began preparing *An Historical Review of the Constitution and Government of Pennsylvania*. Again, how closely William was allied with his father in this project was visible in Franklin's own words, when he proudly told a friend in Philadelphia that in the preparation of the book (which is what it finally became) "Billy afforded great assistance and furnished most of the materials." Franklin called Jackson "one of the best pens in England," but there was one part of *An Historical Review* that was pure Benjamin Franklin—the motto which appeared on the title page. *"Those who would give up essential liberty, to purchase a little temporary safety, deserve neither liberty nor safety."* [18]

To the Penns, the *Historical Review* was a literary bombshell. Franklin wrote cheerfully to Isaac Norris, the Speaker of the Pennsylvania Assembly, shortly after it came out: "The Proprietor is enraged." [19]

In between these labors, which absorbed the better part of a year, Franklin and his son found time to do a little vacationing in the English countryside. One of their most important journeys was a pilgrimage they made to the little village of Ecton, home of their English ancestors. The tour included a stop at the University of Cambridge, where Franklin admitted his "vanity was not a little gratified by the particular regard shown by the Chancellor and Vice Chancellor of the University and the heads of colleges." [20] But Franklin mentioned this only in passing, while he wrote pages to Deborah about the pleasure of retracing, with his son at his side, the quiet country roads and village bypaths which generations of Franklins had trudged before him. Together they examined the Ecton parish register which contained Franklin family records going back 200 years. The wife of the rector at Ecton showed them the family gravestones in the little churchyard. They were so covered with moss that "we could not read the letters till she ordered a hard brush and basin of water, with which Peter scoured them clean, and then Billy copied them," Franklin said.

Best of all, in nearby Wellingborough, they found Mary Fisher, a daughter of Benjamin's uncle, Thomas Franklin. She could remember clearly the departure of Benjamin's father and his wife and two children to New England in the year 1685, and was able to tell them stories of Franklin's father in the years before he emigrated. When she heard that Franklin had paid the rector of Ecton to copy off the names of all the Franklins in the county register, beginning with the first of the line in the middle 1500s, Mrs. Fisher told him, "You have taken more care to preserve the memory of our family than any other person that ever belonged to it." [21]

Franklin was vastly pleased to discover that the old stone building in Ecton where generations of his ancestors had lived was still known as the "Franklin house." He was especially fascinated by stories villagers told him of Thomas Franklin, Mary Fisher's father. On a smaller scale he obviously bore strong comparisons to Benjamin himself. Thomas was "something of a lawyer, clerk of the county courts, and clerk to the Archdeacon in his visitations; a very leading man in all county affairs and very much employed in public business. He set on foot a subscription for erecting chimes in their steeple, and completed it, and we heard them play. He found out an easy method of saving their village meadows from being drowned, as they used to be sometimes by the river, which method is still in being; but when first proposed, nobody could conceive how it could be; but however they said if Franklin says he knows how to do it, it will be done. His advice and opinion was sought for on all occasions by all sorts of people, and he was looked upon she said by some as something of a conjurer." Thomas Franklin died on January 6,

1702, four years to the day before Benjamin Franklin was born. William was so struck by this fact, he gasped: "Had he died on the same day . . . one might have supposed a transmigration." [22]

From Ecton, Benjamin and Billy journeyed on to Coventry and Birmingham, pausing along the way to visit numerous relatives of Deborah. Their favorite was Mrs. Salt, whom Franklin described as "a jolly, lively dame, both Billy and myself agree that was extremely like you, her whole face has the same turn, and exactly the same little blue Birmingham eyes." [23] To his sister, Jane Mecom, in Boston, Franklin reported that he met another relative, Robert Page, widowed husband of their cousin, Jane Franklin. In an old letter from Boston dated July 4, 1723, Page pointed out to Franklin the words, "Your Unkle Josiah has a daughter Jane about twelve years old, a good-humour'd child."

"So Jenny, keep up your character," Franklin wrote, "and don't be angry when you have no letters." [24]

Franklin sent gifts of Madeira and other presents to many of these relatives, by way of thanking them for their hospitality. The whole trip was obviously a profound experience, both for the father and for the son. To see with one's own eyes the deep roots of the Franklin family in the English soil and countryside, to hear a cousin such as Mary Fisher proudly say that the Franklin family had "acted that part well in which Providence had placed it, and for 200 years all the descendents of it have lived with credit, and are to this day without any blot in their escutcheon, which is more than some of the best families, i.e. the richest and highest in title can pretend to," almost certainly deepened that strong sense of unity with the mother country which was an inclination of both Franklin's heart and head. Even more touching were Mary Fisher's words that she was "the last of my father's house remaining in this country" and the obvious pleasure she took to see "so fair hopes" of the family's continuance "in the younger branches." [25] For William Franklin, the experience was perhaps even more meaningful. It provided an emotional, visceral link to the mother country, which he had already found immensely attractive, in its London guise.

The following summer the two Franklins took an even more ambitious journey to Scotland. By now Franklin had become convinced that these summer journeys were good for his health, not only because they relaxed him, but because they enabled him to escape London's perpetual sooty smog. Scotland was almost inevitable as a Franklin destination for several reasons. His closest friend in England, William Strahan, was a

Scotsman, and like all his countrymen who flocked to London by the thousands, he never ceased singing the praises of his native heaths. Even before Franklin came to London, Strahan had glorified Scotland so effulgently that Franklin good-naturedly remarked that if all his fellow printer said was true, he might well move there. Two other close friends, Doctors John Fothergill and John Pringle, were Edinburgh men. Moreover, the University of St. Andrews had awarded Franklin a degree of Doctor of Laws early in 1759, no doubt at the instigation of one, or all, of these influential Scotsmen. He was eager to visit the school, and collect the degree in person.

As Franklin and his son rode out of London on August 8, 1759, the guns of the Tower of London boomed, and from Westminster Abbey the mighty bells pealed triumphantly. Swarms of citizens gathered on corners to discuss the latest war news. English and German troops fighting in Europe under Prince Ferdinand of Brunswick had routed the French Army at Minden. In spite of the fact that the day was clear and hot, victory bonfires were soon burning on almost every street. Drunken mobs celebrated by smashing and robbing the shops of the Quakers who had refused to support the war effort.

Up through Hertfordshire in their chaise rode the two Franklins, reveling in the beauties of the English countryside in its summery prime. Behind them rode Franklin's slave, Peter, on horseback. At Birmingham, they paused to hobnob with the great English printer, John Baskerville, who was just introducing his now-famous typeface.

A few months later, back in London, Franklin would defend the Baskerville typeface by hoaxing a fellow scientist, who insisted that Baskerville's strokes were too thin and narrow, hurt the eye, and would soon blind all the readers in the nation. The man insisted that he could not read a single line of Baskerville type without pain. Franklin stepped into another room, found a sample of a completely different typeface—Caslon—ripped it out of the book and brought it back with him. Handing it to the complainant, he protested that he could not see any of the disproportions he mentioned. The gulled critic went down the page pointing out one instance after another of Baskerville's supposedly too thin and narrow strokes. He even vowed that he could not read the specimen without feeling the acute pain he had mentioned. "I spared him that time the confusion of being told that these were the types he had been reading all his life with so much ease to his eyes . . ." Franklin told the delighted Baskerville.[26]

On to Scotland rolled the Franklins, along the less traveled western road. The route carried them past the fishing village of Whitehaven, where a lad of twelve had just enrolled as a seaman's apprentice for a trading voyage to Virginia. The son of a Scots gardener from Kirkcudbright, his name was John Paul. Later he would add a third name, to give it an English flavor, and call himself John Paul Jones. But the agent of Pennsylvania, not being a seer in spite of his reputation as a conjuror, jogged past, without the smallest notion that some day in the unseen future, he would raise the money to enable this young man to humiliate the English flag which they both currently revered.

At Edinburgh, the city fathers made both Franklins "burgesses and guild brethren of this city in the most ample form." But the Franklins soon left the incredibly dirty and aromatic Scottish metropolis where each night, at ten o'clock, all the residents emptied their "luggies" containing the day's garbage and human offal into the street with the historic cry, "Gardy loo" (Gardez l'eau), while below them frantic pedestrians shrieked, "Haud your hand!" Their destination was Prestonfield, the handsome estate of the noted Scottish physician, Sir Alexander Dick, and his beautiful wife Janet. After a week in this lovely house at the base of Arthur's Seat, with its spectacular view of the Dudingston Loch, the Franklins continued their journey across Scotland to St. Andrews University. If they expected a second Oxford, or the neat, orderly bustle of Harvard or Yale, they were disappointed.

St. Andrews was in an advanced state of decay and the town itself had grass growing in the streets. On all sides were gaunt, wrecked houses where Scottish nobles had once held splendid court. The principal industry seemed to be getting drunk—there were no fewer than forty-two ale houses. The college, founded in 1413, and once the pride of Scotland, had dwindled to a mere twenty students. When Samuel Johnson visited it a few years later, he was appalled to discover that the library was locked and no one could find the key. Fortunately, it was not missing for Franklin's investiture, which took place in the library.

A later rector of St. Andrews has recreated the scene in the ancient room overlooking the college garden with its 200-year-old thorn tree, planted by Mary Queen of Scots. The senior members of the university took their seats in chairs around the graduation stool in the center of the floor. Behind them stood a group of scarlet-gowned students. Franklin knelt on the graduation stool in front of the president of the Senate. While he recited the traditional Latin formula, he placed on Franklin's head the school's historic "graduation cap," a "fragile square of black velvet" which had supposedly belonged to John Knox, and was made the symbol of admission to the university when the Reformation changed Scotland from Catholic to Presbyterian. Then the hood of scarlet silk lined with white satin was draped over the shoulders of the kneeling philosopher and he rose, no longer Mr. Benjamin Franklin, but "Doctor Franklin." [27]

It was a title which Franklin's friends religiously used for the rest of his life. This alone is evidence of how much it meant to him. Franklin moved in a world where so many men had titles handed to them at birth, or had acquired them thanks to their good fortune in being able to afford an expensive education. There is a certain poignancy in the eagerness with which he grasped this tribute from a second-rate college, a hint that for all the honors he received, Franklin never forgot the days when he wandered the streets of Philadelphia and London, a homeless nobody, with only his wits and his muscular energy to recommend him.

From St. Andrews, the two Franklins returned to Edinburgh, where they met still another remarkable Scotsman, Henry Home, Lord Kames, a character so unique he attracted the biographical attention of his fellow Scotsman James Boswell before he became enamored of Samuel Johnson. Kames was sixty-three when he first met Franklin in the Inner House of the Law Courts. Tall, lean, with scarcely a tooth in his head, he was a dedicated practical joker, with a wildly sardonic sense of humor. Once, he presided at the murder trial of Matthew Hay, a friend with whom he used to play chess. When the jury brought in a verdict of guilty, Lord Kames roared from the bench: "That's checkmate for you, Matthew!"

Like Franklin, Kames had been born poor and worked his way to fame, beginning as an indentured clerk. He was a remarkably industrious man, who had educated himself by independently studying mathematics, logic, ethics, metaphysics, natural philosophy, as well as the law. He and Franklin immediately took to each other, and Kames invited Franklin to spend a week with him at his country seat in Berwickshire, on their road back to London. The lovely country house, a few miles from the River Tweed and the English border, is still standing in its beautiful park with its formal gardens rich in trees, including four that Franklin planted during his visit.

Kames and Franklin found each other irresistible. They spent hours together on rides along the River Tweed, and whiled away the evening hours demolishing the Kames House wine cellar. They exchanged their bawdiest stories and tried a few practical jokes on each other. In this department, Franklin dazzled Kames with a stunt which he reserved for a few select victims. As they neared the bottom of a bottle, one night, and Lady Kames began to send dark looks in the direction of her husband, Franklin remarked that the world would be much better off if it followed the Bible's teaching on tolerance.

Kames cocked a Presbyterian-trained eye at Franklin and demanded to know what passage in the Good Book taught that. If anything, the Bible taught intolerance.

Franklin asked for a Bible, assuring Kames that he would find the passage for him in a moment. A Bible was forthwith produced, and Franklin flipped the pages for a minute, then gave a satisfied exclamation, and began to read.

1. *And it came to pass after these Things, that Abraham sat in the Door of his Tent, about the going down of the Sun.*

2. *And behold a Man, bowed with Age, came from the Way of the Wilderness, leaning on a Staff.*

3. *And Abraham arose and met him, and said unto him, Turn in, I pray thee, and wash thy Feet, and tarry all Night, and thou shalt arise early on the Morrow, and go on thy Way.*

4. *And the Man said, Nay, for I will abide under this Tree.*

5. *But Abraham pressed him greatly; so he turned, and they went into the Tent; and Abraham baked unleavened Bread, and they did eat.*

6. *And when Abraham saw that the Man blessed not God, he said unto him, Wherefore dost thou not worship the most high God, Creator of Heaven and Earth?*

7. *And the Man answered and said, I do not worship the God thou speakest of; neither do I call upon his Name; for I have made to myself a God, which abideth alway in mine House and provideth me with all Things.*

In the same carefully cadenced Biblical prose, the story told how Abraham, in a fit of righteousness, drove the old man out of his house. For this, he was sternly rebuked by God and warned that his seed would be afflicted "four hundred years in a strange land."

Kames' long jaw sagged. Lady Kames looked at least as bewildered. As good Presbyterians, they thought they knew every page of their

Bible. Yet not a word of this was familiar to them. Frantically, the Scottish jurist demanded to know from what book of the Bible Franklin was reading.

William Franklin had been sitting quietly to one side, his eyes down, while his father read. Now he looked up, and the two Franklins' eyes met. They both burst out laughing.

In an idle hour Franklin had written this parable on persecution, perfectly imitating the style of the Good Book. He had then committed it to memory. Whenever he wanted to befuddle someone who was too dogmatic in his religious opinions, or too pretentious in his knowledge of the scripture, he treated him to this little performance.[28]

Before they parted, Lord Kames was begging Franklin to send him the entire dossier of his collected works. Franklin was equally charmed by Kames and the other Scotsmen he had met. Back in London he told Kames, "On the whole I must say, I think the time we spent [in Scotland] was six weeks of the *densest* happiness I have met with in any part of my life." [29]

V

In the months between these excursions, Franklin continued his war with the Proprietors. He took advantage of every opening for a blow against their case, however small. When the Assembly of Maryland got into a dispute with the descendants of Lord Baltimore, Franklin published an anonymous letter, attacking Proprietary government in that colony. He had his Philadelphia neighbor Charles Thomson write a history of the diplomacy of the Pennsylvania Proprietors with the Delaware Indian tribe. The heart of the story was the famous Walking Treaty of 1737. The Penns had purchased from the Delawares a tract of land which was, the Indians agreed, to be the extent of a one and a half day's walk. Both the Indians and the agents of the Proprietor knew precisely what this distance meant—the average number of miles an Indian would cover on the trail, moving at a normal pace. The Penns hired two of the best athletes in Pennsylvania, put them through a rugged course of training, and then turned them loose to take the walk. They almost doubled the normal distance, and the Indians, with considerable justice, felt they had been outrageously defrauded. In 1757, the Penns tried to claim some of this disputed land in the Wyoming valley, and began ousting the Indians from the district. In London, Franklin backed the Indians, and the Crown found in their favor.[30]

In the face of this steady, aggressive pressure the Proprietors began giving ground. From an arrogant refusal to permit either taxation or even an inquiry into the net worth of their estates, they grudgingly agreed that Franklin had a right to find out their annual income, and finally, by mid-1760, they were conceding that the estates could be taxed, and their only desire was to see it done "on the same calculation with the estates of other people." [31] This was in itself a major retreat, but they obviously hoped to fight it out along this new line for a good many years by quibbling over the legal process by which the value of their estates would be appraised.

Although he was making progress, Franklin became more and more disgusted with the Penns as human beings. It is an interesting insight into Franklin's psychology. Spacious though his mind was in constructing political theories, he was intensely human in his personal relationships. Once a man lost his respect, he seldom regained it, and he was likely to be treated with surprising ruthlessness. He did not even deign to apologize when he learned that Thomas Penn had gotten his hands on a letter Franklin had written to Isaac Norris in Pennsylvania, describing the scene in which Penn gave up his father's honor in the argument over the charter. Penn was particularly incensed that Franklin said his manner resembled a "low jockey."

Franklin scolded Norris for being so careless with his letters, but he coolly rejected a reproof from Dr. John Fothergill, although he admitted that it had given Penn an excuse to break off negotiations with him. To Norris and other friends, Franklin made it clear that in his opinion negotiating with the Penns was a waste of time. It would be far better to dump them by petitioning the King to turn Pennsylvania into a royal province, directly under the government of the Crown. "The government and property of a province should not be in the same family," he told one of his correspondents. " 'Tis too much weight in one scale." [32]

To Joseph Galloway, his chief political lieutenant, Franklin wrote: "I still see nothing in the letter but what was proper for me to write, as you ought to be acquainted with everything that is important to your affairs and it is of no small importance to know what sort of a man we have to deal with, and how base his principles. I might indeed have spar'd the comparison of Thomas to a *low jockey,* who triumph'd with insolence when a purchaser complain'd of being cheated in a horse . . . but indignation extorted it from me, and I cannot yet say that I much repent of it. It sticks in his liver, I find . . . Let him bear what he so well deserves."

Showing a flash of Poor Richard, Franklin added that by filching private correspondence, Penn had confirmed the old adage, "Listeners seldom hear any good of themselves." [33]

This attitude of course sent the Penns into a frenzy of resentment. From their point of view it was nothing less than revolution. But that was Franklin's way. Once he felt that the moral value of a relationship was undermined, he was ruthlessly ready to dispense with it.

Simultaneously, the two Franklins became involved in another more subtle controversy, emanating from the undercurrent of alienation and misunderstanding that appeared from time to time in the relationships between the colonies and the mother country.

The war in America had drawn the attention of the average English-man to the colonies for the first time in decades, and it also had brought together in often uneasy partnership American and British troops in forays against the French. Like General Braddock, more than a few British officers found the undisciplined Americans irritating, and echoes of their dissatisfaction drifted back to London. William Strahan's paper, *The London Chronicle,* printed several letters purportedly by a British officer who had served in New York and Pennsylvania. The writer as-sailed the Americans mercilessly, reserving some particularly venomous barbs for New Englanders. He accused them of hating the Church of England in the style of their Puritan ancestors, of being boorish and infected with "a leveling spirit" that menaced anyone who grew too rich. As for their soldiering, the Britisher said he would willingly ex-change 6000 American militiamen for 2000 regulars any time. "Three hundred Indians with their yell throw 3000 of them into a panic so total they shoot each other instead of the enemy," he claimed. "For this reason regulars feared to venture into the woods with them on the most trifling expedition."

Boston-born Benjamin Franklin could not let these insults go unanswered. In a long, deliciously acid letter, he demolished these carping critics. It was odd, he said, that they found Americans boorish in dress and language, since they wore nothing but clothes that were made in Britain. As for language, every new book and pamphlet worth reading appeared in America within a few months of its publication in England. As for their fighting abilities, Franklin ticked off one success after another on the American continent, where the vast majority of the troops were Americans. "One ranging captain of a few provincials, Rogers [Robert Rogers], has harassed the enemy more on the frontiers of Canada and destroyed more of their men than the whole army of regulars," Franklin noted. As for Americans growing panicky at the Indian yell—Franklin inevitably pointed to Braddock's disaster, where regulars were thrown into a panic by the "yells of 3 or 400 Indians, in their confusion shot one another, and with five times the force of the enemy, fled before them destroying all their own stores, ammunition, and provisions." The reason regulars hated to venture into the woods, Franklin wryly suggested, was more likely "a concern for their scalps" than the fear that they might be shot by blundering Americans.

Franklin next proceeded to castigate the tendency of the writer to blame all the British disasters on provincials. He recited a roll call of British defeats in the West Indies and on the continent, in this and earlier wars, and sardonically lamented that it was a pity no provincials were involved in them. "Our commanders would have been saved the labor of writing long apologies for their conduct. It might have been sufficient to say, *Provincials were with us!*" Then, in a soothing final paragraph, Franklin called for an end to this kind of bickering.

He pointed out that the province of Massachusetts had voted money to erect a monument to George Lord Howe, killed in the attack on Ticonderoga. Americans admired "the worth and bravery of the British troops." Moreover, he knew that most regular officers were more than willing to allow the provincials their "share of merit." In fact, they were delighted to discover that "the children of Britain retain their native intrepidity to the third and fourth generation in the regions of America; together with that ardent love of liberty and zeal in its defense, which in every age has distinguish'd their progenitors among the rest of mankind." Brave men, fools, wise men, and cowards are intermixed in every nation and in every army and it was silly and unjust to make "national reflections." Panegyrics, on the other hand, were far more acceptable, and

Franklin "boldly" announced that he was ready to say that "the English are brave and wise; the Scotch are brave and wise; and the people of the British colonies, proceeding from both nations—I would say the same of them." [34]

V I

The British victory at Minden was topped a few months later by the triumph of Quebec. Franklin and his son heard the good news when they were in Edinburgh and rode back to a London groggy from another round of celebrations. The war effort, unified and vivified by the driving energies of William Pitt, was producing stupendous victories around the world. The son of an earlier Prime Minister, Horace Walpole, living in foppish splendor at his retreat, Strawberry Hill, told his diary, "Victories come tumbling so over one another from distant parts of the globe, that it looks just like the handiwork of a lady romance writer." In India and in the West Indies, France was also humbled by British fleets and armies.

While the man in the street rejoiced over these triumphs, many powerful nobles, and even King George II himself, regarded them with barely disguised distaste. They hated Pitt far more intensely than they loved their country. The Great Commoner's imperious manner and total disregard of factions, his ruthless honesty, broke all the rules of establishment politics, as they were then played. This malaise among the powerful soon created a strange reaction to Britain's victories. Horace Walpole, ever sensitive to political shifts, caught it in his usual acute if limp-wristed fashion when he told his diary, "It will soon be as shameful to beat a Frenchman as to beat a woman." [35]

Franklin was dismayed by this change in the British mood. He was particularly disturbed to discover that many Englishmen were in favor of returning Canada to the French, and keeping the sugar island of Guadeloupe in the West Indies as part of the terms of an eventual peace. The idea struck Franklin as so absurd that his first reaction was burlesque. He wrote a letter to the London *Chronicle* ridiculing the reasons which he had "with great industry" procured from the pundits who were in favor of giving up this immense territory. Franklin followed this up a few months later with a penetrating pamphlet, "The Interest of Great Britain Considered, With Regard to Her Colonies and the Acquisitions of Canada and Guadeloupe."

By now the dispute over Canada had become a full-scale pamphlet and newspaper war, and in this carefully researched, superbly argued document, Franklin was very serious. He considered the arguments of the anti-Canada writers, one by one, and did his utmost to refute them with logic and facts. Those who claimed that the retention of Canada would be a source of a future war with France were wrong. On the contrary, the present war had started with disputes over territory in America, and if the French remained in Canada, the chances of another war were far greater. "The people that inhabit the frontiers," Franklin said, in an interesting observation from a man who had recently spent some time in the western woods, "are generally the refuse of both nations, often with the worst morals and the least discretion, remote from the eye, the prudence, and the restraint of government. Injuries are therefore frequently, in some part or other of so long a frontier, committed on both sides."

Other writers claimed that if Canada was added to the American colonies, and the continent made British from the coast to the Mississippi, the Americans would soon grow large and strong enough to compete with the mother country as a maritime and manufacturing power. No, said Franklin. Most Americans were farmers, and if they got more land, they would remain farmers for generations to come. Confine them to their thirteen present colonies, however, and they would begin manufacturing in order to give the landless poor a chance to make a living. Drawing facts from his essay on population, he pointed out that exports to the province of Pennsylvania had increased seventeen times in the last twenty-eight years, while the population had increased only four times.

Finally, there were writers who argued that the Americans would eventually form a union with Canada and defy the mother country. In the first place, said Franklin, speaking from harsh experience, it was practically impossible to unite the colonies because of their "different forms of government, different laws, different interests, and some of them different religious persuasions and different manners." They could not agree to unite to defend themselves against the French and Indians who were burning their towns and murdering their people. What could possibly cause them to unite against "their own nation," which "they all love much more than they love one another?" There was only one thing that could unite the colonies—"the most grievous tyranny and oppression." As long as the British government was "mild and just," and important civil and religious rights were secure, Americans would remain "dutiful and obedient." If the British government ever introduced the kind of ruthless religious and political oppression that Spain attempted in the Netherlands, anything could happen, of course. "But this I think I have a right to deem impossible," Franklin said. Summing it up, he reverted to an aphorism worthy of Poor Richard. "The waves do not rise but when the winds blow." [36]

It is, of course, impossible to estimate the impact of Franklin's pamphlet, but it was one of the most thorough arguments on the pro-Canada side and the British government did, finally, decide to keep the Canadian wilderness, and give back Guadeloupe with all its sugary riches to France.

Franklin and his friend Strahan grew equally concerned about the way Pitt's enemies and others who were simply prone to panicky emotionalism were trying to stampede England into a premature disadvantageous peace. To strike a blow against this faction, Franklin resorted to one of his favorite tricks—a literary document supposedly culled from a special source and written in a style that supported the hoax. Thus *The London Chronicle* soberly printed a letter from someone who signed himself "a Briton," introducing an extract "from the famous Jesuit Campanella's discourses addressed to the King of Spain." The writer apologized for the antiquated language. He was using a translation of a 1629 edition, but he thought the material was so apropos to England's present situation "only changing Spain for France" that it was still worth the attention of the public. The Jesuit (who was really a Dominican and actually had written such a book in the seventeenth century) proceeded to advise the King on "the Means of disposing the Enemie to Peace."

The vital thing, he told his sovereign, was to change the minds of the Enemy. How? By spending a few doubloons among "men of learning, ingenious speakers and writers, who are nevertheless in lowe estate and pinched by fortune." These fifth columnists must be instructed in their sermons, discourses, writings, poems and songs to inculcate the following points. "Let them magnify the blessings of peace and enlarge mightily thereon, which is not unbecoming grave Divines and other Christian men; let them expatiate on the miseries of warre, the waste of Christian bloode, the growing scarcitie of labourers and workmen, the dearness of all foreign wares and merchandises, the interruption of commerce by the captures and delay of ships, the increase and great burthen of taxes, and the impossibilities of supplying much longer the expense of the contest." They were also to paint the war as being fought for the advantage of a small clique, to downgrade the victories and conquests as "trivial and of little import." Above all let them "magnifie the great power of Your Majestie and the strength of your Kingdome."

The author of the letter professed to know nothing about the success of "this Jesuit" in his day. But he was sure that "the present age being more enlightened . . . such arts can now hardly prove so generally successful." [37]

In the midst of this vigorous politicking came two rude shocks. The first was personal. Franklin learned that his son William had followed not only the best but the worst of his father's example, and sired an illegitimate son whom he named William Temple Franklin. As he had done after his own misstep, Franklin insisted on William taking complete responsibility for the boy. Unfortunately, William had no income, except the modest sum he received as comptroller of the post office in Philadelphia, and this meant that Franklin had to supply most of the cash. But he did so with no evidence of a complaint, arranging for the child to board with an English family, perhaps recommended by his landlady Mrs. Stevenson, and simultaneously making it clear that he was ready to pay all the bills for the boy's expenses and education, for as long as he lived.

Franklin had hoped to create a romance between William and Polly Stevenson. But William was getting too old to take his father's advice, especially about his personal life. This resistance can also be interpreted as a groping for some way to emerge from his father's formidable shadow. Fathers and sons have been in conflict since civilization began but it was difficult, if not impossible, to sustain this instinctive warfare with a father who was as generous and good-humored as Benjamin Franklin. His account books, which he kept faithfully during his stay in London, are one long stream of loans and gifts of money to William. At one point, perhaps a little appalled by adding up how much he had spent recently, William told his father, "I am extremely obliged to you for your care in supplying me with money and shall ever have a grateful sense of that with the other numberless indulgencies I have received from your paternal affection." William declared he was ready to return to America or "to go to any other part of the world" with his father whenever Benjamin thought it necessary.[38] But this gratitude and spirit of obedience did not extend to marrying the girl of his father's choice.

The only other person with whom both father and son shared the secret of William Temple Franklin's birth was their mutual friend, William Strahan, who a few years later arranged for the boy to be placed in a school in Kensington run by his brother-in-law.

The other jarring intrusion on Franklin's London life was the arrival of William Smith, the clergyman whom Franklin had finally hired as head of the Philadelphia Academy, after seeking in vain to attract several more promising candidates. A small, intense, egotistic man, Smith had thrown himself enthusiastically into the politics of the province, and as an Anglican clergyman, found it easy to oppose the Quakers, and eventually Franklin. He discarded Franklin's original plan for a modern education and inflicted the traditional load of Latin and Greek on the Academy students, to Franklin's intense chagrin. The Propietary Establishment backed him wholeheartedly, and Smith in turn lent them the support of his facile pen in their propaganda wars with the Assembly. After a recent hot exchange, the Assembly had arrested him for libel. He had come to England ostensibly to have the Assembly's verdict overturned in the courts. The Penns embraced him as a useful ally and not only backed his suit, but encouraged him to spread slanders all around London about Franklin.

Smith repeatedly declared that Franklin had lost his popularity at home, thanks to tales other Americans brought back of his luxurious living in London. Even more vicious was Smith's assertion that Franklin's great reputation in electricity was fraudulent. Old Ben had stolen everything he knew from a fellow electrical experimenter, Ebenezer Kinnersley, Smith averred. The climax to this slander campaign came when Smith learned that Oxford University was going to grant Franklin a degree of Doctor of Laws. Smith wrote a letter to the rector of one of the colleges, repeating his assertions about Franklin's thefts from Kinnersley. This was too much, and Franklin, who normally put up with the slings and arrows of political warfare with a calm amounting almost to indifference, exploded and insisted on meeting Smith face to face. The confrontation took place at William Strahan's house. Franklin produced a copy of Smith's letter to the Oxford rector and proceeded to refute it, point by point. Smith collapsed, promised to write a letter of recantation, and escaped into the night. He never wrote the letter, and went back to slandering Franklin assiduously at every opportunity.

When Polly Stevenson heard about some of the things this curious divine was saying about the man she worshipped, she wrote a troubled letter to Franklin. Franklin's reply skewered Smith for all time. "I made that man my enemy by doing him too much kindness. 'Tis the honestest way of acquiring an enemy. And since 'tis convenient to have at least one enemy, who by his readiness to revile one on all occasions may make one careful of one's conduct, I shall keep him an enemy for that purpose." He noted that Polly's mother had once admired "the benevolent spirit" of Dr. Smith's sermons. The best answer to that puzzle, Franklin said, and the best summation of Dr. Smith was written by the poet William Whitehead.

> "Full many a peevish, envious, slanderous elf is,—in his works,— benevolence itself.
> "For all mankind—unknown—his bosom heaves; he only injures those with whom he lives." [39]

In the war with the Penns, everything seemed to be moving smoothly in Franklin's favor. So confident of victory was he that he and William planned a long tour of Ireland in the spring and summer of 1759. Then came dismaying news, teaching Franklin what influence could accomplish in English politics. In April, 1759, the governor, William Denny, had approved a money bill passed by the Pennsylvania Assembly, which taxed the Proprietary estates. When the bill arrived in Great Britain, the Penns opened a highly predictable attack on it, insisting that it exposed their estates to unfair and inequitable treatment. The two Franklins were on the point of departing for Ireland when they heard that the Committee for Plantation Affairs of the King's Privy Council had issued a report, highly favorable to the Proprietors. Hearings were scheduled, but these were almost foreordained to sustain the committee report—unless Benjamin Franklin did something, fast.

Cancelling his travel plans and hastily unpacking his bags, Franklin sent his lawyer scurrying to protest the committee report and rushed a letter to no less than the King's First Minister, William Pitt. For months, Franklin had tried to see Pitt, but the great man was too involved in running the war to worry about this minor quarrel in Pennsylvania. Franklin had finally given up, and contented himself with working through his secretaries. But now, in this crisis, he approached Pitt directly, begging him to protect the province from the rapacity of the Penns. Then, he added a postscript that was a supreme example of Franklin guile.

"Between you and I, it is said, that we may look upon them all to be a pack of d—d R—ls; and that unless we bribe them all higher than our adversaries can do, & condescend to do every piece of dirty work they require, we shall never be able to attain common justice at their hands." This was libel, among other things, but Franklin solved that problem by drawing a line through the words. William Franklin, writing to his friend Joseph Galloway, thought this was one of his father's shrewdest maneuvers. He called it "a new species of rhetoric which (as there is no hanging a man for his thoughts) would be of considerable service to those who write and publish libels, if they could get them printed in that manner." [40]

Simultaneously, Franklin recruited influential merchants who traded with Pennsylvania to petition the Board of Trade to alter the Privy Council decision. They pointed out that 100,000 pounds had already been issued in paper currency based on the money bill, and was in general circulation. If the currency was declared worthless, the finances of the whole province would be thrown into chaos.

Franklin's counteroffensive quickly overwhelmed the Penns. After numerous conferences and hearings, it became obvious to the Privy Council that some kind of compromise had to be worked out. One day, Lord Mansfield, Chief Justice of the King's Bench, asked Franklin to step into a nearby office while the lawyers were arguing.

"Are you really of the opinion that no injury will be done to the Penns' estate in the execution of the act?" Mansfield asked.

"Certainly I am," Franklin said.

"Then," said Lord Mansfield, "you can have little objection to enter into an engagement to insure that point."

"None at all," Franklin replied. [41]

The lawyers were then summoned to a conference, and Franklin and his attorney entered into an agreement, specifying certain safeguards to be amended to the disputed taxation bill, and all future bills, which assured the Penns that their estates would not be taxed at a higher rate than other lands of the same kind. The Committee for Plantation Affairs approved the compromise, and the Privy Council as a whole and the King gave their assent a few days later. Franklin had rescued Pennsylvania from possible disaster, and achieved the main objective of his mission to London.

VII

There was now no real reason for Franklin to remain in London except one—his son William. In the autumn of 1760, in one of those major spins of fate's wheel, George II toppled over in his closet, a victim of apoplexy. George III ascended the throne, and with him a new group of men entered the inner circle of imperial power. The new King was only twenty-two, and was almost pathologically devoted to the man who had been his tutor and second father, Lord Bute, a Scottish peer with pretensions to intellectual achievement and a considerable interest in science. Bute's personal physician, and soon the King's personal physician as well, was John Pringle, an equally close friend of both Franklins. In the summer of 1761, the three men took a leisurely tour of Holland and Belgium together. When they returned, the friendship was even more solidified—and so was the Franklin family ambition. Pringle was a Scotsman, and he drew into the web of influence many of Franklin's intellectual Scots friends. Soon it was only a question of what Crown appointment would be suitable for a young man of William's talents and stature. These were considerably enhanced, early in 1762, when he accompanied his father to Oxford, where Benjamin collected his second Doctor of Laws degree and William, in tribute to the role he had played in his father's electrical experiments, was made a Master of Arts.

In the spring of 1762, one of their influential friends, perhaps Dr. Pringle, sent the Franklins the very exciting news that the governorship of New Jersey was available. Until this point, William's best hope had been an appointment to the government apparatus that controlled colonial trade—perhaps a judge of the admiralty court, or a Customs officer such as his friend John Temple had become. The governorship of New Jersey was almost too ideal to be believed. It meant William would remain close to home, to his father and friends in Philadelphia. At the same time, it was even more prestigious than anything he had dared to hope for. It meant an opportunity to vault into the upper echelon of Crown officials. As governor he would deal directly with the lords who sat on the boards of trade, who held the cabinet secretaryships and places on the Privy Council. Nor was this the only reason for rejoicing. Benjamin Franklin was already convinced that the Penns had to be run out of Pennsylvania, and a royal governor replace them. What better argument for royal government than to be able to point to the honest, stable, peaceful regime of that staunch son of Philadelphia, William Franklin, governor of New Jersey? Then, there was that other, by no means forgotten dream—of founding a colony in the Ohio Valley. This was English territory now. What better way to train his son in the uses of power, to inherit the immense patrimony which this experiment would leave him?

But that was five, perhaps ten years away. The problem now was to seize the immediate prize. Absolute secrecy was necessary, because if Thomas and Richard Penn found out about it, they would turn England inside out and spend half their fortune to block the appointment. The entire negotiation was conducted with the utmost delicacy—perhaps the best possible proof that the Franklins had access to the safest, surest, and most inside route to the summit of royal power. Ordinarily appointments were solicited by a kind of group pressure which inevitably made it the gossip of the city. Franklin was admirably prepared to apply such pressure on William's behalf. But this was no longer necessary, thanks to Pringle's intimacy with Lord Bute. Before the summer of 1762 was over, the good news arrived from St. James's Palace. William Franklin was the next royal governor of New Jersey.[42]

Father, son, John Pringle, and William Strahan undoubtedly made a major inroad into London's supply of Madeira that night. Strahan was as delighted as if William were his own son.

The triumph obviously inspired William to feel that he had come into his manhood, and achieved independence at last. For several years he had pursued what one of his friends called "his West Indian charmer." Her name was Elizabeth Downes. She was from Barbados, and may well have been the reason why William declined to fulfill his father's hopes for him and Mary Stevenson. The difference between the two women tells us something about William Franklin. Mary Stevenson was an extremely intelligent, rather independent girl, with whom Benjamin Franklin exchanged long letters about science and literature, addressing her as an intellectual equal. Elizabeth Downes, on the other hand, was a sweet, lovable but deeply dependent woman, who had led an extremely sheltered life and needed the reassurance of a title and a steady salary before she could say yes to William's long courtship. Although analyzing a man at a distance of 200 years is always dangerous, there would seem to be evidence that William Franklin preferred a dependent, clinging woman to an independent one—a sign that he himself had still not completely resolved the inner insecurity which was an inevitable by-product of his birth.

Franklin was disappointed by the match, although he was too intelligent to assume that he had either the right or the power to select a wife for his son. He said nothing to William, of course, but he did reveal his feelings to Polly Stevenson. He had "once flattered himself," he wrote, that she might "become his own in the tender relation of a child; but can now entertain such pleasing hopes no more." [43]

Franklin did not stay in England to preside at William's marriage. The date was set for September, less than a week after the King had approved the final draft of William's commission as governor. Franklin saw no reason to sit around waiting for the consummation of these formalities. He had told William Strahan in July that he felt "here like a thing out of its place, and useless because it is out of its place. How then can I any longer be happy in England? You have great power of persuasion, and might easily prevail on me to do anything; but not any longer to do nothing. I must go home." [44] There was also the importance, at his age, of sailing before the winter storms made an Atlantic crossing a harrowing and exhausting ordeal.

So within a month Franklin was aboard ship at Portsmouth writing mournful farewell letters to his English and Scottish firends. His parting with Mary Stevenson was particularly sad. The young fatherless girl had come to worship Benjamin Franklin and she wept so violently her mother reproved her for making him unhappy. She wrote him a letter of apology, assuring him that her grief would cease the moment she heard he was safely arrived in Philadelphia. Then it would be enough for her to know she had "so valuable a friend in the world." [45]

Even more touching was a letter Franklin carried with him to his *Gazette* partner, David Hall, from William Strahan. The friendship between the two men had deepened steadily during Franklin's five years in England, until on Strahan's part it had become the most important relationship of his life, outside his family. The letter is a remarkable tribute to Franklin's unique personal powers, as well as a revealing glimpse of how he exercised them. Strahan began by telling "Dear Davie"

(Hall had worked as an apprentice for him before joining Franklin in Philadelphia) that Hall would never have seen Franklin's face on his side of the water "had my power been in any measure equal to my inclination." It was amazing, Strahan went on, the way Franklin with all his remarkable talents and abilities which had won the admiration and affection of "the greatest genuises of this country" was equally beloved by simple businessmen such as himself. Franklin knew how "to level himself for the time to the understandings of his company, and to enter without affectation into their amusements and chitchat." This was how he made people from all walks and levels of life "his affectionate friends." As for himself, Strahan said, "I never found a person in my whole life more thoroughly to my mind. . . . It would much exceed the bounds of a letter to tell you in how many views, and on how many accounts, I esteem and love him. . . . Suffice it to say that I part with him with infinite regret and sorrow. I know not where to find his equal, nor can the chasm his departure leaves in my social enjoyments and happiness ever be filled up. There is something in his leaving us even more cruel than a separation by death; it is like an *untimely death,* where we part with a friend to meet no more, with a *whole heart,* as we say in Scotland." Strahan went on for pages, lamenting "a separation so much the more bitter and agonizing, as it is likely to be endless." [46]

Franklin's affection for Strahan was almost as deep. He told him, in his farewell letter, that he felt so depressed on leaving England he had to admit that Strahan's "persuasions and arguments" had had their effect. "The attraction of reason is at present for the other side of the water, but that of inclination will be for this side. You know which usually prevails. I shall probably make but this one vibration and settle here forever. Nothing will prevent it, if I can, as I hope I can, prevail with Mrs. F. to accompany me." [47]

To Polly Stevenson, he wrote with even more emotion. "Adieu, my dearest child: I will call you so; why should I not call you so, since I love you with all the tenderness, all the fondness of a father? Adieu." [48]

With this tender sigh, Franklin turned his back on England and sailed home in a convoy by the leisurely southern route, stopping at the island of Madeira, and studying the Gulf Stream as they poked along. As he neared Philadelphia, one major worry began to nag at the back of his mind. What if even part of the venomous things William Smith had been saying about him in London were true? Five years was a long time, and perhaps his friends had, finally, forgotten Franklin. He had scarcely set his foot on shore before he found how totally fabricated Smith's stories were. The first friends who greeted him proudly informed him that he had been unanimously elected assemblyman once more, while at sea. Moreover, the Philadelphia Franklinophiles had plans to meet him with 500 horsemen and escort him into town like a returning hero. Franklin issued a firm no to this idea and slipped quietly home before they could assemble this military production. A few weeks later, he proudly reported to Strahan, "My house has been full of a succession of [friends] from morning to night, ever since my arrival, congratulating me on my return with the utmost cordiality and affection. . . . Excuse my vanity in writing this to you, who know what has provoked me to it." [49]

Strahan must have noted glumly that there was not a word in Franklin's letter about returning to England. Nothing is more intoxicating to a man than the combination of political power and admiring affection. This was something England could not give Benjamin Franklin, and for the moment at least, his happy memories of London days faded by comparison. He settled down in his familiar house and looked forward to the arrival of his son, the governor.

Book Three

In Darkest
Politics

I

The two big men, made even bulkier by their heavy fur coats, strode purposefully into the clawing February wind whistling down Philadelphia's Strawberry Alley. Beneath the sign, The Death of the Fox, the New York stagecoach was waiting for them.[1] In a few minutes, the horses were picking their way cautiously down Philadelphia's snow-banked streets and the two travelers looked casually out at the city both of them called home. Their memories were different, although they were father and son. Gaps are inevitable, between every generation.

Benjamin Franklin saw a city that had been good to him from the day the dirty, hungry, sixteen-year-old runaway had landed at the Market Street wharf in 1723. In the next three decades, this city on the Delaware had grown from a muddy colonial port to a sophisticated metropolis, the second or third largest city in the British Empire. Benjamin Franklin had grown with it from triumph to triumph. Now he was riding out of his winter-shrouded, red-brick city to still another triumph—the installation of his son as royal governor of New Jersey.

Beside him, thirty-two-year-old William Franklin saw a city that conformed more closely in his mind to the image of wintry reality before his eyes. No sunny contentment bathed Market Street in an unreal glow. The Philadelphia he remembered, after almost six years in England, was a place which had never wholly accepted him. The snubs he had met from the upper-class Graemes and their friends, the backhand sneers and snickers about his illegitimate birth were not memories he could easily forget, or forgive.

As a sensitive, intelligent man with an intense interest in his family, Benjamin Franklin knew and understood what William felt about these social rebuffs. He hoped that now he had made full amends to his son for the pain he had caused him in earlier years. But this was hardly the dominant motive in Franklin's mind. There is no evidence that Benjamin ever felt much guilt about the facts of William's birth. The eighteenth century was far more tolerant about sexual indiscretion than the nineteenth, or our own supposedly liberated twentieth century. The important thing was accepting full responsibility for the results—and this Benjamin had wholeheartedly done. Now, his dominant emotion was the satisfaction of having scored triumphantly on the Penns and their Proprietary allies in Philadelphia.

At the same time, there is ample evidence that William did not see himself as a mere shadow or symbol of his famous father. Although he was well aware that his father's prestige and influence had done much to win him the governorship, he also knew that he could not have won it without some substantial accomplishments of his own. His ready wit and lively manners had earned him the independent friendship of many of his father's acquaintances, such as William Strahan. The Scottish publisher said William had "a solidity of judgment not very often to be met with in one of his years." He had won his law degree and proven himself a suave but hard-hitting antagonist in the propaganda war with the Penns. Thanks to his five years as clerk of the Pennsylvania Assembly, he knew far more than any other American his own age about the intricacies of colonial politics—an absolute essential for a successful governor. His expert knowledge of military affairs was also an important asset. A governor was often called upon to raise and equip troops. If William Franklin had any moments of doubt about his right to the job— and there is no evidence that he ever did—these facts were more than enough to reassure him.

But these achievements, which won him the admiration of his father's generation, did not seem to elicit similar esteem from his contemporaries. Perhaps William spent too much time associating with older men—perhaps he had suffered too many snubs from Americans his own age. At any rate his manner impressed younger people as condescending. Philip Livingston, a New Jerseyite who was studying law in London, was anything but enchanted to learn that "the high and mighty William Franklin" [2] had become the ruler of his native colony. But the new governor was hardly inclined to worry about such carping. In one leap, he had outdistanced his whole generation, moving into the upper class of colonial America at an age when most men were still struggling to shape their careers. As a citizen of a tough-minded century, he probably took some wry satisfaction in the knowledge that Elizabeth Graeme was reported to be inconsolable over his recent marriage. The repeated assurances of her parents that William was not good enough for her had suddenly begun to ring very hollow.

If William Franklin's thoughts about Philadelphia were cold, he did not blame their temperature on his father. As the stagecoach rumbled down the road to Bristol on the Delaware, the two Franklins were soon enjoying that camaraderie which William Strahan admired. William had inherited a full measure of Benjamin's love for a good laugh, and he told a droll story every bit as well as his father. No doubt he soon had Benjamin chuckling, as he told him the latest news from Craven Street—with special emphasis on how much Polly Stevenson and her friends missed his cheerful pursuit of their kisses. Benjamin in turn soon had William chuckling, as he told him of the excitement caused by his latest invention—a musical instrument called the armonica. A series of glass jars, partially filled with water, revolved on a treadle, it created incredibly beautiful music, and it was already on its way to becoming the rage of Europe. One night, Franklin was playing the model he had brought home with him from England, and Deborah awakened downstairs. Listening to the ethereal music in the darkness, she was convinced that she had died and gone to Heaven.

But joking was soon dropped for serious talk on New Jersey politics. The Penns, who by now all but sprouted hives at the mention of the name Franklin, had been outraged at William's appointment. Obviously hoping to stir up trouble, they wrote to influential friends in New Jersey, lamenting that "the whole of this business has been transacted in so private a manner, that not a tittle of it escaped until it was seen in the public papers; so that there was no opportunity of counteracting, or indeed, doing a single thing that might put a stop to this shameful affair. I make no doubt but the people of New Jersey will make some remonstrance upon this indignity put upon them." [3]

Another English acquaintance of the Franklins wrote to a friend in Connecticut, wryly remarking, "I hear there was some difficulty in his being confirmed in his place, for in our conscientious age many scruples were raised on account of his being illegitimate, which we were strangers to till very lately." [4] Closer friends had written Benjamin, warning him about "unruly spirits" in New Jersey, who might cause William trouble. So there was a double reason for Benjamin to accompany his son on this journey. William still needed the aura of his father's prestige, to guarantee a good reception.

One of the most formidable troublemakers was William Alexander, son of Franklin's old friend James Alexander. Lord Stirling, as the son called himself, insisting on his legal right to the family's ancient Scottish title, was a contentious, argumentative man. Thanks to his knowledge of the family, Franklin was able to give William shrewd advice on how to deal with this touchy character, as well as numerous other New Jerseyites whom he had met on his trips through the state, and his visits to New York. The travelers dined at Bristol on the Delaware and found that swift-running river invisible beneath a thick shell of ice—further testimony to the harshness of winter's grip. With burlap on the wheels and on the horses' hoofs, they crossed where, in summer, a ferry would have awaited them and at Trenton found a bed in a local inn.

The next morning, they were pleasantly surprised by a visit from Sir John St. Clair, General Braddock's ex-Hussar, now retired from the British Army and settled in New Jersey. He offered them his coach, pulled by four fine horses, and they were quick to accept. Later in the morning, the three men rolled through the frozen New Jersey countryside toward New Brunswick. The conversation turned first to England, and Franklin was soon reiterating to St. Clair the deep, almost passionate affection he felt for the mother country. Little more than a month earlier he had written to his friend Strahan: "God bless you and let me find you well and happy when I come again to England; happy England! . . . In two years at farthest I hope to settle all my affairs in such a manner, as that I may then conveniently remove to England, provided we can persuade the good woman to cross the seas." In a letter to another English friend, he exclaimed: "Why should that petty island, which compared to America is but like a stepping stone in a brook, scarce enough of it above water to keep one's shoes dry; why, I say, should that little island, enjoy in almost every neighborhood, more sensible, virtuous and elegant minds, than we can collect in ranging a hundred leagues of our vast forests!" [5]

Sir John wanted to hear all they could tell him about the young king, George III, whose coronation the Franklins had attended. Was he as virtuous and high-minded as people said? Both Franklins emphatically agreed that he was a paragon. All omens, political, personal, and military, pointed toward a reign that would reap an unequalled harvest of glory and prosperity for the people of his stupendous empire. The Seven Years War with France was sputtering to a close with the British flag flying over one-fifth of the globe. Canada was conquered, Havana had just fallen to an Anglo-American army, the vast subcontinent of India and the coasts of Africa had been cleared of their once-proud French enemies.

This talk of victories inevitably made Sir John and the Franklins think back eight years to the days when they had first met. How hopeless things had seemed after Braddock's death, with the frontier towns naked to the Indian's scalping knife, and the French triumphant everywhere! Then William Pitt had taken charge of the British war effort, and victory climaxed victory in dizzying succession, until France was prostrate, and George III became King of the greatest empire since men began to write history.

The travelers slept that night in New Brunswick, the standard stopover for the New York stagecoach. The next morning, on the road to Perth Amboy, they had another pleasant surprise. A half-dozen of the most prominent gentlemen in Middlesex County arrived in their sleighs to pay their respects to the new governor. Then down the snowy road came a glittering spectacle—the Middlesex troop of horse, a local militia unit. The winter light glistened on their plumed helmets and upraised sabers as they saluted the new governor and about faced to escort him into Perth Amboy. By noon they had arrived in that pleasant village of 200 houses, on the shores of Raritan Bay. There they were greeted by the outgoing governor, Josiah Hardy, and several members of his council, as well as the mayor and other officials of the town. New Jersey had two capitals, Amboy for East Jersey, Burlington for West Jersey; the oddity was a relic of earlier days, when the colony had been divided into the separate provinces.

The new governor and his father proceeded to the Governor's Council Room in the courthouse and there his commission was read. The language was redolent with royal authority.

> *George the Third by the grace of God of Great Britain, France, and Ireland King, Defender of the Faith &c. To our trusty and well beloved William Franklin, esq. . . . Know you that we reposing especial trust and confidence in the prudence courage and loyalty of you, the said William Franklin, of our especial grace certain knowledge and meer motion, have thought fit to constitute and appoint and by these presents do constitute and appoint you the said William Franklin to be our Captain General and Governor in Chief in and over our province of Nova Caesarea or New Jersey . . .*[6]

While his father and "a numerous concourse of people" (as one newspaper reported) looked on with smiling approval, William Franklin placed his hand upon a Bible and swore to obey and uphold the authority of George III in the province of New Jersey.

Two days later, after receiving a loyal address from the mayor and

Common Council of the city of Perth Amboy, and replying to it with commendable brevity, the fledgling governor returned to New Brunswick, where he met an equally warm reception. The address of the mayor and "commonalty" was as rich in royal sentiments as the governor's commission. "From His Majesty's known goodness and tender regard for his subjects, even in this distant part of his dominions, we rest satisfied and are persuaded that the reins of government are happily placed in the hands of Your Excellency," they told Franklin. The governor in return congratulated them for their loyalty "to the best of princes."

From New Brunswick, the Franklins rode on to Princeton, where Samuel Finley, the president of the college, welcomed them with an even more eloquent address. "From your being entrusted with so honorable and important a commission by the father of his country, the royal patron of religion, virtue, learning, and whatever is good, and from an education under the influence and direction of the very eminent Doctor Franklin, Your Excellency's honored father, we cannot but assure ourselves, that you will view this institution, erected for the best purposes, with a favorable eye." [7] Finally, the Franklins reached Burlington, the West Jersey capital, where there were still more polite addresses and replies, and cordial personal greetings and congratulations from the leading local citizens.

The trip was a triumph from start to finish. Not a single nasty word was spoken, not a hint that anyone resisted or was inclined to resent the new governor. Contentedly, Benjamin Franklin wrote to his friend William Strahan that he "had the pleasure of seeing [William] received everywhere with the utmost respect and even affection of all ranks of people." As they left Burlington to recross the Delaware on the way back to Philadelphia, Benjamin Franklin must have pondered for a moment the oddity of the way their triumphant procession had retraced much of his first journey across New Jersey as a runaway Boston apprentice. He had landed at Perth Amboy, hungry and feverish after a miserable trip by boat from New York, and trudged the fifty miles to Burlington on foot, in rainy October weather, befriended only by an innkeeper who liked to talk about books, and a lonely old woman who was eager to talk to anybody. What a difference forty years had made.

But Benjamin did not get a chance to share any of these thoughts with William. The excited young governor was much too busy talking about himself, and the relief he felt at the warm reception from his subjects. Already his agile mind was analyzing the intricate local politics of

New Jersey, deciding whom he should name for vacancies on his Council, whether he should establish his residence in Burlington or Perth Amboy. So the contented father and the happy son, two devoted—and well-rewarded—servants of the King, rode back to Philadelphia, mercifully unaware of the years ahead.

I I

In June, Franklin was back in New Jersey, to attend a sumptuous public dinner given to William by the town of Elizabeth. By now the new governor was firmly in the saddle. He had handled with commendable smoothness the trickiest part of his job—getting money out of the colony's Assembly, striking the right balance between authority and cooperation in the bargain. From Elizabeth, Franklin set out on one of his tours of North America, in his role as the King's Deputy Postmaster General. Once more he visited post offices from Boston to Virginia, stopping along the way to renew his acquaintance with the prominent Americans of every state: Jared Ingersoll, prominent Connecticut lawyer whom Franklin had met in London; Cadwallader Colden, now lieutenant governor of New York; Lord Jeffrey Amherst, commander-in-chief of the British Army in North America.

But instead of rejoicing with these leaders over the prospects of a triumphant peace, the talk was the same familiar tale of woe he had heard when he made the same journey to the Albany Congress a decade ago. The colonial frontier was aflame once more, and all anyone could do was lament American disunity. The Peace of Paris, as the treaty that ended the Seven Years War was called, ceded to England not only Canada, but all the immense swath of land between the Alleghenies and the Mississippi River. The Indians, realizing that they had backed the wrong side, decided to make an all-out effort to block the whites from this territory. For the first time they did not fight as isolated tribes, but as an aroused people, under the leadership of Pontiac, chief of the Ottawas. Within a few weeks, beginning in mid-May of 1763, every

British post west of Niagara was destroyed except Detroit and Fort Pitt. Once more the frontier echoed to the chilling howl of the war whoop, and men, women, and children died under the tomahawk and the scalping knife along the western borders of New York, Pennsylvania, and Virginia. Pennsylvania was especially hard hit. Franklin's partner in the printing of *The Pennsylvania Gazette,* David Hall, wrote him early in the summer, telling him that the back-country settlements were already in turmoil. Farms were aflame, families were fleeing to the shelter of nearby forts, and there was a terrifying shortage of arms and ammunition. Hall begged Franklin to "return as soon as possible, as your advice may be of use, in this time of calamity." [8]

Franklin must have grimaced when he read these words. He had no desire to relive those exhausting days in 1754 and '55, when he had organized the colony's defenses after Braddock's defeat. All he had received by way of thanks for risking his capital and his life was vilification from the descendants of William Penn and their local Pennsylvania supporters. This time, Franklin declined to rush to Pennsylvania's rescue. Instead, with his daughter Sally for company, he jogged on his way through Connecticut and Rhode Island to Boston. Now twenty, Sally was a sturdily proportioned girl who had inherited her mother's plainness and her father's genial temper. Franklin thought it was time for her to meet the New England branch of the family. Perhaps, too, he wanted to reassure Deborah Franklin that he was as fond of his daughter as he was of his son.

Even before Franklin set out from New York with Sally, he got a bundle of letters from the English mail packet ship telling about the amazingly chaotic political situation in England. Lord Bute, George III's friend and adviser, who had been responsible for William Franklin's appointment as governor, had turned out to be a disaster as Prime Minister, and had petulantly resigned on April 8, 1763. He had been replaced by George Grenville, and with him came a new cast of characters into the cabinet offices that controlled the destiny of Franklin and his son. Dr. John Pringle, Franklin's good friend, had hustled to ingratiate the new Colonial Secretary, Lord Shelburne, and urge him to continue William's appointment. Pringle told Franklin that Shelburne had heard him "with some indulgence," but had made no promises. "This being the state of that affair, I am persuaded that if you were determined before to return to England," Pringle wrote, "you will now see a good reason for hastening your departure; because your being present yourself, may be a considerable weight in the scale, in case matters should come near to a ballance." [9]

Franklin's reaction to this shift in the political weather was indignation. Like every politician, he did not like to hear that his friends were out and strangers, in position to do him harm, were in power. Much of Lord Bute's troubles had concerned the Peace of Paris which, in the opinion of many Britishers, granted too many concessions to their thoroughly beaten enemy, France. Some of the barbs were flung at young George III, personally, because he had been an outspoken advocate of a peace of reconciliation. Franklin placed himself wholeheartedly behind this royal policy. "The glory of Britain was never higher than at present and I think you never had a better prince," he wrote one English friend. "Why then is he not universally rever'd and belov'd?" [10] He also wrote to his close friend William Strahan, begging him to take a half hour from cribbage and give him a close analysis of the situation. Strahan complied, reassuring Franklin that in his opinion William had "sagacity enough, with your assistance, to deserve and secure" his post.[11] Strahan then renewed his campaign to persuade Franklin to return to England for good, insisting that his arguments were "strong and unanswerable."

Franklin remained noncommittal until he finished his New England tour, but back in Philadelphia he sat down to write Strahan a long letter and suddenly found his yearning for the mother country almost overwhelming. "Now I am returned from my long journeys which have consum'd the whole summer, I shall apply myself to such a settlement of all my affairs, as will enable me to do what your friendship so warmly urges. I have a great opinion of your wisdom (Madeira apart;) and am apt enough to think that what you seem so clear in, and are so earnest about, must be right. Tho' I own, that I sometimes suspect, my love to England and my friends there seduces me a little, and makes *my own* middling reasons for going over; appear very good ones. We shall see in a little time how things will turn out."

From there he swept into new apostrophes to George III. He told Strahan not to fear for "our virtuous young King." Franklin was convinced that "the consciousness of his sincere intentions to make his people happy, will give him firmness and steadiness in his measures, and in the support of the honest friends he has chosen to serve him." Franklin foresaw a reign that would be "happy and truly glorious." [12]

But the one thing that had to be worked out, if this retirement to Eng-

land was to become a reality, was Deborah Franklin's still overwhelming
dread of sea voyages. Although her own husband was living proof that
the Atlantic could be crossed safely, Deborah simply would not consider
it. Soon William Franklin was writing Strahan informing him that his
father had given up his dream of moving to England. He was building a
large expensive house on Market Street in Philadelphia. Deborah Franklin had apparently won her struggle to keep her husband in America.

Obviously, Franklin felt he owed Deborah a great deal for her patient
acceptance of his five-year absence in England, and he was ready to live
out the rest of his life with her, with all the forbearance and tact he
could muster. When Deborah confessed that in a moment of jealousy,
she had opened all of her husband's English mail, while he was touring
New England with Sally, Franklin smoothly replied: "I approve of your
opening all my English letters, as it must give you pleasure to see that
people who knew me there so long and so intimately, retain so sincere
a regard for me." [13]

I I I

But the violent world beyond the horizon of peaceful Philadelphia was
about to destroy this reasonable dream. During the fall of 1763, the
western counties of Pennsylvania had become a chaos of desolation and
terror. A missionary sent out by Philadelphia's Christ Church reported
750 abandoned farms and 200 women and children cowering as desti-
tute refugees in the shelter of Fort Pitt. Frantic pleas for help poured
into the capital. As usual, the Proprietary government reacted with
paralysis. A new governor was in the state house. The Penns, no doubt
in part alarmed by the Franklin power play which had captured New
Jersey, had sent over one of their own, John Penn, a grandson of
founder William Penn. He asked the Assembly to pay for a thousand-
man expedition, which would march into the Ohio territory to punish
the raiding Indians in the spring. But little or nothing was done to
counter the immediate problem—the looting and scalping that was
wrecking the western counties.

As usual, when the government fails to act, men take the law into their own hands, with often disastrous results. Several towns in predominantly German Lancaster County were Irish. Many colonies had made it a policy to invite the Irish to settle on their frontiers, as a kind of border guard or buffer against Indian assaults. Men from two of these Irish towns, Paxton and Donegal, embittered by the bloody losses they had already taken, struck in blind fury at the only Indians they could find—a wholly peaceful remnant of a tribe which had signed a treaty with William Penn and the first settlers, and lived in harmony with the white men ever since. Called the Conestogas, they were only twenty in number, and they made their living from weaving baskets, brooms, and bowls which they sold to their white neighbors. "The Paxton Boys," as they called themselves, descended on this hapless little community in the dawn, slaughtered the six Conestogas they found at home and burned their village to the ground.

Officials in Lancaster hustled the fourteen bewildered survivors into the town's jail, the strongest available building, and assured them that they would be defended by all the power the government could muster. John Penn backed them with a proclamation denouncing the murders and forbidding "all persons whatsoever" to molest or injure any peaceful Indians. But Paxton and Donegal Townships were unimpressed and unabashed by this declaration. On the twenty-seventh of December, the Paxton Boys oiled their muskets, sharpened their hatchets and scalping knives, and mounted their horses once more. Into Lancaster they rode, and not a citizen so much as stuck his head out of a window to oppose them. No one had the nerve to take on these wild Irishmen when their blood was up. To the door of the jail they clattered, and having battered it open, they charged inside and slaughtered the fourteen survivors of the Conestoga tribe. It was barbaric frontier cruelty at its worst. Only seven Conestogas could even remotely be called warriors. The rest were women and little children.[14]

Pennsylvania seethed with an ominous mixture of agitation and horror. Governor Penn issued another proclamation, offering 200 pounds reward for the capture of the Paxton ringleaders. He was like a man shouting into a whirlwind. Nobody listened. On the contrary, more than a few people in the colony rose to defend the murderers. The Paxton Boys were Presbyterians, and the members of that faith found labored arguments in the Bible to support the theory that the Indians were an accursed race, and it was an act of piety to extirpate them. They also got in a few licks against the traditional Pennsylvania policy toward the

Indians, which was dominated by the Quaker philosophy of forbearance. To the frontiersmen who were exposed to the savagery of Indian warriors on the warpath, kindness was synonymous with weakness, and the massacre of the Conestogas, in the minds of these confused, embattled people, was a demand for a new policy based on eye-for-eye vengeance. Benjamin Franklin was appalled to see that more than a few Pennsylvanians, even his Philadelphia neighbors, agreed with this justification of the murderers. He decided to give them an answer.

A few days after the first of the year, the printing press of *The Pennsylvania Gazette* churned out copies of a pamphlet entitled, "A Narrative of the Late Massacres in Lancaster County." It was a masterpiece of verbal destruction. Franklin told how the Conestogas had made a treaty with William Penn that was to last "as long as the sun should shine or the waters run in the rivers." He then went down the list of the victims, giving a brief sketch of the most important.

". . . Shehaes was a very old man, having assisted at the second treaty held with them, by Mr. Penn in 1701, and ever since continued a faithful and affectionate friend to the English; he is said to have been an exceeding good man, considering his education, being naturally of the most kind, benevolent temper.

"Peggy was Shehaes's daughter; she worked for her aged father, continuing to live with him, though married, and attended him with filial duty and tenderness.

"John was another good old man; his son Harry helped to support him.

"John Smith, a valuable young man, of the Cayuga Nation, who became acquainted with Peggy, Shehaes's daughter, some few years since, married her, and settled in that family. They had one child about three years old.

"The reader will observe, that many of their names are English. It is common with the Indians that have an affection for the English, to give themselves, and their children, the names of such English persons as they particularly esteem."

Franklin told how Shehaes, when he was warned that he was in danger of being murdered, replied, "It is impossible, there are Indians, indeed, in the woods who would kill me and mine if they could get at us, for my friendship to the English; but the English will wrap me in their matchcoat and secure me from all danger."

"How unfortunately was he mistaken," Franklin added, and described how the old Indian was "cut to pieces in his bed" in the first massacre at Conestoga. Then Franklin described in heartbreaking terms the final scene in jail. "When the poor wretches saw they had no protection nigh, nor could possibly escape, and being without the least weapon for defense, they divided into their little families, the children clinging to the parents; they fell on their knees, protested their innocence, declared their love to the English, and that, in their whole lives, they had never done them injury; and in this posture they all received the hatchet! Men, women, and little children—were every one inhumanly murdered!—In cold blood!"

Franklin then went on to tell a series of fascinating short stories, which described how the ancient Greeks, the Saracens, the Spaniards, the Negroes of Africa, and the Indians of America invariably practiced mercy toward strangers who by chance or accident happened to wander into their country or to visit them as peaceful guests. "In short it appears," Franklin wrote, "that they [the Indians] would have been safe in any part of the known world, except in the neighborhood of the Christian white savages of Paxton and Donegal."

Sheer castigation was not Franklin's goal. In the final pages of his demolition, he revealed his real purpose. There were 140 other peaceful Indians, most of them converts to Christianity, who had fled to Philadelphia for safety. Already, some Philadelphians were complaining about the expense of maintaining them, and suggesting that they be sent back into the countryside, where they would meet certain death. Franklin asked his neighbors if they could leave these poor people "exposed to the armed madmen of your country? Let us rouze ourselves for shame and redeem the honor of our province from the contempt of its neighbors. . . . Cowards can handle arms, can strike where they are sure to meet with no return, can wound, mangle, and murder; but it belongs to brave men to spare and to protect; for, as the poet says, *Mercy still sways the brave*." [15]

This was strong language, but Franklin knew exactly what he was doing. He was no friend of lawless revolution, and the Paxton Boys showed every sign of turning their vendetta against the Indians into just that. Early in February, word reached Philadelphia that a mob of 800 heavily armed frontiersmen, led by the infuriated Paxtons, was on the march. It was 1755 all over again, with the province defenseless against armed invasion. Once more the governor and his Council, quarreling with the Assembly and with each other, were creating a stew of frantic indecision. According to a merchant just back from the frontier, the rioters' professed purpose was to kill the 140 peaceful Indians who were now living on Province Island in the Delaware. But they also made it clear that they were ready to shoot anyone else who got in their way. The only organized force in the vicinity of the capital was three companies of the Royal American Regiment—about 180 men. In desperation, John Penn turned to the one man whose personal appeal could persuade Philadelphians to do battle with this oncoming army of potential revolutionaries: Benjamin Franklin. He offered Franklin command of any organization he could form—and begged him to form it as soon as possible.

For two consecutive days and nights Franklin sat up with the governor and his Council, planning the defense of the city. Once more the big problem was persuading people to risk their lives to defend the government, when the Quakers still declined to bear arms. Shrewdly Franklin suggested recruiting Quakers to dig ditches around the building in which the Indians were being housed. The Royal American regulars were to man these fortifications. Franklin, meanwhile, called on his fellow Philadelphians to form a military association, and put down his name as the first volunteer. Within hours, almost a thousand citizens had followed his lead, including a surprising number of Quakers, who were probably alarmed at rumors that after the Paxton Boys and their friends finished off the Indians, they were going to settle a few old scores with the Quakers. As Franklin later told an English friend, "The governor offered me the command of them, but I chose to carry a musket, and strengthen his authority by setting an example of obedience to his orders."

About midnight on Monday, February 6, 1764, horsemen came racing into the city to tell Governor Penn that at least 250 Paxtons, hefting their murderous frontier rifles and tomahawks, and swearing Gaelic oaths, were in Germantown, only seven miles away. Once more the governor panicked, and at two o'clock in the morning, Penn and his counselors were pounding on Benjamin Franklin's door. Church bells clanged throughout the city, summoning the Associaters and regular soldiers to arms. Throughout a long cold night they waited for an attack. None came. Toward morning they learned that several clergymen had warned the Paxtons that the city was ready for them, and the frontiersmen had decided to wait at Germantown for reenforcements.

No doubt at Franklin's suggestion, the governor decided to send an official delegation to confer with them. Inevitably, Franklin was asked to head the delegation. He assented without a murmur. A less courageous man might have chosen to stay behind the city's fortifications. To meet eyeball to eyeball with these quick-triggered Irishmen, after he had publicly called them cowards and murderers, was no small matter. But Franklin rode out to the confrontation with his fellow assemblyman, Joseph Galloway, William Logan of the Governor's Council, and Attorney General Benjamin Chew. By the time they arrived, almost 500 Paxtons were swarming through the quiet streets of Germantown and many more were expected. They were talking of 1500, perhaps even 5000 men if they needed them.

Four Paxton leaders met the delegation. At first they were ready to bluster their way into Philadelphia, but Franklin and his companions bluntly told them to come ahead and try it. There were over 1000 men, regulars and volunteers, entrenched and armed with cannon, waiting for them. The reception would be a lot warmer than Lancaster. This "fighting face," as Franklin called it, unnerved the Paxtons. They began claiming they never intended to murder anybody. All they wanted was a chance to air their grievances, to awaken the governor and the Assembly to the deplorable conditions on the frontier. From there, it was easy enough to agree that if their impromptu army dispersed, the governor, his Council, and the Assembly were ready to give a full and fair hearing to the frontiersmen's complaints.[16]

Franklin and the rest of the governor's delegation rode back to Philadelphia that evening, and the militia volunteers were disbanded. Summing up his hectic week, Franklin wrote wryly to a London correspondent, "Within four and twenty hours, your old friend was a common soldier, a counselor, a kind of dictator, an ambassador to the country mob, and on their returning home, *nobody,* again." [17]

In his official residence, a mortified Governor John Penn could not quite agree that Franklin was nobody. He writhed at the thought of how he would have to tell his uncle, Thomas Penn, that he had been forced to beg Benjamin Franklin for help. His counselors, all members of the Proprietary Party, were equally mortified, and almost as soon as the Philadelphia Associaters had disbanded, they began plotting to twist the whole ugly incident into a political weapon that would smash Franklin for good. With an elaborate show of conciliation, the governor saw the Paxton leaders in private. Some of their followers were permitted to come into Philadelphia with their guns, and examine the peaceful Indians in their refuge to see if they could identify any redman who was guilty of a crime. No doubt some of these interrogators were those who had slaughtered the peaceful Conestogas. But Governor Penn said not a word about prosecuting these murderers. His denunciatory proclamation, his reward for those who brought the killers to justice, both were forgotten. When Franklin and his followers in the Pennsylvania Assembly asked the governor for a chance to interrogate the Paxton leaders, Penn curtly rebuffed them.[18] The Paxton Boys swaggered back to their frontier townships making triumphal noises, and a few weeks later the governor issued a proclamation, tailored to their specific demands. Henceforth Pennsylvania would pay 150 dollars for every captive male Indian of a hostile tribe, and 138 dollars for every female captive; for the scalp of a male Indian, 134 dollars; for the scalp of a female Indian, 50 dollars. Not a word was said about the need to supply witnesses that the scalps were taken from hostiles.

To Franklin and his followers this proclamation was an invitation to murder, made doubly disgusting because it was signed by the grandson of William Penn. Simultaneously, the governor abandoned all pretense of working harmoniously with the Franklinite Assembly. He asked it for a militia bill in order to protect the colony from future riots and invasions. The Assembly gave it to him, with a provision which was sacred to American militia at the time—the men had the right to elect their officers, and the officers in turn had a voice in choosing the higher ranks. Governor Penn threw the bill back in their faces, asserting that only he had the right to name officers. When the Assembly passed a 55,000-pound money bill, the governor insisted that the best of the Proprietary lands in Pennsylvania could not be assessed higher than the *lowest* rate for land owned by ordinary taxpayers.[19]

The governor and the Assembly batted the argument back and forth for the better part of a month. Finally, the exasperated Assembly asked Franklin to compose a message to the governor expressing their sense of outrage. He did so, icily informing Penn that he would get neither his militia nor his money. Referring to the governor's crude wooing of the Paxtons and their supporters, Franklin condemned "the steps taken to enflame the minds of unthinking people, and excite tumults against the Assembly . . . to awe us into Proprietary measures." They declined to be awed and replied instead with a threat of their own. "We must for the present depend on ourselves and our friends, and on such protection as the King's troops can afford us, which we hope, by the blessing of

God, will be sufficient to defend us, till his Majesty shall graciously think fit to take this distracted province under his immediate care and protection." [20]

To a friend in England, Franklin wrote, "All hopes of happiness under a Proprietary government are at an end; it has now scarce authority enough left to keep the common peace; and was another mob to come against him, I question whether, tho' a dozen men were sufficient, one could find so many in Philadelphia, willing to rescue him or his attorney general, I won't say from hanging, but from any common insult." [21]

To prove he meant what he said, Franklin wrote and the Assembly passed twenty-six resolutions condemning the governor and his policies, and declaring that they were adjourning to consult their constituents on preparing "a humble address" to the King to oust the Proprietors forever.[22] The distracted Penn was soon writing violent denunciations of Franklin to his Uncle Thomas. "There never will be any prospect of ease and happiness while that villain has the liberty of spreading about the poison of that inveterate malice and ill-nature which is so deeply implanted in his own black heart." [23]

Franklin did nothing to soothe the governor's agitation with another pamphlet, "Cool Thoughts on the Present Situation of Our Public Affairs." It was a smoothly reasoned argument that the province had nothing to lose and possibly something to gain by changing to a royal government. An extensive account of the history of New Jersey, which had switched from Proprietary to royal government long ago, was one of the more telling points. But the issue was not really a change of government, Franklin argued. "It is rather and only a change of *governor,* that is instead of self-interested Proprietaries, a gracious King!" [24]

Not everyone agreed with Franklin's argument. Governor Penn and his followers, of course, were in all-out opposition. But when the Assembly began to debate the petition to the King, the Franklinites found almost as much opposition in the ranks of the Presbyterians, the representatives of the German settlers, and a number of thoughtful men who simply feared that the change might be for the worse. Among these, the most talented was a spare, eloquent young lawyer named John Dickinson. He soon emerged as the leader of the opposition, a role which did no damage to his already large ego.

The debate over the petition was bitter and stormy. Dickinson and others attacked it with all the skill and energy they could muster. But the Franklinite majority was immovable. They were finally and totally disgusted with the Penns, and were convinced that they had to go. Caught in the middle was an old Franklin friend, Isaac Norris, the speaker of the Assembly for fourteen years. His daughter was married to John Dickinson, and he was so distressed by the battle that he resigned. The Assembly immediately elected Franklin to replace him, and the petition was rammed through with a solid majority. As Speaker, Franklin was the man who signed the petition, which he had also written.

Everyone knew that the real battle would take place in October, when elections were held. John Dickinson opened the warfare by publishing a speech he had made in the Assembly, with a long preface written by one of the Proprietary Party, full of effusive eulogies of William Penn and, by implication, his descendants. Franklin replied by publishing a speech by his lieutenant in the Assembly, earnest, argumentative Joseph Galloway. Franklin wrote a preface for it that skewered Dickinson, his prefacer, and the Penns with Franklin's favorite weapon, humor.

Dickinson's prefacer had made the mistake of composing, in the form of a memorial, a hymn of praise to William Penn.

WILLIAM PENN
A man of principles truely humane,
An advocate for
RELIGION and LIBERTY
Possessing a noble spirit
That exerted itself
For the good of mankind

It continued in this lapidary style for another page and a half, ending with the declaration that Penn's good deeds deserved "ever to be remembered" [25]

With
GRATITUDE and AFFECTION
By PENNSYLVANIANS.

Franklin's answer was a counter-memorial to the sons.

Be this a Memorial
Of T[homas] and R[ichard] P[enn],
P[roprietaries] of P[ennsylvania]
Who with Estates immense,
Almost beyond Computation,

When their own Province,
And the whole British Empire
Were engag'd in a bloody and most expensive War
Begun for the Defence of those Estates,
Could yet meanly desire
To have those very Estates
Totally or Partially
Exempted from Taxation,
While their Fellow-Subjects all around them
Groan'd
Under the universal Burthen.
To gain this Point,
They refus'd the necessary Laws
For the Defence of their People,
And suffer'd their Colony to welter in its Blood,
Rather than abate in the least
Of these their dishonest Pretentions.
The Privileges granted by their Father
Wisely and benevolently
To encourage the first Settlers of the Province
They,
Foolishly and cruelly,
Taking Advantage of public Distress,
Have extorted from the Posterity of those Settlers;
And are daily endeavoring to reduce them
To the most abject Slavery:
Tho' to the Virtue and Industry of those People
In Improving their Country,
They owe all that they possess and enjoy.
A striking Instance
Of human Depravity and Ingratitude;
And an irrefragable Proof,
That Wisdom and Goodness
Do not descend with an Inheritance;
But that ineffable Meanness
May be connected with unbounded Fortune.[26]

Simultaneously, Franklin opened a second front in London. William
Franklin sent "Cool Thoughts" and other material to William Strahan,

who gave the Franklin side of the story thorough coverage in his news-paper, *The London Chronicle*. Again, the important role William played in Franklin's over-all battle plan was visible in the way this propaganda praised New Jersey as strongly as it condemned Pennsylvania. Franklin was soon writing cheerfully to Strahan, "I thank you for inserting the messages and resolutions intire. I believe it has had a good effect; for a friend writes me, that 'it is astonishing with what success it was propa-gated in London by the Proprietaries, that the [Assembly's] resolutions were the most indecent and undutiful to the Crown, &c, so that when he saw them, having before heard those reports, he could not believe that they were the same.' " [27]

Back in Philadelphia, meanwhile, Franklin's enemies launched a furious counterattack. Off their press came a pamphlet with the stag-gering title, *"What is SAUCE for a GOOSE is also SAUCE for a GAN-DER. BEING A Small Touch in the LAPIDARY Way. OR TIT for TAT, in Your Own Way. AN EPITAPH on a Certain Great Man. Writ-ten by a Departed Spirit and now Most Humbly Inscribed to all His Dutiful Sons and Children, Who May Hereafter Choose to Distinguish Him by the Name of A PATRIOT."*

Then, written in the same parody-epitaph style Franklin had used to skewer the Penns, came the following blast:

AN EPITAPH &c
TO the much esteem'd Memory of
B———— F———— Esq; LL.D;
The only man of his day
In Pennsylvania
Or perhaps of any age or in any country,
Whose ingrate Disposition *and* Badness of Heart
(These enormous Vices)
Ever introduced to
POPULARITY.

For three pages the Proprietary satirist battered Franklin with every available accusation from revolutionary intentions to William's illegiti-mate birth. Then the memorialist turned to slander and accused Franklin of retaining William's mother as a part-time paramour and maid of all work in his own house for several years.[28]

The tone of the election campaign was set, and nothing said or done

thereafter did anything to improve it. Dr. John Ewing, one of Philadelphia's most prominent clergymen, wrote an apology for the slaughter
of the Conestoga Indians which applauded the Paxtons and denounced
Franklin and the Quakers. "Few but Quakers think that the Lancaster
Indians have suffered anything but their just desserts," he declared
piously. The tactics on election day were in keeping with the rest of the
campaign. Franklin and his friends ran on what they called "the Old
Ticket." Dickinson, the Proprietors, and anyone else they could dragoon,
ran on "the New Ticket." An eyewitness described the scene before City
Hall. "The poll was opened about nine in the morning, the 1st of October, and the steps so crowded, till between eleven and twelve at night,
that at no time a person could get up in less than a quarter of an hour
from his entrance at the bottom, for they could go no faster than the
whole column moved. About three in the morning the advocates for the
New Ticket moved for a close. But (O! fatal mistake!) the old hands
kept it open, as they had a reserve of the aged and lame, which could
not come in the crowd, and were called up and brought out in chairs
and litters . . . between three and six o'clock, about 200 voters. As
both sides took care to have spies all night, the alarm was given to the
New Ticket men! Horsemen and footmen were immediately dispatched
to Germantown and elsewhere; and by nine or ten o'clock they began to
pour in, so that after the move for a close, 7 or 800 votes were procured;
about 500 or near it of which were for the New Ticket . . ." [29]

When the votes were finally counted, the following day, the Proprietary Party and their supporters staged jubilant parades through Philadelphia. Franklin and his lieutenant, Galloway, had been beaten by a
squeaky twenty-five votes. "Mr. Franklin died like a philosopher," declared the reporter who was telling the story to a friend in London. "But
Mr. Galloway agonized in death like a mortal Deist, who has no hopes
of a future existence." The Proprietaries stopped cheering when reports
of the voting in other counties reached the capital. It soon became clear
that the Old Ticket retained a solid majority in the Assembly.

Undaunted by his personal defeat, Franklin grimly proceeded with the
business of getting rid of the Penns. Over repeated protests by John Dickinson, the Assembly named Franklin as its agent in England to press the
petition to the King. Dickinson declared that "no man in Pennsylvania
is at this time so much the object of the public dislike" as Franklin. [30] The
Assembly ignored the orator, and Franklin accepted the post. Eleven

hundred pounds were voted for his expenses, but because the treasury was empty, and even this much money had to be borrowed, Franklin accepted only 500 pounds. Dickinson and his party replied by demanding that a minority protest be inserted in the Assembly minutes. This too was voted down.

Franklin announced he was leaving immediately for England, but he found time, while packing, to hurl a final fusillade at his opponents. His pamphlet, "Remarks on a Late Protest," was a bruising reply to Dickinson's contention that Franklin was the worst possible choice to represent the colony in England. Why was he the wrong man to represent Pennsylvania in London? Had he by speeches and writing "endeavored to make His Majesty's government universally odious in the province?" Thus he neatly turned the Proprietaries' arguments back on them. "If I had harangued by the week to all comers and goers on the pretended injustice and oppressions of royal government and the slavery of the people under it; if I had written traitorous papers to this purpose and got them translated into other languages, to give His Majesty's foreign subjects here those horrible ideas of it; if I had declared, written, and printed that 'the King's little finger we should find heavier than the Proprietors' whole loins' with regard to our liberties; then indeed might [his Majesty's] ministers be supposed to think unfavorably of me. But these are not exploits for a man who holds a profitable office under the Crown, and can expect to hold it no longer than he behaves with the fidelity and duty that becomes every good subject."

He denied that he had "a fixed enmity to the Proprietaries." "Let them do justice to the people of Pennsylvania, act honorably by the citizens of Philadelphia, and become honest men; my enmity, if that's of any consequence, ceases from the very moment, and as soon as I possibly can, I promise to love, honour, and respect them."

Then with the skill of a born writer, he changed pace and became more philosopher than pamphleteer. "I am now to take leave (perhaps the last leave) of the country I love and in which I have spent the greatest part of my life. Esto perpetua. I wish every kind of prosperity to my friends; and I forgive my enemies." [31]

Franklin's friends, meanwhile, were marshaling their forces. They were determined to show Philadelphia and the world that their man was still the hero of the majority. On November seventh, Franklin rode out of Philadelphia, escorted by no less than 300 men on horseback. Down at Chester on the Delaware, the ship King of Prussia was waiting for him.

Cannon, borrowed from the Philadelphia armory, boomed as he went aboard, and the crowd sang an improvised version of "God Save the King":

O LORD our GOD arise,
Scatter our Enemies,
And make them fall.
Confound their Politicks,
Frustrate such Hypocrites,
Franklin, on Thee we fix,
GOD Save us all.
Thy Knowledge rich in Store,
On Pennsylvania pour,
Thou [sic] *great Blessing:*
Long to defend our Laws,
Still give us greater Cause,
To sing with Heart and Voice,
GEORGE and FRANKLIN
GOD Save Great GEORGE our King;
Prosper agent FRANKLIN:
Grant him Success:
Hark how the Vallies ring;
GOD Save our Gracious King,
From whom all Blessings spring,
Our Wrongs redress.[32]

Franklin's faithful political lieutenant, Joseph Galloway, and two other close friends, Thomas Wharton and Abel James, both prominent Philadelphia merchants, went on board ship with him and sailed down the Delaware to New Castle. Franklin was deeply touched by this outpouring of affection and loyalty. On the night of November eighth, alone in his cabin aboard the *King of Prussia,* he had only one worry which still nagged at his mind: his daughter, Sally. At twenty-one, she was almost certain to be exposed to the same kind of humiliating snubs and petty insults which had made William Franklin unhappy. Benjamin had wanted to take Sally with him to England to put her beyond the reach of this malevolence, at least for the year he expected to be gone. But Deborah Franklin had absolutely refused to part with her.

Out of this deep concern, Franklin sat down and wrote one of the tenderest letters a father has ever sent a daughter.

"My dear Child, the natural prudence and goodness of heart that God has blessed you with, make it less necessary for me to be particular in giving you advice; I shall therefore only say, that the more attentively dutiful and tender you are towards your good Mama, the more you will recommend your self to me; But why shou'd I mention *me,* when you have so much higher a promise in the commandment, that such a conduct will recommend you to the favour of God. You know I have many enemies (all indeed on the public account, for I cannot recollect that I have in a private capacity given just cause of offence to any one whatever) yet they are enemies and very bitter ones, and you must expect their enmity will extend in some degree to you, so that your slightest indiscretions will be magnified into crimes, in order the more sensibly to wound and afflict me. It is therefore the more necessary for you to be extreamly circumspect in all your behavior that no advantage may be given to their malevolence. Go constantly to church whoever preaches. The acts of devotion in the common prayer book, are your principal business there; and if properly attended to, will do more towards mending the heart than sermons generally can do. For they were composed by men of much greater piety and wisdom, than our common composers of sermons can pretend to be. And therefore I wish you wou'd never miss the prayer days. Yet I do not mean that you shou'd despise sermons even of the preachers you dislike, for the discourse is often much better than the man, as sweet and clear waters come to us thro' very dirty earth. I am the more particular on this head, as you seem'd to express a little before I came away some inclination to leave our church [The rector of Christ Church was a bitter anti-Franklin man, and often made it clear in his sermons.], which I wou'd not have you do. . . ." [33]

Franklin closed the letter by urging Sally to spend some time acquiring "those useful accomplishments, arithmetick and bookkeeping." Sally was obviously no genius, and with the Philadelphia Establishment so thoroughly aroused against the Franklins, there was not much chance that she would marry a scion. So Franklin was attempting to prepare her for becoming a tradesman's wife, and wanted her to be able to give her husband the kind of valuable help Deborah had given him.

For us, with the comfortable wisdom of hindsight, Franklin's new mission to London is almost top-heavy with irony. He was returning to the England he loved to ask George III and his ministers to become the lawful rulers of Pennsylvania. Franklin was still very much a man of his own time, of those earlier eighteenth-century decades, when England and her colonies stood in sometimes desperate battle array against the power of France and Spain. He had played his part in helping to shape the outlines of the present triumphant empire, and now, like a good citizen, he was seeking a way to perfect it. He spoke and acted out of deep wellsprings of old emotion, and out of a faith that was also part of his time—a belief that men could use the light of reason with which they were illuminating nature's mysteries to bring sanity and order into their political and personal lives. Within this fabric of thought and feeling were intimately woven the intense affections of a husband and father. Benjamin Franklin had no way of knowing he was sailing into a maelstrom that would shred this fabric, and finally destroy the deepest and most important personal relationship in his life.

Book Four

Death

OF A

Dream

I

The *King of Prussia* plowed the wintry Atlantic at a lively pace. Joseph Galloway and the other political friends who had gone aboard ship with Franklin had, in one of their last toasts, wished him thirty days' fair wind. The wish was almost too abundantly granted. The weather was terrible, and the seas mountainous. But the *King of Prussia* did indeed reach the Isle of Wight in exactly thirty days. Franklin promptly dashed off a letter to his worried wife, informing her that he had survived another crossing and admitting that because of the terrible weather he had "often been thankful that our dear Sally was not with me." [1]

Ashore, Franklin made record time to London and went straight to his house of happy memories on Craven Street. He found no one at home but the maid, and he sat in the parlor savoring the expectation of seeing Mrs. Stevenson's face, when she finally arrived. The good woman was suitably astonished to find her old friend, whom she thought was 3000 miles away in Philadelphia, greeting her with a hearty chuckle from his favorite easy chair. Daughter Polly was away visiting friends in the country, but Franklin found time in the next few days to dash off a letter to her telling how "surpriz'd" her "good mama" was to find him in her parlor. To Deborah, he wrote a charming little note which began with the familiar "My dear child," telling her that so far he had done nothing but catch "a most violent cold." He added that all his friends had given him "a most cordial welcome." [2] This was soothing stuff intended for a worried wife. Franklin did not try to burden Deborah with the far more serious news he was learning in London.

To Craven Street came a steady stream of American agents for other colonies, as well as Richard Jackson, the official spokesman for Pennsylvania. With doleful faces and in mournful words, they told the same troubled tale. Parliament was about to pass a new tax, a Stamp Act which would for the first time require Americans to pay direct taxes to Parliament in order to conduct their daily affairs. A royal stamp would be required on every conceivable legal document, from lawyers' certificates to marriage licenses. It was the first time that Parliament had ever taxed Americans internally, to use the language of Franklin and his friends. External taxes—duties on imports and exports—had always been imposed, but they were seen as part of the need to regulate trade throughout the empire, for the eventual advantage of all its citizens, both at home and in the colonies.

Franklin was appalled. Word that the British government was considering such an act had been drifting about America for almost a year. Pennsylvania and several other colonial Assemblies had passed resolutions objecting to it, and declaring their readiness to raise taxes for the Crown in the traditional way—each colony voting a sum proportionate to its resources. But the First Lord of the Treasury, George Grenville, had ignored these mild protestations and gone ahead with his plan for a stamp tax. The situation was, in short, a perfect muddle of political confusion, in unfortunate consistency with the slapdash way with which England had governed the colonies since the beginning.

As was his custom, Franklin did more listening than talking. The other agents told him of their May 17, 1764, meeting with Grenville, in which they had desperately sought to find out from the First Lord of the Treasury such rudimentary facts as how much money he expected to make from his stamp tax, in order that they might give their respective Assemblies some idea of how much cash they would have to raise to forestall the measure. To this Grenville blithely replied that details were unnecessary. Earlier, in a speech in Parliament, Grenville had given the distinct impression that he was willing to consider alternatives to a stamp tax. But the First Lord was obviously talking out of both sides of his mouth. Simultaneously, his secretary, Thomas Whately, was collecting the information from the colonies that he needed to write the act. Richard Jackson, who also served as Grenville's secretary, undoubtedly made this clear to his good friend Franklin. In his May seventeenth conference with the colonial agents, Grenville had offered, with the air of a man making a concession, that he would consult with the agents just before Parliament convened—but only if they would request their Assemblies to agree in advance to the principle of a stamp tax. All this was interlarded with profuse statements of affection for the colonies, and glowing testimonials that the King and the mother country sought nothing but their good and protection.[3]

Was there no opposition organized anywhere against the bill? Franklin asked. He knew how solidly Americans were united against it, and he found it hard to believe that all the letters they had written, all the resolves forwarded by their Assemblies, had not raised any response among friends of America in England. Jasper Mauduit, the Massachusetts agent, shrugged and spoke glumly of a vague spirit of opposition among British merchants. But it was all talk and no action. Not even Grenville's secretaries had been able to change the First Lord's mind. Jackson had been against the bill from the start, and Thomas Whately had reaped an ominous harvest of negative letters when he wrote to America for information. Jared Ingersoll, an old Franklin friend from Connecticut, was in London on private business, and had been invited by the agents and Franklin to join them, no doubt on Franklin's recommendation. "I told Mr. Whately," Ingersoll declared, "that I had heard gentlemen in New England—gentlemen of the greatest property—say very coolly that if the government took such a step, they would immediately remove themselves and their families and fortunes into some foreign kingdom."

Another agent, perhaps South Carolina's Charles Garth, suggested, with a feeble grope for optimism, that at least the tax was not very large. "Large or small is not the point," declared Ingersoll. "Once Parliament lays a tax, no matter how moderate, who can say what will follow?" [4]

There was obviously only one move left. Charles Garth and Jackson, the two members of Parliament who were agents, and Franklin and Ingersoll, as two distinguished men fresh from America, would go to Grenville and make a last desperate attempt to stop the bill.

Down to the office of the First Lord of the Treasury they went on February 2, 1765. It was Franklin's first official meeting with men at the very summit of English power. In his previous years in England, he had met powerful peers socially, but officially he had dealt with sub-ministers and secretaries more directly concerned with colonial affairs, and sought in vain a conference with the First Minister of that era, William Pitt. Thus this meeting between George Grenville and Benjamin Franklin was far more significant in the lives of both men, and in the histories of their countries, than anyone, including the men themselves, realized at the time.

Grenville was an unusual British politician in some respects; he worked at his job with the zeal of a sub-accountant, mastering reams of detail. Unfortunately, he combined this talent with a trait that was more typical of the leading politicians of his era—an overwhelming arrogance, bred of his aristocratic background and a sense of being a leader of the world's most powerful nation. He combined this inner certainty with a languid, rather bored manner which produced almost instant irritation in those who had to listen to him. About a year earlier he had risen in the House of Commons to defend the government's policy of imposing new taxes. A huge debt piled up by the Seven Years War made them a necessity, yet the Members repeatedly objected to specific imposts, with the politician's usual passion to protect the special interests of his constituents. Where were new taxes to be laid? Grenville cried. "I wish gentlemen would show me where to lay them." Again and again he repeated this question in his querulous way, until William Pitt suddenly began mocking him with words from an old song, "Gentle shepherd, tell me where!" Instantly, Grenville became known as the Gentle Shepherd, a name which stuck to him for the rest of his life.

The story also underscored Grenville's favorite political tactic. He operated on the principle that no one else knew quite as much about the machinery of the government as he did, and was notably fond of throwing protests back in the laps of the protesters, with a what-would-you-do-if-you-were-in-my-place cry. At the same time, Grenville considered himself a superior politician. He had boldly sought the job of First Minister, and ruthlessly driven out of influence George III's favorite, Lord Bute. Now he thought he could handle these naive colonials with that most superficial of political arts, ingratiation.

The great man was all smiles as Franklin and his friends sat down in his office. Exuding good cheer, he told them how distressed he was to learn that they were troubled about the stamp tax. He listened with a profusion of tut-tuts and tsk-tsks as the agents detailed their respectful disagreement with his policies. He told them he took "no pleasure" in giving Americans this "uneasiness"—and simultaneously implied that he did not really believe serious unease existed anywhere but in the minds of the agents.

Even if there was uneasiness, Grenville made it clear that it was his duty to balance the books, not merely for America, but for the whole Empire. He again repeated the arguments he had used on the colonial agents the year before. Everybody in England paid a stamp tax without protest. Was there a better way to raise money in America? If so, would they please tell him?

As usual, Franklin let others do most of the talking. Jackson, schooled in the traditions of the House of Commons, showed no hesitation about saying bluntly what he thought. He feared the act was the first of many, which would end by completely demolishing the tradition of representative government in America. Once the home government was able to raise all the revenues its royal governors needed by Parliamentary-imposed taxation, no governor in his right mind would ever summon a colonial assembly. In a few years, they would quietly wither away. The First Lord of the Treasury expressed horror at the thought. He had absolutely no desire of such a goal, nor did he think it was in the mind of any English statesman. Jackson was dealing with fantasy, a monster of his own imagination. The simple truth was that the government had to lay a tax. Can any of you gentlemen tell me a better way to do it?

Once more the Americans renewed their plea to let each colony raise a share of the money through its own internal taxation.

But, gentlemen, cried Grenville, can you agree on the proportion each colony should raise?

Of course they could not agree for reasons which Grenville himself knew perfectly well. In the first place, he had never told them how much money he wanted to raise. If he had been serious about this idea, he should have ordered his secretary, Thomas Whately, to send a circular letter to the colonies, when he began collecting information a year ago, telling them to confer and decide on just proportions, or at least send Whately enough information so that he and Grenville could decide. Franklin and his friends could only mumble that neither they nor any other colonial agent had the power to negotiate such a deal. It was something that only the Assemblies themselves, the tax gathering bodies, could handle.

Grenville now proceeded to top this absurdity by announcing to the delegation that he had "pledged his word" to offer a stamp bill to Parliament. The Gentle Shepherd did not have a very good memory. In his own words, he was proving himself a liar by contradicting what he had said a year ago about having an open mind toward raising money in America. In a different atmosphere, Franklin and his friends might have sharply reminded him of this fact. But neither Franklin nor the other agents were psychologically prepared for such a confrontation. On the contrary, they all shared Franklin's deep reverence for the concept of a united, glorious British Empire, and this man, handed the seals of power by George III in his closet, was the living personification of it. So they could only sit and listen despairingly as Grenville closed their half-hour meeting by calling for "coolness and moderation in America" and expressing a simultaneous hope that there would be no "resentments indecently and unbecomingly expressed." Only when they were in Benjamin Franklin's coach, riding back to Craven Street, did they realize that they had been treated like children.[5]

Conversations with Jackson and other members of Parliament in the ensuing days soon made it clear that there was another, even more dismaying side to the government's insistence on the Stamp Act. The majority of Parliament, from the theoretically independent country gentlemen to the retainers of the powerful party leaders, elected from so-called "rotten boroughs," where only a handful of people had the right to vote, were intensely irritated by the first murmurs of American resistance to the Stamp Act. One member of Parliament haughtily declared that the prime purpose of the Act was to establish the right of Parliament to tax the colonies "by a new execution of it, and in the strongest instance, an internal tax."

The whole experience must have been almost overwhelming for Franklin. The problem that had agitated his mind and the minds of his friends in Pennsylvania for so long—the battle with the Proprietors—vanished in this enormously more important issue. Day after day, Franklin followed the debates in Parliament, as reported in the newspapers, and conferred with his influential friends, such as Pringle and Strahan, on how the battle was going. None of the news he heard was good. Only a relative handful of members opposed the tax, but some of them did it with vigor. Franklin must have noted, with not a little interest, that two of the most spirited opposition spokesmen were Irish. Their country, too, had a colonial status within the empire, and they obviously spoke out with a resentment that he, a thus far contented servant of the King, did not yet feel. Franklin may have been sitting in the gallery of the House of Commons on the day when the debates on the Stamp Act reached a kind of climax. Certainly he read and heard about it in vivid detail from men such as Jared Ingersoll, who wrote an electrifying letter home describing it.

Charles Townshend, a member of Parliament who shared—and in fact propagated—a large measure of the prejudice against Americans, arose to make an incredibly condescending speech about colonial opposition to the Stamp Act. "And now will these Americans, children planted by our care, nourished up by our indulgence until they are grown to a degree of strength and opulence, and protected by our arms, will they grudge to contribute their mite to relieve us from the heavy weight of that burden which we lie under?"

The burden, of course, was the British war debt. Colonel Isaac Barré, an Irishman who had fought in America during the French and Indian War, paid no attention to the financial side of this querulous rhetorical question. It was Townshend's tone that infuriated him, and he leaped to his feet with words that would soon resound throughout the American colonies.

"They planted by your care? No! your oppressions planted 'em in America. They fled from your tyranny to a then uncultivated and un-hospitable country—where they exposed themselves to almost all the hardships to which human nature is liable, and among others to the cruelties of a savage foe, the most subtle and I take upon me to say the most formidable of any people upon the face of God's earth. And yet, actuated by principles of true English lyberty, they met all these hardships with pleasure, compared with those they suffered in their own country, from the hands of those who should have been their friends.

"They nourished by *your* indulgence? they grew by your neglect of em: as soon as you began to care about em, that care was exercised in sending persons to rule over em, in one department and another, who were perhaps the deputies of deputies to some member of this house—sent to spy out their lyberty, to misrepresent their actions and to prey upon em; men whose behaviour on many occasions has caused the blood of those sons of liberty to recoil within them; men promoted to the highest seats of justice, some, who to my knowledge were glad by going to a foreign country to escape being brought to the bar of a court of justice in their own.

"They protected by *your* arms? they have nobly taken up arms in your defence, have exerted a valour amidst their constant and labori-ous industry for the defence of a country, whose frontier, while drench'd in blood, its interior parts have yielded all its little savings to your emolument. And believe me, remember I this day told you so, that same spirit of freedom which actuated that people at first, will accompany them still. —But prudence forbids me to explain myself further. God knows I do not at this time speak from motives of party heat, what I deliver are the genuine sentiments of my heart." [6]

But Parliament was more interested in finances than genuine senti-ments. George Grenville produced figures which argued that the Ameri-can colonies' total public debts were less than a million pounds, only a fraction of England's 129,586,789 pounds of red ink. Various oppo-sition maneuvers, such as a motion to adjourn, were beaten down by

overwhelming votes (245 to 49). When colonial agents tried to present petitions against the bill they were curtly refused. Charles Garth
was soon mournfully writing his employers in South Carolina that "the
power of Parliament was asserted and so universally agreed to, that
no petition disputing it will be received." This aroused the ire of another Irishman, Henry Seymour Conway, who took the floor and asked
the question that Franklin and his friends might have put to George
Grenville, if they had been in a mood for confrontation. What was the
point of postponing the Stamp Act for a year, Conway asked, in order
to give the colonies time to make objections or alternative suggestions,
and then huffily turn them down when they were presented by their legal
representatives? "Shall we shut our ears against that information, which
with an affectation of candor, we allotted sufficient time to reach us?"
Conway thundered. "From whom, unless from ourselves, are we to
learn the circumstances of the colonies and the fatal consequences that
may attend the imposing of this tax?" [7]

Conway could not even arouse enough opposition to call for a vote.
The "readings" given the fifty-five resolutions which made up the bill
were a joke. The Stamp Act became law without another murmur of
dissent. Mournfully, Franklin wrote his friend John Ross in Philadelphia
even before Parliament confirmed the bill, "The Stamp Act, not with-
standing all the opposition we have been able to give it, will pass."
He also added, even more ruefully, "We have been of late so much
engag'd in our general American affairs, that it was necessary to let what
related particularly to our province sleep a little for the present." [8]

Franklin and the rest of his American friends in England submitted
with little more than a sigh of resentment to the Stamp Act. Perhaps
because a similar act had long been in force in England, they paid little
attention to its fantastic complications. The Act's printed text alone
consumed some twenty-five pages. It taxed no less than fifteen different
types of legal documents used in court and included newspapers, almanacs, college diplomas, dice and playing cards. Even the tax on newspapers brought only a mild groan from Franklin, who told Ross, "Every
newspaper advertisement and almanack is severely tax'd" with "every
step in the law" also taxed. He admitted it would "fall particularly hard
on us lawyers and printers." [9]

With his act in hand, George Grenville now decided it was time to
display some more superficial magnanimity. He wrote to the colonial
agents and declared that he had no desire to irritate the colonies still

further by sending strangers from England to collect the stamp tax. On the contrary, he was ready to appoint "respectable" local men and asked Franklin and the other agents for suggestions. Franklin and the other agents readily accepted this conciliatory gesture. Franklin even considered it a triumph in his struggle with the Penns, and Thomas Penn obviously considered it in the same way. He complained mightily when Franklin's candidate, his old friend John Hughes, was named Stamp Commissioner for Pennsylvania. Franklin's friends in Philadelphia had the same reaction. One wrote to tell him how "the Old Ticket was rejoicing at the appointment of their valuable and firm representative to the office of Stamp Commissioner." As for the Proprietary Party, they "speak their chagrin and distress in their very looks." [10]

This attitude makes it easier for us to understand Franklin's submissiveness. It was typical of the feelings of the men in his generation, who found it difficult (for some impossible) to think politically in any terms beyond the framework of the existing empire. Also, Franklin's mind was distinctly practical and positive. He had tried to stop the Stamp Act and failed. What, then, was the next best thing to do? Obviously, it was to find a way for the Americans to pay for it as painlessly as possible. The answer, in Franklin's opinion, was one of his favorite ideas, a well-regulated paper currency for all of the colonies. He had tried to persuade Grenville to accept the idea as a substitute for the Stamp Act. The paper bills were to be purchased at colonial loan offices, which would charge interest, payable to the Crown. Now he renewed his efforts to persuade Parliament to pass such a measure, and found considerable encouragement for the idea among many influential Britishers with whom he talked.

But as the spring of 1765 lengthened into summer, there came rolling into London, at first in a trickle that was hardly more noticeable than a wavelet splashing against a Thames River dock, and finally in a mounting surge that assumed all the roaring proportions of a tidal wave, news that the Americans were not accepting the Stamp Act as temperately as George Grenville had hoped they would. From Boston to Virginia, Assemblies denounced and newspapers fulminated. Most startling were impromptu organizations that had sprung up in every colony, calling themselves "Sons of Liberty" and urging Americans to name towns and children after Barré and Conway.

From the largest and most powerful of the colonies, Virginia, came the most astonishing news of all. The Assembly, in defiance of the

royal governor, had confirmed a set of resolves which bluntly denied
Parliament's power to lay the stamp tax. Moreover, a backwoods fire-
brand named Patrick Henry had made a speech in which he roared,
"Caesar had his Brutus, Charles I his Cromwell, may George III profit
by their example." Cries of treason had shouted him down, and he had
apologized for speaking such words in the heat of passion. The Assembly
had then eliminated two of his more radical resolutions, but the remaining resolves still made the point that Virginians had always handled
their own internal affairs, and taxation without representation was something Americans would not tolerate.

Franklin, of course, had been saying these things privately for years.
But his role as a Crown servant, and his acute awareness of present
political realities in England made him more than dubious about the
value of saying them in public, especially in such blatantly defiant terms.
"The rashness of the Assembly in Virginia is amazing!" he told his
friend John Hughes. "I hope however that ours will keep within the
bounds of prudence and moderation; for that is the only way to lighten
or get clear of our burthens." [11]

But defiant resolves were by no means the only news from America.
In Boston, Newport, New Haven, and other cities, mobs attacked and
in some cases destroyed the homes of the Stamp Commissioners, and
forced them to resign publicly, even before their commissions arrived
from England. Franklin must have blinked in disbelief when he got a
letter from his stamp nominee, John Hughes, reporting that the same
kind of violence was imminent in Pennsylvania.

"You are now from letter to letter to suppose each may be the last
you will receive from your old friend, as the spirit or flame of rebellion
is got to a high pitch among the North Americans; and it seems to me
that a sort of frenzy or madness has got such hold of the people of
all ranks, that I fancy some lives will be lost before this fire is put
out. I am at present much perplext what course to steer: For as I have
given you reason to expect I would endeavour to put the Act in execution, and you no doubt have inform'd the commissioners; I cannot
in point of honour go back, until something or other is done by the
people to render it impossible for me to proceed. But perhaps when a
mob is on foot, my life and interest may fall a sacrifice to an infatuated
multitude.—and I know of no way to prevent it but absolutely declaring
off as all the rest have done to the eastward. But as yet I cannot prevail upon myself, notwithstanding the threats of some, and the per-

suasion of others, to do an act that appears to me neither loyal nor reputable.

"I have hitherto kept matters easy by saying I had nothing to resign, for I have neither received my commission or any other kind of writing from the Stamp Office. But when it is known I have received my commission, I fancy I shall not escape the storm of Presbyterian rage. . . ." [12]

A shaken Franklin could only reply that executing the Act might make Hughes "unpopular for a time." But he assured him that "your acting with coolness and steadiness, and with every circumstance in your power of favor to the people, will by degrees reconcile them. In the meantime a firm loyalty to the Crown and faithful adherence to the government of this nation, which it is the safety as well as honor of the colonies to be connected with, will always be a wise course for you and I to take, whatever may be the madness of the populace or their blind leaders, who can only bring themselves and country into trouble, and draw on greater burthens by acts of rebellious tendency." [13]

Parliament's angry reaction to America's violent resistance destroyed any chance of Franklin's suggestion for a colonial paper currency to become law. But new hope of an even more positive and practical nature appeared on the political horizon early in the summer of 1765. George Grenville had fallen from power, largely because George III had decided he could no longer stand Grenville's overbearing manner. When a policy was proposed to him, complained the King, his agreement was taken for granted. The mounting chaos in America no doubt also played a part in the royal decision to dismiss the Gentle Shepherd.[14]

Into power came a man far more congenial to Franklin's ideas. He was Charles Watson-Wentworth, the second Marquis of Rockingham. Immensely wealthy, he supported a "squadron" of politicians in Parliament, including Edmund Burke, an eloquent Irishman who frequently declared his sympathy for America. Rockingham himself had been one of the few outspoken opponents of the Stamp Act. Equally important, the friends and followers of Lord Bute were once more in a position to exert some influence. Thus Franklin was able to tell John Hughes that he and the other agents were planning an "endeavour" to get the Stamp Act repealed. But as a good politician he warned him that "the success is uncertain," and would take time.[15]

If Franklin needed anything to galvanize him, he got it in letters from other intimate correspondents in America. David Hall, his printing partner, wrote as a worried businessman, wondering what to do. "In my last

. . . I told you that all the papers on the continent, ours excepted, were full of spirited papers against the Stamp Law. . . . Because I did not publish those papers likewise, I was much blamed, got a great deal of ill will. . . . I was in hopes that, that storm would have blown over, and that the people would have been satisfied with the arguments I used for not inserting these pieces; but I find I am much mistaken; for as the time of the law taking place draws nearer, the more the clamours of the people increase against me, for my silence in the paper; alledging that as our *Gazette,* spreads more generally than all the other papers put together on the continent, our not publishing, as the printers of the other papers do, will be an infinite hurt to the liberties of the people."

Even more ominous was the final paragraph of Hall's letter. "I could wish you was on the spot, on many accounts; and yet I should be afraid of your safety, as the spirit of the people is so violent against every one, they think has the least concern with the Stamp Law, and they have imbibed the notion that you had a hand in the framing of it." [16]

Other letters from Joseph Galloway made it clear that Franklin was like a man attempting to dam a flood single-handed. "I cannot describe to you, the indefatiguable industry that have been and are constantly taking by the Prop—y Party and men in power here to prevail on the people to give every kind of opposition to the execution of this law [the Stamp Act], to incense their minds against the King Lords and Commons, and to alienate their affections from the mother country. It is no uncommon thing to hear the judges of the courts of justice from the first to the most Inferior, in the presence of the attending populace, to treat the whole Parliament with the most irreverent abuse. . . . It is already become dangerous to espouse the conduct of the Parliament in some parts of America, in any degree." [17]

More letters from John Hughes made it clear that the danger was rampant in Philadelphia.

"Sept. 12. Our clamours run very high, and I am told my house shall be pull'd down and the stamps burnt. To which I give no other answer than that I will defend my house at the risque of my life. I must say, that all the sensible Quakers behave prudently.

"Sept. 16. in the evening. Common report threat[ens] my house this night, as there are bonfires and rejoicings for the change of ministry. The sober and sensible part of the people are doing every thing towards being in readiness to suppress a mob if there should be any intention of rising. I for my part am well-arm'd with fire-arms, and am determin'd to stand a siege. If I live till tomorrow morning I shall give you a farther account; but as it is now about 8 aclock, I am on my guard, and only write this between whiles, as every noise or bustle of the people calls me off.

"9 aclock. Several friends that patroll between my house and the Coffee House, come in just now, and say, the collection of rabble begins to decrease visibly in the streets, and the appearance of danger seems a good deal less than it did.

"12 aclock. There are now several hundreds of our friends about the street, ready to suppress any mob, if it should attempt to rise, and the rabble are dispersing.

"Sept. 17. 5 in the morning. We are all yet in the land of the living, and our property safe. Thank God." [18]

With these came a letter from Governor William Franklin, ruefully reporting that the man who had been appointed Stamp Commissioner in New Jersey had resigned without warning and with no evidence of any threats being made against him. Obviously the agent had seen the way the wind was blowing in other colonies and decided to preserve himself in advance from mob violence. Governor Franklin complained, "His surrender is not only using the gentleman ill who recommended him to office, but the province in general, as it may subject them to be thought as culpable as the N. England governments." William also complained that he had not received an iota of instructions of how to administer the Stamp Act. Finally he discussed the "outrageous conduct" of the people in Boston, who had destroyed the Stamp Commissioner's house and then "as is usual with mobs when they once feel their own power," they destroyed several other houses, "even of those who were against the Stamp Act." [19] William noted that one of these houses belonged to Lieutenant Governor Thomas Hutchinson, a man whom Franklin knew well and—at this time—admired.

The climax to these letters was one from Deborah Franklin that told her husband in vivid, if badly spelled terms, how she had been forced to defend herself and her house, gun in hand. For nine days, she said, she was kept in "one contineued hurrey" by people urging her to flee with Sally to Governor William Franklin's home in Burlington. When the city heard that the Grenville ministry had fallen, there was "verey graite rejoysing." But when the crowds assembled to celebrate with bonfires and rum, they soon began talking about pulling down the houses of those whom they blamed for the Act. High on the list was

Benjamin Franklin, and Stamp Commissioner John Hughes. But friends
and relatives staunchly supported them. One of Deborah's cousins arrived to tell her that "more than twenty pepel" had told him it was his
duty to stay with her. She told him she was "pleased to receive civility
from aney bodey." Toward nightfall Deborah told her cousin to "fech
a gun or two," and also to summon her brother to assist in the defense.
"We maid one room into a magazin. I ordored sum sorte of defens
up stairs such as I cold manaig my self," Deborah told her husband.
When neighbors again advised her to flee she was adamant. "I sed I
was verey shuer you had dun nothing to hurte aney bodey nor I had
not given aney ofense to aney person att all nor wold I be maid unesey
by aney bodey nor wold I stir or show the leste uneseynis." [20] Deborah
and her two relatives were soon joined by a half dozen of Franklin's
friends and neighbors. These reinforcements, plus the "hundreds of our
friends" mentioned by John Hughes (no doubt many of them ex-
Associaters who turned out once more to fight for their colonel) discouraged the mob and no houses were pulled down in Philadelphia.

If Franklin ever had any doubts about the wisdom of repealing the
Stamp Act, they were gone now. He immediately launched a propaganda offensive. His friend Charles Thomson had written a vigorous
reply to a Franklin letter, mournfully explaining the passage of the
Stamp Act, and urging him to "light candles" against the setting of the
sun of liberty. Franklin persuaded Strahan to publish the relevant portion of his letter, and Thomson's reply, in *The London Chronicle*. The
Irish-born Philadelphian's words should have made every sensible Englishman shiver.

"The sun of liberty is indeed fast setting, if not down already, in
the American colonies: But I much fear instead of candles you mention
being lighted, you will hear of the works of darkness. . . . I really
dread the consequence. The parliament insist on a power over all the
liberties and privileges claimed by the colonies, and hence require a
blind obedience and acquiescence in whatever they do: Should the
behaviour of the colonies happen not to square with these sovereign
notions (as I much fear it will not) what remains but by violence to
compel them to obedience. Violence will beget resentment, and provoke
to acts never dreamt of: But I will not anticipate evil; I pray God
avert it." [21]

It was not enough merely to publicize the American point of view.
Franklin found it also necessary to answer the incredibly arrogant and

opinionated assaults on Americans that began appearing in the English press. One of the worst came from a writer who styled himself "Tom Hint." He called for all-out force to repress and punish the Stamp Act dissidents. Tom Hint was particularly outraged that wealthy Americans had joined in the resistance. Gentlemen, he apparently thought, should be more obedient. He therefore took the opportunity to slander "the most opulent inhabitants of America," calling them "selfish, [of] mean dispositions, void of public spirit" and asserted they had repeatedly obstructed the British war effort, during the recent struggle with France.

Franklin knew Tom Hint's identity; he was a British officer who had served in America. The knowledge made it doubly difficult for him to control his temper and he fired back a scorching reply:

"Stabbing in the dark is unbecoming a soldier and an officer," Franklin fumed. He called upon the writer to put "his own name openly and fairly to his accusation; or take to himself in private the conscious shame" of having abused people who had received him with all the hospitality and courtesy in their power.[22]

No sooner had he disposed of Tom Hint than a new calumniator appeared, signing himself *"Vindex Patria."* He denounced the Americans in vicious terms, calling them "a mixed rabble of Scotch, Irish, and foreign vagabonds, descendents of convicts," whose chief occupation was smuggling. He even castigated America's eating habits, from their breakfasts to their Indian corn. Their cries about taxation without representation were nonsense, since they were "virtually" represented in Parliament. This virtual or fictional representation, as it was frequently called, enabled Englishmen to justify the fact that many of their most populous manufacturing towns were not represented in Parliament, while rotten boroughs with one-fiftieth of these cities' population elected members. One of these rotten boroughs, the Manor of East Greenwich, was mentioned in one of the original grants of territory in America. The Crown had stated that the colonists were "to be beholden of us, our heirs and successors, as of the Manor of East Greenwich in our County of Kent." From a legal point of view, *Vindex* argued, this phraseology meant that all of America lay within the Manor of East Greenwich, and was therefore represented in Parliament.

Writing under a variety of pseudonyms, Franklin skewered *Vindex* with his favorite weapon, sarcasm. He defended American breakfasts under the signature "Homespun," soberly declaring, "We Americans . . . may think it a very serious thing to have the honor of our eating impeached in any particular whatsoever." He wondered how a man could denounce Indian corn when he had never even tasted a single grain of it. "But why should that hinder you writing on it. Have you not written even on politics?"

As for the manor of East Greenwich encompassing America, "I have read that the whale swallowed Jonah; and as that is in Holy Writ, to be sure I ought to believe it. But if I were told, that, in fact, it was Jonah that swallowed the whale, I'd fancy I could myself as easily swallow the whale as the story." [23]

This kind of writing was more fun than indignant reproaches and Franklin enjoyed it so much, he tried it again a few weeks later, appearing in the *Public Advertiser,* disguised as an Englishman called *"Pacificus,"* with a plan that would solve the entire American question. It would, he solemnly wrote, "be entirely consistent with the economy at present so much in vogue. It is so cheap a way of going to work, that even Mr. G— G— [George Grenville], that great oeconomist, could have no reasonable objection to it."

He then suggested in straightforward prose that the Crown recruit 6000 soldiers, plus some Indians, and descending from Canada, lay waste the American colonies, burning all the capitals to the ground and cutting the throats of all the inhabitants—men, women, and children. "No man in his wits, after such terrible military execution, will refuse to purchase stamp'd paper. If anyone should hesitate, five or six hundred lashes on a cold frosty morning would soon bring him to reason." No doubt some goodhearted Britons might object to this massacre. Others might point out the harm it would do to England's commerce. But the temporary loss of American trade would cause so many bankruptcies and so much unemployment among manufacturers and laborers that "together with the felons from our gaols" England would soon be able to transport enough social dropouts to repopulate the colonies with "loyal and submissive people, and be morally certain that no act of Parliament would ever be disputed." [24]

Finally, Franklin released to the press the letters he had written to Governor Shirley over a decade ago. These cool, careful analyses of the relationship between the colonies and the mother country, with recommendations that could have averted, and could now solve, the present crisis, created a sensation in London. As Franklin shrewdly pointed out in a letter of introduction, they showed the sentiments of the Americans

on the subject of a Parliamentary tax *before* the threat of French power
was removed from Canada, and the Stamp Act was passed.

All this literary activity was combined with a day and night personal
effort to influence members of Parliament. Every hour, Franklin told
one correspondent, was spent "in forming, explaining, consulting, disputing" with the Empire's lawmakers. He worked closely with the Rockingham administration, and with a committee of twenty-eight London
merchants, led by Barlow Trecothick, with whom Franklin shared a
common birthplace, Boston. The merchants were vastly alarmed by
news of the next phase in American resistance—non-importation agreements signed by businessmen in New York, Philadelphia, Boston, and
every other major American port, pledging themselves to buy no English
goods until the tax was repealed. The merchants sent circular letters to
twenty other British towns and cities urging them to petition Parliament
to abandon the Stamp Act before it wrecked the British economy.

But even with this formidable support, chances for repeal of the Stamp
Act looked dim, at first. The Rockingham ministry was weak. On the
right, it lacked the support of the Grenvilleites and on the left, the Great
Commoner, William Pitt, had refused to lend it his prestige, because, as
usual, he wanted his own way on everything, or nothing. The Grenvilleites made it clear that they could not care less about the value of the
Stamp Act, either in terms of a revenue bill, or the damage it was doing
to British-American relations. The right of Parliament to lay taxes was
the essential point. One of the more vociferous Grenvilleites, Robert
Nugent, made that clear when he arose in Parliament to declare, "A
peppercorn in acknowledgment of the right was of more value than millions without." [25]

Edmund Burke decided that the answer to the political dilemma was
information. "Ignorance of American affairs," Burke said later, "had
misled Parliament. Knowledge alone could bring it into the right road."
For the better part of six weeks, the Rockingham administration paraded
witnesses to the bar of the House of Commons. Fugitive Stamp Commissioners from Rhode Island and Virginia, driven out of the colonies
by the fury of their fellow citizens, testified. London merchants and
experts from the Board of Trade inundated the Members with data on
the cost of civil government and military defense, and how much money
England made from its trade with the colonies. This avalanche of fact
and opinion could—and probably would—have numbed Parliament's

collective mind. Acutely aware of their own weakness, the Rocking-
hamites were trying almost too hard. But they did one thing right. They
asked Benjamin Franklin to testify. Once he had agreed, Franklin made
sure that his performance would have a climactic impact. With the help
of several Rockingham supporters, he drew up and carefully rehearsed
a list of questions and answers that would refute the Stamp Act, once
and for all. There would, of course, be questions from the Grenvilleites
and other hostile members of Parliament, but Franklin was prepared
to take his chances with them, relying on his native wit and the confidence that he knew more about America than anyone in Parliament,
including George Grenville.

In these days of intense discussion, and despite the personal urgency
he felt, Franklin's sense of humor did not desert him. At one point, a
member of Parliament began upbraiding him for his insistence on the
repeal of the Stamp Act. If he really wanted to help matters, the MP
imperiously declared, he would suggest some amendments to the Act
which might make it tolerable to the colonists.

"I must confess," Franklin gravely replied, "I have thought of one
amendment. If you will make it, the Act may remain, and yet the Americans will be quieted. It is a very small amendment too; it is only the
change of a single word."

The MP and his listening colleagues quivered with anticipation. Was
this the answer to the crisis? The opponent of repeal begged Franklin
to tell him.

"The change is in that clause," Franklin said, "where it is said that
'from and after the 1st day of November, one thousand seven hundred
and sixty-five, there shall be paid, etc.' The amendment I would propose
is for one, read two, and then all the rest of the Act may stand as it
does." [26]

William Pitt, now Lord Chatham, spoke out against the Stamp Act,
calling for its repeal. But he also insisted on "the sovereign authority of
this country over the colonies." Since this, and not the Stamp Act as
such, was the real nub of the problem, Pitt in effect canceled himself out.
Meanwhile, the Grenvilleites and their cohorts fought back with a
battery of logical and emotional arguments, in and out of Parliament.
The chaplain of the Earl of Sandwich, a man who made no secret of his
contempt for Americans, ridiculed the Rockingham ministry's weakness
and warned that if Parliament succumbed to a policy of appeasement,
the Americans would swiftly become ungovernable. "Can it be sup-

posed," he asked, "that the colonists will ever submit to bear any share
in those grievous burdens and taxes, with which we are loaded, when
they find that the government will not, or dare not assert its own authority and power?" [27] On London streets a satirical ballad made the same
point.

> *Who'd stay in musty England,*
> *And work himself to death,*
> *Where, choaked with debts and taxes*
> *No man can fetch his breath*
>   *And to America we'll go &c.*
> *Then to America we'll go,*
> *Where we will merry be;*
> *Since there no taxes need be paid,*
> *And wise men all agree.*
>   *And to America we'll go &c.*
> *Then fare thee well, Old England,*
> *Where honesty can't thrive;*
> *Farewell roast-beef, and bread, and beer,*
> *We'll go to yonder hive.*
>   *And to America we'll go &c.*[28]

In this heated atmosphere, the moment of truth for Parliament and
Franklin arrived on February 13, 1766.

I I

"What is your name and place of abode?"

"Franklin, of Philadelphia."

The calm, quiet voice carried clearly across the packed benches of the
House of Commons. At first glance, the man standing before the bar—
a horizontal piece of wood that blocked the passage into the well of the
House—was unimpressive. Benjamin Franklin wore no royal orders or
ribbons. His clothes were in the simple—but by no means inexpensive—

style of a well-to-do English merchant. He was stout and the white wig he wore was just a little old-fashioned, dropping too low on the shoulders, definitely missing the dash and style which was the mode of upper-class London. But there was a serene self-possession about the man that made the niceties of high fashion inconsequential. He stood there, and his very silence said: important.

His name was, of course, familiar to most members of Parliament. Even the dullest country gentleman, who rarely thought about anything more significant than pursuit of the fox, the most effervescent macaroni, who found it hard to think about anything weightier than the shade of his mulberry waistcoat, at least knew that Benjamin Franklin was the American who had startled the scientific world with his epochal discoveries about the nature of electricity.

For Franklin, this was the most momentous hour of his life. These words, *Franklin of Philadelphia,* tolled in his mind like a solemn sonorous bell. They said things to him that he did not really want to hear. Until this moment— or at least until the few months preceding this moment, which were all part of the same nightmarish experience—he did not think that *Franklin of Philadelphia* set him apart from these men who sat on the crowded benches covered with tacky green cloth, nor from their fellow politicians in their nearby Whitehall Palace offices. As a fellow servant of the Crown, with a son a royal governor, Benjamin Franklin had considered *Franklin of Philadelphia* as no more significant than the set speech he often used when he entered a roadside tavern during his trips around America. "I am Ben Franklin," he would say. "I was born in Boston, now live in Philadelphia, and I have no news. Now what can you give me for dinner?" All his life Ben Franklin had thought of his native land as an essential part of that magnificent, ever-expanding empire known as Great Britain. He had gloried in—and fervently supported—the triumphs which had driven the French off the continent of North America, and made England supreme in India, Africa, the West Indies, and Europe. But now events in America had forced Benjamin Franklin to face a fact which had always squirmed just below the level of his conscious mind. England and her colonies, separated by the immense Atlantic, were not one nation. After almost 150 years of slow maturation, a new nation, or at least a new people, had arisen on the other side of the ocean—Americans. Franklin had predicted it in his essay on population. But he had not foreseen that his people would achieve political maturity long before they reached economic independence. He was facing it now. By one of those fascinating series of coincidences that make thoughtful men wonder whether history is as accidental as it seems at first glance, the man best qualified to speak for this political maturity was here in London in the moment of crisis.

Aside from the problem of convincing these very disgruntled Englishmen that they should humiliate themselves (and to their minds impugn the prestige of Parliament) by voting the Stamp Act's repeal, one other aspect of the scene is worth noting. Speaking before the British Parliament was a harrowing experience for someone who lacked oratorical gifts. The artists who painted or sketched pictures of the House of Commons in the 1760s labored to create the impression that the room's size compared favorably with Britain's imperial power. Actually, the chamber was only sixty feet long, twenty-eight feet wide, and thirty feet high— not much larger than the living rooms of some modern upper middle class American homes. Many speakers experienced acute claustrophobia when they rose, and found themselves practically eyeball to eyeball with a sea of faces. One man, attempting his first (and last) speech, said, "I brought out two or three sentences when a mist seemed to rise before my eyes: I then lost my recollection, and could see nothing but the Speaker's wig which swelled and swelled and swelled until it covered the whole house. I then sank back on my seat and never attempted another speech." [29]

Franklin himself was not a gifted speaker. In fact he freely admitted in his *Autobiography* that he was "a bad speaker, subject to much hesitation in the choice of words." Standing at the bar, confronting the packed, largely hostile house, he must have thanked God that he had had the forethought to plan his performance in advance. James Hewitt, one of the Rockingham members with whom Franklin had planted questions, rose to begin the inquisition. Hewitt was from Coventry, an industrial city hard hit by the American importation boycott.

"Do the Americans pay any considerable taxes among themselves?" he asked.

"Certainly, many and very heavy taxes," Franklin replied.

"What are the present taxes in Pennsylvania, laid by the laws of the colony?"

"There are taxes on all estates, real and personal; a poll tax; a tax on all offices, professions, trades and businesses, according to their profits; an excise on all wine, rum, and other spirits; and a duty of ten pounds per head on all Negroes imported, with some other duties."

"For what purposes are those taxes laid?"

"For the support of the civil and military establishments of the country, and to discharge the heavy debt contracted in the last war."

"How long are those taxes to continue?"

"Those for discharging the debt are to continue until 1772, and longer, if the debt should not be then all discharged. The others must always continue."

"Was it not expected that the debt would have been sooner discharged?"

"It was, when the peace was made with France and Spain. But a fresh war breaking out with the Indians, a fresh load of debt was incurred; and the taxes, of course, continued longer by new law."

"Are not all the people very able to pay those taxes?"

"No. The frontier counties, all along the continent, having been frequently ravaged by the enemy and greatly impoverished, are able to pay very little tax."

Another member, John Huske, one of the few men in Parliament who had been born in America, rose to replace Hewitt as straight man. He asked Franklin questions about the distribution of the stamps, as he saw it in his role as Deputy Postmaster General of North America. In the same casual, deadpan, almost humdrum way, Franklin made it clear that the act was not only unjust, it was totally impractical. In the thinly populated back settlements and in Canada, there was no mail service, and people could not get stamps—which meant they could not marry, make their wills, buy or sell property—without taking long journeys and "spending perhaps three or four pounds, that the Crown might get sixpence."

Suddenly the performance was interrupted by a harsh question from the opposition. "Are not the colonies from their circumstances very able to pay the stamp duty?"

It was a question that might have ruined a less skillful man. But Franklin knew that the Stamp Act had specified the payment was to be made in specie—gold or silver coins which were so scarce in America many colonies had already resorted to issuing paper money. So he neatly evaded the main point in his reply.

"In my opinion, there is not gold and silver enough in the colonies to pay the stamp duty for one year."

Irately, the gentleman made one more slash at Franklin's throat.

"Don't you know that the money arising from the stamps was all to be laid out in America?"

"I know it is appropriated by the Act to the American service; but it will be spent in the conquered colonies [Canada and Florida] where the soldiers are, not in the colonies that pay for it."

The Rockinghams rose to Franklin's rescue with more questions about the population of the colonies, and how much they imported from Britain. Smoothly Franklin delivered the significant statistics. There were 300,000 white men in America between sixteen and sixty—more than enough to make a formidable army. Pennsylvania alone imported 500,000 pounds of British goods each year. The implication was obvious. Not only would a war with these people be dangerous; it would be highly uneconomic.

Then George Grenville, as stubborn as he was arrogant, was on his feet interrupting Franklin's friends to shrill his favorite question. "Do you think it right that America should be protected by this country and pay no part of the expense?"

"That is not the case," Franklin replied. "The colonies raised, clothed, and paid during the last war, near twenty-five thousand men, and spent many millions."

"Were you not reimbursed by Parliament?"

"We were only reimbursed what in your opinion we had advanced beyond our proportion, or beyond what might reasonably be expected from us; and it was a very small part of what we spent. Pennsylvania, in particular, disbursed about five-hundred thousand pounds and the reimbursements in the whole did not exceed sixty thousand pounds."

Grenville sat down, looking very uncomfortable.

On the questions and the answers rolled, in the same zigzag pattern; the Rockinghams drawing from Franklin reams of information that made the Stamp Act look more and more like the greatest piece of idiocy in Parliament's history. Again and again, Franklin cut down obnoxious and difficult questions with blunt facts or subtle evasions.

When someone tried to make him admit that the last war with Spain and France (1739–48) was fought for the sake of America because hostilities began over Spanish captures in American seas, Franklin replied, "Captures of ships carrying on the British trade there with British manufactures."

When another adversary asked him if the colonial Assemblies would indemnify loyal subjects whose property had been damaged by Stamp Act rioters, Franklin mildly replied, "That is a question I cannot answer."

Franklin made it clear that the Americans intended to maintain their opposition to the stamps for years if necessary. He vowed they were ready to begin manufacturing their own clothes, shoes, glass, tableware, farm utensils, and other items they had previously imported from Britain. Always he walked the delicate line between outright defiance, which would have insulted the ticklish tempers of many members, and pliant submission, which might have encouraged the opposition.

One member asked him, "Can anything less than a military force carry the Stamp Act into execution?"

"I do not see how a military force can be applied to that purpose."

"Why not?"

"Suppose a military force sent into America, they will find nobody in arms; what are they then to do? They cannot force a man to take stamps who chooses to do without them. They will not find a rebellion; they may indeed make one."

When a skeptic asked him if the Americans would pay as much for "worse manufactures of their own, and use them preferable to better of ours," Franklin replied with an instantaneous epigram. "People will pay as freely to gratify one passion as another, their resentment as their pride."

Then came the most important planted question—and the most moving moment in Franklin's performance. A Rockingham member asked: "What was the temper of America toward Great Britain before the year 1763?"

"The best in the world," Franklin replied. "They submitted willingly to the government of the Crown, and paid, in their courts, obedience to the acts of Parliament. Numerous as the people are in the several old provinces, they cost you nothing in forts, citadels, garrisons, or armies to keep them in subjection. They were governed by this country at the expense only of a little pen, ink, and paper; they were led by a thread. They had not only a respect, but an affection for Great Britain; for its laws, its customs and manners, and even a fondness for its fashions, that greatly increased the commerce. Natives of Britain were always treated with particular regard. To be an Old-England man was, of itself, a character of some respect, and gave a kind of rank among us."

This was Benjamin Franklin speaking out of the wellsprings of his own experience. The words have a ring which go beyond smooth preparation to the more meaningful realm of personal truth.

"And what is their temper now?"

"Oh, very much altered. . . ."

"If the Act is not repealed, what do you think will be the consequences?"

"A total loss of the respect and affection the people of America bear to this country, and of all the commerce that depends on that respect and affection."

There were some floundering attempts by the opposition to regain the initiative. Most of them were repetitious. Franklin cut one questioner down with a cool "I have answered that." He got a laugh when another somewhat muddled member asked him if the colonies would acquiesce in the authority of Parliament if the Stamp Act was repealed.

"I don't doubt at all that if the legislature repeal the Act the colonies will acquiesce in the authority," said Franklin with a twinkle in his eye.

Finally, his friends rescued him with two questions which were obviously designed to bring down the curtain on his performance.

"What used to be the pride of the Americans?"

"To indulge in the fashions and manufactures of Great Britain."

"What is now their pride?"

"To wear their old clothes over again, till they can make new ones."[30]

III

A week later, the House of Commons voted to repeal the Stamp Act. Benjamin Gerrish, an American then in London, wrote home exultantly that the bill was on its way to the House of Lords. "A bitter pill it will be to them, but swallow they must, in spite of their teeth," he chortled. Another American, Thomas Rushton, wrote in the same cheerful vein. "It was the impossibility of enforcing the Act that influenced the minds of most people, and when Dr. Franklin on his examination asked them, if it took six years to conquer Canada, defended only by five or six

thousand men, with all the colonies to assist them, how would they conquer all the colonies united together, without that assistance, they stared
and were strook silent." [31]

In America, the news of repeal created a wave of euphoria. The
chief beneficiary was Benjamin Franklin. His testimony was reprinted
in almost every colony, and his popularity soared. The Proprietary
Party in Pennsylvania had to eat the slander they had been spreading, that Franklin had aided and abetted the Stamp Act. In London,
the man who made the victory possible was by no means so exultant.
He noted wryly that Parliament had also passed a Declaratory Act,
in which it insisted that it had the right to enact laws binding the
British colonies "in all cases whatsoever." To his friend Charles Thomson in Philadelphia, he wrote, "If I live to see you I will let you know
. . . how much we were obliged to what the profane would call luck
and the pious, Providence." [32]

Parliament demonstrated, only a few days later, why Franklin was
still on his guard. The lawmakers passed an act indemnifying stamp
agents and others who had suffered substantial losses for their loyalty
to the Crown. Grenville and his followers vehemently insisted that the
Americans ought to pay for this damage, or at the very least they should
pay for the government's costs in printing the millions of stamps, which
had now become worthless paper.

In an anonymous letter to a London paper, Franklin ridiculed such
peevish tactics. "Was the harmony and good understanding" achieved
by "a generous total repeal" to be lost for "a pittance?" The idea, he
said, put him in mind of a Frenchman who used to accost English and
other strangers on one of the Seine's bridges brandishing a red-hot iron.
Making a complimentary bow, he would say, "Pray, Monsieur Anglais,
do me the favour to let me have the honour of thrusting this hot iron
into your backside?"

"Zoons, what does the fellow mean!" the agitated Englishman would
cry. "Begone with your iron or I'll break your head!"

"Nay, Monsieur," replied the Frenchman, "if you do not chuse it, I do
not insist upon it. But at least, you will in justice have the goodness to
pay me something for the heating of my iron." [33]

At the same time the zany story was an index of Franklin's cockiness.
His Stamp Act performance was a tremendous triumph, and Benjamin
Franklin probably thought it would become the high point of his life.

The words "If I live" in his letter to Thomson are significant. He was fifty-nine years old in an era when only a handful of men reached the biblical three score and ten. It was distinctly comforting to an elderly politician to learn that he was being toasted and hailed as a hero in taverns and coffee houses up and down the coastline of North America. In the fall of 1766, Benjamin Franklin was a contented man.

I V

In politics, Franklin was no more a prophet than other men. After the climax of the Stamp Act crisis, Anglo-American affairs seemed, for a while at least, to have reached a point of relatively peaceful equilibrium. Franklin's mind inevitably gravitated from thinking large thoughts about the British Empire to thinking about Benjamin Franklin, William Franklin, and their future. The project for which he had returned to England—driving the Penns out of Pennsylvania—was in limbo. No one in Pennsylvania could create any popular enthusiasm for the royal government after the Stamp Act upheaval. Franklin's political party barely survived the debacle, and only then by jettisoning his friend John Hughes. He never again held political office in Pennsylvania. His friend Franklin, on the other hand, thanks to his magnificent performance before the House of Commons, was renominated as Pennsylvania's agent in London. Who else, the Assembly reasoned, could do a better job of protecting their interests in the imperial capital?

Since there was very little Pennsylvania interest to protect, in the diplomatic hiatus, Franklin's thoughts about the future centered more and more around that other dream which he had told his friend George Whitefield he hoped to make the final bright point of his life—the founding of a western colony. More and more it became the logical last step of his career—the one thing he was best fitted to create out of (what seemed to him) the odd twists and turns of his life. What other American could match his fame and influence in England, especially his contacts with all the branches and factions of the British power structure? Moreover, it was a project in which William Franklin was now deeply involved.

William had remained in close touch with trader George Croghan, the man who had introduced him to the West in 1748. After the Peace of Paris in 1763, Croghan was named Deputy Superintendent for Indian Affairs under Sir William Johnson, who lived on a vast estate in upper New York and, thanks to his marriage to an Indian woman, had tremendous influence with the Iroquois and other tribes. Croghan played a vital role in settling the Pontiac Indian war, personally negotiating a treaty of peace with Pontiac and other chiefs. The Pennsylvania trader had the backing of a number of Philadelphia merchants, notably the wealthy Wharton family. Samuel Wharton, an ambitious younger member of this clan, was a good friend of William Franklin, and he and Croghan stopped at the governor's residence in Burlington, New Jersey, on Croghan's return from his peace mission to Pontiac. Croghan showed Franklin a journal he had kept of the trip, describing in detail meadows growing wild grass and hemp ten or twelve feet high. Hemp alone would pay a speculator a profit on these lands. But how to get at them, that was the problem.

Croghan had already made one fruitless trip to London in the hope of obtaining confirmation of a grant of 200,000 acres he had wangled from tribes in the Pittsburgh area. The problem was a proclamation which the British government had issued in 1763, in which the Crown had forbidden further colonization beyond the Alleghenies, reserving the Ohio Valley lands for the Indians. The speculators asked William if the man who had persuaded Parliament to repeal the Stamp Act could persuade them to adjust this invisible boundary. Perhaps, said William Franklin. But the argument had to be something more effective than the hopes of a group of private individuals for personal gain. Far better, suggested Governor Franklin, dusting off his father's idea, was a proposal to found an entire colony, in which they would be the proprietors. The speculators seized on the idea as a creation of pure genius—which to a considerable extent it was.[34] Governor Franklin was commissioned to draw up a plan which he called "Reasons and Proposals for Establishing a British Colony at the Illinois." The colony was to occupy an immense tract of land between the Illinois and Mississippi Rivers. Each of the partners was to bear two-sixteenths of the cost, and share two-sixteenths of the profits. Junior partners, in on a one-sixteenth basis, included Franklin's old friend John Hughes and his political lieutenant, Joseph Galloway. It was agreed that room should be left for adding some influential members in England. First on that list was, of course, Benjamin Franklin.

In London, the agent for Pennsylvania responded with enthusiasm. "I like the project of a colony . . . and will forward it to my utmost here," he told William. But he warned the speculators that they were making a mistake in allowing room for only a few British partners. He pointed out some problems. Although his good friend, William Petty, Lord Shelburne, had become secretary of state for the Southern Department, an equally potent figure was Wills Hill, Lord Hillsborough, a nobleman with immense estates in Ireland, who was head of the powerful Board of Trade. Hillsborough was against western colonization for a very practical reason. He was afraid it would attract too many tenants from his estates in Ireland and reduce his rents. Franklin pointed out to his son that there was an estimated 63,000,000 acres of land in the proposed colony, more than enough to provide for additional partners, who would "increase the weight of interest here." [35]

A few weeks later, Franklin was reporting to William that he had discussed the proposed colony with Shelburne. Unfortunately for the Franklins and their friends, they were dealing with a man who invariably went through torments of indecision before making up his mind. Shelburne proceeded to point out to Franklin arguments he had heard from many people against the founding of such a colony. It was too far inland to be governed easily. It might become a power unto itself, and lure other colonies away from their allegiance to England. There was a shortage of labor in England and in the settled colonies. He himself, Shelburne said, did not think these arguments had "much weight." Franklin assured William that he had tried hard "to invalidate them entirely." But the meeting ended with his Lordship in his usual state of mind: undecided. To nudge him in the right direction, Franklin loaded him with the plan William had drawn up, George Croghan's western journal and a map of the projected colony.

Franklin pursued Shelburne relentlessly throughout the fall and winter of 1766–67. On October 11, 1766, he was reporting that Shelburne "was pleased to say he really approved" William's plan. But there was that old bugaboo which had caused the Stamp Act uproar—a shortage of money. To lend further weight to his arguments, Franklin brought Richard Jackson into the scheme as a partner. Nothing illustrates the web of persuasion Franklin was weaving around Lord Shelburne better than this letter of November 8, 1766, to William. "Mr. Jackson has now come to town. The Ministry have asked his opinion and advice on your plan of a colony in the Illinois, and he has just sent me to peruse his answer in writing, in which he warmly recommends it, and enforces it by strong reasons; which gives me great pleasure, as it corroborates what I have been saying on the same topic, and from him appears less to be suspected of some American bias." [36]

About the same time, Sir William Johnson forwarded a letter favoring the colony to the Secretary of State, and a copy to Benjamin Franklin. This seemed a very sound move to Franklin, who assured William that Johnson was "much relied on in all affairs that may have any relation to the Indians." [37] But the year 1766 trickled away, and 1767 began to follow it, with no action forthcoming from Lord Shelburne, or any other member of the government.

The problem lay in the disorganized state of English politics, and the still-festering wounds of the Stamp Act crisis. Young Lord Rockingham had demonstrated considerable political ability in managing the repeal of the Stamp Act. But thereafter he relapsed into lackadaisical incompetence, displaying little or no energy in leading and disciplining Parliament. His government was soon being described by Parliament's reigning wit, Charles Townshend, as "a lute-string administration, fit only for summer wear." In desperation, the King was forced to ask William Pitt to form a government. Aging and unwell, Pitt nevertheless agreed. But he was scarcely in office when a combination of crippling gout and melancholia assailed him. He absented himself from London for weeks at a time, and the government blundered forward, with no real leader.

Into this vacuum stepped Charles Townshend. As lightheaded as he was witty, Townshend was an artist at talking on both sides of any question. He had voted for the Stamp Act, and for its repeal. But he was an astute politician in his own flighty way and had a shrewd sense of the mood of Parliament. In the first months of 1767, this mood was alarmingly anti-American. The Quartering Act, one of the acts passed by George Grenville's ministry, required local colonial Assemblies to provide money for the support of British troops stationed within their borders. The Assembly of New York resented the fact that the Crown had stationed a heavy proportion of these regiments within its boundaries, simply because the colony was strategically convenient. They declined to vote a money bill for their support. Parliament, egged on by the still-smarting Grenville and his supporters, simmered with righteous indignation. There was talk of sending additional regiments and a battle fleet to extract the Assembly's vote at the point of a gun. The leaderless Chatham Ministry, as it was now called, swayed and almost collapsed underneath this first wave of petulance. There was talk of an imminent reorganization, and Franklin dolefully wrote William: "Great changes being expected keeps men's minds in suspense, and obstructs public affairs of every kind. It is therefore not to be wondered at that so little progress is made in our American schemes. . . ." [38]

V

Charles Townshend, sensing a propitious moment, stepped forward to announce that he had a plan to raise money in America. He would take the Americans at their word, when they declared they only resented internal taxes, but had no objection to external ones. He therefore proposed to lay extra import duties on glass, lead, paints, paper, tea, and a long list of other items imported by the Americans. To guarantee that the duties would be collected, Townshend added to them a bill which created a new system of vice-admiralty courts, whose judges had the power to issue "writs of assistance" which gave treasury agents the right to invade a man's house, warehouse, or ship without a search warrant. Parliament voted resoundingly for the Townshend Acts, and they became law on June 29, 1767.

Franklin could only shudder at this folly. To his chief political lieutenant in Pennsylvania, stolid Joseph Galloway, he commented, "One of the distinctions of party here" was to be an adversary to America. "Those who have in the last two sessions shown a disposition to favor us, being called by way of reproach, Americans. While the others . . . value themselves on being true to the interests of Britain and zealous for maintaining its dignity and sovereignty over the colonies." [39]

The bad temper was not all on the British side. Franklin soon realized he was moving into the same position he had attempted to occupy in

Pennsylvania politics—a moderate who talked sense to both sides. But now, because he had played that role in vain in Pennsylvania, there was a certain note of hopelessness in his remonstrations, especially when they were addressed to the Americans. In another letter to Galloway, he noted that the British merchants who had fought for the repeal of the Stamp Act, and had even chartered a vessel to carry the "joyful news" to North America, had spent 1500 pounds. "For all this, except from the little colony of Rhode Island, they had not received as much as a thank ye." Moreover, circular letters which they had written "with the best intentions" to the merchants of several colonies containing "their best and most friendly advice" (to say and do as little as possible to arouse Parliament) either went unanswered or got contemptuous and insulting replies. The captain of their messenger ship was "everywhere treated with neglect and contempt instead of civility and hospitality; and nowhere more than at Philadelphia," Franklin wrote, adding, "I own I was ashamed to hear all this." [40]

More and more he lamented the instability of the ministry and especially the recklessness of Charles Townshend. He gave Galloway another example of Townshend's circus-rider's approach to politics. One day George Grenville began ridiculing the new duties as trifles. Far better, Grenville declared, to issue paper money for the colonies and collect interest on it for the Crown. "Mr. Townshend, finding the House listened to this and seemed to like it, stood up again and said, 'That was a proposition of his own, which he had intended to make with the rest, but it had slipt his memory, and the gentleman, who must have heard of it, now unfairly would take advantage of that slip and make a merit to himself of a proposition that was another's,' and as proof of it, assured the House a bill was prepared for the purpose, and would be laid before them."

There was, of course, no such bill, and Townshend's fellow ministers were left gasping once more. His statement ruined months of careful work by Franklin and Richard Jackson in favor of a paper money act based on a completely different approach. Grenville's accountant's mind could see nothing wrong with interest-bearing bills, but, as Franklin pointed out in a paper he wrote on the subject, after a few months, the interest would become worth computing, and calculating it on every trifling bill would cause infuriating delays in transacting business in shops and taverns. Moreover, as the interest rose, the paper would be hoarded, and the result would be less business, not more. Franklin's idea, to make paper money "general legal tender" (with the loan offices that issued it paying interest on the total sum to the Crown), was destroyed by Townshend's idiocy. "I fear that imprudencies on both sides may, step by step, bring on the most mischievous consequences," he told Galloway.[41]

To Lord Kames, in another letter about the same time, Franklin returned to the lofty view he had taken in the Albany Congress. Knowing that he was talking to a kindred spirit, he urged him to throw his influence into the dispute. "You may thereby be the happy instrument of great good to the nation, and of preventing much mischief and bloodshed. I am fully persuaded with you, that a consolidating *union* by a fair and equal representation of all parts of this empire in Parliament, is the only firm basis on which its political grandeur and prosperity can be founded." There was once a time, he said, when the colonies would have been delighted to accept such a proposition. "They are now indifferent about it; and if it is delayed much longer . . . will *refuse* it."

Mournfully, Franklin admitted that it was almost a certainty that the offer would be delayed because "the pride in this people cannot bear the thought of it." Then came a most significant line, revealing how much the controversy was affecting Franklin emotionally, "Every man in England seems to consider himself as a piece of a sovereign over America; seems to jostle himself into the throne with the King, and talks of *our subjects in the colonies.*"

This attitude, in Franklin's opinion, flowed from a fundamental misconception. "It is a common, but mistaken notion here, that the colonies were planted at the expence of Parliament, and that therefore the Parliament has a right to tax them &c. The truth is, they were planted at the expence of private adventurers, who went over there to settle, with leave of the King, given by charter. On receiving this leave, and those charters, the adventurers voluntarily engaged to remain the King's subjects, though in a foreign country; a country which had not been conquered by either King or Parliament, but was possessed by a free people." [42]

This paragraph is fundamental to all of Franklin's thinking about the relationship between England and America. Equally important was his fondness for Great Britain. "Upon the whole, I have lived so great a part of my life in Britain," he told Kames, "and have formed so many friendships in it, that I love it, and sincerely wish it prosperity; and therefore wish to see that union, on which alone I think it can be secured and established." But overmastering all facts and feelings was his vision of America's future. "America, an immense territory, favoured by Nature with all advantages of climate, soil, great navigable rivers and lakes, &c, must become a great country, populous and mighty; and will, in a less time than is generally conceived, be able to shake off any shackles that may be imposed on her, and perhaps place them on the imposers." This was a vision rooted not only in sentiment but in science, in Franklin's confidence in his mathematical prediction of America's population growth.

This vision was what made Franklin so sad when he contemplated England's hostile, aggressive mood toward the colonies. "Every act of oppression will sour their tempers, lessen greatly, if not annihilate the profits of your commerce with them," he warned Kames, "and hasten their final revolt; for the seeds of liberty are universally found there, and nothing can eradicate them." [43]

V I

In spite of the discouraging political atmosphere, Franklin continued to press Lord Shelburne and other ministers to gain their backing for the new western colony. On August 28, 1767, he wrote to William Franklin: "Last week I dined at Lord Shelburne's, and had a long conversation with him and Mr. Conway [Henry Seymour Conway, the Irish orator who was now a member of the cabinet] . . . on the subject of reducing American expense." The two ministers talked of turning Indian affairs over to provinces that bordered on the tribal lands. Indian superintendents, such as Sir William Johnson, each thinking he was representing the largesse of George III, had recently executed treaties involving exorbitant sums. Franklin immediately "took the opportunity of urging it as one means of saving expense . . . that a settlement should be made in the Illinois country; expatiated on the various advantages. . . . I mentioned your plan, its being approved by Sir William Johnson, the readiness and ability of the gentlemen concerned to carry the settlement into execution, with very little expense to the Crown, &c. The Secretaries appeared finally to be fully convinced, and there remained no obstacle but the Board of Trade, which was to be brought over privately, before the matter should be referred to them officially."

In this same letter, Franklin added an interesting paragraph about the French ambassador in London, one Monsieur Durand. "He is extremely curious to inform himself in the affairs of America; pretends to have a great esteem for me, on account of the abilities shown in my examination [before the House of Commons during the Stamp Act crisis]; has desired to have all my political writings, invited me to dine with him, was very inquisitive, treated me with great civility, makes me visits, &c. I fancy that intriguing nation would like very well to meddle on occasion, and blow up the coals between Britain and her colonies; but I hope we shall give them no opportunity." [44]

Franklin's reaction to the French ambassador's overtures was entirely in keeping with his hoping-for-the-best but fearing-the-worst mood at the time. A few days later, he left with his good friend, Sir John Pringle, for a summer vacation in France. Someone who views history as a series of intrigues might try to make something sinister of this. But Franklin showed little sign of being anything except an eager, observant tourist.

From Paris he wrote a lively letter back to Polly Stevenson, telling of his adventures along the way. "At Dover," he told her, "a number of passengers who had never been before at sea" insisted on eating a hearty breakfast before they sailed. "Doubtless they thought that when they had paid for their breakfast, they had a right to it, and that when they had swallowed it they were sure of it. But they had scarce been out half an hour, before the sea laid claim to it, and they were oblig'd to deliver it up. So it seems there are uncertainties, even beyond those between the cup and the lip."

In France, Franklin met numerous members of the French Academy of Sciences, for whom he was already a famous name. He was fascinated by a group of French economists, the physiocrats, who argued that the government should have as little as possible to do with business. One of their leaders, Pierre Samuel du Pont de Nemours, eventually moved to America and founded a corporate dynasty. Franklin became even more friendly with a French scholar-scientist, Barbé Dubourg, who spoke excellent English, and expressed a great interest in translating Franklin's writings into French. But the high point of Franklin's visit was his presentation to King Louis XV at Versailles. He told Polly Stevenson about it in vivid detail. The King "spoke to both of us [BF and Dr. Pringle] very graciously and chearfully, is a handsome man, has a very lively look, and appears younger than he is." In the evening the two travelers went to the *Grand Couvert,* at which the royal family dined in public. Franklin and Pringle were brought forward, and stood beside the King and Queen. Knowing Pringle was physician to the English royal family, King Louis asked him a good many questions about his fellow rulers. Franklin added that Louis "did me too the honor of taking some notice of me; that's saying enough, for I would not have you think me so much pleas'd with this King and Queen, as to have a whit less regard than I us'd to have for ours."

Franklin found Versailles "a prodigious mixture of magnificence and negligence, with every kind of elegancy except that of cleanliness, and what we call *tidyness.*" He admired the Parisians' drinking water, which they filtered through sand cisterns, and their clean streets which encouraged people to walk on them, and cut down on the number of coaches and chairs which constantly clogged London's streets. He noted, with his scientist's eye, that a Parisian on foot, even when he was carrying an umbrella, did not take up more than three square feet, while a coach took up 240 square feet. He also admired French manners. "It seems to be a point settled here universally, that strangers are to be treated with respect; and one has the same deference shewn one here by being a stranger, as in England by being a lady. . . . Why don't we practice this urbanity to Frenchmen? Why should they be allowed to outdo us in any thing?"

He freely admitted that he was enjoying France immensely. "Traveling is one way of lengthening life, at least in appearance. It is but about a fortnight since we left London, but the variety of scenes we have gone through makes it seem equal to six months living in one place. Perhaps I have suffered a greater change, too, in my own person, than I could have done in six years at home. I had not been here six days, before my taylor and perruqyier [wig maker] had transform'd me into a Frenchman. Only think what a figure I make in a little bag-wig and naked ears. They told me I was become 20 years younger and look'd very galante;

"So being in Paris where the mode is to be sacredly follow'd I was once very near making love to my friend's wife.

"This letter shall cost you a shilling, and you may consider it cheap, when you reflect, that it has cost me at least 50 guineas to get into the situation, that enables me to write it. Besides, I might, if I had staied at home, have won perhaps two shillings of you at cribbidge." [45]

This charming letter also makes it clear how deeply and intricately Franklin continued to interweave his personal life, his role of husband and father and friend, through the broader web of world affairs and Parliamentary politics in which he was involved. He took as intense an interest in the life and loves of Polly Stevenson, as if he were her own father. In mid-1767, he wrote to Deborah, "Our Polly's match is quite broke off. The difference was about money matters. I am not displeased at it, as I did not much like the man, thinking him a mean-spirited mercenary fellow and not worthy so valuable a girl as she is in every respect: person, fortune, temper, and excellent understanding." [46]

His fondness for Polly Stevenson even inspired Franklin to one of his rare flights of poetry as a birthday present for her. He made fun of his poem in a wry letter that probably had the young lady laughing too hard to read the rather serious sentiments.

Dear Polly,

A muse, you must know, visited me this morning! I see you are surpriz'd, as I was. I never saw one before. And shall never see another. So I took the opportunity of her help to put the answer into verse, because I was some verse in your debt ever since you sent me the last pair of garters.

This muse appear'd to be no housewife. I suppose few of them are. She was drest *(if the expression is allowable) in an* undress, *a kind of slatternly* negligee, *neither neat nor clean, nor well made; and she has given the same sort of dress to my piece. On reviewing it, I would have reform'd the lines, and made them all of a length, as I am told lines ought to be; but I find I can't lengthen the short ones without stretching them on the rack, and I think it would be equally cruel to cut off any part of the long ones. Besides the super-fluity of* these *makes up for the deficiency of* those; *and so, from a principle of justice, I leave them at full length, that I may give you at least in one sense of the word,* good measure. *Adieu, my dear good girl, and believe me ever your affectionate, faithful friend,*

> *You'd have the custom broke, you say,*
> *That marks with festive mirth your natal day,*
> *"Because, as one grows old,*
> *One cannot so be told*
> *How many of one's years have pass'd away."*
> *That reason came not from your heart.*

> *'Tis given in earnest but by those,*
> *The empty belles and emptier beaux*
> *Who justly may suppose*
> *The outward frame to be their better part,*
> *And therefore grieve that time subjects it to decay.*[47]

There are two more stanzas, which are atrociously bad poetry and justified everything Franklin said about his slatternly muse.

Franklin followed with equally close attention the fortunes of his real family in Philadelphia. He advised Deborah minutely on decorating their new house. When Deborah complained that "the Blue Room" was too dark, he told her, "I would have you finish it as soon as you can, thus: paint the wainscot a dead white; paper the walls blue, and tack the gilt border around just above the surbase and under the cornish." Additional instructions included "papier mache musical figures" tacked to the middle of the ceiling. "When this is done," he assured Deborah, "I think it will look very well." [48]

He was not so sure about his daughter Sally's choice of a husband. Deborah let him know in rather strong terms that she approved of young Richard Bache, a Yorkshireman who had emigrated to Philadelphia after Franklin had left on his second mission to Europe. William Franklin clearly disapproved of the young man, who had a somewhat less than successful record in business, and at the age of thirty not much visible means of support. William told his father that most of Franklin's friends were equally dubious about Bache. Franklin feared that the young man was a fortune hunter. But he had enough confidence in Deborah's common sense to let her judgment prevail.

Franklin only pointed out that his partnership with David Hall, under which he had received about 700 pounds a year, had expired in 1766, and Hall had become full owner of *The Pennsylvania Gazette*. There was also the possibility, on the shifting sands of English politics, that he might lose his post office job. This meant they would be reduced to living on a rather narrow scale. He warned Deborah not to "make an expensive feasting wedding" but to conduct everything "with frugality and economy." He hoped that Mr. Bache did not have expectations "of any fortune to be had with our daughter before our death." The most he could see his way clear to do was to fit Sally out "handsomely" in clothes and furniture, to the tune of about 500 pounds. "For the rest, they must depend, as you and I did, on their own industry and care." [49]

Franklin also wrote William, urging him to let Deborah and Sally have their way. The last thing he wanted was a family quarrel when he was too far away to mediate it, and he gathered from Deborah's letters that William was throwing his weight around. William peremptorily denied the implied accusation in his father's advice. In a clear reference to his earlier withdrawal from Deborah's stormy jurisdiction, he wrote: "On the contrary, I can safely say it has been the constant endeavor of my life to avoid all such quarrels, and I have not only pass'd over quietly what I have been told by others, but things of the most provoking nature which I have seen and heard in person." These words implied rather strongly that if anyone was acting up, it was Deborah with her fishwife's tongue. "A regard to your peace & happiness has prevented your being acquainted with these matters," he told Franklin. "Be assur'd . . . you are greatly mistaken in thinking that my mother was 'not angry with our friends for not approving the match, etc.' " William closed the discussion with a sentence which underscored his devotion to his father. "I sincerely wish that you may on your return find that everything has been conducted to your satisfaction, for as to what other people may think it is a matter of no consequence." [50]

Most of the time William and his father discussed politics. In the fall of 1767, William was writing earnestly to his father that the Townshend Acts were arousing widespread opposition throughout America. Boston had led the way with riots and fiery denunciations in the newspapers, while Franklin's old foe, John Dickinson, had produced a pamphlet, *Letters of a Pennsylvania Farmer,* which revised the old colonial distinction between internal and external taxes, and made a further distinction, between taxes to regulate commerce and taxes for revenue. The latter, Dickinson insisted, Parliament had no right to impose. William was grateful that New York, the province with the greatest influence on New Jersey, had accepted the new duties with little or no protest. Proudly, William added that he heard many people in New Jersey and New York praising Benjamin Franklin's efforts on behalf of all of the colonies in this protracted struggle with Parliament.

Franklin replied in a similar spirit, saying he too was delighted with New York's discretion. "I wish the Boston people had been as quiet," he added. Then came a comment that was to take on greater significance in the light of future events. "Governor Bernard [of Boston] has sent over all their violent papers to the Ministry, and wrote them word that he daily expected a rebellion. . . . A certain noble lord expressed himself to me with some disgust and contempt of Bernard on this occasion, saying he ought to have known his people better, than to impute to the whole country sentiments, that perhaps are only scribbled by some madman in a garret; that he appeared to be too fond of contention, and mistook the matter greatly, in supposing such letters as he wrote were acceptable to the ministry." [51]

This "certain noble lord," was probably Lord Shelburne, who was pro-American and disliked seeing a royal governor blacken the character of a whole people. Franklin was dedicated to urging more people on both sides of the quarrel to think the same way. He pointed out to William that if "we Americans wish not to be judged of in the gross, by particular papers written by anonymous scribblers and published in the colonies, it would be well, if we could avoid falling into the same mistake in America, in judging of ministers here by the libels printed against them." He enclosed with his letter "a very abusive" attack on the current Ministry.[52]

VII

But overriding even politics in the letters between father and son was the dream of the western colony. In late 1767 Franklin reported to William with obvious pride and delight that Lord Shelburne had drawn up a paper recommending western settlement and laid it before the King and Privy Council. He had informed this summit of imperial power that the paper represented not only his own sentiments, but the thinking of General Jeffrey Amherst, Dr. Franklin, and Mr. Jackson, "three gentlemen that were allowed to be the best authorities for anything that related to America." The Privy Council's attitude toward the paper was encouraging, and it had been referred to the Board of Trade. Since Franklin had long been in the process of bringing these gentlemen over "privately," as he had told William he would in an earlier letter, there was little opposition left to worry about there.

But all this delicate lobbying would come to naught if a new western boundary could not be rearranged. Sir William Johnson, operating simultaneously as Indian agent and silent partner in the new colony (a deal which the British commander-in-chief in America, General Thomas Gage, had turned down as improper), had already persuaded the Indians to agree to a restructured boundary and had, in fact, reported the new arrangement to the Board of Trade. He was only awaiting approval from London to confirm the treaty. By way of creating additional pressure, William Franklin and Samuel Wharton stimulated a letter-writing campaign from Croghan and other Indian experts, assuring the London bureaucrats that if the treaty was not approved, an Indian war that would make Pontiac's rebellion look like a petty flare-up was certain. Meanwhile, Franklin urged Shelburne to confirm Johnson's treaty, on its merits. The Colonial Secretary reacted with considerable astonishment. He declared that he had never even heard of such a treaty. Shelburne sent Franklin to Lord Clare, latest head of the Board of Trade, where Johnson's letters routinely went. There, Franklin ran into a wall of blue-blooded incompetence. Lord Clare vowed that he had never received any letters from Sir William Johnson concerning the boundary. He would have his secretary search for them. Although Clare was lukewarm to the idea of a western colony, as Shelburne had been at first, Franklin obviously had confidence in his ability to galvanize him. He wrote hopefully to William, "The present ministry seem now likely to continue through this session of Parliament; and perhaps if the new Parliament should not differ greatly in complexion from this, they may be fixed for a number of years, which I earnestly wish, as we have no chance for a better."

But close as he was to the pro-American members of Pitt's chaotic ministry (made even more leaderless by the death of Townshend a few months after he passed his disastrous Acts), Franklin was in no position to predict the outcome of the constant jockeying for power among the rival groups and factions in Parliament, and around the throne. Thus, in the first days of the new year (1768) Franklin dolefully reported to William: "Dear Son. . . . Just when I wrote it was thought the ministry would stand their ground. . . . Lord Shelburne is stripped of the American business which is given to Lord Hillsborough as Secretary of State for America, a new distinct department." Franklin told his son that only time would tell how "these changes may affect us," but he was obviously avoiding the truth to keep up William's spirits. In a letter written the same day to Joseph Galloway, he was more candid. The change in the ministry was almost certain to be a disaster, for both the western colony and English-American relations. Of Lord Hillsborough he said, "I do not think this nobleman in general an enemy to America; but in the affair of paper money he was last winter strongly against us." Hillsborough and several other new ministers, such as Lord Sandwich, were attached to the faction revolving around the Duke of Bedford, "a party that has distinguished itself by exclaiming against us on all late occasions," Franklin gloomily observed.[53]

Boston's riotous defiance had infuriated Parliament and aroused a new wave of anti-Americanism in England. Franklin tried to combat it with a smooth, beautifully written essay, "Causes of the American Discontents before 1768." Essentially it was a plea for a return to the old requisition system of raising money for America. He then examined the various bones of contention on which both sides had been gnawing and analyzed them in a spirit of rational good will. He struck hard, however, at the punishment of the New York Assembly for noncompliance with the Quartering Act. To suspend an Assembly because they declined to raise money as Parliament ordered them meant, to Americans, that they must "obey implicitly" every law made by Parliament to raise money without their consent under threat of losing all their rights and privileges. Nevertheless, Franklin maintained that despite all these resentments, the colonists remained attached to the King by "principle and affection . . . but a new kind of loyalty seems to be required of us, a loyalty to Parliament. . . ." Again Franklin touched here the heart of his conception of American rights—the image of a free people who settled America and then freely consented to continue their membership in the British Empire, through their loyalty to the King, while they retained, through their individual Assemblies, the right to legislate for themselves on domestic matters. It was Parliament's interference in these domestic rights that was at the heart of America's resentment.[54]

William Franklin proudly told his father that readers in America thought "The Causes more to the purpose than all the Farmers' letters put together." But they were scarcely published when the latest news from Massachusetts caused a whole new uproar in Parliament. The radicals had gained control of the Massachusetts Assembly and issued a circular letter calling on all the colonies to boycott every item on which the Townshend Acts laid a duty, and simultaneously to petition the King for their repeal. Resolutions by a Boston town-meeting along similar lines had already aroused "a prodigious clamour" in Parliament, Franklin told William, adding, in an obviously discouraged tone, "I have endeavored to palliate matters for them as well as I can. . . ." [55]

VIII

Even before the news of the Massachusetts circular letter reached London, Franklin was discovering that Lord Hillsborough was anything but friendly either to America or to him. On March 13, 1768, he was writing mournfully to William, "The purpose of settling the new colonies seems at present to be dropped." Instead of backing a surge westward, as Shelburne had done, Lord Hillsborough was more inclined to order a massive withdrawal, leaving Forts Pitt, Oswego, Niagara, and other outposts to the colonies to garrison and keep up. "As to my own sentiments, I am weary of suggesting them to so many different inattentive heads," Franklin said, "though I must continue to do it while I stay among them." The only progress he had to report was that Sir William Johnson's letters about the boundary change, "were at last found and orders were sent over about Christmas for completing the purchase and settlement of it."

Franklin asked Hillsborough to send duplicates to Johnson and urge a speedy execution, using the weapon that William and his friends had created in their letter-writing campaign, the threat of an Indian war. But in the present state of massive dissatisfaction with America, even this weapon had become a two-edged sword. "I can tell you there are many here to whom the news of such a war would give pleasure," Franklin told his son, "who speak of it as a thing to be wished; partly as a chastisement to the colonies, and partly to make them feel the want of protection from this country, and pray for it." Even more ominous was Hillsborough's personal animosity toward Franklin. "My Lord H. mentioned the Farmers' letters to me, said he had read them, that they were well-written, and he believed he could guess who was the author, looking in my face at the same time, as if he thought it was me. He censured the doctrines as extremely wild. . . ." [56]

Meanwhile, Franklin's own thinking on British-American relations was undergoing a gradual change. "I know not what the Boston people mean by the 'subordination' they acknowledge in their assembly to Parliament, while they deny it the power to make laws for them, nor what bounds the Farmer sets to the power he acknowledges in Parliament to regulate the trade of the colonies, it being difficult to draw a line between duties for regulation and those for revenue. . . ." The more he thought and read on the subject, Franklin said, the more he began to think "that no middle doctrine can be well maintained." Something might be made of either extreme—"that Parliament has a power to make *all laws* for us, or that it has a power to make *no laws* for us; and I think the arguments for the latter more numerous and weighty." Franklin's only solution to this dilemma was a legal union between the colonies and Great Britain, similar to the one which joined England and Scotland. But he gloomily admitted "such union is not likely to take place." [57]

I X

Along with these possible visions of the future, Franklin lived very much in the present. He was always aware that his enemies might try to strike at him through his son. One day early in March, 1768, George Grenville complained in the House of Commons that Governor William Franklin of New Jersey and two other governors had callously ignored an order sent to them, to report on the manufactures carried on in their respective provinces. Franklin immediately rushed to the House of Commons and studied the reports of the other governors, hurried back to Craven Street and wrote a warning letter to William. He told him that all the reports were "much in the same strain, that there are no manufactures of any consequence. . . . These accounts are very satisfactory here and induce the Parliament to despise and take no notice of the Boston Resolutions [calling for nonimportation]." He urged William to send in his account before the meeting of the next Parliament.[58]

Franklin found himself first fascinated and then disgusted by the choosing of this Parliament. He wrote wryly to Joseph Galloway that the first record of bribery in a Parliamentary election was in Queen Elizabeth's time, when a man paid four pounds to local officials to send him to Parliament. "The price has monstrously risen since that time, for it is now no less than *4000 pounds!* It is thought, that near two millions will be spent this election." To his political lieutenant, Franklin pictured the whole thing as a gigantic raffle. "But those who understand figures say . . . The Crown has two millions a year in places and pensions to dispose of, and it is well worth while to engage in such a seven years' lottery, though all that have tickets should not get prizes." [59] To William he was more harsh and emotional. "This whole venal nation is now at market," he said, "will be sold for about two millions, and might be bought out of the hands of the present bidders (if you would offer half a million more) by the very devil himself." [60]

A month later, with the elections over, Franklin wrote to William in an even more disgusted tone. "There have been amazing contests all over the kingdom, twenty or thirty thousand pounds of a side spent in several places, and inconceivable mischief done by debauching the people and making them idle, besides the immediate actual mischief done by drunken mad mobs to houses, windows, &c." [61]

Even more repellent to Franklin was Parliament's arrogant treatment of John Wilkes, a radical who had been prosecuted for abusing the King in his newspaper, *The North Briton*, in 1763. Wilkes had fled to France to escape jail, and returned home in 1768 to run for Parliament. He was elected overwhelmingly, and when the government fined him 1000 pounds and sentenced him to jail for twenty-two months, London was engulfed in wild rioting. Troops were needed to restore order. Parliament then nullified Wilkes' election, but he ran again and was reelected. Twice more, Parliament reenacted the farce and finally, in complete desperation, declared Wilkes' opponent elected, even though he had lost by a 5 to 1 majority. By now "Wilkes and Liberty" was the battle cry of the British lower classes, particularly in London. Some radicals in America took up the cry, and named towns and children after Wilkes. But Franklin was not impressed by the lawless mobs of coal heavers and porters, tailors and Thames watermen who roamed the streets of London, wrecking and looting. Wilkes himself, it should

be noted—and Franklin certainly knew this—had no use for these ex-
cesses. "I am not a Wilkite," he insisted. To Franklin the disorder was
only further evidence of how badly the English were governing themselves. "Some punishment seems preparing for a people who are . . .
intent on nothing but luxury, licentiousness, power, places, pensions and
plunder," he said.[62]

On the heels of Wilkes came the letters of Junius. No one has been
able to decide with certainty the identity of this literary mystery man who
supported Wilkes, and for the next three years savagely attacked the
King and other members of the British establishment in the most searing
terms. One thing is certain, Junius was an insider, who knew who was
sleeping with whom, and getting what, and he told it all in blisteringly
specific detail. "Sir," he sneered at George III, "it is the misfortune of
your life . . . that you should never have been acquainted with the
language of truth. . . ." The Duke of Grafton, a pro-American politician, was another favorite Junius target, as was Lord Mansfield, the
anti-American Chief Justice.[63] From an American point of view, Junius
meant little to Franklin. But he could not help absorbing some of the
venom Junius spewed on the men with whom Franklin had to deal in
his day-to-day London life.

The elections strengthened the hand of the anti-American forces in
Parliament. One of their first moves was a threatening gesture toward
Franklin. As he told the story to William in a long letter early in July,
1768, he had received a warning of what was to come, thanks to his
friendship with Grey Cooper, a secretary of the treasury and good friend
of Sir John Pringle. Cooper, Franklin said, "desired me by a little note
to call upon him. . . . Which I did, when he told me that the Duke
of Grafton had mentioned to him some discourse of Lord Sandwich's. . . ." Sandwich was the new Postmaster General, and a close
friend of George Grenville. He had told Grafton, who was now acting
as First Minister in a reorganized cabinet, that the post office in America
was suffering, because of Franklin's long residence in England. "The
Duke had wished him [Mr. Cooper] to mention this to me," Franklin
continued, "and to say to me at the same time that though my going
to my post might remove the objection, yet if I choose rather to reside
in England, my merit was such in his opinion, as to entitle me to something better here, and it should not be his fault if I was not well provided for."

Franklin could have replied that there was another perfectly competent American undersecretary at home on the job, his friend, John Fox-croft of Virginia. But this might have sounded impertinent, so he quietly said that he was thinking of going home but he was also "extremely sensible of the Duke's goodness" and had lived so long in England and felt "a friendship and affection for many persons here" that he was equally willing to stay "some time longer, if not for the rest of my life."

Franklin went on to describe in detail how Cooper had next intro-duced him to Lord North, the pudgy, sleepy-eyed new Chancellor of the Exchequer, who professed himself to be delighted that Franklin "was not unwilling to stay with us" and hoped that "we shall find some way of making it worth your while." Then came a long conference with Mr. Todd, the Secretary of the Post Office, which made Franklin suspect that he was the real author of the move to oust him, because he had a friend who wanted the job. Franklin then made several calls on the Duke of Grafton, but neither a new appointment nor a definite decision to oust him from the post office was forthcoming. Personally, he told William that he did not "think it fit to decline any favor so great a man expressed an inclination to do me, because at court if one shows an unwillingness to be obliged, it is often construed as a mark of mental hostility, and one makes an enemy."

Thus Franklin moved through the political jungle. It was exhausting, frustrating, enervating work. He told William of spending another long night with Lord Clare, head of the Board of Trade. "He took me home from court . . . that I might dine with him as he said alone, and talk over American affairs. . . . He gave me a great deal of flummery, saying that though at my examination [in the Stamp Act crisis] I answered some of his questions a little pertly, yet he liked me, from that day, for the spirit I showed in defense of my country; and at parting, after we had drank a bottle and a half of claret each, he hugged and kissed me, protesting he never in his life met with a man he was so much in love with."

Two days later, Clare was ousted from his job, and Lord Hills-borough took his place, while simultaneously retaining the title and powers of Secretary of State for America. The change, Franklin rue-fully told Joseph Galloway, was "very sudden and unexpected." It was not good news for either the Franklins or America. But there was an even worse possibility in the offing, as Franklin warned William. George Grenville was likely to become First Minister again and this meant that Franklin would definitely refuse "anything that would seem to put me in his power." Grenville was almost certain to bring about "a breach between the two countries"—England and America. The refusal was more certain to give offense for the reason Franklin had just explained. "So that you see a turn of a die may make a great difference in our affairs. We may be either promoted or discarded; one or the other seems likely soon to be the case, but it is hard to divine which."

To William Franklin these words could only have been disturbing. He was doing a first-rate job dealing with a ticklish colonial Assembly during a period of serious unrest. He did not want his future decided by the words and actions of his father, who was deeply and personally involved in the complex politics of London 3000 miles away, especially when Franklin added, "I am myself grown so old as to feel much less than formerly the spur of ambition, and if it were not for the flattering expectation, that by being fixed here I might more effectually serve my country, I should certainly determine for retirement without a moment's hesitation." [64] This was a sentiment which William Franklin could hardly share. His life was far from over. On the contrary, he was dreaming a larger dream. In the same summer that he received this letter, he had journeyed to upper New York State and joined Sir William Johnson and other officials in another conference with the Indians, which affirmed the renegotiated boundary lines and opened millions of additional western acres to settlement. In spite of Benjamin's alertness on behalf of his son in such matters as the missing report on manufacturing in New Jersey, William Franklin could not help wondering if his father was not, in the long run, more of a hindrance than a help to his career. Even the missing report aroused more uneasiness than gratitude. William wrote vehemently that he had indeed submitted a very thorough paper on New Jersey's manufacturing, such as it was, but it had obviously gone the way of Sir William Johnson's boundary letters.

When William returned from the Indian conference there was a letter waiting for him on his desk from Lord Hillsborough, ironically numbered 13, that must have caused his stomach to do several dismayed flips. It was a devastating admonishment, by order (Hillsborough said) of the King. The specific reason for the royal wrath was the failure of the New Jersey Assembly to comply with the exact wording of the Quartering Act when it voted money for supplying troops in the province. On the advice of his council, William had signed the bill, rather than see

A
Franklin Family
Gallery

This painting by Robert Feke gives us a unique glimpse of Franklin the successful Philadelphia businessman, in elegant clothes and an expensive wig. Estimated to be in his early forties here, he soon retired from business and devoted himself to science and public service. He often deprecated "the pursuit of wealth to no purpose." *Fogg Art Museum, Harvard University Portrait Collection.*

This portrait, painted in London in 1759 by Benjamin Wilson, shows Franklin, the Pennsylvania agent and politician, gazing without illusions at life in the imperial capital of the British Empire. *White House Collection.*

The eighteenth century considered scientists somewhat akin to sorcerers, and Franklin, as a man who had penetrated the mysteries of lightning and electricity, was considered to have an especially strong aura of magic and mystery. This engraving by Edward Fisher, after a 1762 London portrait by Mason Chamberlin, definitely hints at dark powers. *The Metropolitan Museum of Art, The Michael Friedsam Collection, 1932.*

A personal favorite of Franklin and his family, this portrait was painted in London in 1767 by David Martin. Called the "thumb portrait," it dramatizes the political and moral philosopher who was trying to reconcile a quarreling England and America. *The Pennsylvania Academy of the Fine Arts.*

"Figure to yourself an old man, with grey hair appearing under a martin fur cap, among the powder'd heads of Paris." Franklin used these words to describe himself to an English friend a few weeks after he arrived in Paris to win French aid for the faltering American revolution. Based on a contemporary French painting, this portrait is by John Trumbull. Franklin found the fur hat an ideal way of dramatizing the American cause. *Yale University Art Gallery.*

One of the best-known paintings of Franklin, this portrait by Joseph Silfrède Duplessis was painted in 1778, the year Franklin was presented to Louis XVI, after he had signed the triumphant Treaty of Alliance with France. The artist's opinion is summed up in the single word he used to title his work. *The Metropolitan Museum of Art, The Michael Friedsam Collection, 1931.*

This bust by the French sculptor Jean Antoine Houdon, modeled in 1778, added to Franklin's fame in France. In 1785 Houdon came to America with Franklin and executed a similar bust of George Washington. *The Metropolitan Museum of Art, Gift of John Bard, 1872.*

Probably the last formal portrait painted of Franklin, this work by Charles Willson Peale was completed in 1787. This was the year when Franklin poured out his last remaining energies in the Constitutional Convention. He is wearing the bifocal spectacles which he invented. *The Historical Society of Pennsylvania.*

Deborah Franklin was a sometimes turbulent but always loyal wife. She resented the presence of William Franklin in her house and eventually drove him out with her sharp tongue. Franklin always appreciated the help she had given him when he was a struggling young tradesman. But she remained a shopkeeper's daughter, as he matured into one of the century's greatest minds. This, as much as politics, explains why Franklin preferred to spend most of the last twenty years of their marriage in England. *Culver Pictures.*

William Franklin was Benjamin Franklin's only surviving son and a central figure in his emotional life. William was illegitimate. Nevertheless his father lavished gifts, attention and education on him, and used his influence to make him royal governor of New Jersey in 1763. In 1775 William refused to join his father in the revolution against royal authority. "Nothing ever affected me with such keen sensations," Franklin later wrote. *Frick Art Reference Library.*

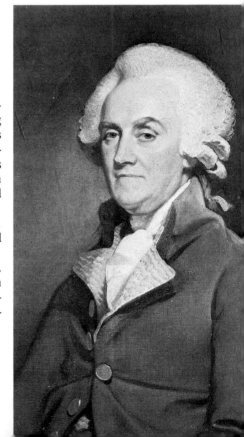

Francis Folger Franklin died of smallpox in 1736 at the age of four. He was the first child born of Franklin's marriage to Deborah Read. "Little Franky" was apparently a very bright, lovable boy. Fifty years later, in France, Franklin wept when he talked of him. "I always thought he would have been the best of all my children," he said. *Frick Art Reference Library.*

Sarah Franklin was Franklin's only daughter. "Sally," as Franklin called her, married English-born Richard Bache, over Franklin's objections. She attempted to play a peacemaker's role in the family. She continued to correspond with her brother William after his defection from the American cause and in the 1790s visited him while on a trip to England. She remained equally loyal to her father, nursing him in his old age. *The Metropolitan Museum of Art, Wolfe Fund, 1901.*

William Temple Franklin was the illegitimate son of William Franklin. Raised in England by his grandfather, "Temple" did not come
to America and meet his father until 1775, when he was sixteen.
He was immediately plunged into the revolutionary turmoil and
forced to choose between Benjamin and William. He yielded to his
grandfather and accompanied him to France as his secretary. But
the experience left him emotionally unstable for the rest of his life.
Yale University Art Gallery.

the troops starve. A wiser man than Hillsborough would not have insisted so pompously on the strict letter of the law—it was a good
example of how trivial the British government in general and Hillsborough in particular were becoming about Great Britain's "rights."
But this was not the only club with which Hillsborough belabored
William. His Majesty (which meant Hillsborough) was also concerned
that the New Jersey Assembly had considered and replied to the Massachusetts circular letter denouncing the Townshend Acts. Hillsborough
had earlier sent a dispatch warning all governors to forbid their Assemblies to consider the Massachusetts circular letter. The warning had
arrived on William's desk too late. The New Jersey Assembly had been
considering the Bay Colony's message for three weeks, and had later
answered it. But Governor Franklin found no evidence in the answer
that New Jersey "had any intentions of uniting farther with . . .
Massachusetts Bay than in petitioning His Majesty." This did not satisfy
Hillsborough at all. "Your entire ignorance of what was passing in the
Assembly, concerning the letter from Mass. Bay . . . for more than
three weeks, betrays a very blameable inattention to your duty; and
declaring, when fully apprized of these proceedings, that you had no
reason to believe there was a disposition in the people to enter any
unwarrantable combination with the Mass. Assembly indicates a disposition that does not correspond with those principles which ought to
be the rule of your conduct."

This sounded as if William should have forbidden the Assembly to
consider the Massachusetts letter—a power which Hillsborough must
have known no governor possessed, and which he should have known
would have instantly aroused the Assembly to rebellious fury. Hillsborough made a great deal of noise about the good behavior of the
Pennsylvania and New York Assemblies, which had not replied to the
circular letter. The implication, of course, was that William, echoing
his father's sentiments, had been whispering rebellion to his Assembly's
ears. Hillsborough closed with more huffing and puffing about "his
Ma'ty's disapprobation of your conduct" and added that he himself
was concerned that he had "occasion for animadversion upon your conduct in so many instances." He hoped that an explanation from William
would enable him to discover "there has not been so just grounds for
it [his concern] as I have too much foundation to apprehend. . . ."

William gave him his explanation, and it was a good one. He did
not cower or cringe, but he was also not defiant. He told Hillsborough

that the Secretary's "animadversion and censures" were "unmerited" and he was confident that he could "prove them so to every impartial person. As such I flatter myself I may address your Lordship. . . ." He then coolly proceeded to point out that whoever told the King that New York and Pennsylvania were setting New Jersey a good example was "greatly mistaken." The Assemblies of both colonies had appointed committees to petition for the repeal of the Townshend Acts within the previous month. He urged Hillsborough to face the fact that there was "scarce an assembly man in America, but what either believes that Parliament has not a right to impose taxes for the purposes of a revenue in America, or thinks that it is contrary to justice, equity and sound policy to exercise that right, under the present circumstances of the colonies, supposing it ever so unquestionable." As for trying to suppress the agitation at the point of a gun—as the Crown was attempting to do in riot-torn Boston with two regiments of regular troops—this was no solution. In words that should have made Hillsborough and every other British official think twice, William declared, "Men's minds are sour'd, a sullen discontent prevails, and in my opinion, no force on earth is sufficient to make the assemblies acknowledge, by any act of theirs, that the Parliament has a right to impose taxes on America. . . ." He then proceeded to answer in precise detail Hillsborough's accusation that he did not know what was going on inside the New Jersey Assembly.

Obviously, William Franklin was Benjamin's son. The letter ran to thirty smoothly written pages, ending with the hope that he had said enough to remove the King's displeasure "than which nothing could affect me more sensibly as I have long valued myself on a strict performance of my duty, and the strongest attachment to my sovereign." [65]

Lord Hillsborough did not deign to reply to William Franklin's defense. He also did not remove him from his governorship. Obviously the ministry was attempting to harass Benjamin Franklin into a more compliant mood by simultaneously tempting him with a better job, and threatening the positions held by him and his son. To make sure he was striking the right political note, William began sending his official dispatches to his father first. It was not just the political tone that concerned William. He also wanted his father to know his exact words, so that he could defend him on the spot against Hillsborough's potential back stabbings. He made no secret of his bitter dislike of Hillsborough. "I suppose the success which has attended the measure of sending troops to Boston, that is, in putting a stop to the riots, & preventing any opposition to the late acts of Parliament, will be a means of establishing Lord H-b in the administration, and I don't doubt but he exults greatly on the occasion. The same spirit, however, still prevails in the colonies, as did before, and nothing can make them acknowledge the right of Parliament to tax them, tho' they may at present acquiesce in it." William also told his father of the numerous petty ways in which Hillsborough was continuing their quarrel. He appointed people to the New Jersey Governor's Council without even bothering to inform William and instead of ending his letters with the usual friendly salutation which gentlemen, particularly Crown officials, used in the eighteenth century, Hillsborough simply said, "I am, sir, etc." There was, William said, "a meanness in this kind of conduct extremely unbecoming one in his station." [66]

When the new Parliament met, Lord Hillsborough showed his true anti-American colors. He took the lead in a heated debate about what course England should follow toward America. Hillsborough introduced a complete program, aiming at nothing less than total repression. It even included a threat to suspend the Massachusetts charter. It was typical of the chaotic state of British politics that the King's First Minister, the Duke of Grafton, opposed the program and persuaded the King to decline his support. But this was the closest the pro-Americans in the government and in Parliament came to a victory. Toward the end of the session, Thomas Pownall, a former colonial governor and a good friend of Franklin, made a motion to repeal the Townshend Acts. The motion was defeated, but it won a substantial number of supporters—proof that the Americans' nonimportation campaign was having its impact.

Franklin did everything in his power to hearten his countrymen in this peaceful but highly effective resistance. He told his old Boston friend, Samuel Cooper, that the anti-American ministers "flatter themselves you cannot long subsist without their manufactures. They believe you have not virtue enough to persist in such agreements—they imagine the colonies will differ among themselves, deceive and desert one another, and quietly one after the other submit to the yoke, and return to the use of British fineries. . . . I have ventured to assert, that they will all find themselves mistaken; and I rely so much on the spirit of my country, as to be confident I shall not be found a false prophet tho' at present not believed." In this same letter, however,

Franklin struck another note, which illustrated the delicate balancing act he was struggling to perform. "I hope nothing that has happened, or may happen, will diminish in the least our loyalty to our sovereign or affection for this nation in general," he told Cooper. "I can scarcely conceive a King of better dispositions, of more exemplary virtues, or more truly desirous of promoting the welfare of all his subjects. . . . The body of this people too, is of a noble and generous nature, loving and honoring the spirit of liberty and hating arbitrary power of all sorts. We have many, very many friends among them.[67]

"But as to the Parliament!" This, Franklin made it clear, was in his opinion the source of all America's woes. He wrote in a similar vein to the Committee of Merchants in Philadelphia, assuring them that "by persisting steadily" they would be "the means under God of recovering and establishing the freedom of our country entire, and of handing it down complete to posterity." [68]

X

About this time, Franklin began taking a tougher line in the propaganda articles he was writing in the English newspapers. Only in recent years have historians become aware of the prodigious number of these pieces. They were published under pseudonyms, and many of the originals were lost when Franklin's papers were scattered after his death. But an exhaustive search of English and American newspapers by Verner W. Crane rediscovered literally dozens of them. His book, which reprints only those which were previously unknown, and does not include the several dozen already printed in earlier collections of Franklin's papers, runs to 283 pages. Day and night, Franklin toiled at his desk, struggling to shed light on the historic argument, to present it as the Americans saw it, and to answer the outrageous calumnies being circulated by anti-American pamphleteers and parliamentarians.

In one of his best efforts, he wrote under the pen name Expositor. He portrayed himself as an Englishman who was considerably alarmed by the mounting acrimony between America and the mother country because he had "considerable" investments as well as several near relations on that side of the water.

"From the epithets of unjust ungenerous rogues, rebels, &c., which are so lavishly bestowed on the Americans, I have been induced to look into those late acts of Parliament, which the colonies refuse to comply with, and to my very great surprize find there is not one single word in those acts for the purpose of raising money to help poor old England, from which I begin to suspect we are all on a wrong scent. How can we justly accuse them of refusing to assist poor old England in her distresses, when we neither ask nor require it of them?" He then went on to point out that all of the controversial acts had specifically declared themselves to be for the purpose of raising money to defend and support the civil government in America. Wasn't this odd, to ask the Americans to raise money to defend themselves "when every enemy is driven out of the country?" As to supporting the civil government, this was something the Americans had always done by raising their own taxes. "My countrymen," Franklin declared, "we are all by the nose: there·is a snake in the grass. . . ." Who or what was it? Franklin suggested the answer was "a very common custom among pick-pockets, i.e., a thief cries catch thief." The people who were hoping to profit from the American revenues were the "friends and favorites" of the ministers in power. "Whoever therefore will give themselves the trouble to look at these acts, which the Americans refuse to comply with, will at once see the whole as a piece of ministerial policy, designed not for the good of Great Britain or her colonies, but for an American establishment, whereby they may be able to provide for friends and favourites.

"The Irish establishment has been much talked of as a sinecure for friends and favourites and cast-off mistresses; but this American establishment promises a more ample provision for such like purposes." [69]

These were harsh words, and since the government had ways of finding out the identity of the various propagandists, Franklin must have known he was risking the enmity of some very powerful men, whom he was boldly calling thieves. Franklin himself never made a particularly serious effort to disguise the source of his newspaper writing. He signed one of his harshest letters "Francis Lynn," and his son William was soon writing him jovially that it was "much admir'd and has been much reprinted, I believe, in all the papers on the continent.

Everybody attributed it to you, and some have had sagacity enough to discover that the signature is a pun on the real name of the author." [70]

If these letters earned Franklin some dangerous enemies, they also won him some enthusiastic friends. In mid-1768, the legislature of Georgia voted to appoint him their London agent, with a salary of 100 pounds sterling yearly. In 1769, the New Jersey legislature, thanks no doubt to some subtle politicking on the part of William Franklin, asked him to handle their legal and diplomatic affairs. With his wealth of contacts in New England, particularly Massachusetts, his solid political base in Pennsylvania and New Jersey, and this unsolicited tribute from Georgia (it took Franklin completely by surprise—he remarked to William that he could not even think of a single person he knew in that colony), Benjamin Franklin was becoming more and more a spokesman for all of America. It did not make him any more popular with the anti-Americans in the ministry. Nor did another typically Franklinesque bit of whimsey which he began practicing about this time. As a Deputy Postmaster General, he had a franking privilege and simply had to write on his letters "Free B. Franklin." But now, particularly on letters he wrote to America, he began writing "B. Free Franklin." [71]

The mounting hostility made it more and more probable that he was under the kind of scrutiny men in power have always been prone to give their enemies. Both Franklins were well aware of the tactic. When William Franklin failed to get the usual letters from his father on a packet boat that arrived early in 1769, he immediately voiced a suspicion that "Lord H. may have given orders to the Postm[r] Gen to stop your letters to me." [72] A year later, Joseph Galloway was warning Franklin that General Thomas Gage, a man "void of principle or virtue," was sending copies of Franklin's letters to the ministry, whenever he could lay his hands on them.

This tougher stance made it much more difficult for Franklin to approach the ministry as a lobbyist for a western colony. The Illinois Company sank into a kind of limbo. William Franklin had already foreseen this fate, and informed his fellow speculators in America accordingly. They swiftly concocted new and, what seemed to them, better plans. They formed an Indiana Company which purported to represent "suffering traders" who had lost great sums of money in goods and buildings during Pontiac's war in 1763. Samuel Wharton, George Croghan, and William Franklin had represented the company at the tribal conference arranged by Sir William Johnson at Fort Stanwix in November, 1768. They claimed that the Indians owed the Indiana Company some 85,000 pounds. Impressed by Sir William Johnson's firm—and apparently disinterested—backing of this claim and pleased by the presents Sir William had lavished on them to the tune of 10,460 pounds, 7 shillings, 3 pence, the chiefs had ceded to the Indiana Company no less than 1,800,000 acres. Sir William violated specific instructions he had received from Whitehall on the limitations of the western boundary to include this vast domain, and as a final fillip made it part of the treaty with the Six Nations, literally "a condition of sale." If the Crown refused to ratify it, the whole treaty would be invalidated and the immense amount of time and money spent to gather the Indians—some 3400 had come to Fort Stanwix—from so many tribes would have to be spent all over again.

Exultantly, Samuel Wharton wrote William Franklin to "urge your father, rather to drop the Illenoise affair than miss succeeding in the restitution." [73] He also urged William in turn to urge Benjamin to warn Lord Hillsborough that any delay in the ratification of the treaty could start another Indian war. There was a twist involved, even in the use of this scare tactic. The Six Nations claimed the lands, but so did the Cherokees and the Shawnees. Wharton argued that hesitation by the Crown would alienate the Iroquois, traditional allies of England, by impugning "their right to the country."

But the steady escalation of the quarrel between the ministry and America made Franklin all but useless with Hillsborough. That noble lord, prejudiced as he was against the whole idea of western expansion, angrily disapproved of Sir William Johnson's helping the Indiana Company execute a private purchase within the terms of a government treaty. He probably knew by then, thanks to Thomas Gage, who resented Johnson's powerful role in Indian affairs, that Johnson was a silent partner of the company, as was Governor William Franklin, also no favorite of Hillsborough's. At the nobleman's instigation, his fellow lords on the Board of Trade voted to censure Johnson.

Franklin's inability to give much help to his son and his partner was undoubtedly part of the reason why energetic Samuel Wharton decided to come to London and lobby for the grant. By the time he got there, Franklin had already hired an attorney, and Hillsborough's opposition was known. The problem was how to circumvent or, even better, overcome this powerful nobleman. To make sure that Lord Hillsborough's spies could not decipher their letters if they intercepted them, Franklin and Wharton worked out a code system in which Franklin became "Moses" and Wharton always referred to himself through false initials.[74]

Franklin advised Wharton to persuade Sir William Johnson to mention "with spirit" the certainty of war with the Six Nations if the treaty and the boundary were not confirmed in entirety. The ministry was so unstable, Franklin reasoned, it would not dare oppose someone with Johnson's prestige.

Franklin must have been well aware that there was a growing desperation in the ranks of his son's partners. Wharton's firm had already gone bankrupt because of their failure to obtain restitution from the Crown for earlier losses in the French and Indian War, as well as in Pontiac's war. George Croghan had mortgaged every house and piece of land he owned. William Franklin had borrowed 3000 pounds—largely on the strength of his father's name—from wealthy friends to finance the trip to London for Wharton. At Fort Stanwix William had also purchased a huge tract of land from the willing Indians—perhaps 50,000 acres— around Lake Otsego in upper New York State, and had borrowed heavily to pay for this as well. He had been borrowing small sums from his father continually since he became governor—his salary was no match for his upper-class tastes—and when Franklin gently reminded him that he was falling rather far in arrears, William begged him to be patient "a little longer till I have got my land patented." [75] He was betting that the western grant would come through before the creditors began calling in the mortgages and loans. Wharton wrote nervously that if they failed "I must pine away the remainder of my days in mortification, beggary and contempt." He undoubtedly displayed the same hysteria to Franklin in their many conversations at his Craven Street lodgings.

But Lord Hillsborough proved much tougher and meaner than Franklin or anyone else had suspected. Reassured by Gage, he scoffed at rumors of an Indian war and frightened Johnson into silence. Meanwhile, he helped to circulate vicious rumors about the Indiana Company, describing it as "a certain junto who . . . have lately pursued such indirect, fraudulent and selfish schemes. . . ." [76]

But Franklin had only begun to fight. A born politician, he loved the shock and clash, the subtle twists and turns of mood and luck that spelled success or failure in the treacherous world of imperial power. When another Indiana partner, William Trent, arrived in England, also on money borrowed from William Franklin, he was awed by Franklin's contacts among "the first people of the nation." He communicated some of this awe to Wharton, who was more inclined to try to fight Hillsborough alone. The two younger men sat down and finally took the advice which Franklin had offered them when the Illinois Company was formed. There was only one way to defeat Hillsborough, and that was by enveloping him. Dissolve the Indiana Company, already blackened by Hillsborough's rumor brush, and resurrect it in another larger company which would include a select group of the "first people."

So, in the summer of 1769, Walpole Associates was formed, absorbing the claims and ambitions of the Indiana Company. Its name was drawn from one of its most prominent partners, banker Thomas Walpole, nephew of the former First Minister, Robert Walpole. The rest of the company read like a *Who's Who* of English society. There was Thomas Pownall, staunch supporter of America in Parliament; Anthony Todd, secretary of the British post office; Charles Pratt, better known as Lord Camden, Lord Chancellor of England; Lord Gower, president of the Privy Council; Lord Rochford, Secretary of State for the Northern Department; and Earl Temple, George Grenville's brother. Richard Stonehewer, private secretary to the Duke of Grafton, the First Minister, was another choice addition. Grey Cooper, a Secretary of the Treasury and a firm Franklin friend, was also there, along with Richard Jackson, William Strahan and his son Andrew. For good measure, there was Thomas Bradshaw, an intimate political lieutenant of the Duke of Grafton. Franklin, of course, was a partner and he made sure William Franklin and Joseph Galloway were also named.

Franklin's letter to Grey Cooper, bringing him into the company, is a perfect example of his skill as a political operator in the imperial capital.

> *An application being about to be made for a grant of lands in the territory on the Ohio lately purchased of the Indians, I cannot omit acquainting you with it, and giving you my opinion, that they will very soon be settled by people from the neighboring provinces, and be of great advantage in a few years to the undertakers. As you have those fine children, and are likely to have many more, I wish for their sakes, you may incline to take this opportunity of making a considerable addition to their future fortunes, as the expence will be a trifle. If therefore you will give me leave, I shall put your name down among us for a share (40,000 acres).*[77]

Hillsborough must have gasped when he saw Franklin's lineup. Walpole Associates represented almost every level of British society, and every political faction. Pro-Americans and anti-Americans were apparently more than willing to sit side by side on the board of directors of a company that seemed likely to make millions out of the American wilderness. Exultantly, Thomas Wharton, Samuel's older brother, told Sir William Johnson, "There are 72 shareholders, among which, are some of the first noble men &c in the kingdom. . . . They are promised a charter on the most ample basis—Capt. Trent writes to his wife . . . that he sho'd finish his business to his entire satisfaction. . . ." [78]

Walpole Associates petitioned the Privy Council for a grant of 2,400,-000 acres within the Fort Stanwix grant. They were prepared to pay the treasury 10,460 pounds, 7 shillings, 3 pence—the exact amount that William Johnson had laid out for presents at the Fort Stanwix tribal conference. The price was a Franklinesque needle that we can be sure was not lost on Lord Hillsborough. The Privy Council referred the request to the Board of Trade.

A committee, led by Franklin, appeared before this body in early December, 1769. Hillsborough, in the chair as president, listened poker-faced to their proposal. He did not even twitch when Franklin again specified the amount of money they were prepared to pay—even though Franklin was in effect threatening him with the humiliation of being forced to ratify a treaty he had denounced. Instead of exploding, Hillsborough amazed Franklin and everyone else by becoming enraptured that such a group of distinguished gentlemen were interested in colonizing America. The only thing wrong with their request, he declared, was that it was too small. "Why not ask for more land? Enough to make a province?" Managed by such distinguished hands, it could not fail to reap honor and profit to the King. In fact, Hillsborough said he was so enthusiastic about the idea he was himself prepared to present the proposition to the lords of the Treasury.

Although Franklin was certainly astonished, he managed to stammer his appreciation and accept his Lordship's generous offer. A meeting of Walpole Associates was instantly convened at the Crown and Anchor Tavern on the twenty-seventh of December. The company was reorganized into the Grand Ohio Company and they decided to ask for 20,000,000 acres. In that same meeting, Franklin and his partners undoubtedly also figured out why Hillsborough had performed his startling about face. He had been shrewd enough to see that Franklin had hopelessly outgunned him with Walpole Associates. He therefore had decided to outsmart the outsmarters by urging them to ask for a province. Even if the Treasury and the Privy Council approved such a huge grant, Hillsborough reasoned that Franklin and his friends could never raise the money to pay for it. This looked like simple arithmetic to Hillsborough. If two and a half million acres were worth 10,460 pounds, 7 shillings, 3 pence, then twenty million acres ought to cost at least 100,000 pounds. Also, at the pace the government usually moved, twenty million acres should take them ten times as long to grant as two million.

On January 4, 1770, Lord Hillsborough got one of the biggest shocks of his life. He had scarcely sat down to dinner when one of his retainers informed him that the Treasury lords had granted the twenty million acres to the Grand Ohio Company, only eight incredible days after the partners had submitted their petition. Even more mortifying was the price—10,460 pounds, 7 shillings, 3 pence. We can be fairly certain that his Lordship's digestion was not very good that night.[79]

But Hillsborough refused to surrender. He lobbied fiercely behind the scenes against the Treasury decision, and in April, 1770, the Treasury lords executed a slight retreat under this pressure. They suddenly announced that they had only approved the purchase price, but they did not have the power to authorize the grant itself. This sent Franklin and his friends back to the Privy Council, who once more referred the matter to the Board of Trade and thus, almost a year later, Franklin was eyeball to eyeball with Lord Hillsborough again.

Hillsborough flourished a petition from another group of speculators, the Mississippi Company, claiming prior rights to the same land. The Mississippi Company was represented by a small, querulous Virginian named Arthur Lee—a name that would some day haunt Benjamin Franklin. Also on the scene with counterclaims was the Ohio Company of Virginia, in which George Washington, among others, was a major stockholder. Lee's father had been a founder of this company, but it was represented by another Virginian, James Mercer. Franklin and his friends had no trouble demolishing the Mississippi Company's case, but Mercer swung the weight of his colony's prestige behind his argument, and it was hard to down Hillsborough when he huffed that he could not approve the grant without getting more information on Virginia's plea. This meant letters to America and a delay of three to six months. To William Franklin and his debt-ridden friends, this was a blow. Creditors in America were pressing them hard, and William wrote angrily to Trent that he had more than one reason "to repent my going to the treaty of F. Stanwix. . . ." There was, however, nothing they could do but wait.[80]

X I

Meanwhile, Parliament was convening, and once more the problem of America was the obsessive subject. As the Grafton administration blundered and blustered and threatened to collapse into complete confusion, Franklin saw a paradoxical sign of hope. He told Joseph Galloway, "Of late a cry begins to arise, can no body propose a plan of conciliation? Must we ruin ourselves by intestine quarrels?—I was asked in company lately by a noble lord if I had no plan of that kind to propose."

" 'Tis easy to propose a plan," Franklin had answered. "Mine may be express'd in a few words; *repeal* the laws, *renounce* the right, *recall* the troops, *refund* the money, and *return to the old method of requisition.*"

The noble lord thought all of these things were possible, except renouncing the right. This, he said, was something to which Parliament would never consent, and he pointed out that "your own little assemblies" were very stubborn about rescinding acts which they had passed.

"If continuing the claim pleases you," Franklin said, "continue it as long as you please, provided you never attempt to execute it; we shall consider it in the same light with the claim of the Spanish monarch to the title of King of Jerusalem." [81]

For a while, the British government showed signs of listening to this witty but wise advice. Grafton persuaded his erratic coalition to abandon all the Townshend duties except the tax on tea, which was retained as a solace to those who felt the Parliament's right to tax had to be upheld. Grafton and his supporters wanted the tea tax withdrawn as well, but Hillsborough and the Bedfordites refused to go along. In a circular letter announcing the government's intention, Hillsborough deliberately left out conciliatory sentences on which the cabinet had agreed, and made nasty references to "legislative authority" and "execution of the law" in a manner certain to wound American feelings. When Grafton did nothing to discipline him, except shrug his shoulders helplessly, the pro-Americans decided it was time to go into opposition.

Chaos threatened, until there appeared on deck a surprising candidate for First Minister—Lord North. As bland as he was pudgy, he appealed to a loose group of men without any really strong opinions about the conflicts that were agitating the empire. They thought of themselves as "the King's friends" and piously declared that above all they wanted a stable government. The years of instability had persuaded a great many eager politicians from various factions to gravitate toward the source of power, the throne. Thus North was able to pull together a government that had a semblance of unity because it represented a wide spectrum of influence. But most of the men in the key jobs were second-raters who had never even achieved leadership in their own groups.

Nevertheless, North was better than someone as crassly anti-American as Hillsborough or Sandwich. The new First Minister proclaimed his intention to go ahead with repealing the Townshend duties, except the tax on tea, and pledged that during his administration the Parliament would lay no new taxes upon the colonies. It was ironic that on the very day that he introduced the repealing bill—March 5, 1770—what Franklin had dreaded finally occurred in Boston. A mob clashed with a squad of British soldiers, a volley of shots was fired, and five men lay dead or dying in the snow. But the Boston Massacre, although it caused a furor in that city, had little or no impact in England or in other colonies because the British government had already taken a major step toward conciliating America.

It did, however, affect Franklin deeply on an emotional level. He was a Bostonian by birth and never forgot it. On June 8, 1770, he wrote an extremely important letter to his friend Samuel Cooper. With the Townshend duties largely out of the way, except the duty on tea, with its "obnoxious preamble" which declared Parliament's right to tax in uncompromising terms, the major remaining issue, as Franklin saw it, was the British policy of maintaining a "standing army . . . among us in time of peace, without the consent of our assemblies." He emphatically declared it was unconstitutional. The King himself could not do it in England, without the consent of Parliament.

Franklin repeated his contention that the colonies were founded by free men and were in effect independent states, united as England and Scotland had been before the Union by having one common sovereign, the King. He boldly called the colonial Assemblies "plantation parliaments" and urged Americans henceforth to refrain from using such expressions as "the supreme authority of Parliament" or "the subordinacy of our assemblies to Parliament" in colonial papers. He maintained that the only way in which the Americans' right to legislate for themselves could be abrogated was by a formal act of union, such as the one that joined Scotland and England. "If Great Britain now think such a union necessary with us, let her propose her terms, and we may consider them. . . .

"This kind of doctrine the Lords and Commons here would deem little less than treason," Franklin warned Cooper. "I unbosom myself thus to you, in confidence of your prudence. . . ." [82]

Franklin knew that the temporary repeals and assertions of rights were no solution to the problem of England's relationship with America. They were merely cheap salve rubbed over a festering wound. In his search for new principles, he evolved the idea of independent commonwealths, on which the British Empire eventually organized itself. In this, as in many other of his ideas, Franklin was too far ahead of his time. Hardly an Englishman alive in the reign of George III was able to perceive the brilliance of the theory Franklin was creating—and the few who did appreciate it had little or no voice in Parliament.

Nevertheless, Franklin's thinking on this all-important subject—particularly as he expressed it in that letter to Samuel Cooper—became a major turning point in Franklin's own life, and in the national lives of England and America. By the fall of 1770, the Massachusetts Assembly had become completely disgusted with Governor Thomas Hutchinson, because among other things he had played such an obviously partisan role in the trials of the British soldiers after the Boston massacre. When the London agent for Massachusetts died, the colony's Assembly plunged into an acrimonious debate over his replacement. One wing suggested Benjamin Franklin. But some of the more radical thinkers in Boston, notably Samuel Adams, suspected Franklin because he was still a royal official. They argued that he could not be trusted to represent them impartially in their disputes with the governor and the Crown.

Samuel Adams supported Arthur Lee, who called himself Junius Americanus, and specialized in circulating vicious slanders about the British ministry to anyone who would listen. Other assemblymen pointed out that Franklin already was agent for three colonies and hardly needed the business of a fourth. But Samuel Cooper produced Franklin's letter describing his theory of the Crown's authority, and a majority instantly voted for the philosopher of electricity. "Your letter came most seasonably," Cooper wrote to Franklin. Because the governor had recently vetoed bills relating to other colony agents, the Assembly rebelliously chose Franklin as their agent, in effect telling the governor to find his own agent in London to represent his diametrically opposite views.

For Franklin, deep in his political struggle to create the western colony, the Massachusetts appointment was a severe embarrassment. He had not sought the job, any more than he had asked to be agent for Georgia. But Georgia was an innocuous cipher in the colonial scheme of things, while Massachusetts was considered by Parliament the fountain-head of rebellion and sedition. For Franklin to be chosen agent by this most radical of all the colonies, was like a contemporary American politician becoming a lobbyist for the Chinese Communists.

Why didn't Franklin turn down the appointment? He was, after all, already agent for three other colonies. Unfortunately, this too was a political impossibility in the wider context of the British-American quarrel. Just as a refusal of an offer from a noble lord implied hostility, so the refusal of an (implied) endorsement from rebellious Massachusetts would quickly be construed by Franklin's American critics as a sign that he was at heart lukewarm to the American cause. Finally and more fundamentally, there was the obvious fact that Franklin was *not* lukewarm to the American cause. On the contrary, he was in many ways more radical at this point in the historic debate than American leaders such as Samuel Adams, who as late as 1771 was still conceding Parliament's right to lay external taxes on America to control the trade of the empire. By this point, Franklin had receded so far from the untenable middle position, as he called it, that he was very close to saying Parliament could not tax Americans at all without the consent of their individual Assemblies.

XII

Throughout the preceding months, Franklin had been vigorously prosecuting his newspaper campaign against the anti-Americans in the government. Again and again, Franklin had struck directly at the men in power, especially Lord Hillsborough. In one newspaper article he wrote, "We are told indeed sometimes that the people of America would generally be quiet, if it were not for their factious demagogues, and that the whole mischief is owing only to two or three restless spirits there. . . . But in truth, the parties are G. G. [George Grenville], L—d H. [Lord Hillsborough], and the D. of B. [The Duke of Bedford] on the one side, and on the other all our fellow-subjects in America." Elsewhere in this attack Franklin stated bluntly, "There is not the smallest probability of an accommodation [between England and the colonies] while the present A—n M—r [American Minister] continues in that department, nor the least prospect of his being removed; but on the contrary, all his rash, ill-judged measures are to be approved, confirmed and pursued."

On January 2, 1770, the newspaper, the *Public Advertiser,* published "NEW FABLES humbly inscribed to the S—y of St—e for the American Department."

FABLE ONE

A herd of cows had long afforded plenty of milk, butter and cheese to an avaricious farmer, who grudged them the grass they subsisted on, and at length mowed it to make money of the hay, leaving them to shift for food as they could, and yet still expected to milk them as before; but the cows, offended with his unreasonableness, resolved for the future to suckle one another.

FABLE TWO

An eagle, king of birds, sailing on his wings aloft over a farmer's yard, saw a cat there basking in the sun, mistook it for a rabbit, swoop'd, seized it and carried it up into the air, intending to prey on it. The cat turning, set her claws into the eagle's breast; who, finding his mistake, opened his talons, and would have let her drop; but puss, unwilling to fall so far, held faster; and the eagle, to get rid of the inconvenience, found it necessary to set her down where he took her up.

FABLE THREE

The lion's whelp was put on board a Guinea ship bound to America as a present to a friend in that country: it was tame and harmless as a kitten, and therefore not confined, but suffered to walk about the ship at pleasure. A stately, full-grown English Mastiff, belonging to the captain, despising the weakness of the young lion, frequently took its food by force, and often turned it out of its lodging box, when he had a mind to repose therein him-

*self. The young lion nevertheless grew daily in size and strength,
and the voyage being long, he became at last a more equal match
for the mastiff; who continuing his insults, received a stunning
blow from the lion's paw that stretched his skin over his ears, and
deterred him from any future contest with such growing strength;
regretting that he had not further secured it's friendship, than provoked it's enmity.*[83]

On that same day in the *Public Advertiser*, Franklin began publishing
a series of essays called "The Colonists' Advocate." These were bold,
hard-hitting pieces, supposedly by an English official who had "some
years service in America." He bluntly called the anti-Americans enemies
of liberty, rejected their arguments as "a most pitiful set of defenses,"
spoke savagely of places for "needy court-danglers," and compared the
ignorance of the ministers to "the savages of Louisiana, who to come at
the fruit, cut down the tree." This was very strong stuff, especially in
an era when the noble lords expected to be approached with bows and
compliments.[84]

Now, Franklin's appointment as agent for Massachusetts meant that
he had to meet his prime target, Lord Hillsborough, face to face. In
order to function as agent, he had to make a formal report of his
appointment to the head of the Board of Trade.

Somewhat nervously, Franklin discussed the prospect of the interview
with his friends. They advised him to wear his friendliest face and pretend that there was no warfare raging on either side. That way, his Lordship might be challenged to match Franklin's civility, and the interview
could be accomplished with a minimum of exacerbation. Franklin, with
his knowledge of human nature, was probably not so optimistic. But on
the morning of January 16, 1771, he set out on his unpleasant errand.

XIII

To Franklin's relief, the porter who guarded his Lordship's door refused
to let him enter. Franklin left his name, regained his coach and drove
off. But before he was out of the square, the porter came crying after

him to halt. "His Lordship will see you, sir," were probably the most unwelcome words Franklin had heard in months.

He was shown into his Lordship's reception room, where he found himself face to face with Sir Francis Bernard, former governor of Massachusetts and the man Lord Shelburne had condemned for needlessly inflaming the province and calumniating the colony's reputation. He was a constant companion of Lord Hillsborough, not a good omen for Franklin and his hopes of a peaceful reception.

A moment later, John Pownall, Secretary of the Board of Trade, invited Franklin into Hillsborough's bedroom. Usually Hillsborough let Franklin sit outside his door for three or four hours waiting his turn. Delighted to save some time he had already considered lost, Franklin found it easier to put on "the open cheerful countenance" that his friends had advised him to wear. His Lordship did not look particularly malevolent as he greeted him. "I was dressing in order to go to court; but hearing that you were at the door, who are a man of business, I determined to see you immediately," he said.

Franklin thanked him and replied that his business for the present was "not much." He was only here to pay his respects to his Lordship and to "acquaint you with my appointment by the House of Representatives of Massachusetts Bay to be their agent here, in which station if I could be of any service—"

A transformation took place on Hillsborough's face at the words *Massachusetts Bay*. With an expression that Franklin later described as "something between a smile and a sneer," he cut him short.

"I must set you right here, Mr. Franklin, you are not agent."

"Why, my Lord?"

"You are not appointed."

"I do not understand, your Lordship. I have the appointment in my pocket."

"You are mistaken. I have later and better advices. I have a letter from Governor Hutchinson. He would not give his assent to the bill."

"There was no bill, my Lord. It was a vote of the House."

"There was a bill presented to the governor for the purpose of appointing you and another, one Dr. Lee, I think he is called, to which the governor refused his assent."

"I cannot understand this, my Lord; I think there must be some mistake. Is your Lordship quite sure that you have such a letter?"

"I will convince you of it directly." Hillsborough rang a bell on a nearby table. "Mr. Pownall will come in and satisfy you."

"It is not necessary that I should now detain your Lordship from dressing for going to court. I will wait on your Lordship another time."

"No, stay," Hillsborough snapped in his most imperious manner. "He will come immediately." When a servant appeared at the door he barked at him, "Tell Mr. Pownall I want him."

A moment later Pownall stood breathless in the doorway. He was the brother of Franklin's good friend, Thomas Pownall, but as a maddening example of the way the issue of America divided men, he had "a strong bias" against Americans.

"Have not you at hand Governor Hutchinson's letter mentioning his refusing his assent to the bill for appointing Dr. Franklin agent?"

"My Lord?" Pownall gasped.

"Is there not such a letter?"

"No, my Lord," said Pownall. "There is a letter relating to some bill for the payment of a salary to Mr. de Berdt and I think to some other agent, to which the governor had refused his assent."

"There is nothing in the letter to the purpose I mention?"

"No, my Lord," said Pownall sadly.

"I thought it could not well be, my Lord," said Franklin, "as my letters are by the last ships, and they mention no such thing. Here is the authentic copy of the vote of the House appointing me, in which there is no mention of any act intended. Will your Lordship please to look at it?"

Hillsborough took the paper from Franklin's hand, as if it were offal, but did not bother to look at it. "An information of this kind is not properly brought to me as Secretary of State," he quibbled. "The Board of Trade is the proper place."

"I will leave the paper then with Mr. Pownall to be—"

"To what end would you leave it with him?" Hillsborough stormed.

"To be entered on the minutes of that Board, as usual."

"It shall not be entered there," Hillsborough roared. "No such paper shall be entered there while I have anything to do with the business of that Board. The House of Representatives has no right to appoint an agent. We shall take no notice of any agents but such as are appointed by acts of the Assembly, to which the governor gives his assent. We have had confusion enough already. Here is one agent appointed by the Council, another by the House of Representatives. Which of these is agent for the province? Who are we to hear in provincial affairs? An agent appointed by act of Assembly we can understand. No other will be attended to for the future, I can assure you."

"I cannot conceive, my Lord," said Franklin calmly in the face of this blue-blooded wrath, "why the consent of the governor should be thought necessary to the appointment of an agent for the people. It seems to me that—"

"I shall not enter into a dispute with you, sir, upon this subject," Hillsborough raged.

"I beg your Lordship's pardon," Franklin said icily. "I do not presume to dispute your Lordship. I would only say that it seems to me that every body of men who cannot appear in person where business relating to them may be transacted, should have a right to appear by an agent. The concurrence of the governor does not seem to be necessary. It is the business of the people that is to be done; he is not one of them; he is himself an agent."

"Whose agent is he?" said Hillsborough, flustered by this new idea.

"The King's, my Lord," said Franklin.

"No such matter," snapped Hillsborough. "He is one of the corporation by the province charter. No agent can be appointed but by an act, nor can any act pass without his assent. Besides, this proceeding is directly contrary to express instructions."

This was a favorite Hillsborough word. As Franklin had pointed out in the public press, these arbitrary instructions had done not a little to set America aflame. But he wisely decided not to suggest this to Hillsborough, now. "I did not know there had been such instructions," he said. "I am not concerned in any offence against them and—"

"Yes," said Hillsborough, interrupting Franklin for the fourth or fifth time, "your offering such a paper to be entered is an offense against them." He folded up Franklin's letter of appointment without having read a word of it. "No such appointment shall be entered. When I came into the administration of American affairs I found them in great disorder. By my firmness they are now something mended; and while I have the honor to hold the seals [of office] I shall continue the same conduct, the same firmness. I think my duty to the master I serve, and to the government of this nation, requires it of me. If that conduct is not approved, they may take my office from me when they please. I shall make them a bow and thank them; I shall resign with pleasure. That gentleman knows it—" Hillsborough pointed to Pownall. "But while I continue in it I shall resolutely persevere in the same firmness."

Franklin, describing this violent scene for Samuel Cooper, said that by now the color had drained from Hillsborough's face. He seemed,

Franklin said, to be "angry at something or somebody besides the agent, and of more consequence to himself."

Calmly Franklin held out his hand for his letter of appointment. Hillsborough returned it to him. "I beg your Lordship's pardon for taking up so much of your time," Franklin said. "It is, I believe, of no great importance whether the appointment is acknowledged or not. For I have not the least conception that an agent can *at present* be of any use to any of the colonies. I shall therefore give your Lordship no further trouble."

Coolly, Franklin made his formal bow and departed.

A few weeks later, Franklin sent the "minutes" of this tense confrontation—a word-for-word, blow-by-blow description which read like a script from a play—to Samuel Cooper. He told Cooper that he had since heard that "his Lordship took great offence at some of my last words, which he calls extremely rude and abusive. He assured a friend of mine, that they were equivalent to telling him to his face that the colonies could expect neither favor nor justice during his administration."

One can almost see the grim smile in Franklin's next words. "I find he did not mistake me." [85]

XIV

Franklin also told Cooper that this was only one of "many instances of his [Hillsborough's] behavior and conduct, that have given me the very mean opinion I entertain of his abilities and fitness for his station. His character is conceit, wrongheadedness, obstinacy and passion." The only consolation and encouragement, Franklin said, was the knowledge that Hillsborough "is not a whit better lik'd by his colleagues in the ministry, than he is by me." [86]

But these bold words concealed from his American friends the deep dismay this open breach with Hillsborough had caused Franklin. An acute depression replaced his usual cheerfulness. He spent more and more time secluded in his Craven Street lodgings. Almost certainly, the reason was the devastating impact Franklin feared the clash would have on the petition of the Grand Ohio Company. Soon William Strahan was writing worriedly to Governor Franklin the first critical words he had ever used against his old friend. Strahan said that Franklin "could not stir in this [Ohio] business as he is not only on bad terms with Lord Hillsborough but with the ministry in general. Besides, his temper has grown so very reserved, which adds greatly to his natural *inactivity,* that there is no getting him to take part in anything." This was a picture of a man hurt and depressed by his inability to achieve the brightest dream of his life, on behalf of his son.

Samuel Wharton was no consolation. He had used Franklin to push his way into the inner circle of London society, and now turned on him for seeming to lose interest in Wharton's one hope of escape from bankruptcy. He even managed to turn Strahan against his old friend. In his letter to William Franklin, Strahan lavishly declared that without Wharton the project would be in a state of collapse. He "hath acquired *better connections* here than *any other American* I know of ever did," Strahan wrote, in an obvious comparison to Franklin. Strahan was a man who liked winners, and his hearty good nature found it hard to understand depression. He added in the same critical tone that he had heard Franklin "at my house propose to Mr. Wharton to strike his name out of the list [of partners] as it might be a prejudice to the undertaking."

His sole motive in writing "thus freely" to William, Strahan said, was "to put you upon your *guard,* & to induce you to be as circumspect in your conduct as possible, as it is imagined here, that you entertain the same political opinions with your father, and are actuated by the same motives with regard to Britain and America." [87]

These words were to become far more ominous in a few years. For the moment William was still inclined to side strongly with his father. In the first draft of his reply to Strahan, he wrote the skeptical sentence, "I have no doubt of Mr. Wharton's activity, sagacity or perseverance in this business . . . but that he should, as you say, without the least *assistance* from any other quarter, find means to connect himself with many of the greatest names in Britain is indeed not a little surprising." William omitted this sentence from the final copy of the letter he sent to Strahan because he feared the printer would "look upon it as a sneer, & that I doubted his veracity. Besides it was probable he would show it to S. W. [Samuel Wharton] which might occasion a coolness." [88] William also did not tell Strahan the whole truth about his feelings toward the Grand Ohio Company. He claimed that if the colony was founded it would give him pleasure, not because it was advantageous to him but only because it would rescue his friends, Croghan, Wharton, and Trent, from their embarrassments. This was less than candid since about the same time Wharton and Trent were writing William from London, begging him to send along another installment of the expense money he had promised them. He was as deeply involved in the project as the Whartons, and in almost as much danger of bankruptcy.

On other matters, William was more revealing to Strahan. Lord Hillsborough, he said, "has no reason (other than the natural connection between us) to imagine that I entertain the same political opinion with my father with regard to the disputes between Britain & America. My sentiments are really in many respects different from those which have yet been published on either side of the question; but as I could not expect the voice of an individual be attended to in the temper both parties were in, I for the most part kept my sentiments to myself, & only endeavored to steer my little bark quietly through all the storms of political contest with which I was everywhere surrounded." [89]

Hillsborough, obviously bent on making as much trouble as possible for the Franklins, persuaded the Board of Trade to write a letter to New Jersey containing strict instructions regarding the appointment of a London agent. The Board hoped that the "House of Reps of N.J. would from the propriety of the thing itself have receded from their claim of the sole right of appointing an agent for the colony . . . as we think such claim is unjust and unwarrantable. . . ." This put William Franklin in a very sticky corner. He promptly notified the Board of Trade that there was no hope that the Assembly would ever agree to such instructions. Then he went to work on his Assembly, and wheedled an agreement out of them. They voted a formal bill, appointing Benjamin Franklin agent for another year, and the governor and the council signed it. In a letter to his father he admitted that he did not expect Benjamin to be "altogether pleased" with this compliance. Defensively promising to explain it in more detail in a future letter, William pleaded that "it really (inter nos) makes no kind of difference, and yet will fortify the My. [Ministry] as it will appear to be a point gained." [90]

Benjamin was in no mood to let Hillsborough gain anything, and he was even more annoyed that William would cooperate in a scheme that was obviously aimed at cowing colonial agents. No doubt on orders from Hillsborough, Governor Thomas Hutchinson of Massachusetts had refused to authorize the payment of Franklin's salary. If agents could only be appointed with the signature of a royal governor, soon there would be no colonial representatives in London except ministerial yes-men. Franklin first threatened to resign rather than serve in "such a suspicious situation." But he finally decided to let his son score his small point with the ministry, and accepted the job of acting as New Jersey's agent for another year.[91]

This was only a small segment of Franklin's clash with Hillsborough. There is evidence in Franklin's papers that this powerful lord was also hard at work among his fellow cabinet members, trying to get Franklin arrested, probably for treason. In fact, a letter from one of Franklin's friends to an English lawyer talks of it not as a possibility, but as a near certainty. "I think when he is arrested his friends will find such security you approve rather than lett him be detained here." [92] Hillsborough was declaiming against Franklin at every London dinner table and club he visited. Even William Strahan, who felt that his newly acquired job as King's printer required him to take a more moderate position on the quarrel, got an earful from his Lordship. Franklin, thundered Hillsborough, "was a factious, turbulent fellow, an enemy to the King's service, a republican." Franklin, on his part, let his Lordship know that he was gathering material to get him impeached.[93]

X V

Partly to escape Hillsborough's threats, and also to shake off his depression, Franklin traveled a great deal during the year 1771. He let Samuel Wharton and Thomas Walpole struggle with the problem of shoving the Grand Ohio Company through Hillsborough's opposition. In the spring he took a tour of the British midlands. He traveled through Birmingham, Sheffield, Leeds, and Manchester—the "clothing towns"—from which England exported wool and cotton goods around the world. The huge mills and intricate weaving machines were fascinating to Franklin's scientific mind. But the other, humane side of his mind was

active too. In this early phase of the industrial revolution, wages were
brutally low. The workers who toiled at the machines for twelve and
fourteen hours a day were filthy, half-starved skeletons, clothed in rags.
The manager of one Norwich factory began boasting to Franklin about
the world-wide range of his exports. He told how Norwich cloth made
suits and stockings and dresses for people in the West Indies, America,
India, and half the countries of Europe. Franklin listened patiently to
this geographical roll call and then, his eyes on a ragged worker, asked:
"And what do you export to Norwich?" [94]

Another trip took him to Twyford House, the country home of Jonathan Shipley, Bishop of St. Asaph. Shipley and Franklin had apparently
met in London, where the Bishop sat in the House of Lords. Their
friendship was quickly cemented by a similarity in disposition and political views—Shipley was an urbane, witty, charming man thoroughly on
the side of the colonies in the great and continuing debate on the "American problem." His red-brick country house was in one of the most
beautiful sections of England, especially in mid-summer, when Franklin
arrived. Named for the village of Twyford, which surrounded it, the
house was only nine miles from Southampton in the heart of a green,
glowing region. Franklin had already spent a few days there and
had written a grateful letter to the Bishop, telling how he was breathing
"with reluctance the smoke of London, when I think of the sweet air of
Twyford."

The Bishop's family was another source of pleasure to Franklin. He
had five beautiful daughters, Anna Maria, Amelia (called Emily), Elizabeth, Georgiana, and Katherine, and, together with his wife, they fussed
over Franklin as if he were a visiting god. It was a perfect consolation for
his bruised spirit, and he responded with a wealth of anecdotes about his
life and times. Perhaps it was one of the girls, or the Bishop who suggested that he ought to write down some of these stories for posterity.
But there is another much more probable explanation, suggested by the
first words he wrote in the secluded red-brick summer house in the
Shipley's sun-drenched garden: "Dear Son." [95]

This opening of what was to become the century's most famous autobiography is a commentary in itself on the main emotional thrust of
Franklin's life. It was no casual act, this book he began, no mere response to an offhand suggestion by one of the charming Shipleys. It was
part of the most fundamental dream of Franklin's life—to found a family
that would honor his name and emulate his example, and carry into that
American future he envisioned so magnificently the wisdom he had

accumulated from his experimental approach to life. Simultaneously it was an attempt to build an emotional bridge of words to this living son, separated from him now for seven years, and not, he sensed, in complete agreement with him on the great political question of their time—America's relationship to England.

He began the book with a memory that was certain to stir William's feelings. "I have ever had a pleasure in obtaining any little anecdotes of my ancestors. You may remember the inquiries I made among the remains of my relations when you were with me in England; and the journey I took for that purpose. Now imagining it may be equally agreeable to you to know the circumstances of *my* life, many of which you are yet unacquainted with; and expecting a few weeks uninterrupted leisure in my present country retirement, I sit down to write them for you."

Then Franklin added words which reflected another equally strong side of his complex character. "Having emerg'd from the poverty and obscurity in which I was born and bred, to a state of affluence and some degree of reputation in the world. . . ." This was the unique aspect of Benjamin Franklin, the thing that made him so extraordinary in his time. It was an era still dominated by aristocracy. For a man to have risen from Franklin's humble birth to his present state of fame, influence, and power was an extraordinary achievement. It has become commonplace for us, but it was nothing less than phenomenal in the eighteenth century. It was one of several reasons why British aristocrats felt an instinctive hostility to Franklin. That habit of reflection on his experience, which had not a little to do with his success, made it inevitable that Franklin would be aware of his uniqueness, and proud of it.

An autobiography was also "the next best thing most like living one's life over again." In fact, it was better to write it than talk about it, "the inclination so natural in old men," since no one "thro' respect to age" need feel obliged to give him a hearing, since "this may be read or not as one pleases."

Perhaps the most charming note in these opening pages was Franklin's cheerful admission that he had enjoyed life so much "that were it offer'd to my choice, I should have no objection to a repetition to the same life from its beginning, only asking the advantage authors have in a second edition to correct some faults of the first." But even if this were denied, he would still "accept the offer." This reminded him of an epitaph he had written for himself, many years ago.

> *The Body of*
> *B. Franklin*
> *Printer;*
> *Like the cover of an old book,*
> *Its contents torn out,*
> *And stripped of its Lettering and Gilding,*
> *Lies here, food for worms*
> *But the work shall not be wholly lost:*
> *For it will, as he believ'd, appear once more,*
> *In a new & more perfect Edition,*
> *Corrected and Amended*
> *By the Author*

From there the story moved swiftly through a brief history of the English Franklins into the heart of the book—Franklin's vivid portrait of himself and his father Josiah in early eighteenth-century Boston, his boyhood in a family where thirteen sat at one time at the dinner table, his apprenticeship as a printer to his bad-tempered brother James, and young Benjamin's flight to Philadelphia. At the end of three weeks, he had brought his story up to 1731, the year of the foundation of Philadelphia's Subscription Library, "the mother of all the N. American subscription libraries now so numerous." Proudly he declared, "These libraries have improv'd the general conversation of the Americans, made the common tradesmen and farmers as intelligent as most gentlemen from other countries, and perhaps have contributed in some degree to the stand so generally made throughout the colonies in defence of their privileges." [96]

XVI

On this harshly contemporary note, Franklin broke off his narrative, and returned to London's political wars. For company on his ride he took the youngest Shipley daughter, Katherine or Kitty, then eleven, who was going back to school. Nothing illustrates the endless diversity of Frank-

lin's mind and character more than the letter which he wrote to Mrs.
Shipley, describing the journey and the delight he took in Kitty's girlish
chatter.

*The first stage we were rather pensive. I tried several topics of
conversation, but none of them would hold. But after breakfast we
began to recover spirits and had a good deal of chat. Would you
hear some of it? We talked of her brother, she wished he was married. And don't you wish your sisters married too? Yes. All but
Emily; I would not have her married. Why? Because I can't spare
her, I can't part with her. The rest may marry as soon as they
please, so they do but get good husbands. We then took upon us
to consider for 'em what sort of husband would be fitted for every
one of them. We began with Georgiana. She thought a country
gentleman who loved traveling and would take her with him, that
loved books and would hear her read to him. I added that had a
good estate and was a member of Parliament and loved to see an
experiment now and then. This she agreed to. So we set him down
for Georgiana and went on to Betsy. Betsy, says I, seems of a sweet
mild temper, and if we should give her a country squire, and he
should happen to be of a rough, passionate turn, and be angry
now and then, it might break her heart! O none of 'em must be so;
for then they would not be good husbands. To make sure of this
point, however, for Betsy, shall we give her a bishop? O no, that
won't do. They all declare against the church, and against the
army; not one of them will marry either a clergyman or an officer;
that they are resolved upon. What can be the reason for that? Why,
you know that when a clergyman or an officer dies, the income
goes with 'em; and then what is there to maintain the family? There
is the point. Then suppose we give her a good, honest, sensible city
merchant who will love her dearly and is very rich? I don't know
but that may do. We proceeded to Emily, her dear Emily. I was
afraid we should hardly find anything good enough for Emily; but
at last, after settling that if she did marry, Kitty was to live a good
deal with her, we agreed that as Emily is very handsome we might
expect an earl for her. So having fix'd her, as I thought, a countess,
we went on to Anna Maria. She, says Kitty, should have a rich
man that has a large family and a great many things to take care
of; for she is very good at managing, helps my mama very much,*

*can look over bills, and order all sorts of family business. Very well,
and as there is a grace and dignity in her manner that would become
the station, what do you think of giving her a duke? O no! I'll have
the duke for Emily. You may give the earl to Anna Maria if you
please: but Emily shall have the duke. I contested this matter some
time; but at length was forced to give up the point, leave Emily in
possession of the duke, and content myself with the earl for Anna
Maria. And now what shall we do for Kitty? We have forgot her, all
this time. Well, and what will you do for her? I suppose that though
the rest have resolved against the army, she may not yet have made
so rash a resolution. Yes, but she has: Unless, now, an old one, an
old general that has done fighting, and is rich, such a one as General
Rufane. I like him a good deal; you must know that I like an old
man, indeed I do. And somehow or other all the old men take to
me; all that come to our house like me better than my other sisters.
I go to 'em and ask 'em how they do, and they like it mightily; and
the maids take notice of it, and say when they see an old man come,
there's a friend of yours, Miss Kitty. But then as you like an old
general, hadn't you better take him while he's a young officer, and
let him grow old upon your hands? Because then you'll like him
better and better every year as he grows older and older? No, that
won't do. He must be an old man of 70 or 80, and take me when
I'm about 30. And then you know I may be a rich young widow.*[97]

Perhaps Franklin's greatest gift was his ability to enjoy precisely what
he was doing, when he was doing it, even to make an art of it, whether
it was making an experiment, testifying before Parliament or chatting
with an eleven-year-old girl.

XVII

In London, Franklin found politics in a state of summer quiescence. All
the noble lords who ran the British government were enjoying the sunny
pleasures of their great estates. Franklin decided to profit by their ex-

ample, and, as he told his wife in a letter, "I am to set out next week with my old friend and fellow traveler, Counselor Jackson." The destination was Ireland and Scotland.

After some visiting in the Midlands, the two travelers made for Holyhead in Wales, where they caught a packet boat for Ireland. The packet's name was *Hillsborough,* and Franklin must have wondered if he ought to risk boarding it. But on the afternoon of Thursday, September 5, 1771, he and Jackson stepped ashore in the little port of Dunleary, four miles from Dublin. Franklin's first impression of Ireland never left him. Toothless, dirty, ragged people, described by one contemporary traveler as "the dregs of creation," stood idly in the doors of their crumbling shacks or shuffled desultorily along the slimy, smelly street. Dunleary, whose name has since been changed to Kingstown, was Irish poverty at its worst. The travelers had to fight their way past hordes of whining beggars and aggressive porters to get their bags aboard the Dublin stagecoach. In the capital, which Dubliners proudly called the second city of the empire, Franklin and Jackson saw some of the reason for the misery they had witnessed at Dunleary. Dublin was being rebuilt on a magnificent scale by Ireland's British overlords. The new Parliament House with its Ionic columns had recently risen, the Royal Exchange in Cork Street was half built, and Trinity College was expanding. The spacious new avenues and squares were considered the equal of any other city in Europe. Best of all, of course, were the stately Georgian mansions of the Anglo-Irish nobility, Moira House on the South Quay, Tyrone House in Marlborough Street, and Leinster House, which was to inspire an Irish architect named Hoban to create prize-winning plans for a house called "The President's Palace" in a yet unborn city named Washington, D.C.

The two travelers were graciously greeted by the Lord Lieutenant of Ireland, George Townshend, brother of the late minister, whose whimsical ways had inflamed the quarrel between England and America. The Viceroy shared his brother's whimsical character, often wandering unescorted through Dublin and helping blind beggars across the busy streets. He invited Franklin and Jackson to dine with him at Dublin Castle.

When they arrived at the Castle, they were shown into a room to await the other members of the party. There, to Franklin's astonishment, they found themselves face to face with none other than Lord Hillsborough. He too was a dinner guest. Franklin was even more amazed to discover his Lordship "was extremely civil, wonderfully so to me whom he had not long before abused to Mr. Strahan as a factious, turbulent fellow, always in mischief, a republican, enemy to the King's service and what not." At the dinner table, Lord Hillsborough's civilities continued. He even raised a bumper of good Madeira, and drank to Dr. Franklin's health. He showered pleasantries on the two visitors and insisted on knowing where they planned to travel in Ireland. If they came north, he hoped they would visit with him on his estate for a few days. Describing the conversation to his son, Franklin said Hillsborough "urged it in so polite a manner that we could not avoid saying that we would wait on him if we went that way. In my own mind I was determined not to go that way." [98]

Franklin soon found himself whirling from dinner party to dinner party in sociable Dublin. Many of the dinners were political. The country was divided between the Courtiers and the Patriots. The Courtiers supported the prerogative of the Crown, not unlike the royalist party in Massachusetts, while the Patriots fought for more independence for Ireland. "The latter [the Patriots] treated me with particular respect," Franklin told William proudly. In fact, he had not a little to do with the creation of what the British government considered a somewhat incendiary publication. The Patriots were all friends of America and Franklin said "everything I could think of to confirm them." He paid particular attention to Dr. Charles Lucas, founder of the *Freeman's Journal* and a member of the Irish Parliament from Dublin City. Eleven days after Franklin arrived, Lucas published an open letter expressing his sympathy for the victims of the Boston Massacre. In fact, Franklin so thoroughly converted Dr. Lucas that at a dinner his toast was "Mr. Bowdoin of Boston."

A few days later, Franklin stood in the Dublin streets and watched the Viceroy ride past in his sumptuous coach to open Parliament. The crowds lining the sidewalks sang a defiant ballad which must have been especially appealing to Franklin.

> *To Albion's ear ye breezes bear*
> *This tale of Ireland's woe*
> *That worth alone exalts a throne*
> *And vices bring it low.*

Later that day, Franklin sat in the gallery of the Parliament building beneath the striking dome, while the Lord Lieutenant read his opening speech. When he began talking about taxes, there was a volley of boos, shouts, and insulting remarks hurled from the galleries, and Lord Townshend, in a pet, threatened to clear the House if he did not get silence. Two days later, Franklin paid the Parliament another visit. The Speaker, Viscount Pery, whom he had met at the Lord Lieutenant's dinner, saw him and Jackson entering the visitors' gallery. What followed had the appearance of the impromptu, but in view of Franklin's political expertise, the viscount may well have been carefully primed for the occasion. Pery suddenly announced that he understood there was in town an "American gentleman of distinguished character and merit" who was "a member or delegate of some of the parliaments of that country." This, of course, was even better music to Franklin's ears than the ballad he had just heard sung on the Dublin streets. He stood silent, carefully concealing his delight, as Pery went on. There was a rule of the House for admitting members of the English Parliament to the floor, and Pery wondered if the House would consider the American assemblies as English parliaments? He hesitated to give an order on it without receiving their directions. Instantly the whole House gave what Franklin proudly called "a loud, unanimous aye." Two members came to the bar where Franklin was now standing, let him in, and gave him a seat of honor near the Speaker's desk.

As Franklin explained it to Thomas Cushing, the Irish were "dispos'd to be friends of America . . . with the expectation that our growing weight might in time be thrown into their scale, and by joining our interest with theirs might be obtained for them as well as for us, a more equitable treatment. . . ." But as for Ireland's weight helping America, Franklin saw small hope. The country was too totally crushed by the ruthless application of English power. "The appearances of general extreme poverty among the lower people are amazing," Franklin told Cushing. "They live in wretched hovels of mud and straw, are clothed in rags, and subsist chiefly on potatoes. Our New England farmers, of the poorest sort, in regard to the enjoyment of all the comforts of life are princes when compared to them. Such is the effect of the discouragements of industry, the nonresidence not only of pensioners, but of many original landlords, who lease their lands in gross to undertakers that rack the tenants and fleece them skin and all to make estates to themselves, while the rents, as well as most of the pensions are spent out of the country."

He told of an English gentleman who began needling Franklin about

America's inability to build up a better export trade. From all he had heard of the good grazing-land in America, and from what he saw of the amount of American flaxseed imported by Ireland, he could not understand why the colonists were not able to share some of the Irish trade in beef and butter and linen to the West Indies and other parts of the Empire.

"I suppose the reason might be," Franklin said dryly, "our people eat beef and butter every day and wear shirts themselves." [99]

After several more days of partying in Dublin, Franklin and Jackson set out for Belfast, where Franklin hoped to catch a ship to Scotland. Their route carried them within calling distance of Hillsboro, the Hill estate, and Jackson did not feel they could pass his Lordship by without offending him. Franklin, thoroughly prepared to do this, proposed that they separate. He would go on to Armagh to visit with Dean Hugh Hamilton, a fellow scientist who had recently written a pamphlet on barometers which had attracted some attention. But when they reached the point in the road where they were to part, there was no carriage available for Franklin, and he was obliged to succumb to Jackson's political necessities and jog onward to Hillsboro. The immense estate was run with military efficiency by his Lordship. Neat, well-kept plantations perched atop the hills the travelers passed, and at the mansion house they were greeted by a castle guard with cocked hats and Dutch breeches in memory of William of Orange "of glorious memory." They were in the north of Ireland now where the Catholics were an utterly crushed minority, without even the freedom to sing rebellious ballads.

Lord Hillsborough greeted them with the same lavish civility he had displayed in Dublin Castle. In fact, like a chameleon he seemed to have absorbed the coloration of the Irish atmosphere, and Franklin could only blink in astonishment as he heard his Lordship "censuring the English government for its narrowness with regard to Ireland, in restraining its commerce, manufactures &c." Franklin, of course, immediately "apply'd his observations to America" and to his further astonishment, Lord Hillsborough agreed that it was "wrong to restrain our manufactures" and avowed that "the subjects in every part of the King's dominions had a natural right to make the best use they could of the production of their country." This was practically a quotation from Franklin's newspaper propaganda. His Lordship went on to declare that he always avoided laying before Parliament reports of colonial manufacturers, unless they were especially called for. He took the credit for a recent bounty declared by Parliament to encourage silk manufacturing in America and asked Franklin to advise him on how to persuade Parliament to vote a similar bounty for the production of wine. And had Franklin any thoughts on Newfoundland, which had now become settled to the point where it needed a "proper form of government?"

This startling request for Franklin's advice did not end his Lordship's kind attentions. He insisted on Franklin's taking a tour of the neighborhood, and summoned his eldest son, Lord Kilwarling, to escort their guest on a forty-mile ramble. It was a chilly day, and his Lordship doffed his greatcoat and put it over Franklin's shoulders with his own hands as the carriage pulled away.

Writing to his son, several weeks later, Franklin was still puzzling over this reversal of form on Hillsborough's part. "Does not all this seem extraordinary to you? I knew not what to make of it, unless that he foresaw a storm on acct of his conduct to America, and was willing to lessen beforehand the acrimony with which the people & friends of that country might possibly pursue him." [100] To Thomas Cushing, in a letter written about the same time, Franklin was even more dubious about Hillsborough's conduct. He pointed out that his Lordship had not repealed any of the offensive instructions, such as forcing the Boston Assembly to sit at Cambridge. He therefore was inclined to think that his Lordship "meant only, by patting and stroaking the horse, to make him more patient, while the reins are drawn tighter, and the spurs set deeper into his sides." [101]

Back in London, after renewing his friendship with Lord Kames, Alexander Dick and other auld acquaintances in Scotland, Franklin hastened to pay his respects to Lord Hillsborough and thank him for his hospitality in Ireland. Before Franklin could get out of his coach, the porter curtly told him that his Lordship was not at home. He left his card and returned a second time, to receive the same answer. This time Franklin knew it was a blatant lie, because one of his good friends was with Hillsborough, by appointment. The following week he made another visit and got the same blunt answer. Persevering, he came back a week later on a levee day—a day on which his Lordship saw visitors by the dozen. There were numerous carriages parked around the square, and Franklin's coachman did not bother to ask whether his Lordship was at home. He was opening the coach door when Hillsborough's porter came bawling out at him. How dare he open his door before he had inquired whether my Lord was at home! Then he turned to Franklin and said in his most insolent tone, "My Lord is not at home."

That was Franklin's last visit. Thereafter, as he told his son William, he and Hillsborough "only abused one another at a distance." [102]

XVIII

But Franklin declined to let Lord Hillsborough ruin the good spirits he had regained as a result of his three months' jog through Ireland and Scotland. A decided plus to his happiness was a meeting with his son-in-law, Richard Bache, who had returned to England to meet his father-in-law and visit his aging mother. Bache had brought along with him 1000 pounds which he hoped Franklin would be willing to distribute in the right places to buy him a government job. Franklin declined flatly. Instead, he advised Bache to take the money and buy goods to sell in Philadelphia on a cash and carry basis. If he would thus "sit down to business in Philadelphia," Franklin thought he might "by quick returns, get forward in the world." Rather pointedly, Franklin wrote to his son, "I wish to see all I am connected with in an independent situation, supported by their own industry." [103]

Bache took his father-in-law's advice, and Franklin, pleased with his son-in-law on this and all other points, added 200 pounds of his own money to his capital.

About the same time, Franklin got a cheerful letter from his "adopted daughter," Polly Stevenson, who had married a young doctor named Hewson and given birth to her first child. She had made Franklin his godfather. Polly told him that the young man resembled his godfather in many interesting ways. "He is generally serious, no great talker, but sometimes laughs very hearty; he is fond of being in his birthday suit, and has not the least apprehension of catching cold in it; he is never troubled with the aerophobia, but always seems delighted with fresh air." [104]

Franklin jovially replied: "His being like me in so many particulars pleases me prodigiously; and I am persuaded there is another, which you have omitted, tho' it must have occurr'd to you while you were putting them down."

He proceeded to give Polly some impromptu advice on raising the young man. "Pray let him have everything he likes; I think it of great consequence while the features of the countenance are forming; it gives them a pleasant air, and, that being once become natural and fix'd by habit, the face is ever after the handsomer for it, and on that much of a person's good fortune and success in life may depend. Had I been cross'd as much in my infant likings and inclinations as you know I have been of late years [a reference to the kisses Franklin was always trying to steal from Polly and her young friends] I should have been, I was going to say, not near so handsome; but as the vanity of that expression would offend other folks' vanity, I change it, out of regard to them, and say a great deal more homely."

In the same letter Polly teasingly warned him that her mother was seeing another man in his absence. Franklin declared he was hardly surprised. "I have been us'd to rivals, and scarce ever had a friend or a mistress in my whole life, that other people did not like as well as myself." His only problem, he said, was trying to figure out who the enterprising stranger was. At first he suspected a certain duke, having read in the paper that that gentleman was visiting of late "an old lady not many miles from Craven Street." But then he read that Prince Charles had vanished from Rome on a mysterious journey, and decided it was he who had taken the opportunity to "solace himself." [105]

XIX

This renewed energy and *joie de vivre* inspired Franklin to do more than simply abuse Lord Hillsborough at a distance. He made it well-known at dinner tables around London that he was preparing an exhaustive critique of Hillsborough's administration, which would demolish that gentleman once and for all. Simultaneously, through the other influential members of the Grand Ohio Company, he put more and more pressure on Hillsborough to issue a report on the petition for the new colony.

Hillsborough had used up every excuse for delay. The Virginians had been bought out and merged their interest with the Grand Ohio people, numerous petitions had poured in from the frontier (stimulated by Samuel Wharton and his friends) warning of the need for formal government and of preventing a new Indian war. Franklin had spent almost two decades weaving a web of intimate political contacts, and he now used all of his resources on the shaky Irish Lord. William Strahan wrote a letter to his (and Franklin's) friend, the philosopher David Hume, asking for his help. Hume in turn wrote to Lord Hertford, the King's chamberlain, who in turn spoke to the King, and soon Hillsborough was shaken to the soles of his feet by a direct inquiry from George III himself about the strange delays which seemed to beset plans for the new western colony.

The cornered Hillsborough at last issued a report from the Board of Trade condemning the proposition. Lord Gower, the president of the Privy Council, who also was a partner in the Grand Ohio Company, arranged for a public hearing on the petition. Samuel Wharton was chosen to make the verbal presentation, but it is almost a certainty that most of his devastating arguments, entitled "Observations on, and Answers to the Foregoing Report," were composed by Benjamin Franklin.[106] Wharton was no mean talker, and he put on a magnificent performance before the Privy Council's Committee for Plantation Affairs. Less than a month later, the Committee recommended to the Privy Council that the Board of Trade's report be set aside and a new colony be created as soon as possible.

Seldom had an English politician been more mortified than Lord Hillsborough. The Committee's decision was a cruel blow to his prestige. He had only one alternative: resignation.

Exultantly, Franklin wrote to William, "At length we have got rid of Lord Hillsborough . . . to the great satisfaction of all the friends of America. You will hear it said among you, I suppose, that the interest of the Ohio planters has ousted him; but the truth is, what I wrote you long since, that all his brother ministers disliked him extremely, and wished for a fair occasion of tripping up his heels; so, seeing that he made a point of defeating our scheme, they made another of supporting it on purpose to mortify him, which they knew his pride could not bear. I do not mean that they would have done this if they had thought our proposal bad in itself, or his opposition well founded; but I believe if he had been on good terms with them they would not have differed with him for so small a matter. The King, too, was tired of him and of his administration, which had weakened the affection and the respect of the colonies for the royal government, of which (I may say it to you) I used proper means from time to time that His Majesty would have due information and convincing proofs. . . .

"The King's dislike made the others more firmly united in the resolution of disgracing Hillsborough, by setting at nought his famous report."

Did this mean that the Grand Ohio Company was at last about to triumph? Franklin was too experienced a politician to make so rash a prediction. "Now that the business is done, perhaps our affair may be less regarded in the Cabinet, and suffered to linger, and possibly may yet miscarry. Therefore, let us beware of every word and action that may betray a confidence in its success lest we render ourselves ridiculous in case of disappointment. We are now pushing for a completion of the business; but the time is unfavorable, everybody gone or going into the country, which gives room for accidents. . . ." [107]

X X

Not only had he gotten rid of Lord Hillsborough; Franklin also played no small part in choosing his successor. As he told the story to William, "A friend at Court," possibly the American artist, Benjamin West, who had just been made historical painter to the King, told Franklin, "We Americans were represented by Hillsborough as an unquiet people, not easily satisfied with any ministry; that, however, it was thought too much occasion had been given us to dislike the present." The friend then asked Franklin, if Hillsborough were removed, who would be more acceptable. "There is Lord Dartmouth," Franklin replied. "We liked him very well when he was at the head of the Board [of Trade] formerly, and probably should like him again." [108]

To Franklin's scarcely concealed delight, Henry Legge, first Earl of Dartmouth, became Secretary of State for the American Colonies and President of the Board of Trade, a few weeks after Hillsborough resigned. In personality he was the total opposite of Hillsborough. Dartmouth was a sensitive, deeply religious man with a staunchly pro-American attitude and record. Thanks to his generosity, the college of Dartmouth had been founded in New Hampshire, and his Lordship had patented 100,000 acres of land in east Florida for his sons, and some 40,000 acres in the Ohio country for himself. Everything about him seemed to presage a benevolent administration and a favorable attitude toward the creation of the new colony.

The apparent totality of his victory dazzled Franklin into a surge of unparalleled optimism. "As to my situation here," he told Governor Franklin, "nothing can be more agreeable. . . . A general respect paid me by the learned, a number of friends and acquaintance among them with whom I have a pleasing intercourse; a character of so much weight that it has protected me when some in power would have done me injury, and continued me in an office they would have deprived me of; my company so much desired that I seldom dine at home in winter, and could spend the whole summer in the country-houses of inviting friends if I chose it. Learned and ingenious foreigners who come to England almost all make a point of visiting me; for my reputation is still higher abroad than here. Several of the foreign ambassadors have assiduously cultivated my acquaintance, treating me as one of their *corps*, partly I believe from the desire they have, from time to time, of hearing something of American affairs, an object become of importance in foreign courts, who begin to hope Britain's alarming power will be diminished by the defection of her colonies; and partly that they may have an opportunity of introducing me to the gentlemen of their country who desire it. The King, too, has lately been heard to speak of me with great regard. . . ."

Only one thing troubled him for the moment—a violent longing for home that sometimes seized him, and which he managed to subdue only by "promising myself a return next spring or next fall and so forth." Now, however, the encouraging change in the government "being thrown into the balance" persuaded him to "stay another winter." [109]

XXI

The remark about balance refers to Franklin's ingenious way of making decisions. About this same time, Joseph Priestley, a young English scientist whom Franklin had befriended and helped to write his *History and Present State of Electricity,* asked his advice on a job offer. Lord Shelburne wanted him to become his librarian, and Priestley, who was teaching school, could not decide whether the job would give him more or less time for his writing and scientific activity. Franklin replied that for want of sufficient information he couldn't really tell him *what* to decide, but he could tell him how. "When these difficult cases occur, they are difficult chiefly because while we have them under consideration, all the reasons pro and con are not present to the mind at the same time; but sometimes one set present themselves, and at other times another, the first being out of sight. Hence . . . the uncertainty that perplexes us.

"To get over this, my way is to divide half a sheet of paper by a line into two columns; writing over the one pro and over the other con, Then during three or four days of consideration I put down under the different heads short hints of the different motives that at different times occur to me, for or against the measure. When I have thus got them all together in one view, I endeavour to estimate their respective weights; and where I find two (one on each side) that seem equal, I strike them both out. If I find a reason pro equal to some two reasons con, I strike out the three . . . and thus proceeding I find at length where the balance lies; and if after a day or two of farther consideration, nothing new that is of importance occurs on either side, I come to a determination accordingly. . . . I have found great advantage from this . . . moral or prudential algebra." [110]

Priestley was one of a group of liberal young scientists whom Franklin gathered around him during the 1770s in London. They were all as interested in politics as they were in science, a by no means unusual phenomenon in those days, and they were also effective writers and speakers. Not surprisingly, Franklin swiftly enlisted them on America's side of the battle for public opinion.

Another young man who caught Franklin's eye was Benjamin Vaughan, born in the West Indies, American in blood and sympathies, thanks to his Boston-born mother. Vaughan was something of a walking encyclopedia, interested in everything from science to agriculture. A third member of the circle, young in spirit although some years older, was Richard Price, an expert on economics, who longed to reform England's mercantile system, with its antiquated state controls. But the man who seems to have engendered the most enthusiasm in Franklin was suave, engaging Edward Bancroft. Connecticut born, he had emigrated to England, married an English wife, and made a modest fortune running a plantation in Surinam. There he had become a pioneer in the art and science of vegetable dyes, and a student, among other things, of tropical poisons. Bancroft wrote some very effective pro-American propaganda under Franklin's tutelage, and impressed the older man both with his ardor for his country's cause and with his shrewd penetrating mind.

In a very loose, unstructured way, these and other men of similar political inclinations revolved around Franklin's old friend from the colonial office, Lord Shelburne. Franklin himself continued to maintain a close friendship with this immensely wealthy nobleman. Shelburne was a people collector, who enjoyed entertaining diverse personalities at his handsome country house, Bowood, outside of London. During one Franklin visit the other guests were Colonel Isaac Barré, the defender of American rights in Parliament; David Garrick, the noted actor; and Abbé André Morellet, a free-thinking French priest, who had spent some time in the Bastille for defending the liberal French *philosophes* against powerful conservatives. The abbé was deeply interested in politics and government, as well as science, and he found Franklin fascinating. In bad French and broken English they agreed on the need to promote freedom of commerce in the world, discussed population trends and exchanged favorite drinking songs.

With two such potent talkers as Barré and Garrick, Franklin said little when the party was general. But he quietly upstaged even the great Garrick with a performance of his own, while they were strolling through the park of the Bowood estate. Donning his conjuror's mantle, Franklin mysteriously declared that his study of science had given him powers which he seldom revealed. For instance, he said, pointing to a nearby stream, where a brisk breeze was causing a good deal of turbulence, he had learned how to calm storm-tossed waters. The remark inspired instant skepticism in the company. Leaving them where they stood, about 200 paces from the water, Franklin advanced to the edge of the stream and made a series of magical passes over it with his cane. Suddenly, to the disbelieving eyes of the spectators, the surface of the water subsided and became as smooth and glassy as a sheltered puddle. Morellet, Shelburne, and the others rushed to the bank but they saw nothing that explained the miracle. A workman who happened to be standing nearby was so awe-struck he was convinced that Franklin had supernatural powers. "What am I to believe?" he cried.

"Only what you see," said Franklin.

After letting his friends rack their brains for an hour or two, Franklin smilingly revealed his secret. In the hollow bottom of his cane, he had taken to carrying a small vial of clear oil. He had been experimenting for two years on calming water by pouring oil on it. Trials in the ocean inclined him to think that it was not, as he had at first hoped, a technique that might preserve a ship at sea, during a storm. But it worked quite well on smaller bodies of water.[111]

XXII

Franklin's optimism about Lord Dartmouth's ministry increased tenfold when he attended his first levee, early in November, 1772. Dartmouth received him with the cordiality of an old friend, and, Franklin told William in a letter written the same day, his first order of business was "to recommend my son to his protection, who, says I, is one of your governors in America." John Pownall, still one of the ministerial secretaries, was with them and he added, "And a very good governor he is."

"Yes," said Lord Dartmouth, "he has been a good governor and has kept his province in good order during times of difficulty." [112]

Franklin wisely decided that it would be better to bring up the Ohio Company some other time, and bowed his way out with a remark that he would wait on his Lordship another day on business. Dartmouth graciously replied that he would always be ready to hear him and glad to see him.

"I shall attend his levee again today, on some New England affairs, and hope we may now go on more smoothly," Franklin said. "But time will show." As for the "Ohio affair," as he called it, the Boards were meeting again, and the partners hoped to push it forward with all possible speed. A few hours later, Franklin added a postscript to this hopeful letter. He was just back from Dartmouth's levee, and delightedly reported that his Lordship had shown him "particular respect in sending for me out of the crowd long before my turn, and apologizing for having kept me so long. . . ." He also made no objection to Franklin's acting as agent for Massachusetts without the governor's approval. Whether this would continue would depend on whether he could resist pressure from his secretaries, John Pownall and William Knox, both thoroughly anti-American, who would undoubtedly urge him to continue, as a matter of honor, Hillsborough's objections to Franklin's agency.

But Franklin was soon to discover that Lord Dartmouth was more symbol than reality. Even out of office, Lord Hillsborough remained a close friend and influential ally of the First Minister, Lord North. Not a few of the members of the Privy Council who had voted against Hillsborough were hoping that the blow would knock out North as well, and that a new ministry, under the political heirs of the Duke of Bedford (now dead), would come into power. Lord Gower, the Privy Council president, was head of the Bedfordites, and this was as much his motive for knifing Hillsborough as was his partnership in the Grand Ohio Company. Hillsborough thus had no difficulty poisoning North's complaisant second-rate mind against Franklin. During a visit to the country estate of a mutual friend, North and Franklin ate dinner, supper, and breakfast together without exchanging more than three sentences. Franklin was soon reporting mournfully to his son that Lord Dartmouth was "truly a good man and wishes sincerely a good understanding with the colonies, but does not seem to have strength equal to his wishes." [113]

XXIII

Although the rest of America was comparatively quiet, something close to open warfare still raged between the Massachusetts Assembly and Governor Thomas Hutchinson. Thus Franklin spent more and more time representing and defending Massachusetts, and his standing with Dartmouth began to slip steadily. This in turn had an adverse effect on the progress of the new colony, which now had been named Vandalia in honor of Queen Charlotte's Germanic ancestors. A draft constitution had been drawn up and approved by the Board of Trade and on May 19, 1773, the Privy Council ordered Edward Thurlow, the attorney general, and Alexander Wedderburn, the solicitor general, to draw up the final papers for the grant.

But these two tough Scotsmen were purchased friends of Lord North's and they proceeded to find dozens of objections to various legal aspects of the project. Lord Dartmouth himself began to voice uneasiness about the colony. Lord North and Dartmouth were half-brothers, North's father having married Dartmouth's widowed mother.

These delays strained the nerves of the younger speculators to the snapping point. Samuel Wharton complained bitterly to George Croghan, bankrupt and hounded by creditors back in America, that "all we were thought to believe [about Benjamin Franklin] *before* I left America, was bluff and declamation." Wharton's business partners, Baynton and Morgan, accused him of swindling them because he had failed to name them as partners in the Grand Ohio Company. William Franklin warned his father that he suspected Wharton was opening their mail. Franklin was more inclined to suspect William Knox, the anti-American under-secretary in Dartmouth's office.

Franklin himself took a philosophic attitude toward the Ohio Company's lack of progress, and spiced it, as he so often did, with humor. He told Joseph Galloway, "I begin to be a little of the sailor's mind when they were handing a cable out of a store into a ship, and one of 'em said, ' 'Tis a long, heavy cable. I wish we could see the end of it.' 'D—n,' says another, 'if I believe it has any end; somebody has cut it off.' " [114]

Even before he wrote these soothing words, Franklin had taken a step which was to sink the Grand Ohio Company forever and arouse his enemies in the British government as never before. On December 2, 1772, in a letter to Thomas Cushing, Franklin wrote the following fateful words: "On this occasion I think it fit to acquaint you, that there has lately fallen into my hands part of a correspondence that I have reason to believe laid the foundation of most if not all our present grievances. I am not at liberty to tell thro' what channel I received it; and I have engag'd that it shall not be printed, nor copies taken of the whole, or any part of it; but I am allow'd to let it be seen by some men of worth in the province, for their satisfaction only. In confidence of your preserving inviolably my engagement, I send you inclosed the original letters, to obviate every pretense of unfairness in copying, interpolation or omission." [115]

These letters which Franklin sent to Boston had been written by Governor Thomas Hutchinson and his lieutenant governor, Andrew Oliver, in 1768–69, during the riots in Boston over the Townshend duties. They described the state of the province in terms that suggested anarchy was imminent, and urged the Crown to send troops to cow the Boston mobs. Hutchinson wrote: "There must be some abridgement of what is called English liberty." Oliver suggested that officers of the Crown ought to be made "in some measure independent" of the Assembly. Franklin had heard about these letters in the summer or early fall of 1772. He was talking with "a gentleman of character and distinction," as he told it several years later, and was complaining about the numerous grievances which the Hillsborough administration had inflicted on Massachusetts, particularly the quartering of troops in Boston. To his "great surprise" the gentleman assured him that this measure and all the other grievances could be traced not to the British government in London, but to Americans in Boston. The measures had been "projected, proposed to administration, solicited, and obtained by some of the most respectable among the Americans themselves," the gentleman avowed, "as necessary measures for the welfare of that country." Franklin was unconvinced, until the gentleman called on him "some days after and produced to me these very letters from Lieut.-Gov. Hutchinson, Secry. Oliver, and others." [116]

Who was this "gentleman of character and distinction"? It may have been John Temple, the relative of the powerful Temple clan whom Benjamin and William Franklin had met in 1757 on their voyage to London. Temple had achieved the purpose of his journey to the imperial capital. His kinship to the Temples, which genealogists now consider somewhat dubious, won him a post as surveyor-general of Customs in North America, with a salary of 1000 pounds a year. This was not a job that was designed to win a man much popularity in America, but as a Boston-born man himself, Temple was emotionally, if not legally, on the American side of the quarrel with England. An additional impetus to this commitment was his marriage to the daughter of Franklin's good friend, James Bowdoin.

Temple's fellow Customs' officers in Boston hated him intensely, and they accused him of falsifying his accounts. Recalled, he was cleared of their slanderous charges, but the government declined to send him again to America. Instead, he was given a lucrative office in the British Customs Service. But he had expressed bitter regret at being forced to leave "my native country which I sincerely love," and he was, like Franklin, convinced that a handful of wrongheaded men on both sides of the Atlantic were responsible for igniting the quarrel between America and the mother country. High on his list, for personal and political reasons, were Hutchinson and Oliver, who had supported and perhaps even connived in his expulsion from the American Customs Service.[117]

While he was in Boston, Temple had been, in the routine of his office, a constant correspondent of Thomas Whately, the Joint Secretary of the Treasury, to whom Hutchinson and Oliver wrote their letters. Whately had died intestate in May, 1772, and his estate, including his voluminous correspondence, had been placed in the hands of his brother, banker William Whately. It would have been a fairly simple matter for Temple to ask Whately's permission to go through his brother's papers, to extract some of his own letters. In the process, it would have been equally easy for him to purloin those of Hutchinson and Oliver.

Franklin's motive in sending off the letters to Boston could only have been what he stated in his covering letter—the hope that the Boston patriots would find less reason to hate England when they discovered that the British government had been acting on misrepresentations, sent to them by fellow Bostonians. But there was also in this tangled web the sudden surge of optimism and the new sense of power which Franklin had felt when Lord Dartmouth came into office. Almost certainly Franklin recalled the attitude of Lord Shelburne, the previous American secretary who had favorable feelings toward the colonies, when Governor Francis Bernard had written violently negative letters home. Franklin would never have taken such a serious step without the comfortable reassurance in the back of his mind that Lord Dartmouth would agree with his stand and support him in the face of possible censure. Forgetting his recent lament about Dartmouth's lack of strength, Franklin was dangerously overestimating the American secretary's power, as well as his fondness for Benjamin Franklin.

XXIV

Events moved slowly in the eighteenth century, especially when the principal actors were separated by 3000 miles of ocean. Franklin spent the next few months peacefully enough, visiting friends in the countryside and watching the British government as it attempted to solve a new overseas problem: India. The British East India Company, a semi-public organization that operated with almost complete independence from the English government, was in severe financial difficulty. Its stock plummeted on the London exchange, and in January, 1773, it requested from the government a loan of 1,500,000 pounds to stave off imminent bankruptcy. Part, but by no means all, of its troubles were the losses it had suffered in exporting tea, one of its chief sources of profit, to America. Americans were still drinking prodigious quantities of this favorite beverage, but much of it was being smuggled from the Dutch and French West Indies. Not only was it more profitable, but it was a patriotic gesture of defiance against the North ministry's insistence on keeping the tax on tea to "maintain the right." In a letter to William Franklin, Benjamin reported that the company had imported "great quantities in the faith that that agreement [the nonimportation agreement] could not hold; and now they [the East India Company] can neither pay their debts nor dividends." The ensuing "shock to credit" caused a recession in the manufacturing districts, and thousands of British workers were "now starving, or subsisting on charity." All, Franklin noted wryly, "the blessed effects of pride, pique and passion in government, which should have no passions." [118]

For a while the North ministry played around with the idea of having the company "save its honor by petitioning for the repeal of that duty," Franklin told Joseph Galloway, adding, "A fine hobble they are all got into by their unjust and blundering politics with regard to the Colonies." [119] But North, although he was personally inclined to avoid trouble, was too much in the grip of the anti-Americans in the cabinet to accept this solution. So, after a great deal of wrangling, the government imposed another solution on the reluctant East India Company. Henceforth, the government would have much more say in regulating the company's internal affairs. In return, the government would help them get rid of their surplus tea, by repealing the English duty on it and setting up a special agency to sell the tea in America at a price which would be even cheaper than the smuggled products of their competitors. Simultaneously, of course, the ministers expected to enjoy the pleasant spectacle of seeing Americans pay the hated duty in order to get cheaper tea. Thus Parliament's right would be simultaneously affirmed, and the British economy rescued from the "hobble."

Franklin was disgusted with this solution, and immediately made this clear to his friends in Boston. "It was thought at the beginning of the session, that the American duty on tea would be taken off," he told Thomas Cushing, "but now the wise scheme is to take off so much duty here, as will make tea cheaper in America than foreigners can supply us, and to confine the duty there to keep up the exercises of the right. They have no idea that any people can act from any other principle but that of interest; and they believe, that 3d [pence] in a lb. of tea of which one does not perhaps drink ten in a year, is sufficient to overcome all the patriotism of an American." [120]

The cynical attitude of the British ministry infuriated Franklin, and, as always, when emotion flowed in him, he reached for his pen. Soon there appeared in the newspapers the boldest piece of propaganda he had yet produced.

RULES
BY WHICH
A GREAT EMPIRE MAY BE REDUCED TO A SMALL ONE
PRESENTED TO A LATE MINISTER
WHEN HE ENTERED UPON HIS ADMINISTRATION

The last line of the title was a dig at Lord Hillsborough, but Franklin made it clear in his opening paragraph that he was addressing himself "to all ministers who have the management of extensive dominions." He then proceeded to give them twenty satiric rules for wrecking the empire.

I. *In the first place, gentlemen, you are to consider, that a great empire, like a great cake, is most easily diminished at the edges. Turn your attention, therefore, first to your remotest provinces; that, as you get rid of them, the next may follow in order.*

II. *That the possibility of this separation may always exist, take special care the provinces are never incorporated with the mother country; that they do not enjoy the same common rights, the same privileges in commerce; and that they are governed by severer laws, all of your enacting, without allowing them any share in the choice of the legislators. By carefully making and preserving such distinctions, you will (to keep to my simile of the cake) act like a wise gingerbread maker, who, to facilitate a division, cuts his dough half through in those places where, when baked, he would have it broken to pieces.*

No reader could miss the immediate application of these and the rules that followed:

However peaceably your colonies have submitted to your government, shewn their affection to your interests, and patiently borne their grievances; you are to suppose them always inclined to revolt and treat them accordingly. Quarter troops among them, who by their insolence may provoke the rising of mobs, and by their bullets and bayonets suppress them. By this means, like the husband who uses his wife ill from suspicion, you may in time convert your suspicions into realities.

Rule V suggested sending out as governors and other royal officials, *"prodigals who have ruined their fortunes, broken gamesters or stock jobbers . . . wrangling proctors and pettifogging lawyers."* Next came a slam at Francis Bernard, who had been recalled as governor of Massachusetts and made a baronet. *"When such governors have crammed their coffers, and made themselves so odious to the people that they can no longer remain among them, with safety to their persons, recall and reward them with pensions. You may make them baronets too, if that respectable order should not think fit to resent it."* This, Franklin assured them, *"will contribute to encourage new governors in the same practice, and make the supreme government, detestable."*

Next came a series of wry advices on how to lay taxes in the worst possible way, and make them as odious as possible. After that came a blast at the harsh British enforcement of the Customs laws. *"Convert the brave, honest officers of your Navy into pimping tide-waiters and colony officers of the Customs. Let those, who in time of war fought gallantly in defense of the commerce of their countrymen, in peace be taught to prey upon it. Let them learn to be corrupted by great and real smugglers; but (to shew their diligence) scour with armed boats every bay, harbor, river, creek, cove or nook throughout the coast of your colonies; stop and detain every coaster, every wood boat, every fisherman, tumble their cargoes and even their ballast inside out and upside down; and, if a penn'orth of pins is found un-entered, let the whole be seized and confiscated. Thus shall the trade of your colonists suffer more from their friends in time of peace, than it did from their enemies in war."* [121]

A few days later, in the *Public Advertiser* another story appeared. It was introduced by what passed in the eighteenth century for a sensational headline.

> The Subject of the following Article of
> ### THAT FOREIGN INTELLIGENCE
> Being Exceedingly Extraordinary, is the
> Reason of Its being Separated from the Usual
> Articles of Foreign News
> ### AN EDICT
> ### BY THE KING OF PRUSSIA

In ceremoniously regal language, Frederick the Great, the King of Prussia, proceeded to proclaim that it was "well known to all the world" that England was a colony of Germany. The first settlers in

England had been Germans under Hengist, Horsa, and others of "our renowned ducal ancestors." Since the colony had "hitherto yielded little profit," Frederick was imposing a four and a half percent duty on all goods and foodstuffs exported or imported from England. All ships bound from Great Britain to any other part of the world would henceforth be forced to touch at the port of Königsberg, "there to be unladened, searched and charged with said duties." The edict went on to forbid the smelting of iron and other forms of manufacturing in Great Britain, banned the weaving of woolen cloth and the making of hats, and finally ordered *"that all the thieves, highway and street robbers, housebreakers, forgers, murderers . . . and villains of every denomination, who have forfeited their lives to the law in Prussia; but whom we, in our great clemency do not think fit here to hang, shall be emptied out of our gaols into the said island of Great Britain, for the better peopling of that country."*

The King flattered himself "that these our royal regulations and commands will be thought just and reasonable by our much favored colonists in England," and proceeded to cite statutes justifying them from laws made by the British Parliament or from instructions given by their kings "for the good government of their own colonies in Ireland and America."

For a final acid touch, the King blandly declared that *"all persons in the said island are hereby cautioned not to oppose in any wise the execution of this our edict, or any part thereof, such opposition being high treason; of which all who are suspected shall be transported in fetters from Britain to Prussia, there to be tried and executed according to the Prussian law."* [122]

X X V

As he often did when he was sticking his neck out dangerously, Franklin absented himself from London during the days when these two articles appeared. He had become friendly with Lord Le Despencer, the new

Postmaster General, and had spent several vacations at his palatial estate in West Wycombe. Franklin was sitting in the breakfast room, chatting with his Lordship and several other guests when the London papers arrived. Paul Whitehead, a well-known writer of the time, had a habit of scanning the papers and then reading aloud the choice bits of gossip and news to the company. This morning he burst into the breakfast room breathless with excitement.

"Here! Here's news for ye! Here's the King of Prussia claiming a right to this kingdom!"

Consternation. Everyone stared in total disbelief. Franklin, no mean actor, managed to look as goggle-eyed as the next man. Whitehead read two or three paragraphs, and one of the listeners burst into violent denunciation of the Prussian King. "Damn his impudence, I dare say, we shall hear by next post that he is upon his march with one hundred thousand men to back this."

But as Whitehead read on, he began to notice the exact correspondence between the Prussian King's claims and Parliament's asserted rights over America. Suddenly he looked Franklin in the eye and said, "I'll be hanged if this is not some of your American jokes upon us."

Franklin smilingly confessed, knowing he was in pro-American company. Whitehead finished the article, amid roars of laughter from the audience. Everyone agreed, Franklin said, "that it was a fair hit." Lord Le Despencer liked it so much he ordered the piece cut out of the paper and preserved in his library.[123]

London readers liked it even more. Both satires sold out the papers in which they were published, and were printed a half-dozen times in other publications. In a letter to his son, Franklin apologized for not being able to send him a copy of the "Edict." He had sent his clerk the next morning to the printers and wherever the papers were sold. "They were all gone but two." Franklin preferred the "Rules by which a Great Empire May be Reduced," probably because it was clearer and bolder in its attack. But most English readers preferred the "Edict." He told William, with not a little satisfaction, that one of the chief anti-Americans in the government, Lord Mansfield, called it "very able and very artful" and gloweringly predicted that it would "do mischief by giving . . . a bad impression of the measures of government; and in the colonies by encouraging them in their contumacy."

There was another reason for this new boldness in Franklin. Typically it appeared first in a letter to his son, in mid-July, 1773, and it was obviously the result of his growing disappointment with Dartmouth's ministry, and his attempt to understand why this good man was so powerless. "Between you and I, the late measures [the Tea Act] have been, I suspect, very much the King's own, and he has in some cases a great share of what his friends call *firmness*." Only if we remember how much weight Franklin placed on the person and the role of the King in maintaining the unity of the empire can we grasp how serious this statement was, to him. Yet he remained hopeful that "by some painstaking and proper management, the wrong impressions he has received may be removed, which is perhaps the only chance America has for obtaining *soon* the redress she aims at." Underscoring his seriousness, he added, "This entirely to yourself." [124]

Another reason for his boldness was also intimately connected with his son. The Boston political leaders had disregarded Franklin's instructions, made copies of Hutchinson's letters, and finally arranged to have them printed in the papers. William Franklin wrote to his father, expressing the natural distaste that he, a governor, would feel upon seeing a fellow official's private correspondence made public in such a manner. He told his father that Governor Hutchinson was accusing Franklin of writing letters to the Boston patriots, advising them to insist on independence. Obviously William half believed this and anxiously asked his father for an explanation.

In a tense letter, Franklin replied that he had done no such thing. He wasn't sure which of his letters Hutchinson had intercepted, but he supposed "he has sent copies of them hither, having heard some whisperings about them." He assured William that he would "be able at any time to justify every thing I have written"; he had "uniformly" advised the people of Boston that "they should carefully avoid all tumults and every violent measure, and content themselves with verbally keeping up their claims, and holding forth their rights whenever occasion requires; secure, that, from the growing importance of America, those claims will erelong be attended to and acknowledged."

Then, he bluntly told William Franklin where he stood on the heart of the historic argument. "From a long and thorough consideration of the subject, I am indeed of opinion, that the Parliament has no right to make any law whatever, binding on the colonies; that the King, and not the King, Lords, and Commons collectively is their sovereign; and that the King, with their respective Parliaments is their only legislator." Then came the point of tension. "I know your sentiments differ from mine on these subjects. You are a thorough government man, which I do not wonder at, nor do I aim at converting you. I only wish you to act uprightly and steadily, avoiding that duplicity, which in Hutchinson, adds contempt to indignation. If you can promote the prosperity of your people, and leave them happier than you found them, whatever your political principles are, your memory will be honoured." [125]

But Franklin did not reveal to his son the full contents of the extraordinary letter which he wrote to Thomas Cushing on July 7, 1773. By now, Lord Dartmouth had been in office almost a year, and it was clear to Franklin that there was no hope that he would ever redress the balance of power within the North cabinet. In fact, North had not even tried to prevent powerful anti-American politicians in the cabinet from blithely assuming much of the jurisdiction over America originally centered in Dartmouth's ministry. As Franklin had already told William, it was becoming equally obvious to him that indolent, bumbling Lord North could not possibly maintain any policy, much less a harsh and repressive one, for two weeks without some very firm backing from the man who held the real executive power in his royal hands: George III.

"The question then arises, how are we to obtain redress?" Franklin wrote to Cushing. His answer was drastic. The Parliamentary history of England gave him the clue. Only by "withholding aids when the sovereign was in distress" were the people able to force the King and his lords to redress their grievances. This was the heart of the reason why the House of Commons always insisted on keeping control of all money bills, not even permitting the House of Lords to interfere in this crucial area. All right, Franklin reasoned, "this country pretends to be collectively our sovereign. It is now deeply in debt. Its funds are far short of recovering their par since the last war: Another would distress it still more. Its people are diminished, as well as its credit. Men will be wanted, as well as money." The next time a war comes to the Empire, and England turns to America for aid and friendship, "then is the time to say, *Redress our grievances.*"

Franklin noted that in 1770, when Britain almost went to war with Spain over a dispute about the ownership of the Falkland Islands, "some great men here" put on a very "different countenance . . . towards those who were thought to have a little influence in America." He was confident that if the war had taken place, Lord Hillsborough "would have been immediately dismiss'd, all his measures revers'd and every step taken to recover our affection and procure our assistance." [126]

This may not have been advice to create political independence in the literal sense, but to an officer of the British government, such confrontation tactics must have seemed very close to advising a kind of independence that was little short of treason. There is, moreover, a very strong probability that the British government read every word Franklin wrote. A copy of another letter to Cushing, in the same tough vein, was filed in Lord Dartmouth's office with the ominous notation: "Very remarkable and requires no commentary." [127]

By thus bringing "the dispute to a crisis" Franklin felt that the colonies would then be able to negotiate "on equitable terms" to create a genuine political union with the mother country. Franklin still saw advantages to this on both sides. Britain would have America's resources in time of war, and America would have Britain to act as "a common umpire in our disputes, thereby preventing wars we might otherwise have with each other." He then used a metaphor which obviously was much on his mind at the time. If the Americans would "bear a little with the infirmities" of the British government, "as we would with those of an aged parent, tho' firmly asserting our privileges," he thought, "this advantageous union may still be long continued."

He reiterated his belief that America had "many friends and well-wishers" among the British people. They included numerous merchants and manufacturers, and even some of the country gentlemen. The members of the dissenting (non-Anglican) churches were all on America's side. But he admitted that only "a few members of Parliament in both houses, and perhaps some in high office, have in a degree the same ideas" and none of these "seem willing as yet to be active in our favor, lest adversaries . . . charge it upon them as betraying the interest of this nation."

Because they were in such a minority, "the friends of liberty" in England were even beginning to wonder if this rule by the King's friends, which so swiftly was becoming personal rule by George III himself, was not endangering the traditions of English liberty. That was another reason why they wished Americans "may long preserve it on our side of the water, that they may find it there if adverse events should destroy it here." But they were "anxious and afraid, lest we should hazard it by premature attempts in its favor. They think we may risque much by violent measures, and that the risque is unnecessary, since a little time must infallibly bring us all we demand or desire, and bring it us in peace and safety."

Then came two more sentences which must have raised Lord Dartmouth's eyebrows when he read a copy of this letter. "I do not presume to advise," Franklin said, "there are many wiser men among you, and I hope you will be directed by a still superior Wisdom." Cryptically, was Franklin admitting here that although he was not in favor of a violent solution, other Americans might justifiably decide it was the best answer? [128]

One thing is clear from these words, and from others Franklin wrote about this time: he was growing more and more impatient with the interminable quarrel between England and America, and growing more and more determined to settle it, one way or another. In a letter he wrote to William Franklin in November, 1773, he implicitly renewed his defense of tough tactics. Telling William that his "Rules" satire had been reprinted several weeks later in the same paper as a result of the "earnest request of many private persons, and some respectable societies," he added, "Such papers may seem to have a tendency to increase our divisions; but I intend a contrary effect, and hope by comprising in little room, and setting in a strong light the grievances of the colonies, more attention will be paid to them by our administration, and that when their unreasonableness is generally seen, some of them will be removed to the restoration of harmony between us."

About this time, Franklin wrote a song that revived the image of England as an aging parent, with some of his best satirical touches. It is easy to see him, surrounded by his pro-American friends, singing in his sitting room at Craven Street.

> *We have an old mother that peevish is grown*
> *She snubs us like children that scarce walk alone*
> *She forgets we've grown up and have sense of our own:*
>   Which nobody can deny, deny
>   Which nobody can deny.
>
> *If we don't obey orders, whatever the case;*
> *She frowns, and she chides, and she loses all patience,*
>   *and sometimes she hits us a slap in the face,*
>   Which nobody can deny, &c.

Her orders so odd are, we often suspect
That age has impaired her sound intellect;
But still an old mother should have due respect,
    Which nobody can deny, &c.

Let's bear with her humours as well as we can:
But why should we bear the abuse of her man?
When servants make mischief, they earn the rattan,
    Which nobody should deny, &c.

Know too, ye bad neighbours, who aim to divide
The sons from the mother, that still she's our pride;
And if ye attack her we're all of her side,
    Which nobody can deny, &c.

We'll join in her lawsuits, to baffle all those,
Who, to get what she has, will be often her foes:
But we know it must all be our own, when she goes,
    Which nobody can deny, deny,
        Which nobody can deny.[129]

XXVI

But the old mother was about to display a kind of impatience that went beyond all of Franklin's calculations. He had hoped to confine the Hutchinson-Oliver letters to a small circle of Boston leaders. But they were soon so well known among those hostile to the British Ministry that Benjamin Edes boldly printed them in his Boston *Gazette*. This set the smoldering dispute between the governor and the people aflame again, and in a formal resolution forwarded to Franklin, the Assembly petitioned the King for the removal of the governor and lieutenant governor. As the Assembly's agent, Franklin had the ticklish duty of submitting this explosive 'document to Lord Dartmouth. His Lordship made no immediate comment to Franklin; in fact he ignored the petition for the better part of two months. But Dartmouth made it clear to Hutchinson that he thoroughly condemned the whole idea of the petition and assured him that "these proceedings . . . will soon be fully examined and considered here, and I have not the least doubt that the result of such consideration will be to your honor and satisfaction." [130]

When Franklin called to inquire about the petition in December, 1773, he was told that a committee of the Privy Council would soon consider it. But he gathered "by the turn of his [Dartmouth's] conversation" that the petition did not have a prayer. Then Dartmouth donned his conciliator's mantle and expressed his fervent wish that the differences between England and America could be accommodated. "Perhaps," Franklin wrote wryly, reporting on the interview to Thomas Cushing in Massachusetts, "his good wishes are all that are in his power." [131]

But there were other more serious consequences to these purloined letters elsewhere in London. William Whately, as executor of his brother's estate, accused the Franklins' friend John Temple of stealing the letters, which had by now been printed in the London papers. From verbal insults, Whately and Temple descended to exchanging scurrilities in the newspapers, and Temple finally decided that his honor could be preserved only by the sight of Whately's blood. They began by exchanging a round each from pistols, then drew swords and went to work. As an ex-Customs officer, Temple was reasonably skillful in the use of this weapon, but banker Whately had obviously never handled a sword before in his life. He flailed at Temple in utterly ridiculous fashion, frustrating his attempt to end the battle by pinking Whately in the sword arm. Finally Temple managed to deliver a flesh wound in the side, and Whately cried for quarter. But Temple was unfortunately rather deaf and, infuriated by what seemed like Whately's brainless resistance, he aimed a thrust at the banker's shoulder. The frantic Whately tried to duck, slipped and fell on his face, taking the point of the blade in the back part of the shoulder as he went down. The two men parted totally unsatisfied, with Whately resolving to take fencing lessons and have another crack at Temple as soon as his wounds healed. Temple, defending himself against the rumor that he had stabbed Whately in the back as he lay on the ground, published a long account of the duel in the *Public Advertiser,* in which he reiterated his denial of Whately's charge, that he was the man who stole the letters.

About the same time (mid-December, 1773), Franklin returned to London from Lord Le Despencer's country house and realized that someone was almost certain to be killed if Temple and Whately met for a second time. So, on Christmas Day, 1773, he published in the *Public Advertiser* a fateful note.

> *Finding that two gentlemen have been unfortunately engaged in a duel about a transaction and its circumstances of which both of them are totally ignorant and innocent, I think it incumbent upon me to declare (for the prevention of further mischief, as far as such a declaration may contribute to prevent it) that I alone am the person who obtained and transmitted to Boston the letters in question. . . .*

Franklin added a brief defense, claiming that the letters were "not of the nature of *private* letters between friends. They were written by public officers to persons in public stations, on public affairs, and intended to procure public measures. . . ." He claimed that they had been passed from hand to hand among many public persons in England, and the only "caution" expressed with regard to their privacy was to keep them away from colonial agents, who might return them, or copies of them, to America.[132]

Fourteen days later, Franklin was mildly astonished to discover that the petition of the Massachusetts Assembly was to receive a formal hearing before the Privy Council's Committee for Plantation Affairs on the following Tuesday, January eleventh. This was unusual in itself. As Franklin explained in a later letter to Thomas Cushing, since the petition did not demand that the governors be either punished or censured, Franklin had assumed that the King would consider it "in his Cabinet"—in private consultation with the Privy Council. Hastily Franklin rushed to consult Arthur Lee, who had horned his way into a sort of sub-agent status, and William Bollan, who represented the Massachusetts Governors' Council in London. Lee was out of town, and Bollan advised Franklin that there was no point in retaining a lawyer; it was almost impossible to find a good one willing to risk offending the Privy Council, the *crème de la crème* of the British establishment. On Monday, the day before the meeting, "very late in the afternoon," Franklin was informed that Israel Mauduit, who acted as agent for Governor Hutchinson and Lieutenant Governor Oliver, had obtained the Council's permission to be represented by a lawyer. "This very short notice seemed intended to surprise us," Franklin grimly observed.[133]

On Tuesday morning at twelve, Franklin and Bollan walked to the Cockpit, a section of Whitehall Palace which had once actually served as an arena for fighting cocks, in the days of Henry VIII. It was now the building in which the Privy Council regularly met and the Prime Minister conferred with his cabinet. It was used as an address when state papers were issued, much as 10 Downing Street is today. The Lords in Council met in a spacious chamber, built in drawing-room style with an open fireplace at one end. The long table at which the wigged and ribboned nobles sat ran from the fireplace to the opposite end of the room. Through the windows, at that end, one could look out on St. James's Palace.

When Franklin entered the room, a single glance down this table made it clear that the atmosphere of the hearing would be frigid. Standing beside the chair of the Lord President of the Council, Lord Gower, was Alexander Wedderburn, the King's solicitor general. This was the counsel "hired" to defend Governors Hutchinson and Oliver. A lean, cold-eyed Scotsman with a savage tongue, Wedderburn had once been an outspoken foe of the North ministry. George III and Lord North had purchased him as casually as they might have acquired a piece of minor statuary for St. James's Palace. A week after winning an ovation from London Whigs for a speech on behalf of their radical champion, John Wilkes, Wedderburn became solicitor general, and Lord North's most vociferous supporter in Parliament. He had, Lord North remarked, an "invaluable gift of an accommodating conscience." [134] Junius, the wielder of history's wickedest political pen, commented that there was "something about him that even treachery cannot trust." A historian of the present century summed up Wedderburn as a combination of "cupidity and meanness which, if we were dealing with fiction, would be condemned as the intrusion of unconvincing melodrama." [135]

It was bad enough to be confronted by such a man on the basis of a purely political enmity. But Franklin undoubtedly knew there was a special circumstance which was bound to intensify Wedderburn's gift for vicious invective: Thomas Whately had been one of the few genuine friends Wedderburn ever possessed. They had shared bachelors' quarters in London for years and Wedderburn made no secret of the fact that he regarded Franklin's use of the controversial letters as nothing less than a violation of his dead friend's honor.

The tone of the hearing was set almost immediately, when Franklin asked permission for Mr. Bollan, who was a barrister, to speak on behalf of the petition. Permission was peremptorily refused by the Lord President and Franklin was told to do his own talking. Calmly he stepped forward and presented the petition, backing it up with the resolutions of the Assembly and the Hutchinson-Oliver letters. In his mildest manner, Franklin remarked, "It is some surprise to me, My Lords, to find counsel employed against the petition."

"Had you not notice sent you?" asked Lord Chief Justice William De Grey.

"Not till late yesterday afternoon," replied Franklin drily. In the same even calm voice, he attempted to place the petition in the proper perspective. He did not see how "anything could possibly arise out of the petition, any point of law or of right, that might require the discussion of lawyers." On the contrary, "this matter before Your Lordships is rather a question of civil or political prudence, whether, on the state of the fact that the governors have lost all trust and confidence with the people and become universally obnoxious, it will be for the interest of His Majesty's service to continue them in those stations in that province." There was no point in listening to the arguments of lawyers. It was a question of national policy, which the Privy Council was perfectly equipped to decide.

Chief Justice De Grey replied as if he had not heard a word Franklin had said. "Where a charge is brought, the parties have a right to be heard by counsel, or not, as they choose."

"Will Mr. Mauduit waive his right to be heard by counsel," Franklin asked, "in order that Your Lordship may proceed immediately to consider the petition?"

Mauduit hastily declined to compete. "I know well Dr. Franklin's abilities and wish to put the defense of my friends upon a parity with the attack," he said. "He will not therefore wonder that I choose to appear before Your Lordships with the assistance of counsel."

The Chief Justice asked Franklin if he wished to go on without counsel, anyway.

"I desire to have counsel," Franklin replied, almost curtly.

"What time do you want?"

"Three weeks."

The Chief Justice postponed "further proceedings" until Saturday, the twenty-ninth of January.

Before Lord De Grey could close the meeting, Wedderburn added an ominous postscript. "I reserve the right," he said, "when the matter comes on again, to ask certain questions, such as how the Assembly came into possession of [the letters], through what hands, and by what means they were procured."

"Certainly," said the Chief Justice, "and to whom they were directed; for the perfect understanding of the passages may depend on that and other such circumstances. We can receive no charge against a man founded on letters directed to nobody, and perhaps received by nobody. The laws of this country have no such practice."

The meeting broke up. As Franklin was picking up his papers Lord President Gower sidled up to him and asked in mocking terms if he planned to answer Wedderburn's questions.

Coolly Franklin replied, "In that I shall take counsel." [136]

XXVII

London was soon aswirl with excited rumors about Franklin's fate. Wedderburn continued to proclaim his intention to tear him apart. The King and the Privy Council were supposedly in hearty agreement with this plan. They were convinced that Franklin was an incendiary, the center of an intrigue against the government itself. "Hints," as Franklin called them, reached Craven Street in the form of verbal messages and letters that some members of the Council were recommending that he be seized as a common criminal and sent to Newgate. There was also very strong talk that they had already decided to fire him as Deputy Postmaster General. In the hearing, after Franklin was thoroughly "blackened," the Massachusetts petition was to be rejected with "epithets." [137]

Pro-ministry writers smeared Franklin with mud in the newspapers. One of the more talented among them used rhymes in the *General Evening-Post* on January 11, 1774.

TO D—R F——N
Thou base, ungrateful, cunning, upstart thing!
False to thy country first, then to thy King;

> *To gain thy selfish and ambitious ends,*
> *Betraying secret letters writ to friends:*
> *May no more letters through thy hands be past,*
> *But may thy last year's office be thy last.*[138]

Among Franklin's first thoughts was the fate of the Grand Ohio Company. There had been rumors that one of the reasons Solicitor General Wedderburn and his fellow Scot, Attorney General Edward Thurlow, delayed the charter for the province of Vandalia was Franklin's name among the list of stockholders. They maintained that he was "unworthy the favors of the Crown," because of his opposition to the ministry. Now they had a far more devastating accusation to back up this argument. A few hours after the meeting at the Privy Council, Franklin met with Thomas Walpole and the two men decided it would be best for him to write a public letter, resigning from the company. It was a cleverly worded document, which managed to work in a good bit of propaganda for the company, along with the resignation.

> *Sir: Being told that some persons in Administration have suggested that my conduct in affairs between this Kingdom and North America do not by any means entitle me to such a mark of favor from Government, as that of being a proprietor in the grant of land on the Ohio, to be made to yourself and Associates, I think it necessary to inform you, that I never considered the agreement with the Treasury for these lands as a matter of favor, unless it was such from us to Government, by showing them that the lands that they used to give away might produce something to the publick Treasury.*
> *. . . I do therefore desire that you will strike my name out of the list of our Associates, and hereafter not look upon me as one of them—I wish you however all success in your hazardous undertaking. . . .*[139]

Walpole now had something in his hand to silence Thurlow and Wedderburn. Privately, however, he and Franklin concluded another agreement, whereby Franklin retained his full rights to his two of the company's seventy-two shares of stock.

Then came an event that sent the blaze of ministerial wrath over the Hutchinson letters into an uncontrollable conflagration and doomed the Grand Ohio Company to extinction. On January 19, 1774, the British ship *Hayley* reached Dover with news that was undoubtedly rushed overland to Whitehall. On the night of December 16, 1773, forty or fifty Bostonians disguised as Indians had stormed aboard the British ships

Dartmouth, Eleanor, and *Beaver* in Boston harbor and dumped some 300 chests of East India tea into the salt water. On January 22, the St. James's *Chronicle* printed a complete description of the Tea Party, taken from Boston newspapers carried by the *Hayley.* Two days later, Lord Dartmouth asked the captain of the *Hayley* to come to his office and give him a complete report of the riot. The following day, the ship *Polly* docked at Gravesend with the doleful news that its cargo of tea destined for Philadelphia was still in the hold. That other center of Franklin influence had defiantly refused to allow either the tea or the East India Company agent to land. Finally, on Thursday, the twenty-seventh of January, Governor Hutchinson's official report of the assault on British property arrived and Lord North and the cabinet met in the Cockpit that evening to ponder the crisis.[140]

In such an atmosphere, any lingering hope Franklin might have entertained for the Massachusetts Assembly petition evaporated. Franklin was "half inclined" to waive the use of counsel and save the colony the money. But William Bollan was now in a near panic of apprehension and urged Franklin to hire the best available lawyer. Through Arthur Lee, Franklin attempted to hire Sergeant Glynn, famous for his successful defense of the agitator, John Wilkes. But Glynn was incapacitated by a fit of the gout, and Franklin instead hired John Dunning, a lawyer who was also a legend in his own way. By the sheer brilliance of his mind, he had triumphed over a uniquely ugly face and feeble body, as well as a toneless voice that was frequently choked by phlegm. To overcome Dunning's personal deficiencies, Franklin hired another lawyer, John Lee, who was not so bright, but had a far more engaging voice and appearance.

In the midst of all these conferences and consultations, Franklin found himself dunned in a lawsuit brought by William Whately. This was particularly galling because only a month before the affair of the letters had erupted Franklin had gone to a great deal of trouble to assist Whately in securing title to some land in Pennsylvania—worth 5000 pounds— claimed by both him and the powerful Penns. Franklin had also voluntarily drawn the imperial lightning to himself to save Whately from an almost certainly fatal second duel with John Temple. Whately was, Franklin knew, a banker who handled a considerable amount of government pension money. It was easy enough to see why he was bringing the suit, which claimed that Franklin, in his trade as a printer, had made money out of stealing and publishing the Hutchinson-Oliver letters.

The absurd charge was obviously designed to do nothing but harass him.

As the twenty-ninth of January drew nearer, Franklin nevertheless remained somehow optimistic. In a way the uproar over the tea increased this optimism. The violence in Boston had finally brought the argument between America and Great Britain to a simple, brutal point of confrontation. The ministry, in the hearing on the twenty-ninth, had an unparalleled opportunity to demonstrate that they were, in spite of strong provocations, still determined to settle the quarrel peacefully. As for himself, Franklin anticipated less danger from Mr. Wedderburn. With the empire in crisis, he "could not believe that the solicitor general would be permitted to wander from the question before their lordships" —the petition from the Massachusetts Assembly. Where and how Franklin had gotten the letters really had nothing to do with the business at hand—business which events had suddenly made momentous.[141]

But on the twenty-ninth of January, when he arrived at the Cockpit for the hearing, Franklin instantly realized that his optimism was wishful thinking. Never before in the history of any living Londoner had so many lords attended a Privy Council meeting—thirty-six, all in their most gorgeous finery, resplendent with Stars of the Garter and other royal Orders. Around the table swarmed a crowd of courtiers and politicians, most of them with greedily excited looks on their faces. Glancing across the room, Franklin saw dozens of faces he knew. Lord Gower, of course, the Council president, and Lord Rochford, both partners in the Ohio Company, and Lord Sandwich, and Lord Le Despencer, who may have given him a small cautious smile of friendship. Near the chair of the Council president, Franklin saw his good friends Joseph Priestley and Edmund Burke. A newcomer from America, wealthy Ralph Izard of South Carolina, had also managed to squeeze into the room which was soon so crowded that when Lord North arrived late, no chair could be brought in for him to sit at the table and he stood, in his usual pudgy somnolence, beside Lord Gower's chair. Franklin stepped into one of the recesses of the fireplace only a few feet away. Subtracting the worried looks on the faces of the handful of his friends, there was a holiday atmosphere in the room. Obviously, as Franklin later wrote, all the courtiers had been invited "as to an entertainment."

Fortunately, Franklin had dressed well for the occasion. He was wearing one of his best suits, a dark-brown outfit made of a spotted material known as Manchester velvet. His wig was long and old-fashioned, as it was when he appeared before Parliament during the Stamp Act crisis. But no one expected a man of sixty-eight to wear the latest styles. Not that Franklin acted like an old man. An eyewitness described him as standing "conspicuously erect without the slightest movement of any part of his body. The muscles of his face had been previously composed, so as to afford a placid, tranquil expression. . . ." [142]

The meeting opened with Franklin's lawyers repeating what he himself had stated three weeks earlier—the question before the Council was not a legal matter. It was an appeal to the wisdom and goodness of the King and his Councillors. Unfortunately, Dunning had a bad cold, which made his normally husky voice almost inaudible. But John Lee did his best to make up for this deficiency, with oratory in a more popular style.

Lee made his bow and retired. There was a moment of restless, expectant silence in the room. Then Alexander Wedderburn stepped forward, until he could place his hand on the Privy Council table, and began his speech.

This was no simple petition under consideration here, no request for a minor favor from the King, he intoned. No, the question went to the very heart of Britain's imperial policy. Could the British government now or in the future hope to employ men of proven loyalty to administer its colonies?

The answer, Wedderburn thundered, was NO if the Privy Council seriously entertained the petition of the Massachusetts Assembly, which Dr. Franklin was presenting. Governor Thomas Hutchinson and Lieutenant Governor Andrew Oliver had written nothing in their letters that any loyal servant of the Crown could not admit, with pride. Moreover, there was nothing in their official conduct since they had assumed the governorship on which grounds for dismissal could be argued. Wedderburn proceeded to eulogize Hutchinson as a noteworthy Crown servant. There was not "one single act of misconduct" to which the Massachusetts Assembly could point during his four years as governor. Yet they were asking the King to dismiss him and his lieutenant governor, "because they have lost the confidence of the people."

Why had they lost this confidence? Wedderburn piously ignored the fact that Hutchinson and Oliver had been feuding with the Assembly almost continuously since they took office. The sole reason for this supposed loss of confidence, he thundered, was the letters Franklin had sent to Boston.

Wedderburn now turned on Franklin the full force of his savage, mer-

cenary rhetoric, his natural violence enhanced by the opportunity of performing before such an elite political audience, and enhanced again by
his friendship with the late Thomas Whately. "Dr. Franklin, therefore,
stands in the light of the first mover and *prime conductor* of this whole
contrivance against His Majesty's two governors; and having, by the help
of his own special confidants and party leaders, first made the Assembly
his agents in carrying on his own secret designs, he now appears before
Your Lordships to give the finishing stroke to the work of his own
hands."

What made Franklin's tactics especially odious, Wedderburn roared,
was the use of private letters. The solicitor general's voice throbbed with
emotion as he read the half-dozen lines in the letters that did in fact
allude to relatively private concerns. Whately had been hospitable to
some friends of Hutchinson and Oliver when they were visiting in London, and the writers thanked him for his trouble.

"How these letters came into the possession of anyone but the right
owners is a mystery for Dr. Franklin to explain," Wedderburn cried.
"They who know the affectionate regard which the Whatelys had for each
other, and the tender concern they felt for the honor of their brother's
memory as well as their own, can witness the distress which this occasioned. My Lords, the late Mr. Whately was most scrupulously cautious
about his letters. We lived for many years in the strictest intimacy; and
in all those years I never saw a single letter written to him. These letters,
I believe, were in his custody at his death. . . . Nothing, then, will
acquit Dr. Franklin of the charge of obtaining them by fraudulent or
corrupt means for the most malignant purposes, unless he stole them
from the person who stole them. This argument is irrefragable.

"I hope, My Lords, you will mark and *brand* the man, for the honor
of this country, of Europe, and of mankind," urged Wedderburn on
behalf of a government which had been rifling Franklin's mail for years.
"Private correspondence has hitherto been held sacred in times of the
greatest party rage, not only in politics but religion. He has forfeited all
the respect of societies and of men. Into what companies will he hereafter
go with an unembarrassed face, or the honest intrepidity of virtue? Men
will watch him with a jealous eye; they will hide their papers from him,
and lock up their escritoires. He will henceforth esteem it a libel to be
called a man of letters; this man of *three* letters."

Smiles and snickers had been emanating from the Privy Council table
at Wedderburn's acrid sarcasm. This last line brought a wholesale guf-

faw. Every well-educated man of the time got the joke, which was from a play by the Roman playwright, Plautus, in which a character spoke of a thief as a "trium litterarum homo"—a man of three letters, *fur*.

"Wherein had my late worthy friend or his family offended Dr. Franklin," Wedderburn cried, "that he should first do so great an injury to the memory of the dead brother, by secreting and sending away his letters; and then, conscious of what he had done, should keep himself concealed, until he had nearly, very nearly, occasioned the murder of the other? After the mischiefs of this concealment had been left for five months to have their full operation, at length comes out a letter, which is impossible to read without horror, expressive of the coolest and most deliberate malevolence. My Lords, what poetic fiction only had penned for the heart of a cruel African, Dr. Franklin has realized, and transcribed from his own. His too, is the language of a Zanga.

> *"Know then 'twas—I*
> *I forg'd the letter—I dispos'd the picture—*
> *I hated, I despised, and I destroyed."*

Zanga was the Negro villain in a popular tragedy of the time, *Revenge*. Wedderburn now proceeded to explain Franklin's motives. His ego had become so inflated by the way the newspapers mentioned his arrivals and departures, and his cordial reception in the best houses of England, he had become drunk with absurd notions of power. He began to think of himself as the minister for "the great American republic," an independent power for whom he alone was qualified to speak. Finally, Wedderburn said with a sneer in Franklin's direction, he began acting like a foreign ambassador who . . . "when residing here, just before the breaking out of a war, or upon particular occasions, may bribe a villain to steal or betray any state papers; he is under the command of another state, and is not amenable to the laws of the country where he resides; and the secure exemption from punishment may induce a laxer morality. But Dr. Franklin, whatever he may teach the people at Boston, while he is *here* at least is a subject; and if a subject injure a subject, he is answerable to the law. And the Court of Chancery will not much attend to his new self-created importance."

As he roared out this threat, Wedderburn brought his fist down upon a cushion on the table, to the right of the Lord President. Jeremy Bentham, not yet famous as a political economist, was standing nearby. "I would, not for double the greatest fee the orator could on that occasion have received, been in the place of that cushion," he later said. "The ear was stunned at every blow. . . . The table groaned under the assault."

Along with Franklin's swollen ego there was another more vicious motive, Wedderburn howled. He wanted the governorship of Massachusetts for himself. "It was not easy before this to give credit to such surmises," roared the solicitor general, "but nothing surely but a too eager attention to an ambition of this sort, could have betrayed a wise man into such conduct as we have now seen." And what kind of government would Franklin and his willing tools in Boston create? "A tyranny greater than the Roman," Wedderburn bellowed. Had they not heard, in the past few days, the latest news from the "good men of Boston?" [143]

For almost an hour, Franklin had to endure this scurrilous abuse, while the Cockpit rocked with laughter at Wedderburn's best sallies, and the lords of the Privy Council studied him with mocking, haughty eyes. Many of the spectators did not believe any man could remain silent under such treatment. Ralph Izard, with his hot South Carolina blood, said, "Had it been me that was so grossly insulted, I should instantly have repelled the attack, in defiance of every consequence." Yet Franklin achieved the seemingly impossible. He remained, in Jeremy Bentham's words, "the whole time like a rock, in the same posture, his head resting on his left hand, and in that attitude abiding the pelting of the pitiless storm." It was in fact more than a storm. It was a political and emotional catastrophe, which makes Franklin's self-control all the more remarkable. He was seeing the death of all his hopes of reconciliation between England and America, for which he had labored ten years. All the wishful thinking he had done about the eventual good sense of the English people asserting itself, all the deep affection for England and Englishmen which he had acquired over so many years, one might even say the essential structure of his life, was being demolished in front of his eyes. That these men, most of whom he knew personally, could scheme to make him the spectacle of such a crude sideshow, allow him to become the target of a man as despicable as Wedderburn, was almost beyond belief. A profound, even immense personal resentment was thus added to the natural impetus to rage. Franklin's self-control in the face of such provocation was certainly one of the most remarkable achievements of his life.

But his masterful silence did not mean that Franklin intended to forgive or forget the outrage which Lord North and his ministers had perpetrated against him. As the meeting broke up, and the crowd flowed out of the Council chamber into an anteroom, Franklin found himself walking beside his tormentor, Wedderburn. Gently, Franklin took the orator by the arm and whispered in his ear, "I will make your master a little king for this." [144]

XXVIII

While the courtiers swarmed around Wedderburn in the anteroom of the Cockpit, Franklin went quietly home to Craven Street. The next day he received a letter from the government informing him that he had been dismissed as Deputy Postmaster General for America. In another twenty-four hours, another letter arrived ordering him to submit his accounts to his successor, who had already been appointed. His only consolation for the moment was the numerous friends, such as Joseph Priestley, who rushed to Craven Street to let him know that they were standing by him, no matter how reckless the ministry in their rage might become. But Franklin's first thoughts were not of himself, or of his own safety. Instead, his emotions raced across the ocean to Governor William Franklin. After this crushing and total repudiation by the Ministry, with the obvious consent of the King, how could his son have any future in the service of the British government?

> *Dear Son:—This line is just to acquaint you that I am well, and that my office of Deputy-Postmaster is taken from me. As there is no prospect of your being ever promoted to a better government, and that you hold has never defray'd its expenses, I wish you were well settled in your farm. 'Tis an honester and more honourable because a more independent employment. You will hear from others the treatment I have receiv'd. I leave you to your own reflections and determinations upon it, and remain ever your affectionate Father.*[145]

Franklin told Priestley, who breakfasted with him the following morning, "that he had never before been so sensible of the power of a good conscience; for that, if he had not considered the thing for which he had been so much insulted, as one of the best acts of his life, and what he should certainly do again in the same circumstances, he could not have supported it."

That same day, February 2, 1774, Franklin wrote another letter to Thomas Cushing, Samuel Adams, and other leading Boston patriots, urging them to offer to pay the East India Company for the ruined tea. "This all our friends here wish with me; and that if war is finally to be made upon us, which some threaten, an act of violent injustice on our part, unrectified, may not give a colourable pretense for it. A speedy reparation will immediately set us right in the opinion of all Europe." He pointed out that Parliament had frequently made similar grants from the public treasury when private property was destroyed by rioting mobs in England and America.[146]

Not until February fifteenth, more than two full weeks after the ordeal in the Cockpit, did Franklin sit down to write a full account of it to his friends in Masachusetts. He obviously wanted time to let his emotions cool. But even after two weeks, there was more than a little acid in his description of Wedderburn's speech. He told how the solicitor general had "bestowed plenty of abuse" upon the people of Massachusetts. "But the favorite part of his discourse was leveled at your Agent, who stood there the butt of his invective ribaldry for near an hour, not a single Lord adverting to the impropriety and indecency of treating a public messenger in so ignominious a manner, who was present only as the person delivering your petition, with the consideration of which no part of his conduct had any concern." Franklin then added words that can only be described as incendiary. "When I see, that all petitions and complaints of grievances are so odious to government, that even the mere pipe which conveys them becomes obnoxious, I am at a loss to know how peace and union are to be maintained or restored between the different parts of the Empire. Grievances cannot be redressed unless they are known; and they cannot be known but through complaints and petitions. If these are deemed affronts, and the messengers punished as offenders, who will henceforth send petitions? And who will deliver them? . . . Where complaining is a crime, hope becomes despair." [147]

He then told of his dismissal as Deputy Postmaster, and warned that henceforth the American Postmaster General was no longer permitted to fill vacancies without awaiting instructions from the government. This meant that in the future these vacancies would probably be filled by ministers' lackeys. "How safe the correspondence of our Assembly committees along the continent will be through the hands of such officers may now be worth consideration, especially as the Postoffice Act of Parliament allows a postmaster to open letters, if warranted to do so by the order of a Secretary of State, and every provincial secretary may be deemed a Secretary of State in his own province." [148] This letter was all the Americans needed to hear. Within a few months, the British postal service in the colonies had been virtually abandoned, and an independent post office organized. It was one of the first—if not the first—agencies of the British government to be discarded by the Americans—a fact which must have given Franklin considerable satisfaction.

This was hardly the voice of moderation and conciliation, which Franklin has so long been pictured as personifying during his years in England. It was true, that at one point Franklin tried to espouse this role. But over the last few years, his patience and his generous feelings for England had been steadily eroded by persistent collision with the stupidity, venality, stubbornness and arrogance of the rulers of England's empire. Two years before the Continental Congress voted with anguish and hesitation for independence, Franklin had arrived at this momentous conclusion in England—at least on the level of his emotions. Intellectually he permitted his cool head to talk hopefully of some basis for a future settlement. But already he was thinking ahead, toward a new political order, when he sat down to write two more letters, one to Joseph Galloway, and the second to William Franklin.

To Galloway he carefully explained his motives for sending the Hutchinson-Oliver letters to Massachusetts. Franklin reiterated his belief that if the ministry "had been dispos'd to a reconciliation, as they sometimes pretend to be, they could have chosen this opportunity to demonstrate it." Instead, they let the solicitor general wander into "a long studied invective against me." He added that Wedderburn's speech had since been printed in a heavily edited version. "Compar'd to the verbal speech, the printed one is perfectly decent," Franklin said. "I shall soon answer it & give this Court my farewell."

In recent letters, Galloway had discussed with Franklin the possibility of creating a constitution that would specify America's rights within the empire. Basically, it was an elaboration by his legal mind of Franklin's

Albany Plan of Union. Franklin agreed on the importance of such a document but he was wryly pessimistic about the chances of anyone in England helping to work out such an understanding. "If 'tis to be settled, it must settle itself, no body here caring for the trouble of thinking on't.

"I long to be with you & to converse with you on these important heads. A few months I hope will bring us together. In the calm retirement of Trevose [Galloway's country estate] perhaps we may spend some hours usefully. I am sure they will be spent agreeably too, dear friend." Then Franklin added a postscript which did nothing to raise Galloway's spirits. "The ship Ohio still aground." [149]

On the same day, Franklin wrote another letter to William, in which he reversed the advice he had given him on the second of February.

> *Some tell me that it is determined to displace you likewise, but I do not know it as certain. . . . Perhaps they may expect that your resentment of their treatment of me may induce you to resign, and save them the shame of depriving you when they ought to promote. But this I would not advise you to do. Let them take your place if they want it, tho' in truth I think it scarce worth your keeping, since it has not afforded you sufficient to prevent your running every year behindhand with me. But one may make something of an injury, nothing of a resignation.*[150]

That superb last line is clear proof that Franklin the philosopher was once more in charge of his mental and emotional house. He did, as he promised Galloway, write a rebuttal to Wedderburn's speech, defending his motives and role in the Hutchinson-Oliver letters affair. But after it was finished, he decided not to publish it. Meanwhile, the British government was demonstrating that their intemperate attack on Franklin was no accident. They proceeded to display the same reckless attitude toward the colony of Massachusetts and America in general.

The North ministry rammed through Parliament a series of punitive laws. The port of Boston was peremptorily closed to all shipping until the destroyed tea had been paid for and the revenue officers compensated for the duties owed them. Next came an act "for regulating the government in the Province of Massachusetts Bay." Most of the powers acquired over the generations by the Assembly and courts of Massachusetts were removed. "I propose in this bill, to take the executive power from the hands of the democratic part of the government," Lord North candidly admitted. The Regulating Acts, as they were called, also authorized

British officers to quarter their troops in the homes of private citizens in Massachusetts. As a new governor, to make sure that the colonists got the message, the King appointed General Thomas Gage, heretofore commander-in-chief of the British Army in North America.

The debate on these bills could only have enraged Franklin. John Dunning, Franklin's ex-attorney, condemned the Regulating Acts in a two-hour speech that was a devastating analysis of their aggressive aims. The Acts were intended to provoke the colonists into rebellion by taking away their charters, he declared, while empowering the government to authorize ruthless wholesale repression when that rebellion occurred. Edmund Burke followed Dunning and spoke for almost two hours, calling for conciliation instead of punishment. But the North majority shouted down these voices of moderation with the most extreme sentiments. "I say stand and deliver to the Americans," roared Richard Rigby, speaking for the followers of the Duke of Bedford. A North supporter, John St. John, working hard for the lucrative sinecure, Surveyor General of Inland Revenue, scorned the idea that America could do anything about the punitive acts. " 'Tis said that America will be exasperated. Will she then take arms? 'Tis not as yet, thank God, the strength of America which we dread when put in competition with this country. She has neither army, navy, money, or men. . . . Shall we then fear the destruction of our trade? Believe it not; while it is her interest to trade with us, so long she will in spite of her resentment." The non-importation agreements which the colonists were attempting to construct in support of Massachusetts were "cobweb confederacies" that self-interest would soon destroy. In despair, as the North squadrons rolled over them, West Indian born Rose Fuller, another leading member of the Opposition, lamented, "It is not an error of the Ministry, it is an error of the nation: I see it wherever I go. People are of the opinion that these measures ought to be carried into execution." [151]

But the final and most devastating blow, for Franklin personally, was yet to come. On May second, Lord Dartmouth presented to the House of Lords a bill "making more effectual provision for the government of the province of Quebec." This was a measure which had been discussed in various cabinets for the better part of a decade. The problem of governing Canada, with its predominantly French-speaking Catholic population, had baffled successive administrations. The first portions of the Quebec Act, as the law came to be called, were reasonable enough. The British had learned something from their centuries of trouble in

Ireland, and had decided not to ram their culture and religion down the throats of the French-Canadians, who outnumbered the English in Canada, 400 to 1. Lord North told the Commons that the bill gave the French-Canadians the right to live under French civil laws and practice the Roman Catholic religion. Rule by a governor and an appointed council, in the traditional French style, was to be preferred to the elected Assemblies of the English colonies. This was statesmanship, and at another time most Americans would have accepted such a policy amicably enough. Only the most vociferous and aggressive Protestant dissenters might have complained to see their old enemy, the Roman Catholic Church, established in the northern half of the continent. Certainly Benjamin Franklin, as an apostle of tolerance, would have warmly approved.

The timing of the Quebec Act, however, made even these clauses subject to strong criticism, in both England and America. People were quick to point out that Lord North was granting French Catholics the right to live under laws of their own choosing, while he was denying Massachusetts that privilege. The contrast inspired one English observer to explode at North. "How it is possible for a man to derive strength even from the whole world if he will not know his own mind for a quarter of an hour together?" [152] But it was the fourth clause of the Quebec Act which patently revealed the North ministry's intention to use this long-overdue measure to punish its American enemies. The boundary of Quebec was suddenly extended southward to the Ohio River, and west to the Mississippi.

A glance into the interior of the British government makes it clear that this was a blow aimed directly at Franklin and the Grand Ohio Company. The man who concocted this idea was William Knox, Dartmouth's undersecretary of state. While Knox and his fellow undersecretary, John Pownall, were rushing to put together background material for the Quebec Act (and complaining mightily that "after so many years of neglect of the business of Quebec, everything is now to be done in a hurry") [153] Knox slipped a memorandum on the boundary in front of Lord Dartmouth. It described how his old political boss, the late George Grenville (dead now three years), had hoped to place this immense tract of wilderness "under one general control & regulation by act of Parliament." It conveniently omitted the story of how Lord Hillsborough, who had taken up Grenville's fallen mantle as chief anti-American in the government, had fought his losing battle with the Grand Ohio Company to keep English and American settlers out of this wilderness. Instead, Knox merely lamented that Grenville's plan had proved "abortive" and talked at length about the numbers of *French* that were in this region, outside the protection and control of British civil government. On the basis of this single memorandum, without making the slightest investigation of its allegations, Dartmouth permitted Knox to add the boundary clause to the Quebec Act. It was typical of the haphazard, absentee way Dartmouth ran his office.[154]

In the debate on the bill in the House of Commons, the Opposition forced the North ministry to tell some brutal truths in public. Isaac Barré accused them of having "some secret purpose" in extending the boundaries of Quebec. Alexander Wedderburn arose to admit that the primary purpose was to give the British colonies "little temptation to stretch themselves" into the interior. It was, Wedderburn declared, "the ancient policy of the country" to keep the colonies along the lines of the sea and rivers. He insisted that this was the best and only way of maintaining control over them. Wedderburn, a dedicated proponent of rule by force, had no compunction about being so frank. Lord North, who like Dartmouth was torn between conciliation and repression, revealed a much more agitated state of mind about the bill. When one member of Parliament insinuated that the First Minister's real aims were concealed, and his methods devious, Lord North rose and said he "cared not what the hon. gentleman thought of him; that he never paid any respect to what a passionate and prejudiced person said; that he knew the hon. gentleman had an ill opinion of him, and he was welcome to think so still." Another member of the opposition wryly remarked that North was showing far more passion than his accuser.[155]

As he watched these disheartening developments with the eyes of an insider, Franklin's contempt for the government deepened steadily. He stopped urging Massachusetts to pay for the tea and applauded the decision of the Americans to meet in congress in Philadelphia in early September, 1774, to discuss the crisis. To Thomas Cushing he wrote, "I rejoice to find that the whole continent have so wisely, justly and unanimously taken up our [Massachusetts] cause as their own. This is an unexpected blow to the Ministry, who relied on our being neglected by every other colony; this they depended on as another circumstance that must force our immediate submission. . . . They are now a little disconcerted." [156]

Franklin was far less encouraged—in fact he was deeply distressed—

by the way politics intruded on his relationship with his son. The governor had written to Franklin telling him that many people wished he was a delegate to the Congress. William had in the meantime made an independent move to create a body that might negotiate a reconciliation. He called for a Congress of Royal Governors and some members of their councils and Assemblies who might meet with "some gentlemen of abilities, moderation, and candour from Great Britain commissioned by His Majesty for the purpose." He told his father he had sent this suggestion to Lord Dartmouth. Then, turning to the situation in Boston, he told his father he thought it was "very extraordinary that neither the Assembly of Mass. Bay nor the town of Boston have so much as intimated any intention or desire of making Satisfaction to the E. India Company and the officers of the customs, when by doing these two things which are consistent with strict justice, and by declaring that they will not hereafter attempt to hinder the landing at Boston any goods legally imported, they might get their port opened in a few months. . . . they ought first to do justice before they ask it of others." [157]

Franklin's reply to this comment, which was little more than he himself had recommended earlier in the year, showed how far the spirit of moderation had dwindled in his breast. He began by abruptly telling William that "no person . . . in America has given me the least intimation" that his presence was wished for at the Congress. "It is thought by the great friends of the Colonies here, that I ought to stay till the result of the Congress arrives, when my presence here may be of use." He dismissed William's idea for a governors' congress with a single line. "I hear nothing of the proposal you have made for a congress of governors, etc." Then he tore into William's sentiments on Boston. "I do not so much as you do wonder that the Massachusetts have not offered payment for the tea: one, because of the uncertainty of the act, which gives them no surety that the port shall be opened on their making that payment. Two, no specific sum is demanded. Three, no one knows what will satisfy the custom-house officers. . . . As to 'doing justice before they ask it,' that should have been thought of by the legislature here, before they demanded it of the Bostonians. They have extorted many thousand pounds from America unconstitutionally, under colour of Acts of Parliament, and with an armed force. Of this money they ought to make restitution. They might first have taken out payment for the tea, &c., and return'd the rest. But you, who are a thorough courtier, see every thing with government eyes." [158]

Franklin ended his letter with a brief comment on the current state of
the Grand Ohio Company. Thomas Walpole had presented another
memorial to the Privy Council in August and still professed optimism
that "sooner or later it must succeed." But William had already come
close to abandoning his hopes of rivaling the Penns in a western province.
On May 25, 1774, six weeks before he wrote to his father, he had told
Sir William Johnson that his last letters from England mentioned "that
the Ohio affair stands still, the present rage against America making it
improper to be moved. . . . As I see no prospect of that rage being
lessened, for some years at least, I think the matter may, if it depends
on that circumstance, be almost as well given up." [159]

Thus one of the strongest links by which Franklin attempted to maintain his role as paternal dispenser of gifts and power to his son was
already broken. He did not realize it, but an even more fundamental
bond was being severely strained. On May 31, 1774, William had
written to Lord Dartmouth a report on the political situation in New
Jersey. He ended it with words that were to have anguished significance
in a few more months. "His Majesty may be assured that I shall omit
nothing in my power to keep this province quiet, and that, let the event
be what it may, no attachments or connections shall ever make me swerve
from the duty of my station." [160]

There was one strong bond which still linked the two Franklins:
William Temple Franklin. The boy was now fifteen, and was spending
more and more time with his grandfather at Craven Street. He had
grown up as William Temple, without the right to use the name Franklin. But now, as Benjamin's thoughts turned more and more toward
home, he decided it was time to bring Temple boldly into the family,
and give him the full recognition which he deserved. He wrote to
William informing him of this decision. It was also time to think of a
profession for the boy, ". . . that the remainder of his education may
have some relation to it. I have thought he may make an expert lawyer,
as he has good memory, quick parts, and ready elocution. He would
certainly make an excellent painter, having a vast fondness for drawing,
which he pursues with unwearied industry, and has made great pro-
ficiency. But I do not find that he thinks of it as a business. The only
hint of inclination he has given is that of being a surgeon; but it was
slightly mentioned." Franklin then added some words that came close
to saying William's whole career was a mistake. "It is indeed my wish

that he might learn some art by which he could at any time procure a subsistence; and after that, if anything better could be done for him [politically], well and good. But posts and places are precarious dependencies. I would have him a free man. Upon the whole, in my opinion we should turn him to the law. . . ." [161]

For the time being, Franklin declined to take his son's advice about coming home immediately. He stubbornly maintained his outpost in Craven Street, in spite of a new swirl of ministerial threats. In the middle of the spring, he had told Thomas Cushing, "It is given out that copies of several letters of mine to you are sent over here to the ministers, and that their contents are treasonable, for which I should be prosecuted if copies could be made evidence." It was possible, Franklin said, although he was not conscious of any treasonable intentions. He had already been condemned by "high authority" for actions he considered good, so he was not inclined "to wonder if less than a small lump in my forehead is voted a horn." [162] Although he had decided not to publish a defense of his use of the Hutchinson letters in England, he made sure that a long account of the affair and its lurid aftermath in the Cockpit was published in the Boston papers. He also wrote a devastating third person account of his ordeal in the Cockpit for the Pennsylvania *Gazette*. It was published as "Extract of a Letter from a Gentleman in London" and described how Franklin was abused "to the great entertainment of 35 Lords of the Privy-Council, who had been purposely invited as to a bull-baiting." [163]

How deeply Franklin still felt the humiliation of the Cockpit—and his resentment of more recent slanders by the ministry—was vividly visible when he wrote to his sister, Jane Mecom, in the summer of 1774. She had heard a report that Franklin had offered to desert the American cause if the government gave him back his postmastership. Since he was getting only about 300 pounds a year as postmaster, while he was being paid 1000 to 1200 a year as agent for Pennsylvania, New Jersey, Georgia, and Massachusetts, this added stupidity to the malice of the rumor, and he made it clear that he resented both aspects, in this blazing letter.

Dear Sister. . . . The report you mention that I offered to desert my constituents, and banish myself if I might continue in place,

*is an infamous falsehood, as you supposed. —And as ridiculous
as false, since it implies that I have not arithmetic enough to
calculate the difference between 300 & 1000. —They are every
now & then reporting here that I am using means to get again
into office. Perhaps they wish I would. —But they may expect
it till doomsday. For God knows my heart, I would not accept
the best office the King has to bestow, while such tyrannic measures are taken against my country. —Be assured I shall do nothing
that will prejudice me in your opinion, or be inconsistent with the
honest public character I have hitherto maintained. I kept my
former post indeed till it was taken from me, because I did not
receive it as a favour from Government, but rose to it in the course
of office from seniority join'd with merit. I therefore thought I had
a right to it, and I did not chuse to compliment them with a resignation, rather liking that they should take upon themselves the
shame of depriving me. They have done me honour by turning me
out, and I will take care they shall not disgrace me by putting me
in again.*[164]

Franklin also continued to skirmish briskly in the newspapers with
government writers and speakers. In one letter he called for the re-
printing of "The Rules by which a Great Empire may be Reduced
to a Small One" because, "I apprehend that this plan is at present
under the consideration of the House of Commons." [165] But his favorite theme during these months was British military arrogance. Both
in and out of Parliament, the British were telling themselves that
Americans were poltroons who could not possibly resist Britain's
professional army. One night, visiting at Sir John Pringle's, Franklin
heard Colonel Thomas Clarke, aide-de-camp to the King, blandly
declare that with a thousand British grenadiers he would undertake
to go from one end of America to the other, and geld all the males
"partly by force and partly by a little coaxing." This remark inspired
Franklin to write one of his most savage satires, "On Humbling Our
Rebellious Vassals," in which he recommended attaching a corps
of sow gelders to the British. Army and marching them throughout
America, to perform the task Clarke had suggested. "The advantages
arising from this scheme . . . are obvious," Franklin wrote. "In the
course of fifty years it is probable we shall not have one rebellious

subject in North America. This will be laying the axe to the root of the tree." [166]

When Colonel James Grant assured Parliament that Americans were hopeless soldiers, useful only as beasts of burden, Franklin published an imaginary speech to him, in which he recalled that during the French and Indian War, Grant had commanded a mixed body of British and American troops who were ambushed by the enemy. The British had fled, leaving the Americans to cover their retreat. Equally scalding was an open letter he wrote to Lord North, giving him advice on setting up a military government in America. After they had squeezed the colonists for their last shilling, and made them complete slaves, he advised the King's First Minister to sell them to "the best bidder." He recommended Spain, "as their power hath more of the ready than France." With a little luck, the ministry could probably get 2,000,000 pounds for the soil and the people upon it. This could then be applied "toward the payment of one-hundredth part of the national debt," and bring down on North "the blessing of the poor" by enabling him "to take off the halfpenny duty on porter." [167]

At the same time, Franklin wrote tough advice to the Continental Congress and arranged for this too to be published in American newspapers, from Massachusetts to Georgia. He told them to "specify every oppressive act of Parliament" since 1764 so that the English friends of America could have a ready supply of arguments. But he warned them not to rely on any support "on this side of the water." America's main hope must be "in your own virtue, unanimity and steadiness; temper and resolution must be joined." He warned Boston "not to enter into any violent measures" without the strictest concert with the other colonies, particularly Maryland, Virginia, and the Carolinas, because only a total refusal to trade with Britain would have the impact needed to bring the British government to its senses.

But grim proof that neither the government nor the people of Great Britain were inclined to listen to reason came in the fall of 1774, when Lord North dissolved Parliament and the country plunged into a frenzy of electioneering. This took on a personal dimension for Franklin, when he learned that his old friend Strahan had decided to insure his job as King's printer, and run for Parliament as a ministry man. As the holder of a post that increased his income by two or three thousand pounds a year, he was naturally expected to purchase his seat and he did so without demur, being elected as a member for Malmesbury. With such intimate knowledge of how the system worked, Franklin was hardly optimistic that the new Parliament would swing to the American side. The prestige, power, and cash of George III were the crucial factors in the British power structure. As Franklin explained it to Thomas Cushing, "most of the members are bribing or purchasing to get in." This meant "that there was little doubt of selling their votes to the Minister for the time being, to reimburse themselves. Luxury introduces necessity even among those that make the most splendid figures here; this brings most of the Commons as well as Lords to market." He added sardonically, "If America would save for 3 or 4 years the money she spends in fashions & fineries & fopperies of this country, she might buy the whole Parliament minister and all." [168]

A few days later, he wrote to Joseph Galloway in the same disenchanted spirit. "Many think the new Parliament will be for reversing the late proceedings; but that depends on the court, on which every Parliament seems to be dependent; so much so, that I begin to think of Parliament here of little use to the people. '. . . They could afford to govern us cheaper, the Parliament being a very expensive machine that requires a vast deal of oiling and greasing at the people's charge; for they finally pay all the enormous salaries of places, the pensions and the bribes, now by custom become necessary to induce the members to vote according to their consciences." [169]

Around this time Franklin met an Englishman who was equally disgusted with British society—a lean, hawk-nosed tax collector named Thomas Paine. At thirty-seven he was a failure at almost everything he had tried, from marriage to corset-making to civil service. He had recently given up a hopeless struggle to convince the British government that the salaries of excisemen should be raised, and decided to emigrate to America. Franklin gave him letters of introduction to his son-in-law and numerous other Philadelphians.

Franklin stayed on outpost duty at Craven Street, acutely conscious of ministerial hostility. "My situation here is thought by many to be a little hazardous," he told Galloway, "for that if by some accident, the troops and people of N. E. [New England] should come to blows, I should probably be taken up; the ministerial people affecting everywhere to represent me as the cause of all the misunderstandings. . . ." But he said that he would stand his ground until he heard the results of the Continental Congress. [170]

XXIX

Fresh evidence of how far the ministry was prepared to go came in a most unpleasant way, from Franklin's friend Strahan. Governor William Franklin had unwisely written Strahan a letter, criticizing both the ministry and the radical wing of the American patriots. Strahan edited out the relatively innocuous remarks on the ministry, exhibited the Royalist parts of the letter to numerous people in London, and finally sent it to Philadelphia for publication in one of the newspapers. He was obviously willing to embarrass his old friend with his fellow Americans, in the hope of influencing some colonists with the magic of the Franklin name. Strahan had helped to print much of Franklin's earlier propaganda. But now he closed his paper, *The London Chronicle,* to him. Although his friendship for Franklin made him still wish for reconciliation, Strahan was like most Englishmen thoroughly out of patience with America's obstreperous defiance, and convinced that one way or another the wayward colonists must be disciplined and forced to submit to Parliament's supremacy.

Time was running out much faster than anyone, even Franklin, suspected. This was evident to one of the few men in England whose politics matched Franklin's breadth and vision, William Pitt, now Lord Chatham. Toward the end of August in 1774, Franklin was visiting in the neighborhood of the great statesman's house and was invited to call. For years Chatham, harassed by gout and episodes of black depression, had played little or no part in British politics. Now, he told Franklin, he was preparing to emerge from semi-retirement to rescue the empire he had done so much to create. He deplored the severity of the laws the North ministry had passed to punish Massachusetts, and he hoped that the people of that colony "would continue firm and united, defending by all legal and peaceful means their constitutional rights."

Franklin assured him that he had "no doubt they would do so." Then Chatham brought up something that obviously worried him

263

a great deal. Many Englishmen feared that "America aimed at setting up for itself as an independent state." Was it true?

Earnestly Franklin told him that he had traveled more than once from one end of the continent to the other and kept a great variety of company, eating, drinking, and conversing with them freely. "I never heard in any conversation from any person drunk or sober, the least expression of a wish for a separation or hint that such a thing would be advantageous to America." [171]

The magisterial Chatham expressed delight at hearing these words. He told Franklin that he would be glad to see him again, as often as he was inclined to visit. It was a notable moment in Franklin's life, to hear these words from a man whom he admired more than any other English statesman. His mind must have flashed back to those first years in England when Chatham had been First Minister of a triumphant empire, and Benjamin Franklin of Pennsylvania had sought in vain for an interview with him.

Franklin, speaking more and more as an American ambassador, had given an astutely diplomatic reply to Chatham's question about independence. It carefully masked his real feelings on the subject, now, and carried the whole thing back to those halcyon days before the Stamp Act. What he really felt about the American cause at this time is far more evident in the letters and journals of young Josiah Quincy, Jr., who arrived in London on November seventeenth. The son of an old Franklin friend, Quincy was a fervent, whole-souled idealist who had helped John Adams defend the British soldiers involved in the Boston Massacre. Part of his mission was, incredible as it may seem, to check on Franklin's loyalty.

The more aggressive Boston leaders, such as Samuel Adams, still entertained severe doubts about Franklin. The chief reason for their suspicions was Arthur Lee. This strange Virginian espoused the most extreme radical views and hobnobbed with John Wilkes and his friends. But Lee's radicalism lay, not in a considered judgment of the English government, based on experience, such as Franklin was making, but in a bitter, twisted suspicion that no man in power or out of it was sincere or trustworthy. He found a congenial peer in Samuel Adams when he applied this philosophy to the British government, and this in turn aroused Lee's hopes that he might become Massachusetts' sole agent in London.

When Franklin got the job, Lee had proceeded to spread nasty rumors about his loyalty to the American cause. As early as 1771, he criticized Franklin's "temporizing conduct" and pointed out that he had "the possession of a profitable office at will . . . a son in a high post at pleasure," which made it hard for Lee to see how "in an open contest between an oppressive administration and a free people, Dr. Franklin can be a faithful advocate for the latter." [172] He frequently hinted, and at one point blatantly stated, that Franklin was taking bribes or had a price which the North ministry had not yet decided to pay. While Franklin was writing to friends in Boston that he was in danger of being arrested, one of his ship-captain friends handed him a Boston paper in which the writer solemnly reported that Franklin had been restored to royal favor and was on the point of receiving a far more lucrative job than the Deputy Postmastership he had lost. Such rumors inspired the Bostonians to send young Quincy on his errand. He was also commissioned to function as a kind of special envoy, and bring back a realistic report of what Great Britain was thinking and feeling about America.

Quincy had tea in Craven Street only a few hours after he landed. The entries in his diary are an interesting indication of the magic Franklin worked on his convictions. The first entry read, "Waited upon Dr. Franklin and drank tea with him. He appears to be in good health and spirits, and seems warm in our cause and confident of success." Later the same day he wrote, "Dr. Franklin appears the staunch friend of America." Ten days later he was writing, "Dr. Franklin is an American, heart and soul. You may trust him . . . he is explicit and bold." [173] The sight of Quincy and Franklin arm in arm in the lobby of Parliament enraged Lord Hillsborough and confirmed his long-standing conviction that Franklin was the evil genius behind Massachusetts' insubordination. His Lordship rose in the House of Lords to thunder that there were "men walking in the streets of London who ought to be in Newgate or at Tyburn."

While extremists like Hillsborough spluttered in their obstinate, bellicose ways, the North ministry was developing a serious case of the jitters. They had confidently told themselves that the punitive acts would quickly bring Massachusetts to its knees; the precise opposite had happened. The province now seemed united in defiance, almost to the last man. The ministers had also told themselves that the Americans were not united, but the gifts of money and goods pouring into Boston from every province and now the first meeting of the

Continental Congress exploded this assumption. North, Dartmouth, and the other ministers who yearned for conciliation became more and more uneasy, and less inclined to listen to the cabinet's war hawks. Desperately they began looking for some way out of their dilemma. From all points of the compass, only one name and face seemed to confront them: Benjamin Franklin, the man the government had humiliated and done its utmost to disgrace.

Under the circumstances these noble lords could hardly come to Franklin and apologize. They still saw themselves as the personification of England's dignity and honor. The possibility of being rebuffed by a mere ex-tradesman filled them with horror. Nevertheless, the fact remained that Franklin was the only man in England who had even a semblance of authority to speak for America. So, swallowing their mortification, they had to ignore "the cool, sullen silence" (Franklin's own words) he had maintained toward them. No matter that he had not attended a single one of their levees or receptions since that fateful twenty-ninth of January. They would have to approach him in ways devious enough to preserve their pride of station, yet practical enough to offer a hope at least of averting catastrophe.

X X X

One day in late November, a friend approached Franklin at a meeting of the Royal Society and told him there was a noble lady who had heard of his prowess as a chess player and yearned to test her skill against him. Her name was Miss Howe, and Franklin, of course, knew immediately who she was—the sister of George Augustus Lord Howe, who had died fighting beside Americans at Fort Ticonderoga in the French and Indian War. Miss Howe had two other brothers, Sir William Howe and Richard Lord Howe, both members of Parliament and known to be, to some extent at least, friends of America.

At the same time Franklin was approached more directly by two Quaker friends, David Barclay, a banker and merchant with extensive business in America, and Dr. John Fothergill, Franklin's old adviser on Pennsylvania, who was Lord Dartmouth's personal physician. Barclay made the first overture and arranged a conference with Fothergill. By this time, Franklin had begun playing chess with Miss Howe and found her a most agreeable and worthy opponent. On the day he was to meet Fothergill and Barclay, he played several matches with her and afterwards had a charming and seemingly offhand conversation.

"What is to be done with this dispute between Great Britain and the colonies? I hope we are not to have a civil war," Miss Howe said.

"They should kiss and be friends," said Franklin. "What can they do better? Quarreling can be of service to neither, but is ruin to both."

"I have often said," replied Miss Howe, "that I wished government would employ you to settle the dispute for 'em. I am sure nobody could do it so well. Do you not think that the thing is practicable?"

"Undoubtedly, Madam," said Franklin, "if the parties are disposed to reconciliation; for the two countries have really no clashing interests to differ about. 'Tis rather a matter of punctilio which two or three reasonable people might settle in half an hour." He thanked her for her good opinion of him as a peacemaker. "But the ministers will never think of employing me in that good work, they choose rather to abuse me."

"Ay," said Miss Howe, "they have behaved shamefully to you. And indeed some of them are now ashamed of it themselves." [174]

Little more than an hour later, Franklin was at Fothergill's house, hearing him say remarkably similar things about the ministry. When Franklin declared that he could see not the slightest sign of a disposition toward accommodation, Fothergill said he was mistaken. "Whatever was the violence of some," he had reason, he said, *"good reason,* to believe others were differently disposed." Earnestly the two peace-loving Quakers urged Franklin to draw up a plan which they might communicate to "the most moderate among the ministers," who, they assured Franklin, "would consider it with attention."

Franklin reluctantly agreed, although he pointed out that anything he said might be abrogated by the results of the Continental Congress, which were expected to arrive daily. He jotted down seventeen points which he called "Hints for a Conversation upon the Subject of Terms that Might Probably Produce a Durable Union Between Britain and the Colonies." They ranged from paying for the destroyed tea to repealing all the punitive acts to Parliament's disclaiming all powers of internal legislation in the colonies. Taxation was to be by requisitions only, on the request of the King, and limited to time of war. Barclay and Franklin conferred at length over the articles and modified the wording of several of them to make them more palatable to the ministry.

A week later, the petition from the Continental Congress to the King arrived. With it came a covering letter addressed to Franklin and the other London agents asking them to submit it to his Majesty and then make it public through the press. Franklin immediately conferred with other colonial agents, attempting to line them up in a united front to present the petition to the government. Instead, he got his first glimpse of the painful separations which the conflict was to cause. Most of the agents hastily left town, or came down with sudden illnesses, or claimed that they had no instructions from their respective colonies which empowered them to have anything to do with such a potentially treasonous document. One of the most rapid retreaters was Paul Wentworth, the glib, extremely clever agent for New Hampshire. Franklin did not know it at the time, but Wentworth was soon meeting with British Secret Service chiefs and signing up as a spy.[175]

As copies of the American petition circulated privately, London was aswirl with rumors. The impression on the people, as far as Franklin could see, "was greatly in our favor." The administration "seemed to be staggered"—a deduction Franklin made from their nervous, uncertain silence and the frantic attempts they made to find out the details of the petition and when and how it was to be submitted, before Franklin acted. The war hawks inside the North cabinet had been huffing that no petition from the Congress could be received, because it was an illegal body. But Lord Dartmouth received it from Franklin's hands, perused it for a day, and then told Franklin it was "a decent and proper petition," and presented it to the King. Afterward he told Franklin and the other agents that his Majesty had received it "very graciously" and promised to lay it before the two houses of Parliament as soon as they met. This prompted a rumor that the entire dispute had been resolved. Stocks soared on the London exchange and one frantic speculator wrote Franklin the following letter:

Mr. Neate presents his most respectful compliments to Dr. Franklin, and as a report prevailed yesterday evening that all the disputes between Great Britain and the American colonies were, thro' his application and influence with Lord North, amicably

settled conformable to the wishes and desire of the late Congress,
W. N. desires the favor of Dr. Franklin to inform him by a line,
per the bearer, whether there is any credit to be given to the re-
port.[176]

Meanwhile, at the Howe mansion, Franklin became involved in
something far more serious than chess. With that same studied innocence, Miss Howe began telling him how much her brother, the
admiral, admired Dr. Franklin and wished to meet him.

Franklin said he would be "proud of the honor" of an introduction
to his Lordship.

"He is but just by," said Miss Howe. "Will you give me leave to
send for him?"

"By all means, Madam, if you think it proper."

Miss Howe rang for a servant, wrote a note, and a moment later
Lord Howe was exchanging bows with Franklin, a charming smile on
his swarthy countenance. He was the kind of man Franklin instantly
liked: tough yet generous, with a cool head and a warm heart. In
battle he was as ferocious as he was skillful. In 1759 he had been
one of the captains who had led the English fleet into rock-strewn
Quiberon Bay on the French coast to annihilate the French fleet that
had taken refuge there. After a battle, Howe was famous for his solici-
tude for the wounded, down to the lowliest seaman, often sharing with
them the provisions of his own mess, a rarity in an age when most
noblemen thought they could ignore the needs and feelings of the
common man with impunity.

After a somewhat fulsome exchange of compliments, Franklin and
Howe got down to business. Although he said he was "unconnected
with the ministry" it was soon obvious that he was functioning as an
unofficial envoy to explore the possibility of a reconciliation. Like his
sister before him, he lamented Franklin's treatment in the Cockpit
and assured him that some of the ministers "were ashamed of it, and
sorry it had happened." Nevertheless, he admitted that Franklin might
still decline to have any direct communication with the ministry, and
he offered himself as a channel of indirect communication, with a
guarantee that he would "keep perfectly secret" everything Franklin
said.

This was a little too thick for Franklin's taste. He knew that the
conciliators in the ministry—primarily Lord North and Lord Dart-

mouth—were just as anxious to keep the negotiations a secret to protect themselves from attack by the hawks in the cabinet and Parliament. He also resented the tendency to place all the blame for his
estrangement on the imbroglio in the Cockpit—as if he were a petulant little boy who had pushed the empire to the brink of civil war
because his feelings had been hurt.

"Give me credit for a sincere desire of healing the breach between
the countries," he asked Lord Howe. "I would cheerfully and heartily
do everything in my small power to accomplish it." But as far as he
could see, "from the measures talked of as well as those already determined on, no intention or disposition of the kind existed in the
present ministry, and therefore no accommodation could be expected
until we saw a change." As for the personal injuries done him, Franklin
said that those done his country were so much greater that he did not
think the other, at this time, worth mentioning. He went even further,
adding that it was "a fixed rule with me not to mix my private affairs
with those of the public. I could join with my personal enemy in
serving the public, or, when it was for its interests, with the public in
serving that enemy." [177]

Behind these superb sentiments, there was, of course, a subtle,
crucial struggle for personal advantage. The two men, although they
liked and respected each other on sight, were nevertheless antagonists,
duelists almost, in the struggle for the high ground of statesmanship
and magnanimity. Lord Howe had tried to maneuver Franklin into
negotiating as a man transcending personal resentments—and thus
more likely to make concessions. Franklin had firmly and serenely
restored the balance to his favor by claiming that personal resentment
as such did not exist in his mind. Howe could only express delight at
such a sentiment and asked Franklin to draw up in writing some
propositions that might form the basis of a negotiation. He then practically admitted the ministry's vulnerability by suggesting that it might
be better if Franklin was not seen at his house, or he at Craven Street.
It would be wiser, he blandly suggested, if they continued to meet here,
at his sister's house, where people were now used to seeing Franklin
come and go for his chess matches.

Franklin agreed. A few nights later, the ministry made another pass
at him, this time through his old friend, Thomas Pownall, ex-governor
of Massachusetts. Pownall was now in Parliament, forlornly calling for
a full reform of colonial administration. He told Franklin that Lord North

did not personally approve of the punitive acts; he had sponsored them in compliance with the majority of the cabinet who favored repression. Pownall tried to make points by discussing how hard he was working to change Lord North's mind about Franklin. His Lordship, according to Pownall, looked on Franklin "as the great fomenter of the opposition in America, and as a great adversary to any accommodation." Pownall's solution was an envoy or commissioner to America to settle the differences. He envisioned himself as the man and hoped to have Franklin beside him, to cast an authentic aura of pro-Americanism about him.[178]

At his next meeting with Lord Howe, Franklin saw more evidence of the web the ministry was attempting to weave around him. Howe began by assuring him "of a certainty" that there was "a sincere disposition" in Lord North and Lord Dartmouth to accommodate the differences with America. He then asked Franklin what he thought of sending "some person or persons over, commissioned to inquire into the grievances of America upon the spot." Franklin said he thought that "a person of rank and dignity who had a character of candor, integrity and wisdom might possibly, if employed in that service, be of great use." Miss Howe, who was present once more as what modern diplomats might call the negotiators' cover, said, "I wish, brother, you were to be sent thither on such a service; I should like that much better than General Howe's going to command the army there."

This was probably not the first time that Franklin heard the strong rumor that the family's youngest brother, William Howe, was to be commissioned a major general and sent to Boston to bolster the government's military posture there.

"I think, Madam," said Franklin, "they ought to provide for General Howe some more honourable employment."

With a smile, Lord Howe now took from his pocket a paper and said, "If it is not an unfair question, may I ask whether you know anything of this paper?"

A glance told Franklin it was a copy of his Hints, in David Barclay's handwriting. He readily admitted he was the author. Instantly Lord Howe became grave. He said he was "rather sorry" to find that Franklin had written it, because it had lowered his hopes of a reconciliation. There was no likelihood that most of the propositions in the "Hints" would ever be accepted by Parliament. Lord Howe begged Franklin to reconsider the subject and form a more acceptable plan, waxing eloquent on the service the creator of such a plan would do for the nation and adding, although he did not think of influencing Franklin "by any selfish motives," he could expect "any reward in the power of government to bestow."

This reappearance of the ugly British opinion that every man had his price made Franklin recoil. In telling the story later, he called it "spitting in the soup." [179] Nevertheless, he agreed to draw "some sketch of a plan." Verging on supersecrecy, and hoping that he had wrung the promise of a concession from Franklin, Howe said it might be best to send it to his sister, who would copy it and send the copy to him and return the original to Franklin. This way, Franklin need have no fear that his "constituents in America, with whom he had to keep well" might someday in the style of the Hutchinson letters see written proof that Franklin had sold them out.

But Franklin was much too shrewd to place such a weapon in his enemy's hands. No matter what he said, he would never trust the North ministry with such a document, even if it was an unsigned copy. Moreover, the British, after having first underestimated Franklin's importance, were now ballooning him into a superman, who really had the power to speak for all of America. Actually, Franklin's instructions from the Continental Congress extended only to submitting the petition to Parliament. Everything else he said was entirely unofficial. But overriding both these realities was the undoubted fact that Franklin was in whole-souled agreement with the spirit of American resistance. If he still had a dwindling hope of avoiding war, and keeping America within the structure of the empire, he was determined to make sure it was on a footing of total equality.

A few days later he sent a paper to Miss Howe which is one of the saddest and also one of the greatest he ever wrote. It is both a state paper and a moving personal testament to Franklin's wisdom and humanity. No previous Franklin biographer has ever printed it in full. It deserves to be read, not only for the purity of its language, but also because no other document so totally (if indirectly) indicts the rulers of Great Britain in 1775 as men of monumental stupidity and blindness. Nothing else satisfactorily explains how they could have read—and ignored—such advice.

It is supposed to be the wish on both sides not merely to put a stop to the mischief at present threatening the general welfare, but to cement a cordial union, and remove, not only every real grievance, but every cause of jealousy and suspicion.

With this view, the first thing necessary is to know what is, by the different parties in the dispute, thought essentially necessary for the obtaining such a union.

The American Congress in their petition to the King have been explicit, declaring that by a repeal of the oppressive acts therein complained of, the harmony between Great Britain and the colonies, so necessary to the happiness of both and so ardently desired of them, will, with the usual intercourse, be immediately restored.

If it has been thought reasonable here to expect that, previous to an alteration of measures, the colonies should make some declaration respecting their future conduct, they have also done that by adding: That when the causes of their apprehensions are removed, their future conduct will prove them not unworthy of the regard they have been accustomed in their happier days to enjoy.

For their sincerity in these declarations, they solemnly call to witness the Searcher of all hearts.

If Britain can have any reliance on these declarations (and perhaps none to be extorted by force can be more relied on than these, which are thus freely made), she may without hazard to herself try the expedient proposed, since if it fails she has it in her power at any time to resume her present measures.

It is then proposed: That Britain should show some confidence in these declarations, by repealing all the laws, or parts of laws, that are requested to be repealed in the petition of the Congress to the King;

And that at the same time, orders should be given to withdraw the fleet from Boston, and remove all the troops to Quebec or the Floridas, that the colonies may be left at perfect liberty in their future stipulations.

That this may, for the honour of Britain, appear not the effect of any apprehension from the measures entered into and recommended to the people by the Congress, but from good will, and a change of disposition towards the colonies, with a sincere desire of reconciliation, let some of their other grievances, which in their petition they have left to the magnanimity and justice of the King and Parliament, be at the same time removed, such as those relating to the payment of governors' and judges' salaries, and the instructions for dissolving Assemblies, etc.

*And to give the colonies an immediate opportunity of demon-
strating the reality of their professions, let their proposed ensuing
Congress be authorized by government (as was that held at Albany in 1754), and a person of weight and dignity of character
be appointed to preside at it on behalf of the Crown.*

*And then let requisition be made to the Congress, of such points
as government wishes to obtain for its future security, for aids,
for the advantage of general commerce, for reparation to the India
Company, etc., etc.*

*A generous confidence thus placed in the colonies will give
ground to the friends of government there, in their endeavours to
procure from America every reasonable concession or engagement, and every substantial aid that can fairly be desired.*[180]

Mournfully, a few days later, Howe sent a note to his sister, that
from the "sentiments" of Franklin's message, "the desired accommodation threatens to be attended with much greater difficulty than
I had flattered myself . . . there would be reason to apprehend."
Howe said he would forward Franklin's message to the ministry, but
obviously with very little hope. A week later—early in January, 1775—
another message came from Howe. He asked, again through his sister,
if Franklin would personally "engage" to pay for the tea "as a preliminary." He also wanted to know if the idea of Congress supplying
England with aid in the form of requisitions was still a viable idea.
Franklin replied that the requisition idea was still very much alive.
But as for the tea, the people of Boston were hardly likely to approve
of paying now, when "twenty times as much injury" has been done
to them by blocking up the port.[181]

XXXI

In the meantime, the newly elected Parliament convened for its first
session. Franklin had been in communication with Lord Chatham. He
had gone to Hays, Chatham's country estate, to show him the pe-

tition of the Continental Congress, almost as soon as it arrived, and the statesman had expressed enthusiastic approval of the American proceedings. Now he received a card from Lord Stanhope, a country neighbor of Chatham, asking him to attend the House of Lords the following day. Lord Chatham was to make a motion concerning America and had specifically asked his friend to bring Franklin to witness the debate. At the door Chatham created a considerable stir when he loudly declared, "This is Dr. Franklin, whom I would have admitted into the house." Political tipsters rushed in all directions to spread the news that the great man and Benjamin Franklin had formed an alliance. While Franklin watched tensely, Chatham arose and submitted a resolution calling on the King to withdraw the troops from Boston before "any sudden and fatal catastrophe" occurred. A close associate of Chatham, Lord Camden, rose to support him and won Franklin's praise as "another wonderfully good speaker and clear close reasoner." [182]

From the ministry came an angry denunciation of the motion, in words that were not likely to brighten Franklin's already dim optimism. Lord Suffolk rose to insist that "the mother country should never relax till America confessed her supremacy. . . . Any concession on our parts, to the right on which all our pretensions were founded, . . . would be to the last degree impolitic, pusillanimous and absurd." It was, he thundered, "high time for the mother country to exert her authority, or forever relinquish it. . . . I should scorn to continue one of His Majesty's ministers, and not advise coercive measures, when I was so firmly and fully convinced of their necessity; and I take a particular pride in avowing those sentiments; and mean steadily to abide by them at all events." He closed by broadening his personal rejection and speaking for the whole North cabinet, declaring "the ministerial resolution of enforcing obedience by arms." [183]

The motion was rejected. "Sixteen Scotch peers and twenty-four bishops, with all the Lords in possession or expectation of places, when they vote together unanimously, as they generally do for ministerial measures, make a dead majority," Franklin said. All the eloquence of Chatham and Camden and several others who joined them, "availed no more than the whistling of the winds." After some tepid debate, the House of Commons also refused to consider the petition from the Continental Congress on the grounds that the Congress was not a legally constituted body. Permission for Franklin to submit it was refused by 218 to 68.

In spite of his disappointment, Franklin was deeply moved by Chatham's courageous stand on America's behalf. He was even more touched when Lord Stanhope, at Chatham's request, sent him the copy of the original paper from which he had read the motion. Franklin sat down and dashed off the following note:

> *Dr. Franklin presents his best respects to Lord Stanhope, with many thanks to His Lordship and Lord Chatham for the communication of so authentic a copy of the motion. Dr. F. is filled with admiration of that truly great man. He has seen, in the course of life, sometimes eloquence without wisdom, and often wisdom without eloquence; in the present instance he sees both united, and both as he thinks, in the highest degree possible.*[184]

At one point during the debate on the motion, one of the ministry's spokesmen had scornfully remarked that it was easy to criticize their measures, but no one had proposed anything better. Lord Chatham had arisen to declare that he was not one of those "idle censurers" and he solemnly informed the ministers that he planned to lay before the Parliament a comprehensive program for healing America's differences and restoring peace to the empire. In the next week, Chatham discussed this plan with only two persons, Lord Camden, who checked it for legality, and Benjamin Franklin, to make sure that in substance at least, it would be acceptable to America.

Franklin did not agree with all aspects of the plan. It emphasized in sweeping terms the imperial authority of the British Parliament, although it surrendered to Americans the exclusive right to levy their own taxes. Chatham twice called on Franklin in Craven Street, a high honor which Franklin admitted "flattered not a little my vanity." His second call was on Sunday, January 29, 1775, and he stayed nearly two hours, his coach practically filling the narrow street. All London was abuzz with the news before the day was over. That particular visit, Franklin said, "gave me the more pleasure as it happened on the very day twelve-month that the ministry had taken so much pains to disgrace me before the Privy Council." [185] Although Franklin tried hard to deny the wound, it was still there.

He had little or no success in altering Lord Chatham's plan. On Tuesday, January thirty-first, at their last conference, Franklin went out to his country mansion and stayed "near four hours." The great orator overwhelmed Franklin with a flow of words that was so elo-

quent, Franklin admitted, "I found little inclination to interrupt him."
He covered barely half the points he wanted to correct, and even those
he covered were left unchanged because it was more important, at a
first reading, to meet the prevailing prejudices of Parliament. In the
blank Lord Chatham had left, for the titles of the American acts
Chatham wished repealed, Franklin copied for him a list from the
proceedings of the Continental Congress—a task he dismissed as
something that might have been done "by any copying clerk." But it
must have given him considerable pleasure. The next day Lord Stanhope once more brought Franklin down to the House of Lords and
Lord Chatham laid his plan before the House, which was crowded
with both peers and members of the Commons, all of them conscious
that a climactic moment in the crisis was at hand.

Flattering as Chatham's tactics were to Franklin, showing his bill
to only two people before he introduced it was not good parliamentary
politics. The members of the Opposition, most of whom were either in-
dependents or grouped around other peers such as Lord Rockingham,
were totally uninformed and inevitably disorganized. Few politicians
are content to obey the dictates of a leader as imperious as Chatham
unless the country is imminently threatened with destruction. In what
Franklin called "an excellent speech," Chatham presented his plan.
Along with his somewhat contradictory assertion of Parliamentary
supremacy and America's exclusive right to tax itself, he called on
Parliament to recognize the Philadelphia Congress as a lawful assembly,
and remove most of the other grievances that were alienating the
Americans.

What happened next revealed in the starkest possible terms the
schizophrenia within the North ministry. Lord Dartmouth, as the
American secretary, rose first to reply to Chatham. He showed how
much he yearned to make even a gesture of conciliation by saying
that the plan contained "matter of such weight and magnitude as to
require much consideration; he therefore hoped the noble Earl would
not expect their lordships to decide upon it by an immediate vote."
Lord Chatham quickly replied that he "expected nothing more."

Up sprang Lord Sandwich, perhaps the most bellicose man in North's
ministry. In what Franklin called a "petulant, vehement speech" he
called for the immediate rejection of Chatham's plan "with the contempt it deserved." Shrilly Sandwich declaimed that he could never
believe the plan "to be the production of any British peer." On the

contrary, it appeared to him "rather the work of some *American.*" As he said these words he turned his haughty sallow face toward Franklin, who was leaning on the bar of the house. Yes, Sandwich shrilled, he fancied he had in his eye the very person who had drawn it up, "one of the bitterest and most mischievous enemies this country had ever known." Almost every eye in this august conclave of England's nobility was instantly fastened on Franklin. But as in his earlier ordeal at the Privy Council, he maintained an expression "as immovable as if my features had been made of wood."

"The wise Lord Hillsborough," as Franklin wryly described him, now arose to strongly second Sandwich's call for rejection. Members of the Opposition, including Lord Shelburne and Lord Camden, insisted that the plan ought to be considered, either on its merits or at the very least for the character and dignity of the House. But one of these lords made the mistake of mentioning that Lord Dartmouth, speaking for the ministry, had also recommended consideration of the plan. Dartmouth rose, his soft, feminine eyes clouded with agitation, his bow lips petulant at being divided from his fellow ministers, and humbly ate his own words. He had altered his mind, he said, after having heard the opinions of so many lords against the plan and he too recommended rejecting it immediately.

Lord Chatham now rose and coolly replied to Sandwich. He said the plan was entirely his own—a declaration he felt he was obliged to make since so many of their lordships appeared to have such a mean opinion of it. If it was to be censured, it was unjust to let any blame for it fall on another individual. In the past, people had said his greatest fault was his unwillingness to take advice. But now he did not hesitate to say that if he was the First Minister of this country, and had "the care of settling this momentous business," he would not be ashamed "of publicly calling to his assistance a person so perfectly acquainted with the whole of American affairs" as the gentleman Sandwich had alluded to and "so injuriously reflected on." He was a man "whom all Europe held in high estimation for his knowledge and wisdom" and ranked with England's Boyle and Newton. He was an honor, not to the English nation only, but to human nature.

Franklin again struggled to maintain a wooden face and succeeded. What he saw happen next in that conclave of Britain's bluest and supposedly best blood was shocking enough to freeze anyone's features. Sandwich's motion to reject passed 61 to 32. "Lord Chatham's bill,"

Franklin told Charles Thomson in a letter four days later, "tho' on so important a subject, and offered by so great a character, and supported by such able and learned speakers . . . was treated with as much contempt as they could have shown to a ballad offered by a drunken porter." [186]

XXXII

A few days later, Franklin received bad news of a more disturbing personal nature. William Franklin wrote to tell him that Deborah was dead. She had suffered a stroke almost a year ago, which left her enfeebled in both mind and body. A second stroke had carried her into eternity, on December 19, 1774, and William had struggled through snow drifts to arrive, barely a half hour before her funeral, to pay the respects which duty, if not inclination, required of him. Deprived of her fiery spirit, Deborah must have been a rather pitiful sight in her last days. Even William forgot his animosity and spoke of her as "my poor old mother." The news shook Franklin in several ways. He reproached himself for not having gone home sooner—especially when he heard that Deborah had lamented bitterly his decision to stay another year after the Cockpit humiliation. She had wept and said the news meant she would never see her Pappy alive again. Moreover, there was now no one to superintend his considerable capital and property in Pennsylvania, and with a war threatening, it was all the more imperative to put his financial house in order. He decided to leave as soon as possible.

Nothing that happened in England, during the next few weeks, inclined him to change his mind. The House of Commons voted down or ignored petition after petition from London and Liverpool merchants, the manufacturers of Manchester and the traders of Wolverhampton, begging them to avert the crisis that was certain to disrupt Great Britain's economy. Lord North rose in the Commons to propose an address to the King in which the state of affairs in Massachusetts

Bay would be called a rebellion, and begged his Majesty to take immediate action to insure obedience to the laws and sovereignty of England. Only a passing reference was made to the government's willingness to show the Americans "every just and reasonable indulgence" if they made "proper application."

Then, in one of those inexplicable reversals, which can only be explained by Lord North's incoherent, divided mind, the ministry suddenly announced that they were prepared to make a conciliatory proposal. On February twentieth, North appeared in Parliament to announce that any colony that agreed to contribute by vote of their Assembly "their proportion to the common defense," and also agreed to raise money for the salaries of the governor and the courts, would henceforth be exempt from all further taxation, except duties imposed for the regulation of commerce, and even the monies raised by these duties would be deposited to the account of each colony for their individual use. It was nothing more than Franklin's old idea of raising money by requisition. If the proposition had been put to the Continental Congress, and the ministry had abandoned its insistence on the technicality that the Congress was not a legal body, something might have come of it. But in the present situation, it sounded like an attempt to bribe individual colonies away from their loyalty to Congress.

Franklin, through his private sources, reported that North had intended to make a much more generous and elaborate offer, but the extremists in the cabinet threatened to revolt and bring down the ministry. They accepted the watered-down proposition North finally offered because, Franklin was certain, they "rely upon [it] as a means of dividing, and by that means subduing us." Fervently he wrote to friends in America, urging them to stand together. "The eyes of all Christendom are now upon us," he told James Bowdoin, "and our honour as a people has become a matter of the utmost consequence to be taken care of. If we tamely give up our rights in this contest, a century to come will not restore us in the opinion of the world; we shall be stamped with the character of dastards, poltroons and fools; and be despised and trampled upon, not by this haughty, insolent nation only, but by all mankind." [187]

As his own hopes of compromise plummeted to zero, he became uncomfortably aware that he was being separated from friends who had over the years followed his original lead. The gap between him and his son William was already acutely evident. In the same letter that contained his almost tender comments on Deborah's death, William Franklin had turned to politics and tried to give his father some advice. He told him to give up squabbling with the ministry and come home. The advice was almost paternal on William's part. Perhaps seeing Deborah dwindle into enfeeblement and death made him think of his father as equally old and almost as helpless. "If there was any prospect," he wrote, "of your being able to bring the people in power to your way of thinking, or those of your way of thinking being brought into power, I should not think so much of your stay. But as you have had by this time pretty strong proofs that neither can be reasonably expected, and that you are looked upon with an evil eye in that country, and are in no small danger of being brought into trouble for your political conduct, you had certainly better return while you are able to bear the fatigues of the voyage, to a country where the people revere you, and are inclined to pay a deference to your opinions. I wonder none of them, as you say, requested your attendance at the late Congress, for I heard from all quarters that your return was ardently wished for at that time, and I have since heard it lamented by many that you were not at that meeting; as they imagined, had you been there, you would have framed some plan for accommodation of our differences that would have met with the approbation of a majority of the delegates, though it would not have coincided with the deep designs of those who influence that majority. However mad you may think the measures of the ministry are, yet I trust you have candour enough to acknowledge that we are noways behindhand with them in madness on this side of the water. . . ." [188]

Next Joseph Galloway wrote to him, enclosing a copy of the plan of union which he had proposed in the Continental Congress. It was more or less the same plan he had urged on Franklin a year ago, the descendant of Franklin's Albany Plan. It had been voted down by Congress 6 to 5. Deeply hurt by this rejection of what he felt was the only hope of compromise, Galloway retreated to his country estate, and would have nothing more to do with Congress. He sent the plan to London, in the hope that it might inspire some action from that side of the Atlantic. Regretfully Franklin had to tell him that he no longer believed in his own brainchild. "I have not heard what objections were made to the plan in the Congress, nor would I make more than this one, that when I consider the extream corruption prevalent among all orders of men in this old rotten state, and the glorious publick virtue so predominant in our rising country, I cannot but apprehend more mischief than benefit from a closer union. I fear they will drag us after them in all the plundering wars, which their desperate circumstances, injustice and rapacity may prompt them to undertake; and their wide, wasting prodigality and profusion is a gulph that will swallow up every aid we may distress ourselves to afford them. . . . However, I would try anything, and bear anything that can be borne with safety to our just liberties, rather than engage in a war with such near relations, unless compelled to it by dire necessity in our own defense." [189]

In this divided spirit, Franklin continued to negotiate behind the scenes with Barclay, Fothergill, and Howe. For the first time, the steady drift toward war began to affect his nerves. At one point, when Lord Howe told him that the ministry was definitely swinging toward reconciliation, and would soon send him as a peace commissioner to America, with Franklin at his side, Franklin lost control of himself and wept with joy. But like so many of North's and Dartmouth's ideas, it was nine-tenths wish and one-tenth will, and it soon dissolved in the glare of Sandwich-Suffolk belligerence. Franklin for the first time in his life, found himself unable to sleep, and this worried him. "Whatever robs an old man of his sleep, soon demolishes him," he said.[190]

In his desperation, Franklin agreed to risk his popularity in America, and promise on his own authority that in spite of all the injuries they had since received, Boston would agree to pay for the tea. But he insisted if the ministry demanded such a dangerous concession from him, the least he could expect from them was an equally large retreat—rescinding the punitive acts. This the ministry refused to do, and the two Quakers sadly advised Franklin to withdraw his offer. Lord Howe, after raising Franklin's hopes so high, mournfully reported that he too was empty-handed. There was no immediate hope of his appointment as a peace commissioner, and when Franklin explained that he must leave for America as soon as possible, the admiral mournfully told him to go.

In Parliament, the North ministry swung, like a ship without a rudder, into the prevailing current of arrogant belligerence. A bill for restraining all of New England's trade passed 215 to 61. The friends of America in the opposition denounced it as certain to cause war—a war that England could not possibly win. In a distinctly Franklinesque echo, Lord Camden cited the number of men America could put in the field. Lord Sandwich rose to reply. "I cannot think the noble Lord can be serious on this matter," he said. "Suppose the colonies do abound in men, what does that signify? They are raw, undisciplined, cowardly men. I wish instead of 40 or 50,000 of these brave fellows, they would produce in the field at least 200,000, the more the better, the easier would be the conquest; if they did not run away, they would starve themselves into compliance with our measures."

This was typical of the almost incredible contempt for America that Franklin heard in Parliament, in clubs, and in private homes during these last weeks in England. William Strahan came to him with a story about a Scotch sergeant in Boston who had captured forty American militiamen single-handed and marched them into captivity at the point of his bayonet.[191] The climax came for Franklin in a debate he attended at the House of Lords. Lord Camden rose to defend America and called for reconciliation. The ministry replied with "base reflections on American courage, religion, understanding, &c.," in which Franklin heard his countrymen treated "with the utmost contempt, as the lowest of mankind, and almost of a different species from the English of Britain." American honesty was particularly abused. Several of the lords asserted that the whole dispute was a pretext to avoid paying just debts.

An enraged Franklin went home and drew up a Memorial to present to Lord Dartmouth. It was a wholesale attack on the punitive acts, in which he demanded "satisfaction" for the accumulated damage the laws had done to Massachusetts and New England. Fortunately, he had the good sense to take it to his friend Thomas Walpole, head of the Grand Ohio Company, and ask him his opinion. Walpole, who was a member of the House of Commons, read the wild accusatory words with growing astonishment. He looked at the paper, looked at Franklin, and then at the paper again, as if he could not quite believe his own eyes. The violent, intemperate prose was completely foreign to the Benjamin Franklin he knew. When he saw Walpole was speechless, Franklin asked him to show it to Lord Camden, who lived nearby, and hurried off to continue his packing. The next day, Franklin got the Memorial back with a note advising him that both Walpole and Camden thought it "might be attended with dangerous consequences to your person, and contribute to exasperate the nation." The next day, when Walpole called at Craven Street, he found that Franklin had gone to the House of Lords. He was so worried about Franklin's emotional state that he followed him there, took him aside, and begged him not to deliver the paper to Lord Dartmouth. Since he had no instructions to make such a protest, it would only draw the ministerial lightning in

Franklin's direction once more. They would call it "a national affront" and possibly arrange another, even worse ordeal before the Privy Council.[192]

By this time Franklin had reserved a cabin aboard the Pennsylvania packet, had taken William Temple Franklin out of school, and was within a few days of departing. The lawsuit between him and William Whately was still dragging through the courts, and he knew that this in itself would give the government the right to detain him if they were so inclined. So Franklin took Walpole's advice and decided not to deliver his last roar of defiance.

On one of his final days in London, he conferred for hours with Edmund Burke, the intellectual leader of the Rockingham wing of the opposition. Burke was planning to make a major speech on conciliating the colonies and, like Lord Chatham, he wanted to make sure it was as realistic as possible, from an American point of view. That night Franklin received a last mournful letter from Dr. Fothergill. The Quaker urged Franklin to gather the leading Philadelphians together and inform them "that whatever specious pretences are offered, they are all hollow; and that to get a larger field on which to fatten a herd of worthless parasites, is all that is regarded." This was grim confirmation of Franklin's old accusation, that the British government's attempt to broaden its jurisdiction in America was primarily motivated by a hunger for more patronage. The efforts he, Franklin, and Barclay had made for peace would, Fothergill hoped, "stun at least, if not convince, the most worthy that nothing very favourable is intended, if more unfavourable articles cannot be obtained." [193]

War was very close, and Franklin knew it. It filled him with dread, not only because it was a war which had raged inside his own mind and body for almost ten years. Again and again he had struggled to compose and suppress the violence, to subdue it behind the mask of philosophic serenity he yearned to wear. But now it had broken out in his own mind. The raging defiance he had felt as he wrote that last Memorial, the astonished dismay on his friend Thomas Walpole's face as he read it, made that clear. This was agony enough, this loss of his sense of place in the world, this division between an England and an America whom he had long loved equally. But there was an even more appalling division, a more painful loss, threatening him on the other side of the Atlantic. What would William Franklin think and do if war broke out?

A long time ago, Franklin had seen, intellectually, that there was really no middle ground in this contest. Now he saw even more starkly that once blood was spilled, no man would be permitted to hold the middle ground that his son and Galloway were attempting to maintain without being called a traitor.

On that last day in London, Franklin also spent some time with his old friend Joseph Priestley. They went over a bundle of newspapers recently arrived from America, and Franklin pointed out to Priestley the articles that might do America the most good if they were reprinted in English papers. Perhaps it was this last attempt to play the propagandist on America's behalf, a role in which he had tragically failed, that overwhelmed him. "He was frequently not able to proceed for the tears literally running down his cheeks," Priestley said.[194]

XXXIII

The source of these tears and the best possible proof of the intricate connection between the personal and the political in Franklin's mind were the first words he wrote on board the Pennsylvania packet. On the same day Edmund Burke was delivering to a temporarily hypnotized House of Commons his magnificent speech on reconciling America. "The proposition is peace. Not peace through the medium of war; not peace to be hunted through the labyrinth of intricate and endless negotiations; not peace to arise out of universal discord, fomented from principle in all parts of the Empire; . . . It is simple peace; sought in its natural course, and in its ordinary haunts. It is peace sought in the spirit of peace, and laid in principles purely pacific." [195]

While Burke stunned the Tory majority with the majesty of his rolling periods, Franklin began the longest letter he ever wrote with two simple words: "Dear Son." [196]

Day after day, as the Pennsylvania packet plowed through seas so calm that a London barge would have found them no more troublesome than the Thames, Franklin wrote the detailed history of his secret negotiations with the British government. Not even young Josiah Quincy, who had sailed for Boston two weeks before, his delicate frame racked by the consumption that would kill him before he reached home, knew about this hidden tangle of hopes, hints, and frustrations. Perhaps Franklin feared to reawaken the suspicions of him Quincy had brought from Boston. At any rate, what he hesitated to reveal to the young idealist, who was literally sacrificing his life for the Cause, Franklin told in infinite detail to the man he had already called a "thorough courtier." He was prepared to take the risk because in his own spacious mind, the truth was the most powerful of all arguments. So, day after day he wrote and wrote, until the words that flowed out from that opening "Dear Son" ran to ninety-seven extraordinary pages. Today they remain a masterpiece of diplomatic reporting. But almost no previous Franklin biographer has paid sufficient attention to their other face— the anguished, sometimes bitter personal argument which lies embedded in the narrative like splotches of blood on a beautifully woven rug.

Discussing Lord North's conciliatory proposal, Franklin compared it to the request of "a highwayman, who presents his pistol and hat at a coach window, demanding no specific sum, but if you will give all your money or what he is pleas'd to think sufficient, he will civilly omit putting his own hands into your pockets; if not, there is his pistol." [197] Describing Dartmouth's about-face on Chatham's proposal, Franklin noted savagely, "I am the more particular in this, as it is a trait of that nobleman's character, who from his office is suppos'd to have so great a share in American affairs, but who has in reality no will or judgment of his own, being with dispositions for the best measures, easily prevail'd with to join in the worst." He was even more devastating in his description of the ministry's attack on Lord Chatham's plan. "To hear so many of these *hereditary* legislators declaiming so vehemently against, not the adopting merely, but even the consideration of a proposal so important in its nature, . . . gave me an exceeding mean opinion of their abilities, and made their claim of sovereignty over three millions of virtuous, sensible people in America seem the greatest of absurdities, since they appear'd to have scarce discretion enough to govern a herd of swine. *Hereditary legislators!* thought I. There would be more propriety, because less hazard of mischief, in having (as in some university of Germany) *hereditary professors of mathematicks!* But this was a hasty reflection: For the *elected* House of Commons is no better, nor ever will be while the electors receive money for their votes, and pay money wherewith ministers may bribe their representatives when chosen." [198]

Not even the seekers after peace, Howe, Barclay and Fothergill, came off unscathed. Franklin spoke in scornful terms of Howe's repeated attempts to offer him the "favors" of the government in return for his cooperation. At another point, he told how Barclay and Fothergill disagreed with him when Franklin insisted that Parliament had to give up their asserted right to alter colonial charters and constitutions at their pleasure. America would never feel safe or secure as long as this pretension was maintained. The two Englishmen apparently could not resist pointing out that America was not very safe right now. Somewhat too smugly, they reminded Franklin that it would be easy for Britain to order the fleet to burn every seaport on the American continent. Franklin exploded. "I grew warm," he told William, "said that the chief part of my little property consisted of houses in those towns; that they might make bonfires of them whenever they pleased; that the fear of losing them would never alter my resolution to resist to the last that claim of Parliament." [199]

With equally obvious pride, he stressed Lord Chatham's praise of the Continental Congress. He quoted the great man as saying that the Americans had acted "with so much temper, moderation and wisdom," that he thought it "the most honourable assembly of statesmen since those of the ancient Greeks and Romans, in the most virtuous times." A born writer, Franklin gave the narrative the pace and emotional structure of a novel, building it from the "cool, sullen silence" that he was maintaining at the opening of the story to the exasperated fury of his insulting Memorial to Lord Dartmouth at the close, with Fothergill's final crushing letter as an abrupt, dramatic coda.

To relieve his mind and calm his nerves while writing this 30,000-word letter, Franklin studied the Gulf Stream. He had discussed this strange ocean river with several American captains, and observed it in an offhand way on his earlier crossings. Now he dropped thermometers over the side as they sailed through it, took samples of the water, and noted it was far less phosphorescent in the dark than the rest of the sea. Years before, one of his Nantucket cousins had told him that American captains made better time than British captains because they understood how to use the Gulf Stream's current when they were sailing with it, and avoided it when they were sailing in the other direction. Franklin now concluded that they were right. He decided that the best way to find out whether a ship was in the Gulf Stream or not was to equip it with thermometers. This was a scientific discovery of the first rank, but it would be a long time before Franklin decided it was wise to confide the news to the world.[200]

On the fifth of May, when the packet dropped anchor in the Delaware opposite Philadelphia, the first news Franklin heard from those who came aboard was what he dreaded most: war had begun. Sixteen days before, General Gage had sent a military expedition to Concord, Massachusetts, to seize cannon, gunpowder, and other supplies stored there. Fighting had erupted on the Lexington green at dawn on April nineteenth, and before the day was over forty-nine Americans had been killed and thirty-four wounded. The British in their running retreat from Concord lost 273—killed, wounded, and missing. Franklin could only think wearily of the ninety-seven-page letter in his trunk and wonder if he had come home too late to send it to the royal governor of New Jersey.

Book Five

Trauma
of Birth

I

Franklin found Philadelphia in a frenzy of military preparation. Associated companies, recruited as Franklin had raised militia in the past, were drilling in every open field and yard. The Continental Congress was to meet in five days. Franklin, once he was settled in his house, after a joyous welcome from his daughter Sally, his son-in-law Richard Bache, and their three sons, asked the question that was paramount in his mind: has William resigned?

Faces fell. The answer was no. William maintained, the last time they heard from him, that he felt "obligated" to the ministry for their permitting him to retain his post, in spite of his father's disagreements with them. He still argued that there was "madness" on both sides of the water, and struggled to maintain some kind of middle position.

The next day, the Pennsylvania Assembly voted to appoint Franklin as an additional member of the colony's delegation to the Continental Congress. He immediately accepted. This was a high honor, but that same day he got more bad news. Joseph Galloway, who had also been elected a member of the delegation, had declared he would not serve. This meant that the leading voice in Pennsylvania was Franklin's old foe, John Dickinson. Few previous biographers have tried to assess the impact of these double blows to Franklin's hopes and plans.[1] Galloway's desertion meant that Franklin was politically isolated in Pennsylvania. Instead of being able to sit in Congress as the spokesman for the host state, and give Pennsylvania an equal voice in Congress with the other two large states, Massachusetts and Virginia, he represented no one and nothing but himself.

On May 8, 1775, Franklin wrote a letter to Galloway, expressing his deep concern at his old friend's "resolution of quitting publick life at a time when your abilities are so much wanted." He told Galloway that William Franklin would be at Burlington on May fifteenth to meet with the New Jersey Assembly. If William could not "conveniently come hither" to meet him before that date, he proposed seeing him there, and

then swinging down to Trevose to see Galloway on the way back. He
signed the letter "With unalterable esteem and affection." Galloway
was extremely anxious to talk with Franklin, and had offered to send
his carriage to bring him directly to Trevose. Franklin explained that
he was "so taken up with people coming in continually I cannot stir,"
but he was tempted by the offer.[2] Sometime within the next ten days,
the three men met. As Galloway recalled the scene later, they sat up
late, and bottles of Madeira went around and around while they talked
about happier days, when the three of them were like a father and two
sons, running Pennsylvania and New Jersey and planning even more
magnificent colonies in the West, under the protection of a benevolent
empire. Finally, Franklin, hoping he had bridged their eleven-year separation, raised the question they all hesitated to discuss. Where did they
stand?

Tensely, William tried to explain to his father the sense of obligation
he felt to the King and to the ministry, which prevented him from resigning. He denounced with equal fervor the stupidity of Thomas Gage,
for sending his troops into the country on a brainless, needless expedition
and the "violent men" in Massachusetts and in the Continental Congress.
He even attempted to argue that his father should at the very least feel
enough obligation to the British government to avoid playing more than
a neutral spectator's role.

While William Franklin nodded approval, Galloway talked bitterly
about mechanics and tradesmen trying to be statesmen, under the leadership of Charles Thomson, who had become his chief political foe in
Pennsylvania. He was so blinded by local politics, and the blow to his
pride when Congress made Thomson its secretary, and then rejected his
plan of union, that he simply could not see the larger struggle with any
kind of perspective. Galloway's temper rose as he described the treatment he had received from the radicals in the Pennsylvania Assembly.
He had attempted to bypass the Continental Congress, and persuade
the Assembly to petition the King directly. A box with a noose and a
threatening letter in it was left in his lodgings. This, of course, made it
easy for him to tell himself he was opposing "lawless measures." [3]

With a harsh sigh, Franklin told them where he stood. He was for
independence. The two younger men could only gasp and shake their
heads. They could not quite believe that the man who was for them a
symbol of moderation and rational compromise could embrace this
doctrine, which thus far only a few extremists dared to whisper in
private. In desperation, Franklin read the two men parts of the ninety-

seven-page letter to William that he had composed on board ship. Nothing changed their minds. They were both convinced that the Continental Congress was as wrongheaded and foolhardy as the British ministry, with the worse handicap that it had no legal right to exist and issue orders or resolutions.

Galloway retired to Trevose and William went back to Perth Amboy, where the government had recently built him a handsome new mansion. But for the Franklins, political separation could not mean personal separation. Especially now, when there was a new link between them: William Temple Franklin. Childless all these years, the governor was almost pathetically overjoyed to claim Temple as his son, and he swiftly exerted his formidable charm to win the handsome sixteen-year-old boy's affection. When he returned to Perth Amboy, William took Temple with him. Franklin, as he often did when he was emotionally distressed, reached for his pen to continue the argument. The letter almost seems to pick up in the middle of a sentence, and constitute a reply that Franklin thought of giving his son, and forebore to say, perhaps because he would not have been able to control his temper.

> *I don't understand it as any favour to me or to you, the being continued in an office by which, with all your prudence, you cannot avoid running behindhand if you live suitably to your station. While you are in it I know you will execute it with fidelity to your royal master, but I think independence more honourable than any service, and that in the state of American affairs, which, from the present arbitrary measures is likely soon to take place, you will find yourself in no comfortable situation, and perhaps wish you had soon disengaged yourself.*[4]

The next day, Franklin wrote a similar letter to Galloway, urging him to serve in the Continental Congress. Once more his old lieutenant stonily refused. On May twelfth, the Pennsylvania Assembly finally acceded to his request, and excused Galloway from his appointment. He published a statement in the newspapers, denying the "malevolent reports" that were circulating about his loyalty, and permanently retired to Trevose.

Franklin took his seat in the Continental Congress on the tenth of May. In political terms he was the loneliest man in the crowded chamber of the Pennsylvania State House, where sixty-three delegates from the still widely divided thirteen colonies met to discuss the crisis. Embarrassed by the abstention of both his son and his political lieutenant, and unsure of his fellow congressmen, Franklin maintained a discreet, somewhat mournful silence. Most of the congressmen were strangers to him. They were a generation, some of them two generations, younger. Most of his contemporaries, such as Mather Byles in Massachusetts, fellow Stamp Act opponent Jared Ingersoll in Connecticut, Thomas Vernon in Rhode Island, Cadwallader Colden in New York and John Foxcroft in Virginia, were either taking the King's side or retreating to a bewildered, pitiful neutrality.

Almost immediately it was evident to Franklin that few in Congress shared his defiant spirit. Only some New England delegates were really ready for independence. Massachusetts had been invaded, her people shot, her houses burned by British troops. British warships were seizing American ships, largely from New England, on the high seas. But the delegates from other states, most of whom had yet to see a hostile British soldier or warship, were not so inclined to regard ship seizures or the outburst of violence at Lexington and Concord as a signal for all-out war. They were quick to point out that the British troops had retreated inside Boston and remained on the defensive since that time, making no effort to attack the improvised militia army from Massachusetts and the other New England colonies that was besieging them. There was, these congressmen argued, still some hope for peace. To Franklin's considerable mortification, the leading spokesman for this point of view was his old political enemy, John Dickinson. Meanwhile William Franklin's ambiguous position gave Philadelphia rumormongers a chance to whisper that his father had sold out to the British and was operating as a Parliamentary spy. Others said he was waiting for the right moment to submit a plan of reconciliation coauthored by himself and Lord Chatham. Richard Henry Lee, brother of Arthur Lee, exhibiting that mania for suspicion which was one of his family's less endearing traits, announced that he was launching a one-man investigation to find out if Franklin was really a traitor. Young James Madison, not yet a delegate from Virginia, succumbed to a highly uncharacteristic tendency to accept the story at face value. He told the Philadelphia printer, William Bradford, nephew of Franklin's old newspaper competitor, and an eager disseminator of this slander, that "the bare suspicion of his guilt amounts very nearly to a proof of its reality." [5]

There is some evidence that at first Franklin still entertained some faint hopes for peace. He wrote to his friend, Bishop Shipley, saying, "A war has commenced which the youngest of us may not see the end of.

My endeavours will be if possible to quench it, as I know yours will be; the satisfaction of endeavouring to do good is perhaps all we can obtain or effect." [6] But this pacific spirit was soon eroded by the news of what was happening to the citizens of Boston.

With food running short, the British were turning out all superfluous mouths. People were being forced to flee into the country with whatever they could carry in wagons and on their backs. Franklin's widowed sister, Jane Mecom, sixty-three and asthmatic, was one of these refugees, and she wrote a heartbreaking letter to Franklin, telling him of her travails. She had no man to assist her. Eventually, after some frantic negotiating, she managed to hire a wagon and, with the help of a granddaughter, packed it with "what I expected to have liberty to carry out, intending to seek my fortune with hundreds of others not knowing whither." At this point of desperation, Franklin's old friend Catherine Ray, married to a Rhode Islander, William Greene, invited Mrs. Mecom to take refuge with her. "I brought out what I could pack up in trunks and chests," she mournfully told her brother, but she had to leave behind all her furniture. At Warwick she found the Greene house already jammed with refugees. Along with William and Catherine Greene and their five children, there were ten other Boston relatives in the eight-room house, and six more expected the day Jane arrived. [7]

Jane's plight was doubly disturbing to Franklin, because she not only was his favorite sister, but had already endured a life of almost unparalleled grief and disappointment. Her husband had died of a lingering illness, and of the nine children she raised to maturity, all were dead except a daughter and two sons, and both of the sons were insane. Franklin had been paying for the care of the older boy, Edward, for almost fifteen years; the second victim, Benjamin, had broken down more recently, after years of trying to make a living as a printer, frequently with his uncle's help. Franklin was paying for his care, too, on a New Jersey farm. "I sympathize most sincerely with you and the people of my native town and country. Your account of the distresses attending their removal affects me greatly," Franklin wrote. He urged Jane to join him in Philadelphia, or accept an invitation William had sent to her to enjoy the hospitality of his spacious new house in Perth Amboy, New Jersey. "Perhaps that may be a retreat less liable to disturbance than this: God only knows," Franklin said. [8] Obviously he still regarded William as one of the family, in spite of their widening political breach.

Franklin wrote this letter on June seventeenth—a fateful day for the people of his native town and country. Hoping to thwart a British plan to launch an attack on the besieging American army, the Yankees seized high ground, known as Breed's Hill and Bunker's Hill, on Charlestown Heights north of Boston. The British attacked them and a full-scale battle erupted, totally different in form and far more bloody than the running skirmishes of the retreat from Concord and Lexington on April nineteenth. The British finally drove the Americans off both hills, but it cost them 1150 men—about forty percent of their attacking force. The Americans lost an estimated 441 men. At the height of the battle, the British fired hot shot from nearby men-of-war into the village of Charlestown, just below Breed's Hill, and some 300 houses were destroyed in the conflagration that swiftly followed.

Listening to this carnage described in vivid terms to the assembled Congress on the twenty-sixth of June, Franklin was filled with a wrath and disgust beyond anything he had felt thus far. Yet he was forced to remain silent while his old enemy John Dickinson brought forward a humble petition to the King. As the spokesman for the pivotal state of Pennsylvania, Dickinson had a weight and power that made it essential for Congress to listen to him. Franklin must have writhed in frustration as he watched the performance, thinking what he could have accomplished if William Franklin were sitting beside him as the head of New Jersey's delegation, and Galloway were on hand to rally Pennsylvania. Between them they could have created a bloc of influence that radiated into Maryland, Delaware, and New York—and dominated the Congress with results far different from what Dickinson's muddleheaded, wishful-thinking leadership was achieving.[9]

If Franklin had been Pennsylvania's leader there would have been no "olive branch petition" to the King. The same day that Congress adopted this second plea for reconciliation, Franklin went home to Market Street and wrote a letter to his old friend William Strahan.

> *Philadelphia, July 5, 1775*
>
> *Mr. Strahan: You are a member of Parliament and one of that majority which has doomed my country to destruction. You have begun to burn our towns and murder our people. Look upon your hands! They are stained with the blood of your relations! You and I were long friends. You are now my enemy, and I am*
>
> *Yours,*
>
> *B. Franklin*

The letter was never mailed. Probably Franklin never intended to mail it, but he made sure it was widely reprinted throughout America and Europe.[10]

Two days later he wrote a bitter letter to his friend, Bishop Shipley, describing the battle and the burning of Charlestown. "In all our wars from our first settlement in America to the present time, we never received so much damage from the Indian savages as in this one day. . . . Perhaps ministers may think this a means of disposing us to reconciliation. I feel and see everywhere the reverse. . . . I am not half so reconcilable now as I was a month ago. The Congress will send one more petition to the King which I suppose will be treated as the former was, and therefore will be the last. . . . You see I am warm; and if a temper naturally cool and phlegmatic can, in old age, which often cools the warmest, be thus heated, you will judge by that of the general temper here, which is now little short of madness." [11]

I I

After Bunker Hill, Franklin had no doubt whatsoever that all-out war had begun. It was time to form a nation out of the thirteen colonies. As the man who had created the original idea for an American union, Franklin was ideally qualified to draft the master plan. So, a full year before the Congress took the fateful step, Franklin wrote a declaration of independence.

> *Whereas the British nation, through great corruption of manners and extreme dissipation and profusion, both private and public, have found all honest resources insufficient to supply their excessive luxury and prodigality, and thereby have been driven to the practice of every injustice, which avarice could dictate or rapacity execute; And whereas, not satisfied with the immense plunder of the East, obtained by sacrificing millions of the human species, they have*

*lately turned their eyes to the West, and, grudging us the peaceable
enjoyment of the fruits of our hard labour and virtuous industry,
have for years past been endeavouring to extort the same from us,
under colour of laws regulating trade, and have thereby actually
succeeded in draining us of large sums, to our great loss and detri-
ment; And whereas, impatient to seize the whole, they have at
length proceeded to open robbery, declaring by a solemn act of
Parliament, that all our estates are theirs, and all our property
found upon the sea divisible among such of their armed plunderers
as shall take the same; And have even dared in the same act to
declare, that all the spoilings, thefts, burnings of houses and towns,
and murders of innocent people, perpetrated by their wicked and
inhuman corsairs on our coasts, previous to any war declared
against us, were just actions, and shall be so deemed, contrary to
several of the commandments of God (which by this act they presume to repeal), and to all the principles of right, and all the ideas
of justice, entertained heretofore by every other nation, savage as
well as civilized; thereby manifesting themselves to be* hostes
humani generis; *And whereas it is not possible for the people of
America to subsist under such continual ravages without making
some reprisals; Therefore, Resolved, &c.*[12]

Franklin was keenly aware that the crucial issue was not independence
but union. British barbarism might create a mood of alienation, but
only American statesmanship could create a union out of the thirteen
diverse colonies, whose sharply different lifestyles were obvious from
the moment the blunt, plainly dressed puritans of New England sat
down beside the subtle, laced and ruffled planters of Virginia and South
Carolina. So, as an integral part of his declaration of independence,
Franklin added "Articles of Confederation and Perpetual Union" for
"the United Colonies of North America." Thirteen in number, the articles
created a "confederacy" in which each colony retained "its own present
laws, customs, rights, privileges and peculiar jurisdictions" within its
own limits but surrendered to Congress the power to wage war and
make peace, enter into alliances and regulate such matters of general
concern as the post office, currency and the army and navy. Congress
would also have the responsibility for settling disputes among the colonies, and "the planting of new colonies when proper." Franklin had not
forgotten the potential riches of the Ohio Valley. Representation in the

general Congress was to be proportionate, based on one delegate for every 5000 votes.[13]

Before he introduced his proposal Franklin attempted to do some preliminary politicking. He showed the Declaration and Articles to several delegates. Among them was Thomas Jefferson, a tall redheaded young Virginian, also a newcomer to Congress. Already a vigorous defier of British pretensions, Jefferson gave the plan his enthusiastic approval. But he noted that "others were revolted at it." Franklin soon found that the proposal had no hope of passing. Most of the delegates were so antagonistic to the idea that they warned Franklin not to propose it from the floor. They did not want such a revolutionary item entered in the Congressional journal. Franklin was reduced to asking for permission to present his paper, not as a finished plan, but only as food for thought which the Congressmen might digest and use at some later date. On the twenty-first of July, 1775, Franklin made this feeble gesture, with the understanding that the Articles were accepted as a purely informal individual offering, and no reference was made to them in the regular journal. It was painful evidence of Franklin's political isolation, and his Pennsylvania enemies, John Dickinson and the other members of the old Proprietary Party, must have chortled that night over Franklin the political cipher.[14]

Franklin was simply not in intimate contact with the majority of Congress, the way stumpy, contumacious John Adams of Massachusetts was. Only a few days after Bunker Hill, he was writing to a friend in Massachusetts, "Secret and confidential, as the saying is, the Congress is not yet so much alarmed as it ought to be. . . . You will see a strange oscillation between love and hatred, between war and peace—preparations for war and negotiations for peace. . . ." Adams was wholeheartedly with Franklin in favor of independence and confederation. Three days after Congress unofficially accepted—and totally disregarded—Franklin's call for independence and union, Adams was writing to that same friend in Massachusetts, "We ought to have had in our hands a month ago the whole legislative, executive and judicial of the whole continent, and have completely modeled a constitution; to, have raised a naval power, and opened all our ports wide. . . ." But Adams added another suggestion which Franklin would have found harder to accept. Congress should, Adams said, ". . . have arrested every friend to [British] government on the continent and held them as hostages for the poor victims in Boston." [15]

III

Franklin was still hoping that the escalation of violence would force William to abandon his unrealistic middle position, and choose the side of his country in the impending struggle. No doubt he was able to understand a little better William's refusal to make the leap toward independence when a majority of the Continental Congress were still following John Dickinson and his olive branch. There was also a more and more pressing personal reason to avoid a break, if it was humanly possible. William Temple Franklin was spending the summer with his father and stepmother in Perth Amboy and was enjoying himself immensely. William had apparently found no difficulty inducing his wife Elizabeth to welcome Temple as a son. The motherless boy had responded with deep affection to her kindness, and he swiftly became a full-fledged member of his father's family. William was delighted with his son, and made it clear to his father that he was deeply grateful for the care and attention the elder Franklin had shown Temple during his years in London.

A lively well-to-do society clustered around the governor in his fine new house. The move from Burlington was, as Benjamin Franklin no doubt knew, in itself a political gesture. William had deserted New Jersey's western capital and the fine 500-acre farm he had purchased in its vicinity, to settle in Amboy, with its heavy concentration of Tories.

Franklin was obviously more than a little worried about the impact of this society on Temple's young mind. When several letters from Temple finally arrived, Franklin replied almost immediately. "I wonder'd it was so long before I heard from you. The [mail] packet, it seems, was brought down to Philadelphia, and carry'd back to Burlington before it came hither. I am glad to learn by your letters that you are happy in your new situation, and that tho' you ride out sometimes, you do not neglect your studies." He added that he had a letter from Mrs. Stevenson who "sends her love to her dear boy. . . . Mr. & Mrs. Bache send their love to you. The young gentlemen [the Bache grandsons] are well and pleas'd with your remembering them. Will has got a little gun, marches with it, and whistles at the same time by way of fife." [16]

It was a quiet, by no means ineffective way of reminding Temple that there were others who loved him too, and even toddlers were aware that war was brewing.

In other letters, Benjamin discussed Temple's future with William. They finally decided to enroll him in the university at Philadelphia in the fall. But even when the subject was something as innocent as Temple, the underlying political tension could not be concealed. Regarding Temple's return, William wanted to know "whether you approve of my coming [with him] to Philad." or "if I may expect you here." [17]

With congressmen such as John Adams already talking about arresting loyalists, the sight of William in Philadelphia would only make Franklin's political influence in Congress even smaller than it already was. He quickly told William that he preferred to come to Perth Amboy. Late in August, Franklin made the trip. As he jogged across New Jersey, he must have recalled with something close to bewilderment the triumphant journey he and William had made little more than a decade ago to install him as the royal governor. Incredible, that twelve years could turn a whole world upside down. How could he make William see that this revolution in the order of things was right and just, a natural process as inevitable as the growth of a child and his departure from the home? Alas, shrewd as he was in understanding men and motives, Franklin, with the limited psychology of his century, simply did not comprehend the drives that were forcing William to oppose his father in this, the greatest crisis of both their lives.

At such critical turning points, the totality of a man's life and nature rushes into the narrow moments of his decision, and his freedom to choose is reduced to the vanishing point. In the seclusion of the governor's house at Perth Amboy, the two men confronted each other in a final test of strength.

Franklin pointed to the steady escalation of the conflict—and its continental nature. George Washington of Virginia was now in Massachusetts, in command of the "Grand American Army" besieging Boston. Franklin described the burning of Charlestown, the cruelty and venality with which the British were treating the Americans inside occupied Boston, the latest news from Europe, that the British were hiring troops in Germany to bolster their army. While William shook his head in disagreement, Franklin told him that it was impossible for Britain to conquer America. The most they could do was establish a few enclaves on the coasts. They would never penetrate into the interior. What did it matter if the British blockaded every port on the continent, a task which would require an immense fleet? They could deprive a farming nation such as America of nothing essential. America would hold out for twenty years. Lord North and his ministers would not last a year, once Parliament saw what the war was costing.

But the heart of Franklin's argument was the importance of William's acting now. Timing was all important. In the next few months, Congress would be appointing numerous generals to George Washington's Army. As one of the few Americans who had some military experience, one of these posts was William's for the asking. Congress had appointed Benjamin Postmaster General. He had already appointed William's brother-in-law, Richard Bache, his chief deputy. There were dozens of other jobs in the department, and the other branches of this new government where his services would be welcomed and valued.

Once more William Franklin shook his head and argued back. He contended with passionate conviction that most of the people were not for independence. Only a small faction were in favor of this drastic, treasonous step and they were beguiling and hoodwinking the mass of the people, while simultaneously their war-like insurrectionary acts were forcing the British government into acts of war on their side, which, William freely admitted, worsened the situation. To bolster his argument about the majority of the people disdaining independence, the governor offered his father evidence from the last two meetings of the New Jersey Assembly. To prove that the British government was not the aggressor, ruthlessly ignoring every hope of conciliation, William flourished instructions from Lord Dartmouth ordering him to place Lord North's conciliatory proposal before the New Jersey Assembly. Dartmouth's letter was full of expressions of hope that war could be averted. Finally, if war did come, it was absurd to think that America, a country that could barely find enough money to pay its governors' salaries, could hope to conduct a war that would cost millions, against the richest, most powerful nation in the world. It was madness to think that raw provincials, untrained militiamen, could stand up against British regulars in a protracted war. They had fought well from entrenchments at Bunker

Hill. But wars were not won by fighting from entrenchments. In the authoritative tone of a semiprofessional soldier, William lectured his father about battle strategy and British invincibility.

It was a hopeless debate from the start. Both men rested their cases on what they had seen and heard in the past ten years. But beneath this arraignment of evidence there was a fundamental difference between father and son—a difference of spirit. Franklin was a living embodiment of the free, risking, venturing spirit that had brought men to America in the first place. His life had been a series of new beginnings, and the bold self-discipline of his open, experimental mind found it easy to contemplate one more, even at the age of seventy. William Franklin's experience had been totally opposite. Alienated from a sense of belonging in America by the accident of his birth (for which unconsciously he could not help blaming his father) he had found genuine acceptance and a new sense of achievement in England. He could not escape England's grip upon him, because he did not want to escape it. It was his emotional home, this stamp of royalty, this title which he bore at the King's pleasure. This old man, confronting him across the wine bottles, could not compete with it. Although his father's vigor must have amazed him, William insisted upon seeing him as old. In a year or two he would be dead. What then with Galloway gone and Dickinson in charge in Pennsylvania, what sort of future was there for a man of forty-four with no profession beyond a law degree which he had never exercised? Politics was not for William Franklin an avocation, practiced out of a sense of gratitude to a nation that had given him so much. Politics was William's profession, his livelihood, and it was simply too late, too risky to make a fresh beginning in a new political order, among men who had more reason to suspect him than trust him.

Finally there was, for William, the golden gleam of the western colony, which still beckoned—and simultaneously sharpened his resentment against his father, who had done so much to wreck it. In the letter he wrote a few weeks before Benjamin came down to Perth Amboy for their climactic confrontation he commented bitterly on a letter which Benjamin had received from Thomas Walpole and his associates in the Ohio Company. "I . . . observed that since you left England they have received the *strongest assurances* that as soon as the present great dispute is settled *our grant shall be perfected.*" William did his own underlining, and the two sets of words comprise a cry of anguish and anger. On his part, Benjamin Franklin obviously rejected with contempt the hint that he should lend his prestige and talents to settling the "great dispute" in order to make himself and his son rich.[18]

Wearily, after their long night of argument, father and son parted. Franklin rode back to Philadelphia with Temple. A few days later, William sent him the minutes of the New Jersey Assembly's last two meetings and those official papers from London which he found so hopeful. Mournfully, he signed the letter "Your ever dutiful and affectionate son." [19]

I V

A month later, Franklin was a member of a committee sent to Cambridge, Massachusetts, to confer with George Washington on reorganizing and supporting the American Army. In a letter he wrote to Richard Bache, from Cambridge, there is a hint of the conflict which the argument with William was creating in Franklin's spirit. "I am not terrified by the expense of this war should it continue ever so long," he grimly avowed. But a few lines later he admitted that he wished "most earnestly for peace, this war being a truly unnatural and mischievous one." [20]

On his way back from Cambridge, Franklin stopped at Warwick, Rhode Island, and picked up his sister Jane Mecom, who was still living in Catherine Ray Greene's crowded house. He took her back with him to Philadelphia. The pleasure this tragedy-ridden woman found in her brother's company was evident in Jane's letter to Catherine Greene. "My seat [in the coach] was exceeding easy and journey very pleasant. My dear brother's conversation was more than an equivalent to all the fine weather imaginable." Only once on the journey did Jane's touchy temper manifest itself. They were supposed to dine at Wethersfield, Connecticut, where Mrs. John Hancock was living. Jane no doubt looked forward to dazzling one of the grande dames of Boston society by appearing with her famous brother. But the two Franklins became so involved in their agreeable conversation that they forgot to tell the stagecoach driver to turn off at Wethersfield, and when they discovered their mistake, they were several miles beyond it, and the driver refused to go back. For Jane this was a "mortification." [21]

The two older Franklins stopped overnight at Perth Amboy, but Jane mentioned no additional mortification from that meeting. Father and son apparently forebore to continue their grim debate in front of Aunt Jane, who was burdened with so many troubles already. Writing back to Catherine Ray Greene, Jane described William's house as "very magnificient." Elizabeth Franklin wrote to Temple, toiling over his school books in Philadelphia, that they "had the happiness of my father's and Aunt Mecom's company last Tuesday night; we would willingly have detained them longer, but Pappa was anxious to get home. . . ." [22] There was not a hint in the letters of these two women about the ominous, ever-widening division between father and son. But William Franklin must have discussed with his father the momentous decision he had already made—to convene the New Jersey Assembly on November 15, 1775.

Other royal governors had either fled or been driven from their posts. But William Franklin had many advantages they lacked. One was the prestige of his name. Another was his long tenure in office. A third was his frequent declarations that the rights of the people and the prerogatives of the Crown were equally dear to him. Largely rural, with no major city in which agitators could prosper, and no newspaper to fan the flames, New Jersey had never had a strong revolutionary movement. When the revolutionary provincial congress laid taxes and drafted men into the militia, a reaction had swept the province during the fall of 1775 which made it difficult for the patriots to interfere with the governor's summons to the Assembly. Thus the colony relapsed into political schizophrenia, and William Franklin seized the opportunity to speak with a new, very dangerous voice.

Appearing before the assemblymen in Burlington on November 16, 1775, Governor Franklin discoursed on "the present unhappy situation of publick affairs," proclaiming his wish to say nothing to "endanger the harmony of the present session." He then proceeded to say a great deal that endangered the harmony of the entire American Revolution. He told the Assembly that "His Majesty laments your neglecting the resolution of the Commons of last February twentieth"—Lord North's conciliatory resolution, which the governor's father had already described as about as conciliatory as a highwayman brandishing a pistol in a stagecoach window. Boldly, Governor Franklin now proceeded to explain to the Assembly why he had not imitated other royal officials and fled to the protection of the nearest British warship. He did not wish the King to think that New Jersey was in "actual rebellion" as other states obviously were. The King was taking "all necessary steps" for putting down that rebellion, and Governor Franklin solemnly averred that he shuddered at the thought of exposing New Jersey to the royal heel. He begged the Assembly to "exert your influence likewise with the people, that they may not . . . give cause for the bringing such calamities on the province."

If they did not agree with him, and wanted him to get out, all they had to do was tell him. With a frankness which dazzled the uneasy legislators, he let them know he was well aware that "sentiments of independency are . . . openly avowed, and essays are already appearing in the publick papers to ridicule the people's fears of that horrid measure." Then, leading them artfully in his direction, he added, "If, as I hope, you have an abhorrence of such design, you will do your country an essential service by declaring it in so full and explicit terms as may discourage the attempt." [23]

Not a word was spoken by the Assembly against these sentiments from the royal governor. In part they were undoubtedly disarmed by William's frankness. But a more practical reason for their good humor soon became apparent. He announced that the King had finally granted a plea that New Jersey had been making annually for the better part of a decade—the province now had royal permission to print 100,000 pounds in bills of credit, which would serve as badly needed paper money. Part of this influx of cash was to be used to raise the salary of the governor and other civil servants in the province, and to help pay for the governor's new residence. On the twenty-ninth of November, the Assembly reacted to this royal munificence by appointing a committee to petition George III. Governor Franklin suggested they urge the King to "use his interposition to prevent the effusion of blood and to express the great desire this house hath to restoration of peace and harmony with the parent state on constitutional principles." Even more startling were resolutions of the Assembly, sent to the New Jersey delegates in the Continental Congress. One directed these delegates "not to give their assent to . . . any propositions . . . that may separate this colony from the mother country or change the form of government thereof." [24]

V

It was a truly incredible performance, and an enormous tribute to William Franklin's talents as a politician, to extract these measures from an American Assembly, sitting less than a half day's journey from the Continental Congress in Philadelphia. There, the business of the day was largely consumed in approving the Franklin Committee report reorganizing and enlarging George Washington's army, and worrying over the ominous report of another committee, surveying the situation of the American army that was attempting to bring Canada into the continental confederacy. Congress was also advising several colonies, among them New Hampshire, South Carolina, and Virginia, to go ahead and form their own local governments, and take no more orders from royal officials, who had either fled or, as in Virginia's case, had declared martial law and were attempting to organize a local army to suppress rebellion. Engulfed in this ever swifter current toward independence, the congressmen could not quite believe their ears when they heard what Governor Franklin and his Assembly were doing just across the Delaware River in Burlington. If New Jersey's petition got to the King, and he received it graciously and bestowed still more proofs of his generosity from his ample exchequer, the chances were all too good that other wavering colonies, such as New York and Maryland (both of whom had forbidden their delegates to vote for independence), would have second thoughts about their loyalty to the penniless Continental Congress.

John Adams, the American who had the keenest eye on the question, later estimated that about one-third of the people were for independence, one-third were opposed, and one-third were indifferent. At this point in the struggle, the pro-independent people were much fewer, probably no more than one-quarter, possibly one-fifth. If the King had even one or two opportunities to demonstrate his good will (which was to him dependent, of course, on a colony's "submission"), the deep wellsprings of feeling for England which were still a living reality in almost every American might have swiftly swept the independence men into a tiny, impotent minority.

Even more probable was the instantaneous jealousy that would seize every colony if New Jersey, then New York, then Maryland made separate petitions and won special favors from the King. The continental union, already demonstrably so fragile that Benjamin Franklin could not even persuade them to consider his Articles of Confederation, could vanish in the smoke of mutual recrimination, overnight. Almost single-handedly, William Franklin was daring to duel his father and the rest of the Continental Congress for the control of a continent. Seldom have men played for higher political and personal stakes. If he won, William Franklin could expect from a grateful King and Parliament those "highest favors" Lord Howe had dangled in front of his father. Simultaneously, he could enjoy the gratifying vision of himself as a peacemaker, albeit a submissive one.

But the men meeting in Congress at Philadelphia were equally aware of the stakes. Although they by no means agreed on whither they were marching—toward independence or eventual reconciliation—they were in total agreement on the necessity of maintaining a united front. The very day they heard the news of the New Jersey Assembly's petition and resolution, they forthwith:

> RESOLVED UNANIMOUSLY, *That in the present situation of affairs, it will be very dangerous to the liberties and welfare of America, if any Colony should separately petition the King or either House of Parliament.*[25]

Congress appointed a three-man committee, and ordered them to leave for New Jersey without delay to persuade the legislature to abandon their petition. The members of the committee were John Dickinson of Pennsylvania, George Wythe of Virginia and John Jay of New York.

If there was a low point in Franklin's life, it was December 4, 1775, the day this committee was formed. His chief political foe in Pennsylvania, John Dickinson, had been assigned by his fellow Americans to rescue the revolution (Franklin, at least, had no doubt that it was a revolution) from his Tory son. It reduced Franklin's political power in Pennsylvania—and in Congress—to something very close to zero. A man who could not persuade his own son to join the Cause—or at least stop him from threatening the entire fabric of American resistance— could hardly be respected as a political leader.

Dickinson, Wythe, and Jay appeared in Burlington, to William Franklin's vast rage and resentment, on December fifth, the day after they were appointed. They asked for permission to address the Assembly. Behind the scenes, Governor Franklin frantically lobbied with influential members, to persuade the assemblymen to refuse to listen. But this was asking too much of American legislators in late 1775. The Assembly granted permission, and Dickinson and his two companions took the floor. A highly effective orator, Dickinson begged the assemblymen to withdraw the petition, arguing that it was a capitulation to the British policy of divide and conquer. Only if they convinced Britain that they were not "a rope of sand" would Americans ever redress their grievances. Young John Jay made a more subtle suggestion. He pointed out that Congress had already presented Dickinson's "olive branch" petition to the King. Wouldn't it be better to wait and see what his Majesty did with that perfectly respectable plea before making one of their own? The assemblymen, not a little uncomfortable at being the subject of a unanimous rebuke from the Philadelphia Congress, seized on Jay's idea as a perfect out. They promptly resolved that their petition to the King "be referred" until the King replied to the olive-branch plea. Governor Franklin could only watch in silent frustration, while his daring attempt to build a backfire against independence flickered out. His consolation, a very minor one, was the prompt adjournment of the legislature, which left on the record the resolutions forbidding the state's congressional delegates to vote for independence.[26]

V I

Benjamin Franklin, meanwhile, was adding the power of his potent pen to his grim resolve to fight to a finish. He sent some witty statistics to his friend Joseph Priestley in England, knowing he would swiftly spread the story as a Franklin *bon mot*. "Britain, at the expense of three millions, has killed 150 Yankees this campaign which is 20,000 pounds a head. . . . During the same time 60,000 children have been born in America." He urged Priestley to have their mutual friend, Richard Price, apply "his mathematical head" to calculating "the time and expense necessary to kill us all." To Member of Parliament David Hartley, he warned, "You are insensible of the Italian adage, that there is no *little enemy. . . . ."* [27]

On December 14, 1775, the Pennsylvania *Evening Post* published a news item which summed up better than anything else Franklin's personal attitude toward the struggle. It was his favorite propaganda device, the hoax.

> *The following inscription was made out three years ago on the cannon near which the ashes of President Bradshaw were lodged, on the top of a high hill near Martha Bray in Jamaica, to avoid the rage against the Regicides exhibited at the Restoration:*

STRANGER
Ere thou pass, contemplate this cannon,
Nor regardless be told
That near its base lies deposited
the dust of
JOHN BRADSHAW,
Who, nobly superior to all selfish regard,
Despising alike the pageantry of courtly splendour,
The blast of calumny and the terrors of royal vengeance,
Presided in the illustrious band
of heroes and patriots
who fairly and openly judged
CHARLES STUART
Tyrant of England
To a public and exemplary death;
Thereby presenting to the amazed world,
And transmitting down, through applauding ages,
The most glorious example
Of unshaken virtue, love of freedom and impartial justice,
Ever exhibited on the blood-stained theatre of human action.
O, reader!
Pass not on till thou has blessed his memory,
And never—never forget
THAT REBELLION TO TYRANTS IS OBEDIENCE TO GOD. [28]

John Bradshaw was not even buried in Jamaica. But the hoax was so successful it passed into history books, and was quoted as fact by numerous historians in the nineteenth century. Franklin admitted his authorship only to a handful of like-minded contemporaries, such as Thomas Jefferson and John Adams. Jefferson later adopted the last line for his personal seal.

Franklin did more than write tough letters and brilliant propaganda during that same month of December, 1775, when his son was doing his utmost to torpedo the American cause. Ever since his return home, he had been working at a pace which might have killed a far younger man. He was a member of the Committee of Safety for the State of Pennsylvania, responsible for putting the province in a state of defense against potential British incursions. In this guise he bought powder and conferred on the manufacture of saltpetre, and pondered the problem of blocking the Delaware River with underwater barriers made of logs and iron, which he also probably designed. In Congress, he served on no less than ten different committees, in addition to his duties as America's first Postmaster General. He had to worry about the Indians of "the Middle Department" along Pennsylvania's and Virginia's borders, advise Congress on ways and means to protect the trade of the colonies, draw up a report on Lord North's conciliatory proposition, and confer with generals and engineers on supplying and equipping the American Army. Americans were so short of powder, Franklin recommended the use of pikes and bows and arrows. A well-aimed arrow, he observed, was at least as accurate as the contemporary musket, which was grossly unreliable except at point-blank range. "My time," Franklin told Priestley, "was never more fully employed. In the morning at six, I am at the Committee of Safety . . . which holds till near nine, when I am at the Congress, and that sits till after four in the afternoon." [29] No wonder John Adams noted that Franklin, during the sessions of Congress, was "a great part of the time fast asleep in his chair."

V I I

By far the most important committee on which Franklin served began its work during that same painful month of December, 1775. In the closing days of November, Congress had appointed Franklin, Benjamin

Harrison of Virginia, Thomas Johnson of Maryland, John Dickinson of
Pennsylvania, and John Jay of New York to a secret committee with
"the sole purpose of corresponding with our friends in Great Britain,
Ireland and other parts of the world." Another secret group, the Committee of Commerce, headed by Robert Morris, was to handle the business of buying war materiel. Both were momentous steps for Congress.
Franklin had thought about seeking foreign aid more than once, and
expressed grave doubts as to its wisdom. In London, he had advised
Josiah Quincy, Jr., against it. The logical country from whom to seek
aid was France, and Franklin had been an Englishman too long to look
on such an alliance with equanimity. Twice in his long life, he had helped
fight the French. He had seen first-hand the French and Indian slaughter
on Pennsylvania's frontiers. But he had warned several English friends,
such as Priestley, that it was "natural" to think of a foreign alliance "if
we are pressed." News from England, in December, 1775, made it clear
that immense pressure was on its way. The British were, in fact, hiring
German troops to bolster their army. The King had rejected the olive-
branch petition and declared the colonies in rebellion. There seemed to
be no longer the slightest doubt that all-out war had begun.

A few days after—or perhaps before—this news arrived, Francis
Daymon, the French-born librarian of the Philadelphia Library, paid a
discreet call on Dr. Franklin to inform him that there was another
Frenchman, one Achard de Bonvouloir, in Philadelphia, who was
anxious to meet him. Although he called himself an "Antwerp merchant"
and insisted he had come to America "out of curiosity," Daymon's
raised eyebrows made it clear to Franklin that there was much more to
Mr. Bonvouloir than his public image. There was a strong probability
that he was an agent of the French government. Franklin instantly arranged for a clandestine meeting between the Frenchman and the secret
committee of foreign correspondence. Philadelphia was swarming with
British sympathizers and the touchy feelings of so many people about
the question of independence made dealing with the representative of a
foreign power—particularly France—doubly dangerous. The Americans
and the secret agent met by night, each man traveling alone to the
rendezvous by a different route.

The conversation, as Bonvouloir reported it, was thick with evasions
and subterfuges. The first thing the Americans wanted to see was some
written instructions, to make sure this man was not a British agent, collecting information that could hang them. Alas, Bonvouloir had only

verbal instructions, and even these were so vague that he could make them no offers. He could only promise "to render them every service that could *depend* on him, without making himself in any way responsible for events." Bonvouloir spoke of "acquaintances" to whom he could pass on requests, with the assurance that these mystery men would keep everything confidential.

Franklin, as the chief spokesman for the committee, ignored this cloud of diplomatic chaff and got to the point. Would France help America? What would be the conditions under which she would give aid?

Again, the secret agent zigzagged. He thought "France wished them well." Whether she would aid them—"that might happen." But he knew nothing about terms. If they were inclined to make proposals, his "reliable acquaintances" would be happy to present them—but nothing more.

What about sending a deputy with full powers to France? This made Monsieur Bonvouloir very nervous. The idea was "precipitous, and even hazardous. . . . It was slippery business in the face of the English." But he was willing to pass on the inquiry, and ". . . perhaps obtain a response which would determine which course to pursue." He reiterated that he was only a private individual, "a traveler out of curiosity." If his "acquaintances" could be of any service, he would be "much pleased." But he could guarantee only one thing—his ability to keep a secret.

Three times during the month of December, Franklin and the committee met by night with this master of double talk. In spite of the fact that he produced not a scrap of written credentials, Franklin decided that candor was worth the risk and gave him a remarkable insider's view of the crisis at this point in time. The Americans thought they had men and munitions enough to withstand the British Army. But they desperately wished for naval protection against the British fleet. In October, the British had followed up their destruction of Charlestown by burning Falmouth, Massachusetts. Only France or Spain could give them protection against British ships of the line. Franklin shrewdly intimated that they had not quite made up their mind which one to ask.

This almost made Bonvouloir shed his curious traveler's cover. He argued vehemently against Spain and discoursed on the numerous advantages that France could offer. Franklin, more certain than ever that he was dealing with an authentic agent, told him that it was too soon to seek France's aid openly. At the moment, it would "excite un-

easiness to have a foreign nation interfere." Better to wait until the beginning of the campaign when the people saw British warships and
armies on the attack. That will soon change everyone's mind, and make
them "feel the necessity of being helped." All they wanted for the moment from France was as many muskets as possible and two good en-
gineering officers to help them construct fortifications.

Bonvouloir replied that two engineers, and even more, would be no
problem. As for the muskets and even ammunition, that was "a matter
between one merchant and another" and he saw "no great difficulty
about it." But he reiterated that he could guarantee nothing. He was
"nobody." He had "serviceable acquaintances—that was all." [30]

Franklin was too shrewd to bet all his money on this evasive gentleman. While he and the rest of the secret committee were conferring with
Bonvouloir, he was simultaneously writing to Arthur Lee in London,
telling him of the committee's formation and asking him to find out
"the disposition of foreign powers towards us." Franklin put Lee in
touch with an old friend, Charles W. F. Dumas, a Swiss intellectual who
lived at The Hague, in Holland, and was an expert on international
law. Franklin asked him to serve as a transmitter of Lee's dispatches.
Franklin knew that it would soon be impossible for Lee to send information directly from England to America. He also asked Dumas to set
up a listening post in The Hague, to find out if "there is any state or
power in Europe who would be willing to enter into an alliance with us
for the benefit of our commerce, which amounted, before the war, near
seven million sterling per annum." As for arms and ammunition, "any
merchant who would venture to send ships laden with those articles
might make great profit; such is the demand in every colony." [31]

VIII

While Frankin launched these first probes toward Europe, Congress
was attacking other problems. On January 2, 1776, they passed a resolution which was to cause Franklin acute personal pain. They called on

local authorities in the various colonies to "frustrate the mischievous machinations and restrain the wicked practices" of those "unworthy Americans" who persisted in supporting the royal government. Three days after this resolution passed, it was in the hands of William Alexander, the son of Franklin's old friend, who was now commanding the militia in eastern New Jersey. Alexander, who still claimed the Scottish title of Lord Stirling, yet paradoxically supported the American cause, had a personal grudge against Governor William Franklin. They had engaged in an acrimonious public debate when Stirling accepted his commission in the state militia. Governor Franklin had ordered him to resign from his council, thereby forcing Alexander to commit himself wholeheartedly to the revolutionary cause. This made him resent intensely Governor Franklin's fence straddling, and the moment he saw the Congressional resolution, he ordered his men to seize the governor's mail. Before nightfall, a fat packet addressed to Lord Dartmouth, the colonial secretary, and marked "Secret and Confidential," was in Alexander's hands.

To a vehement pro-American—and by now the pugnacious Alexander was definitely in that category—the governor's mail was most alarming reading. William told the colonial secretary that independence was a plot by a small minority which was being conducted "by such degrees and under such pretences as not to be perceived by the people in general till too late for resistance." Also enclosed was a thorough report of the New Jersey Assembly's meeting, including the resolutions against independence, and summaries of the speeches Dickinson, Jay, and Wythe had made to persuade the assemblymen to retract their petition for reconciliation. There were also extracts from the proceedings of the New Jersey Provincial Congress and a great deal of material from colonial newspapers, underscoring the prevalence of radical propaganda. Much of this was hanging evidence if the British won the war.[32]

Alexander immediately ordered a contingent of militia to head for Perth Amboy. About 2 A.M. on the night of January eighth, the colonel in command, apparently on Alexander's orders, turned out all his men, surrounded the governor's house as if it were a fortress under siege and demanded a guarantee from the governor that he would not leave the town. William assured him that he had no intention of leaving "unless compelled by violence."

On January ninth, William's correspondence with the colonial secretary and Alexander's report were laid before the Continental Congress.

Also included in the packet was a letter from another Perth Amboy citizen, Cortlandt Skinner, which contained strong loyalist sentiments. Congress ordered Skinner seized for interrogation by the New Jersey Committee of Safety. But they did nothing whatsoever about Governor Franklin. The Congressmen were apparently as baffled and embarrassed by the situation as Benjamin Franklin himself. After some talk by Alexander about confining William in a private home in Elizabeth, he was permitted to remain in his own residence in Perth Amboy.[33]

Franklin apparently said nothing about the mortifying incident to anyone at home. William Temple Franklin wrote a chatty letter to his father on January fifteenth without a single mention of his difficulties. He got back a bitter blast, describing the whole nasty episode in detail. Instinctively, William dueled his father for Temple's loyalty by stressing Elizabeth Franklin's reaction to "being awakened with a violent knocking at the door about two o'clock in the morning and seeing the house surrounded by a large party of men armed with guns and bayonets." Her fright had "nearly deprived her of her life. She is not yet perfectly recovered . . . and I am really apprehensive that another alarm of the like nature will put an end to her life." William said he had tried to "prevail on her to go either to Barbados or England where she has friends and relatives who will treat her with that kindness and respect she has always treated mine. But she is not willing to leave me on any consideration. She has no relatives of her own in this country to whom she can resort, or from whom she can receive any comfort in a time of distress; and she cannot but take notice that mine do not at present seem disposed to give themselves any concern about her." By now Temple must have known the story of his father's birth and unhappy childhood. There was more than an echo of it in his words, when he told Temple, "It gives me pleasure to find you inquire so affectionately for Mrs. Franklin. She has a very sincere regard for you, and you cannot but have seen that she is happy in every opportunity of expressing it. Let what will happen, I hope you will never be wanting in a grateful sense of her kindness to you." [34]

Temple was deeply disturbed by his father's letter, and wrote an immediate answer, full of apologies and sympathy. But Benjamin Franklin did not communicate with his stubborn son. He had obviously decided that the political chasm separating them could only be filled by cold, absolute silence.

IX

That chasm widened in the next month. Thomas Paine, the bankrupt ex-tax collector and corset maker whom Franklin had recommended to friends in Philadelphia as "an ingenious, worthy young man," published on January 10, 1776, a two-shilling pamphlet of forty-seven pages called "Common Sense." It was a devastating attack on the two ideas that still prevented most Americans from voting for independence— loyalty to the King and the British Constitution. The pamphlet was a sensational success. In less than three months, 120,000 copies were sold. Many people thought Franklin had written it, but he vehemently denied it. The idea was, however, suggested to Paine by young Dr. Benjamin Rush of Philadelphia, a Franklin disciple, and Paine sent Franklin the first copy off the press.

Sensing a strong swing in public opinion, Franklin once more tried to seize the leadership of Congress by offering, on February fifteenth, a resolution to open the ports of America to ships of all nations. But it was voted down because, in John Adams' words, too many members considered it as "a bold step to independence." Nevertheless, Franklin and other members of both secret committees negotiated with another Frenchman, a merchant named Penet, who had arrived in Philadelphia as a private entrepreneur, eager to sell guns and ammunition to the Americans. Unlike John Adams and Samuel Adams and other members of Congress, who filled their diaries and letters with lamentations over Congressional timidity and hesitation on the subject of independence, Franklin maintained a calm silence on the subject. He never seems to have had the slightest doubt that independence would come in due time, once the King and his ministers fully revealed how little genuine interest they had in reconciliation on any other basis but total submission. Another, perhaps stronger reason for Franklin's certainty was the knowledge that he and the other members of the secret committees (on which the Adamses, because of their unpopularity, did not serve) were already conducting themselves as representatives of an independent state.

On March third, Franklin's committee took another large stride in this direction by appointing Silas Deane to go abroad and negotiate directly with the French. Deane was a Connecticut merchant who had served in the first two sessions of Congress, but had not been reelected to the current session. Energetic, with a reputation as a shrewd business-man, Deane was thirty-nine, and an apparently dedicated independ-ence man. Franklin wrote his diplomatic instructions. They were vivid testimony to the almost total dependence of Congress on Benjamin Franklin's contacts abroad. Appearing in the character of a "merchant," Deane was told to confer with Franklin's French friends, notably Barbé Dubourg, translator and editor of Franklin's works. Franklin had already written Dubourg asking his help, and he assured Deane that he would find him "a man prudent, faithful, secret, intelligent in affairs, and capable of giving you very sage advice." He would help Deane apply for an interview with the Count de Vergennes, the French foreign minister.

Deane was ordered to tell the Count that "there is a great appearance we shall come to a total separation from Great Britain" and, therefore, Congress regarded France as "the power whose friendship it would be fittest for us to obtain and cultivate." Deane was to dangle in front of Vergennes the prospect of winning a "great part of our commerce" which had contributed so much to Britain's "late wealth and impor-tance." If Deane found Vergennes reserved, under no circumstances was he to press him. Here Franklin had to descend to minutia. If an aggressive Connecticut Yankee such as Deane displayed the sense of equality he undoubtedly felt toward a European nobleman, the results would be disastrous. Deane was told "to shorten your visit," tell the Count where he was staying in Paris, and assure him "knowing how precious his time is, you do not presume to ask another audience; but that, if he should have commands for you, you will, upon the least notice, immediately wait upon him." Finally, Deane was told to contact Charles Dumas in Holland, and Edward Bancroft in London. Obviously Franklin was forced to function as a combination secretary of state and tutor.[35]

X

Congress next handed Franklin another diplomatic assignment. Affairs in Canada seemed to be sliding toward chaos and total collapse. The American Army had been repulsed in a New Year's Eve attack on Quebec, and that city was still holding out against a siege. But the Americans were getting neither food nor reinforcements from the 80,000 French-Canadians in the province, who seemed to suspect the Americans were military adventurers at best, and potential enemies—because of their religious differences—at worst. Congress had done nothing to allay this latter suspicion—and was, in fact, largely responsible for it. In protesting the Quebec Act in the address to the people of Great Britain (October 21, 1774) Congress had declared, "Nor can we suppress our astonishment that a British Parliament should ever consent to establish in that country a religion that has deluged your island in blood and dispersed impiety, bigotry, persecution, murder and rebellion through every part of the world." Five days later, Congress had about-faced and issued an address to the Canadians, declaring they could not imagine how "difference of religion will prejudice you against a hearty amity with us." Such double talk failed to convince the leading French-Canadians, particularly the "noblesse" and the clergy.

Congress decided that the only hope of clearing up the unfortunate misunderstanding was a direct appeal from a Congress committee. Franklin was chosen for his knowledge of the French language and his reputation in France. With him was elected Samuel Chase of Maryland, as a representative of a province where the Catholic religion was tolerated. The third member was another Marylander, Charles Carroll, a wealthy Catholic who was an enthusiastic patriot. To further bolster the committee's appeal, Charles Carroll was asked to persuade his cousin, the Reverend John Carroll, a priest who was living on the family estates, to go along. Both the Carrolls had been educated in France and spoke fluent French.

The appointment caused Franklin to make a decision he had been thinking about for some time. He resigned from the Pennsylvania Committee of Safety, and from the State Assembly, to which he had also been elected. He said he was "unequal to so much business," but later developments suggest that there may also have been a subtle political motive in this resignation. John Dickinson was firmly in control of the State Assembly and was punctiliously insisting that no man could be seated without first taking his oath of allegiance to the King. It was one of several symptoms that Dickinson had begun to display, suggesting that when it came to a crunch on the issue of independence, he was not dependable. Franklin, who served with him on the secret committee and had ample opportunity to know through numerous mutual acquaintances that Dickinson's wife and mother were both urging him to back still another gesture of reconciliation, had no desire to give his old enemy a chance to use his name and prestige. It was bad enough to be voted into oblivion as a minority voice on the Pennsylvania delegation to Congress. Why should he let Dickinson be able to say that the Assembly, speaking as the voice of the people of Pennsylvania, backed his wavering stance, even though Benjamin Franklin was a member? In such a situation, it was far better to abstain and let Dickinson go his unsteady way, alone.

Before he left for Canada, Franklin presided at a highly unusual gathering which took place at the Indian Queen Tavern on March 20, 1776. It was a meeting of the American division of the Grand Ohio Company. It was not, really, strictly speaking, the Grand Ohio Company any longer. As the breach between the two countries widened, the American members decided to revive the old Indiana Company, Ohio's predecessor, and use that façade to press their claims to the million and a half acres of land the Iroquois had ceded them. With America and England on the brink of war, one might think that this relic of Franklin's last triumph in British politics would have been abandoned. But the speculators, particularly Samuel Wharton and William Trent, insisted that the corpse was still alive, or could at least be restored to life by the breath of that new source of power, the Continental Congress. Wharton remained in England to maintain communication with Thomas Walpole and his friends. Trent returned to America, and busily collected opinions from Congressmen, such as Patrick Henry, supporting the Ohio Company's claims. Trent was also authorized by Wharton to offer eight members of Congress a half share each if they would promote the idea that the company had a right to the land, not only on the basis of the cession of the Privy Council, but on the undoubted fact that they had already purchased it from the Indians. They flourished legal opinions from prominent English lawyers, such as Sergeant Glynn, maintaining that the Indians were the ones who owned the land and any cession on their part constituted a clear title. [36]

Absent, of course, was William Franklin, under virtual house arrest in Perth Amboy. But he would have boycotted the meeting anyway. He was convinced that this new policy was a mistake and would only injure their chances of winning the grant from the Crown. He still clung to the King as the fountainhead of wealth and power. But his father and the other American members of the company were now indifferent to the largesse of George III. Briskly, Joseph Galloway was elected president and Thomas Wharton, vice president. George Morgan was appointed secretary of a land office and empowered to sell 400-acre lots.

The meeting was a commentary on the state of suspended animation in which England and America were poised, during the first six months of 1776. Thomas Paine's denunciation of kings and two-house Parliaments was sweeping the continent, and the King had declared the colonies outside his protection, forbidden all nations to trade with them and authorized the seizure of American ships on the high seas. Yet all these events were words, not actions. Franklin, who was probably doing more than any other man except George Washington to turn the words into acts, saw no conflict in transferring the idea of a western colony from the sovereignty of England to the sovereignty of the United States. He was probably skeptical about its chances, and he certainly no longer had any vision of himself or his son presiding over it. At seventy, he obviously looked upon the project as part of the inheritance he hoped to leave his grandchildren. He arranged to have his son-in-law, Richard Bache, made one of the company's three trustees.

A few days later he departed for Canada with the two Maryland Carrolls and Samuel Chase. The two Catholics must have wondered how they would be treated by Dr. Franklin, who had, like most other eighteenth-century men of science, a reputation as a freethinker. They soon found out that Franklin was the last man in the world to feel, much less exhibit, any kind of religious prejudice. When he heard from Chase the stirring story of Charles Carroll's role in spurring Maryland's spirit of resistance (which included burning a tea ship—something not even Boston had dared to do, and which, to Maryland's chagrin, is rarely mentioned in Revolutionary histories), they became instant friends. Soon Charles Carroll was writing home to his father, "Docr. Franklin is a most engaging and entertaining companion of a sweet, even and lively temper, full of facetious stories and always applied with judgment and introduced apropos—He is a man of extensive reading, deep thought and curious in all his inquiries: his political knowledge is not inferior to his literary and philosophical. In short, I am quite charmed with him: even his age makes all these happy endowments more interesting, uncommon and captivating. . . ." [37]

The good talk and abundant Irish wit provided by Franklin's traveling companions were the only pleasant aspect of the trip. Otherwise, for Franklin it was a nightmare from the day they began plowing up the Hudson in a cramped sloop, a chill northeast wind blowing cold gusts of rain in their faces. Near present-day Tarrytown, a particularly violent gust split the mainsail, and they had to spend a day and a half huddling below decks in Thunder Hill Bay. It took five weary days to reach Albany, where Major General Philip Schuyler greeted them and offered them the hospitality of his handsome town house. The sight of the general's two daughters, Betsy and Peggy, described by Charles Carroll as "lively, agreeable, black-eyed girls," revived Franklin momentarily, but the following day the general insisted on dragging the commissioners thirty-six miles in a wagon over unbelievably wretched roads to his country home in Saratoga.

Already worn down by his dawn-to-dusk schedule during the past six months on the Pennsylvania Committee of Safety, and in Congress, Franklin all but collapsed with exhaustion at Saratoga. For a few days he thought he was dying and wrote letters of farewell to old friends, such as Josiah Quincy, Sr., of Boston.[38] A stopover of seven days and the constant attention of the charming Mrs. Schuyler restored his strength somewhat. But a few days before they resumed the journey, no less than six inches of April snow fell, and it was still lying thick on the hills when they slogged forward on horseback for two days to reach the shores of Lake George. There they boarded thirty-foot open boats, fitted with awnings, and began a fifteen-day trip up Lake George and Lake Champlain through waters that were frequently thick with ice. Not until the twenty-ninth of April did they arrive in Montreal, the last day spent in jolting local carriages known as caleches. "I never traveled through worse roads or in worse carriages," Charles Carroll wrote in his journal.[39]

The man who greeted them on behalf of the American Army was Benedict Arnold, recently made a brigadier general. After several pleasant hours of tea-drinking and an elegant supper which the commissioners were too weary to appreciate, they retired to the home of Mr. and Mrs. Thomas Walker, ardent advocates of America's cause.

The next day the commissioners had a conference with General Arnold and his staff, and it was instantly apparent that they had traveled over five hundred miles in vain. The French-Canadians were daily growing more hostile, and the appearance of a Congressional committee sporting a leading Catholic layman and a Catholic priest was not going to change their minds. Bishop Jean Briant, the ruling Catholic prelate, had remained inside Quebec throughout the American siege, issuing strident pastorals forbidding the sacraments to any Catholic who sided with the *Bostonnais,* his favorite term for the American rebels. The Bishop repeatedly told his people that the Americans were traitors and religious hypocrites. The actions of more than a few Americans had done nothing to erase this accusation. General David Wooster of Connecticut had closed Montreal's churches on Christmas Eve and informed the committee of Catholics who called on him, "I regard you all as enemies and rascals." Bishop Briant had forbidden any priest to show the slightest courtesy to Father John Carroll. He had a letter of introduction to the Reverend Pierre Floquet, who had, along with Carroll, been a member of the recently abolished Jesuit order. Floquet invited Father Carroll to dinner and permitted him to say Mass in his house. The French priest was instantly suspended by the bishop—which meant that he was unable to say Mass or hear confessions—because of his *"Bostonnais* heart." [40]

Franklin donated 353 pounds of his own money in gold to the starving American Army. But they needed something more in the order of 20,000 pounds. The men were in rags, shivering in the harsh cold of the wintry Canadian spring. Franklin himself found the cold almost unbearable. He bought a marten fur hat to replace his tricorn, but it did him little good. His sturdy old body began to show signs of breaking down under the physical and mental stress. His legs swelled alarmingly, and boils broke out in a number of places. Twelve days after he arrived, he acknowledged the total hopelessness of the situation by deciding to go home. His two younger cohorts, Samuel Chase and Charles Carroll, could stay behind and make whatever decisions needed making to rescue the American Army from disaster.

Sick as he obviously was, Franklin nevertheless left Montreal immediately to make the exhausting journey back down the lakes and the Hudson, alone. The next day, while he was waiting in acute misery at the

American-held fort of St. John's, at the head of Lake Champlain, Father John Carroll arrived and quietly asked Franklin if he could accompany him home. The affection he had won from these two Catholics had, one suspects, not a little to do with this decision. Father Carroll acted as nurse as well as companion as the open boats beat their way down Lake Champlain and Lake George to Saratoga. At Albany the hospitality of the Schuyler family restored Franklin again. He and Father Carroll finally reached New York on May 27, 1776. He wrote the commissioners they had left behind in Canada, "I . . . think I could hardly have got along so far, but for Mr. Carroll's friendly assistance and tender care of me." [41]

He continued to be tormented by boils, but the swelling in his legs began to disappear, to be replaced by an attack of the gout. However, he was not too sick to have tea with an old friend in New York, a Mrs. Barrow, whose husband had joined the loyalists aboard the King's ships in the harbor. Franklin had paid her a visit on the way to Canada, and she had told him that she feared her house and person might be abused by the Americans because of her husband's politics. Franklin had interceded with George Washington to make sure she was not molested, and now he called again to ask "how our people had behaved to her." She told him everyone had treated her with the utmost decorum and respect.

"I'm glad of that," said Franklin. "Why, if they had used you ill I would have turned Tory."

"In that case," she said, with a twinkle in her eye, "I wish they had." [42]

X I

In Philadelphia, Franklin could only reiterate to Congress what he had already told them in a letter from Canada—that unless the army got money immediately, it would have either to "starve, plunder, or surrender." Although in his exhausted condition, and with his gouty feet, he could do little in Congress, he undoubtedly listened with enthusiasm to the news of what had been happening there. On April sixth, Congress had taken a major step toward independence by opening American ports to the commerce and ships of all nations, except those of Great Britain and her dependencies. On May tenth, they had passed an even more significant resolution—one that was to have special consequences for Franklin. After more than a year of warfare, Congress declared "it was absolutely irreconcilable to reason and good conscience for the people of these colonies now to take the oaths and affirmations necessary for the support of any government under the Crown of Great Britain, and it is necessary that the exercise of every kind of authority under the said Crown should be totally suppressed, and all the powers of government exerted under the authority of the people of the colonies . . ." [43] This swept away with one breath every vestige of royal government, from governors to Assemblies, because all of them required an oath of loyalty to the King. From all over the continent, Tom Paine's propaganda and the unyielding menaces of Great Britain were producing a "torrent" (in John Adams' words) of letters calling on Congress to declare America's independence.

But in New Jersey, William Franklin, still under what amounted to house arrest, declined to agree with either Congress or the American people. Instead, on May thirtieth, he issued a call for the New Jersey Assembly to meet in Perth Amboy on June twentieth. He had received word from the new colonial secretary, Lord George Germain, that commissioners empowered to negotiate a peace were en route from England. Playing the old game of divide and conquer, Germain did not bother to inform the Continental Congress, but instead hoped that each colony would negotiate with the commissioners separately. Unfortunately for Governor Franklin, the third Provincial Congress of New Jersey convened on June tenth and promptly resolved that the "late Governor's proclamation was null and void." The following day they resolved that William's proclamation was "in direct contempt and violation of the resolve of the Continental Congress." This meant he was "an enemy of the liberties of this country" and should be placed under arrest. His salary which, astonishingly, he was still being paid by New Jersey was ordered "from henceforth to cease." Then, shifting to a more humane tone, Congress urged the arresting officers to conduct themselves "with all the delicacy and tenderness which the nature of the business could possibly admit." If Governor Franklin agreed to sign a parole, guaranteeing his good conduct, he would be permitted to live unmolested on his farm at Rancocas Creek below Burlington.

But Governor Franklin was totally uncooperative. He told the militia officer who arrested him that he rejected the parole "with the contempt such an insult deserved from one who has the honor to represent His Majesty." [44] The militia men took him to Burlington for a hearing before a committee of the Congress. He warned his escort that they were acting "at their peril," and refused to answer questions before this "illegal assembly which had usurped the government of the King." He told the committee of the Assembly, chaired by the Reverend John Witherspoon, president of Princeton, that they could "do as you please and make the best of it." The assemblymen informed the Continental Congress that William was "a virulent enemy to this country" and described his "gross and insolent" behavior in detail. On Monday, June twenty-fourth, the Continental Congress resolved that "William Franklin be sent under guard to Governor Trumbull [Connecticut]." By this time, William, though still defiant, was physically sick. The New Jersey Congress refused to admit that he was too ill to travel, and the governor wrote a bitter letter to his son Temple, telling the boy that their "low mightinesses with great difficulty were persuaded by some friends of mine to postpone my departure till tomorrow morning, when I must go (I suppose) dead or alive. Two of their members, who are doctors, came to examine me to see if my sickness was not feigned. Hypocrites always suspect hypocrisy in others.

"God bless you, my dear boy; be dutiful and attentive to your grandfather, to whom you owe great obligations. Love Mrs. Franklin for she loves you, and will do all she can for you if I should never return more. If we survive the present storm, we may all meet and enjoy the sweets of peace with greater relish." [45]

The governor was obviously still fighting for Temple's allegiance, and there is considerable evidence that he was winning, even before his arrest. While Benjamin Franklin was in Canada, Temple complained to his father that numerous people in Philadelphia, including Franklin's son-in-law, Richard Bache, treated him with something less than cordiality. Apparently Temple had made the mistake of expressing some support for his father's stand. The boy had spent the spring recess in Perth Amboy with William and Elizabeth, and thereafter sent them a steady stream of letters from Philadelphia, as well as newspapers and pamphlets arguing both sides of the crisis.

Throughout the last two weeks in June, while William was being arrested and transported to Connecticut, Benjamin Franklin used his gout as a good excuse to avoid attending Congress. He took little or no part in the strenuous politicking that raged throughout that month, as pro-independence men, led by John Adams, struggled to line up the votes needed to pass a declaration. On June seventh, Richard Henry Lee of Virginia had introduced a resolution declaring "that these united colonies are and of right ought to be, free and independent states." But after two days of argument, it was evident that there was still no unanimity on the issue, and further debate was postponed until July first. In the meantime, a committee was directed to prepare a declaration of independence. Franklin was named one of the members of that committee, and because of his worldwide reputation, both as a scientist and an author, he might, at first glance, seem to have been the logical man to write it. But the embarrassment of his Tory son seriously damaged his appeal as a revolutionary spokesman. So the committee members decided it made more political sense to give the job to thirty-three-year-old Thomas Jefferson of Virginia, the largest of the thirteen colonies, and a delegate without personal liabilities.

Other things were happening in Pennsylvania that Franklin must have watched with the greatest interest. Knowing his penchant for working behind the scenes, it is almost impossible to believe that he did not, in fact, have something to do with these local events. Mass meetings and other forms of public pressure had battered the Pennsylvania Assembly throughout the month of June, until John Dickinson lost complete control and on June fourteenth, the Assembly resolved to permit Pennsylvania's Congressional delegates to vote as they saw fit on independence. But by this time, independence-minded Pennsylvanians were so disgusted with the Assembly that they began organizing a movement for a Constitutional Convention to meet in July.

This upheaval swept away almost the entire base of John Dickinson's political support, and when he rose in Congress on July first to give a fervent speech against a vote for independence at this time, everyone was keenly aware that the Assembly, which had sent him and his hand-picked delegation (except for Franklin) to Congress, was practically abolished, and most Pennsylvanians had shown themselves to be wholeheartedly in favor of independence. On the morning of July second, when it became apparent that the Pennsylvania delegation to Congress was the only group still in opposition (New York abstained because it had no instructions from its Assembly), Dickinson conceded his political impotence by staying home, and Robert Morris, one of his followers, did likewise. Meanwhile, Franklin had persuaded staid John Morton, an old acquaintance who had served many years in the Pennsylvania Assembly with him, to swing his vote to join him and James Wilson and declare Pennsylvania for independence by a majority of three to two. Ironically, Morton had, only a month before, written a letter which contained a reference to Benjamin Franklin's personal situation. "The contest is horrid. Parents against children, children against parents." [46] But now, under the weight of Franklin's example, and the arguments of John Adams, he voted, in a voice tight with anguish, for independence.

Next Congress turned to the Declaration that Thomas Jefferson had been preparing. Jefferson had shown his draft of the Declaration to the other members of the committee. Franklin had made only a few minor changes in the wording. Perhaps the most important was where Jefferson had said, "We hold these truths to be sacred and undeniable—" Franklin crossed out "sacred and undeniable" and substituted "self-evident."

Franklin made several other changes, equally brief and effective, but most of these were eliminated in the ruthless editing job Congress performed on Jefferson's masterpiece. A long passage condemning the slave trade was struck out at the insistence of the Deep South, and an even longer diatribe against the British people was excised because it was deemed impolitic to alienate American supporters in England. A sharp rebuke aimed at the use of "Scottish mercenaries" was eliminated when several Scottish-Americans in Congress expressed their indignation. Franklin happened to be sitting beside Jefferson while this verbal surgery was being performed, and he could see that the sensitive young Virginian was undergoing severe mental anguish over what seemed to him crass mutilation of his document.

When it was over, and the final, considerably shortened version, had won a vote of approval, Franklin tried to console the mortified Jefferson. "I have made it a rule," he said, "whenever in my power to avoid becoming the draftsman of papers to be reviewed by a public body." To explain why, he told Jefferson a story from his journeyman printer days. One of his friends, an apprentice hatter, had decided to open a shop for himself. "His first concern was to have a handsome signboard with a proper inscription. He composed it in these words: *John Thompson, hatter, makes and sells hats for ready money,* with a figure of a hat subjoined. But he thought he would submit it to his friends for their amendments." The first man he showed it to thought the word "hatter" was superfluous because it was followed by the words "makes hats." Thompson agreed and struck it out. The next friend observed that the word "makes" might as well be omitted, because the customers would not care who made the hats, as long as they were good ones. Thompson agreed and struck it out. A third friend suggested eliminating "for ready money" because none of the local merchants sold on credit. Again Thompson bowed to the will of the majority, and now he had a sign which said: "John Thompson sells hats." "Sells hats," said his next friend, "why nobody will expect you to give them away. What then is the use of that word?" Again poor Thompson conceded. Moments later, the word "hats" went into oblivion when another friend pointed out that there was one painted on the board. And so he was left with a sign that said: "John Thompson" beneath the painted hat.[47]

It was like Franklin to tell a joke at the moment when he was voting for a declaration that would make him a traitor, liable to be hanged, drawn and quartered under English law. Contrary to the myth, however, no one actually signed the Declaration on July fourth. Instead, it was publicly proclaimed in the State House Yard on July eighth. Not until August second was a final copy, engrossed on parchment, signed by the members of Congress. Then, Franklin is supposed to have made another witticism that is more imperishably connected with his name. John Hancock, after placing his large scrawl at the head of the document, reportedly said, "We must be unanimous; there must be no pulling different ways; we must all hang together."

"Yes," Franklin replied, "we must indeed all hang together, or most assuredly we shall all hang separately."

It is something Franklin may well have said, but long years of searching by dozens of historians have exhumed no credible evidence for it. It was undoubtedly current in Philadelphia at the time. On April 14, 1776, Carter Braxton of Virginia wrote to a friend: "It is a true saying of a wit—We must hang together or hang separately." [48]

Such humor came naturally to Franklin. But there is another more profound explanation for the way it appeared in a new and more effervescent way now and in the years to come. The farther he went down the road toward independence, the more totally he turned his back on the two great but essentially egotistic dreams of his life—founding a Western colony, and creating a family dynasty. Independence meant the death blow to both these dreams, and by letting them go, opening himself at seventy to an unknown future, Franklin drew on resources of the spirit which only those who have experienced freedom in all its mysterious depths can understand. He had been born a free man, but now he was freeing himself from those self-imposed ambitions that had narrowed the political and emotional side of his life. True, he had served the public for many years out of a sense of gratitude for early good fortune. But there was little or no risk or loss involved in these previous years of public service. Now he was risking everything—the modest estate he had accumulated, the reputation he had so painfully constructed. If England won the war, his property would be confiscated, his reputation as a philosopher and public servant besmirched forever by the King's condemnation as a traitor and rebel. This risk, this ultimate commitment to freedom without hope of personal gain, simply because he knew it was right, because he felt embodied in his soul the cause of America, now and in future centuries, was a unique, soaring emotion that made the risks of punishment, the burdens of Congress and Pennsylvania politics seem mere bubbles to be laughed away.

X I I

The proponents of independence had predicted that it would inspire Americans everywhere with new resolution and fresh energy. It certainly seemed to have that effect on Franklin. For a man who less than a month before had been describing himself as old and feeble, he now plunged into a whirl of state and national politics that would have exhausted two men half his age. He accepted the presidency of the Pennsylvania Constitutional Convention, as well as the leadership of the new state delegation to the Continental Congress. John Adams exulted to his wife, "Dr. Franklin will be governor of Pennsylvania! The new members from this city are all in this taste—chosen because of their inflexible zeal for independence." [49] The triumph of the Independence Party, which coincided with the publication of the Declaration, was celebrated in Philadelphia by "bonfires, bells and other great demonstrations of joy," according to one local diarist.

Franklin did not participate to any great extent in the debates of the Pennsylvania Constitutional Congress. But his influence was amply evident in its results. Instead of a governor, the state chose to be guided by an executive council, and instead of a two-house legislature, they chose a single chamber. Both these ideas were the results of Franklin's meditation on his long years of political experience. He thought a plural executive reduced the danger of dictatorial one-man rule, while a single legislative chamber made the law-making body more responsive to the will of the people. When one man asked Franklin why he was against a two-house legislature, he responded with a story about a snake with two heads and one body. "The snake was going to a brook to drink," Franklin said, "and on her way was to pass through a hedge, a twig of which opposed her direct course. One head chose to go on the right side of the twig, the other on the left. . . . Before the decision was completed the poor snake died with thirst." [50]

Independence may have galvanized Franklin. It is also obvious that regaining political power in Pennsylvania added not a little to his energy. His long months of silence were over. Throughout the hot, humid weeks of July and August he was on his feet in Congress day after day, participating vigorously in the debates, trying to make muddleheaded delegates think clearly about creating a union that would endure. But the victory of independence was followed by almost complete frustration on union.

Congress, in one of its typical fits of waywardness, had formed a committee to draw up plans for a confederation about the same time that it commissioned a declaration of independence. They had made John Dickinson the chairman and had handed to him Franklin's long-ignored Articles of Confederation. A more idiotic combination of man and document could not have been devised. The name Franklin instantly raised prickles on Dickinson's skin, and he felt compelled to overhaul the Articles of Confederation along different, if not superior, lines. The most important—and disastrous—change Dickinson made was throwing out Franklin's idea of proportional representation, based on the number of male voters in each colony between the ages of sixteen and sixty. Each delegate in Franklin's Congress was to have one vote. Each *colony* in Dickinson's version had one vote.

This was nothing less than an invitation to chaos. Again and again Franklin warned that the larger states such as Pennsylvania and Massachusetts and Virginia would soon grow disgusted with being reduced to equality with mini-states such as Rhode Island and would pull out of the confederacy. "Let the smaller colonies," Franklin said, "give equal money and men, and then have an equal vote. But if they have an equal vote without bearing equal burdens, a confederation upon such iniquitous principles will never last long." [51]

The smaller colonies protested that if the big states had their full weight in Congress, the smaller states would become "vassals." Such strong imagery produced violent emotions in many of the members, and revived some of the fears that had originally made Congress abhor the idea of independence. Most of the proponents of independence had been from the two largest states, Massachusetts and Virginia, and Franklin, once more in the saddle in Pennsylvania, had also been an independence man. Now all three were fighting for proportional representation. John Adams, with his usual intransigence, insisted, "Reason, justice and equity never had weight enough on the face of the earth to govern the councils of men. It is interest alone which does it, and it is interest alone which can be trusted. . . . Therefore the interests within doors should be the mathematical representatives of the interests without doors." The individuality of a colony, which the small states revered, "was a mere sound. Does the individuality of a colony increase its wealth and numbers? If it does, pay equally." [52]

For a while it looked as if the British were right, and the unity of the Americans was a rope of sand. Many smaller-state men were so angry that it seemed they might walk out. Franklin arose to spread some oil on the waters. He told them a story he had heard in England about the opposition of Scottish peers to the union between England and Scotland. One nobleman predicted "that as the whale had swallowed Jonah, so Scotland would be swallowed by England." But there were soon so many Scotsmen in high places in the English government "that it was in event that Jonah had swallowed the whale." An admiring Jefferson later recalled: "This little story produced a general laugh and restored good humor." [53]

But neither humor nor reason could persuade the Congressmen to agree. The small states clung fiercely to Dickinson's unworkable plan. They could not even agree on how to count heads, if they accepted proportional representation. Dickinson was for counting every man, woman, and child in a colony, which missed Franklin's point, that by counting only men from sixteen to sixty, they would get a good index of a state's productive capacity, which in turn suggested what proportion of the federal taxes they could pay. Then Southerners began arguing against counting their slaves as people. Thomas Lynch of South Carolina blandly declaimed: "Our slaves being our property, why should they be taxed more than the land, sheep, cattle, horses, etc? "

Franklin cut him down by pointing out that there was "some difference" between slaves and sheep—"Sheep will never make any insurrections." [54]

For the first three weeks of August, the Congress wrangled day and night without coming even close to agreement. They seemed mesmerized by another Dickinson change in Franklin's original Articles. Franklin had, with his usual reasonableness, pointed out that nothing in this world is perfect, things changed, and therefore amendments could be proposed to the Articles by Congress, and approved by a majority of the colonial Assemblies. Dickinson insisted that alterations could only be made "in an assembly of the united states" (a Constitutional Convention) and "be afterwards confirmed by the legislatures of *every* colony."

The Congressmen were also paralyzed by a conviction, which Franklin himself shared, that the war would not last more than another year. On August twenty-eighth, Franklin wrote to Horatio Gates, now in command of the Northern Department along the Canadian border: "My last advices from England say, that the ministry . . . cannot find means next year to go on with the war." [55] This idea made the fear of their brother states loom larger in the minds of many Congressmen than the specter of British conquest. Samuel Chase of Maryland went home in disgust, denouncing all the taxation plans he had heard thus far. Other Congressmen followed him, lured, as he was, by the politics of their native states, and the dismal sensation that Congress was getting nowhere.

At the end of five weeks, the Congressmen had agreed on nothing, neither taxation, representation nor executive powers. On top of this appalling failure came news from the fighting front that was even more dismaying. On August twenty-seventh, George Washington and his largely amateur army had given battle on Long Island to the superbly trained and equipped British host commanded by Major General William Howe, and had been murderously thrashed. Only a near miraculous combination of British overconfidence and foggy weather had enabled Washington to escape with the bulk of his army to Manhattan Island, by night.

XIII

At this worst of all possible moments, there arrived on Congress's doorstep a new offer for reconciliation from England.

Franklin's old friend, Lord Howe, had arrived in New York, armed with his long-sought commission to make peace. He was also armed with a less peaceful title—Commander-in-Chief of His Majesty's Royal Navy. His brother, Major General William Howe, was also a member of this strangely ambiguous peace commission. Late in July, Howe had written Franklin a letter informing him of his commission and urging a parley. Franklin had written a scorching, highly personal reply, informing Howe that the "atrocious injuries" already inflicted by the British "had extinguished every remaining spark of affection for that parent country we once held so dear." If Lord Howe was prepared to negotiate a peace "between Britain and America as distinct states now at war," Franklin thought that was "not yet quite impracticable, before we enter into foreign alliances." His esteem for Howe made it "painful to me to see you engage in conducting a war . . . both unjust and unwise." He warned Howe that "even success will not save from some degree of dishonor those, who voluntarily engaged to conduct it." [56]

Lord Howe refused to be discouraged by this blast and after the battle of Long Island had demonstrated, so he thought, the clear superiority of the British over the American Army, he sent a captured American general, John Sullivan, to Philadelphia to suggest a parley with some members of Congress, on a purely private, unofficial basis. Howe was forced to make this foredoomed approach because he had been strictly forbidden by the British ministry to recognize Congress.

Shaken by the defeat on Long Island and their own failure to confederate, Congress decided that they could not afford to ignore Lord Howe's offer. While John Adams fumed that General Sullivan was "a decoy duck," and wished that the first bullet fired on Long Island had gone through his head, Congress appointed a committee of three to meet Howe. Franklin was the logical first choice. So was Adams, to calm the fears of the independence men. Edward Rutledge of South Carolina, a vigorous opponent of independence until the very last moment, represented the Congressional doves.

The three men journeyed to South Amboy, where they had trouble getting beds at a very crowded inn. The roads were swarming with soldiers en route to reinforce Washington in New York. Franklin and John Adams had to share one small, lumpy bed. Although they were in wholehearted agreement on the subject of independence, the two men were temperamentally and physically opposites in almost every other way. Adams was a hypochondriac, who always saw himself in danger of a deadly disease. He had a special dread of the night air, shared by many people, including numerous distinguished physicians of the era. Franklin, proponent of air baths and ventilation, was horrified when Adams slammed tight the only window in their tiny room.

"Don't shut the window, we shall be suffocated," Franklin said.

Adams explained that he was "an invalid" and the night air would be his death.

"The air within the chamber will soon be, and indeed is now, worse than that without doors," Franklin said. "Come open the window and come to bed, and I will convince you. I believe you are not acquainted with my theory of colds."

A reluctant Adams opened the window and crept into bed with Franklin.

Cool air, night air, moist air, none of these things caused colds, as most people then believed, Franklin declared. "People often catch cold from one another when shut up together in closed rooms, coaches, &c., and when sitting near and conversing so as to breathe in each other's transpiration." He also suspected "too full living, with too little exercise." But he was absolutely convinced that no one ever caught cold from being cold. "Traveling in our severe winters, I have suffered cold sometimes to an extremity only short of freezing, but this did not make me *catch cold*. Boys never get cold by swimming. Dampness may indeed assist in producing the disorder we call a cold; but of itself can never by a little addition of moisture . . . hurt a body . . . filled with watery fluids . . . from head to foot . . ."

Adams fell asleep, he said, in the middle of the Doctor's explanation, and the last words he heard from Franklin had a very sleepy sound to them.[57]

The next day the negotiators were in Perth Amboy. The sight of his son's handsome new house must have been painful to Franklin, especially since Elizabeth Franklin was still living in it, growing steadily more depressed and distraught. Her husband had been confined to the town of Wallingford, Connecticut. All summer she had written tearful letters to Temple, telling how soldiers delighted in being "rude, insolent and abusive" to the royal governor's wife. She was desperate for money since William's salary had been cut off, and none of his debtors would pay her a cent. Early in August, Temple had come down to spend the rest of the summer with her, and had brought her sixty dollars which he had extracted from his grandfather. Franklin had also sent Elizabeth a brief but not unkind note; he sympathized with her unhappiness, but he reminded her that thousands of people who had been forced to flee from occupied Boston and threatened New York were equally unhappy, and suffering more than she was. Elizabeth's reply was full of self-pity and bad humor. Her troubles "were really more than so weak a frame" could support. Moreover, it was "generally in your power to relieve them." [58] She could not see why Franklin did not use his influence to persuade Congress to let William live in his own home. She seemed to have forgotten that William had rejected the offer of a parole on his Burlington County farm and had practically forced the state to arrest him.

Franklin had suggested William's house as a possible meeting place for the conference with Howe. Perhaps he was hoping he would thus have an excuse to see Elizabeth Franklin and Temple, without drawing public attention to his visit. But the admiral preferred a safer (for him) house on British-occupied Staten Island, just opposite Amboy. A barge sent by Lord Howe met the committee on the Jersey shore. In it was an officer who informed the Americans he had been sent as a hostage to guarantee their safe return. John Adams for once overcame his suspicious nature and suggested the arrangement was childish and undignified. In his diary, Adams gives himself full credit for the suggestion, but it is hard to believe that Franklin did not feel the same way the moment he saw the hostage. He knew Lord Howe too well to suspect him of such crude treachery.

On Staten Island, Lord Howe had a regiment of Hessians drawn up in a double line from the shore to the door of the big stone mansion known as the Billopp House. When he saw his officer in the boat, Howe exclaimed, "Gentlemen, you make me a very high compliment and you may depend upon it I will consider it the most sacred of things." He shook Franklin's hand with special cordiality and displayed all the vaunted Howe charm he could muster in greeting Adams and Rutledge. But the Hessian guard, looking, in Adams' words, "fierce as ten furies," was a silent commentary on the other role which the admiral was playing. Strictly speaking, they were a guard of honor, but there was more than a suggestion of a threat in their presence, as well. The admiral, conforming to the letter of his instructions from the King, was proffering both the olive branch and the sword.

Inside the house, which had been plundered and wrecked by the Hessians, the delegation found one room hung with moss and branches and a table spread with a cold meal of ham, tongue, mutton, and claret. Lunch was all good-natured small talk, and only after the table had been cleared did Lord Howe turn to the somber subject that brought them together. He began by declaring that he felt for America "as for a brother, and if America should fall, I should feel and lament it like the loss of a brother."

"My Lord," Franklin said with a small smile, "we will use our utmost endeavors to save your Lordship that mortification."

Howe's face darkened, and for a moment he almost lost his temper. "I suppose you will endeavor to give us employment in Europe."

This was an obvious bit of fishing, in pursuit of Franklin's remark in his letter about making foreign alliances. Franklin was much too smart to say anything. He just kept on smiling. With a visible effort, Lord Howe tried to regain his tone of compassionate moderation. He told them how he had sought out his peace commission, hoping to "proceed straight to Philadelphia and meet the Congress face to face." But the King and his ministers had declined to recognize Congress, and even now, Howe confessed considerable nervousness that he was not exceeding his powers if they insisted on considering themselves as a committee of the Congress. "I hope you will not, by any implication, commit me upon that point."

"Your Lordship may consider us in any view you think proper," Franklin replied. "We, on our part, are at liberty to consider ourselves in our real character. But there is, really, no necessity on this occasion to distinguish between members of Congress and individuals. The conversation may be held as among friends."

John Adams, with his inimitable talent for ruffling tempers, said that he agreed. In fact, he would be willing "to consider myself for a few moments in any character which would be agreeable to you, Your Lordship, except that of a British subject."

"Mr. Adams is a decided character," said his Lordship, swallowing hard. Howe begged the three Americans to consider the possibility, at least, of giving up the Declaration of Independence. In an eloquent description which contained considerably less truth than poetry, he said his powers were "to restore peace and grant pardons, to attend to complaints and representations, and to confer upon the means of a reunion upon terms honorable and advantageous to the colonies and to Great Britain." Almost plaintively he added, "You know, gentlemen, that we expect aid from America; our dispute seems only to be concerning the mode of obtaining it."

"Aid we never refused upon *requisition,*" Franklin shot back.

"Your money, let me assure you, is the smallest consideration. America can confer upon Great Britain more solid advantages; it is her commerce, her strength, her men that we chiefly want."

"Aye, my Lord," said Franklin, delighted to have this opportunity to beat his favorite drum, "we have in America a pretty considerable manufactory of men."

But he was totally serious when Howe asked him to comment on the situation. Franklin repeated what he had already said in his letter. "All former attachments are obliterated. America cannot return to the domination of Great Britain, and I imagine that Great Britain means to rest it upon force." Adams and Rutledge concurred, both of them pointing out that Congress had declared independence in response to an overwhelming demand by the American people. They could not repeal the Declaration, even if they were inclined to do so.

Lord Howe was crushed by this intransigence. "I have not the authority, nor do I ever expect to have, to treat with the colonies as states independent of the Crown of Great Britain," he said.

Franklin suggested writing home to England to get it. It would take the same length of time for his Lordship to do that as it would for the Americans to find out from their thirteen state legislatures whether they would consider a repeal.

Howe gloomily shook his head. "It is vain to think of my receiving instructions to treat upon that ground."

There was a mournful silence. Then Franklin said, "Well, my Lord, as America is to expect nothing but upon unconditional submission—"

"No, Dr. Franklin," Lord Howe said, "Great Britain does not require unconditional submission. I think that what I have already said proves the contrary, and I desire, gentlemen, that you will not go away with such an idea."

Franklin declined to argue with him. Instead he asked his Lordship if he was authorized to receive propositions from Congress to Great Britain.

Howe, wary of the trap into which Franklin was trying to lead him—recognizing Congress—zigzagged and said, "I do not know that I could avoid receiving any papers that should be put into my hand, though I am doubtful of the propriety of transmitting them home. Still, I do not say that I would decline doing so." [59]

Two days later, Franklin, Adams, and Rutledge turned in a report of their conversation to Congress. It dismissed the poetry in Lord Howe's description of his peace commission, and declared that his only authority was to grant pardons and declare "the King's peace," in various parts of America, "upon submission." Congress collectively shuddered at this more or less expected news.

In the next few days, dispatches, letters, and rumors pouring in from New York made the possibility of submission loom large. Admiral Howe's brother, informed of the failure of the peace commission, unleashed his redcoats on George Washington once more. On September 15, 1776, they swept ashore at Kip's Bay behind a curtain of fire from Admiral Howe's ships. The raw Americans panicked and ran, leaving a thunderstruck Washington practically alone on the battlefield. Congress, for that matter, looked as decimated as Washington's army. The dispute over the confederation had emptied numerous seats. Some states were not even represented. In this atmosphere of military and political disarray Franklin found himself faced with a loyalist uprising within his own family.

X I V

On September sixteenth, William Temple Franklin wrote to his grandfather, asking permission to take a trip to Connecticut to see his father. The ostensible reason was Elizabeth Franklin's desire to send a letter to her husband. She declined to trust it to the American post

office fearing it would be opened. Franklin refused to give the boy
_____ _____ ____ ____ ____ Elizabeth write to William care of
_____ _t instead. Temple answered with
_____ is grandfather of distrusting him,
_____ carry "dangerous intelligence" to his

_____ telling Temple he was talking non-
_____ dangerous intelligence to his father,
_____ he could make no use of it. . . . You
_____ right if you could have suspected me
_____ your welfare, on acct of the length of
_____ inexperience, the number of sick return-
_____ infectious camp distemper, which makes
_____ with the loss of time in your studies, of
_____ to grow tired." He could not believe that
_____ to risk her stepson's life on such a journey,
_____ not want to ask Governor Trumbull the small
_____ letter. "I rather think the project takes its rise
_____ ination to a ramble, & disinclination for returning
_____ ith a desire I do not blame of seeing a father you
nave so mucn reason to love." He offered to send Elizabeth some
franked letters addressed to Governor Trumbull which would enable
her to correspond with her husband, free of charge.[60]

In Congress, Franklin was involved in a far different and more
momentous debate. After long months of silence, the embattled
Americans had finally heard from someone in Europe. Barbé Dubourg
had written Franklin a long letter assuring him that the French government and the French people were sympathetic to the American cause,
but among the King's ministers, "none will espouse it with warmth."
France was "over head and ears in debt." Moreover, Dubourg sadly
admitted that his best friend in the Cabinet, the economist Turgot,
had just been fired. The only really good news Dubourg sent was the
ease with which he was recruiting French artillerymen and engineers for
the American Army.

At the rate things were going, there might not be an American
Army for them to serve in, or a Congress to pay them. From their
other emissaries in Europe, Congress had not heard a word in months.
Silas Deane was totally silent. The only information they had had
from Arthur Lee was the fact that he did not trust two members of

Places
and People

Franklin's residence on Craven Street, just off the fashionable Strand, is still standing in London. He rented four rooms in this building from a widow, Margaret Stevenson. He soon converted her and her young daughter Polly into a second family.

The House of Commons as seen from the bar. Although artists attempted to make the room seem imposingly large, in keeping with England's imperial power, it was in reality only 68 feet long, 28 feet wide, and 30 feet high. More than one member got acute claustrophobia when he rose to speak. This is the view which Franklin had as he testified against the Stamp Act in 1766. *Copyright: Radio Times Hulton Picture Library.*

Peter Collinson, a Quaker merchant with a strong interest in science, was the channel through which Franklin's discoveries in electricity were reported to the Royal Society and eventually to all of Europe. *The Metropolitan Museum of Art, Gift of William H. Huntington, William Henry Huntington Collection.*

Frederick Lord North, the second Earl of Guilford, was the British Prime Minister whose muddled policies brought on the Revolution. Franklin and he cordially despised each other, long before hostilities broke out. On one weekend they ate breakfast, dinner and supper at a mutual friend's country house without exchanging more than three sentences. *Copyright: National Portrait Gallery, London.*

Edward Gibbon, myopic author of *The History of the Decline and Fall of the Roman Empire,* refused to have dinner with Franklin in France. Franklin told him he would be happy to give him "ample materials" on the decline of the British Empire. *Copyright: National Portrait Gallery, London.*

Jonathan Shipley, the Bishop of St. Asaph, was one of the few members of the English hierarchy to oppose the war with America. The origin of his opposition was his close friendship with Benjamin Franklin. It cost Shipley his chance to become Archbishop of Canterbury. *Benjamin Franklin Collection, Sterling Memorial Library, Yale University.*

William Strahan was Franklin's closest friend in England. A fellow printer, he was the publisher of Samuel Johnson, Gibbon, Hume and other famous writers. As a member of Parliament, he voted for war against America, and Franklin wrote him a scorching letter after Bunker Hill. But they were quickly reconciled when hostilities ceased. *The Metropolitan Museum of Art, Gift of Georgiana W. Sargent in Memory of John Osborne Sargent.*

Irish-born Edmund Burke was one of the leading opponents of the American war in Parliament. A brilliant orator, he consulted Franklin closely while preparing his great speech on the reconciliation of the colonies. *Benjamin Franklin Collection, Sterling Memorial Library, Yale University.*

William Petty, Lord Shelburne, was another prominent member of the British Opposition. A brilliant political thinker, unappreciated in his time, he was a good friend of Franklin. Because of his subtle mind, his enemies called Shelburne "the Jesuit of Berkeley Square." He was the Prime Minister who negotiated the treaty of peace with America. *Copyright: National Portrait Gallery, London.*

William Pitt, the first Earl of Chatham, was the English statesman Franklin most admired. The architect of victory in the Seven Years War, he struggled to prevent the break with America and frequently conferred with Franklin on how to resolve the crisis. In 1778 he collapsed and was carried dying from the House of Lords after a final effort to bring down the North ministry. *Copyright: National Portrait Gallery, London.*

Joseph Galloway was Franklin's chief political lieutenant in Pennsylvania. A gifted but legalistic thinker, he wavered between the Revolution and the King, first serving and then withdrawing from the Continental Congress. He had a strong influence on the thinking of William Franklin. Eventually, late in 1776, Galloway fled to New York and became a leader of the Loyalists. *Benjamin Franklin Collection, Sterling Memorial Library, Yale University.*

Charles Gravier, the Count de Vergennes, was the Foreign Minister of France and the architect of the policy that brought his nation to the aid of America. Aloof and reserved, he was primarily interested in humbling England to redress the European balance of power. Unlike other American diplomats, Franklin was unbothered by his motives, as long as he kept supplying the money and weapons America so badly needed. *Benjamin Franklin Collection, Sterling Memorial Library, Yale University.*

Silas Deane was a Connecticut merchant who preceded Franklin to France as America's representative and became deeply involved in the purchase of war materiel. An unstable temperament, a soaring ambition and accusations of fellow Americans turned him into a liability and finally into a traitor. *Culver Pictures.*

CAP.ᴺ
CUNINGHAM.

ngraved from the Original Sketch which was taken by an Artist of

Gustavus Conyngham, a fighting Irishman from Donegal, was one of the first captains Franklin commissioned to prey on English shipping in European waters. Although he never achieved the fame of John Paul Jones, he did almost as much damage. *Beinecke Rare Book and Manuscript Library, Yale University.*

ARTHUR LEE . 1790.

Virginia-born Arthur Lee was Franklin's hair shirt in France. One of the commissioners nominated by Congress to negotiate the Treaty of Alliance, he quarreled with everyone and accused Franklin and Deane of robbing millions. When Congress replied by making Franklin sole ambassador, Lee went home and spent the rest of his life smearing mud on Franklin's reputation. Franklin considered him insane. *Yale University Art Gallery.*

John Adams replaced Lee as American commissioner in France and at the end of the war returned to join Franklin in negotiating the treaty of peace. He was almost as contentious as Arthur Lee, and he soon fell to vilifying Franklin. Franklin said he was "always an honest man, often a wise one, but sometimes, and in some things, absolutely out of his senses." *Culver Pictures.*

John Jay joined Franklin and Adams in the peace negotiations. A New York Huguenot, he allowed his anti-French emotions to run amok. His intransigence and headstrong tactics destroyed Franklin's carefully laid plans to persuade the English to cede Canada to the United States in the final treaty. *Culver Pictures.*

Anne-Catherine de Ligniville, Madame Helvetius, was Franklin's neighbor in France. Franklin was fascinated by her unique mixture of bohemian abandon and aristocratic hauteur. In 1779 he asked her to marry him. She refused, as she had refused numerous offers from other men, because of her devotion to her late husband, the philosopher Claude Adrien Helvetius. Franklin told her that he visited Paradise in a dream and found Helvetius married to his wife, Deborah. "Come, let us *revenge* ourselves," he said. *Archives Photographiques, Paris.*

Franklin stands before the privy council on January 29, 1774, calmly enduring the titanic wrath of the British ministry, after the news of the Boston Tea Party arrived in England. The lords and ladies were invited "as to an entertainment," he wrote, to to hear the Solicitor General of England tear him apart. He made no attempt to defend himself. But four years later, when he signed the Treaty of Alliance with France, he wore the same suit he had worn on this fateful day. "To give it a little revenge," he said. *Henry E. Huntington Library and Art Gallery.*

Franklin stands on the right, in this John Trumbull painting, as the Declaration of Independence is presented to Congress on July 1, 1776. He made only a few minor word changes in Jefferson's document. Were it not for the defection of his Loyalist son, Franklin might have been asked to write this crucial document. *Yale University Art Gallery.*

the secret committee, John Jay and Benjamin Franklin. The debacle in Canada, and the signs of an even worse debacle in New York, made it clear that America needed help, massive amounts of help, fast. This kind of talk was painful to Franklin, who had been so confident that America could and would defend herself successfully. He reiterated his dislike of pleading for help. America, he said, was a virgin state and "a virgin state should preserve the virgin character, not go about suitoring for alliances, but wait with decent dignity for the application of others." [61]

Congress declined to take this advice. It may have been sound diplomacy, but from where they sat, the finer points of the diplomatic art would have to be ignored. It was time to seek France's help, with the utmost urgency. In an atmosphere of intense secrecy, the depleted Congress voted to send a major embassy to France. On the first ballot, they unanimously chose the American most likely to impress the Old World: Benjamin Franklin.

The decision filled Franklin's mind with gloom. It meant a winter voyage across the Atlantic, which, for a man his age, might be a death sentence in itself. The Atlantic also swarmed with British cruisers, and if one captured him on such a mission, a traitor's death at the end of a Tyburn rope would be a certainty. But his total commitment to the American cause spoke when he turned to young Dr. Benjamin Rush, who sat next to him. "I am old and good for nothing; but, as the storekeepers say of their remnants of cloth, 'I am but a fag end, and you may have me for what you please,' just so my country may command my services in any way they choose." [62]

His profound, intense paternalism was also still very much alive. His first thoughts, as he planned his voyage, were of William Temple Franklin. If he left him behind in America, the boy would almost certainly drift into his father's and stepmother's loyalist orbit, with possibly fatal consequences. Grimly Franklin decided to take Temple with him. Even if they were captured, the British would not harm the boy, and numerous friends in England would care for him and see that he completed his education. Franklin dashed off a note to Temple, urging him to return to Philadelphia immediately. "I hope . . . that your mother will make no objection to it, something offering here that will be much to your advantage if you are not out of the way." Temple was back in Philadelphia by October third, and he talked no more of visiting his father, or even bothered to answer letters from his stepmother. We can be sure that Franklin, with his talent for words, made a sojourn in France sound like a fabulous adventure to this high-spirited seventeen-year-old.[63]

More extraordinary was another family decision Franklin made— to take his six-year-old grandson, Benjamin Franklin Bache, with him. It was apparently based on the boy's obviously high intelligence and the probability that the war would disrupt his education if he stayed behind in Philadelphia. Young Benny was already writing letters under his grandfather's benevolent eye. Earlier in September, he had addressed one to Temple that his grandfather humorously decided not to send. He said it was "too full of pothooks & hangers, and so unintelligible by the dividing words in the middle and joining ends of some to beginnings of others, that if it had fallen into the hands of some committee it might have given them . . . a suspicion of its containing treason, especially as directed to a Tory house." [64]

Four days after Congress had voted to send Franklin to France, supposedly under a double bond of absolute secrecy (all deliberations of Congress were supposed to be secret, but about Franklin's mission an absolute silence was enjoined), a friend of Robert Morris stopped him in the street and asked whether Dr. Franklin and other ambassadors were really going to France. That same day, Thomas Story, an American who had carried the secret committee's letters to Arthur Lee a year ago, returned to Philadelphia with hopeful information from Lee. He had been in touch with a French agent in London who informed him that the French were prepared to ship 200,000 pounds' sterling worth of arms and ammunition to their islands in the West Indies, where American ships could pick them up. Franklin and Robert Morris, the only two members of the secret committees in town, instantly drew up a memorandum recording this good news, but decided, with the concurrence of one or two other congressmen whom they trusted, to keep it a secret for the time being. Only if an "unexampled misfortune should befall the states of America so as to depress the spirits of Congress" would Morris take the risk of cheering them up with the news before the goods were safely in American hands.

This was the only hopeful note in a month of otherwise mounting gloom. Washington was forced to evacuate New York and retreated to White Plains with the British Army in pursuit, moving in, so it seemed, for the kill. Franklin, as a last gesture of defiance and dedication, pledged his valuable property in Philadelphia and raised all the money he could borrow—some 4000 pounds, which he lent to Congress, in the hope that other men would do likewise. Knowing that Philadelphia would almost certainly be a prime British target, Franklin had a last conference with his old friend Joseph Galloway. Where did he stand now? The wary Galloway told Franklin that he was rapidly becoming a convert to the Revolutionary cause. In fact, he was about to raise a regiment and offer his services to Washington's army. Delighted by the news, Franklin asked him if he could store his personal papers—the records of his lifetime—at Trevose. Galloway readily consented, and wished Franklin Godspeed on his mission.

The following day, Franklin said what he probably thought was his last goodbye to his daughter and son-in-law, and rode with his two grandsons to Chester, where they stayed overnight. The next morning they rode another three miles down the river to Marcus Hook, where boats took them aboard the sloop *Reprisal.* It was a perfect name for the ship that was to carry Franklin toward that "bright point" with which he longed to end his life. The realist who could write, "In the affairs of this world men are saved, not by faith, but by the want of it," was acting now out of a faith in the destiny of this new breed of men, called Americans, which he in so many ways personified.

It was as yet a frail vessel, this infant republic, as frail as the tiny *Reprisal,* with her sixteen pitiful guns, sailing out onto an Atlantic patrolled by Lord Howe's 1200-gun fleet. Like Franklin himself, the Americans at this point seemed to have little on which to rest this faith in their destiny, beyond an inner conviction that free men, and a nation committed to freedom, have a special mission in this world, and the creator of the universe would somehow stretch forth his sheltering hand to them. This was Franklin's prayer, as the little *Reprisal* weighed anchor and thrust its bow into the gray swells of the wintry Atlantic. In a letter he wrote the day before he sailed, he put this faith into unforgettable words. "I hope our people will keep up their courage. I have no doubt of their finally succeeding by the blessing of God, nor have I any doubt that so good a cause will fail of that blessing." [65]

Book Six

Bon Homme Richard

I

The *Reprisal* was small, but she was a lean, full-rigged ship, in that daring tradition which would eventually spawn the mighty American clipper ships that ruled the seas of the nineteenth century. She breasted the cold billows of the Atlantic with a speed that considerably lessened the danger of Franklin's suffering an ignominious end at Tyburn. More than once, British cruisers appeared on the horizon. Grim-eyed, taciturn Captain Lambert Wickes beat to quarters, and the hundred-man crew turned out with a military precision that Franklin thought "equal to anything of the kind in the best ships of the King's fleet." [1] A Marylander who had given up a profitable career in privateering to join the infant U.S. Navy, Captain Wickes was a fighting sailor whom Franklin filed in his ample memory for future use.

Otherwise the voyage contained little in the way of amusement or consolation. The food was terrible, nothing but salt beef and ship's biscuits. The seas were mountainous, confining Franklin to his cramped cabin most of the time. Once a day he braved wind and waves to take the temperature of the Gulf Stream. This was an almost pathetic gesture. For the rest of the time, all he could do was suffer. Shivering in the raw cold, he took to wearing the fur hat he had acquired in Canada. But it did little good. The boils that had tormented him in Canada broke out again, and he felt himself growing more and more feeble. His only hope was the assurance from Captain Wickes that they were making remarkably good time.

One day, toward the end of the fourth week, Wickes burst into Franklin's cabin and asked with considerable excitement if he would come on deck. There was a ship coming toward them, and it was obvious from the cut of her sails and the slow, wallowing gait that she was not a man-of-war. Wickes was under orders from Congress to take no prizes and avoid all encounters with the enemy until he had deposited Franklin safely in France. But this plodding merchantman was a tempting plum. The captain did not have to plead. Franklin nodded, and moments later the crew of the *Reprisal* was racing to quarters. The British ship, a brigantine out of Bordeaux heading for Cork, surrendered without a shot. A prize crew was swiftly put aboard her. The same day they repeated the performance with another brig from Hull. Dangerous as such forays were, Franklin could not resist the opportunity to strike a blow at England the moment he got within range.

Two days later, they were in Quiberon Bay, and after waiting four days for a favorable wind to carry the ship up the Loire to Nantes, Franklin landed at the fishing village of Auray. He was so exhausted he could barely stand, but his indomitable spirit was unquenched. He immediately fired off a letter to Silas Deane in Paris, reporting his arrival. "I am weak, but hope that the good air which I breathe on land will soon re-establish me," he said, "that I may travel with speed to join you in Paris." He also asked Deane to notify Arthur Lee, in London, that he had been nominated as a third commissioner. Thomas Jefferson, Congress's first choice (after Franklin), had regretfully refused because of his wife's health. Fortunately, Franklin had no inkling of the enormous headache that this seemingly simple substitution would create for him.[2]

Auray has changed little since Franklin landed there on December 3, 1776. The same rickety bridge arches over the placid river, the same steep gables overlook the wharf. The Breton fishermen who manned the little boat that put them ashore still speak the same strange mixture of French and Gaelic. No one in the village had ever heard of the famous Dr. Franklin, and they greeted him with little more than the curious stares country bumpkins give a stranger from another country. The weather was cold and raw, and Franklin continued to wear his fur hat. After a twenty-four-hour delay, a wreck of a carriage and two tired horses finally arrived from a neighboring town, and they started down the Nantes road which, the driver politely informed them, was infested with bandits. Only two weeks ago several travelers had been robbed and murdered along the route.

They reached Nantes unscathed, to find themselves the center of a tremendous social uproar. Someone, probably the messenger whom Franklin had hired to carry his letter to Silas Deane, had notified the city that he was coming. Nantes was already a passionate convert to the American cause. Many of its merchants had been trading with

America for decades. Monsieur Penet, the entrepreneur who had turned up in Philadelphia, was at the head of an entourage that greeted Franklin as if he had already won the Revolution, single-handed. The exhausted envoy had to attend an immense public dinner given by "friends of America." Then Penet and his partner, Monsieur Pliarne, whisked him out to the country house of their associate, Monsieur Gruel. These gentlemen did their utmost to assure him of their vast enthusiasm for the American cause. But Franklin was not too exhausted to detect, almost instantly, that they were somewhat less than respectable. Perhaps he found this out in a private conversation with his friend Sieur Montaudoin, one of the city's great merchants, long a specialist in American trade. Montaudoin hailed Franklin's arrival by writing a poem in his honor and by purchasing a Dutch clipper which he renamed the *Benjamin Franklin*. Meanwhile, Captain Wickes arrived with his two prizes and sold them immediately. This news was almost enough, in itself, to restore Franklin's strength. One of the reasons he had allowed Wickes to take the prizes was to test French willingness to permit American privateers and ships of war to use their ports.

Meanwhile, he was coping with a stream of distinguished visitors from the city and the surrounding countryside, all eager to pay their respects to Franklin and express their enthusiasm for the American cause. Franklin was deeply touched and flattered. While he maintained a cool, noncommittal face to the world, he revealed his private feelings, as he often did, to his sister Jane. "You can have no conception of the respect with which I am receiv'd and treated here by the first people, in my private character; for as yet I have assum'd no public one—" [3]

While Franklin recuperated at Nantes, the two greatest cities in Europe were abuzz with excited rumors and speculations about his totally unexpected appearance. George III was more than ever convinced that Franklin was the evil genius behind the rebellion. His ministers and their hired writers swiftly passed the word that the philosopher had fled before the imminent collapse of the American cause. Word of Howe's victories on Long Island and in New York had led the North ministry to half believe this propaganda. Franklin's friends in England angrily defended him. "I never will believe," said Edmund Burke, "that he is going to conclude a long life, which has brightened

every hour it has continued, with so foul and dishonorable a flight."
Lord Rockingham told Burke that he considered the presence of
Franklin at the French court "much more than a balance for the few
additional acres which the English had gained by the conquest of
Manhattan Island." [4]

I I

Paris was in an even wilder ferment of expectation. Horace Walpole,
who loved to collect the latest gossip from both capitals, was informed
by his favorite Paris correspondent, "No one can tell whether he [Frank-
lin] is actually in Paris or not. For three or four days it has been said
in the morning that he had arrived, and in the evening that he had
not yet come." Finally, at two o'clock in the afternoon on the twenty-
first of December, Franklin stepped from his coach and vanished into
the Hotel de Hambourg on the Rue de l'Université. He was still wearing his marten fur hat, and Paris buzzed with the news of his arrival
and the uniqueness of his appearance. In style-conscious France it was
simply incredible for the representative of a foreign state to appear
in public wearing such a costume.

But Franklin knew precisely what he was doing. Thanks to the
translation by Barbé Dubourg, he was already well known in France
as *Bon Homme Richard,* the author of *The Way to Wealth,* which had
won an enthusiastic reception among the tightfisted French bourgeoi-
sie. In his introduction, Dubourg had pictured Franklin as the supreme
example of France's idealized vision of America, compounded from
the writings of Voltaire and Rousseau.

Voltaire, the guiding spirit of the French *philosophes,* the apostles
of the Enlightenment, had written extensively about a Pennsylvania
he had never visited. He pictured it as a world of idyllic social perfection, overflowing with religious toleration, prosperity and virtue.
In this rhapsody, the philosopher extolled the Good Quaker, who embodied all of Pennsylvania's virtues, above all the simplicity of manner

and style which France, entangled in the rituals of Catholicism and aristocracy, conspicuously lacked. Rousseau called for a return to the soil, to the supposed nobility of the savage, the purity of primitive man. Both these ideas reflected France's almost total ignorance of America and savages. But Franklin intuitively sensed that, myths or facts, they were a superb opportunity for him to dramatize America's cause.

The opportunity also coincided with a most uncomfortable physical condition, which his month-long ordeal aboard the *Reprisal* had worsened. Off and on throughout his life, Franklin seems to have been bothered by periodic attacks of a skin disease similar to psoriasis. We know from a sporadic journal he kept on his health that it was extremely bad during his first weeks in Paris. It not only covered much of his body, but invaded his hair, and made wearing a wig very uncomfortable.[5] When he heard echoes of the excitement caused by his fur cap, he decided to make it a symbol of American simplicity and wear it everywhere, instead of a wig.

On January 15, 1777, the Abbé de Flamarens, who wrote a kind of newsletter from Paris for his friends in the provinces and abroad, described Franklin as follows: "This Quaker is in the complete costume of his sect. He has handsome features, spectacles always over his eyes, little hair, a fur cap which he wears constantly, no powder but a very clean air, extremely white linen, a brown suit completes his apparel." [6] Another Frenchman who noted his impressions of Franklin in these first weeks said: "Everything in him announces the simplicity and innocence of primitive morals. . . . Such a person was made to excite the curiosity of Paris. The people clustered around as he passed and asked, 'Who is this old peasant who has such a noble air?' " [7]

Meanwhile, in the Hotel de Hambourg, Franklin was absorbing the current political situation and meeting the men with whom he would live and work in the months to come. Inevitably, he did most of his talking with Silas Deane and Edward Bancroft, who had been in Paris since July, 1776, and had, at first glance, accomplished a great deal. Deane proudly reeled off to Franklin a dizzying list of distinguished European soldiers whom he had sent to America with his recommendations. He talked excitedly of no less than eight ships loaded with guns, ammunition, clothing, which had sailed or were ready to sail. Deane had accomplished this apparent miracle without any financial support from America. Swiftly, he introduced to Franklin the two Frenchmen who had been instrumental in making it possible.

First was Caron de Beaumarchais, a swaggering, mustachioed figure almost too flamboyant to be true. A playwright of some note, a former French foreign agent in the confidential service of both Louis XV and the present King, an expert in the art and science of blackmail, Beaumarchais poured out his enthusiasm for the American cause. He claimed, with some reason, to have played a crucial role in persuading Louis XVI to cooperate with the French foreign minister, Count de Vergennes, by making funds available to the trading company which Beaumarchais had set up, Hortalez et Cie. The King of France and the King of Spain had advanced two million livres—about 200,000 dollars—to finance the Hortalez operation. Beaumarchais, who only a few months earlier had been bankrupt and on the run from squadrons of creditors, moved into a splendid Paris residence and began living like a duke. Everything about Beaumarchais challenged belief; it was hard to understand why a great power would entrust such a delicate task to an effervescent playwright. Franklin's friend, Barbé Dubourg, undoubtedly filled his ear with a good deal of private information about Beaumarchais. Dubourg had been so upset when the playwright was made the chief channel of French secret aid that he had rushed to Versailles and begged Vergennes to abandon the idea. But Deane was completely hypnotized by Beaumarchais' abundant, if superficial, charm.

Franklin was less impressed. He preferred the second major French supporter of the American cause, who rushed to the Hotel de Hambourg to meet him. Stocky, energetic Jacques-Donatien Leray de Chaumont was one of the most successful businessmen in France. Born in a middle-class family in Nantes, he had made a fortune in the East Indian trade, bought the fifteenth-century chateau of Chaumont, and become overseer of the King's forests and commissary of the French Army. He was the kind of man to whom Franklin instinctively responded—solid, dependable, with an established character in the world of business and politics—not a backstairs palace adventurer like Beaumarchais. Chaumont had advanced 1,000,000 livres to Deane on credit, and was briskly involved in acting as the middle man in funneling much of the guns, uniforms, and ammunition through Hortalez et Cie.

It was Chaumont who undertook the job of helping to sell Franklin to the French people. He did it with a vigor and talent worthy of modern-day Madison Avenue at its best. On his Chaumont estate, this jovial merchant-prince had built a ceramics factory and imported from Italy a well-known artist, Giovanni-Batista Nini. But the artist was at work down in the Loire valley, and Chaumont wanted to move fast. Was there a sketch of Franklin that the artist could use? Franklin produced a drawing done by the son of Thomas Walpole, the English banker who had been one of the mainstays of the Grand Ohio venture. This was rushed to Nini at Chaumont, and there the artist, hearing about the rage for the fur cap, added one modeled not on Franklin's Canadian chapeau but a more famous (to the French) one worn by Jean Jacques Rousseau. Chaumont had the sketch, swiftly approved, printed on terracotta medallions and produced by the thousands in the ovens at his chateau.[8]

Neither Chaumont, Deane, nor Beaumarchais made any secret of the fact that along with an enthusiasm for the American cause, they hoped to make a great deal of money from the war. Beaumarchais made much of the point that he had, by October, 1776, spent a staggering 5,600,000 livres (over 1,000,000 dollars)—600,000 for equipping ships and paying seamen, 2,500,000 for munitions and guns, and an equal sum for clothing, largely supplied by Chaumont. Today American politicians would look askance at Deane, especially, and cry conflict of interest. But the idea barely existed in 1776. Just as few thought it strange to appoint relatives to jobs at their disposal, as Franklin invariably did, even fewer were in the least disturbed by the fact that a merchant-prince, such as Robert Morris, the man Deane yearned to emulate, was operating his private business with one hand and running the government's business with the other. It was part of the eighteenth-century's realistic attitude toward that fundamental factor in human affairs which they called "interest." Ideally, of course, the man was supposed to strike a rational balance between his own and the public's interest. If he rapaciously neglected the public side of the job, he would be open to censure.

Not only did Franklin tolerate Deane's enthusiastic participation in Beaumarchais' and Chaumont's dreams of financial glory, he persuaded him to appoint his Boston-born grandnephew, Jonathan Williams, who had hurried from London to meet his famous granduncle, as a special agent in Nantes to handle both private and public business. Aside from the fact that he did not trust Mr. Penet and wanted to keep an eye on him, Franklin was trying to solve another unpleasant dilemma that confronted him. Thomas Morris, the half-brother of Robert Morris, had been appointed commercial agent for the United States in Europe and had arrived from London looking and acting like a hopeless alcoholic. Soon a British agent was describing him as "the greatest drunkard in Europe." Franklin hoped that somehow Williams, who spoke French fluently and was an expert accountant and totally trustworthy, would prevent the chaos that was, in fact, already developing at Nantes and other ports because of the slapdash way that Beaumarchais did business.[9]

I I I

With this one gesture toward the business side of the operation, Franklin wisely withdrew from it. For one thing, he had no experience in operating on the grand multi-million-dollar scale which obviously suited the temperament and (Franklin hoped) the abilities of Deane. Besides, it was simply too exhausting. Haggling over contracts and contractors, worrying over delivery dates and shipping schedules, and roistering wth hard-drinking ship captains had Deane and his volunteer American assistant, young William Carmichael, on the run from 5 A.M. in the morning until midnight. It was no job for a man of seventy. Early in March, Franklin moved out of the Hotel de Hambourg and retreated to the village of Passy. Now a residential district of Paris, distinguished largely by its high-rent apartment houses, Passy then was a charming suburb, surrounded by forests, with a beautiful view of the Seine. There, Franklin accepted the invitation of the Chaumonts to live rent-free in one of the pavilions of their spacious villa, the Hotel de Valentinois. Franklin described his situation in a letter to his sister Jane Mecom. "I live in a fine airy house upon a hill, which has a large garden with fine walks in it, about a half an hour's drive from the city of Paris." [10]

Significantly, Passy was on the road to Versailles. This was perhaps its main attraction to Franklin, aside from his desire to escape the pandemonium of the Hotel de Hambourg. From what Deane had told him, it was evident that the diplomatic side of the American mission had been badly neglected. France was, if anything, moving away from an alliance with America as the grim news of the American Army's defeats in Canada and on Long Island filtered across the Atlantic. Permission to export the remaining war materiel purchased by Deane and Beaumarchais was abruptly revoked. This made Silas Deane profoundly angry and disillusioned with France.

Like too many other Americans, Deane had wildly idealistic notions about the motivation of men and nations. He was outraged to discover that France was helping America largely with a view to helping herself and with an absolute minimum of risks. He would have been even more outraged if he could have read the secret memoranda which Count de Vergennes had been depositing in the Foreign Office files since 1774, carefully analyzing the risks and advantages of France's intervening in the quarrel between England and her colonies. Franklin, on the other hand, was totally unsurprised by France's cold-blooded approach. He had had more than a hint of their attitude in his dinners with the French ambassador in London. Twenty years of hobnobbing with the men who ran the British Empire had long since extinguished any fanciful hope that statesmen were motivated by anything but national self-interest. While Deane and Carmichael went into frenzies because the French, with a jumpy eye on England, revoked permission for Beaumarchais' supply ships to sail, Franklin coolly went about the business of playing the bittersweet game of great power diplomacy on France's terms.[11]

On the twenty-eighth of December, 1776, Franklin, Deane, and the third American commissioner, Arthur Lee, who had rushed from London to join them, had their first interview with the French foreign minister, Charles Gravier, the Count de Vergennes. In his fifty-seventh year, this suave, reserved diplomat was the veteran of a lifetime in European capitals, ranging from Constantinople to Stockholm. Cold and aloof in manner, he was a solidly built, rather plump-faced man with a commanding, even a patronizing air. His basic tactic in diplomatic confrontations was one which Franklin had long since mastered: to say as little as possible. In this first meeting, he let Franklin do most of the talking. It was a superb study of one professional coolly taking the measure of another.

What America needed, more than anything else, was a French military alliance. But Franklin never even mentioned it throughout the interview. Instead, he talked only about America's willingness to sign a commercial treaty with France which would give the French the benefit of the thirteen colonies' substantial trade. Vergennes, who knew what America wanted and needed as well as Franklin, found himself forced to admire the American commissioner's skill. "I don't know whether Mr. Franklin told me everything," he wrote somewhat ruefully to the Count Montmorin, the French ambassador in Madrid, "but what he did say is not very interesting." The foreign minister found the petition for a commercial treaty so "modest" that he could not help wondering if there were "political considerations" behind it. With a shrewdness that matched Franklin's guile, Vergennes went to the heart of the war. Franklin wanted France as an ally. But he wanted to deal with her as an equal, not a supplicating beggar. The commercial treaty was Franklin's way of saying that America had something very important to offer in exchange for French aid. Even more important, by playing the commercial treaty as his opening card, Franklin was also informing Vergennes that he was not prepared to pay the high price France might exact for a military treaty—a formal alliance which would involve America in all of France's future wars.[12]

Eight days later, Franklin followed up this interview with a masterful letter, which made it clear that he thoroughly understood the game Vergennes was playing. Franklin began by asking for what he knew he could not get—eight ships of the line, completely manned, which the Americans wanted to hire in the same way that George III was hiring Hessians and other German soldiers. This, of course, might lead France into war with England. But Franklin was sure that by "the united force of France, Spain [allied to France by the so-called Bourbon family compact], and America, she [England] will lose all her possessions in the West Indies, much the greatest part of that commerce which has rendered her so opulent, and be reduced to that state of weakness and humiliation which she has, by her perfidy, her insolence, and her cruelty, both in the East and the West, so justly merited." This was not a bad summation of Vergennes' war aims. It could only have stirred the veteran diplomat to fresh admiration of Franklin's diplomacy. He also undoubtedly appreciated the way Franklin referred to "the private purchase made by Mr. Deane"—and then squirmed as Franklin pointed out that since the exportation of Deane's "articles" was forbidden, he wished to buy in the name of the American Congress "twenty or thirty thousand muskets and bayonets and a large quantity of ammunition and brass field pieces, to be sent under convoy."

Then, with the same suave serenity, Franklin laid a warning card on the table. "While the English are masters of the American seas, and can, without fear of interruption, transport with such ease their army from one part of our extensive coast to another, and we can only meet them by land marches, we may possibly, unless some powerful aid is given us or some strong diversion be made in our favor, be so harassed and be put to such immense distress, as that finally our people will find themselves reduced to the necessity of ending the war by an accommodation." Finally Franklin dangled even more boldly the bait of America's commerce, "which in time will be immense." The opportunity, if neglected, "may never return again; and we cannot help suggesting that a considerable delay may be attended with fatal consequences." [13]

Vergennes was much too shrewd to answer this letter in any formal way. Instead, he sent his undersecretary, Conrad Alexandre Gerard, to reply verbally. The eight ships were out of the question. The French Navy could not spare them. Even with the addition of the Spanish fleet, the Bourbon allies were not yet equal to Great Britain on the ocean. By the end of the year, they hoped to achieve naval parity—and perhaps supremacy. Then, if all went well, France might speak boldly on behalf of America. For the time being, aid must continue to be secret. But in a few days, the commissioners would see "proofs" of France's sincerity.

Within a week, King Louis XVI approved an additional loan of 2,000,000 livres to the Americans, and the French Farmers General—the government trading company which handled the imports of staples such as tobacco and wheat—advanced another million. The absolute necessity to keep the aid secret was so strictly enjoined that Franklin did not even tell the truth in a dispatch he wrote a few days later to the secret committee of Congress. He explained the loan as the result of "the inclination of the wealthy here to assist us," and added, to make sure the committee got the message, "We have accepted this generous and noble benefaction." [14]

Unfortunately, the British ambassador in Paris, Lord Stormont, knew about the loan, and in fact about every detail of France's secret aid long before Congress heard about it. George III spent 80,000 pounds a year on the British Secret Service. The French ports swarmed with British agents checking on the cargoes and destinations of French ships. But the best return the King (he read the reports of most of the agents personally) got on his money was the 500 pounds a year he paid Edward Bancroft. The man whom Franklin trusted so implicitly—whose name he had given Silas Deane in the original instructions for the American mission in Paris, and who was working as Deane's personal secretary—had been on the British payroll for over a year. By the time Franklin arrived in Paris, Bancroft had probably corrupted Silas Deane as well. But the nature of this corruption was as peculiar as the kind of war the Americans were fighting.

During the summer of 1776, Deane had collaborated with an English fanatic, known as John the Painter, to burn the naval dockyards at Portsmouth. The fugitive fled to Bancroft's house in London for refuge, with the British secret police in angry pursuit. The terrified Bancroft got rid of the Painter only hours before he was seized and duly hanged. This and other evidence suggests that Deane's corruption, at least, was more motivated by the opportunity Bancroft dangled before him to speculate on the British stock market, using their insider's knowledge. By slipping the British a little "harmless" information now and then, Bancroft would have the right to move freely between England and France. Bancroft himself may have thought he could play this murky game in the beginning. During 1775 and 1776, when the quarrel remained inside the family of the British Empire, it was easy to see right and wrong on both sides. Morally, a kind of twilight quality prevailed. But as the conflict escalated into all-out war, and independence became America's aim, it was impossible to straddle the political fence, and Bancroft, already compromised, became a full-time spy. Whether Deane knew everything or, compromised himself, only half-dreaded, half-feared, and tried to ignore the worst possibilities, is a mystery which will remain unsolved forever. Many of Deane's papers were destroyed, and Bancroft's grandson, on the discovery of his treason, burned his papers. But we now know, thanks to our access to the British Secret Service files, that Bancroft was feeding the enemy comprehensive reports on everything about the Americans in Paris, from their weapons shipments to William Carmichael's taste for expensive tarts.[15]

I V

Enmeshed in such a web of moral and political duplicity, Franklin's mission would seem to have been doomed from the day he landed. But Franklin had a priceless asset on his side: he had no illusions about his friends and he knew his enemy. His years in England had enabled him to acquire a unique insight into the way the British government operated and the British mind worked. When a Philadelphia woman, living in France as a chaperone to five English girls, wrote Franklin a note warning him that the British Secret Service had eyes and ears everywhere, he replied that he had no doubt her information was "well-founded." Then he coolly revealed the tactics that were to frustrate George III and his 80,000-pound-a-year Secret Service payroll.

"It is impossible to discover in every case the falsity of pretended friends who would know our affairs," Franklin serenely declared, "and more so to prevent being watched by spies." The only solution was a rule "which prevents any inconvenience from such practices." What was the rule? Franklin, who was conducting secret negotiations in violation of solemnly signed treaties between France and England, summed it up as "simply this: to be concerned in no affairs I would blush to have made public, and to do nothing but what spies may see and welcome. . . . If I was sure, therefore, that my valet de place was a spy, as probably he is, I think I should not discharge him for that, if in other respects I liked him." [16]

This was, of course, pure nonsense from a man of Franklin's age and experience. As he demonstrated when he was fighting Lord Hillsborough for the Ohio colony, and negotiating with the British government on the eve of the war, he knew as much about operating secretly as the most seasoned European statesman. But with that intuitive intelligence that went to the heart of every problem from science to politics, Franklin had already seen why he could afford to ignore

George III's spies—and even use them against him. Vergennes might want to keep French aid as secret as possible because it was not yet clear in his mind—or in the mind of his King—whether the American cause was worth a war with England. But Franklin, thinking of America first, saw it was to his country's *advantage* if the English knew as much as possible about what he and Deane and the other members of his mission were doing in France. The more George III found out, the more his gorge would rise, and the more likely would be an English declaration of war on France.

It did not matter to Franklin whether England did the declaring or France. His mission was to get France into the war on the American side, and the quicker the better. Of course, he continued to play the game of formal secrecy with Vergennes, but he did it hoping and praying that there was a British agent close enough to hear every word that was being spoken—which, in the person of Edward Bancroft, for all practical effects there was.

The excitement of this sport was like champagne to Franklin. His letters in these first months practically bubble. To Polly Stevenson Hewson, still in London, he wrote: "My dear, dear Polly: Figure to yourself an old man with grey hair appearing under a marten fur cap, among the powdered heads of Paris. It is this odd figure that salutes you, with handfuls of blessing on you and your dear little ones. . . . I have with me here my young grandson, Benjamin Franklin Bache, a special good boy. I shall give him a little French language and address, and send him over to pay his respects to Miss Hewson [Polly's daughter]." In a postscript he added: "I must contrive to get you to America. I want all my friends out of that wicked country. I have just seen in the papers seven paragraphs about me, of which six were lies." [17]

To an older English lady, Emma Thompson, who had written him from St. Omer, he was even more high-spirited. "You are too early, *hussy,* as well as too saucy, in calling me rebel: you should wait for the event which will determine whether it is a rebellion or only a revolution." Mrs. Thompson, a widow, was bored at St. Omer and was thinking of moving to Brussels, but wondered if she could afford it. Franklin told her that a single woman with an income of 200 pounds a year ought to be able to maintain herself comfortably anywhere— "and me into the bargain. Do not invite me in earnest, however, to come and live with you; for, being posted here, I ought not to comply, and I am not sure I should be able to refuse."

As for winning the war, he had a unique plan which he was sure Mrs. Thompson would appreciate. If every lady and gentleman in France "would only be so obliging as to follow my fashion, comb their own heads as I do mine, dismiss their *friseurs* and pay me half the money they pay to them" he would be able to finance the American war effort painlessly. Moreover, he would then enlist these *friseurs,* who were at least a hundred thousand strong, turn them into an army, and "make a visit with them to England, and dress the heads of your ministers and privy councillors; which I conceive at present to be *un peu dérangées."* [18]

Meanwhile, stories about Franklin and his mission swirled through France. One whisper had him allying France and an independent America, another had him negotiating a truce with England which guaranteed American independence, another had him weaving all Europe into a war against English arrogance. He was a scientist conferring with fellow French savants on new weapons, he was a magician who had already hypnotized Vergennes and was now working on the King, he was in secret communication with Frederick the Great in Prussia, an avowed English-hater, and Catherine the Great in Russia, who supposedly had troops for sale. Franklin contradicted none of these wild tales. As he told the American lady who had warned him against spies, "The various conjectures concerning my business here . . . do me no harm, and therefore it is not necessary that I should take the least pains to rectify them." The more people talked about him, Franklin knew, the more outraged the British would become.

Already the British ambassador, Lord Stormont, had strenuously protested Franklin's very presence in Paris, warning Vergennes that tolerating him was an unfriendly act. The foreign minister had earnestly assured Lord Stormont that, as far as he knew, Franklin was in Paris as a private citizen.

Behind the façade, Franklin maintained his pressure on Vergennes. On February 1, 1777, he went beyond his original offer of a commerical treaty and offered France a military alliance. A long letter had arrived from Robert Morris, the head of the secret committee on commerce, warning the envoys that from where he sat the future looked ominous. The Continental dollar was depreciating, trade was at a standstill, thanks to the British blockade, and there was alarming evidence that England was girding for a tremendous effort to end the war in 1777.[19] But Vergennes, like the master diplomat he was, parried Franklin's offer and did the same thing with a memoire from Congress asking for a two million pound loan.

Undaunted, Franklin decided that the best thing to do, if he wanted to start a conflagration, was strike a few sparks on his own. Poker-faced, he asked Vergennes if there was any objection against Captain Lambert Wickes doing a little cruising against British vessels, and possibly bringing his prizes into French ports. The British ambassador had protested violently over Wickes' first experiment in this department, when he brought Franklin to France. Vergennes, trapped between prudence and aggression, had to admit that there was no objection if Wickes' ship was "a vessel in distress." As for the prizes, that would depend on how loudly the British yelled. Captain Wickes promptly stood out of Nantes and in a matter of days picked off four small British merchantmen. Next, on direct orders from Franklin, he captured the royal mail packet to Lisbon, the HMS *Swallow*. Then he opened his seacocks until there was enough water in his hold to prove his "distress" and sailed his prizes back into Nantes.

The seizure of the *Swallow* was one more escalation in the psychological war Franklin was conducting against George III and his ministers. He knew that the one thing they could not bear was humiliation (an experience he did not particularly like himself) and for the monarch of the ocean to have one of his official packets captured on the high seas by these rebels his ministers had so often scorned in his palace and Parliament was humiliation to the nth degree—especially when the insult took place only a few miles from the headquarters of the British home fleet.

Once more Lord Stormont protested wildly. Vergennes cooled him off by ordering Wickes and his prizes out of French waters within twenty-four hours. Of course by this time all the prizes had been sold, taken offshore and hastily repainted, and their cargoes transferred to other ships. In a deadpan report to Congress, Franklin, with Deane as a cosigner, admitted that Wickes had given "some trouble & uneasiness to the [French] court." But in the very next sentence they coolly added, "We have ordered him to make another cruize before he returns to America." [20]

Before Wickes put to sea again, Franklin found an even likelier candidate for splashing salt water into the royal eye. His name was

Gustavus Conyngham. A hot-headed daredevil from County Donegal, he had a score to settle with the British. Their protests had forced him to abandon his ship, *The Charming Peggy,* loaded with war materiel, in Dutch waters, and corrupt Dutch officials had seized it and sold it for next to nothing. Franklin put Conyngham in command of a lugger, the *Surprise,* which had been fitted out in Dunkirk. On May 3, 1777, he captured an even more juicy diplomatic prize—the British packet, *Prince of Orange,* loaded with the confidential mail the government was sending to its ambassadors in Europe. He also snapped up a brig loaded with wine, lemons, and oranges.

This time Lord Stormont almost went berserk. Conyngham had made the mistake of taking his prizes back into Dunkirk, a port which the British partially controlled, thanks to a concession wrung from the French at the end of the Seven Years' War. Stormont insisted that Conyngham was nothing but a pirate and demanded his surrender for public hanging. Vergennes, badly shaken by Stormont's threats of war, tried to soothe the foaming British lion by arresting Conyngham and his crew. But he managed to avoid surrendering them as pirates.[21]

Meanwhile, Franklin and Deane were exultantly reading the secret correspondence of the British government. They noted how strenuously the British were telling all their ambassadors that the war in America was practically over. This passionate desire to stifle the facts was aimed, of course, at discouraging other European nations from backing the American cause. It inspired Franklin to one of his best *bon mots.* Lord Stormont, being in the most sensitive capital, was the most assiduous spreader of slander about the defiant Americans. One day a French friend rushed to Franklin to repeat the latest story about America's collapse, which he had heard from the British ambassador. Six battalions in Washington's army had laid down their arms. Was it true? the Frenchman asked.

"Oh, no," replied Franklin gravely, "it is not the truth, it is only a Stormont."

Within a day the story had swept Paris, and *stormonter* became a new Gallic synonym for lying. Lord Stormont grew so agitated that one day he wrote no less than nine letters to London about Franklin's activities.[22]

About the same time, Franklin destroyed another member of the British establishment with his wit. Edward Gibbon, who had already published (on William Strahan's presses) the early volumes of his magnificent *Decline and Fall of the Roman Empire,* was visiting Paris and happened to find himself eating at the same inn with Franklin. The American envoy invited the historian to join him at his table. Gibbon, a stumpy, myopic little man who was a member of Parliament voting blindly with the North majority at the time, primly replied that a servant of the King could not have any conversation with a rebel. Franklin sent back his regrets—and then could not resist adding that if Mr. Gibbon ever decided to write a book on the decline and fall of the British Empire, he would be happy to supply him with "ample materials." [23]

V

Using French funds, Franklin now equipped Captains Conyngham and Wickes with ships and guns to carry the war into England's home waters. Wickes, commanding a squadron of three ships, destroyed ten vessels and seized eight prizes off the Irish coast. But this was only a warmup for Conyngham's next voyage. Standing out in a cutter aptly called the *Revenge,* Conyngham cruised for two months, seizing and sometimes destroying British ships in the North Sea and the Baltic and on all the coasts of England and Ireland. He sailed completely around the British Isles, even landing once on the northwest coast of Ireland to replenish his water supply, and then hauled off for the Spanish port of Cap Ferrol. Insurance rates in London soared, and panicky British merchants began using French ships. Franklin chortled with delight when he heard that there were no less than forty French vessels in the Thames, taking on cargo—a sight that must have driven First Lord of the Admiralty Sandwich almost mad with exasperation.

Even more exasperated, if possible, was Lord Stormont, in Paris. He accused Vergennes of allowing Conyngham to sail on another pirate cruise, of outfitting and arming his ship, and, in short, of making war on British commerce. Furious, Stormont threatened to resign and thus break off diplomatic relations—which was exactly what Franklin was hoping he would do. An agitated Vergennes wrote a stiff letter to Franklin and Deane, warning them that the conduct of their privateering captains "affects the dignity of the King, my master, at the same time it offends the neutrality which His Majesty professes." [24] As for Conyngham, Vergennes showed the aggrieved Stormont the port records, which stated that the *Revenge* had been sold by its American owner, one William Hodge, to a British subject named Richard Allen, who had declared the ship was leaving on a commercial cruise.

When this palpable dodge did not stand up—Allen was a common seaman who had shipped out with Conyngham as part of his crew— Vergennes had Hodge arrested at his hotel and escorted to the Bastille. Hodge was an agent for the commercial committee of Congress, and hence a part of the American mission in Paris. Franklin promptly had influential French friends intercede for him, but Vergennes, desperate to keep up appearances, replied stiffly that it was "a very serious fault to tell the King a falsehood," and kept him in jail.[25]

Franklin and Deane did their best to play along with Vergennes. Deane solemnly avowed that Conyngham had sailed with written instructions not to attack the enemy, but that his men had mutinied and forced him to turn privateer. Nevertheless, Hodge stayed in the Bastille until the French fishing fleet was safely home from Newfoundland's Grand Banks. If Stormont had resigned and called for war, this irreplaceable source of French sailors, not to mention a fortune in ships and fish, would have been instantly devoured by the British fleet.

The naval war was by no means the only way in which Franklin made George III and his ministers squirm. When he heard the good news that Washington had reversed the tide of defeat by storming into Trenton on Christmas night to capture almost a thousand Hessians, Franklin was inspired to write one of his satiric masterpieces. It was entitled "From the Count de Shaumbergh to the Baron Hohendorf Commanding the Hessian Troops in America."

Dated from Rome, it was supposedly a letter from the Count to the Baron, in which he rapturously discusses the Hessian casualties at Trenton. "You cannot imagine my joy in being told that of the 1950 Hessians engaged in the fight, but 345 escaped. There were just 1605 men killed, and I cannot sufficiently commend your prudence in sending an exact list of the dead to my minister in London." Like all the petty German princes who had sold troops to the British, the

Count was getting paid per casualty, and the English had listed only 1455 dead, maintaining that there were a hundred wounded who ought not to be included on the dead list. But the count had no worries on this score. "I trust you will not overlook my instructions to you on quitting Cassel and that you will not have tried by human succor to recall to life the unfortunates whose days could not be lengthened but by the loss of a leg or an arm." He was thus looking forward to collecting 643,500 florins from the British Exchequer.

"I am about to send you some new recruits," crowed the Count. "Don't economize them." The Count's trip to Italy had cost him "enormously" and he had contracted for a "grand Italian opera" which was going to cost even more. It was absolutely necessary to encourage as much mortality as possible. "You will, therefore, promise promotion to all who expose themselves; you will exhort them to seek glory in the midst of dangers. . . . Meantime, I pray God, my dear Baron de Hohendorf, to have you in his holy and gracious keeping." [26]

Franklin also turned out numerous other propaganda pieces on American credit and the English national debt (if laid out in shilling pieces, he computed it would be 9572 miles more than twice around the whole circumference of the earth) with the implication that America was a sterling financial risk for European bankers and England was on the verge of financial collapse. Perhaps even more alarming to the English was the information, supplied by Paul Wentworth, ex-agent for New Hampshire and now England's Secret Service chief in France, that Franklin was corresponding with the leading members of the British opposition, Lord Shelburne and Lord Rockingham, as well as with his old friend, banker Thomas Walpole, who was close to Lord Chatham. Edward Bancroft was probably the channel through which these letters passed. Even though he made copies of the letters to pass on to Wentworth, the spy had to deliver them. Thus Franklin, without realizing it in this case, got another dividend out of George III's espionage budget.

Then, from George III's point of view, came an even more alarming development. Benjamin Vaughan, now Lord Shelburne's secretary, appeared in Paris in September, 1777, with messages for Franklin that his master did not choose to commit to paper. Almost certainly Vaughan was attempting to find out what terms, if any, Franklin was prepared to offer in truce negotiations. This made Franklin uneasy—or so he pretended. He did not want the French public to see him meeting openly with a British emissary. He could not have had any illusions about Ver-

gennes and the rest of the French government finding out about it. Their
spy system was almost as efficient and at least as numerous as the
British. To avoid "speculation" Franklin told Vaughan to meet him in
"a large white wooden building upon a boat in the river opposite to the
Tuilleries." Here Franklin and Parisians who were swimming enthusiasts
took to the water two or three times a week. The bathing attendants did
not know Franklin's name. Vaughan was told to ask for "an old Englishman with grey hair." [27]

There is no record of what Franklin told Vaughan, but he probably
got the same reply Franklin made by mail to another member of the
English Opposition, David Hartley, who had written to him, hoping to
get some glimmer of hope that peace could be speedily restored. Both
Vaughan and Hartley were thinking of a peace based on the old colonial
arrangement. Franklin swiftly demonstrated that when the interests of his
country were at stake, peace at any price was not one of his solutions.
"As to our submitting to the government of Great Britain," he told
Hartley, "it is vain to think of it. She has given us by her numberless
barbarities . . . in the prosecution of the war and in the treatment of
prisoners [in England] . . . so deep an impression of her depravity,
that we never again can trust her in the management of our affairs and
interests." He even went so far as to tell Hartley that not merely the
ministers and the members of Parliament were now detested by Americans, but the whole British people were considered equally guilty because
of their "public rejoicings on occasion of any news of the slaughter of an
innocent and virtuous people, fighting only in defense of their just rights."

Grimly Franklin added that if he could draw his friends and the friends
of liberty and virtue out of England, he would prefer to continue the
war "to the ruin of the rest." But since such a withdrawal was impossible,
he was prepared to admit a "wish" for peace. But this wish would be
ineffective unless the British showed some sign of mending their vicious
ways. The best and first thing they could do, Franklin told Hartley, was
permit the Americans to send a commissary, or hire one, to supply the
numerous American prisoners in British jails with decent food and warm
clothing. Most of them were captured seamen, and some of them, he
pointed out wrathfully, had been sold to the African and East India Companies. This might inspire Americans to sell some captured British "to
the Moors." [28]

While he undoubtedly meant every word of it on one level, Franklin,
who was always capable of thinking on three or four levels simultaneously, also had shrewd diplomatic reasons for this bellow of defiance.

He was mentally preparing for the possibility that he might yet have to negotiate some kind of truce with the English.

On the French side of his diplomatic tightrope act, things were looking grim. Although Washington had checked the British at Trenton and Princeton, there were ominous signs that in the next campaign George III and his generals were making the immense effort to crush the rebellion predicted by Robert Morris. One British army, commanded by Major General John Burgoyne, was slated to descend from Canada along the lakes and the Hudson River, and cut off New England from the middle states. Major General Howe, meanwhile, was to attack Washington's main army and capture Philadelphia.

Practically none of the supplies Deane and Beaumarchais had purchased with the King's money had reached Washington's troops. The seas off the French coast swarmed with British cruisers and the American coast was equally well patrolled. Even Dutch ships were searched and seized in European waters as well as in the Caribbean. Neither the French nor the Dutch had the stomach to challenge Great Britain by sending American cargoes under armed convoy to the West Indies. In Versailles, the French government revealed its profound caution in other ways. Vergennes assured Ambassador Stormont that the King had ordered him and the Minister of Marine to maintain "strictest obedience" to French neutrality agreements. Franklin was told to make himself as invisible as possible by ceasing to appear in public. When a publisher dedicated a book about a French scientist to Franklin, he routinely asked royal permission. At first the King gave his blessing. But when the Americans started losing, the royal imprimatur was cryptically revoked.[29]

V I

As usual, Franklin declined to lose his head. He understood precisely why the French were nervous, and he did his best to humor them. He stated his philosophy in a letter to Arthur Lee. "While we are asking aids, it is necessary to gratify the desires, and in some sort comply with the humours of those we apply to." [30] But Franklin did not comply to the point of cringing submission. He continued to let Vergennes know in numerous shrewd and subtle ways that his policy of watchful waiting was unwise. One day in July, Franklin casually mentioned how much he would like to see two plays by Molière. The *Comédie Française* heard about it—not by accident, we can be sure—and instantly announced a command performance for "Bon Homme Richard." By four in the afternoon the performance was sold out.

Elsewhere, Franklin used his wit, knowing that every word he said would be carried swiftly back to Vergennes. When a dinner companion remarked to him, "One must admit, monsieur, that it is a great and superb spectacle which America offers us today," Franklin replied, "Yes. But the spectators do not pay." As the year 1777 drew to a close, and nothing but bad news arrived from America, Franklin grew more blunt. One night in September, at another dinner party with an influential French nobleman, he deliberately drank more wine than usual. Then he turned to his host and said, "There is nothing better to do here than to drink; how can we flatter ourselves . . . that a monarchy will help republicans revolted against their monarch." [31]

Franklin was playing a truly desperate game, and in that gloomy fall of 1777, even he must have wondered if he was holding a losing hand. Along with the French stand-pat policy and mounting English pressure, there was the dismal prospect of American bankruptcy. The cargoes of tobacco and wheat that were to have financed their mission could not penetrate the British blockade. The French loan to the commissioners was exhausted, and Hortalez et Cie, to the vast agitation of Beaumarchais, was also awash in red ink. Franklin and Deane discussed the possibility of selling some of the unshipped guns and uniforms they had already bought, to keep the mission going.

The news from America continued to be bad. Arthur Lee read the commissioners a paragraph from his Congressman brother, Richard Henry Lee, morosely predicting that without an alliance with France and Spain and an immense loan, it would be "difficult to maintain . . . independence." The swarm of spies inside and outside the Paris mission also took their toll. When they presented a memoire to Versailles, asking for an additional loan of 14,000,000 livres and the recognition of American independence, Vergennes told them that his immediate superior, the aged and timid Count de Maurepas, had been warned by Ambassador Stormont that the memoire was coming before it even arrived.

From America in that same gloom-ridden fall of 1777 came bad news of a more personal kind. William Franklin had been caught signing and smuggling out of Connecticut official pardons, which the British were using to regain wavering New Jerseyites who had taken an oath of allegiance to Congress. Negotiations for his exchange with the British for an American prisoner of equal rank were abruptly suspended, and William was confined to the town jail in Litchfield, Connecticut. It was on the second floor above the local tavern, making sleep almost impossible. William's cell was minute, with only one tiny window. Meanwhile, the British Army abandoned New Jersey and took William's wife Elizabeth with them. Adrift in a New York already jammed with loyalist refugees, without funds or friends, Elizabeth collapsed both mentally and physically. Friends got word to William that she was dying, and he begged Washington's permission to go to her side. The tenderhearted Virginian was inclined to grant his request, but when he referred it to Congress, it was icily refused. So poor Elizabeth Franklin died, bewildered and alone.[32] Her sweet, compliant nature had won Jane Mecom's affection, and she wrote to Franklin, lamenting how much Elizabeth must have "suffered . . . how attentive soever those about her might have been to do all that was necessary for her. . . . She is seldom out of my mind. I loved her greatly." Then she added words that were even more poignant to Franklin. "Temple will mourn for her much." [33] For Temple, life had indeed become a series of losses, and the death of the only mother he had ever known was undoubtedly a major factor in the emotional instability he was soon to reveal.

Not quite as distressing, personally, but unsettling in other ways, was the news of Joseph Galloway's about-face. Forgetting his tall talk about raising an American regiment, Galloway had given up straddling the fence, and fled to the protection of the British Army late in 1776, when they looked like sure winners. With a pang, Franklin must have instantly wondered what happened to the trunk full of his personal papers which he had left with his indecisive friend before sailing to France. Not only all the correspondence of his twenty years in England, was in it, but also the only existing copy of the *Autobiography* he had written for William during those tranquil weeks at Twyford House with the Shipleys.

Nevertheless, Franklin struggled to keep up his own spirits and those of the other Americans. In a long talk with Arthur Lee, he reiterated his faith that America would survive. What had been accomplished already—the achievement of national unity and the Declaration of Independence—was "such a miracle in human affairs" that if he had not been in the midst of it, and seen all the developments, he would never have believed it possible. Then late in November came news that seemed to demolish even this theoretical optimism. Sir William Howe had captured Philadelphia. Congress had fled first to Baltimore, and then to York, Pennsylvania. For all of the Americans in Paris it was a devastating blow. But for Franklin, the disaster was not only political but personal. All his property, most of his personal wealth and—as far as he knew—his daughter, her husband, and his beloved grandchildren were in British hands.

But Franklin was not the sort of man who let his personal anguish disturb his public face. A few days later at a dinner party, someone said to him with obvious malice in his voice, "Well, Doctor, Howe has taken Philadelphia."

"I beg your pardon, sir," said Franklin, "Philadelphia has taken Howe." [34]

There was truth as well as wit in this answer. Philadelphia was, from a strategic point of view, useless to the British, and Franklin with his chess player's eye saw this clearly. The Delaware River was a thin, tenuous lifeline on which the British had to depend for supplies. They were surrounded by a sea of hostile Americans. Philadelphia was a symbolic conquest—not a real one.

But diplomats deal in symbols, and to the American mission in Paris the news was disheartening. On November twenty-seventh, they gathered for a grim conference. Silas Deane wanted to categorically inform the French government that the Americans demanded an immediate alliance, or they would begin negotiations for a settlement with Great Britain. Franklin refused to throw in his hand so recklessly. He insisted America could "maintain the contest and successfully too without any European assistance." The danger was that France might construe such an ultimatum as a threat and "abandon us in despair or in anger." Lee sided with Franklin. The disconsolate envoys ended the conference by agreeing that the most they could hope for at the moment was that France would continue to pay the interest on their debts, which would at least keep them out of jail.

Less than a week after this dismal decision, a rumor came drifting into Paris from Nantes. An American ship had arrived with a messenger carrying important dispatches for the commissioners in Paris. Like starving men, Franklin and his confreres gnawed on this crumb of hope. Perhaps the story of Howe's capture of Philadelphia was another British fiction. The three commissioners and their French friends,

Beaumarchais and Chaumont, gathered at Franklin's house in Passy to await the arrival of the courier.

The moment a chaise was heard rattling over the cobblestones of the courtyard of the Hotel Valentinois, Franklin and the others rushed out of the house. Thirty-year-old Jonathan Loring Austin of Boston, secretary of the Massachusetts Board of War, barely had time to introduce himself before Franklin asked, "Sir, *is* Philadelphia taken?"

"Yes, sir," replied Austin.

Franklin's great head drooped. With a sigh he clasped his hands and turned away, obviously crushed by the official confirmation of the news he had dreaded to hear. He had taken perhaps two steps toward the house when young Austin spoke again.

"But, sir, I have greater news than that. General Burgoyne and his whole army are prisoners of war!" [35]

The news was, in Silas Deane's words, "like a sovereign cordial to the dying." Franklin rushed Austin into the house and with shaking hands ripped his dispatches from his bags. Beaumarchais leaped into his carriage and thundered away toward Paris to spread the news. He declined to slow down for a curve in the road and found himself head over heels in the ditch. For the next few days he spread the news with his arm in a sling. Undoubtedly, he made a great deal of one aspect of Burgoyne's defeat, which must have also delighted Franklin and Deane. Many of the guns and much of the ammunition on the American side at the battle of Saratoga had come from the hold of the *Amphitrite,* a Beaumarchais ship that had broken through the British blockade and unloaded her deadly cargo at Portsmouth, New Hampshire.

VII

At Passy, Franklin and his fellow commissioners worked day and night preparing dispatches spreading the official news to other European countries that Burgoyne was a captive and the British offensive shattered. The most important communication went to Count de Vergennes at Versailles.

In two days, they had an encouraging answer. Monsieur Gerard, undersecretary for foreign affairs, paid the envoys a personal call to convey Vergennes' congratulations. More important, the undersecretary said that the Count thought the time was ripe for the envoys to renew their proposals for an alliance. Franklin prepared the document, had it signed and approved by his fellow envoys, and sent Temple Franklin rushing to Versailles with it. He came dashing back breathlessly to repeat Vergennes' words: "In two days an answer shall be sent to you and you will see how much disposed I am to serve the cause of America." That night at dinner, George Grand, brother of their French banker, Ferdinand Grand, told Franklin that the foreign minister had spoken of the envoys as "our friends" instead of "your friends"—the diplomatic subterfuge he had used in the past.

Four days later, Franklin, Deane, and Lee played the Secret Service game of changing carriages and sneaking out back doors to meet Vergennes and Gerard in a house a half-mile outside of Versailles. There, the cresting wave on which they seemed to be riding to victory suddenly began to falter. Vergennes was still playing a cautious game. He discussed in detail the possible treaty that France might make with the Americans. But then he coolly announced that it was impossible to sign it unless Spain concurred. The King of Spain was a Bourbon uncle of Louis XVI of France. Their "family compact" forbade them to enter into wars or alliances without mutual approval.

Franklin instantly saw that this could and probably would lead to some serious foot-dragging. He had already sent Arthur Lee to Spain in an attempt to bring her over to the American side, and the Spanish had been so lukewarm they declined even to let Lee into the country. He had conducted a series of fruitless conferences with the Spanish foreign minister in a border town.

But there was a way of building a fire under the French, and Franklin had already taken the first steps to convert George III into his carrier of wood. The news of Burgoyne's disaster sent a wave of hysteria churning through the British ministry. Lord North persuaded a reluctant George III that the time had come to offer massive conciliation to the Americans, to head off a French alliance. Secret agent Paul Wentworth now was sent hustling to Paris to find Franklin and Deane and talk about the possibility of a truce.

Franklin let Deane smoke out the British offer. The French police and Vergennes' secret agents, of course, knew precisely what Wentworth's mission was. The mere fact that Deane had agreed to see the British spy threw them into a panic. Gerard rushed to Deane even before he met Wentworth and told him that the French had decided not to wait for word from Spain. They were ready to give the United States formal recognition if they promised not to conclude a separate peace with England. Meanwhile, Franklin himself played the war-of-nerves game with Vergennes, turning over to the French minister a letter from London asking him if the Americans would accept something "a little short of absolute independency." At dinner, Wentworth found Deane, carefully rehearsed by Franklin, performing like a master diplomat. The discouraged Wentworth reported to his Secret Service chief in England that Deane was "vain, desultory and subtle" and utterly uninterested in the "honours and emoluments" which he dangled in front of him if he became a cooperative peacemaker.[36]

On December thirty-first, the news Franklin had feared finally arrived from Spain. King Charles III was not inclined to fight for American independence at present. Five more days passed with nothing but silence from Versailles. Franklin decided it was time to raise the pressure on Vergennes to the maximum level. After three weeks of dodging dinner invitations from Wentworth, he suddenly agreed to an interview, with Deane present as a witness. In advance Franklin laid down one stern requirement. There was to be no talk of "rewards or emoluments."

On January 6, 1778, the master spy spent two hours with Franklin. He tried flattery, argument, persuasion, and appeals to history. He urged Franklin to forget his private resentments and help make Britain and America "the greatest empire on earth." Franklin's reply was independence or nothing. Wentworth produced an unsigned letter from William Eden, his Secret Service boss, declaring that Britain was ready to fight for another ten years rather than grant America independence.

"America," Franklin snapped, "is ready to fight fifty years to win it."

The rest of the letter, full of conciliatory sentiments, Franklin found sensible enough. Knowing that Wentworth would report the interview to his royal superiors, Franklin could not resist a dig at Lord North and George III. He was glad, he said, "to find honour and zeal so near the throne." Here and throughout the interview, Wentworth was baffled to find Franklin dodging every proposition he offered him. "I never knew him to be so eccentric," reported the harassed spy.[37]

The next day, a baffled Wentworth went back to London, and Franklin added one final touch to his scenario. He simply neglected to report to Vergennes that he had seen the spy. The jittery foreign minister, remembering how faithfully Franklin had reported previous British overtures, convened the French Council of Ministers and warned them that England was clearly upping the ante and it was time for France to act. The Council instantly voted for an alliance.

The next day, the commissioners were asked to gather at Deane's lodgings in Paris for a conference with Gerard. Nervously Gerard asked them, "What is necessary to be done to give such satisfaction to the American commissioners as to engage them not to listen to any propositions from England for a new connection with that country?"

After a brief conference with his fellow commissioners, Franklin wrote out a formal answer. "The commissioners have long since proposed a treaty of amity and commerce which is not yet concluded. The immediate conclusion of that treaty will remove the uncertainty they are under with regard to it and give them such a reliance on the friendship of France as to reject firmly all propositions made to them of peace from England which have not for their basis the entire freedom and independence of America, both in matters of government and commerce."

Solemnly Gerard read the answer, and then informed the commissioners that the Council of Ministers had confirmed the alliance and King Louis XVI had given his personal pledge to sign the treaty, no matter what his Spanish uncle thought of it. Benjamin Franklin had proved himself the equal if not the superior of the best diplomats in Europe.

One final touch remained. On the fifth of February, the details of the treaty were finally worked out and Franklin and his fellow envoys were invited to the office of the Ministry for Foreign Affairs for a formal signing. Edward Bancroft noticed that Franklin dressed for the occasion in a suit of Manchester velvet which was vaguely familiar. Just as they were about to depart for the signing, they received word from Undersecretary Gerard that he was ill with a heavy cold and would prefer to postpone the ceremony until the following day. The Americans, of course, complied, and the next day Bancroft noticed that Franklin was wearing the same suit once more. Then he re-

membered where he had seen it—it was the outfit Franklin had worn
when Solicitor General Wedderburn had humiliated him before the
Lords in Council at the Cockpit. Bancroft remarked on the coincidence
to Silas Deane, and the Yankee trader asked Franklin why he was
wearing it. Franklin smiled and said: "To give it a little revenge." [38]

VIII

The Treaty of Alliance meant almost certain war between England and
France. But Franklin, with his triple-decker mind, was already thinking
about peace. The chief obstacle, in his view, was the ministry of yes-
men around George III. Get rid of them, he reasoned, and there was
a good possibility that he and his numerous friends in the opposition
might be able to work out a settlement based on free trade and American independence. So he boldly began playing British politics once
more. Using Edward Bancroft as his emissary, Franklin got word to
his old friend of the Grand Ohio days, banker Thomas Walpole, that
the treaty with France was signed, and he urged him to make the
best possible use of the news. On December 23, 1777, Walpole had
told Franklin that he had been having conversations with Lord Chatham and was "certain he would concede everything necessary for the
security of America and begin the business at the right end as you
may judge for a cessation of arms & recalling the troops. He & Lord
Camden desire their best compliments to you. . . ." [39] Walpole leaked
the news of the treaty to Charles James Fox, the most explosive member
of the Opposition and a Parliamentary debater of rare talent.

When the House of Commons convened on February 17, 1778, Lord
North promptly introduced conciliatory acts which granted America
the terms Franklin had suggested two short years before in his negotiations with Lord Howe—the repeal of all the obnoxious legislation
back to 1763, the recognition of the Continental Congress, and the
virtual independence of America, within the framework of the empire.
Fox allowed North to pose as a peacemaker for the better part of two
hours. He even remained silent when the Prime Minister declared his

concessions "were from reason and propriety, not from necessity." [40] Fox then arose and ironically congratulated Lord North for joining the opposition. Then, like the expert verbal duelist that he was, he pinned the First Minister to his bench by asking whether America had signed a treaty with France within the last ten days.

Waspish Horace Walpole, who may have been let in on the secret by his cousin Thomas, described the ensuing scene in his diary. "Lord North was thunderstruck and would not rise. . . . Burke called on his Lordship to answer to the fact of the treaty. Still the Minister was silent, till Sir G. Saville rose, and told him that it would be criminal to withhold a reply, and a matter of impeachment, and ended with crying, 'An answer! An answer! An answer!' Lord North, thus forced up, owned he had heard a report of the treaty, but desired to give no answer to the house at that moment. . . . Such evasive answers rather convinced everybody of the truth of the report." [41] In fact, a copy of the treaty (courtesy of Edward Bancroft) was on North's desk at that moment. But to have admitted it would have also meant admitting that his conciliatory proposals were not inspired by "reason and propriety" but frantic necessity.

Franklin was obviously hoping to make a fool out of North in the House of Commons and bring down the ministry. How close he came was evident from the Secret Service reports which Beaumarchais sent Vergennes from his agents in England. At the end of February, Beaumarchais was predicting, "Within a week Lord Chatham will be entrusted with affairs and Lord North dismissed." North himself revealed his desperation by begging the King to let him resign. "The anxiety of his mind for the last two months has deprived Lord North of his memory and understanding," he told his royal master. Meanwhile, he was sending relays of negotiators to Franklin in a last hysterical try to appease the man he and his friends had insulted and humiliated.

First came a Moravian churchman, James Hutton, an old neighbor from Craven Street. Then Franklin's Parliamentary correspondent, David Hartley, and then another member of Parliament, William Pulteney. What Franklin told them was not likely to restore Lord North's memory and understanding. He reiterated that independence was non-negotiable. To Hutton he suggested that if England wanted to regain America's good will, she might throw in Canada, Nova Scotia, and Florida in the treaty of peace. To Hartley, he wrote, "Whenever you shall be disposed to make peace upon equal and reasonable terms, you will find little difficulty, if you get first an honest ministry. The present have all along acted so deceitfully and treacherously as well as inhumanly toward the Americans, that I imagine, the absolute want of all confidence in them, will make a treaty at present, between them and the Congress impracticable." [42] Pulteney, operating like a secret agent under an assumed name, made the mistake of telling Franklin that he came in a semi-official capacity and was prepared to offer peace terms. Franklin instantly showed him the door. To have said another word to him would have violated the treaty with France, in spirit if not in fact. Franklin then immediately informed Vergennes of North's approach.

Pressing what he thought was an advantage, Franklin now took the offensive and dispatched Jonathan Loring Austin to England, where he became a semi-permanent boarder with Lord Shelburne and attended Parliament as a guest of the Opposition, dined regularly in public with them, and thus made it clear that Franklin was as willing to do business with the Opposition as he was loath to negotiate with Lord North. He was, in effect, telling Parliament: If you want peace, get rid of North and his toadies. It was nothing less than a peace offensive, with Franklin simultaneously working all his avenues to the seat of power. On February twenty-sixth, he wrote David Hartley, "I am of opinion, that if wise and honest men, such as Sir George Saville, the Bishop of St. Asaph, and yourself were to come over here immediately with powers to treat, you might not only obtain peace with America, but prevent a war with France." [43]

Pitting himself so boldly against the men in control of the most powerful nation in the world was not without its dangers. At one point, Hartley, during these tense weeks, sent Franklin a nervous message that he was in danger of being assassinated. This was certainly not beyond the power of the British Secret Service or beneath their ethics. More and more, George III was coming to view the entire war as a contest between himself and Benjamin Franklin. When a King acquires such a fixation, there are always a few dutiful servants in the wings, eager to relieve His Majesty of his tormentor. But Franklin refused to scare. Instead of blustering defiance, he sent Hartley a reply which may well have given the British second thoughts: "I thank you for your kind caution, but having nearly finished a long life, I set but little value on what remains of it. . . . Perhaps the best use such an old fellow can be put to is to make a martyr of him." [44]

But George III was a very stubborn man. Although he was fundamentally obtuse, there was a streak of cunning in his nature that enabled him to control more gifted men. Late in 1777, he had taken the precaution of purchasing Lord North by giving him 20,000 pounds to settle his debts. This made the pliant First Minister his political slave, unable to resign in the face of total disaster. With a similar use of royal funds and favors, the King kept his grip on the majority in Parliament, in spite of fulminations from the Franklin favored Opposition. The closest they came to victory was on a budgetary vote early in March which the ministry carried by only six votes in a House of 288. Horace Walpole, watching the King's blunders from the sidelines, became so agitated that he gasped: "Unless sudden inspiration should seize the whole island of Britain and make it with one voice invite Dr. Franklin to come over and new model the government, it will crumble away in the hands that still hold it." [45] But neither so extravagant a summons nor any other kind of serious gesture was made by George III or his ministers to avert the inevitable confrontation.

I X

It came on March 20, 1778, when King Louis XVI formally received Franklin and his fellow envoys at Versailles. A week before, Vergennes had notified Ambassador Stormont of the existence of the treaty, and the French ambassador in London had handed a similar note to the British foreign secretary. But the King's personal reception was the ultimate stamp of approval, and Franklin was deeply aware of the momentous nature of the day. The admittedly small hope he had entertained for a manipulated peace was gone. Calmly he resumed the role he had played so well during his first months in France—the symbol of republican simplicity. For the visit to Versailles, he carried this performance to the level of consummate daring by choosing to appear before the King without a wig, sans sword or any other accouterment but a simple brown suit, spotless white stockings and plain shoes with silver buckles. It is hard for us to realize that this was daring—but dress at the court of Versailles was as carefully regulated as all the other bits of etiquette that surrounded the King. There were even prescribed styles for each season. It was not at all unusual for the royal chamberlain to bar those who were out of costume.

As his carriage rolled into the immense courtyard of Versailles, Franklin must have felt a surge of contradictory emotions. He was about to pledge America's faith to a nation that he had been born to suspect and even hate. For weeks, in letters and in person, his English friends had been warning him not to make the mistake of trusting France. The game he had played to bring down the North ministry, the numerous remarks he had made about the inadvisability of a virgin state suitoring for alliances, were further indications of the deep reluctance he had had to overcome within himself before achieving this diplomatic triumph. Only a few weeks before he had told David Hartley that America was "a virtuous daughter . . . forc'd and driven into the arms of France." [46] Now those arms were about to officially embrace her. Perhaps there was in Franklin's bold choice of costume an unspoken compromise with these uneasy echoes in his mind. It was a way of announcing to the French in the most subtle and yet declaratory terms that America *was* independent and meant to stay that way.

In the courtyard, crowds of Parisians swarmed around the envoys' coaches. A gasp ran through the crowd when Franklin alighted. "He is dressed like a Quaker," went the half-frightened whisper through the spectators. From Vergennes' apartment in a wing of the palace, Franklin and his fellow envoys were led down the seemingly endless corridors to the monumental doors of the royal apartments. Noblemen and noblewomen lined the walls, murmuring their admiration of Franklin's daring. But the Frenchman who almost went into shock was the royal chamberlain. There was an agonizing moment when, in the opinion of one American who was present, this functionary debated a protest. But his nerve failed him, and Franklin swept serenely into the King's dressing room, where Louis XVI greeted him with a lack of ceremony which was in perfect harmony with the tone Franklin had set. In a loose robe, with his hair hanging down to his shoulders, the young King was warm and relaxed. "Firmly assure Congress," he said, "of my friendship. I hope that this will be for the good of the two nations." He added that he was "exceedingly satisfied, in particular, with your own conduct during your residence in my kingdom." Franklin replied, "Your Majesty may count on the gratitude of Congress and its faithful observance of the pledge it now takes." [47]

As Franklin returned to the courtyard, the sight of him inspired the spectators there to abandon the strict requirements of palace etiquette, and they burst into a tremendous cheer. There is a tradition that Franklin was so moved by it, he wept. Certainly the spontaneous affection of these warm-hearted people was enough to make him all but banish his inherited fears and prejudices, and rejoice in the certainty that he had found a good husband for the "virtuous daughter" that England had driven out of her house.

X

The following day a sullen Lord Stormont slunk out of Paris without paying his respects to the King. It was practically a declaration of war. In England, the Opposition gathered around Lord Chatham for one last attempt to bring down the North ministry. Desperately ill, the great statesman was practically carried into the House of Lords and there rose to excoriate the ministry. Just as the debate began, with every evidence that North and his followers were on the brink of rout, Chatham collapsed and was carried out of the chamber, a dying man. The Opposition was left in total disarray, and North bumbled on in the service of the relentless King.

Franklin was soon too busy coping with an outbreak of political madness in the American mission to pay much attention to what was happening in England. Instead of uniting the three commissioners in a euphoria of triumph, the French alliance became a signal for an unbelievably mean and fratricidal war of words. The evil genius was Arthur Lee.

At first, Lee had tried to overcome his old envy of Franklin, born in the days when the man from Philadelphia had so thoroughly demolished him in the Grand Ohio fight and in the competition for the Massachusetts agency. When Lee first arrived in Paris, he wrote glow-

ingly of Franklin to Lord Shelburne, calling him "our Pater Patriae"—
the father of his country—several years before anyone had fastened
the title on George Washington.[48] In his sour, savage way, Lee was
a dedicated American. But like too many radicals, he was primarily a
hater. This emotion, so foreign to Franklin's spirit, was like a bubbling
corrosive in Lee's soul, constantly threatening to spill over onto his
friends as well as his enemies.

Lee was also an immensely vain, egotistical man, imbued with an
enormous sense of personal and family esteem. The longer he stayed
in France, the more mortified he became by Franklin's popularity. How
could the French shower such adulation on the son of a tallow candler
and treat Arthur Lee, scion of the Lees of Virginia, as if he were
practically invisible? This was the underlying, fundamental cause of
Lee's torment. But at first he controlled this basic emotion and aimed
his spleen at a lesser target—Silas Deane.

While Lee was in England, he had met Beaumarchais and the ebullient dramatist had talked wildly to him, in his usual extravagant terms,
about the prospects of French aid for America. At the time, Lee got
the distinct impression that this aid was to be a free gift of the French
King. By the time Silas Deane arrived in Europe, and Beaumarchais
had got down to serious negotiations with Vergennes, the scheme of
Hortalez et Cie had been born, and this free gift idea had been abandoned for both diplomatic and financial reasons.

Louis XVI was one of the great cheapskates of history, and if he
could possibly avoid giving anything away, he was eager to do it.
There was also the wisdom of forcing Americans to pay for the aid
in foodstuffs and raw material, thus enlarging the embryo commerce
between the two nations. In fact, once Beaumarchais got his initial
royal backing, he borrowed money wherever he could find it and invited numerous wealthy friends and speculators to join him in Hortalez
et Cie, with the prospect of making millions. This Arthur Lee righteously refused to believe. With his basic inclination to suspect treachery
and corruption everywhere, he instantly decided that Beaumarchais was
a crook who was mulcting Americans for goods and services the King
was giving away, and Silas Deane was even worse than a crook, he
was a traitor in the game for all he could rob from his country.

Never hesitant about putting his opinions on paper, Arthur Lee soon
began writing these slanders to the Continental Congress. There he had
some powerful correspondents. His two brothers, Richard Henry Lee

and Francis Lightfoot Lee, were influential members from Virginia. Richard was a fervent admirer and constant colleague of Samuel Adams of Massachusetts, who was not far behind Arthur Lee when it came to suspecting the worst of people. Thus Lee had support from the two most powerful states in the confederation. Serenely certain of his own rectitude, he was soon outlining a plan whereby the "Ls & As" could take over the whole war. The first thing he did was persuade Congress to send him reinforcements. He got his brother, William Lee, appointed commercial agent for America in France, replacing the previous commissioner, Thomas Morris, drunken half-brother of financier Robert Morris. Thomas needed replacing; he had allowed the slippery French merchant Penet, to swindle thousands from the American government. William Lee was cut from the same contumacious cloth as Arthur; in fact he was even more of an anomaly as an American diplomat because he was also still an alderman of the city of London—a post he declined to resign.[49] Although Franklin's son was in jail in Connecticut for trying to straddle the fence between rebel and loyalist, William Lee did not for a moment allow his strange political stance to deter him from joining Arthur in his mudslinging campaign. "You can't at this time be unacquainted with the faithless principles, the low, dirty intrigue, the selfish views & the wicked arts of a certain race of men, & believe me, a full crop of these qualities you sent in the first instance from Philadelphia to Paris," he told his correspondents in America. Meanwhile, Arthur was telling Samuel Adams and Richard Henry Lee how to rearrange America's diplomats in Europe. "France remains the center of political activity, and here, therefore, I should choose to be employed." He proposed sending Franklin to Vienna, a post that was "respectable and quiet" and thus eminently suited for an old man. Silas Deane could be shipped to Holland, and "the Alderman"—brother William—was slated for Berlin. But he reiterated that France, "the great wheel that moves them all," was to be reserved for his unique genius.[50]

To achieve this goal, Lee found fault with everything. He professed to be horrified when he discovered that Silas Deane alone, without consultation with the other commissioners, was sending orders to Franklin's nephew, Jonathan Williams, in Nantes. Lee made it seem a crime that Deane was doing private business on the side, sometimes investing his own money as well as the government's money in outfitting a privateer or in buying goods and hiring a ship to transport them to America. It did not trouble him in the least that Deane lacked the Lee family's patriarchal estates and hundreds of slaves and had only his business connections to keep him and his family solvent. The British ministry, eager to repay Franklin for the headaches he had had been giving them by feeding inside information to the Opposition, was delighted to fill Lee's head with stories, some of them true, about Deane and Edward Bancroft gambling in British stocks. Lee got this information from Major John Thornton, a self-styled humanitarian who had come to Paris on behalf of American prisoners of war in British jails. Lee hired Thornton as his secretary, never suspecting he was a British spy.

While Thornton was picking him clean, Lee fulminated over Bancroft's frequent trips to England, which aroused his suspicions to the point of frenzy. Considering the fact that he was guilty, Bancroft did a remarkable job of facing Lee down, boldly calling on him for proof and pointing to the secret information (most of it rather trifling) which he brought back from England as proof of his loyalty to the patriot cause. But lack of proof never troubled Arthur Lee. In the feverish world of his imagination, he was capable of conjuring up evidence that did not exist and then writing about it as if it were a reality he had seen and even touched. Bancroft became an excuse to widen his circle of malevolence to include Franklin. He began by accusing the Doctor of spending too much time in the salons and dining rooms of Paris. Since he himself, thanks to his sour and humorless ways, was rarely invited into French homes, he was soon conjuring up visions of unspeakable orgies in which Franklin was indulging himself, while his country was perishing.

Although neither Deane nor Franklin had any idea of what Lee was writing home, it was easy enough to gather from Lee's touchy manner that all was not harmonious within the mission. Franklin struggled to maintain at least a semblance of good feeling. One day when Deane and Lee were dining with him, one of their French neighbors sent in a large cake with the inscription, *Le digne Franklin* (The worthy Franklin).

"As usual, Doctor," Deane said, "we have to thank you for our accommodation and to appropriate your present to our joint use."

Franklin, no doubt seeing the sour look on Arthur Lee's face, said, "Not at all. This must be intended for all the commissioners; only these French people cannot write English. They mean, no doubt, Lee, Deane, Franklin."

"That might answer," growled the humorless Lee, "but we know that whenever they remember us at all, they always put you first." [51]

Unfortunately for Silas Deane, Lee's attack on him coincided with widespread criticism of both the quality and the number of the foreign officers Deane had recruited to serve in the American Army. Too many of these men arrived in America with a contract signed by Deane, guaranteeing them commands and ranks already held by Americans. Congress was forced either to buy them out and ship them home at American expense, or order Washington to give them commands, at the risk of alienating some of the best officers in the American Army. Franklin did his best to intercede for Deane. He knew from first-hand experience the immense pressure under which Deane had worked, as well as his inexperience in such matters. Franklin told Congressman James Lovell of the Committee for Foreign Affairs, "I, who am upon the spot and know the infinite difficulty of resisting the powerful solicitations of great men, who if disobliged might have it in their power to obstruct the supplies he was then obtaining do not wonder . . . he was at first prevailed on to make some such agreements." All of the men were recommended as "Caesars, each of whom would have been a valuable acquisition to America." He assured Lovell that Deane had "long since corrected that mistake, and daily approves himself to my certain knowledge an able, active and extremely useful servant of the publick." [52]

Sensing he had Deane on the defensive, Lee became even more impossible to deal with during the negotiations for the Treaty of Alliance. Vergennes made it clear that Lee was *persona non grata* to him, and hence he was frequently left out of the highly secret diplomatic maneuverings. This threw Lee into frenzies of resentment. He called for reinforcements on his fellow Southerner, Ralph Izard, who had been appointed ambassador to the court of the Grand Duke of Tuscany. Izard was immensely wealthy and had many of the mannerisms and attitudes of an English lord. Pontifically, he insisted on intruding himself into the delicate negotiations and was outraged when Franklin declined to consult him. At one point, Lee, with Izard's headstrong backing, threatened to wreck the treaty by refusing to sign it, because he and Izard did not like a minor clause waiving export duties on goods shipped to the French West Indies in return for a French waiver on the exportation of molasses to the United States. Only a last-minute concession by the French, which allowed Congress to be the final arbiter of this agreement, rescued Franklin from acute embarrassment.

Izard wrote Franklin a haughty letter, declaring he felt himself hurt by Franklin's lack of consultation with him during the negotiations, and demanding an interview with him. Franklin's reply must have made it clear to the South Carolina aristocrat that he was not dealing with a man in his dotage. Tersely he said he had no time to give a full answer to Izard's letter. "I must submit to remain some days under the opinion you appear to have formed, not only of my poor understanding in the general interest of America, but of my defects in sincerity, politeness and attention to your instructions. . . . You mentioned that you feel yourself hurt. Permit me to offer you a maxim, which has thro life been of use to me, and may be so to you, in preventing such imaginary hurts. It is, 'always to suppose one's friends may be right till one finds them wrong, rather than to suppose them wrong till one finds them right.' " [53]

Hotheaded and impulsive, Deane was almost too willing to feud with Arthur Lee. Franklin attempted to cool him off by imputing Lee's habits of mind to incipient insanity. "It is very charitable to impute to insanity what proceeds from the malignity of his heart," Deane told Jonathan Williams. "But the Doctor insists upon it that it is really his case, & I am every day more & more inclined to give in to it." [54] But when Congress recalled Deane (on November 21, 1777) and replaced him with John Adams, there was no doubt that Lee had triumphed at home. The unstable Deane alternated between rage and self-pity, and at first threatened to quit politics and refuse to return to America.

But Beaumarchais announced that he could make Deane's return a triumph if he let the dramatist write the scenario. Beaumarchais arranged with Vergennes for Deane to return aboard a French fleet, escorting the first French ambassador to the United States. The King gave him a portrait framed in diamonds, Vergennes wrote a letter of glowing praise, and Franklin added another personal note to Henry Laurens, the president of Congress.

More important, Franklin agreed, at Vergennes' request, to say nothing to Arthur Lee about the identity or departure of the new

French ambassador, their good friend Monsieur Gerard, the foreign office undersecretary with whom Franklin had conducted most of the negotiations. Deane, of course, found no difficulty in keeping his mouth shut, since he knew that Lee would put his busy pen to work immediately and arouse his cohorts in Congress to prime their rhetorical artillery. So, on March 31, 1778, Deane said farewell to Franklin and slipped out of Paris secretly. That night he joined Gerard somewhere along the highway south, and they headed for the naval base at Toulon, where the French fleet was ready to sail.

This was all very comforting to Deane. But it left Franklin alone to face the spiteful wrath of the Lees. Arthur Lee went into a tantrum when he found out that he had been deceived. Lee knew, of course, that Deane had been recalled, and he had peremptorily insisted that his public accounts be settled, under his (Lee's) authoritative eye before Deane departed. On the day Deane left Paris, Lee had written Franklin a haughty letter demanding "that the earliest day may be appointed" to tackle this formidable job. Franklin had coolly rebuffed him: "There is a stile in some of your letters, I observe it particularly in the last, whereby superior merit is assumed to yourself in point of care and attention to business, and blame is insinuated on your colleagues without making yourself accountable by a direct charge of negligence." The tactic, Franklin said, "was as artful as it is unkind." He then informed Lee that Deane had departed, leaving with him "the publick papers." [55]

Lee exploded. "Had you studied to deceive the most distrusted and dangerous enemy of the public, you could not have done it more effectually," he shrilled. ". . . I trust, sir, you will not treat this letter as you have done many others with the indignity of not answering it."

Like William Franklin, Arthur Lee seemed to have a confirmed opinion that Franklin was in his dotage. To Lee, this meant he could be lectured and chastised almost at will. Franklin's letter of April third must have changed his mind.

> SIR,
> It is true I have omitted answering some of your letters. I do not like to answer angry letters. I hate disputes. I am old, cannot have long to live, have much to do and no time for altercation. If I have often receiv'd and borne your magisterial snubbings and rebukes without reply, ascribe it to the right causes, my concern for

the honour & success of our mission, which would be hurt by our
quarrelling, my love of peace, my respect for your good qualities,
and my pity of your sick mind, which is forever tormenting itself,
with its jealousies, suspicions & fancies that others mean you ill,
wrong you, or fail in respect for you.—If you do not cure your self
of this temper it will end in insanity, of which it is the symptomatick
forerunner, as I have seen in several instances. God preserve you
from so terrible an evil: and for his sake pray suffer me to live in
quiet.

The following day Franklin wrote Lee a longer letter, answering
his accusations in detail and adding an even more stinging rebuke.
"You ask me, why I act so inconsistent with my duty to the publick?
This is a heavy charge, sir, which I have not deserved. But it is to
the publick, that I am accountable and not to you. I have been a
servant to many publicks thro' a long life; have serv'd them with
fidelity, and have been honoured by their approbation: there is not
a single instance of my ever being accus'd before of acting contrary
to their interest or my duty. I shall account to the Congress when
call'd upon for this my terrible offense of being silent to you about
Mr. Deane's and M. Gerard's departure. And I have no doubt of
their equity in acquitting me." [56]

Some historians doubt that Franklin sent these letters to Lee. But he
may have read them to him, as he read to William his long letter on his
negotiations in England. He obviously wanted a tough reply to Lee
on the record. Franklin took Lee seriously because he realized the
damage the testy Virginian could do to the American cause with his
connections in Congress. Moreover, he was, technically, Franklin's
equal in the American mission in Paris. Izard, on the other hand,
although he was a friend of Henry Laurens, the president of Congress,
Franklin treated as comedy. For one thing, his diplomatic assignment
to the Grand Duke of Tuscany was an absurdity. The Grand Duke,
from whom Congress hoped to extract a loan, would not even let
the ambassador into his country. But Izard, by a close reading of his
commission, persuaded himself that he was empowered to remain in
Paris and serve as a fourth wheel on the American mission there.
Franklin did not agree, and ignored him. This produced an endless
series of angry expostulations and explosions. Izard styled himself
"the voice of the truth" and lectured Franklin on everything he did,

even down to Franklin's having his grandson copy the Treaty of Alliance instead of letting Lee or Izard do it. At one point, he accused Franklin of acting like the tyrant Kouli Khan who cut the tendons of a man's legs with his sword and then afterwards compelled him to dance.[57]

Izard had a habit of sending his secretary, one John Julius Pringle, to Franklin with ultimata which Franklin was supposed to answer on the spot. One day in April of 1778, Pringle, who was as imperious as his employer, appeared in Franklin's study with one of these missives. Obviously enjoying himself, Franklin singled out Izard's favorite objection—that no one had sent him a copy of the treaty with France, which he very badly needed to study as a model for the treaty he hoped to negotiate with Tuscany. The implication was that Franklin was guilty of delaying this immensely important mission. "Has not the treaty been sent to him? Did he go into Tuscany?" Franklin asked, knowing perfectly well that Izard was still sitting in Paris, with his wife and children, living off the American mission.

Pringle could only puff that Izard had "good reasons for staying." Izard proceeded to stay for another eight months, and then had the gall to ask Franklin for more money to support himself and his family in their accustomed style. Wryly, Franklin pointed out to him that he had received 2000 guineas—over 10,000 dollars—less than a year before to equip him for his trip to Tuscany, and "you have not incurr'd the expence of that journey." Then Franklin grew blunt. "You are a gentleman of fortune. You did not come to France with any dependence on being maintained here with your family at the expence of the United States in the time of their distress." Instead of drawing more money from his country's debt-riddled exchequer, Franklin suggested Izard reimburse the United States the money he had been paid for services never rendered.[58]

To complete the demolition of Izard, Franklin wrote one of his smaller satiric masterpieces, *Petition of the Letter Z*. It was the story, complete with dialogue, of a demand by "the letter Z, commonly called Ezzard, Zed, or Izard," against being treated "with disrespect and indignity." Z insists on being placed at the head of the alphabet, and substituted for S in the word *wise*. But the other letters vote him down. He is admonished "to be content with his station, forbear reflections upon his brother letters, and remember his own small usefulness, and the little occasion there is for him in the republic of letters." [59]

To make Izard squirm a little more, Franklin, when he asked him for the government's money, said he needed it to buy food and clothing for some 300 American prisoners who had escaped from British jails and were completely dependent on the American mission for food and clothing. These seamen were one more of Franklin's many harassments. As a descendant on his mother's side of Nantucket sailors, he had an instinctive sympathy for salt-water men, which seven crossings of the Atlantic had only deepened. He used his many contacts in England, particularly with the sympathetic David Hartley, to set up a fund to buy warm clothing and decent food for the sailors still in British prisons. There were almost 1000 of these unfortunate men in jail at one point during the war.

Technically they were not Franklin's responsibility, but he fretted and worried over them as if they were his own children. Arthur Lee intruded his incompetent hands into the business, with the help of his talebearing spy-secretary, Major Thornton. Certain as usual that only a Lee could do things right, Arthur personally selected a Maryland merchant, Thomas Digges, who was operating as Lee's private secret agent in London. Like almost everyone else around Lee, Digges was on the British payroll. He was also a first-class scoundrel. He took 400 pounds which Franklin sent to David Hartley and, instead of passing it on to the prisoners in weekly stipends, kept it in his own pocket.

Franklin's condemnation of Digges is one of his lesser known classics. "He that robs the rich even of a single guinea is a villain; but what is he who can break his sacred trust, by robbing a poor man and a prisoner of 18 pence given in charity for his relief and repeat that crime as often as there are weeks in a winter, and multiply it by robbing as many poor men every week as make up the number of near 600? We have no name in our language for such atrocious wickedness. If such a fellow is not damned, it is not worthwhile to keep a devil." [60]

Along with being hounded and harassed by his countrymen, Franklin was ceaselessly bombarded with appeals for interviews and letters of recommendation from Frenchmen. He told James Lovell of the Committee on Foreign Affairs, "You can have no conception how we are . . . besieged and worried on this head, our time cut to pieces. . . ." [61] His old friend Barbé Dubourg was frequently guilty of sending total strangers to Franklin. Finally Franklin could stand it no longer, and spoke his mind with undiplomatic bluntness. "These applications are my perpetual torment. . . . All my friends are sought out and teiz'd to teize me. Great officers in all ranks, in all departments; ladies great and small . . . worry me from morning to night. The noise of every coach now that enters my court terrifies me. I am afraid to accept an invitation to dine abroad, being almost sure of meeting with some officer or officer's friend, who, as soon as I am put in good humour by a glass or two of champaign, begins his attack upon me. . . . If therefore, you have the least remaining kindness for me, if you would not help to drive me out of France, for God's sake, my dear friend, let this your twenty-third application be your last." [62]

As usual, Franklin kept his sanity by seeing both the funny and the serious side of the situation. One day, not long after Barbé Dubourg's twenty-third application, Franklin cooked up a "Model of a Letter of Recommendation of a Person You Are Unacquainted With."

The bearer of this, who is going to America, presses me to give him a letter of recommendation, tho' I know nothing of him, not even his name. This may seem extraordinary, but I assure you it is not uncommon here. Sometimes indeed, one unknown person brings another equally unknown, to recommend him; and sometimes they recommend one another! As for this gentleman, I must refer you to himself for his character and merits, with which he is certainly better acquainted than I can possibly be. I recommend him however to those civilities which every stranger of whom one knows no harm has a right to; and I request you will do him all the good offices and show him all the favour that, on further acquaintance, you shall find him to deserve. [63]

Perhaps because of his aversion to the whole business of recommendation, Franklin never met the Marquis de Lafayette before that symbolic hero of Franco-American cooperation departed from France. But he did respond to pleas from friends of Lafayette's powerful family and write a letter to George Washington, asking him to take the impulsive, twenty-year-old romantic militarist under his personal care. Only when Lafayette returned to France in 1779 to lead a projected French invasion of England did the now thoroughly certified young hero meet Franklin. Then, of course, they became instantaneous friends, and for a while Temple Franklin was so enraptured by Lafayette's military ardor that he donned a uniform and served as his aide-de-camp.

About this time came some comic relief from England. George III, acting out his paranoid conviction that Franklin was the evil genius behind the war, listened with great attention when a local electrical scientist, one Benjamin Wilson, assured him that Franklin's pointed lightning conductors were inferior to blunt ones. The King asked Franklin's old friend, Sir John Pringle, for his opinion, and Pringle replied tartly that natural laws were not changeable by royal pleasure. George flew into a rage, fired Pringle as physician to the Queen, removed him as president of the Royal Society, and banished him from the court. He then threw himself into Wilson's arms and replaced all the pointed conductors on St. James's Palace with blunt ones.

The wrangle inspired the following verse from a London wit:

> *While you, great George, for safety hunt*
> *And sharp conductors change for blunt*
> *The nation's out of joint:*
> *Franklin a wiser course pursues,*
> *And all your thunder fearless views,*
> *By keeping to the* point.

Chuckling over the story in Paris, Franklin commented that he wished the King had rejected all kinds of lightning rods. Then he might worry about whether he and his family were safe from the "thunder of Heaven" and stop using "his own thunder in destroying his innocent subjects." [64]

XII

Another creator of headaches soon arrived in Paris to challenge Franklin's good humor. John Adams, Silas Deane's replacement, was allied by blood and instinct to the "Ls & As" on which Arthur Lee's schemes and hopes depended. Yet Adams' stubborn New England honesty would not permit him to condemn Franklin out of hand. His diary supplies us with a fascinating study of a man slowly rationalizing his prejudices. It also explains why Franklin, for all his fame and geniality, had numerous enemies. Adams personified a type of man, still very much among us today, who insists that life should be far more simple and literal than it really is or ever will be. Essentially it is a moral approach to life, a demand that all activities have a direct and obvious relationship to some purpose, preferably large and important. A candor amounting to self-confession, regardless of the consequences, is another trait highly prized by such people. Franklin, who preferred to work behind the scenes, believed that indirect influence usually achieved far more than confrontation and was constantly ready to exploit the humorous or satiric potentialities in every situation, inevitably outraged the Lees and Adamses of his world, and even today arouses a kind of sniping enmity among a wide range of writers and historians.

Almost anywhere, Adams would have found it hard to get along with Franklin, but the situation in France multiplied his bafflement and irritation. One of the more amusing things about these moralists, who are so quick to find fault with those around them, are their rather large egos. Adams was constantly fretting in his diary over his role in history. He struggled against considerable limitations to model himself into a great man, and as the leader of the fight for independence, he had won a justifiably large reputation among his own countrymen. But when he arrived in France, he got a shock from which his ego never quite recovered.

There was only one American name on everyone's lips: Franklin. "His name was familiar to government and people," Adams groused, "to foreign courtiers, nobility, clergy and philosophers, as well, as plebeians, to such a degree that there was scarcely a peasant or a citizen, a valet de chambre, coachman or footman, a lady's chambermaid or scullion in a kitchen who did not consider him a friend. . . ." Chaumont's publicity campaign, in which Franklin had so cheerfully joined, had obviously been a huge success. What Adams could not stand was the unabashed pleasure that Franklin took in the publicity, and the enthusiasm with which he aided and abetted it. This, declared Adams' puritan conscience, was egotism and vanity. It made it easy for him to resent the French tendency to attribute near miraculous powers to Franklin. "When they spoke of him they seemed to think he was to restore the Golden Age," Adams humphed. "His plans and his example would abolish monarchy, aristocracy and hierarchy throughout the world." [65]

Franklin greeted Adams warmly as an old compatriot from the Continental Congress, personally introduced him to Vergennes, and for the first two weeks took him with him to dinner nightly, giving him an opportunity to become acquainted with a veritable *Who's Who* of French society. Adams met everyone from the noted philosopher Condorcet to Monsieur de Sartine, the powerful Minister of Marine, and Madame de Maurepas, wife of the French Prime Minister and a lady of enormous influence. Adams missed the point completely. He simply had no idea that these sophisticated people combined diplomacy, champagne, wit and duck à la bigarade. Instead of being grateful to Franklin for giving him in two weeks an entré into the French Establishment which Arthur Lee had failed to achieve in two years, Adams wrote in his autobiography: "These incessant dinners and dissipations were not the objects of my mission to France."

Adams was equally obtuse when he observed Franklin's daily routine. He called it "a scene of continual dissipation." Franklin breakfasted too late, he complained, "and as soon as breakfast was over a crowd of carriages came to his levee." The visitors were "philosophers, academicians and economists . . . but by far the greater part were women and children come to have the honor to see the great Franklin, and to have the pleasure of telling stories about his simplicity, his bald head and scattering straight hairs." It never seemed to dawn on the bilious little man from Boston that Franklin was continuing that love affair between himself and the French people which had played no small part in making the alliance possible. Instead of realizing that Franklin had concentrated on this side of the mission, and let Deane handle the commercial and shipping problems, the resentful New Englander groaned: "I found that the business of the commission would never be done unless I did it." [66]

With this air of self-pitying martyrdom, Adams took charge of putting the commission's books and papers in order. There is no doubt that here he performed a much-needed service. Franklin was not a very orderly man. When he attempted to convert himself into a paragon of moral perfection by practicing his list of virtues, order was the one that had baffled him most. Perhaps this was an inevitable result of his multiple talents. In France a certain amount of pride was also probably involved. At the age of seventy, when you are one of the most famous men in the world, it is difficult to turn bookkeeper. Unfortunately he got little help from those around him. William Temple Franklin was more interested in becoming a playboy than an efficient secretary, and Edward Bancroft, who was supposed to be the general secretary of the mission, spent most of his time living it up in Paris with Silas Deane, William Carmichael, and their ship captains.

By refusing to divide the business of the mission, and by succumbing to Arthur Lee's injunction that all official papers must be signed by all three commissioners, Adams found himself pursuing Franklin for days to get his signature on a single document. Adams raged to his diary about Franklin's dislike for doing anything until it absolutely needed doing and he complained even more sourly over Franklin's reluctance to speak out in public. Adams seemed to think that Franklin should have an American opinion on every aspect of the war, and that he should trumpet these day and night. He decried what he considered Franklin's subservience to the French, never seeming to realize that America was totally dependent on France for money, guns, ships of the line, and all the other sinews of war, except men. Adams, with his puritanical insistence on bellowing the truth as he saw it, no matter what the consequences, simply could not see the wisdom of Franklin's dictum about the need to "comply with humors" of people who were providing the wherewithal for the war effort.

If Adams was annoyed by Franklin, he was honest enough to admit that he was appalled by Arthur Lee. By the summer of 1778, the madness which Franklin had predicted for Lee seemed close to erupting. He was completely irrational on the subject of Benjamin Franklin, spewing forth venomous slander and denunciatory diatribes to Adams

and to correspondents in America. Lee made the preposterous suggestion that his house in Paris be set up as the central office of the
commissioners, and all the papers of the mission kept there. Why the
youngest member of the mission should make the oldest travel two
to three hours each day to discuss their affairs and sign a few papers
was hard to rationalize. "Dr. Franklin's age," Adams wrote Lee, "his
rank in the commission . . . his character in the world," made it a
rather strange proposition. Moreover, "nine-tenths of the public letters
are constantly brought to this house [Adams was living at Passy with
Franklin] and will ever be carried where Dr. Franklin is." This un-
arguable truth was, of course, wormwood for Arthur Lee, and when
Adams suggested that Lee abandon his expensive separate quarters
in Paris and move in with him and Franklin at Passy, the Virginian
declared that he did not trust their host, Monsieur Chaumont. Adams
suggested, by way of a final compromise, that they meet regularly at
nine o'clock in the morning at Passy. This would catch Franklin before
he began his daily social whirl. Lee replied that he could not possibly
get there before eleven.[67]

In a moment of instinctive candor, Adams summed up Lee and
Izard in words that explain for all time Franklin's antipathy to them.
Lee's countenance, Adams said, "is disquieting, his air not pleasing,
his manners not engaging, his temper . . . harsh, sour and fiery, and
his judgment of men and things is often wrong. . . . Izard is still
worse." But when Adams heard the latest news from America about
Silas Deane, his emotions took charge, and he went berserk.

Deane, after waiting in vain for Congress to give him the triumphal
reception he felt he deserved, gradually realized he was an accused
man. When Congress was slow about giving him a hearing, he took
to the newspapers and recklessly attacked Arthur Lee and his friends.
Adams rushed to Franklin and told him that Deane's public self-
defense was "one of the most wicked and abominable productions that
ever sprang from a human heart!" All his latent hostility for Franklin
poured out. "No evil could be greater, nor any government worse than
the toleration of such conduct," he shouted.[68]

Franklin said nothing. He had lent the prestige of his name to Deane,
and the Connecticut man had obviously misused it. Deane's judgment
of men and events had been poor from the first, and that was another
reason why Franklin had carefully withdrawn from his circle of commercial activities. But he always thought that Deane was basically a

patriot, which he may well have been in his own erratic mind. Alas, historians digging through the British state papers have uncovered evidence that shortly before Deane went home he began doing business with the British, through Paul Wentworth. In return for information about American activities, George III had approved a shipment of British goods that would be sold in New York, and the profits slipped to Deane's brother, Barnabas, in Connecticut.[69] This compromise, whether born of Deane's disgust with Arthur Lee's poisonous politics or his desperate desire to become a great merchant, may well have been the reason for his reckless declamatory conduct before Congress. If there was genuine treachery involved—no one knows precisely what information Deane gave the British—not a little of the reason for Deane's defection could be traced to Arthur Lee. No one has ever proved that Deane was dishonest on the vast million-dollar scale Arthur Lee righteously described. Franklin continued to defend Deane as a basically honest man, though after his outburst against Congress, he was cautious about giving him any broad endorsement as a politician or a diplomat.

The wisdom of keeping as far away from the commercial side of the mission as possible became doubly clear to Franklin. When John Adams, at Arthur Lee's rancorous instigation, recommended that Franklin's nephew, Jonathan Williams, be barred from handling any of the government's commercial business at Nantes, Franklin, to Adams' surprise, agreed without a murmur of argument. But when Franklin was going through some back bills and came across a notation on one of them from Arthur Lee accusing Williams of peculating 100,000 livres, Franklin wrathfully told Lee to prove it or withdraw the charge. "A rogue living in a family is a greater disgrace to it than one *hang'd* out of it," he declared. As usual, Lee had no proof beyond the vaporings of his feverish imagination.[70]

The imbroglio over Deane created a tremendous conflagration in Congress—the Lee and Adams wing, determined to achieve an impossible purity in all aspects of the government, launched a bitter attack on the dominance of Robert Morris and the middle-states men around him who were handling the commercial affairs of the Revolution. The wrangling reached such violent proportions that one exasperated Congressman declared: "We are plagued to death . . . with our commissioners abroad; these men will involve the continent in perdition." [71] Inevitably, Arthur Lee's brothers did their best to fan some of the flames in Franklin's direction. They strove mightily to destroy him so that Arthur could reign in single splendor as the American ambassador in Paris. Richard Henry Lee called Franklin "that wicked old man" who had made his headquarters in France "a corrupt hotbed of vice . . . how long must the dignity, honor and interest of these United States be sacrificed to the bad passions of that old man under the idea of his being a philosopher?" [72]

They also attacked Franklin with a whispering campaign insinuating that Temple Franklin was disloyal. This was a low blow that struck home. The wound inflicted by William's defection bled once more. Bitterly Franklin asked his son-in-law, Richard Bache, who had warned him that Temple was under attack, "It is enough that I have lost my *son;* would they add my grandson?" The patriarchal nature of Franklin's family feeling flowed into his pen as he wrote. "I am continued here in a foreign country, where, if I am sick, his filial attention comforts me, and, if I die, I have a child to close my eyes, and take care of my remains." To his daughter, Sally, Franklin added, "I should not part with the child, but with the employment." [73]

Meanwhile, all three commissioners had advised Congress to resolve their quarrels by appointing one man as ambassador to France. Doughty John Adams, with that remarkably honest intellect which sometimes overcame his mean prejudices, made it clear that Franklin was the only possible choice. Franklin himself, of course, declined to recommend anyone.

On September 14, 1778, Congress voted on a new ambassador to France. Franklin won, 12 states to 1, but the vote was far from unanimous within the state delegations. Franklin was stunned to discover that his own state, Pennsylvania, was the only one that had cast a majority against him. This was a tribute to the intensity of the battle over Deane which took place in Philadelphia, and thus had a more direct impact on Pennsylvanians. But this defection was for Franklin little more than a temporary pang. A 12 to 1 majority was, after all, an endorsement sweeping enough to satisfy any reasonable man, and Franklin was eminently reasonable. To his nephew, Jonathan Williams, he wrote, "This mark of public confidence is the more agreeable to me as it was not obtained by any solicitation or intrigue on my part, nor have I ever written a syllable to any person, in or out of Congress, magnifying my own services or diminishing those of others." [74]

It is hard to believe that Franklin was able to suppress a chuckle at the discomfiture of the Lee brothers. "America has . . . struggled to a fine purpose to make a Ben. instead of a Geo. her absolute lord and master," squawked William to Arthur Lee. Richard Henry Lee wrote from Philadelphia attempting to soothe Arthur's scalded soul. "The Doctor is old and must soon be called to account for his misdeeds; therefore bear with him, if possible." [75]

Franklin immediately called on Arthur Lee to deliver to him all the official papers in his possession. Lee haughtily replied that he had no papers relating to any business conducted by the sole plenipotentiary to the court of Versailles. As for papers relating to the previous three-man American mission, he intended to retain every scrap in his files. Only a few weeks later, Franklin found himself with a delicious opportunity to revenge this final effrontery from his defeated enemy.

Patrick Henry, the governor of Virginia, wrote to the new ambassador, asking him what had happened to an order he had sent to William Lee, requesting him to buy arms and military stores for Virginia on credit. Franklin calmly reported that he had taken the matter into his own hands, because William Lee had been absent when the order arrived. He had immediately found three merchants who were all ready to sell the war materiel on credit. Then Arthur Lee had taken charge of the business, and all three merchants had immediately withdrawn. The merchants Lee finally selected quarreled with him and complained to Franklin. "But I cannot remedy them, for I cannot change Mr. Lee's temper," Franklin said. So a full year later, the order was unfilled. Thus Franklin demolished Lee's standing with the most powerful politician in Virginia.[76]

XIII

Another task which Franklin took up with enthusiasm, even before he finally got rid of Arthur Lee and company, concerned Commodore John Paul Jones. This born sea warrior arrived in France early in 1778 and immediately sought Franklin's help in obtaining command of a ship—and hopefully a squadron—to harry British commerce in home waters. Franklin threw all his influence and prestige behind him. Jones was vain, difficult, argumentative, and enormously ambitious. At one point he threatened to challenge the French Minister of Marine, Gabriel de Sartine, to a duel because he failed to give him the ship Jones wanted. The commodore was also a notorious ladies' man. No sooner had he established himself in the household at Passy than he became Madame Chaumont's lover. But Jones' furious zeal to make the British squirm easily persuaded Franklin to forgive him all his personal foibles.

In the summer of 1778, Jones boldly sailed his little sloop *Ranger* into the British port of Whitehaven and only bad luck prevented him from burning all 300 ships in the harbor. He then proceeded to scour the Irish Sea, capturing seven prizes and winning a fierce one-hour battle with the British sloop *Drake*. Franklin then wangled command of an old East Indiaman for him, and Jones, in gratitude for Franklin's help, renamed the ship the *Bon Homme Richard* in his honor. On August 14, 1779, Jones put to sea commanding a flotilla of five ships, mostly manned by French seamen and officers.

Before Jones sailed on this expedition, Franklin wrote out his instructions. He cautioned Jones to be "particularly attentive" toward any prisoners which he might take, and "although the English wantonly burnt many defenseless towns in America," he forbade Jones to follow the same example, unless a "reasonable ransom" was refused. Even then, he was ordered to give "sick and ancient persons, women and children" time to escape. Jones' reply was a unique tribute to Franklin. "Your liberal and noble-minded instructions would make a coward brave." [77]

Jones sailed around the British Isles, up the west coast of Ireland, around Scotland, and down to the coast of Yorkshire, capturing seventeen ships and throwing the kingdom into a wild panic. As Franklin gleefully reported it to his sister Jane, "We have occasioned a good deal of terror & bustle . . . as they imagined our Commodore Jones had 4000 troops with him for descent." [78] The climax of this voyage was the famous battle between the *Bon Homme Richard* and the British frigate *Serapis,* watched by thousands of British on the shore. With his ship battered and sinking, Jones uttered his historic defiance: "I have not yet begun to fight." Combining sheer guts and magnificent seamanship, he forced the British captain to strike his colors, and sailed the captured *Serapis* into port, leaving the shattered *Richard* to sink at sea.

Although Jones did little more fighting for Franklin, the Ambassador was by no means through playing admiral. His prime motivation, aside from inflicting wounds on English commerce, was the American prisoners still in British jails. Jones had brought more than 500 prisoners into Holland, but the arrogant English declined to exchange Americans for Britons held in a neutral country. They were betting on the probability that Holland would expel Jones and his captives, and British warships waiting off the Dutch coast could easily repossess them. But Franklin worked out a chess-player's solution to this trap. He arranged for Jones to turn his prisoners over to the French ambassador in Holland, and he exchanged them for Frenchmen the British were holding. Meanwhile, in France, Vergennes arranged to turn over 500 British prisoners to Franklin. Nevertheless, the delays were maddening, and while he was plowing through the red tape, Franklin decided to add to his supply of Englishmen. So, he commissioned two Irish smugglers, Luke Ryan and Edward McCatter, as privateers under the American flag. Sailing out in the *Black Prince* and *Black Princess,* and once in a ship called the *Fearnot,* these doughty Gaels accounted for 114 British vessels captured, burned, scuttled, or ransomed. They brought 161 prisoners into French ports and accounted for five times that number aboard ships which they captured and then paroled. The British refused to count the paroled sailors as valid for exchange, but the dividend in captured and destroyed British ships more than made up for the disappointment on the score of prisoners. In the course of this business, Franklin had to spend endless hours functioning as an admiralty judge, worrying over the disposition of prize money between captains, privateer owners, and crews, dickering endlessly with the French court, and port and admiralty officers of the French government. It was wearisome, exhausting work, and Franklin, grappling with the thousand and one other details of his job as minister plenipotentiary, frequently wished that he had never heard of Luke Ryan or the *Black Prince* or *Black Princess.* Yet he grimly applied himself to thickets of French and English legal verbiage, for only one reason, which he concisely stated to Vergennes: "I have no other interest in those armaments than the advantage of some prisoners to exchange for my countrymen." [79]

XIV

A note of desperation became visible in the continued efforts of various Englishmen to tempt the Americans into returning to the imperial fold. One of the strangest approaches was a letter tossed into Franklin's doorway early in the summer of 1778 signed by a certain Charles de Weissenstein. The missive offered reconciliation to the Americans based upon virtual independence. The names of the American leaders, including Washington and Franklin, were listed, and there was a space left blank beside them, in which they could fill in the price for which they were prepared to sell out their country. On July sixth between 12 and 1 P.M., there would be a messenger waiting beside the iron gates of the choir of the cathedral of Notre Dame, ready to pick up Franklin's reply. He would be wearing a rose in his hat or buttonhole. The language of the letter, which exuded an air of total assurance—there was no talk of obtaining the King's permission or the government's approval—convinced Franklin that the author was George III himself. He therefore went out of his way to make his reply as brutally insulting as possible.

Franklin dug out of a library a book on government which he knew the King had studied as a young man, and read him a lesson from it about a tricky King who encouraged his subjects to revolt prematurely, knowing he had the strength to suppress them. "These are the principles of your nation," Franklin said, and that is why he considered it "vain to treat with you." As for trusting in reconciliation based on an act of Parliament, Franklin sneered, "Good God, an act of Parliament! This demonstrates that you do not yet know us, and that you fancy that we do not know you." He was even less impressed with the "places, pensions and peerages" which Weissenstein offered. "These, judging from yourselves, you think are motives irresistible." Then, in a typical Franklinesque touch, he added that as things now stood in America, no one could accept a King's pension "without deserving, and perhaps obtaining, a SUS-pension." [80]

Franklin was much too shrewd to deliver this letter personally. As he pointed out, he was "one of the most remarkable [well-known] figures in Paris" and it would be difficult for him to appear at Notre Dame where he could not have "any conceivable business" without attracting a great deal of attention. So he forwarded Weissenstein's letter and his answer to Vergennes, obviously hoping that the foreign minister would contrive to deliver it to London. But Vergennes was too much the professional diplomat to indulge himself, as Franklin occasionally did, in the release of personal emotion. He turned the letter over to the French Secret Service, who sent some operatives to Notre Dame on the appointed day and did in fact find a British agent with a rose in his buttonhole strolling up and down, hoping in vain to see Ambassador Franklin enter with a letter in his hand.

To further frustrate George III, Franklin cheerfully continued his personal publicity campaign on behalf of his country. Houdon, the greatest sculptor of the age, executed his bust and the great economist, Turgot, titillated the French appetite for epigrams with a Latin classic: *"Eripuit caelo fulmen sceptrumque tyrannis*—He snatched the lightning from the sky and the scepter from tyrants." When Voltaire, the greatest living French author and the father of the French Enlightenment, returned to Paris to die, after an exile of twenty-eight years, Franklin immediately arranged an interview. He took with him Temple Franklin, and soon all Paris was buzzing with the news that the dying sage had given the young American his blessing in two momentous words, "God and liberty." When Voltaire was initiated into the influential Nine Sisters Masonic Lodge, it was Franklin, not Turgot or some other leading French intellectual, who had the honor of escorting him. Still later, they met once more at the Academy of Sciences and in this unlikely place, there were wild shouts, *"Il faut s'embrasser, à la française*—You must embrace French fashion." So the two old men (Voltaire was eighty-four) walked to the center of the room and put their arms around each other and kissed each other's cheeks. Once again, the French went into raptures of emotion about the spectacle of "Solon and Sophocles embracing."

Although Adams accused Franklin of being motivated by a swollen ego, there is ample evidence that Franklin never lost his perspective on what he was doing. Writing to his sister late in 1779, he referred to "the vogue I am in here." This popularity, he said, "has occasioned so many paintings, bustos, medals & prints to be made of me, and distributed throughout the kingdom, that my face is now almost as well-known as that of the moon. But one is not to expect being always in fashion." [81] Franklin also knew where to draw the line. One artist created an allegorical picture called *L'Amerique Independante* which showed Franklin in a toga with a laurel wreath on his head and a wand in his hand, standing between symbolical America and France, while their enemies lay prostrate before them. Franklin instantly wrote the artist, ordering him to change the identity of the figure in the toga to "The Congress." Attributing to Benjamin Franklin the chief responsibility for the conduct of the war, "would be unjust to the numbers of wise and brave men, who by their arms and counsels have shared in the enterprise and contributed to its success (as far as it has yet succeeded) at the hazard of their lives and fortunes." [82]

Perhaps the most amazing aspect of this popularity was the fact that Franklin had achieved it in a country where he could barely speak or write the language. Although he could read French well enough, he never learned to use it fluently, and if more than two or three people began speaking in a group, he admitted that his impression of what was being said was a blur. More than once, this lack of facility was responsible for some rather amusing gaffes. Once, at a large gathering, a lady arose to make an impromptu speech. Again and again the audience burst into applause, and Franklin cheerfully joined them. Later, Temple Franklin told him that he had been applauding praise of himself.

"If you Frenchmen would only talk no more than four at a time, I might understand you and would not come out of an interesting party without knowing what you were talking about," he complained to one French friend. In large groups, Franklin made it a policy to remain silent—a tactic which the voluble French immediately elevated into another Franklin virtue.

X V

There was one aspect of his popularity which Franklin freely admitted to his sister Jane he hoped to preserve as long as he stayed in France— "the regard . . . of the French ladies, for their society and conversation when I have time to enjoy it, is extreamly agreeable." [83]

Franklin had long since perceived one of the fundamental facts of French society—that women played an extremely important role in forming and creating public opinion, and even in influencing political decisions. They promptly became one of the prime targets of his publicity campaign. Simultaneously, he found himself delighted by their wit and intelligence, and their enormous enthusiasm for him. This reciprocal flow of electricity created the historical phenomenon of a man of seventy becoming something close to a matinee idol. To puritanical Americans such as John Adams, always ready to suspect the worst, this automatically made Franklin a lecher. But it is hard to believe that a man of seventy—even a Franklin—could be orgiastic on the scale that Adams intimated. Nor does it seem likely, if he was in continual pursuit of sexual pleasure, that he could have discussed it so offhandedly with his deeply religious sister, among others.

To a Boston niece Franklin wrote cheerfully, "You mention the kindness of the French ladies to me. I must explain that matter. This is the civilest nation upon earth. Your first acquaintances endeavour to find out what you like, and they tell others. If 'tis understood that you like mutton, dine where you will you find mutton. Somebody, it seems, gave it out that I lov'd ladies; and then every body presented me their ladies (or the ladies presented themselves) to be embrac'd, that is to have their necks kiss'd. For as to kissing of lips or cheeks, it is not the mode here, the first is reckon'd rude & the other may rub off the paint. The French ladies have, however, 1000 other ways of rendering themselves agreeable; by their various attentions and civilities, & their sensible conversation. 'Tis a delightful people to live with." [84]

There were times when this female enthusiasm became almost overwhelming. Once, no less than 300 ladies swarmed around Franklin, crowned his head with laurels, and chose the prettiest among them to kiss him on both cheeks. A French neighbor of Franklin's in Passy said the women "flocked to see him, to speak to him for hours on end, without realizing that he did not understand much of what they said, because of his scant knowledge of our language." But Franklin was, in spite of this handicap, equal to the challenge. The shrewd French neighbor noted that "he greeted each one of them with a kind of amiable coquettishness that they loved." Whenever one madame or mademoiselle asked him if he did not care for them more than any of the others, Franklin had an answer that was a diplomatic masterpiece. "Yes, when you are closest to me, because of the force of attraction." [85]

Along with this sophisticated badinage, Franklin created a family out of the circle of French women who lived near him in Passy. Again, the phenomenon sounds that note of almost compulsive paternalism, that enormous authority which enabled Franklin to bind others to him emotionally, with all the force and permanence of a blood relationship. It was a repetition of his life in Craven Street, where he had created a similar bond between himself and the Stevensons. But in Passy the atmosphere was more supercharged, thanks to the added ingredient of French wit and emotion. French women responded instinctively to Franklin's fondness for playing romantic games with words, and, occasionally, with other equally available resources.

His first and closest friend was Madame Brillon de Jouy, an exquisitely beautiful woman of thirty-five who was considered one of the most talented amateur pianists in Europe. Some of the leading musicians of the era dedicated compositions to her, and she composed her own sonatas for the harpsichord and the piano. She was married to a tall, hearty French treasury official, who was twenty-four years older than she. This, plus a moody, artistic temperament and an overwhelming devotion to a father who had recently died, left her vaguely restless and discontented, in that plaintive romantic manner that was gradually becoming the vogue in Europe. She first attracted Franklin with her music. He began visiting her house, which was only a short distance away from the Hotel Valentinois, to hear her play the piano and listen to her two pretty daughters sing. Franklin was soon calling these visits "my opera." [86] They found other things in common—a fondness for chess and religious discussion.

But the erotic was never far from Franklin's mind, even when he talked religion, and Madame Brillon, being French, found herself more than disposed to play the same titillating game. One night, as they sat on the terrace of the Brillon mansion, with its hundred steps running down into a peaceful garden, Franklin soberly informed Madame Brillon that if the Catholic religion was true, he felt himself damned because he was constantly committing one or another of the seven deadly sins—pride, covetousness, lust, anger, gluttony, envy, and sloth. Gaily, Madame Brillon replied that he needed a spiritual director, such as all devout Catholics of that time—and even a few today—depended upon to win salvation. Would Madame Brillon be his spiritual director? Franklin playfully asked. Why not, said the lovely lady, and forthwith heard his "confession"—in which he described to her his sins, placing special emphasis on his weakness for pretty women. The next day, she sent him a delightful absolution. "I will not be stern. I know my penitent's weak spot, I shall tolerate it! As long as he loves God, America and me above all things, I absolve him of all his sins, present, past and future; and I promise him paradise where I shall lead him along a path strewn with roses." [87]

Franklin replied by shifting his ground from the capital sins to the Ten Commandments. He told Madame Brillon that he believed there were twelve. The two extras were: Increase and multiply and Love one another. "Come to think of it, they are a bit misplaced, and shouldn't the last have been first," he said. "However, I never made any difficulty about that, but was always willing to obey them both, whenever I had an opportunity."

Then, the Ambassador took the offensive. "Pray tell me, my dear casuist, whether my keeping religiously these two commandments, though not in the Decalogue, may not be accepted in compensation for my breaking so often one of the ten? I mean that which forbids coveting my neighbor's wife, and which I confess I break constantly. . . ." There was, he added, an opinion of a certain father of the church that the best way to get rid of temptation was to give in to it. "Pray instruct me how far I may venture to practice upon this principle."

Madame Brillon responded with witty finesse. She told him that she was inclined to pardon him but she felt that she should consult "that neighbor whose wife you covet, because he is a far better casuist than I am. And then too, as Poor Richard would say, in weighty matters two heads are better than one." [88]

But Franklin was hard to discourage. He returned with a whole list of sins, all in the coveting and pursuing category—of other women. He argued that the sort of friendship she was imposing on him could be divided ad infinitum without being unfaithful. He compared it to "the sweet sounds brought forth from the pianoforte by your clever hands." Twenty people could enjoy this music if they happened to be within hearing, in spite of the fact that Madame Brillon intended it only for Franklin. The same was true of his affection or tenderness. Her only fault, Franklin told her, "was this kind of avarice which leads you to seek a monopoly on all my affections, and not to allow me any for the agreeable ladies of your country." [89] Obviously, Franklin was hoping that jealousy would succeed where curiosity had failed. But the lady was immovable. "My heart, while capable of great love, has chosen few objects on which to bestow it; it has chosen them well, you are at the head of the list," she insisted.

Gradually but inevitably, the relationship between this remarkable woman and equally remarkable man shifted from gaily erotic fooling to something much deeper and more profound. Madame Brillon began calling Franklin *mon cher Papa*—my dear Papa—and he began calling her his daughter. Gently, with perfect delicacy, he retreated from his first tone of physical urgency, but he knew too much about women ever to abandon it completely. She in turn continued to give him her kisses, and she sat on his lap so often, several local gossips began talking about it. Franklin retaliated by tempting her with the story of an archbishop who refused to give even a farthing to a beggar. He accused Madame Brillon of being equally niggardly. "You who are as rich as an archbishop in all Christian and moral virtues, you could sacrifice for my sake a little portion of those virtues without the loss being sensible, but you tell me it is asking too much. Such is your charity toward an unfortunate who used to enjoy plenty and is now reduced to begging your alms." But Madame Brillon was immovable. "My dear Papa, your bishop was a rascal," she said.[90]

Then, in mid-1779, came a crisis which, if Franklin had been a dedicated lecher, would have given him what he kept saying he wanted so badly. Madame Brillon discovered that her husband was having an affair with her daughters' governess. It was a blow that almost destroyed her mental and physical health. Frantically she turned to the only person in whom she could confide—Franklin. "My soul is very sick," she cried. "You are my father. It is the father's love that I need more than ever." [91] Like a patient going to a psychiatrist, she made an appointment with Franklin for ten in the morning, and poured out her agony. Franklin's response refutes forever the musical-comedy caricature that has him leaping from bed to bed throughout his years in Paris. No one is easier to seduce than a wife who has been wronged, but such an unscrupulous act would have completely destroyed this fragile woman, with her acute Catholic conscience. She was groping for spiritual strength, and Franklin gave it to her, out of his rich reserve.

He urged her to forgive her husband, to continue to be a "good mother, good wife, good friend, good neighbor, good Christian, etc.

(without forgetting to be a good daughter to your Papa) and to neglect and forget, if you can, the wrongs you may be suffering at present." He urged on her his old doctrine, which he had written in *Poor Richard's Almanack* in 1749 and practiced throughout his life, in personal quarrels. "Doing an injury puts you below your enemy; revenging one makes you but even with him; forgiving it sets you above him." [92] To teach her a more philosophic attitude toward life, he told his old story of the whistle, and what he had learned from it as a boy. The best thing, he advised her, was to get all the good we can from this world, and not waste our time pursuing whistles, whether they be high honors, riches, or in Madame Brillon's case, recrimination and revenge.

The ironic, essentially spiritual nature of Franklin's relationship with Madame Brillon was summed up for all time in an essay he wrote for her, after a visit to a lovely island in the Seine called Moulin Joli. During their strolls around the island, they had seen swarms of a little fly called *Ephemera* who lived only a day. Espousing his magician's role, Franklin told Madame Brillon, "You know that I understand all the inferior animal tongues." Poking fun at himself, he added, "My too great application to the study of them is the best excuse I can give for the little progress I have made in your charming language." Franklin told how he had listened to a conversation among a group of *Ephemerae*, who were arguing about the merits of two foreign musicians—not unlike the French of that decade, who were bitterly divided over the virtues of Gluck and Piccini—but he was more interested in the discourse of an old gray-headed *Ephemera*, who was sitting alone on another leaf, talking to himself.

It was, said he, the opinion of learned philosophers of our race, who lived and flourished long before my time, that this vast world, the Moulin Joli, could not itself subsist more than eighteen hours; and I think there was some foundation for that opinion, since, by the apparent motion of the great luminary that gives life to all nature, and which in my time has evidently declined considerably toward the ocean at the end of our earth, it must then finish its course, be extinguished in the waters that surround us, and leave the world in cold and darkness, necessarily producing universal death and destruction. I have lived seven of those hours, a great age, being no less than four hundred and twenty minutes of time.

How few of us continue so long! I have seen generations born, flourish, and expire. My present friends are the children and grandchildren of the friends of my youth, who are now, alas, no more! And I must soon follow them; for by the course of nature, though still in health, I cannot expect to live above seven or eight minutes longer. What now avails all my toil and labour in amassing honeydew on this leaf, which I cannot live to enjoy! What the political struggles I have been engag'd in for the good of my compatriot inhabitants of this bush, or my philosophical studies for the benefit of our race in general! For in politics what can laws do without morals? Our present race of Ephemerae *will in a course of minutes become corrupt, like those of other and older bushes, and consequently as wretched. And in philosophy how small our progress! Alas! art is long, and life is short! My friends would comfort me with the idea of a name they say I shall leave behind me; and they tell me I have lived long enough to nature and to glory. But what will fame be to an* Ephemera *who no longer exists? And what will become of all history, in the eighteenth hour, when the world itself, even the whole Moulin Joli, shall come to its end and be buried in universal ruin?*

To me, after all my eager pursuits, no solid pleasures now remain but the reflection of a long life spent in meaning well, the sensible conversation of a few good lady Ephemerae, *and now and then a kind smile and a tune from the ever amiable Brillante. . . .*[93]

X V I

Nearby, in the village of Auteuil, lived a totally different kind of woman, with whom Franklin had a very unpaternal relationship. Aristocratic Anne-Catherine de Ligniville d'Autricourt, daughter of one of the royal families of Lorraine and widow of Claude Adrian Helvetius, one of France's leading intellectuals, was a woman who ruled men with an imperious will and a flashing temper. In her late fifties, she was no longer a great beauty—her enemies called her "the ruins of Palmyra"—but she was a quintessential French type, spawned by the best traditions of the *ancien régime,* which gave to gifted women a role they had not achieved in any other society. Madame Helvetius ran a unique household in Auteuil. It consisted of two free-thinking abbés, André Morellet, whom Franklin had met at Lord Shelburne's house in England a decade earlier, and Martin Lefebvre de la Roche, a handsome ex-Benedictine in his late thirties who was a disciple of the late Helvetius's decidedly atheistic philosophy. Also aboard was Pierre Georges Cabanis, a twenty-two-year-old student of medical theory.

The economist Turgot, who was deeply in love with Madame Helvetius and who had twice proposed in vain, brought Franklin to Auteuil. He was instantly captivated with this rare woman who combined the hauteur of the aristocrat with the abandon of the bohemian. Her household was in a continuous state of chaotic disorder. Her three acres of gardens were thronged with flowers in the erratic romantic English manner, in deliberate contrast to France's traditional formality. The house and grounds literally crawled with animals—cats, dogs, chickens, ducks, pigeons, deer, and a veritable zoo of birds in huge aviaries. Add to this a stream of brilliant, important guests who wandered in and out for impromptu lunches, teas, and dinners, and you quickly see what Franklin perceived and loved—the house at Auteuil was more than a house—it was a world presided over by a kind of goddess. He promptly gave the goddess a slightly blasphemous name—"Notre Dame d'Auteuil."

Never before in his life had Franklin had the opportunity to meet such a woman intimately. His analytic mind groped to explain the source of her fascination to "statesmen, philosophers, historians, poets and men of learning" who attached themselves to her "as straws to a fine piece of amber." She had no pretensions to learning. She could not even spell correctly. She made no attempt to charm them. "Artless simplicity" was the "striking part" of her character. He could only decide that there was something about her—a kind of vital life force—that made simply being in her company such a pleasure, that all these men of genius were not only pleased with her, "but better pleased with one another and with themselves." [94]

What Franklin liked most aside from the lady of the house was the talk. The Abbé Morellet won every argument with outrageously specious reasoning, while spooning ninety percent of the cream into his coffee or onto his fruit. The house could burn down all around Abbé de la Roche, and he would not even notice the flames, until they reached the book he was reading. He was the solemn, serious young straight man who saw himself trying to bring some order into the chaos, but actually spent most of his time talking to Franklin and nibbling sweetmeats. Cabanis played the role of Franklin's intellectual son, prying endless stories of his boyhood and youth from him. Franklin immediately plunged into this melee, dealing out insults, compliments, and jokes and epigrams with magnificent abandonment.

But for Franklin the dominant note soon became his adoration of the lady in charge. Accepting an invitation to a party from Abbé de la Roche, he wrote: "M. Franklin never forgets any party at which Madame Helvetius is to appear. He even believes that if he were to go to Paradise that morning, he would beg to be allowed to remain on earth until half past one, to receive the embrace she was kind enough to promise him at their last meeting in M. Turgot's house." [95]

There was none of Madame Brillon's coyness about Madame Helvetius. "Do you want, my dear friend, to have dinner with me on Wednesday?" she would write to Franklin. "I have the greatest desire to see you and embrace you—and a little bit your son [Temple] too." Franklin would instantly accept with an equally bold note. "I get too much pleasure from seeing you, hearing you, too much happiness from holding you in my arms, to forget such a precious invitation."

Throughout 1779, Franklin's fascination escalated, and so did his daring. Knowing that nothing was sacred in Auteuil, Franklin used Cabanis and the abbés as message bearers. He told the young doctor, "If Notre Dame is pleased to spend her days with Franklin, he would be just as pleased to spend his nights with her; and since he has already given her so many of his days, although he has so few left to give, she seems very ungrateful in never giving him one of her nights, which keep passing as a pure loss without making anyone happy except Poupon [the cat]." [96] Soon he was warning Cabanis that he planned to capture Madame for life. Then came a delicious essay, an appeal from the flies of the apartment of Monsieur Franklin.

Bizz, izzz ouizz z ouizzz izzzzzzzzz, etc. We have long lived under the hospitable roof of the said bonhomme F. He has given us free lodgings; we have also eaten and drunk the whole year at his ex-

pense without its having cost us anything. Often, when his friends and himself have used up a bowl of punch, he has left a sufficient quantity to intoxicate a hundred of us flies.

We have drunk freely from it, and after that we have made our sallies, our circles and our cotillions in the air of his bedroom, and have gaily consummated our little loves under his nose.

Finally, we would have been the happiest people in the world, if he had not permitted to remain over the top of his wainscoting a number of our declared enemies, who stretched their nets to capture us, and who tore us pitilessly to pieces. People of a disposition both subtle and fierce, abominable combination!

You, very excellent Lady, had the goodness to order that all these assassins with their habitations and their snares be swept; and your orders, as they always ought to be, were carried out immediately. Since that time we have lived happily, and have enjoyed the beneficence of the said bonhomme F. without fear.

There only remains one thing for us to wish in order to assure the stability of our fortune; permit us to say it,

Bizz izzz ouizz z ouizzzz izzzzzzzzzz etc.

It is to see both of you forming at last but one menage.[97]

Finally, as the year 1779 drew to a close, the Ambassador lost his philosophic detachment completely and asked Madame Helvetius, in all seriousness, to marry him. She told him what she had already told Turgot—that she had made a resolve to remain single, out of her devotion to her late husband. Franklin went home to Passy and, undiscouraged, wrote one of his most famous essays. He said that he "fell on my bed, and believing myself dead, found myself in the Elysian fields." It took him only a few moments to find Monsieur Helvetius, who received him with great courtesy. He asked Franklin a thousand questions about France, but never mentioned Madame Helvetius. The late philosopher explained that during several of his early years in Paradise he thought only of her. But now he had taken another wife, "the most like her that I could find." The new wife was, he admitted, "not so completely beautiful, but she has as much good sense, a little more of spirit, and she loves me infinitely. Her continual study is to please me; and she has actually gone to hunt the best nectar and the best ambrosia in order to regale me this evening; remain with me and you will see her."

"I perceive," Franklin said, "that your old friend is more faithful than you; for several good offers have been made her, all of which she has refused. I confess to you that I myself have loved her to the point of distraction; but she was hard-hearted to my regard, and has absolutely rejected me for love of you."

The detached ex-husband proceeded to give Franklin some advice. "If you had won over the Abbé M. (with coffee and cream) to speak for you, perhaps you would have succeeded; for he is a subtle logician like Duns Scotus or Saint Thomas; he places his arguments in such good order that they become nearly irresistible. Also, if the Abbé de la R. had been bribed (by some beautiful edition of an old classic) to speak against you, that would have been better: for I have always observed, that when he advises something, she has a very strong penchant to do the reverse. . . ."

Just then, the new Madame Helvetius entered with the evening's nectar. Franklin was astonished to find that she was none other than his late lamented wife, Deborah. When he indignantly tried to claim her, she told him coldly, "I have been your good wife forty-nine years and four months, nearly half a century; be content with that. Here I have formed a new connection which will endure to eternity."

"Offended by this refusal of my Eurydice," Franklin told Madame Helvetius, "I suddenly decided to leave these ungrateful spirits, to return to the good earth, to see again the sunshine and you. Here I am! Let us *revenge* ourselves." [98]

Madame Helvetius at first professed no more than amusement at Franklin's impudence. But when she realized his marriage proposal was, although clothed in banter, fundamentally serious, she became deeply disturbed and fled for advice to her old friend Turgot. The portly economist in turn paid a visit to Franklin to calm his "agitated" head, so he told another friend. But the evidence would seem to suggest that Franklin was not so agitated as he was determined, and that most of the agitation occurred in the breast of Madame Helvetius. So severe did it become that the lady was forced to abandon her little kingdom at Auteuil, and spent the summer at Tours. Franklin, in the meantime, accepted her unalterable resolution to remain single and printed his visit to the Elysian fields on a small press he had set up at Passy. He sent copies of it to numerous friends, thus giving everyone the impression that the whole thing was a joke. Some people have argued that he did this to evade the humiliation of rejection by Madame Helvetius, but it can be equally argued that he was trying to save Notre Dame d'Auteuil herself from embarrassment.

XVII

Most of these emotional crises were crowded into the year 1779, when Franklin's spirits were soaring and the war looked as if it would soon be over. The French fleet had driven the British out of Philadelphia, leaving them with only two small enclaves on the American coast at Newport and New York, just as Franklin had predicted to his son William. Spain entered the war against England, and another French fleet, assisted by a Spanish armada, was poised to seize naval superiority in European waters, enabling the French Army to invade England. Rampant optimism prevailed in both France and America. On February 17, 1779, Congress considered the report of the committee to propose peace terms, and on September twenty-seventh they commissioned John Adams to return to Europe and negotiate a peace treaty with Britain.

But the year ended in disillusion and frustration on a political and military scale almost as acute as the personal pangs Franklin suffered with Madame Helvetius. The invasion of England was abandoned when the Franco-Spanish fleet succumbed to an epidemic of typhus and other diseases. After the recapture of Philadelphia, Franco-American cooperation in the New World faltered badly, and attempts to storm Newport and Savannah, Georgia (seized by the British in late 1778), ended in near-fiasco.

Both Congress and their constituents, intoxicated by the French alliance, had fallen into a kind of wishful lethargy in 1779. "People here [Pennsylvania] are fast asleep," exclaimed a Continental officer. "It's as perfect a peace as it was in '73 & there is nothing that will rouze them but British guns & drums." Another patriot compared

America to a great beauty who had landed a husband. "We have grown careless in our dress and sluttish in our manner." For Franklin, the first signs of carelessness were financial. Bills began raining in upon him from all over Europe and America, in the merry confidence that somehow he would persuade the French to pay. The Committee of Commerce blithely sent him orders for goods amounting to a staggering 12,000,000 livres—a sum he could not possibly raise. "Too much is expected of me," he lamented to William Carmichael, who was representing America in Madrid. "Not only the Congress draw upon me, often unexpectedly, for large sums, but all the agents of the Committee of Commerce in Europe and America think they may do the same when pinched." [99]

As a businessman, Franklin knew only too well the disastrous consequences of the failure of American credit. When John Jay, sent to Madrid to negotiate a loan from Spain, told Franklin that in Cadiz reports prevailed that American bills were not being honored, Franklin instantly responded that such stories were "wicked falsehoods." So vital did he consider America's financial reputation, he rushed to his banker, Ferdinand Grand, and enclosed in his letter to Jay a "certificate" from that gentleman, certifying that the reports were "calumnies." [100]

Everywhere else Franklin looked, things seemed to be going wrong. John Paul Jones and his fellow captain, Pierre Landais, called upon Franklin to settle a quarrel between them, left over from the battle with the *Serapis*. Landais was a seagoing Arthur Lee, who quarreled with everyone and was a miserable fighting man in the bargain. During the battle with the *Serapis,* he had become so confused that he fired a broadside into the *Bon Homme Richard.* Jones accused him of doing it deliberately. Franklin tried to solve the mess by relieving Landais of his command of the frigate *Alliance* and giving the ship to Jones. But Arthur Lee, who had finally been recalled from Europe by Congress, had booked passage in the *Alliance,* and he encouraged Landais to lead a revolt among the crew, seize the ship, and sail it back to the United States. Before the voyage was over, Landais had threatened Lee with a carving knife for serving himself ahead of the captain at dinner and had shown so many other symptoms of instability that the crew had deposed him and elected one of the lieutenants as captain, to get the ship home in one piece.

Franklin soon found that getting rid of Lee was by no means a panacea that guaranteed him peace of mind. Silas Deane had also vanished, and this meant that Franklin had to cope with the business side of the American mission. Along with endless arguments over the ownership of captured ships and the distribution of prize money, there were even more nightmarish involvements with Beaumarchais and Chaumont. Beaumarchais never did balance his books. There were a million livres for which he never accounted. Chaumont turned out to be as much of a plunger as Beaumarchais, and was soon on the edge of bankruptcy. He demanded favors and concessions from Franklin that the Ambassador, ever conscious of Arthur Lee's evil eye, was unable to grant. Morosely, Franklin complained to Jonathan Williams: "I, in all these mercantile matters am like a man walking in the dark. I stumble often and frequently get my shins broke."

Meanwhile, from William Carmichael, from his son-in-law Richard Bache and even from his sister Jane Mecom, Franklin heard stories of the venom that Lee and Izard were spewing against him in America. Franklin told Carmichael that these charges were "so frivolous, so ill-founded and amount to so little, I esteem them rather as paneygyrics upon me." [101] He was justified in using such language to dismiss Lee's charges that he and Deane had made themselves millions out of the American mission to France. But not a little of Franklin's troubles at home were emanating from one of his few serious errors of judgment, which was supplying his enemies with excellent ammunition.

In February, 1780, Samuel Wharton had turned up at Passy with an exciting story about his hairbreadth escape from England a step ahead of the British Secret Service, who wanted his head for sending information to Franklin. There was strong suspicion that the whole affair was staged by his powerful friend Thomas Walpole, in order to enable Wharton to transfer his allegiance to the American cause. Harassed with so many other concerns, Franklin probably gave little thought to Wharton, who was still absorbed in his Grand Ohio Company dreams of glory. Nothing much had come of the attempt of the American wing of the company to persuade Congress to confirm the Privy Council grant, and Wharton was now on his way to America to lend his more formidable energies to the effort. Although Franklin, soon after he arrived in France, had withdrawn the funds he had left with Walpole to pay for his continuing role in the company, he still considered himself a member of the enterprise, in a general way. In 1778, he had, through Edward Bancroft, regained the letter of resignation he had written to Thomas Walpole in 1774. Franklin had placed it in his papers, with a memorandum, explaining the circumstances in which he wrote it, with an endorsement: "Paper that may be of consequence to my posterity." [102] Now, he signed a memorial drawn up by Wharton, urging Congress to confirm the grant. With this in his pocket, Wharton was soon flaunting Franklin's name more publicly in a pamphlet, *Plain Facts*. "The glorious revolution of these states was not made to destroy but among other things to protect private property and as the grant to Messrs. Franklin, etc., would have passed under the British government . . . can it be supposed that the Congress of America will be less sensible to the influence of justice than the King of England was?" [103] Later in the year, Wharton persuaded Tom Paine to write a pamphlet, entitled "Public Good," supporting the proposition, in return for 300 shares in the company. Wharton also got himself elected to Congress, so he could not only lobby but vote for his scheme. Naturally, Arthur Lee, who had an insider's knowledge of the history of the entire Indiana Company-Grand Ohio speculation, was one of the fiercest opponents, and undoubtedly took delight in pointing out how Franklin was trying to use his high office and prestige to make a fortune for himself, his family, and his friends. Later, when his son-in-law, Richard Bache, obviously uneasy because of the turmoil being stirred up, asked Franklin's opinion of the Wharton-Paine pamphlets, Franklin replied, "Justice is, I think, on the side of those who contracted for the lands. But moral and political rights sometimes differ, and sometimes are both subdued by might." [104] This was hardly a passionate endorsement of Wharton's cause, and it strongly suggests that Franklin was already having second thoughts about the wisdom of allowing the intriguing Philadelphian to use his name.

Knowing the unstable moods of legislative bodies, Franklin could not help but wonder if the Lee-Adams axis might suddenly seize control of Congress. As a man who had long yearned to end his days on a bright point, Franklin had no desire to be fired from his job with odium and imputed disgrace. His worries about Congress were not assuaged by the almost total lack of communication between them and him. Nor was his state of mind improved by the sudden reappearance of John Adams in Paris. Adams came as the extremely premature commissioner in charge of peace negotiations and did not even have the good grace to tell Franklin why he was on the scene. Franklin told Carmichael, "We live upon good terms with each other, but he [Adams] . . . never communicated anything of his business to me and

I have made no inquiries of him, nor have I any letter from Congress explaining it so that I am in utter ignorance." [105]

Diplomatically, John Adams' position was an absurdity. He was empowered to negotiate peace with a nation that was not showing the least interest in the subject. In fact, the British were on the offensive in America and in the West Indies. Vergennes, as a seasoned diplomat, practically ordered Adams to keep his mouth shut, lest he make himself and his country ridiculous. With nothing better to do, Adams proceeded to pick a quarrel with Vergennes. Congress, trying desperately to control the runaway depreciation of American currency, decided to redeem earlier bank notes at a ratio of 40 to 1. Vergennes thought that this was fair enough if it applied only to American citizens, but foreigners, particularly French merchants, ought to be indemnified since they had accepted the original notes in good faith. The French Foreign Minister pointed out that his countrymen had run considerable risks to help the Americans, and shortchanging them was hardly what he called gratitude. With an almost incredible lack of diplomacy, Adams replied that it was France who should be grateful to America for enabling her to humble Great Britain.

More than a little irked, Vergennes called on Franklin for support, and he did his best to explain away Adams' conduct. Meanwhile, Honest John, as he called himself, proceeded to lecture Vergennes on naval and military strategy, demanding a French fleet to support Washington's army. Vergennes coldly informed him that the King, "without having been solicited by Congress," had already made plans to send an expeditionary force to bolster the American cause. Adams took it upon himself to resent these words and wrote Vergennes another long lecture on why France should be grateful to the United States. Grandly, this burlesque of a diplomat declared, "I am determined to omit no opportunity of communicating my sentiments to your Excellency upon everything that appears to me of importance to the common cause." [106]

This was too much for Vergennes. Stiffly he informed Adams that "Mr. Franklin being the sole person who has letters of credence to the King for the United States, it is with him only that I ought and can treat of matters which concern them." A thoroughly angry Vergennes called in Franklin and handed over to him the correspondence with Adams, requesting him to forward it to Congress, "That they may judge whether he is endowed, as Congress no doubt desires, with that conciliating spirit which is necessary for the important and delicate business with which he is entrusted." [107]

Numerous people had told Franklin that Adams was his secret enemy. Certainly Adams had talked loosely and vindictively against Franklin to a wide range of people, including members of Congress and even the new French ambassador to the United States, the Chevalier de la Luzerne. If Franklin wanted to destroy Adams' reputation as a diplomat and politician, he now had all the ammunition he needed. But like Washington, Franklin was too committed to the American cause to permit animosity to cloud his judgment. He saw Adams for precisely what he was, and summed him up in a line (written at a later date) that simultaneously describes and explains his erratic role in American history: "He means well for his country, is always an honest man, often a wise one, but sometimes, and in some things, absolutely out of his senses." [108]

Now Franklin passed on the correspondence Vergennes had given him with the gentlest kind of criticism of Adams' blundering conduct. ". . . . He seems to have endeavoured to supply what he may suppose my negotiations defective in," Franklin told the president of Congress. "He thinks, as he tells me himself, that America has been too free in expressions of gratitude to France; for that she is more oblig'd to us than we to her; and that we should show spirit in our applications. I apprehend, that he mistakes his ground and that this Court is to be treated with decency and delicacy." Franklin pointed out that the King took "pleasure" in his benevolence in assisting "an oppressed people." Franklin thought it was good policy to increase this pleasure with expressions of gratitude, which, he pointed out, "is not only our duty, but our interest."

Whether Adams' boldness or Franklin's smooth complaisance was the better course, "it is for Congress to judge." [109] Later, when Adams' letters and Franklin's covering dispatch were about to depart for America, Franklin generously informed Adams of the whole transaction and offered him an opportunity to enclose a letter defending his own point of view. Adams preferred to let the matter stand, but in his hypersensitive soul, the mere fact that Franklin was the transmitter of Vergennes' rebuke was one more black mark against the American Ambassador.

While Adams was making trouble on the European side of the

Atlantic, disturbing news came from America. Extending their southern offensive, the British captured Charleston, South Carolina, and an entire American army in May, 1780, and three months later annihilated a second American army at Camden, South Carolina. With just a trace of discouragement in his words, Franklin wrote to Adams, who had gone to Holland to solicit a loan from that neutral but British-leaning country, "Our credit and weight in Europe depend more on what we do than on what we say; and I have long been humiliated with the idea of our running about from court to court begging for money and friendship, which are the more withheld, the more eagerly they are solicited, and would perhaps have been offer'd if they had not been ask'd. . . . The proverb says God helps them that help themselves. And the world, too, in this sense is very godly." [110]

In another moment of discouragement, he told Georgiana Shipley, who continued to correspond with Franklin, although her father as a Bishop sat in the House of Lords, "There has been enough blood spilt." He yearned, he said, for "a peace solid and everlasting." But even when his spirits were low, he could still joke. "It is a great while since I have heard anything of the *good Bishop,*" he told Georgiana. "Strange, that so simple a character should sufficiently distinguish one of that sacred body!" [111] Shipley was the only member of the British hierarchy who steadfastly opposed the war, and it cost him his chance to become Archbishop of Canterbury.

XVIII

On top of all these political and diplomatic woes, Franklin's health broke down. In October, 1780, he took to his bed with the worst attack of gout he had ever suffered. For six weeks he was prostrate and in severe pain, and even when he pronounced himself recovered, he was so weak and his feet and knees so tender that he was unable to attend diplomatic ceremonies at Versailles. "Going up and down stairs is exceedingly difficult and inconvenient to me," he told his friend Charles W. F. Dumas, who was still laboring on behalf of the United States in Holland.[112]

From America came more bad news of a depressing personal sort. William Franklin had been exchanged late in 1778 and had spent the next eighteen months in New York, vainly attempting to persuade the British Army to let him play a role in the war. Finally, thanks largely to pressure from England, the Army had permitted William to form a "Board of Associated Loyalists" of which he had become president. It was a guerrilla organization, committed to that most hateful brand of warfare, and they were soon launching raids against fellow Americans loyal to Congress in New Jersey, New York, and Connecticut. The news could only have intensified the bitter pain Franklin still felt at William's defection. Now he was not only a political enemy, he was spilling the blood of fellow Americans, the blood of men who were loyal to the cause that Franklin was leading. Perhaps one needs to experience leadership, to understand the intense solidarity which the leader, particularly a man as paternal as Franklin, feels for those who follow him. The news that his son had taken up the gun, the knife, and the torch of the midnight raider in distant New York was as dismaying to Franklin as if William and his guerrillas had appeared in Passy to attack his French friends and neighbors. In Franklin's mind it destroyed all hope of ever again bridging the gulf which had opened between them.

Then came more dismaying news from America. Ralph Izard had joined Arthur Lee in Congress, and he persuaded a fellow member from South Carolina to introduce a motion to recall Franklin. Izard, seconding the demand, declared, "The political salvation of America depends upon the recalling of Dr. Franklin." Arthur Lee backed it with a pamphlet, accusing Franklin of mulcting millions from American funds in France. The recall motion was put to a vote, and lost, 11 to 2, but it must have caused Franklin a pang to learn that Massachusetts, the state of his birth, for whom he had risked so much as an agent in England, and which he still called "my country," had voted against him. But even more humiliating news was to come. Congress was sending Colonel John Laurens, one of Washington's aides and a son of the former president of Congress, as an envoy extraordinary to plead for additional help from France.

The very name Laurens instantly raised Franklin's hackles. The father, Henry Laurens, had sided with the Lees and Adams in Congress so blatantly that the members had finally made it clear that they had lost confidence in him and he had resigned as president. He had then accepted an assignment to negotiate a treaty with Holland and had been captured on the high seas, with all his confidential papers. The British had used the papers as a pretext for declaring war on Holland, largely to give them a chance to seize Dutch West Indies islands which the Americans were using to transship war supplies. Laurens himself was thrown into the Tower of London, where he became another Franklin headache. Through his liberal friends in Parliament, the Ambassador lobbied and pressured for humane treatment of Laurens, completely ignoring the fact that he had been a political adversary.

It was hard for Franklin to see the appointment of Laurens' son as anything but a grim sign that Congress had lost confidence in its Ambassador's effectiveness. It was time to counterattack, or surrender. Franklin disliked surrenders. He proceeded to write a letter to Vergennes that was a diplomatic tour de force. There was nothing new in handing Vergennes another appeal from Congress for money. Franklin had shuffled so many of these across his desk that it was certain to produce nothing more than a yawn of boredom from the French diplomat. So, after a brief mention that Congress was begging for money once more, Franklin unveiled two authorities that were far more likely to make the Count sit up and listen. "The Marquis de la Fayette writes to me that it is impossible to conceive, without seeing it, the distress the [American] troops have suffer'd for want of clothing; and the following is a paragraph of a letter from General Washington, which I ought not to keep back from Your Excellency, viz. '. . . . Our present situation makes one of two things essential to us; a peace, or the most vigorous aid of our allies, particularly in the article of *money.*' "

Then Franklin added the weight of his own prestige, with an elegiac touch that made it personal and more likely to penetrate the Count's defenses. "I am grown old. I feel myself much enfeebled by my late long illness, and it is probable I shall not long have any more concern in these affairs. I therefore take this occasion to express my opinion to Your Excellency, that the present conjuncture is critical; that there is some danger lest the Congress should lose its influence over the people, if it is found unable to procure the aids that are wanted; and that the whole system of the new govern't in America may thereby be shaken . . ." Franklin ended with a note of somber warning.

If the British recovered America, the opportunity for separating the colonies and the mother country "may not occur again in the course of ages." And in a decade or two, the English might draw from America's commerce and soaring population the wealth, the seamen, and the soldiers that ". . . will enable them to become the *terror of Europe.*" [113]

Franklin followed up this letter with a note, two weeks later, that was practically an ultimatum. Vessels were sailing for America, and he insisted on having an answer to the "application" for supplies and money. Vergennes instantly granted an interview and, after lecturing Franklin on the difficulty France had raising money for its own expenses in the war, informed him that the King had decided to grant America 6,000,000 livres, not as a loan, but as a free gift. "This sum," Franklin proudly informed the president of Congress, "was exclusive of the three millions which he had before obtained for me to pay the Congress's drafts for interest &c. expected in the current year." Thus, without a hint of rebuke or acrimony, Franklin coolly informed the Congress that he had obtained—as a free gift—at least as much as Colonel Laurens had hoped to borrow before the envoy extraordinary even arrived.[114]

Franklin now unleashed a little psychological warfare on his fellow Americans. In the same letter that announced his diplomatic triumph in the matter of French aid, he resigned as Ambassador to the court of Versailles. "I have passed my seventy-fifth year," he wrote, "and I find the long and severe fit of gout, which I had the last winter, has shaken me exceedingly, and I am yet far from having recovered the bodily strength I before enjoyed. I do not know that my mental faculties are impaired; perhaps I shall be the last to discover that; but I am sensible of great diminution of my activity, a quality I think particularly necessary in your minister for this Court." With just a touch of pride, and a neat reminder in the bargain, he added, "I have been engag'd in public affairs, and enjoyed public confidence, in some shape or other, during the long term of fifty years, and honours sufficient to satisfy any reasonable ambition; and I have no other left but that of repose, which I hope the Congress will grant me." He insisted that the resignation was not prompted by "the least doubt of . . . success in the glorious Cause, nor any disgust" received in its service. Since his health did not permit him to risk a sea voyage, he planned to remain in France, and was ready to assist the new

Ambassador "with any influence I may be supposed to have, or counsel that may be desired of me." With his usual combination of shrewdness and personal diplomacy, Franklin tried to pick his successor. His choice was young John Jay, who was vainly trying to persuade the Spaniards in Madrid to part with some of their money for the American cause. Franklin sent a copy of his letter of resignation to Jay, telling him, "I wish you to succeed me here. No copy of the letter is yet gone from France . . . nor have I mentioned my intention to anyone here: If therefore the change would be agreeable to you, you may write to your friends accordingly." [115]

Franklin knew only too well that when a man in high office is under attack, the perfect way to silence his enemies is to proffer his resignation and force the issue to an immediate decision. This was precisely what happened. The moment word of Franklin's request became known, a chorus of supporters rallied to his side. From Madrid, John Jay proved himself a disinterested patriot, by writing an alarmed letter to Congress, urging them to reject the resignation. He corresponded with Franklin regularly, Jay avowed, and there was not an iota of senility in his letters. More important, there was simply no one who could match his enormous prestige in Europe. "I confess," wrote Jay, "it would mortify my pride as an American, if his constituents should be the only people to whom his character is known that should deny his merit and services the testimony given them by other nations." [116] John Laurens, the envoy extraordinary, who finally arrived in Paris and conducted a whirlwind campaign to supplement the gift Franklin had obtained with an additional loan, was even more impressed by the vigorous cooperation Franklin gave him in every possible way. Although Laurens failed, except to persuade the French (with Franklin's help) to let him bring back to America with him 2,500,000 livres in cash, the young colonel returned to Congress to inform them that if they accepted Franklin's resignation, they were out of their minds. What Franklin needed was not a replacement, but help. Laurens told the Congressmen that they were asking a seventy-five-year-old man to function simultaneously as an ambassador and admiralty judge and the American Army's purchasing agent, with no one to assist him but a twenty-year-old boy. What he needed was a competent staff to handle the million and one details that inundated the embassy. The result was almost a foregone conclusion. Congress voted overwhelmingly to refuse Franklin's resignation.

The lack of anguish the Ambassador displayed on hearing this news, in August, 1781, makes it clear that he had hardly expected or desired a contrary answer. "I must therefore buckle again to business," he wrote to William Carmichael, "and thank God that my health and spirits are of late improved. I fancy it may have been a double mortification to those enemies you have mentioned to me, that I should ask as a favour what they hoped to vex me by taking from me; and that I should nevertheless be continued. . . . I call this continuance an honour, and I really esteem it to be a greater than my first appointment, when I consider that all the interest of my enemies, united with my own request, were not sufficient to prevent it." [117]

But as always, Franklin's sense of humor and unillusioned view of human nature saved him from a swollen head. When another friend congratulated him on his reappointment and called him the keystone of the American arch, he turned the compliment aside with a funny story. It reminded him, he said, of a farmer in Pennsylvania who sent two servants to borrow a harrow from a neighbor. They were about to pick it up and lug it home when one of them said, "What could our master mean by sending only two men to bring this harrow. No two men upon earth are strong enough to carry it." "Poh!" said the other, who considered himself the local strong man. "What do you talk of two men, one man may carry it. Help it upon my shoulders and see." So the muscular boobie staggered home with the harrow on his shoulders, while his shrewd friend followed him exclaiming, "Zounds, how strong you are. I could not have thought it. Why you are a Samson." Franklin was pointing out that Congress was paying him the same kind of compliment, by reappointing him to his job—and its headaches.[118]

XIX

Less than a month later, Franklin was telling Superintendent of Finances Robert Morris that the continued blizzard of bills from Congress, coupled with a stern letter from Vergennes that there was a limit to

French generosity, "terrifies me." He had promised Vergennes that Congress would draw no more bills on Europe after March, 1781. But now the Ambassador was seeing bills drawn as late as June twenty-second. He told Morris that he could not possibly pay these since he had promised Vergennes that he had enough money to end the year "with honour." To Thomas McKean, the new president of Congress, Franklin sent an earnest warning. The French were still good friends of America, he said, "but the best of friends may be overburthened . . . by too frequent, too large and too importunate demands." [119]

When a merchant named John de Neufville, with whom John Adams was doing business in Holland, seized 50,000 pounds' worth of war supplies which Adams had purchased and refused to deliver them until the Americans paid a petty damage claim, Franklin exploded with the wrath of a man who was determined to suffer no more financial embarrassments. "I would not be compell'd to pay whatever he may please to demand, because he has our goods in possession," Franklin told Adams. "We have, you observe, our hands in the lyons mouth; but if Mr. N. is a lyon, I am a bear, and I think I can hug & gripe him until he lets go our hands." [120]

Franklin's touchiness on money matters was no doubt explained in part by the mental, emotional, and political collapse of Silas Deane. After waiting in vain for Congress to reimburse him for the money he had spent on America's behalf in Paris, he had returned to Europe as a private citizen, hoping to have the accounts he left there audited. When he arrived, he found out that the man whom Congress had appointed to do the job had declined, and this meant an inevitable delay of six months to a year. Desperate for money, deeply embittered by the treatment he had received in Philadelphia, and already compromised through his ties to Bancroft, Deane retreated to Ghent, Holland, and sold out completely to the English. In return for 3000 pounds in goods, to be delivered in America on his account, he wrote a series of letters denouncing the French alliance and urging America to sign a truce with England.

The letters were supposedly to a private friend in America, and Deane arranged for the British to intercept them. George III thought they had "too much the appearance of being concerted with this country," but he had them published in Rivington's *Royal Gazette* in New York anyway. People who had defended Deane in Congress, such as John Jay and Robert R. Livingston, could not believe the letters were genuine. But Franklin, replying to an inquiry from Livingston, now foreign secretary, mournfully reported, "There is no doubt of their being all genuine. . . . He has sent me a letter of twenty full pages, recapitulating those letters, and threatening to write and publish an account of the treatment he has receiv'd from Congress, &c. He resides at Ghent, is distressed both in mind and circumstances, raves and writes abundance, and I imagine it will end in his going over to join his friend Arnold in England." [121]

Franklin refused to back down on his judgment of the Silas Deane he had known in 1776. "I believe he was then sincere and hearty in our Cause," he said. A few days later, he wrote a mournful farewell to "the Honble. Silas Deane, Esq." He declined to enter into a political debate with him. "To me it appears that your resentments and passions have overcome your reason and judgment; and tho my ancient esteem & affection for you induce me to make all the allowances possible . . . yet the length you have gone in endeavouring to discourage and diminish the number of the friends of our country and cause in Europe and America and to encourage our enemies . . . make it impossible for me to say with the same truth & cordiality as formerly that I am

> *Your affectionate friend*
> *& humble servant,*
> *B. Franklin"* [122]

X X

About a month after he was reconfirmed as Ambassador, Franklin received an even more momentous honor from Congress—he was appointed, along with John Jay and John Adams, a member of a new five-man peace commission that replaced John Adams' one-man mission. Franklin immediately wrote to the touchy Adams, who was still in Holland, telling him that he esteemed it "an honour to be joined with you in so important a business." With humorous wisdom, he added that he had never known a peace made, even the most advantageous, that was not criticized and the makers condemned as injudicious or corrupt. " 'Blessed are the peacemakers' is, I suppose, to be understood in the other world," Franklin warned, "for in this they are frequently curs'd." [123]

As for peace negotiations, Franklin doubted that they "shall happen in my time." A few weeks later he advised the president of Congress that "peace is not to be expected" as long as the English kept telling themselves that the Americans were "weary of the contest, and on the point of submission." [124]

On the night of November twentieth, a special messenger arrived at Passy with a letter from Versailles. With his mind full of financial worries, Franklin may well have opened it with trepidation. Was it an angry blast from Vergennes about America's apparently endless improvidence? No, it was good news—the best possible news, the most incredible news. George Washington and Count de Rochambeau, Commander of the French Expeditionary Army, had joined forces with the French fleet and trapped the best army Britain had in America at the little tobacco port of Yorktown, Virginia. Eight thousand Redcoats and their commander, Charles Lord Cornwallis, were prisoners of war. Before dawn, Franklin was up sending letters to his neighbors at Passy and Auteuil and to special friends in Paris, announcing the glorious news. He took special care of the reply he sent to Versailles. Louis XVI, he declared, had "riveted the affections" of the American people to his reign and "made millions happy." The King was, Franklin declared, "Le plus grand faiseur d'heureux [The greatest creator of happiness] that this world affords." [125] Writing about the good news to his compatriot Adams, Franklin soared into poetry. "The infant Hercules in his cradle has now strangled his second serpent and gives hopes that his future history will be answerable." [126]

But the most glowing words he wrote on Yorktown were to George Washington. "No news could possibly make me more happy," Franklin said. "All the world agrees that no expedition was ever better planned or better executed." He assured Washington that Yorktown had "made a great addition to the military reputation you had already acquired, and brightens the glory that surrounds your name, and that must accompany it to our latest posterity." [127]

Franklin and Washington did not exchange many letters. But when they did write, the enormous respect which these two giants of the Revolution felt for each other was instantly apparent. Washington's greatest letter to Franklin was yet to come. But Franklin had already written to Washington a letter which no American can read without

emotion. Not only is it a rare glimpse of greatness speaking to greatness, it is also a unique blend of political wisdom and American faith.

> Should peace arrive after another campaign or two, and afford
> us a little leisure, I should be happy to see Your Excellency in
> Europe, and to accompany you, if my age and strength would
> permit, in visiting some of its ancient and most famous kingdoms.
> You would, on this side of the sea, enjoy the great reputation you
> have acquir'd, pure and free from those little shades that the
> jealousy and envy of a man's countrymen and contemporaries are
> ever endeavouring to cast over living merit. Here you would know,
> and enjoy, what posterity will say of Washington. For one thousand
> leagues have nearly the same effect with one thousand years. The
> feeble voice of those groveling passions cannot extend so far either
> in time or distance. At present I enjoy that pleasure for you, as I
> frequently hear the old generals of this martial country (who study
> the maps of America and mark upon them all your operations)
> speak with sincere approbation and great applause of your conduct;
> and join in giving you the character of one of the greatest captains
> of the age.

> I must soon quit this scene, but you may live to see our country
> flourish, as it will amazingly and rapidly after the war is over. Like
> a field of young Indian corn, which long fair weather and sunshine
> had enfeebled and discoloured, and which in that weak state, by a
> thunder gust of violent wind, hail, and rain, seem'd to be threaten'd
> with absolute destruction; yet the storm being past, it recovers fresh
> verdure, shoots up with double vigour, and delights the eye, not of
> its owner only, but of every observing traveler.[128]

XXI

Within three days of receiving the news of Yorktown, Franklin brushed
off a peace feeler from his old friend, Thomas Pownall. He said he
despaired of seeing "this curs'd war . . . finish'd in my time." For
this he blamed England. "Your thirsty nation has not yet drank enough

of our blood." But then he added words which he knew would travel swiftly to the ears of the Opposition in London. "I am authoriz'd to treat of peace whenever she [England] is dispos'd to it." Two weeks later, he wrote to his old friend William Strahan, who was still sitting in Parliament voting blindly with the King's friends. After several paragraphs about the excellence of French and Spanish printing, he assured him that he hoped their "ancient private friendship" still existed, "tho at present divided by public circumstances." [129] Since he had made a point of calling Strahan his enemy in public, this too was almost certain to be interpreted as an encouraging sign by the growing number of Englishmen who yearned for peace.

Franklin was back at his old game of trying to bring down the North ministry. But for the moment, he was pessimistic. More than once he had remarked that when it came to predicting future English moves, the best way to do it was by selecting the most prudent choice and assuming that George III would choose the precise opposite. A new year—1782—dawned, and still there was no official move from the English government. The indefatigable David Hartley appeared in Passy via the mails on January fifteenth, asking Franklin if it was true that "America was disposed to enter into a separate treaty with Great Britain." He enclosed a manuscript of a "conciliatory bill," which he hoped to introduce into Parliament, calling for a ten years' truce with America, while England continued to fight France.

Franklin's reply was ferociously negative. There was not a man in America, he told Hartley, "that would not spurn at the thought of deserting a noble and generous friend, for the sake of a truce with an unjust and cruel enemy." But he made a point of informing Hartley that he, Adams, Jay, and Henry Laurens had "a special commission" to negotiate a treaty of peace. He added some advice which peace-makers of every era would do well to remember. He urged Hartley to keep out of his communications "invidious expressions." There was no point in declaring that England would fight to the last man and the last shilling, rather than "be dictated to by France," or that England would never agree to a recognition of American independence "at the haughty command of France." If every proposition for peace was construed as an insult, "no treaty of peace is possible." Then, with that incomparable tact which seldom failed him, Franklin added, "Whatever may be the fate of our poor countries, let you and I die as we have lived, in peace with each other." [130]

Franklin and Hartley continued to correspond, while the British

Parliament churned with promising unrest. The North ministry beat off
by a single vote a resolution calling for an end to the war. To buy off
some of the critics, the King dumped Lord George Germain, the American secretary who had been in charge of prosecuting the war. Franklin,
watching all this closely through the reports from his English correspondents and European newspapers, concluded "the nation is sick of
it, but the King is obstinate." Franklin warned Congress to place no
confidence whatsoever in the British declaration that henceforth the
war in America would be defensive. "It is only thrown out to lull us,"
he said. "Depend upon it, the King hates us cordially, and will be
content with nothing short of our extirpation." If Lord North was able
to get a money bill through the House of Commons, Franklin saw
"but little probability" of peace negotiations for another year.[131] Again
and again, Franklin urged Americans to oil their guns for another
campaign, and not be lulled by hopes of peace. There was no doubt
that the English were "somewhat humbled at present," but a little success may make them as insolent as ever. He recalled that when he
was "a boxing boy" it was allowed, even after an opponent said he
had had enough, and was struggling groggily to his feet, to give him
"a rising blow." Let ours, Franklin said, "be a douser." [132]

On Thursday evening, March 21, 1782, a messenger brought an
interesting letter to Franklin's door at Passy.

> *Lord Cholmondely's compliments to Dr. Franklin; he sets out
> for London tomorrow evening, and should be glad to see him for
> five minutes before he went. Ld C. will call upon him at any time
> in the morning he shall pleased to appoint.*

Franklin replied that he would be happy to see his Lordship, whom
he had never met. The next morning there appeared in his study a
young English nobleman carrying a letter of introduction from Madame
Brillon. Franklin's "daughter" was spending the winter at Nice for her
health, and she had met Lord Cholmondely there. Her letter introduced him as an amiable young man, who was interested in the cause
of peace. Then she nervously added that he was probably a spy. But
the young nobleman tried to pry no secrets out of Franklin. Instead
they discussed the obvious swing in Parliament toward peace, and
Lord Cholmondely remarked that he was a friend of Lord Shelburne,
and he wondered if Franklin might want to send a message to this
leader of the Opposition. Franklin accepted the offer and wrote a brief

note congratulating Shelburne on "the late resolutions of the Commons." He said he hoped they would tend "to produce a general peace, which I am sure your Lp with all good men desires, which I wish to see before I die, and to which I shall, with infinite pleasure, contribute every thing in my power."

Franklin wrote this with the hope of placing one more weapon in the hands of the Opposition. By the time Lord Cholmondely arrived in England, a political revolution had occurred in Parliament. Lord North had at last persuaded George III to let him resign, and Lord Rockingham had become First Minister—and named Lord Shelburne, colonial secretary of state. "Great Affairs," Franklin noted dryly in a journal which he began keeping around this time, "sometimes take their rise from small circumstances." [133]

Within two weeks, a new visitor appeared on Franklin's doorstep in Passy. His name was Richard Oswald, and he carried with him a letter from Lord Shelburne. A Scottish merchant who was one year older than Franklin, with no previous diplomatic experience, Oswald was, at first glance, a rather strange choice for a peacemaker. He was a repulsively ugly old man, with only one eye. But he made up for these physical deficiencies with a remarkably engaging manner, and—it soon became apparent—a strong sympathy for the American point of view. Moreover he had the confidence of Shelburne and before the war had been a business associate of Henry Laurens, who had finally been released from the Tower of London, thanks in no small part to Franklin's efforts. Shelburne enigmatically told Franklin in his letter of introduction that Oswald was "an honest man" whom he had selected "after consulting some of our common friends." Shelburne vowed that Oswald was "fully appriz'd of my mind" and that he, Shelburne, had "few or no secrets." He insisted that he wished to retain "the same simplicity and good faith which subsisted between us in transactions of less importance." In a separate letter Laurens told Franklin that he had assured Oswald that "when the Doctor converses or treats with a man of candour, there is no one more candid than himself." [134]

If anyone believed this eyewash, it was certainly not Franklin. He was already aware that in the closing days of the North ministry the British had sent emissaries to John Adams in Holland, and to Vergennes, in the hope of creating discord between the various negotiators. A larger cloud looming over the peace negotiations was the instructions sent by Congress to the American delegates. They were told to insist on independence—but in all aspects of the negotiations to rely on the leadership and advice of the ministers of Louis XVI. This bit of legerdemain was the work of the French minister to the United States, the Chevalier de la Luzerne, who liberally disbursed livres among the members of Congress to get it. Both John Jay and Adams threatened to resign when they saw this proviso in their commissions. Franklin made no such protest, and the supporters of John Adams, then and in future eras, have argued that the reason was his almost slavish dependence on the French court. But Franklin's silence was equally explainable as part of his fundamental policy of keeping his mouth shut as much as possible about issues that might endanger the all-important French alliance.

Although he was well aware of his confreres' opinion of the structure of the peace negotiations, Franklin lost no time reporting the British offer and urging John Jay and John Adams to come to Paris as soon as possible to join him. Jay complied almost immediately, but Adams, deep in the process of negotiating a Dutch loan, declined to show up for months. Simultaneously, Franklin informed Vergennes of Oswald's arrival, and its significance. The French Foreign Minister decided he would like to take a look at England's peace ambassador, and Franklin brought Oswald to Versailles for an interview. Vergennes immediately warned Oswald that there was no hope of making a separate peace with any one of the four allies now in the war—France, Spain, Holland, and the United States. While Franklin nodded assent, Vergennes pointed out to the aged emissary that it was impossible for him or any other belligerent to make peace propositions independently, while England, being alone in the war, could and should make the "first propositions" much more easily.

Franklin made no objection whatsoever to this diplomatic marriage of America and France, while he was sitting in Vergennes' office in Versailles. But the next day at Passy, when he saw Oswald in private, he showed a completely different attitude toward the instructions from Congress about subordinating American policy to France. Oswald was en route back to London, to report to Shelburne. Franklin gave him a letter to his Lordship, warmly endorsing Oswald. "I desire no other channel of communication between us," he told Shelburne, "than that of Mr. Oswald, which I think Your Lordship has chosen with much judgment." He called Oswald "a wise and honest man" and vowed that in his negotiations with him, he would act "with all the simplicity and good faith, which you do me the honour to expect from me." He ended with a brief appeal to Shelburne on behalf of American prisoners in England.[135]

Franklin let Oswald read the letter before he sealed it, and then while the old Scot was glowing with pleasure at the compliments, Franklin serenely suggested that since they were in such hearty agreement with each other, it might be a good idea to indulge in a little "free communication of sentiments" on some possible clauses in a treaty of peace. He urged Oswald to think in terms of "reconciliation with America" not "a mere peace." He reminded him of the enormous damage England had done in America—the towns burned, the people scalped by Indian raiding parties. If England wanted to achieve a reconciliation, it behooved her to offer something by way of reparation. Why not, along with independence for the thirteen colonies, throw in Canada and Nova Scotia? By selling these vast empty lands to future settlers, the American government could raise enough money to compensate those who had suffered from British troops and their Indians. It might also be possible to indemnify the loyalists for the confiscation of their estates.

This suggestion to surrender another third of the British Empire sent Oswald into ecstasy. He told Franklin that "nothing . . . could be clearer, more satisfactory, and convincing" than his reasoning. Franklin had jotted down on paper the main outlines of his argument, which he called "Notes for Conversation." He stated carefully at the bottom of the page, "This is mere conversation matter between Mr. O. and Mr. F., as the former is not entitled to make propositions, and the latter cannot make any without the concurrence of his colleagues." This was a formality similar to the signs that highway builders put up warning drivers that the road is legally closed and they are proceeding at their own risk. Franklin knew the rules of the diplomatic game too well to believe (or expect Vergennes to believe) that any proposition made by a legally empowered peace commissioner was less than serious. Oswald regarded the proposition as so important that he talked Franklin into letting him take the "Notes" back to England with him to show Lord Shelburne.[136]

Significantly, Franklin wrote to Adams reporting his conversation with Oswald and sending him copies of several documents, such as Shelburne's letter. But he did not include a copy of his "Notes for Conversation," nor tell Adams that he had given the paper to Oswald. Franklin stated his reason candidly in his journal. On reflection, "he was not pleas'd" with having favored reparation for the loyalists. The reason was the old and still-bleeding wound of William's defection. Acutely aware of his enemies in Congress, Franklin was hypersensitive to the possibility that someone might accuse him of using his high office to benefit his Tory son. "I was," he admitted, "a little asham'd of my weakness in permitting the paper to go out of my hands." [137]

Less honorable men than Shelburne or Oswald might have used the paper to drive a wedge between Franklin and Vergennes, and even between Franklin and the touchy Adams, who would almost certainly have frowned on Franklin's negotiating behind his back. Franklin relied not only on the nobleman's honor but on his own insight into Shelburne's policy, which was aimed at persuading America to drop out of the war so that England could then get the best possible bargain on peace terms with France. The French had made significant conquests in the West Indies, Africa, and India, which the British wanted very much to regain at the bargaining table, without dispatching expeditionary forces. In terms of immediate cash value, these other possessions were worth much more than Canada, and Franklin, tempting the British to throw the fourteenth colony into the peace pot, was drawing on his insider's knowledge of the strong lobby which West and East Indian merchants and planters had in Parliament.

Franklin also knew that Canada was one item in the bargaining which France did not want America to win. Vergennes felt that the presence of British power on America's borders would be a powerful force impelling an independent America into the arms of France. But the knowledge of this fact did not prevent Franklin, the supposed "slave" of Versailles' policies, from boldly propositioning Oswald.

In Shelburne, Franklin had an adversary who could play the game of double-think and even triple-think as well as double-talk, as skillfully as anyone in the world. While he was avowing to Franklin that he was in favor of peace, simplicity and plain dealing, the earl was shipping secret negotiators in all directions to find a crack in the American front. One was rushed to New York to find out if Congress could be persuaded to shift its ground behind Franklin's back. Henry Laurens, released from the Tower of London on parole, was sent to France to discuss the possibility of a separate peace with John Adams. He rebuffed him emphatically. Adams immediately informed Franklin of what the Ambassador had undoubtedly suspected from the first. "Lord Shelburne still flatters the King with ideas of conciliation and a separate peace." [138] Adams accused Shelburne of nothing more than political maneuvers to raise the stocks and shore up British finances. "If you agree to it," Adams said, showing the same deference to Franklin that Franklin had been showing to him, "I will also agree never to see another messenger that is not a plenipotentiary"—that is, an emissary fully empowered by the British government to negotiate peace.

Franklin's doubts about Shelburne increased drastically when Oswald returned on the fourth of May with a letter from the colonial secretary which said nothing whatsoever about peace terms beyond vagaries about "a happy conclusion of all our public differences." Oswald was still functioning as nothing more than a confidential messenger, with no official commission from the British government. Verbally he conveyed to Franklin a reiteration of Shelburne's confidence in his "character for open and honest dealings." Then, more significantly, Oswald added, "It was also generally believ'd" that Franklin had "still remaining some part of [his] ancient affection and regard for Old England."

To add to the confusion, Oswald informed Franklin that a second peace emissary was on his way to Paris. He represented Charles James Fox, who was functioning as foreign secretary in the Rockingham cabinet. Although they had been fellow politicians in Opposition, Fox and Shelburne disliked each other intensely. Fox claimed the right to send his own ambassador to do business with France, which was outside the bounds of Shelburne's Colonial Department. There was no doubt that Fox was bidding to take over the peace negotiations. But in his choice of an emissary, he demonstrated that lack of judgment which was ultimately to wreck his career as a Parliamentary politician. Fox chose Thomas Grenville, son of Franklin's old archenemy, George Grenville, whose stamp tax had begun the quarrel between England and America.

Inevitably, young Grenville had mental reservations about Franklin, and Franklin had even more about him. Fox strove to overcome this obstacle by giving Grenville a letter to Franklin in which he said, "I know your liberality of mind too well to be afraid, lest any prejudices against Mr. Grenville's *name* may prevent you from esteeming those excellent qualities of heart and head, which belong to him." Franklin invited young Grenville to dinner and with "a good deal of general conversation" probed his mind and opinions, and the next day escorted him to Versailles to meet Vergennes. There, as Franklin had anticipated, the new peace emissary made his first move. In return for granting America independence, he coolly informed Vergennes that Great Britain expected the return of all the captured British islands.

Vergennes gave Grenville a diplomatic smile and said he did not think the independence of America was something Britain possessed to trade. "America," he said, "does not ask it of you: there is Mr. Franklin, he will answer you as to that point."

"We do not consider ourselves as under any necessity of bargaining for a thing that is our own," Franklin informed the discomfited envoy, "and which we have bought at the expense of much blood and treasure, and which we are in full possession of."

Feebly Grenville protested that the war had been provoked by the encouragement France had given to the American Revolution. With one eye on Franklin, Vergennes indignantly denied that any such encouragement had ever been given. "The breach had been made, and independence declared, long before America received the least encouragement from France," declared the French foreign minister. He defied the world to give the smallest proof to the contrary. "There sits Dr. Franklin," he said, "who knows the facts, and can contradict me if I do not speak the truth."

Franklin, who had conferred with French agents in Philadelphia a year before independence was declared, solemnly nodded his assent. Between these two seasoned professionals, beginner Grenville was like a shuttlecock in a championship badminton game. Back in Passy, Franklin wryly noted in his journal, "Mr. G. express'd himself as not quite satisfy'd with some part of the Count de Vergennes discourse, and was thoughtful." [139]

Simultaneously, while he backed Vergennes in his diplomatic confrontation with the enemy, Franklin was listening and thinking for himself. Vergennes had done more than reject American independence as a bargaining point. He had also candidly revealed the self-interest which had led France into the war in the first place. France wanted a drastic revision of the humiliating treaty of 1763, hoped to break the British stranglehold on India, and sought better guarantees of French fishing rights off Newfoundland's Grand Banks. There were also the war aims of Spain, which was seeking to wrest Gibraltar from the English. Holland too was going to want some compensation for the damage Britain had wreaked on her possessions in the West Indies. Even a man with one-third of Franklin's sagacity could see, in Vergennes' own testimony, the indubitable fact that self-interest was a major motivating force among all the allies.

The next day, Grenville paid Franklin a visit and tried far more vigorously than Oswald to detach him from the French alliance. Franklin replied with a swatch of logic that left the fledgling diplomat gasping. It was nothing less than a little sermon on the nature of international obligations, couched in those personal terms that Franklin loved. "A, a stranger to B, sees him about to be imprison'd for theft by a merciless creditor; he lends the sum necessary to preserve his liberty," Franklin said. If B later repays the money, has he discharged the obligation that he owes to A? "No," Franklin said, "he has discharged the money debt but the obligation remains, and he is a debtor of a kindness of A, in lending him the sum so seasonably." Even if B later lent A money in the same circumstances, he would still only have discharged a part of the obligation of gratitude he owed to A.

France, of course, was A and America was B, and Franklin was saying that America should stand by France even after she achieved her independence and repaid her loans. Grenville protested desperately that this was "carrying gratitude very far" and reiterated his argument that France was the one who was profiting most from the war by separating America from England. Franklin told him bluntly that "the generous and noble manner" in which France had given America help "without exacting or stipulating for a single privilege or particular advantage to herself" made it impossible for him, and he hoped "and indeed did not doubt . . . my countrymen," to listen to such an argument. Thus Grenville "gain'd nothing of the point he came to push," Franklin noted in his journal.[140]

Franklin was playing an extremely delicate, crucially important game. Without betraying Vergennes, he was attempting to tease the British into conceding American independence—and after that concession begin the bargaining that would maneuver Shelburne into surrendering Canada. Reports from both Oswald and Grenville to their chiefs in London emphasized Franklin's hints that once independence was granted, America might be tempted to make some kind of separate peace. But the more Franklin talked with Grenville, the more convinced he became that he was the wrong tool to execute this subtle operation. At twenty-six, he was too eager to make a name for himself as a diplomat by driving the hardest possible bargain. Oswald, on the other hand, was too old to have such personal ambitions, and there was some basis for believing him when he said he wanted nothing more than peace. So Franklin calmly proceeded to eliminate Grenville.

Franklin became convinced that Grenville had to go when he discovered from the Marquis de Lafayette, who was acting as a liaison man between Versailles and Passy, that Grenville's instructions from London empowered him to treat only with France. Vergennes confirmed this, telling Franklin, "They want to treat with us for you. But this the King will not agree to. He thinks it not consistent with the dignity of your state. You will treat for yourselves: and every one of the powers at war with England will make its own treaty. All that is necessary to be observ'd for our common security is, that the treaties go hand in hand, and are sign'd on the same day." These were welcome words for Franklin. They not only authorized him to do what he had already been doing; they gave him another weapon to use against the hapless Mr. Grenville.[141]

Franklin made an appointment with the already jittery young diplomat at Passy and challenged him on the validity of his powers to negotiate with America. Grenville swore that he would get his commission reworded to include America as soon as possible, and informed Franklin confidentially that he had instructions from Fox to acknowledge the independence of America previous to the commencement of negotiating a treaty. Desperately Grenville loaded Franklin with compliments, vowing that all of England believed that Franklin was the only living man who could reconcile the two countries. He damned North and his ministers in vivid terms, in effect condemning his own father, whose American policies the North ministry had generally followed. Franklin practically yawned in his face. "Such flattering language from great men" might have affected him in his younger days, he confided to his journal. But now he was too old to worry about anything but leaving behind him "the tolerably good character [reputation]" he had thus far achieved.[142]

Events suddenly made Grenville's removal from the scene all the more urgent. From the West Indies came the dismaying news that Admiral de Grasse, the keystone of the allied victory at Yorktown, had been badly thrashed by a revived British fleet off the Saints Islands. The Admiral himself and his hundred-gun flagship had been captured, along with four other ships. Although Grenville insisted that the victory did not alter Britain's desire for peace, Franklin sensed potential foul play in the involved instructions that Grenville obtained from London. The most he could get his diplomatic masters to state was an authorization for him to treat with *France and her allies*. This was not good enough for Franklin, and he bluntly insisted on the specific mention of America as one of these allies. Almost curtly, he refused to give Grenville any assurance that, when independence was granted, America would not make any exertions on behalf of the claims of Spain or Holland.

The frustration in Grenville's letters to Fox, reporting his conversations with Franklin, make it clear that the American Ambassador had read the young diplomat's mind. He was getting nowhere, Grenville moaned—revealing the ambition that the somewhere he wanted to get was a promise from Franklin that independence was a tradable item, which America was prepared to buy at the expense of her allies. Meanwhile, Franklin was writing to Shelburne, urging him to send Oswald back to Paris with powers to negotiate with America. On June thirtieth, the old Scot returned and put on a plaintive performance, obviously intended to touch Franklin's heart. Great Britain was bankrupt, sighed Oswald. They were even considering a decision to stop paying interest on their national debt. "Our enemies may now do what they please with us," he cried. "They have the ball at their foot." All the thinking people of England looked only to one man to extricate the nation from its present desperate situation—Benjamin Franklin. Never before in history had a single man an opportunity to do so much good. Whether or not this was true, it must have been at least amusing to Franklin to hear himself being proclaimed a savior by the nation that had spent the last seven years reviling him.

Oswald showed Franklin a memorandum from Shelburne which empowered Franklin to write Oswald's commission, with an automatic stamp of approval guaranteed from the colonial secretary. Oswald then proceeded to stand there agreeing with Franklin, while the Doctor repealed his original hint of compensating the loyalists. He did not even object when Franklin went so far as to offer the opinion that neither England nor America owed them anything since it "was by their misrepresentations and bad counsels" that the war had begun. Cheerfully Oswald informed Franklin that he had also recommended surrendering Canada, and "Mr. Fox appeared to be startled at the proposition." [143]

Oswald was almost too good to be true. A few days later, one of the periodic packets of London papers arrived and gave Franklin the weapon he needed to give Grenville the coup de grace. There was a story in the London *Evening Post* of May 30, 1782, in which Grenville was purported to claim that he had "gained a considerable point of information" from Franklin about the possibility of America concluding a separate peace. It made a great deal of the fact that Franklin had shown Grenville a copy of the 1778 Treaty of Alliance, which had been printed in the London newspapers when Grenville was a lad of twenty-two.

The next time Grenville showed up at Passy, excitedly informing Franklin that he had finally obtained from London a new commission which gave him full powers to treat with both France and America, Franklin finished him off. He told Grenville that he was very much unimpressed with the new commission, which merely added that Grenville was empowered to treat with any other *state* besides France. Thus far, he pointed out, the British had not been in the habit of referring to America as a state, preferring to consider the thirteen colonies as thirteen separate groups of rebellious subjects. Then Franklin showed him the London paper and curtly declared that when his conversations were so badly misrepresented, it would be "hazardous" to make any further propositions to Mr. Grenville.[144]

Completely discomfited, Grenville conferred with Oswald, who until now he had been grandly disregarding. Oswald, perhaps deliberately, and perhaps even at Franklin's suggestion, told Grenville how thoroughly he agreed with the propositions Franklin had made him, including the cession of Canada. Grenville rushed to his writing table and dashed off a furious letter to Fox, telling him that Oswald was giving away everything but George III's throne to Franklin. Once and for all, Grenville demanded that Fox resolve the division of authority between himself and Shelburne, or he, Grenville, was giving up.

On June 17, 1782, Parliament passed "the Enabling Act," which gave the ministry power to negotiate "a peace or truce" with America. Fox, impulsive as always, promptly challenged Shelburne's right to conduct the negotiations. The cabinet declined to eliminate Shelburne. A few days later, the head of the government, Lord Rockingham, died of influenza. With Fox in disarray, there was only one logical man to succeed him—Lord Shelburne. The disgruntled Fox quit the cabinet, and Shelburne became the new First Minister. Grenville went home to London to nurse his diplomatic wounds, and Mr. Oswald was swiftly confirmed as the commissioner in charge of negotiating peace with America. Once more, Franklin's insider's knowledge of English politics had won a breakthrough victory.

X X I I

Unfortunately, Shelburne the Prime Minister was even more of a double-talker than Shelburne the colonial secretary. In a speech in the House of Lords shortly after he took office, he declared himself still a follower of

Lord Chatham, who had opposed American independence from the first day he heard the word. Shelburne called it "a dreadful blow to the greatness of this country" and "a fatal necessity" to which he might be forced to yield. But "nothing short of necessity" would extract it from him. Franklin immediately began warning Congress and other American correspondents to keep up their guard against "our insidious enemies." He told Robert R. Livingston, current secretary for foreign affairs, that absolute and total independence was America's only real safeguard. "The King hates us most cordially . . . once admitted to any degree of power and government among us," George would continue his war against liberty "by corruption, artifice and force, until we are reduced to absolute subjection." [145]

To Franklin's relief, John Jay finally arrived in Paris, giving him a colleague whom he thought he could trust. But Jay, little more than a week after he had arrived, was prostrated by the influenza that had killed Lord Rockingham and was epidemic throughout Europe. Franklin had had a bout with the bug in the latter part of June, but his sturdy constitution had thrown off the disease in only a few days. Poor Jay was flattened for much of the summer, and once more Franklin found himself the sole negotiator.

On July tenth, he again demonstrated his ample independence from French influence by meeting with Oswald and in a two-hour session, sketching out virtually an entire peace treaty. There were four necessary terms. At the top of the list was full and complete independence and the withdrawal of all British troops from America. Next came a settlement of the boundaries. Third was a specific insistence on a return of the Canadian boundary to the old Great Lakes line. Although he was no longer contending for a private company, Franklin had never lost his vision of those rich western lands, which the Quebec Act of 1774 had swallowed by extending the Canadian border south to the Ohio. The fourth necessary point was the right of Americans to fish in freedom and safety on the Newfoundland Grand Banks.

Then, in a highly unorthodox diplomatic move, which attempted to utilize the noble sentiments Shelburne and Oswald had uttered about reconciliation, Franklin added four "advisable" articles. First, the British ought to make some gesture of reparation to towns such as Norfolk, Virginia, and Falmouth, Massachusetts, which they had burned. Second, Parliament ought to issue nothing less than an apology for its barbarous conduct of the war. "A few words of that kind," Franklin assured Oswald, "would do more good than people would imagine." Next, the treaty ought to include total reciprocity in import and export duties and shipping privileges, explicitly abandoning the old colonial system by which England had attempted to maintain monopolistic advantages in trading with America. Finally, Franklin recommended once more the cession of Canada, which would remove once and for all the threat of hostile British troops on American borders.[146]

Franklin said that the advisable articles were not "absolutely demanded," but speaking "as a friend," he urged Oswald and Shelburne to take his advice if they really wanted America's friendship. Their reward would not only be permanent peace, but a healthy, profitable share of America's trade, and perhaps even, in some unspecified future decade, a federal union of some sort between the two countries. All this, of course, made Oswald salivate. Franklin even showed him the exact accounting of the aid America had received from France and, doing a complete about face from the position he had taken with Grenville, hinted that once these debts were paid, America owed France nothing "except gratitude."

With these bold proposals, which he did not discuss with Vergennes, Franklin gave the ball Oswald had placed against his foot a mighty boot toward the public goal of peace—and his private goal, American control of the North American continent. Like the good gamesman he was, Franklin knew that by eliminating Grenville, he had seized the initiative in the negotiations, and he was determined to maintain his momentum. There was another reason for his urgency, which sprang from his insider's knowledge of English politics. He knew that Lord Shelburne had only a tenuous grip on Parliament. It was imperative to strike a bargain with him as soon as possible because the chances were all too good that any minister who replaced him would be a more compliant tool of George III, hence far more hostile to American claims.

Simultaneously Franklin made it clear that he was not going to be an apostle of reconciliation, trusting in the triumph of sweetness and light, without some clear-cut gestures of reciprocity from Shelburne. When the Prime Minister dragged his feet on sending Oswald an official commission to act as peace commissioner, Franklin forbade the old Scot to mention his eight-point offer and demanded a specific assurance that Shelburne was prepared to concede American independence. To reassure the Doctor, Shelburne sent across the Channel one of Franklin's most ardent English admirers, young Benjamin Vaughan. He had published an edition of Franklin's scientific writings in London in 1779, a neat bit of propaganda on America's behalf. Arriving in Paris, Vaughan went straight to Passy and handed over to Franklin copies of several secret dispatches which Shelburne had sent at the same time by courier to Oswald. These included a concession of Franklin's four necessary articles. Now he was ready to begin escalating the advisable articles into necessary ones—especially the article on Canada.

In a carefully understated, routine way, Franklin sent Shelburne's communications to Vergennes. The reaction of the French foreign minister reflected his fear—and no doubt his amazement—that Franklin was moving so fast. The French had barely opened their negotiations. If Franklin maintained his momentum—he had already obtained more than Vergennes ever dreamt the English were ready to concede—it seemed more than ever likely that the Americans might sign a separate peace which would make them independent of both Britain and France. So the Count sent Franklin a terse warning that Shelburne's prime goal was still "producing a division between the King and the United States." [147] Franklin was prepared to ignore this warning with equanimity. He had already demonstrated his intention—and his ability—to negotiate independently. But momentum, Canada, even peace itself, were suddenly imperilled by the return of John Jay to the negotiating table.

XXIII

The hawk-nosed, thin-lipped puritan from New York recovered from his influenza just in time to greet Richard Oswald, returning from London with his commission to negotiate a treaty. The wording of the commission was not much better than the equivocal phraseology young Grenville had obtained—and to which Franklin had objected so strenuously. Oswald was empowered to treat for peace "with the said colonies or any of them or any parts thereof." Shelburne, with one eye on the hawks in Parliament, was making a desperate effort not to concede American independence in advance. Jay angrily declined to tolerate this omission. He absolutely refused to negotiate another step unless Oswald obtained a commission specifically recognizing the United States of America.

It was legalism at its worst. Franklin had objected to Grenville's commission to get rid of Grenville as a negotiator. Now he had the man he wanted, Oswald, who agreed with almost every word he said. But he did not dare to contradict the vehement Jay without opening the American delegation to the kind of acrimony that Franklin had come to dread, thanks to Arthur Lee. After wrangling with Oswald over the wording for the better part of a week, Franklin persuaded Jay to discuss the problem with Vergennes. The French foreign minister smoothly assured Jay that he was quibbling over a technicality. Why not exchange full powers with Oswald? Once he accepted the Americans' commissions as plenipotentiaries of the United States of America, Britain would have *de facto* admitted American independence. Jay frowned and shook his head, his dissatisfaction still all too evident. Vergennes turned to Franklin, and with studied reluctance Franklin said that this formula "would do." He was not inwardly disagreeing and outwardly capitulating to Vergennes. Instead, he was forced to simulate enough reluctance to avoid including himself in Jay's super-suspicious view of the situation. Franklin knew Jay was in communication with John Adams, and he knew, too, that Adams was already convinced that Franklin was a Vergennes tool.[148]

From the argument over recognition, Jay and Vergennes passed to discussing an even more disagreeable issue. During Jay's negotiations in Madrid he had learned that the Spaniards were claiming all the territory between the Appalachians and the Mississippi, from the Gulf of Mexico north to the Ohio River. Jay had insistently rebutted this claim and written to Franklin for help. He had backed Jay wholeheartedly. He would not sell a drop of the Mississippi's waters. "A neighbor might as well ask me to sell my street door," he told Jay.[149] Now, through the Spanish ambassador in Paris, the Spaniards were renewing this claim, which ran directly counter to Franklin's goal of gaining the maximum territory possible for the United States. In fact, on August 12, 1782, he wrote Robert R. Livingston, explicitly declaring: "I hope Congress will insist on the Mississippi as the boundary, and the free navigation of the river."

In the interview with Jay, Vergennes did not commit himself either way, but his confidential secretary, Gerard de Rayneval, who was present as a translator, made it clear that in his opinion the Americans were asking too much. Back at Passy, a few hours later, this French reluctance to support American claims inspired Jay to a wild outburst of invective against Vergennes and France. Franklin listened in silence while Jay ranted that the French were playing the Spanish game and were out to keep America as small and impotent as possible. They were not even wholehearted supporters of American independence, Jay insisted, although Vergennes had told him that he would stipulate in all his negotiations with the British that American independence would be the first article in any treaty. After Jay had exhausted his invective against France, Franklin calmly conceded that Spain wanted to "coop us up within the Allegheny Mountains" [150]—something both he and Jay had known for two years. But until he saw some proof that France was playing this game, he preferred to apply the principle he usually followed in such cases—to assume a friend was honest until hard evidence was presented to the contrary. As for Jay's accusation that France was deliberately slowing down the negotiations, everything Vergennes had suggested in their conference seemed aimed at speeding them up.

What Franklin might have added, but did not dare tell his contentious young colleague, was the simple fact that he understood Vergennes' position. Caught between the counterclaims of two allies, the Count instinctively groped for some kind of compromise. It was hardly even surprising that the French foreign minister should lean toward Spain since Spain was a far more important and influential ally to France than America. This was part of the diplomatic game, which was played on a field of shifting grays, not the absolute blacks and whites which the moralistic, literalistic Jay seemed to insist upon. What counted with Franklin was the fact that Vergennes had given the Americans a free hand in negotiating independently with the English, and Franklin had more than demonstrated that he construed this to mean he was free to drive the best bargain he could get from England. What counted even more, Franklin knew from his insider's knowledge of English politics, was maintaining the initiative and momentum that he had already built up with Oswald and Shelburne.

When Oswald visited him the next day (August eleventh) at Passy, Franklin talked about almost nothing but Canada. He discoursed on the "stretch of frontier" it occupied along America's borders and vowed that there could be no hope of a lasting peace until England handed it over. How thoroughly he was succeeding, Oswald revealed in his letters to his superiors in England. After that conversation, he confessed he was ready to yield "the whole territory."

But the next time Oswald saw Jay, he found the younger American wearing a startlingly different face. The truculent and negative manner of their first meeting had vanished. Now Jay suddenly seemed, not merely reasonable, but almost friendly on all points, except one—his insistence on a prior recognition of independence. Jay even drafted a patent or deed for George III, which he argued the King could sign without an act of Parliament, and urged Oswald to forward it to London. Franklin joined Oswald in talking him out of this absurdity, but other members of the British diplomatic mission were soon reporting to London that Jay was "much more open and unreserved" than Franklin.[151]

This shift was deliberate on Jay's part. Over Franklin's objections, he had decided to disregard Vergennes' advice—and the clear instructions of Congress to rely on it—and push for unilateral absolute recognition of American independence, prior to any negotiation. To prove his point, that he was willing to ignore his instructions from Congress, Jay, according to family legend, flung his pipe into Franklin's fireplace at Passy, defiantly declaring that he would break any instructions, in the same way, that forced him to compromise the dignity and honor of America. From The Hague, John Adams, another lawyer in love with legalistic affirmations—and even more in love with anything that Franklin disliked—backed Jay.

Some historians have attempted to convert Jay into a hero by this bullheaded all-or-nothing demand for independence. There is no doubt that it has a noble, patriotic aura, but as the French general remarked, watching the charge of the Light Brigade, "Magnificent—but it is not war." One can only say of the New Yorker's patriotic intransigence— "It is not diplomacy." [152] Jay was letting his ancestral Huguenot prejudices against Catholic France run amok. Instead of playing the game like a chess champion, Franklin style, masking long-range goals, forcing the other side to make the first move, Jay practically gave away all his bargaining power by telling Oswald, "You have only to cut the knot of independence" and Americans would "take care" to be independent of all other nations. This was veering perilously close to violating the treaty with France, which Jay had vowed to Franklin he would never do. But puritans such as Jay and Adams never doubt their own integrity—only the integrity of others.

Canada, and every other point on Franklin's advisable list, vanished from the horizon, and peace itself seemed to recede as this wrangle over "the point of independence" consumed the month of August. Then came a blow which knocked Franklin completely out of the negotiations for the better part of a month—his first severe attack of bladder stone.[153] Jay was left alone on the field.

The British, encouraged by Jay's loose remarks about a separate peace, decided to give him what he wanted and sent Oswald fresh instructions, agreeing that the King would recommend to Parliament an act acknowledging American independence. But by the time this concession arrived in Paris, Jay had allowed his paranoia about France to get completely out of control. He told Oswald that all he wanted, really, was a change in his phraseology, "constructively" recognizing American independence by empowering him to treat with the "commissioners of the United States of America." Next, Jay, immensely disturbed by learning that Gerard de Rayneval had gone to London for personal conferences with Shelburne, persuaded Benjamin Vaughan to become a private courier to the Prime Minister, without Franklin's knowledge. Jay's purpose, in his own mind, was twofold. He was anxious to rebut what he suspected Rayneval was asking Shelburne to do—join France and Spain in limiting American claims to western lands and the Newfoundland fisheries.

To some extent Jay was correct in this suspicion. Although American claims were not the main purpose of Rayneval's mission—he was sent to discuss peace terms between France and England—the subject did come up in the course of his conversations with Shelburne. Playing the game of placating Spain, the French envoy let Shelburne know that France thought American claims to the western lands were excessive. Shelburne casually agreed. But no deal was made, nothing was signed or even verbally arranged. Rayneval was simply fishing for British support if it came to the crunch on this question with the Americans. There was no secret agreement, or even a secret understanding arrived at. The whole situation remained immensely more fluid than Jay, with his rigidly suspicious mind, saw it.

No matter what France or Spain wanted to do about American claims, they were relatively powerless. Shelburne, dealing alone with four belligerents, was the only man who had the power to make decisive choices, as Franklin had seen from the start—and acted upon by negotiating boldly with him for the highest stakes. So Jay's first message to Shelburne, urging him to back American claims to the fisheries and western lands, was largely superfluous.

Shelburne was far more interested in the second message which Vaughan carried from the American negotiator. On Jay's behalf, Vaughan urged Shelburne to "cut the cords" which tied America to France. As Jay explained it to Robert R. Livingston, he made it clear that America intended "faithfully to fulfill our treaty and engagements with this Court," but he pointed out that "it was a different thing to be guided by their or our construction of it." [154] Why this is heralded by some historians as a kind of breakthrough or departure from the policy laid down by Franklin is something of a mystery. It is precisely what he had been doing—and assuming that Vergennes had been doing—from the beginning of the negotiations.

But Jay's words made the possibility of concluding a separate peace with the Americans begin to dance even more brightly before British eyes. Shelburne immediately rephrased Oswald's commission, giving him power to "treat with the commissioners appointed by the colonys, under the title of 13 United States." This was still equivocal phraseology, but Jay accepted this watery reassurance and finally, on September twenty-seventh, six weeks after they should have begun bargaining, he began drafting peace propositions. But before he could give them to Oswald, news from a battlefront arrived, underscoring the urgency Franklin had felt about time and momentum.

A joint French-Spanish attack on Gibraltar had been beaten off with heavy losses, and a relieving British fleet, under the leadership of Admiral Lord Howe, had slipped through the French and Spanish blockade to bring the fortress enough food and ammunition to guarantee its survival for another year at least. The threat to Gibraltar had been perhaps the key reason why the British had been panting to sign a separate peace with the Americans, to get them out of the war. Capture of the Rock, which the British had held since 1704, had been the prime goal of the Spanish war effort.

By way of peace propositions, Jay had nothing to propose but Franklin's four necessary articles with refinements specifying boundaries. There is no evidence that Oswald used Gibraltar as an argument to exclude Canada—but this hardly proves that it had no influence on the negotiations. Defeat at Gibraltar made it all the more likely that Spain might press her territorial claims in the Mississippi Valley to get something out of the war, and Jay grew so jittery about this that he offered the English free navigation of the Mississippi River in return for backing American claims beyond the Alleghenies. Canada vanished from the peace negotiations, never to be mentioned again. The initiative had been lost and the momentum was now definitely in the hands of the British.

X X I V

At this point, into Paris rode John Adams, with one of his few real diplomatic triumphs in his pocket. He had negotiated both a commercial treaty and a loan with Holland. His ego immensely inflated by this success, Adams saw himself arriving in France just in time to rescue his country from Franklin's craven duplicity. He disapproved of everything Franklin had done, such as negotiating with Oswald before he had an official commission. Corresponding with gossips in Paris who fed his delusions, Adams added to his already incredible list of diary indiscretions by declaring that he could feel for Franklin "no other sentiment than contempt or abhorrence." [155] When Adams heard about the American acceptance of Oswald's watery, altered commission, he had instantly leaped to the conclusion that Franklin's finesse was at work, and wrote a violent letter to the American foreign secretary, threatening to resign from the peace commission. He deleted his threat from the final draft of his letter when he found out that the acceptance was John Jay's decision. But Adams did not remove the conviction from his mind that Franklin was in the business of betraying his country for France.

The first thing Adams did in Paris was to listen to another talebearer, a Marylander named Matthew Ridley, who assured him that Franklin was selling America down the Seine. Adams was also fuming over what he considered a personal affront—the appointment of William Temple Franklin as the secretary of the commission, without consulting John Adams. This same Ridley assured Adams that Franklin had duped Jay into this appointment while Jay was still in

Madrid—a total lie which Jay swiftly corrected. To his diary, Adams confided the following absurdity: "Between two as subtle spirits as any in this world, the one malicious, the other I think honest, I shall have a delicate, a nice, a critical part to act. Franklin's cunning will be to divide us . . ." [156]

Perhaps the most ridiculous thing Adams confided to this perennially revealing confessional is the following: "The present conduct of England and America resembles that of the eagle and the cat. An eagle scaling over a farmer's yard espied a creature that he thought a hare; he pounced upon him and took him up in the air. . . ." Adams proceeded to tell the fable of the eagle that is forced to stoop and set the cat down, never realizing that he was simply paraphrasing Benjamin Franklin.

When Adams finally had a private conversation with John Jay, even he was appalled by the depth of Jay's French paranoia. "Mr. Jay likes Frenchmen as little as Mr. Lee and Mr. Izard did. He says they are not a moral people; and they know not what it is; he don't like any Frenchmen; the Marquis de Lafayette is clever, but he is a Frenchman. Our allies don't play fair, he told me. . . ." [157]

His heart palpitating with anticipation, Adams, four days after he arrived in Paris, having spent most of the intervening time talking to nobodies like Ridley, finally found the good grace to call on Franklin. Most of the visit was consumed by a typical Adams harangue. "I told him without reserve my opinion of the policy of this Court, and of the principles, wisdom and firmness with which Mr. Jay had conducted the negotiation in his sickness and my absence, and that I was determined to support Mr. Jay to the utmost of my power in the pursuit of the same system. The Doctor heard me patiently, but said nothing." [158] As Adams was leaving, however, Franklin quietly reminded him that he had been in Paris almost a week, and had yet to call on Vergennes—a diplomatic gaffe of the first order.

Here was the foremost of several reasons why Franklin made no attempt to restrain the headstrong moralism of his two colleagues. Jay and Adams acted as if the French alliance were a mere bagatelle which America could discard with a shrug. Franklin, with frantic letters on his desk from Congress urging him to negotiate another loan of 20,000,000 dollars, knew that the alliance was the only thing that was keeping the helter-skelter American government alive. To have revealed the vitriolic attitudes of Adams and Jay toward France might well have wrecked the alliance, and would have almost certainly sabotaged the desperately needed loan. Moreover, if Franklin had pulled out of the peace negotiations, the entire structure would have come tumbling down. He was the cornerstone around whom Shelburne had built his entire negotiation—at least in the spring and early summer of 1782, when England was desperate for peace. Finally, the important thing *was* peace, even if it was short of the continental triumph which Franklin had been constructing before Jay and Adams arrived on the scene. So the next morning, when Franklin met with his two fellow commissioners, he told them the decision he had reached, during the night. "I am of your opinion, and will go on with these gentlemen in the business without consulting this Court." [159]

But now the three Americans faced an entirely different game. With the news of Gibraltar in their hands, the British were the ones who were on the offensive, and the four necessary articles which Jay had proposed as the complete treaty came flying back from London, with no confirmation and a tough new negotiator to stiffen Oswald's spine. His name was Henry Strachey. Franklin and Adams had met him when they conferred with Lord Howe in 1776 on Staten Island. The oldest clerk in the foreign office, he was, in Adams' opinion, "as artful and insinuating a man as they could send; he pushes and presses every point as far as it can possibly go." Henceforth, the Americans were on the defensive, fighting to hold onto what they could legitimately claim, and beating off a ferocious British effort to compensate the loyalists. This was vital to Shelburne's political existence. London was thronged with loyalists who were besieging every politician in Parliament, insisting that their claims for compensation for their confiscated estates in America be honored in some way. The British were almost as insistent on a clause that excluded the Americans from all but the most minimal use of the Newfoundland fisheries. They were also determined to guarantee the payment of American debts to British merchants in honest money. As a final bite, almost as if they wanted to show their renewed cockiness, they announced that eastern Massachusetts, practically the entire present-day state of Maine, belonged to the province of Nova Scotia.

For six consecutive days, from early in the morning until well after dark, the negotiators argued bitterly and sometimes violently over the first two demands. The Americans agreed readily enough to the clause on prewar debts. John Adams, having once been assigned by

Massachusetts to set the Maine boundary, thoroughly refuted Strachey on that point.

In the argument over the fisheries, Franklin played a key role. As a Massachusetts man, John Adams ought to have taken the lead, but as he noted in his diary, he knew "nothing myself, but as an hearsay witness." Franklin put him in touch with Jonathan Williams at Nantes, who obtained from a Marblehead man at the port a detailed account of the rights that America had hitherto exercised off the Grand Banks. Adams then did most of the talking—and later took all the credit for winning most of what the Americans wanted, although the word "right" was diluted to "liberty"—a loss which caused some problems in future years.

But when the argument turned to the loyalists, Franklin took charge of the American delegation. At first both Jay and Adams wavered toward concession. Franklin blazingly refused to countenance any kind of compensation.

There was an explanation for Franklin's intransigence which no other biographer has heretofore noted. Ex-Governor William Franklin had arrived in London to rescue what he could from the wreckage of his life.[160] He had left New York under a very odious cloud. As president of the Board of Associated Loyalists, he was responsible for planning the numerous small but savage raids which the loyalists had executed against their fellow Americans in New York and vicinity. On one of these, they had captured a fort at Toms River, New Jersey, and had taken prisoner an American captain named Joshua Huddy, a member of the New Jersey militia. The loyalists accused Huddy and his friends of killing one of their partisans, Philip White, and on April 12, 1782, they hanged Huddy from a tree in Monmouth County.

The repercussions of this brutal episode soon reached all the way to Europe, and involved Franklin in an intensely embarrassing gaffe. The outraged Americans demanded that the loyalist officer in charge of the hanging, Captain Richard Lippencot, be handed over to them, or they would exact eye-for-eye vengeance on a British prisoner of equal rank. Under direct orders from Congress, Washington selected by lot Captain Charles Asgill, son of a wealthy and influential English family, and informed the British high command that if Lippencot was not surrendered forthwith, young Asgill—he was only nineteen—would soon be swinging from the end of a rope. Asgill's mother and father used every iota of their formidable influence to extricate their son. They bombarded George III and Louis XVI with memorials and petitions. Vergennes asked Franklin to intercede, and Shelburne instructed Oswald to make an even more fervent appeal to him.

Tartly, Franklin replied, "The situation of Captain Asgill and his family afflicts me, but I do not see what can be done by anyone here to relieve them. It cannot be supposed, that General Washington has the least desire of taking the life of that gentleman. His aim is to obtain the punishment of a deliberate murder, committed on a prisoner in cold blood, by Captain Lippencot. If the English refuse to deliver up or punish this murderer, it is saying that they choose to preserve him rather than Captain Asgill. It seems to me, therefore, that the application should be made to the English ministers for positive orders, directing General Carleton [the new British commander-in-chief in America] to deliver up Lippencot; which orders, being obtained, should be despatched immediately by a swift sailing vessel. I do not think any other means can produce the effect desired." [161]

Meanwhile, in New York, Carleton had arrested Lippencot and court-martialed him. But the board of officers who heard his case acquitted him on the grounds that he had only obeyed orders. Where had these orders come from? From the Board of Associated Loyalists. This soon led to a demand by the Americans for William Franklin's head, and the ex-governor decided it might be just as well if he got out of the country. The war was obviously lost anyway, and when a group of loyalists asked him to be their official representative in London, and in that role to present a petition to the King, begging his Majesty to make good the financial losses they had suffered, William seized the opportunity to depart with at least a semblance of dignity.

It must have been deeply humiliating—and infuriating—for Franklin to discover that the murderer he was calling upon the British to deliver up in such tough style in his letter to Oswald was his own son. Asgill was finally extricated by a direct appeal from Louis XVI to Congress, and Washington let him go with obvious relief. The incident, coming as it did so close to the end of the war, when most of the bloodshed had ended, had enormous emotional impact throughout America and probably did more than any single event to make the Tories odious to the patriots, for decades to come.

William Franklin arrived in London late in September just as the really hard bargaining over terms for the loyalists began in Paris.

We know that Franklin was aware of William's arrival because Benjamin Vaughan, Shelburne's agent, wrote a strong letter urging the Prime Minister to do something handsome for the ex-governor. The source of his plea was none other than William Temple Franklin, who had talked to Vaughan behind his grandfather's back. Vaughan completely swallowed Temple's argument that "a compliment in that quarter" would have a "seasonable effect . . . upon your American affairs."

Both Vaughan and Temple miscalculated the depth of Franklin's bitterness toward William. The knowledge that his son was to be the chief negotiating agent for the defeated loyalists made it inevitable that Franklin would fight giving them even a shilling of compensation. There was also a stringent political issue involved. As John Adams pointed out in his letters and diaries, if the Americans agreed to a thoroughgoing compensation for the loyalists, they would in effect be admitting that the American rebellion was unjust and that the loyalists, by getting full value for their confiscated estates, were the honest upholders of law and order which they styled themselves. Before the eyes of the civilized world, the Revolution would be clouded with a virtual confession of illegality. But as the bargaining grew fiercer, both Adams and Jay inclined toward some palliative form of compensation. Not Franklin. He remained absolutely and totally opposed to the idea, and since he had gone along with the reckless, not to say brainless diplomacy of his two colleagues in regard to Canada, they had to go along with him now. "Dr. Franklin is very staunch against the Tories," Adams told his diary, with just a touch of bewilderment.[162]

Not being a psychologist—in fact, being the very opposite of one— John Adams was totally incapable of analyzing Franklin's motives. The real reason never dawned on him or the bewildered Vaughan. Shelburne did take the trouble to see William Franklin sometime during October, 1782, and he expressed deep sympathy both for the ex-governor personally and for the sad plight of all the loyalists. It must have been doubly galling to William to learn from the Prime Minister that his negotiators were making an all-out effort on behalf of him and his friends and that the man who stood immovably in their path was Benjamin Franklin.

For a final blow, William soon learned that the treaty called for the surrender of the western lands between the Alleghenies and the Mississippi—which meant the annihilation of whatever hopes he had had for making a profit on his Vandalia stock. Later William angrily asked

Richard Oswald why he had given away a fifth of the continent to the Americans.

"Your father, Dr. Franklin," Oswald said, "insisted on a boundary being drawn. The Doctor ran his finger along the map to indicate the desired boundaries. And what could *I* object to a man of Dr. Franklin's influence and authority?" [163]

On November twenty-ninth, only the loyalists stood between the negotiators and complete agreement. Two days earlier, Benjamin Vaughan had returned from London, where he had thoroughly discussed all aspects of the treaty with Shelburne. Parliament, after having been prorogued twice by the jittery Prime Minister, was about to meet. If he did not have at least a preliminary peace with the Americans to show the back-benchers, almost certainly he would be voted out of office. "We have liberal American commissioners in Paris, a liberal English commissioner, and a liberal First Minister for England," Vaughan pleaded. "All these circumstances may vanish tomorrow, if this treaty blows over." Adams suggested sending a courier to London for more instructions. The British replied that would mean having "all laid loose before Parliament . . . it was going to sea again." [164]

Then Franklin unleashed a thunderbolt. "If another messenger is to be sent London," he said, "he ought to carry something more respecting a compensation to the sufferers in America."

He took from his pocket a paper, and began to read: "It is agreed, that His Britannic Majesty will earnestly recommend it to his Parliament, to provide for and make a compensation to the merchants and shopkeepers of Boston, whose goods and merchandise was seized and taken out of their stores, warehouses and shops by order of General Gage, and others of his commanders and officers there; and also to the inhabitants of Philadelphia for the goods taken away by his army there; and to make compensation also, for the tobacco, rice, indigo and Negroes, &c., seized and carried off by his armies, under Generals Arnold, Cornwallis and others from the states of Virginia, North and South Carolina and Georgia, and also for all vessels and cargoes belonging to the inhabitants of the said United States, which were stopped, seized or taken, either in the ports, or on the seas, by governors, or his ships of war, before the declaration of war against the said states. And it is further agreed, that His Britannic Majesty will also earnestly recommend it to his Parliament, to make compensation for all the towns, villages, and farms, burnt and destroyed by his troops or adherents, in the said United States." [165]

The English commissioners stared at each other for a moment in uneasy silence. They then withdrew to a nearby room for a hurried conference. A few minutes later, they returned, and Allyne Fitzherbert, the diplomat who had been negotiating with the French, and who had joined the American negotiations as they neared the climax, quietly agreed to accept the treaty, as it stood. They only asked one favor, as a sop to British public opinion. Would the Americans agree to insert in the treaty a promise that Congress would petition the states to restore or at least make compensation for the seized property of loyalists who had not made themselves obnoxious to their fellow Americans? This idea came from Oswald, and perhaps he, who was closer to Franklin than any other negotiator, had finally divined what was going on in Franklin's mind. Since Jay and Adams were already inclined to give the loyalists even more than this minimal gesture, the deal was made, when Franklin agreed. Both sides knew that it meant nothing, since dealing with the loyalists was a prerogative which Congress had left entirely to the states. Even so, Franklin saw to it that the agreement specified that loyalists who had "borne arms against the said United States" were excluded. This, of course, applied directly to William Franklin.

The next morning, the four American commissioners—Henry Laurens had joined them at the last moment—met in Oswald's room and signed the "preliminary articles." As a bow to the French alliance, the treaty's preface specified that it was not to be concluded "until terms of peace shall be agreed upon between Great Britain and France." The same day, Franklin sent a copy of the treaty to Vergennes at Versailles, and then invited his two colleagues to join him for dinner at Passy. Everyone was in an ebullient mood. Adams confided to his diary, as if it was an amazing revelation, that Franklin had "gone on with us with entire harmony and unanimity throughout, and has been able and useful, both by his sagacity and his reputation, in the whole negotiation." But Honest John could not forbear writing one more of his absurdities. He noted that a Frenchman had called him "the Washington of the negotiation," but he felt that the title ought more justly to go to John Jay.[166] With Washingtons like Jay and Adams, the American Revolution would have ended in 1776. The combined diplomatic accomplishment of their seven years in two European capitals was two puny loans and a minor treaty (with Holland), negotiated after Yorktown.

No one can question the zeal and energy these men gave to their country's cause. Both made major contributions to the founding of the nation, in other areas of the revolutionary struggle. The austere Jay never succumbed to Adams' childish jealousy; he remained an admirer of Franklin for the rest of his life. But his children and grandchildren entered the historical lists on his behalf, and did their utmost to build his reputation at Franklin's expense. Adams went on slandering Franklin for the rest of his long life, and his descendants continued throwing mud unto the fourth generation. Yet there remains the inextinguishable fact, for anyone who looks dispassionately at the record. There *was* a Washington of negotiation. His name was Benjamin Franklin.

X X V

With peace almost secured, Franklin had the sticky task of placating France and wringing from her one more desperately needed loan. The days went by, and nothing but a frigid silence emanated from Vergennes' office in Versailles. Cautiously Franklin paid him a personal call. The two men, friends as well as diplomatic allies, discussed the American treaty in an atmosphere of perfect politeness. But Vergennes made it clear to Franklin that the Americans' "abrupt signature" of their treaty without prior consultation "had little in it which could be agreeable to the King." Franklin defended himself and his colleagues by pointing to the preliminary clause, which specified that the treaty would not become effective until France completed her negotiations. He undoubtedly quoted for Vergennes the frantic statements Vaughan had made about the precarious state of the Shelburne ministry. Vergennes, with his army of spies in London and in the other courts of Europe, knew this as well as Franklin. But the Count made his continuing displeasure evident by doing nothing about Franklin's plea for more money.

Finally, on December 15, 1782, Franklin was forced to send him a delicate ultimatum. The American ship *Washington* was about to sail for America, carrying the Preliminary Articles. The ship had a British passport. Franklin knew that the Count would instantly see this as a hint that Britain and America were drifting toward reconciliation. It would also arouse fears that the British would use the ship to circulate anti-French propaganda about the preliminary treaty throughout America. In the teeth of the foreign minister's certain wrath, Franklin calmly asked him for a first installment on a loan, which he had not yet promised to give. "I fear the Congress will be reduced to despair when they find that nothing is yet obtained," Franklin said. This was both a threat and a warning that America might well drop out of the war.

For once the Count lost his famous self-control. "I am at a loss, sir," he wrote Franklin, "to explain your conduct and that of your colleagues on this occasion. You have concluded your Preliminary Articles without any communication between us, although the instructions from Congress prescribed that nothing shall be done without the participation of the King. You are about to hold out a certain hope of peace to America, without even informing yourself on the state of the negotiation on our part. You are wise and discreet, sir; you perfectly understand what is due to propriety; you have all your life performed your duties. I pray you to consider how you propose to fulfill those, which are due to the King! I am not desirous of enlarging these reflections; I commit them to your own integrity. When you shall be pleased to relieve my uncertainty, I will entreat the King to enable me to answer your demands."

Franklin pondered this challenge for a day and a half, and then answered it in a letter which was a masterpiece of diplomatic *double entendre*—a reply that neither sacrificed American dignity nor the French alliance, that neither crawled nor pleaded, but was rooted in that personal independence that was the essence of his spirit. He began by assuring Vergennes that he had not requested the British passport for the *Washington*. They had sent it voluntarily. Nor were the Americans letting them use the ship to send any letters of their own which might "convey inconvenient expectations into America." He reminded Vergennes once more that "nothing has been agreed in the preliminaries contrary to the interests of France; and no peace is to take place between us and England, till you have concluded yours." Nevertheless, he smoothly admitted that the Count's observation "is however, apparently just, that, in not consulting you before they were signed, we have been guilty of neglecting a point of bienséance [propriety]. But, as this was not from want of respect for the King, whom we all love and honour, we hope it will be excused, and that the great work, which has hitherto been so happily conducted, is so nearly brought to perfection, and is so glorious to his reign, will not be ruined by a single indiscretion of ours. And certainly the whole edifice sinks to the ground immediately, if you refuse on that account to give us any further assistance."

They would hold the ship until Friday, Franklin said, and he would visit him on that day for his answer. Once more Franklin reiterated the gratitude which he and "every American" felt for the "great benefits and favours" the King had bestowed upon them. Then, once more, came the hinted threat. *"The English, I just now learn, flatter themselves they have already divided us,"* Franklin underlined the sentence, as if the idea had just been whispered to him for the first time in his study at Passy. "I hope this little misunderstanding will therefore be kept a secret, and that they will find themselves totally mistaken." 167

A few days later, Franklin was able to tell Robert Morris, the frantic Superintendent of Finances, that the "little misunderstanding" between America and France had been "got over" and the *Washington* had sailed with 600,000 livres in her hold. The balance of a 6,000,000 livre loan would be paid quarterly, throughout 1783. Franklin had done the almost impossible—he had reconciled such opposites as John Adams and John Jay and the Count de Vergennes. Independence had been won, and bankruptcy averted. For a final touch, the British passport for the *Washington* was made out to the "United States of America" and signed by George III—his first acknowledgment in writing that such a nation existed.

Less than a month later, the French and British agreed on terms, and Vergennes invited Franklin and Adams to join him in signing the document—one more hint that the Count was still smarting over his exclusion from the American signing. The ceremony was brief and matter-of-fact. The "mighty system" of a world war was, John Adams noted in his diary, terminated "as perfunctorily as a marriage settlement." 168 But it did mean that the war was, for all effects, over. Later that day, when Franklin arrived at the home of the Duke de la Rochefoucauld for dinner, he could not restrain his joy. He threw his arms around this staunch supporter of America and exclaimed, "My friend, could I have hoped, at my age, to enjoy such a happiness?" [169]

XXVI

Although he was practically certain that peace had at last been won, Franklin warned Congress to keep America's guard up. They had only signed the Preliminary Articles, which had to be ratified by Parliament. Success on another battlefront, such as the West Indies, might well turn England's "giddy" head and reawaken her dreams of conquest. The wisdom of this warning became grimly evident when Shelburne's government crumpled under violent attack by diehards such as Lord Stormont and Lord Hillsborough and harassment from fellow liberals such as Charles James Fox. Shelburne did himself no favors by talking on all sides of the issue of independence, declaring it "equivocal" until the treaty was ratified and insisting that it was granted only as a price of peace, not a prior gift to the Americans. Meanwhile, in the House of Commons, his lieutenant, young William Pitt, was saying the precise opposite. Pitt was looking at the situation with the *de facto* eyes of a realist, not a legalist. But the struggle with Jay over prior recognition, which Shelburne had won, made him hypersensitive on the point. The House of Lords approved the treaty by thirteen votes, thanks largely to Shelburne's eloquent self-defense. In the Commons, after an all-night debate, peace and American independence were accepted, but Shelburne's government was censured by a vote of 207 to 190, for making too many concessions to the belligerents—especially the Americans.

Out of office went Shelburne, and into power came the most unlikely political marriage in British history, Lord North and Charles James Fox, in a kind of tandem ministry. These very strange bedfellows proceeded to do exactly what Shelburne had done when he first opened negotiations. They found a man who was personally ac-

ceptable to Benjamin Franklin. Their choice was Franklin's old friend,
David Hartley, who had been corresponding with him about peace
since the war began. Hartley soon became almost as much a Franklin
mouthpiece as Oswald had been. He agreed wholeheartedly with Franklin on the need for complete freedom of trade between the two
countries, and even succumbed to Franklin's favorite siren song and
recommended that England throw in Canada.

But in England the political mood was running strongly against the
liberal spirit. Fox, a politician first and a liberal second, followed the
tide and suppressed all thought of gestures aimed at reconciliation.
This hard line toward America also demolished Franklin's hopes of
creating in the final peace treaty a new approach to war. Franklin had
urged on Oswald, and now on Hartley, a clause that would end all
privateering, and another clause that would exempt ships carrying non-
combat materiel from destruction by belligerents. But England was too
embittered by defeat to do more than concede what she had already
lost. So the Preliminary Articles became the final Treaty of Peace,
signed on September 3, 1783.

Throughout this second summer of frustrating negotiations, Franklin
had to cope with the problem of John Adams, who became more and
more hysterical on the subject of France and Franklin. "One of my
colleagues," Franklin told Robert Livingston, "thinks the French Minister one of the greatest enemies of our country; that he would have
straitened our boundaries, to prevent the growth of our people; contracted our fishery, to obstruct the increase of our seamen; and retained the Royalists among us, to keep us divided; that he privately
opposes all our negotiations with foreign Courts, and afforded us,
during the war, the assistance we receiv'd, only to keep it alive, that
we might be so much the more weaken'd by it; that to think of gratitude to France is the greatest of follies, and that to be influenced by
it would ruin us. He makes no secret of having these opinions, ex-
presses them publicly, sometimes in the presence of the English Ministers, and speaks of hundreds of instances which he could produce
in proof of them. None of them, however, have yet appeared to
me. . . ." [170]

Behind Franklin's back, Adams was doing some verbal knife-work
worthy of Arthur Lee. He told one correspondent that the mere fact that
Franklin was "trumpeted" by Versailles was proof of his dishonesty. On
September 3, 1783, the very day that peace was signed, Adams struck

an even lower blow. "The moment an American minister gives a loose to his passion for women, that moment he is undone; he is instantly at the mercy of the spies of the court, and the tool of the most profligate of the human race." The contentious puritan then enunciated a principle which was final proof of his incapacity as a diplomat. "No man will ever be pleasing at a court in general, who is not depraved in his morals or warped from [America's] interests." [171]

To Robert Morris, Franklin had earlier written a confidential letter saying that he hoped "the ravings of a certain mischievous madman" against France would not damage the alliance, "which is indeed the solid foundation of our present importance in Europe." [172] Franklin showed, moreover, that he was very much alert to the attacks Adams was making on his reputation among friends in America. On September 10, 1783, he told John Jay that he had received a letter "from a very respectable person in America" saying that "it was entirely owing to the firmness, sagacity and disinterestedness of Mr. Adams, with whom Mr. Jay united" that the western lands and the fishing rights were obtained by the negotiators. "It is not my purpose to dispute any share of the honor of that treaty," Franklin said, but he refused to tolerate "an accusation which falls little short of treason to my country." Jay promptly replied, affirming that Franklin had fought beside them every step of the way. Adams, after three days of silence, replied with a much more perfunctory letter, saying the same thing in a cold, unfriendly way. Grimly, in a letter to another Massachusetts friend, Josiah Quincy, Franklin remarked "that his adversaries may find they presum'd a little too much" upon his age and weakness when they attacked him.[173]

XXVII

But Franklin was much too intelligent to carry such a petty feud beyond the absolute minimum required to protect his reputation. With peace, his spirits soared, and his letters abounded with good humor. To David Hartley he wrote proposing "a family compact" between England,

France, and America to guarantee the world against future wars. "America would be as happy as the Sabine girls, if she could be the means of uniting in perpetual peace her father and her husband," he declared. As for Hartley's concern that America might fall apart, because the government under the Articles of Confederation was so weak, Franklin told him that America's domestic quarrels were "monstrously magnified by your microscopic newspapers." Anyone who judged from them that Americans were tottering into anarchy was like a man who was shown sunspots through a telescope, and concluded that "the whole disk would soon be overspread by them, and that there wou'd be an end of daylight. The great body of intelligence among our people surrounds and overpowers our petty dissensions, as the sun's great mass of fire diminishes and destroys his spots." [174]

When John Jay wrote to tell Franklin that he had many enemies in England, Franklin replied that the fact did not trouble him. "They are my enemies as an American." He added that he also had two or three enemies in America "who are my enemies as a minister." But he was able to thank God "there are not in the whole world any who are my enemies as a *man;* for by His grace, thro a long life, I have been enabled so to conduct myself, that there does not exist a human being who can justly say, 'Ben. Franklin has wrong'd me.' " [175]

William Strahan wrote to Franklin lamenting the political instability which was bringing down one British ministry after another. Franklin told him not to despair. "We have some remains of affection for you, and shall always be ready to receive and take care of you in case of distress. So if you have not sense and virtue enough to govern yourselves . . . dissolve your present old crazy Constitution, and *send members to Congress.*" [176]

Henry Laurens wrote again from England, lamenting the British regulations inhibiting American trade in the West Indies. Franklin professed to be unbothered, confident that a growing America would soon force John Bull to regret his selfishness. "Those who at present wish to kick the hedge-hog, will grow tired of that sport when they find that their own toes bleed." In his letter, Laurens also assured Franklin that, although he did not think Franklin was infallible, as long as he lived he would never cease defending him against the untruths that Adams was spreading against him. Franklin thanked him and then added the following inimitable comment: "As to my infallibility, which you do not undertake to maintain, I am too modest myself to claim it, that is, *in general;*

tho when we come *to particulars,* I, like other people, give it up with difficulty. Steele says that the difference between the Church of Rome and the Church of England on that point, is only this; that the one pretends to be infallible and the other to be *never in the wrong.* In this latter sense, we are most of us Church of England men, though few of us confess it. . . ." [177]

Franklin had in his years at the court of Versailles developed a rather powerful political connection with the Church of Rome. The papal legate was utterly charmed by him, and about this time he gave Franklin a chance to repay an old debt of gratitude. The clerical diplomat told the Ambassador that America's independence had convinced the Pope that the church in the New World was ready to take a major step toward maturity. It was time to appoint an American bishop. Did he have any suggestions? Franklin had only one—his old friend Father John Carroll, who had saved his life on the trip down the lakes from Canada in 1776. The legate passed on Franklin's recommendation to Rome, and the long arm of coincidence soon reached across the ocean, making the ex-Jesuit the first American bishop.

Meanwhile, Franklin was enjoying himself hugely with a new scientific interest—balloons. The French had begun filling silk bags, first with heated air, then with hydrogen, which Franklin called "inflamable air," and Franklin was privileged to witness the beginning of the great adventure which may yet carry men to the distant stars. He sent to fellow scientists in England and America exquisitely detailed reports on these first balloon flights. As with the American trip to the moon, there were numerous croakers who decried the expense and labor (it took two days and nights to fill a balloon) and demanded to know what was the point of ballooning, what good did it do the average man? Franklin gave them a classic reply. "What good is a newborn baby?" he asked. [178]

To Franklin's delight, Congress had finally sent to Europe a politician with whom he was completely compatible. Thomas Jefferson had arrived in Paris on August 6, 1784, and Franklin immediately introduced him into French society, as he had John Adams. But there was never a hint of self-righteous recrimination about high living from the easy-going intellectual giant from Virginia. His already profound admiration for Franklin only grew deeper as he watched him in this twilight of his diplomatic career. Later Jefferson would contemptuously dismiss the charge that Franklin had been under undue French influence. If anything, he said, the French "were more under his influence than he under theirs." [179]

Jefferson especially enjoyed Franklin's triumph over the French scientist, Abbé Guillaume Raynal, who was a supporter of the then popular theory that animals and even men degenerated in the New World, were smaller in stature, and by implication weaker in intellect. One day at the Passy dinner table, Franklin was entertaining the abbé and several of his French friends, along with three or four Americans. The abbé began holding forth in favor of the degeneracy theory with unparalleled eloquence and presumption. Franklin let him talk for a while. Then he said, "Come, Monsieur l'Abbé, we are here one-half American and one-half French, and it happens that the Americans have placed themselves on one side of the table and our French friends on the other. Let both parties rise and we will see on which side nature has degenerated." Up rose Franklin, in all his imposing bulk, beside him were William Carmichael and David Humphreys, Washington's ex-aide, both burly six-footers. The French, on the other hand, Jefferson said gleefully, "were remarkably diminutive, and the abbé himself particularly was a mere shrimp." [180]

Another subject on which Jefferson and Franklin agreed was the Society of the Cincinnati. Created by Washington's officers, it announced itself as a hereditary organization. Both Franklin and Jefferson denounced the idea as a dangerous tendency toward aristocracy. Franklin's comments were by far the more devastating. He showed how absurd it was to imagine one could pass along qualities of mind or spirit to descendants. In nine generations, the blood of the original "Knight" of the Cincinnati would have passed through 1021 other men and women. To get 1000 of these Knights, would require, in round numbers 1,000,000 Americans, and Franklin wondered how with "a reasonable estimation of the number of rogues, and fools, and royalists, and scoundrels, and prostitutes, that are mix'd with, and help to make up necessarily their million of predecessors, posterity will have much reason to boast of the noble blood of the then existing set of Chevaliers de Cincinnatus." Franklin grew so warm on the subject that he even wrote a pamphlet attacking the whole idea of aristocracy. His French friends persuaded him not to publish it, lest it should get him into serious trouble with Versailles.[181]

But Franklin was not in the least inhibited in stating his anti-blue blood opinions to French aristocrats. One day he took on a whole roomful of them. Their spokesman insisted that the majority could not possibly rule in a state because they were uneducated and ill-informed. Only the educated and well-informed minority should govern. Finally the nobleman attempted to trump Franklin by appealing to the others in the room. He asked all those who agreed with him to rise. Everyone stood up, leaving Franklin alone in his chair. Totally unabashed, he declared himself the winner. "According to your own principles," he said, "you represent the ignorant majority, and I the wise minority, decide that you are wrong and must yield." [182]

At Auteuil, the tête-à-têtes between Franklin and Madame Helvetius, the abbés and Cabanis became even more rollicking. Notes and songs flowed back and forth, to be added to the collection of witty essays, such as the *Ephemerae*. Franklin called these his "bagatelles" and printed them on the small press which he had set up in the Hotel de Valentinois. Sometimes Franklin and the abbés would borrow Madame Brillon's piano and have an evening of "good music and tea with ice." Abbé Morellet wrote a song which argued that the American Revolution had really started because Franklin had grown tired of English beer and decided to switch to French wine.

> *In all history there never was*
> *A better braver cause*
> *Independence was the goal*
> *So French wine could soothe the soul*
> *I am told*
> *Of Benjamin.*

The Ambassador replied with a mad essay in praise of wine which he signed Abbé Franklin. It abounded with puns on the word *vin,* French for wine. Before Noah, Franklin pointed out, men had only water to drink and that is why they went astray and became "abominably wicked." So God gave Noah the secret of wine, and he in turn discovered some of the secrets of living. Hence the origin of the word divine—"to discover by means of wine." Solemnly he lectured the Abbé Morellet on putting water into wine, which was then the fashion in France. Franklin did not approve of it. "Offer water only to children," he advised, and pointed out that Saint Paul advised Timothy to put some wine into his water for his health's sake, but "not one of the Apostles nor any of the Holy Fathers have ever recommended putting water into wine." To further prove the divine origin of wine, Franklin noted the position of the elbow, which God had placed precisely in the middle of the arm, enabling a man to lift a glass of wine to his mouth without the slightest difficulty. There

was only one conclusion. "Let us adore then, glass in hand, this benevolent wisdom; let us adore and drink." [183]

Another day Franklin sent over an old song he had written forty years
before on the same subject. The verses contained not a little of his
mellow philosophy.

SINGER

Fair Venus calls; her voice obey
In beauty's arms spend night and day
The joys of love all joys excel,
And loving's certainly doing well.

CHORUS

O! No!
Not so!
For honest souls know,
Friends and a bottle still bear the bell.

SINGER

Then let us get money, like bees lay up honey;
We'll build us new hives, and store each cell.
The sight of our treasure shall yield us great pleasure.
We'll count it, and chink it, and jingle it well.

CHORUS

O! No!
Not so!
For honest souls know,
Friends and a bottle still bear the bell.

SINGER

If this does not fit ye, let's govern the city.
In power is pleasure no tongue can tell.
By crowds tho you're teased, your pride shall be pleased,
And this can make Lucifer happy in hell!

CHORUS

O! No!
Not so!
For honest souls know,
Friends and a bottle still bear the bell.

SINGER

Then toss off your glasses, and scorn the dull asses
Who, missing the kernel, still gnaw the shell;
What's love, rule or riches: Wise Solomon teaches,
They're vanity, vanity, vanity still.

CHORUS

That's true;
He knew;
He tried them all through;
Friends and a bottle still bore the bell.[184]

XXVIII

There was in all this gaiety a bittersweet undertone of sadness. Franklin had decided to go home. The great victory won, and the peace restored, his thoughts turned inevitably to America. Madame Helvetius begged him to spend the rest of his life in France, where so many people loved him. "I want to be buried in my own country," he replied, sounding more and more like a patriarch of old. He sent a veritable stream of letters to Congress, begging them to dismiss him. In almost every one of these letters he added a plea for William Temple Franklin. He expatiated on the long years of service Temple had given him and the country in the French mission, acting as his secretary, and then as secretary of the peace commission. Franklin urged that he be rewarded by being appointed secretary of the legation or a chargé d'affaires in some other American legation in Europe.

For eighteen months, he got no answer to either request. Congress was in a state of political desuetude, moving haphazardly from city to city, with scarcely enough money to pay its dinner bills. In it there was still a sprinkling of Franklin enemies, who delighted in striking at him through his grandson. Unfortunately, Temple gave them a tempting target. He seemed to have inherited very little of his grandfather's talent or stability. His favorite sport was strolling the boulevards of Paris with French friends his own age, dressed in the high style of the day. He liked to shock people by extravagant public performances, such as coming late to dinner and going around the table, kissing every woman in the room.

True to one Franklin tradition, Temple had had an illegitimate child by Blanchette Caillot, the wife of a Passy neighbor. The baby died of smallpox a few months after it was placed in the care of a country family. Instead of sympathizing with the broken-hearted mother, who worshipped her "Franklinet," Temple coldly reproached her for her carelessness and broke off the affair. While he could be charming, there would seem to have been an underlying emotional emptiness in Temple that made it difficult for him to achieve any really satisfactory human relationship. Various visitors to Passy noted that he seemed, at times, to treat his grandfather with considerable discourtesy. Between them there always stood an absent figure—the father whom Franklin had defeated so totally.

In mid-August, 1784, Franklin received a letter from William, a cautious, tentative, but hopeful inquiry to his "Dear and honoured father," asking if they could "revive that affectionate intercourse and connexion which till the commencement of the late troubles had been the pride and happiness of my life." Although he was beaten, William refused to admit that he was wrong. "If I have been mistaken, I cannot help it," he said. "It is an error of judgment that the maturest reflection I am capable of cannot rectify; and I verily believe were the same circumstances to occur again tomorrow, my conduct would be exactly similar to what it was heretofore, notwithstanding the cruel suffering, scandalous neglect and ill-treatment which we poor unfortunate loyalists have in general experienced. . . ." [185]

Having "broken the ice," William wondered if he could come to Paris to see his father and discuss "private family affairs of a very important nature." Franklin answered the letter almost immediately, declaring that he would be glad to "revive the affectionate intercourse." He said it would be "very agreeable" to him. But the next sentence betrayed how difficult this resumption would be. "Indeed nothing has ever hurt me so much and affected me with such keen sensations, as to find myself deserted in my old age by my only son; and not only deserted, but to find him taking up arms against me, in a cause, wherein my good fame, fortune, and life were all at stake." Then, struggling to control himself, Franklin added, "I ought not to blame you for differing in sentiment with me in public affairs. We are men all subject to errors. Our opinions are not in our own power; they are form'd and govern'd much by circumstances, that are often as inexplicable as they are irresistible. Your situation was such that few would have censured your remaining neuter. . . ." Then the bitterness burst through again in the next line, which Franklin underlined: *"Tho there are natural duties which precede political ones, and cannot be extinguish'd by them."*

Franklin added, in the most perfunctory language, "I shall be glad to see you when convenient." But now was not convenient. He would "not have you come here at present." Temple was coming to London at his father's invitation, and Franklin told William to confide "to your son the family affairs you wished to confer upon with me." Tensely, he warned William, "I trust that you will prudently avoid introducing him to company, that it may be improper for him to be seen with." [186]

Temple went to London, and Franklin promptly became a grouchy, miserable grandfather, demanding letters from him by every post, and insisting that Temple clear every move he made with him.[187] At twenty-four Temple must have found it rather humiliating to ask his grandfather's permission to go to the seashore with his father. When he asked for an extension of his visit, Franklin conceded it with an absolute minimum of grace. Then a month passed without a letter from Temple, and Franklin erupted with petulant wrath. He told Temple that "he waited with impatience the arrival of every post. But not a word. All your acquaintance are continually inquiring what news from you. I have none. Judge what I must feel, what they must think, and tell me what I am to think of such neglect." Temple coolly replied by asking for an extension of his stay.[188]

Temple finally returned in December, but the experience did nothing to bridge the chasm between Franklin and his son; if anything it widened it. On neither side was there any attempt to resume a correspondence. William was absorbed in helping loyalists present their claims to the British government for their losses. On his own behalf he presented a bill for 48,000 pounds. Franklin, who was seeing a stream of influential Englishmen, including such potent politicians as young William Pitt, never murmured so much as a word on William's behalf. Lord Shelburne intervened with Louis XVI to obtain a royal pension for his old friend Abbé Morellet without impugning his political integrity. Franklin could certainly have done something for William, in a discreet and unofficial way, if he chose. Instead, William became the victim of a whispering campaign among American loyalists, who accused him of deliberately choosing the King's side as a prearranged plot with his father, so that no matter who won, a Franklin would be on the safe side of the quarrel. This may well have had something to do with the almost brutal way that the Parliamentary commission disposed of William's claims. They granted him only 1800 pounds, and disallowed the rest of his 48,000-pound plea. Other loyalists of his stature received settlements as high as 24,000 pounds. The government did allow him a pension of 800 pounds a year—50 pounds more than the salary he had received as New Jersey's governor. But this, compared to the life-style to which William aspired, was genteel poverty.[189]

Franklin paid a price, within himself, and within his family, for leading America to nationhood. It exceeded in many ways the sacrifice of Biblical Abraham. Franklin had been forced to strike down not just his first born, but his only son, and no intervening deity withheld his hand. Instead, as in most family tragedies, he was forced to relive the emotion again and again for the rest of his life. One day about this time, Franklin was walking in the Bois de Boulogne with a French friend. The conversation turned to children, and Franklin suddenly began describing, in the most emotional terms, his lost little Francis Folger Franklin, dead now more than fifty years. Tears filled his eyes, and he choked, "I always thought he would have been the best of all my children." [190]

But Franklin's mind was too supple, his wisdom too deep, to allow these family emotions to torment him day and night. Most of the time, he took a cheerfully ironic, philosophic attitude toward himself. Writing to a friend in England about his health and present circumstances, he noted how often in his life he had sung a song called "The Old Man's Wish," in which the singer hopes for a warm house in a country town, an easy horse, some good old authors, ingenious and cheerful companions, a pudding on Sundays with stout ale and a bottle of burgundy. Each stanza ended with a refrain.

> May I govern my passions with an absolute sway,
> Grow wiser and better as my strength wears away,
> Without gout or stone, by a gentle decay.

"But what signifies our wishing?" Franklin asked. "Things happen, after all, as they will happen. I have sung that wishing song a thousand times, when I was young, and now find, at fourscore, that the three contraries have befallen me, being subject to the gout and the stone, and not being yet master of all my passions." He reminded himself, Franklin said, of a "proud girl" in Pennsylvania, who regularly proclaimed that she would never marry a parson nor a Presbyterian nor an Irishman and ended by being married to an Irish Presbyterian parson.[191]

XXIX

Finally Congress sent permission to go home. Through Jonathan Williams, Franklin hired an English ship, and after weeks of packing, he started for the coast. He traveled in a royal litter, drawn by the King's mules, because his bladder stone gave him unendurable pain in a jolting carriage. In Passy, Madame Brillon wept after begging him, "If it ever pleases you to remember the woman who loved you the most, think of me." Even her husband added a postscript: "My very dear Papa, I have nothing to add, and even if I wanted to, my tears would not let me see." For Madame Helvetius, the pain was even more intense. Only at the very end did she realize that she alone had had the power to keep Franklin in France. In the middle of his journey to the coast, she suddenly reached out, with almost guilty emotion, begging him to return. "I fear you are in pain, that the road will tire you and make you more uncomfortable. If such is the case, come back, my dear friend, come back to us." As he boarded the ship in Le Havre, Franklin's last thoughts were of her. "I am not sure that I shall be happy in America, but I must go back. I feel sometimes that things are badly arranged in this world when I consider that people so well matched to be happy together are forc'd to separate.

"I will not tell you of my love. For one would say that there is nothing remarkable or praiseworthy about it, since everybody loves you. I only hope that you will always love me some. . . ."[192]

At Southampton, a small coterie of Franklinites gathered to say goodbye. Bishop Shipley and his daughter Katherine were there, as well as Benjamin Vaughan, one of the architects of the peace, now busily engaged in publishing Franklin's collected writings in London. Jonathan Williams arrived to join them for the voyage back to America. Other old friends hurried down from London. For four days they dined and drank together at the Star Tavern. But there was one other visitor to the Star who did not join in these happy hours: William Franklin.

Face to face, Franklin found it even more impossible to forgive his son. He could not forget that William was wanted for murder—the murder of a fellow American. Their conversation together was a cold and matter-of-fact discussion of business matters. Aware now that Congress was probably not going to do anything for Temple, Franklin was becoming more and more anxious about his future. He decided to buy for Temple the substantial farm which William still owned in New Jersey. Unlike the property of other loyalists, it had never been confiscated, almost certainly because it belonged to Benjamin Franklin's son.

Franklin drove the hardest possible bargain. Although he was later to note that land values had tripled in Philadelphia since 1776, he forced William to sell the farm for 227 pounds, 11.5 shillings less than he had paid for it in the 1760s. Nor was this the worst blow. Franklin presented William with a bill for 1500 pounds—the money he had advanced to him during his governorship years. He knew that William, with his claims before the Parliamentary commission still unsettled (it took another year for him to get the bad news), could not possibly pay in cash. Bitterly, William later remarked that he had reason "to believe that had I not taken an active part on the side of government, the debt would never have been demanded by my father." [193] So William was forced to deed over to Temple all the lands he owned in New York State, acquired when he was helping to launch the ill-fated Grand Ohio Company. Thus, on the sourest possible note, Franklin wiped out William's last connection with America.

On the twenty-seventh of July, Franklin entertained the Shipleys and a few other English friends in the cabin of the ship. It was a merry party, which lasted until four A.M. Franklin went to bed, and when he awoke in the morning, the guests had gone and the ship was already under sail. England had vanished beyond the eastern horizon. The ending of his long struggle with the Old World was as offhand and casual as its beginning. Always, and wherever possible, Franklin loved to reduce large ideas and great movements to personal terms.

To his old friend David Hartley, who had not been able to come to Southampton, he wrote a farewell letter which beautifully summed up this approach. "I cannot quit the coasts of Europe without taking leave of my ever dear friend Mr. Hartley. We were long fellow labourers in the best of all works, the work of peace. I leave you still in the field, but having finished my day's work, *I am going home to go to bed!* Wish me a good night's rest, as I do you a pleasant evening. Adieu!" [194]

Book Seven

A Rising
AND A
Setting Sun

I

On the trip home, Franklin wrote his long delayed report on his study of the Gulf Stream. Now that the information would be valuable only to peaceful merchantmen, and not to British men-of-war, he told how ships could shorten their passage from America to England by as much as two weeks by using the three-mile-an-hour current of this great ten-mile-wide ocean river. Similarly, by avoiding it on the passage from Europe to America, they could save as much as sixty to seventy miles a day. Franklin recommended equipping ships with thermometers in order to enable captains to quickly identify the whereabouts of the Stream. He also noted other characteristics—"the Gulf weed with which it is interspersed . . . and that it does not sparkle in the night." [1] Modern scientists have not forgotten Franklin's discovery. The special submarine which began exploring the Gulf Stream from top to bottom in 1969 is named the *Benjamin Franklin*.

But on the six-week voyage Franklin did no work on the project that all his friends had urged on him—his autobiography. One of his Philadelphian Quaker friends, Abel James, had rescued the original manuscript, which he had left with Joseph Galloway in his trunk full of personal papers. Galloway's house had been plundered, ironically, by British soldiers during the fighting around Philadelphia and most of the papers had been lost. James's rescue of the *Autobiography* seemed almost miraculous, and when it appeared on Franklin's desk in Passy, with an urgent plea from his old friend to complete it, Franklin had been inspired to write a small section, largely concerned with his attempt to achieve moral perfection. But aboard ship, he made no effort to carry the narrative forward. Some think that he felt that he could not undertake the more complex story of his political career in Philadelphia and England, without his papers. There may have been another reason for his delay. He could not decide what kind of autobiography he should write. If the attacks of his enemies had made his reputation as odious among his fellow Americans as some people said, it would have to be an apologia. During his period of indecision, when he debated with his French friends whether or not to go home, this rumored unpopularity was one of the arguments they had used against the idea—that a return would only expose him to the irritation of petty envy and malice, which, at a distance of 3000 miles, he could afford to ignore. He had admitted to Madame Helvetius that he was not sure whether he would be happy in America. In his angry letter to John Jay he had remarked that after fifty years in the public service, he had only one ambition, that of carrying a good reputation to the grave with him. Now he was going home, to find out how that reputation stood among his countrymen.

On September 13, 1785, Franklin awoke to find the Cape May lighthouse in full view. Soon they were in Delaware Bay, with "water smooth, air cool, day fair and fine." [2] They worked their way up the Delaware for the rest of the day, anchoring off Red Bank, near sunset. In the morning a light breeze carried them above Gloucester Point, and there in full view was, as Franklin called it in his diary, "dear Philadelphia." The health officer arrived to clear them through quarantine, and soon after him came Richard Bache, with a boat for the whole Franklin party. Another ship had outrun Franklin's vessel with the news that he was on his way, and all of Philadelphia was ready for him. As they landed at the Market Street wharf, an enormous crowd of people lined the streets, roaring a joyous welcome for the only man who equalled George Washington in the hearts of his countrymen. Tears ran down Temple Franklin's cheeks and the young man "was not the only one thus moved." The huge crowd watched with delight while Franklin's daughter Sally embraced him at his street door. No one could possibly have wished for a more triumphant homecoming, and the patriarch closed his travel diary with a moving "God be praised and thanked for all His mercies." [3]

I I

He had come home, he had vowed to his friends in Europe, to spend his few remaining days in leisure, to work on his autobiography, to amuse himself with scientific investigations. But within twenty-four hours, he found that there was no hope of his escaping from politics. Pennsylvania was torn by factions fighting for control of the state, and they all rushed to enlist Franklin. He was wary at first. "My principal merit, if I may claim any, in publick affairs," he told them, "is that of having been always ready and willing to receive and follow good advice." Espousing once more his favorite role, that of the peacemaker, Franklin accepted the nomination to the Supreme Executive Council of Pennsylvania from each of the three factions contending for control. Within a month of his arrival from Europe, he was elected to the Council and promptly chosen Council president. The Assembly then elected him president of the state—the office which corresponds to some extent with the present-day governorship.

Franklin pretended, with some friends, to rebel against this return to public service. He complained that his fellow citizens had "eaten my flesh, and seem resolved now to pick my bones." But he was obviously proud of the honor, which reassured him once and for all that his reputation had survived the attacks of the Lees, the Izards, and the Adamses. He made a point of telling his politically minded European friends that he had been "plac'd at the head of my country by its unanimous voice." [4]

Another reason why he accepted the burden was to refute the rumors that were rampant throughout Europe about the imminent collapse of the United States. The British were telling everyone that the leaders of the Revolution were being repudiated by the people, and intimated that anarchy was only a step away. Franklin knew that the sight of him at the head of the state of Pennsylvania would do much to demolish these lies. He added some facts of his own in letters to friends such as David Hartley. "Your newspapers are filled with accounts of distresses and miseries that these states are plunged into since their separation from Britain. You may believe me when I tell you, that there is no truth in those accounts. I find all property and lands and houses augmented vastly in value; that of houses in towns at least fourfold. The crops have been plentiful, and yet the produce sells high, to the great profit of the farmer. . . . Working people have plenty of employ, and high pay for their labour." [5]

This may have been true in Pennsylvania, but in some other states there was serious unrest. An ex-Revolutionary officer named Daniel Shays led an uprising of farmers in western Massachusetts that for a few weeks threatened to grow into a full-scale revolution. Relations between the states had deteriorated alarmingly, too. There was a tendency to ignore Congress almost completely and pursue independent economic and political paths. It became more and more obvious to Franklin and all thinking men that the Articles of Confederation were almost as bad as no federal government at all. Disgustedly Franklin told one American friend that Congress had not been able to assemble delegates from more than seven or eight states during the whole winter. To Edward Bancroft, Franklin admitted, "We discover, indeed, some errors in our general and particular constitution; which is no wonder they should have, the time in which they were formed being considered. But these we shall mend." [6] A few months later he was writing to his successor in France, Thomas Jefferson, "Our federal constitution is generally thought defective, and a convention, first proposed by Virginia, and since recommended by Congress, is to assemble here next month, to revise it and propose amendments. The delegates generally appointed, as far as I have heard of them, are men of character for prudence and ability, so that I hope good from their meeting." [7]

To those he trusted, Franklin did not hesitate to admit the crucial nature of the Constitutional Convention which met in Philadelphia in May of 1787. "Indeed if it does not do good, it must do harm," he told Jefferson, "as it will show that we have not wisdom enough among us to govern ourselves; and will strengthen the opinion of some political writers, that popular governments cannot long support themselves." Franklin himself rallied all his strength in a last expression of commitment to the cause for which he had already sacrificed so much. At the age of eighty-two, for four consecutive months he trudged almost daily from his house to the Pennsylvania State House, and spent hours wrangling and debating over how to reconcile poor states and rich states, large states and small states, slave states and free states, and the hundred and one other questions confronted by the men who made the Constitution.

From the first day, Franklin personified the spirit of compromise that was essential, if the convention was to succeed. Only he could have challenged George Washington for the chairmanship of the conclave. Franklin deliberately stepped aside and, on the opening day, was prepared to personally nominate Washington for the job. Unfortunately, he was ill and could not attend, but another member of the Pennsylvania delegation nominated Washington, thus making it clear that Franklin was not in competition.

The wrangling between the small states and large states soon grew so intense that it looked as if the convention might break up. Franklin rose and reminded the assembled politicians that in this same room, when the Continental Congress met, prayers were offered daily—prayers that were "graciously answered." He urged the revival of the practice, now. The motion did not carry, largely because men like Alexander Hamilton feared that it would be taken by the public as a sign of "embarrassments and dissensions within the Convention," which indeed it was. But the suggestion did inject a note of profound faith into the bellicose wrangling and enabled Franklin to warn the delegates that if they allowed themselves to be "divided by our little partial local interests," they would become "a reproach and a bye-word down to future ages." [8]

How to reconcile the interests of the large states and the small states was the rock on which the Articles of Confederation had foundered, and if Franklin's resolution did nothing else, it reminded the delegates that the time had come to act as statesmen, rather than partisan horse traders. Unable to solve the problem in the committee of the whole, Congress elected a "Grand Committee," consisting of one delegate from each state, to ponder the dilemma. Franklin had already urged that "both sides must part with some of their demands" and now he made a motion in this Grand Committee, recommending that one house in Congress have equal representation, and the second house be represented in proportion to population. The second house would have control of passing all money bills, so that each state would pay in proportion to its power, the sine qua non which Franklin had urged again and again in the Continental Congress. The two-house arrangement was not original with Franklin. Several delegates from Connecticut had suggested it, and his old foe, John Dickinson, representing Delaware, had supported it in earlier debates. But no one had the weight to persuade the large-state delegates, except Franklin, who was one of them. The crucial importance of Franklin's influence was evident in the squeaky margin of victory by which the foundation stone of American federalism won approval—5 to 4, with one state (Massachusetts) divided.

This was the turning point in the Federal Convention. Once the small states felt their interests were protected, they swiftly became moderate nationalists, and the Convention moved ahead with a minimum of acrimony.

One of Franklin's finer but lesser known moments at the Convention occurred during the debate over whether the Constitution should set property-owning qualifications for service in the new government. This was strenuously endorsed by many of the southern nabobs. Among the most outspoken was Charles Pinckney of South Carolina, who was inordinately proud not only of his wealth, but of his youth, and even lied about his age, pretending to be twenty-four so that he could pose as the youngest man in Congress. Pinckney declared that no one should be elected President who was not worth at least 100,000 dollars and judges and legislators should possess half of that sum. Franklin calmly rose to express his dislike "of everything that tended to debase the spirit of the common people." Pinckney's motion was voted down in a negative roar, so ferocious that Chairman Washington did not even bother to poll the states.[9]

Throughout the Convention, Franklin consistently fought measures that tended to limit freedom and implant a spirit of distrust between different groups of Americans. He opposed the suggestion that immigrants be barred from holding public office for fourteen years. Franklin suggested four. He was even more opposed to the idea of limiting the right to vote to "freeholders"—men who owned property. He heartily approved an amendment which specified that conviction for treason required the testimony of two witnesses "to the same overt act." He also earnestly defended the clause which gave Congress the power to impeach the President. Again, his stand was part of his intense desire to see Americans use the freedom that they had achieved with responsibility and discretion. He pointed out that in the past, when the "chief magistrate rendered himself obnoxious," the people had no recourse but "assassination, in which he was not only deprived of his life but of the opportunity of vindicating his character." He used a similar reason in calling for two witnesses in treason trials. "Prosecutions for treason were generally virulent and perjury too easily made use of against innocence." Elsewhere, the delegates largely ignored Franklin's opinions on specific points. He favored a one-house legislature and a Presidency limited to a single seven-year term without the right of re-election. He thought that the Chief of State should be supplemented by a council, who would serve as a check on a bad President and be a source of support for a good one. These ideas were either voted down or discarded in the days of hectic debate and discussion.

As the Convention neared a close, it became apparent to most of the delegates that the real danger now lay in the possibility that the Constitution would be repudiated by the states. So many of the compromises had passed by thin majorities, and many of the advocates on both sides of the numerous arguments were still disgruntled and unreconciled. A formula was needed, to create at least a façade of unanimity. George Washington, as the presiding officer, could hardly make the plea without implying that he had a low opinion of the final document. So inevitably the leaders of the Convention turned to Franklin.

On September 17, 1787, the delegates assembled for the last time, and the secretary of the Convention, William Jackson, read the final version of the Constitution which they were now called upon to sign. Then Franklin rose with a speech in his hand. Because his bladder stone made it difficult for him to stand without pain, he simply asked for permission to speak and then handed the paper to James Wilson of Pennsylvania to read. Wilson, who had been among the most intransigent large-staters, was a shrewd choice as a mouthpiece. But the words he read were the important thing.

Mr. President:

I confess, that I do not entirely approve of this Constitution at present; but, sir, I am not sure I shall never approve it; for, having lived long, I have experienced many instances of being oblig'd, by better information or fuller consideration, to change my opinions even on important subjects, which I once thought right, but found to be otherwise. . . . Thus I consent, sir, to this Constitution because I expect no better, and because I am not sure that it is not the best. The opinions I have had of its errors I sacrifice to the public good. I have never whispered a syllable of them abroad. Within these walls they were born, and here they shall die. If every one of us, in returning to our constituents, were to report the objections he has had to it, and endeavour to gain partisans in support of them, we might prevent its being generally received, and thereby lose all the salutary effects and great advantages resulting naturally in our favour among foreign nations, as well as among ourselves, from our real or apparent unanimity. Much of the strength and efficiency of any government, in procuring and securing happiness to the people, depends on opinion, *on a general opinion of the goodness of that government, as well as of the wis-*

*dom and integrity of its governors. I hope, therefore, for our own
sakes, as a part of the people, and for the sake of our posterity,
that we shall act heartily and unanimously in recommending this
Constitution, wherever our influence may extend, and turn our
future thoughts and endeavours to the means of having it well
administered.*

*On the whole, sir, I cannot help expressing a wish, that every
member of the Convention who may still have objections to it,
would with me on this occasion doubt a little of his own infallibility, and to make manifest our unanimity, put his name to this
instrument.*[10]

Franklin then made a motion, which had been suggested to him by
Gouverneur Morris, of New York, that all the delegates should sign
as witnesses to "the unanimous consent of the *states*." After some last
minute wrangling from dissidents, the motion carried 10 to 0, and the
illusion of unanimity was achieved.

One by one, the delegates walked to the president's table to sign
the historic document. Franklin, watching them, turned to those who
were sitting near him, and pointed to the president's chair where a sun
happened to be painted. "I have," he said, "often and often in the
course of this session . . . looked at that . . . without being able
to tell whether it was rising or setting: but now at length I have the
happiness to know that it is a rising and not a setting sun." [11]

I I I

Franklin now threw all his influence into the fight for the Constitution's
ratification. His closing speech, by the tacit consent of the other delegates, was widely reprinted, violating the strict secrecy rule of the Convention. In Pennsylvania, Franklin lent his unique prestige by appearing in person before the General Assembly to present a copy of the
Constitution to that body, calling upon them to take the necessary steps

to ratify it as soon as possible. Washington's support of the Constitution was a crucial influence in persuading many reluctant states,
especially his own Virginia, to ratify it. Not so many historians have
recalled that his name was regularly linked with Franklin's in newspaper arguments in its behalf.

Nine months after the Convention ended, Franklin was able to tell
one of his French friends proudly: "Eight states have now agreed to
the proposed new Constitution, . . . one more agreeing, it will be carried into execution." But he would not be "taking a share in the management of it." His "age and infirmities render him as unfit for the
business, as the business would be for him. . . . General Washington
is the man that all eyes are fixed on for President, and what little influence I might have, is devoted to him." [12]

Franklin continued to watch with fascination while the first national
elections were held. In this same period he accepted a third term as
president of Pennsylvania. He admitted to Jane Mecom that he should
have turned the job down. Humorously, he noted that his old friend
Dr. Cooper, when Franklin complained that the electorate was resolved to pick his bones, replied that he approved their taste because,
"the nearer the bone, the sweeter the meat." To someone he trusted
so intimately as Jane, Franklin could not resist admitting the pride he
felt in this third election. "It is no small pleasure to me, and I suppose
it will give my sister pleasure, that after such a long trial of me, I
should be elected a third time by my fellow citizens, without a dissenting vote but my own, to fill the most honourable post in their
power to bestow. This universal and unbounded confidence of a whole
people flatters my vanity much more than a peerage could do." [13]

But Franklin was able to give little time to the job. His health deteriorated rapidly after the last great effort of the Constitutional Convention. The bladder stone gave him more and more pain, and he was
forced to take opium, which made it difficult for him to concentrate
on reading or writing. He managed to finish a few more pages of the
autobiography, but he stopped at his arrival in England in 1757, when
his really significant public career began. He bore his bouts of pain with
amazing fortitude, even preferring it to the opium because he wanted to
keep his mind clear.

As France began to move toward its revolution, he followed the
ominous signs of trouble to come there with growing concern. But he

was largely worried about the fate of personal friends, such as the Duke de la Rochefoucauld, who would die at the hands of the mob, and others, such as Abbé Morellet, who would be driven into exile in the years to come. It was the steady progress of the American government that absorbed Franklin's mind and heart.

In his last letter to George Washington, Franklin unmistakably revealed the source of his will to live. He congratulated the first President "on the growing strength of our new government under your administration." Then he added, "For my own personal ease, I should have died two years ago; but tho these years have been spent in excruciating pain, I am pleased that I have lived them, since they have brought me to see our present situation. I am now finishing my 84th, and probably with it my career in this life; but in whatever state of existence I am plac'd hereafter, if I retain any memory of what has pass'd here, I shall with it retain the esteem, respect and affection with which I have long been, my dear friend, yours most sincerely." [14]

Washington's reply was perhaps the finest tribute ever paid to Franklin—and incidentally refutes the notion that the father of his country was an emotionless statue.

> *Would to God, my dear sir, that I could congratulate you upon the removal of that excruciating pain, under which you labor, and that your existence might close with as much ease to yourself, as its continuance has been beneficial to our country and useful to mankind; or, if the united wishes of a free people, joined with the earnest prayers of every friend to science and humanity, could relieve the body from pains or infirmities, that you could claim an exemption on this score. But this cannot be, and you have within yourself the only resource to which we can confidently apply for relief,* a philosophic mind.
>
> *If to be venerated for benevolence, if to be admired for talents, if to be esteemed for patriotism, if to be beloved for philanthropy, can gratify the human mind, you must have the pleasing consolation to know, that you have not lived in vain. And I flatter myself that it will not be ranked among the least grateful occurrences of your life to be assured that, so long as I retain my memory, you will be thought of with respect, veneration and affection by your sincere friend,*
>
> *George Washington* [15]

I V

At home, Franklin was surrounded by a warm and loving circle. Sarah Bache and her seven children lived in the same house with him. Widowed Polly Stevenson Hewson took his advice and came to America with her three children, to be near the man who was her spiritual and intellectual father. She visited him constantly, read to him and nursed him with tireless affection. Only Temple Franklin worried his grandfather. He was utterly bored with a farmer's life and neglected his 500 New Jersey acres to spend most of his time in Philadelphia. Franklin made one last try to obtain some favor for him from the new Congress, through his old friend Charles Carroll, now Senator from Maryland, but it came to nothing. Embittered by this rejection, in 1791 Temple was to fulfill Franklin's forebodings by contemptuously abandoning America and going to live with his father in England. William had by this time remarried. His wife was Mary D'Evelin, the daughter of a well-to-do Irish family. Her sister, Ellen, lived with them in London, and Temple, although he violently resisted the idea of marriage, had apparently no compunctions about making her his mistress. A daughter, Ellen Franklin, was baptized in St. James Church, London, on May 16, 1798. After a violent quarrel with his father, Temple abandoned both mother and child and departed for France, where he lived the life of a dilettante with an English mistress, Hannah Collier. William raised Ellen as his own daughter, and she lived with him until his death in 1813. Hannah finally browbeat Temple into marrying her in the Paris house of the British ambassador, in 1823.[16] He died a few months later, childless, extinguishing forever Franklin's hope of founding a family line. Temple also failed Franklin in a more direct and disastrous way. Instead of publishing a thorough and complete edition of his papers, which would have replaced the autobiography Franklin never wrote, and enabled nineteenth-century historians to better appraise Franklin's role in the founding of the nation, it took Temple twenty years to get around to throwing together a very inadequate slapdash edition, which did Frank-

489

lin's reputation more harm than good. Most of the precious documents Temple carelessly abandoned.

Franklin himself, in making his will, could not stifle one more expression of the pain William had caused him. He left to "my son William Franklin, late governor of the Jerseys, all the lands I hold or have a right to in the province of Nova Scotia"—a claim which was vague at best. Franklin also gave him "all my books and papers which he has in his possession, and all debts standing against him on my account books"—an item which he had already settled with William in their meeting in Southampton. Then came the last exhalation of bitterness. "The part he acted against me in the late war, which is of public notoriety, will account for my leaving him no more of an estate [than] he endeavoured to deprive me of." [17]

To others, who had given him love and received it in abundance from him, he began writing gentle farewells. To Catherine Ray Greene in Rhode Island, he said, "Among the felicities of my life I reckon your friendship." [18] To fellow peacemaker David Hartley, he wrote one of his noblest sentiments. "God grant that not only the love of liberty, but a thorough knowledge of the rights of man, may pervade all the nations of the earth, so that a philosopher may set his foot anywhere on its surface and say: This is my country." [19]

For Madame Helvetius, who had aroused such deep feelings in him, he transported himself back in time for one last visit to sunny Auteuil. "I cannot let this chance go by, my dear friend, without telling you that I love you always, and that I am feeling well. I think endlessly of the pleasures I enjoyed in the sweet society of Auteuil. And often, in my dreams, I dine with you, I sit beside you, on one of your thousand sofas, or I walk with you in your beautiful garden." By now, Madame Helvetius spoke of her love for him with the same frankness he used with her. ". . . I am getting old, my dear, but I don't mind it, I am coming closer to you, we will meet again all the sooner." [20]

Finally, there was time for one last cause. Franklin accepted the presidency of "the Pennsylvania Society for Promoting the Abolition of Slavery, and the Relief of Free Negroes Unlawfully Held in Bondage." The Society presented a memorial to the first Congress, urging an immediate repudiation of slavery. James Jackson of Georgia led an attack on the proposal, presenting arguments that would eventually grow grossly familiar—that slavery was sanctioned by the Bible, and the Negroes were better off and happier as slaves. This inspired Franklin to play one last hoax with his facile pen. He sent to the *Federal Gazette* an essay which he said was an authentic statement by one Sidi Mehemet Ibrahim, a leading member of the Algerian government a hundred years ago. It was Sidi's reply to a sect called the Erika, or purists, who urged on the Algerians the need to abolish piracy and their nasty habit of enslaving white Christians.

With logic that marvelously paralleled Jackson's speech in Congress, Sidi argued that the Algerians could not afford to free their white slaves to gratify a whimsical sect. He pointed out that Christians were far better off as slaves. They lived lives of perfect safety, they were well-fed, lodged, and clothed. "They are not liable to be impressed for soldiers, and forced to cut one another's Christian throats, as in the wars of their own countries." He quoted the Koran to prove that slavery had the blessing of Allah and convinced the government of Algiers that "the doctrine, that plundering and enslaving the Christians is unjust, is at best problematical; but that it is the interest of this state to continue the practice, is clear." [21]

Numerous Philadelphians were so thoroughly hoaxed that they ransacked the bookstores and libraries of the city, searching for the volume Franklin had cited as his source, "Martin's Account of His Counselship, Anno 1687."

About the same time, Ezra Stiles, one of Franklin's old New England friends, now president of Yale, wrote to him asking him confidentially about his religious beliefs. After making Stiles promise to keep absolute silence, Franklin told him that he still could not subscribe to the teaching of any current sect. But he believed "in one God, the creator of the universe. That He governs it by His providence. That He ought to be worshiped. That the most acceptable service we render to Him is doing good to His other children. That the soul of man is immortal, and will be treated with justice in another life respecting its conduct in this. These I take to be the fundamental points in all sound religion, and I regard them as you do in whatever sect I meet with them." [22]

Early in April, 1790, Franklin complained of a pain in his chest. He became feverish, and it was soon evident that he was suffering an attack of pleurisy. After almost ten days of agonizing pain, he seemed, momentarily, to recover. His cough vanished, and he even arose from his bed. But it was to let his daughter Sally make the bed so that he might "die in a decent manner." When Sally said that she was praying that he would get well and live many more years, Franklin quietly replied: "I hope not." A few hours later, an abscess in his lungs burst, and it became more and more difficult for him to breathe. At 11 P.M. on April 17, 1790, he passed quietly into history.

His sorrowing family stood at his bedside, dutiful daughter Sally and stolid, dependable Richard Bache; grandson Benjamin Franklin Bache, already on his way to becoming a brilliant newspaper editor; and William Temple Franklin. That last face, not unhandsome, but somehow diminished, could only remind the dying man of another dearer face, lost through words spoken and unspoken, through emotions that have tormented fathers and sons since history began; ultimately lost here by a son's inability to grasp the deep and daring dimensions of a new ingredient in the ancient instinctive quarrel—American freedom.

Father and son, the two Franklins had dared the lightning together and won. But American freedom, with its inevitable turmoil and upheaval, had been a more formidable force. Perhaps the best evidence of the value Franklin placed on this freedom was the personal price he paid for it. In those last sinking hours, we can be sure that his regrets were balanced by the knowledge that a whole people had become his spiritual heirs, committed to this questing experimental freedom as the central value of their nationhood. Today's Americans, struggling to cope with this still vital, often unruly heritage in a threatening world, may find some answers in the mature Franklin's life, with its unique blend of faith and realism, laughter and courage. It is for us to reclaim this Franklin and bring him into the mainstream of American life and thought.

NOTES

The author would like to thank the following collectors of Benjamin Franklin papers for permission to cite from letters and other documents they have contributed to the Yale University edition of *The Papers of Benjamin Franklin,* edited by Leonard W. Labaree, Whitfield J. Bell, Jr., *et al* (in many cases he would also like to acknowledge their assistance in directing him to and for providing him with photocopies and Xeroxes of documents from their collections, covering the years beyond those reached by the fourteen volumes of the Papers published thus far): The American Philosophical Society; The Library of Congress; Mason-Franklin Collection, Yale University Library; Manuscript Collection, the New York Public Library, Astor, Lenox and Tilden Foundations; Henry E. Huntington Library and Art Gallery; William L. Clements Library, University of Michigan; The Historical Society of Pennsylvania; Massachusetts Historical Society; New York Historical Society; Cornell University Library; André de Coppet Collection of American Historical Manuscripts in the Princeton University Library; Pierpont Morgan Library; The American Academy of Arts and Sciences; The British Museum; the Public Record Office, London; The John F. Rylands Library, Manchester, England.

The author would also like to thank Janet M. Dick-Cynungham and Mrs. Arthur Loeb for permission to quote from Franklin letters in their possession.

BOOK ONE

1. *Benjamin Franklin's Experiments: A New Edition of Franklin's Experiments and Observation on Electricity,* ed. I. Bernard Cohen (Cambridge, Mass., 1941), *passim.* A recent and remarkable tribute to Franklin is in *Peter Kapitsa on Life and Science* (New York, 1968), a collection of nontechnical speeches and writings by the great Russian nuclear physicist: "Franklin was the first man to understand correctly the essence of electrical phenomena . . ." Kapitsa compares Franklin's breakthrough to the discovery of radioactivity in 1896.

2. *The Papers of Benjamin Franklin* (hereafter referred to as *PBF*), ed. Leonard W. Labaree *et al* (New Haven, 1959–), IV (1961), pp. 366–367.

3. *PBF,* IV, p. 369.

4. Introduction to *The Autobiography of Benjamin Franklin,* ed. Leonard W. Labaree *et al* (New Haven, 1964), pp. 7, 13–15.

5. William Carlos Williams, *In the American Grain* (New York, 1925), pp. 144–157; John P. Sisk, "Making It in America," *Atlantic Monthly,* CCXXIV (December, 1969), p. 63. Williams' attack is almost unbelievably wrongheaded and uninformed about the real Franklin.

6. *PBF,* V (1962), pp. 155n, 219–221.

7. *PBF,* IV, pp. 408–409.

8. *Ibid.,* pp. 466–467.

9. *The Writings of Benjamin Franklin,* ed. Albert Henry Smyth (New York, 1905–1907), V, p. 421.

10. *PBF,* IV, pp. 82–83.

11. *PBF,* II (1960), pp. 128–129.

12. *PBF,* I (1959), pp. 234–235.

13. *Ibid.,* p. 184.

14. *Ibid.,* p. 372.

15. *Ibid.,* pp. 249–250.

16. *Ibid.,* pp. 288, 311.

17. *PBF,* II, pp. 226–227.

18. *Ibid.,* p. 3.

19. *PBF,* I, pp. 255–258.

20. *Autobiography,* p. 143.

21. Smyth, IX, pp. 190, 208–210.

22. "Notes," *Pennsylvania Magazine of History and Biography,* XLVIII, No. 192 (October, 1924), p. 383.

23. *Autobiography,* pp. 155–156.

24. *Franklin's Wit and Folly: The Bagatelles,* ed. Richard E. Amacher (New Brunswick, N.J., 1943), pp. 44–47.

25. Alfred Owen Aldridge, *Benjamin Franklin and His French Contemporaries* (New York, 1957), p. 200.

26. *PBF,* IV, p. 68; III, p. 383.

27. *PBF,* VI (1963), p. 217.

28. "Extracts from the Diary of Daniel Fisher, 1755," *Pennsylvania Magazine of History and Biography,* XVII (1893), p. 276.

29. *PBF,* II, pp. 353–354.

30. William H. Mariboe, "The Life of William Franklin, 1730(1)–1813." Unpublished doctoral dissertation, University of Pennsylvania, 1962, pp. 44–45.

31. *Autobiography,* pp. 186–187.

32. *Ibid.,* pp. 171–172.

33. *PBF,* VI, p. 86.

34. Aldridge, *op. cit.*, p. 198.
35. *PBF*, IV, p. 195.
36. *Ibid.*, p. 74.
37. *Autobiography*, pp. 83–87, 121–122.
38. *PBF*, IV, pp. 227–234.
39. *PBF*, V, pp. 273–275.
40. *Ibid.*, p. 337.
41. *Ibid.*, pp. 357–360.
42. *Ibid.*, p. 490.
43. *Ibid.*, p. 454.
44. *Autobiography*, p. 212.
45. *PBF*, V, p. 438.
46. *Ibid.*, pp. 443–447.
47. *Ibid.*, pp. 449–450.
48. *Ibid.*, p. 473.
49. *Ibid.*, p. 503.
50. *PBF*, VI, p. 183.
51. *Ibid.*, p. 225.
52. *Ibid.*, p. 494.
53. *Ibid.*, p. 183.
54. *PBF*, V, p. 454.
55. *Autobiography*, p. 217.
56. *PBF*, VI, pp. 19–22.
57. *Ibid.*, p. 22n.
58. *Autobiography*, p. 224.
59. *Ibid.*, p. 228.
60. *Ibid.*, p. 229.
61. *PBF*, VI, p. 305.
62. *Ibid.*, p. 365.
63. *Autobiography*, p. 232.
64. J. Bennett Nolan, *General Benjamin Franklin: The Military Career of a Philosopher* (Philadelphia, 1956), pp. 34–35. Also: *PBF*, VI, pp. 313–314.
65. *PBF*, VI, p. 354.
66. *Ibid.*, p. 381.
67. *Autobiography*, p. 235.
68. *PBF*, VI, pp. 364–365, 379.
69. *Autobiography*, pp. 234–235.
70. Nolan, pp. 82–85.
71. *Ibid.*, pp. 91–93.
72. *PBF*, VII, p. 14.
73. *Autobiography*, pp. 177–178.
74. *PBF*, VI, pp. 382–383.
75. *Ibid.*, pp. 468–469.
76. *Autobiography*, pp. 246–247.

77. *PBF*, VII, pp. 107, 110.
78. Mariboe, pp. 67–69.
79. *PBF*, VII, p. 76.

BOOK TWO

1. *Dictionary of National Biography*, ed. Sir Leslie Stephen and Sir Sidney Lee (London, 1937–1938), XX, p. 553.
2. J. T. and H. M. Temple, *The Temple Memoirs* (London, 1925).
3. *PBF*, VII, pp. 340–350.
4. *Autobiography*, pp. 258–259.
5. *PBF*, VII, p. 243.
6. *Ibid.*, pp. 243–244.
7. *Ibid.*, p. 245.
8. *Ibid.*, pp. 115–116.
9. *Ibid.*, p. 246.
10. *Ibid.*, p. 247n.
11. *Dictionary of American Biography*, ed. Dumas Malone (New York, 1935), XV, p. 331. Ralph might well be called America's first professional writer.
12. Paul Leicester Ford, *The Many-Sided Franklin* (New York, 1899), p. 215.
13. *Autobiography*, pp. 261–262.
14. Mariboe, p. 90, cites William Franklin Papers, mss, Gratz Collection, Historical Society of Pennsylvania.
15. This scene is based on a letter which Franklin wrote to Isaac Norris, Jan. 14, 1758. *PBF*, VII, pp. 360–362.
16. *PBF*, VII, pp. 295–297.
17. *Ibid.*, pp. 380–381.
18. *Letters and Papers of Benjamin Franklin and Richard Jackson, 1752–1785*, ed. Carl Van Doren (Philadelphia, Pa., 1947), p. 8.
19. *PBF*, VIII, p. 402.
20. *Ibid.*, p. 134.
21. *Ibid.*, p. 121.
22. *Ibid.*, pp. 136–138; *Autobiography*, p. 47.
23. *Ibid.*, p. 144.
24. *Ibid.*, p. 153.
25. *Ibid.*, p. 121.
26. *PBF*, IX, pp. 259–260.
27. J. Bennett Nolan, *Benjamin Franklin in Scotland and Ireland: 1759 and 1771* (Philadelphia, 1956), pp. 78–79.
28. *PBF*, VI, pp. 114–124.
29. *PBF*, IX, p. 9.
30. *PBF*, VII, pp. 19, 111–112.
31. Penn Papers, Historical Society of Pennsylvania, quoted in *PBF*, IX, p. 200.

32. *PBF*, VIII, p. 299.
33. *Ibid.*, p. 313.
34. *Ibid.*, pp. 340–356.
35. Walpole's letters, ed. John Wright (London, 1840), p. 7.
36. *PBF*, IX, pp. 59–100.
37. *Ibid.*, pp. 342–347.
38. *PBF*, VIII, p. 132.
39. *PBF*, X (1966), p. 234.
40. *PBF*, IX, pp. 188–192.
41. *Autobiography*, pp. 265–266.
42. Mariboe has a good analysis of the political wheeling and dealing to win William's appointment. Interesting sidelights are also in *PBF*, X, p. 147. At first William tried for the job of Deputy Secretary of South Carolina.
43. *PBF*, X, p. 142.
44. *Ibid.*, p. 133.
45. *Ibid.*, p. 140.
46. *Ibid.*, pp. 141–142.
47. *Ibid.*, p. 149.
48. *Ibid.*, p. 143.
49. *Ibid.*, pp. 161–162.

BOOK THREE

1. William A. Whitehead, *Contributions to the Early History of Perth Amboy and Adjoining Country* (New York, 1856), p. 282.
2. William Alexander Duer, *The Life of William Alexander, Earl of Stirling* (New York, 1847), p. 68.
3. Duer, p. 70.
4. *PBF*, X, p. 147n.
5. *Ibid.*, pp. 169, 232.
6. *New Jersey Archives*, First Series (Newark, N.J., 1885), IX, pp. 368–370.
7. *N.J. Archives*, First Series (Paterson, N.J., 1902), XXIV, pp. 144, 146–154.
8. *PBF*, X, p. 294.
9. *Ibid.*, p. 268.
10. *Ibid.*, p. 302.
11. *Ibid.*, pp. 330–331.
12. *Ibid.*, pp. 406–407.
13. *Ibid.*, p. 291.
14. *PBF*, XI, pp. 22–26, 47–52.
15. *Ibid.*, pp. 42–69.
16. *Ibid.*, p. 77.
17. *Ibid.*, pp. 103–104.
18. *Ibid.*, p. 107.

19. *Ibid.*, pp. 111–122.

20. *Ibid.*, pp. 121–122.

21. *Ibid.*, pp. 104–105.

22. *Ibid.*, p. 132.

23. *Ibid.*, p. 173n.

24. *Ibid.*, p. 171.

25. *Ibid.*, p. 298n.

26. *Ibid.*, pp. 298–299.

27. *Ibid.*, p. 354.

28. *Ibid.*, pp. 380–384.

29. William B. Reed, *Life and Correspondence of Joseph Reed* (Philadelphia, 1847), I, pp. 36–37, quoted in *PBF,* XI, p. 391.

30. *The Works of Benjamin Franklin,* ed. Jared Sparks, rev. ed. (Philadelphia, 1840), VII, p. 268n.

31. *PBF,* XI, pp. 429–441.

32. *Ibid.*, pp. 447–448.

33. *Ibid.*, pp. 449–450.

BOOK FOUR

1. *PBF,* XI, p. 517.

2. *Ibid.*, pp. 521, 534.

3. The preceding is condensed from the latest and most authoritative treatment of the Stamp Act, *The Stamp Act Crisis: Prologue to Revolution,* by Edmund S. and Helen M. Morgan, rev. ed. (New York, 1962). Equally valuable is the companion volume assembled by E. S. Morgan, *Prologue to Revolution: Sources and Documents on the Stamp Act Crisis, 1764–1766* (Chapel Hill, N.C., 1959).

4. This dialogue is based upon the letter which Ingersoll wrote to Whately, July 6, 1764. Morgan, *Stamp Act Crisis,* pp. 86–87.

5. The preceding scene is based upon a letter describing it, written by Jared Ingersoll to the Governor of Connecticut, February 11, 1765. Morgan, *Prologue to Revolution,* pp. 31–34.

6. Morgan, *Prologue,* p. 32.

7. *Ibid.*, p. 35.

8. *PBF,* XII (1968), pp. 67–68.

9. *Ibid.*, p. 68.

10. *Ibid.*, p. 145.

11. *Ibid.*, p. 234.

12. *Ibid.*, p. 264.

13. *Ibid.*, p. 235.

14. J. Steven Watson, *The Reign of George III* (Oxford, 1960), pp. 109–111.

15. *PBF,* XII, p. 234.

16. *Ibid.*, pp. 258–259.

17. *Ibid.*, pp. 217–218.

18. *Ibid.*, p. 266.

19. *Ibid.*, pp. 260–262.

20. *Ibid.*, pp. 270–271.

21. *Benjamin Franklin's Letters to the Press, 1758–1775,* collected and ed. Verner W. Crane (Chapel Hill, N.C., 1950), pp. 37–38.

22. Crane, p. 39.

23. *Ibid.*, pp. 42–47, 50–52.

24. *Ibid.*, pp. 54–57.

25. Morgan, *Stamp Act Crisis,* p. 334.

26. *PBF,* XIII (1969), p. 132n.

27. Morgan, *Prologue,* pp. 99–100.

28. *Ibid.*, pp. 156–157.

29. Maurice Hastings, *Parliament House* (London, 1950), p. 84.

30. This account of Franklin's climactic appearance before Parliament is based on the carefully annotated version printed in the most recent volume of *The Papers of Benjamin Franklin,* XIII, pp. 124–162. The numerous previous citations make it clear how much the author is indebted to this magnificent work of American scholarship.

31. Alan Valentine, *Lord North* (Norman, Okla., 1967), Vol. I, pp. 130–131.

32. *PBF,* XIII, p. 428.

33. *Ibid.*, pp. 182–184.

34. Mariboe, *op. cit.,* describes in part the buildup of this idea; so also does C. W. Alvord in *The New Regime* and N. B. Wainwright in *George Croghan, Wilderness Diplomat,* to cite a few of the books which have dealt with the American West before the Revolution.

35. *PBF,* XIII, pp. 276, 414–415.

36. *Ibid.*, p. 486.

37. *Ibid.*, p. 415.

38. *Benjamin Franklin's Autobiographical Writings,* ed. Carl Van Doren (New York, 1945), p. 160.

38. *Ibid.*, p. 160.

39. Smyth, V, p. 41.

40. *Ibid.*, pp. 28–29.

41. *Ibid.*, pp. 26, 29.

42. *Ibid.*, pp. 17, 19–20.

43. *Ibid.*, pp. 45–47.

44. *Ibid.*, pp. 48–54.

45. *Ibid.*

46. *Ibid.*, p. 33.

47. *Ibid.*, pp. 30–31; Van Doren, p. 164.

48. Smyth, V, pp. 33–34.

49. *Ibid.*, pp. 31–33.

50. Benjamin Franklin Papers, mss, II, 2, #126, American Philosophical Society (hereafter referred to as APS).

51. Smyth, V, p. 66.

52. *Ibid.*, pp. 68–69.

53. *Ibid.*, pp. 89–91.

54. *Ibid.*, pp. 78–89.

55. *Ibid.*, p. 90.

56. *Ibid.*, pp. 113–114.

57. *Ibid.*, pp. 114–115.

58. *Ibid.*, pp. 116–117.

59. *Ibid.*, p. 112.

60. *Ibid.*, p. 117.

61. *Ibid.*, p. 121.

62. Smyth, X, p. 245.

63. *The Letters of Junius* . . . (Dublin, 1787), I, pp. 69, 214.

64. All the preceding quotations are from BF's letter to William Franklin, Smyth, V, pp. 142–148.

65. *N.J. Archives,* First Series, X, pp. 45–48, 64–95.

66. Benjamin Franklin Papers, II, 2, #156, APS.

67. Smyth, V, pp. 203–204.

68. *Ibid.*, p. 220.

69. Crane, pp. 132–134.

70. *Ibid.*, p. 138.

71. BF to John Ross, April 11, 1767. Bancroft Transcripts, Vol. 339, NYPL.

72. Benjamin Franklin Papers, II, 2, #164, APS.

73. Cecil B. Currey, *Road to Revolution, Benjamin Franklin in England, 1765–75* (New York, 1968), p. 236.

74. Thomas Walpole to Bancroft, July 1, 1778, Harkness Collection of Autograph Letters, New York Public Library.

75. Benjamin Franklin Papers, II, 2, #156, APS.

76. Albert T. Volwiler, *George Croghan and the Westward Movement: 1741–1782* (Cleveland, 1926), p. 270.

77. Sewell Elias Slick, *William Trent and the West* (Harrisburg, Pa., 1947), pp. 140–141; Thomas P. Abernethy, *Western Lands and the American Revolution* (New York, 1937), p. 45. The letter to Cooper is from the collection of the late Albert M. Greenfield.

78. *Papers of Sir William Johnson,* ed. Department of Archives and History, University of the State of New York (Albany, N.Y., 1921–1965), Vol. 7, pp. 591–592.

79. Jack M. Sosin, *Whitehall and the Wilderness* (Lincoln, Neb., 1961), pp. 187–188.

80. *N.J. Archives,* First Series, X, p. 228.

81. Van Doren, *Writings,* p. 188.

82. Smyth, V, pp. 259–262.

83. Crane, pp. 166–167.

84. *Ibid.*, p. 329f.

85. The preceding scene is reconstructed from the letter Franklin wrote to Cooper, in which he quoted both himself and Hillsborough at length. Smyth, V, pp. 298–304.

86. Smyth, V, pp. 298–299.

87. Benjamin Franklin Papers, mss, Vol. 48, #139a, APS.

88. Benjamin Franklin Papers, mss, Vol. 48, 2, #139b, APS.

89. Hart, C. R., "Letters from William Franklin to William Strahan," *Pennsylvania Magazine of Biography and History,* Vol. XXXV, pp. 446–450.

90. Benjamin Franklin Papers, II, 2, #84, APS.

91. Smyth, V, pp. 380–381.

92. Currey, p. 277; cites Edward Hughes to Joshua Sharpe, Sheerness, April 28, 1771, Franklin Papers, Film 54–61, Frame 201, Miscellaneous Manuscripts Collection, APS.

93. Smyth, V, p. 378.

94. Alfred Owen Aldridge, *Benjamin Franklin, Philosopher and Man* (Philadelphia, 1965), p. 217.

95. *Autobiography,* p. 43.

96. *Ibid.,* pp. 130–131.

97. Van Doren, *Writings,* pp. 268–269.

98. *Ibid.,* pp. 272–273.

99. Smyth, V, pp. 367–368.

100. Van Doren, *Writings,* pp. 272–273.

101. Smyth, V, p. 366.

102. *Ibid.,* p. 413.

103. Van Doren, *Writings,* p. 274.

104. Polly Hewson to BF, Nov. 2, 1771, APS, quoted by Alfred Owen Aldridge, *Benjamin Franklin, Philosopher and Man* (Philadelphia, 1965), p. 224.

105. Smyth, V, pp. 345–346.

106. C. W. Alvord, author of *The Mississippi Valley in British Politics* (Cleveland, 1917), in an article in *The Nation,* August 20, 1914, argues that Wharton wrote this speech, which was soon reprinted as a pamphlet. The only evidence he cites is a passing comment by William Knox, Hillsborough's undersecretary. Yet John Almon, *Biographical, Literary and Political Anecdotes* (London, 1797), II, p. 339, says that Franklin wrote it. Since Almon printed the speech, it seems far more likely that he would know the writer more accurately than Knox, who cordially hated Franklin, and would be happy to record any gossip that detracted from his fame. An interior examination of the speech inclines this writer to credit Franklin, if not for the authorship, at least for much of the substance of the argument. It draws heavily on decisions and policies from earlier ministries, about which Wharton could not have known, firsthand. The references to the Shelburne ministry, especially, have a tone of authority and confidence that only someone as intimate with Shelburne as Franklin could have possessed.

107. Van Doren, *Writings,* p. 277.

108. *Ibid.,* p. 279.

109. *Ibid.,* pp. 279–280.

110. *Ibid.,* pp. 280–281.

111. Carl Van Doren, *Benjamin Franklin* (New York, 1938), p. 419.

112. Smyth, V, pp. 444–445.

113. Van Doren, *Writings,* p. 292.

114. Smyth, VI, pp. 33–34.

115. *Ibid.,* p. 265.

116. *Ibid.,* pp. 262–263.

117. The best summary of Temple's career is the essay on him by Lewis Einstein in his book, *Divided Loyalties* (Boston, 1933).

118. Smyth, VI, pp. 12–13.

119. *Ibid.,* p. 19.

120. *Ibid.,* p. 57.

121. *Ibid.,* pp. 127–137.

122. Crane, p. 237; Smyth, VI, pp. 118–124.

123. Smyth, VI, p. 146.

124. *Ibid.,* p. 98.

125. *Ibid.,* pp. 144–145.

126. *Ibid.,* pp. 75–76.

127. Smyth, V, pp. 363ff.

128. Smyth, VI, pp. 77–79.

129. *PBF,* XII, pp. 431–432.

130. Bernard Donoughue, *British Politics and the American Revolution: The Path to War, 1773–75* (London, 1964), p. 28.

131. Smyth, VI, p. 172.

132. *Ibid.,* p. 284.

133. *Ibid.,* p. 182.

134. Alan Valentine, *Lord North, op. cit.,* I, p. 222.

135. *Ibid.,* p. 222. For Junius' comment, see *The Historical and Posthumous Memoirs of Sir Nathaniel Wraxall, 1771–84,* ed. H. B. Wheatley (London, 1884), II, p. 6.

136. The preceding scene is reconstructed from Franklin's letter to Thomas Cushing, Smyth, VI, pp. 182–186.

137. Smyth, VI, p. 186.

138. Crane, p. 239.

139. BF to Thomas Walpole, London, Jan. 12, 1774, Harkness Collection, NYPL.

140. Donoughue, *op. cit.,* pp. 29–31.

141. Smyth, VI, p. 188.

142. Sparks, IV, pp. 441–445.

143. These quotations from Wedderburn's speech are taken from the two versions subsequently published. The official version is in *The Letters of Governor Hutchinson and Lieut. Gov. Oliver . . . and Remarks Thereon—Together with the Substance of Mr. Wedderburn's Speech,* ed. Israel Mauduit (London, 1774); the version by Franklin's friends is in *Political, Miscellaneous and Philosophical Pieces written by Benjamin Franklin,* ed. Benjamin Vaughan (London, 1779).

144. Aldridge, *Benjamin Franklin, Philosopher and Man* (Philadelphia, 1965), p. 237.

145. Smyth, VI, p. 176.

146. *Ibid.,* p. 179.

147. *Ibid.,* pp. 189–191.

148. *Ibid.,* pp. 191–192.

149. *Ibid.,* pp. 194–197.

150. *Ibid.,* p. 197.

151. Donoughue, pp. 96–99.

152. Sir William Meredith, quoted in Valentine, I, p. 327.

153. Valentine, I, p. 326.

154. Sosin, *Whitehall and the Wilderness* (Lincoln, Neb., 1961), p. 242.

155. Valentine, I, p. 327.

156. Smyth, VI, pp. 244–245.

157. Benjamin Franklin Papers, mss, Vol. 58, 1, #45, APS.

158. Smyth, VI, pp. 240–241.

159. Johnson, *Papers,* VIII, p. 1159.

160. *N.J. Archives,* First Series, X, pp. 457–459.

161. Van Doren, *Writings,* pp. 339–340.

162. Smyth, VI, pp. 229–230.

163. Crane, p. 245.

164. Van Doren, *Writings,* pp. 338–339.

165. Crane, p. 258.

166. *Ibid.,* pp. 262–264.

167. *Ibid.,* pp. 258–262.

168. Smyth, VI, pp. 251–252.

169. *Ibid.,* pp. 253–254.

170. *Ibid.,* p. 254.

171. The preceding interview is based on Franklin's letter to William Franklin, Smyth, VI, pp. 321–324.

172. R. H. Lee, *Life of Arthur Lee LL.D.* (Boston, 1829), pp. 216–217, letter to Samuel Adams, June 10, 1771.

173. Journal of Josiah Quincy, Jr., in *Memoir of the Life of Josiah Quincy, Jun.,* by Josiah Quincy (Boston, 1825), pp. 228, 229, 250.

174. Smyth, VI, pp. 324–327.

175. Einstein, p. 17.

176. Smyth, VI, p. 345.

177. *Ibid.,* pp. 345–358.

178. *Ibid.,* pp. 348–349.

179. *Ibid.,* pp. 352–354.

180. *Ibid.,* pp. 354–356.

181. *Ibid.,* pp. 356–358.

182. *Ibid.,* pp. 360–362.

183. Donoughue, pp. 232–233.

184. Smyth, VI, p. 363.

185. *Ibid.,* pp. 363–365.

186. *Ibid.,* pp. 306, 367–371.

187. *Ibid.,* p. 310.

188. William Duane, *Letters to Benjamin Franklin from his Family and Friends, 1751–1790* (New York, 1859), pp. 59–62.

189. Smyth, VI, pp. 311–312.

190. Aldridge, p. 247.

191. Smyth, IX, p. 261.

192. Smyth, VI, pp. 396–399.

193. *Ibid.,* p. 399.

194. Van Doren, *Benjamin Franklin,* p. 521.

195. Edmund Burke, *Speeches and Letters on American Affairs* (London, 1908, 1945), pp. 76–141.

196. Smyth, VI, p. 318.

197. *Ibid.,* p. 392.

198. *Ibid.,* pp. 369–371.

199. *Ibid.,* pp. 373–374.

200. Goodman, pp. 129–135; Smyth, IX, pp. 407–411.

BOOK FIVE

1. See, for example, Aldridge, *Benjamin Franklin, Philosopher and Man,* pp. 252–264; Carl Van Doren, *Benjamin Franklin,* pp. 527–588; Bernard Fay, *Benjamin Franklin, the Apostle of Modern Times,* p. 383; James Parton, *Life and Times of Benjamin Franklin,* II, pp. 81–88.

2. BF to Joseph Galloway, May 8, 1775; Mason-Franklin Collection, Yale University Library (loaned by Mrs. Arthur Loeb).

3. Oliver C. Kuntzleman, *Joseph Galloway, Loyalist* (Philadelphia, 1941), p. 132.

4. Smyth, VI, p. 399.

5. *The Papers of James Madison,* ed. William T. Hutchinson and William M. E. Rachal (Chicago, 1962), I, p. 151.

6. Van Doren, *Writings,* p. 404.

7. *The Letters of Benjamin Franklin & Jane Mecon,* ed. Carl Van Doren (Princeton, 1950), pp. 154, 159.

8. Van Doren, *Writings,* p. 405.

9. "A certain great fortune and piddling genius, whose fame has been trumpeted so loudly, has given a silly cast to our whole doings," wrote John Adams of Dickinson, in a letter to James Warren, July 24, 1775. *Warren-Adams Letters* (Boston, 1917), I, p. 88.

10. Van Doren, *Writings,* p. 406.

11. *Ibid.,* pp. 406–409.

12. Smyth, VI, pp. 419–420n.

13. *Ibid.,* pp. 420–426.

14. Edmund Cody Burnett, *The Continental Congress* (New York, 1941), p. 90.

15. Page Smith, *John Adams* (New York, 1962), I, pp. 204, 206; Burnett, p. 84.

16. Smyth, VI, pp. 405–406.

17. Benjamin Franklin Papers, mss, IV, 1, #66, APS.

18. *Ibid.*

19. Benjamin Franklin Papers, IV, 1, #68, APS.

20. *Historical Magazine,* Series 1, Vol. 5, p. 313.

21. Van Doren, *Letters,* p. 165.

22. Benjamin Franklin Papers, mss, 101, #10, APS.

23. *N.J. Archives,* First Series, XVIII, pp. 565–567.

24. Mariboe, p. 444.

25. Burnett, p. 125.

26. *Ibid.*

27. Smyth, VI, pp. 430–431.

28. Van Doren, *Writings,* pp. 412–413.

29. Smyth, VI, p. 409.

30. *New Materials for the History of the American* . . . Transl. and ed. John Durand (New York, 1889), I, p. 16; *The Revolutionary Diplomatic Correspondence of the United States,* ed. Francis Wharton (Washington, D.C., 1889), I, pp. 334–335.

31. Wharton, II, pp. 64–67.

32. Mariboe, pp. 447–448.

33. *Ibid.,* p. 452.

34. Benjamin Franklin Papers, mss, Vol. 101, #10, APS.

35. Wharton, II, pp. 78–80.

36. George E. Lewis, *The Indiana Company* (Glendale, Calif., 1941), pp. 190, 215.

37. Ellen Hart Smith, *Charles Carroll of Carrollton* (Cambridge, Mass., 1942), p. 140.

38. Smyth, VI, pp. 445–446.

39. Kate Mason Rowland, *Life of Charles Carroll of Carrollton with his Correspondence and Public Papers* (New York, 1898), I, p. 391.

40. Peter Guilday, *The Life and Times of John Carroll* (Westminster, Md., 1954), pp. 122–123.

41. Smyth, VI, p. 449.

42. Van Doren, *Writings,* p. 427; BF to Mrs. Emma Thompson, from Paris, Feb. 8, 1777.

43. "Recommendation by the Congress to Establish Governments in the Several Colonies," *American Archives* . . ., Fourth Series, ed. Peter Force (Washington, D.C., 1846), VI, p. 660.

44. Benjamin Franklin Papers, mss, Vol. 76, #42, APS.

45. Benjamin Franklin Papers, mss, Vol. 101, #18, APS.

46. Edmund Cody Burnett, *Letters of Members of the Continental Congress* (Washington, D.C., 1921–36), I, p. 114.

47. *The Writings of Thomas Jefferson,* ed. Andrew A. Lipscomb and Albert Ellery Bergh (Washington, D.C., 1903–04), XVIII, pp. 169–170.

48. E. C. Burnett, *op. cit.*, p. 420.

49. *Familiar Letters of John Adams and His Wife Abigail Adams . . .* , ed. Charles Francis Adams (Boston, 1875), p. 198.

50. Smyth, X, pp. 57–58.

51. *The Adams Papers: Diary and Autobiography of John Adams,* ed. L. H. Butterfield *et al* (Cambridge, Mass., 1961), II, p. 245.

52. Jefferson, *Writings*, I, p. 49.

53. Jefferson, *Writings*, XVIII, p. 47.

54. *Adams Papers,* II, p. 246.

55. Smyth, VI, p. 452.

56. *Ibid.*, pp. 459–461.

57. *The Ingenious Dr. Franklin . . .*, ed. Nathan G. Goodman (Philadelphia, 1956), pp. 155–156; *Adams Papers,* III, p. 418.

58. Benjamin Franklin Papers, mss, F85ba, APS.

59. This scene is based upon the account of the negotiations and letters in Smyth, VI, pp. 457–466; John Adams' diary, *Adams Papers,* III, pp. 417–431; and minutes of the meeting taken by Howe's secretary, Henry Strachey, reprinted in "Lord Howe's Commission to Pacify the Colonies," by Paul Leicester Ford, *Atlantic Monthly,* LXXVII (June. 1896), pp. 758–762.

60. Smyth, VI, pp. 468–469.

61. Smyth, VII, p. 35.

62. "Excerpts from the Papers of Dr. Benjamin Rush," *Pennsylvania Magazine of History and Biography,* XXIX (1905), p. 29.

63. Benjamin Franklin Papers, mss, Vol. 69, #5, APS.

64. Smyth, VI, p. 468.

65. Van Doren, *Writings,* p. 462.

BOOK SIX

1. Wharton, II, p. 223.

2. Smyth, VII, pp. 470–472.

3. Van Doren, *Writings,* p. 425.

4. Burke, p. 154.

5. Van Doren, *Writings,* pp. 455–457.

6. Charles Coleman Sellers, *Benjamin Franklin in Portraiture* (New Haven, 1962), p. 98, cites *L'Espion Anglois, ou Correspondance Secrete entre Milord All'eye et Milord All'ear* (London, 1785), V, pp. 5–6.

7. Aldridge, *Franklin and His French Contemporaries,* p. 43.

8. Sellers, pp. 103–105.

9. Julian P. Boyd, "Silas Deane: Death by a Kindly Teacher of Treason?" *William and Mary Quarterly,* Third Series, XVI, pp. 321–322n.

10. Van Doren, *Writings,* p. 430.

11. *The Deane Papers,* I, pp. 465–467. In his letter of Jan. 21,

1777, Carmichael tells C. W. F. Dumas that he looks on Kings and servants of Kings "as swine."

12. Aldridge, *Benjamin Franklin*, p. 269.

13. Wharton, II, pp. 245–246.

14. *Ibid.*, p. 250.

15. The best account of the Bancroft-Deane relationship is Julian P. Boyd's series of articles in the *William and Mary Quarterly*, April ff., 1959. Boyd argues Bancroft not only corrupted Deane; he murdered him after the war.

16. Van Doren, *Writings*, p. 426.

17. *Ibid.*, pp. 425–426.

18. *Ibid.*, pp. 427–428.

19. Wharton, II, pp. 231–238, 257–258.

20. *Ibid.*, p. 287.

21. "Narrative of Gustavus Conyngham, U.S.N., while in Command of the 'Surprise' and 'Revenge,' 1777–1779," *Pennsylvania Magazine of History and Biography*, XXII (1898), pp. 479–488.

22. Richard W. Van Alstyne, "Great Britain, the War for Independence, and the 'Gathering Storm' in Europe, 1775–1778," *Huntington Library Quarterly*, XXVII (August, 1964), p. 322.

23. Sir Gavin de Beer, *Gibbon and His World* (New York, 1968), p. 77.

24. Wharton, II, pp. 364–365.

25. *Ibid.*, p. 377.

26. Smyth, VII, pp. 27–29.

27. Van Doren, *Writings*, p. 430.

28. Smyth, VII, pp. 68–72.

29. Aldridge, *Franklin and His French Contemporaries*, pp. 64–65.

30. Smyth, VII, p. 35.

31. B. F. Stevens Facsimiles (London, 1893), Vol. 18, No. 1691.

32. Mariboe, p. 478.

33. Van Doren, *Letters*, p. 170.

34. "Papers of Dr. Benjamin Rush," *PMHB*, XXIX (1905), pp. 27–28.

35. "Memoir of Jonathan Loring Austin," *Boston Monthly Magazine*, Vol. 2, No. 2, July 1826, p. 59.

36. Samuel Flagg Bemis, "British Secret Service and the French-American Alliance," *American Historical Review*, XXIX, April 1924, pp. 474–495.

37. Bemis, S. F., *op. cit.*, pp. 484–490, Stevens, V, No. 489.

38. Richard Meade Bache, "Franklin's Ceremonial Coat," *PMHB*, XXIII (1899), pp. 444–452; Rush Papers, *PMHB*, XXIX (1905), pp. 27–28.

39. Richard W. Van Alstyne, "Thomas Walpole's Letters to the Duke of Grafton on American Affairs, 1776–1778," *Huntington Library Quarterly*, XXX (November, 1966), p. 32.

40. Valentine, I, p. 505.

41. Horace Walpole, *Journal of the Reign of George the Third* (London, 1859), II, 207–209.

42. Smyth, VII, p. 103.

43. *Ibid.,* p. 109.

44. *Ibid.,* p. 143.

45. *Horace Walpole's Correspondence with William Mason,* ed. W. S. Lewis, Grover Cronin, Jr., and Charles H. Bennett (New Haven, 1955), I, p. 394, May 12, 1778.

46. Smyth, VII, p. 103.

47. Van Doren, *Franklin,* p. 595.

48. Wharton, II, p. 239.

49. Silas Deane makes some savage comments on Lee's fence-straddling, in his letter to Jonathan Williams, Jan. 13, 1778. *Deane Papers,* II, pp. 327–330.

50. *Deane Papers,* II, p. 99; Richard Henry Lee, *Life of Arthur Lee LL.D.* (Boston, 1829), II, pp. 113, 115.

51. Parton, II, p. 296.

52. Van Doren, *Writings,* pp. 431–432.

53. Smyth, VII, p. 98.

54. *Deane Papers,* II, p. 327.

55. Smyth, VII, pp. 129–130.

56. *Ibid.,* pp. 132, 135–136.

57. Wharton, II, pp. 623–624.

58. Smyth, VII, pp. 216–217; Wharton, II, p. 564 (for Pringle).

59. Smyth, V, pp. 550–551.

60. Smyth, VIII, p. 231.

61. Smyth, VII, p. 77.

62. *Ibid.,* pp. 81–82.

63. Van Doren, *Writings,* pp. 433–434.

64. F. L. Lucas, *The Art of Living: Four Eighteenth Century Minds* (New York, 1960), p. 252; Smyth, VII, p. 65.

65. *The Works of John Adams,* ed. Charles Francis Adams (Boston, 1856), I, pp. 660, 663.

66. *Adams Papers,* IV, p. 118.

67. Wharton, II, pp. 781–782.

68. *Adams Papers,* II, p. 345.

69. Boyd, pp. 167–168 fn.

70. Wharton, III, p. 102.

71. Burnett, p. 363.

72. John C. Miller, *Triumph of Freedom* (Boston, 1948), p. 377.

73. Smyth, VII, pp. 345–348.

74. *Ibid.,* p. 230.

75. *Deane Papers,* III, p. 389; Burnett, p. 358.

76. Smyth, VII, pp. 238–240.

77. *Ibid.,* pp. 298–299; 299–300n.

78. Van Doren, *Writings,* p. 472.

79. William Bell Clark, *Ben Franklin's Privateers* (Baton Rouge, La., 1956), p. 172.

80. Smyth, VII, pp. 166–172.

81. Van Doren, *Writings,* p. 472.

82. *Ibid.,* p. 446.

83. *Ibid.,* p. 472.

84. Smyth, VII, pp. 393–394.

85. Gilbert Chinard, "Abbé Lefebvre de la Roche's Recollections of Benjamin Franklin," *Proceedings of the American Philosophical Society,* XLIV (1950), p. 219.

86. Smyth, VII, p. 100.

87. Claude-Anne Lopez, *Mon Cher Papa: Franklin and the Ladies of Paris* (New Haven, 1966), p. 38. This sensitive study of Franklin's relationships in France, by one of the editors of the Benjamin Franklin Papers, utilizes many hitherto unpublished and untranslated letters.

88. Van Doren, *Writings,* pp. 436–437; Lopez, pp. 40–41.

89. Lopez, p. 44.

90. *Ibid.,* p. 58.

91. *Ibid.,* p. 61.

92. *Ibid.,* pp. 64–65.

93. Amacher, pp. 50–52.

94. Smyth, X, pp. 441ff.

95. Lopez, p. 256.

96. *Ibid.,* pp. 258–259; Smyth, VII, p. 375.

97. Amacher, pp. 58–59.

98. *Ibid.,* pp. 54–56.

99. Smyth, VIII, p. 52.

100. *Ibid.,* pp. 56–57.

101. *Ibid.,* p. 52.

102. BF to Thomas Walpole, London, Jan. 12, 1774; Harkness Collection, NYPL; Smyth, VIII, pp. 270–271.

103. Samuel Wharton, *Plain Facts* . . . (Philadelphia, 1781), Appendix I, pp. 161–162, quoted in Lewis, pp. 242–243.

104. Smyth, VIII, p. 304.

105. *Ibid.,* p. 53.

106. Wharton, III, p. 871; IV, pp. 12–13.

107. Wharton, IV, pp. 18–19.

108. Smyth, IX, p. 62.

109. Smyth, VIII, p. 127.

110. Wharton, IV, p. 74.

111. Smyth, VIII, p. 149.

112. *Ibid.,* p. 195.

113. *Ibid.,* pp. 208–210.

114. Wharton, IV, p. 281.

115. Smyth, VIII, pp. 220–221. Franklin to Jay: Feinstone Collection, APS.

116. Sparks, IX, p. 43n.

117. Smyth, VIII, pp. 294–295.
118. Wharton, IV, p. 659n.
119. Smyth, VIII, p. 327.
120. *Ibid.,* pp. 332–333.
121. Smyth, VII, p. 393.
122. Van Doren, *Writings,* p. 513.
123. Smyth, VIII, p. 316.
124. *Ibid.,* p. 325.
125. *Ibid.,* pp. 328–329.
126. *Ibid.,* p. 333.
127. *Ibid.,* p. 411.
128. *Ibid.,* pp. 27–29.
129. *Ibid.,* pp. 330, 336.
130. *Ibid.,* pp. 358–361.
131. *Ibid.,* pp. 390–394.
132. *Ibid.,* p. 397.
133. *Ibid.,* pp. 459–461.
134. *Ibid.,* pp. 461–462.
135. *Ibid.,* pp. 465–468.
136. *Ibid.,* pp. 469–473.
137. *Ibid.,* p. 473.
138. *Ibid.,* pp. 477–478.
139. Almost all of the preceding material is from Franklin's journal. *Ibid.,* pp. 483–492.
140. *Ibid.,* pp. 497–499.
141. *Ibid.,* p. 513.
142. *Ibid.,* pp. 516–518.
143. *Ibid.,* p. 527.
144. *Ibid.,* pp. 533–534, 541–543.
145. *Ibid.,* p. 557.
146. Gerald Stourzh, in the best recent study of Franklin's diplomacy, *Franklin and American Foreign Policy* (Chicago, 1954), underscores how important the acquisition of Canada was in Franklin's thinking.
147. Wharton, V, pp. 616–617.
148. Edward E. Hale and Edward E. Hale, Jr., *Franklin in France* (Boston, 1888), II, pp. 155–159.
149. Smyth, VIII, p. 144.
150. Wharton, V, p. 657.
151. Richard B. Morris, *The Peacemakers* (New York, 1965), pp. 312, 315.
152. *Ibid.,* p. 312. I am conscious that I differ here with the conclusions drawn by Richard B. Morris in his prize-winning study of the peace negotiations, *The Peacemakers.* As anyone who has read this superb work of historical research will recognize, I am indebted to Dr. Morris for many details in my own narrative of this crucial episode in American his-

tory. His immensely diligent search of European archives has given us a far deeper, more three-dimensional image of the negotiations than we had before. But information is one thing, and evidence that supports a historical judgment is another. Useful and interesting as his access to the John Jay papers has been for giving us a better view of Jay's role in the diplomacy of the American Revolution, I fail to see how it justifies his attempt to elevate Jay—or Adams—to equal status with Franklin. This attempt forces Mr. Morris into some extremely curious statements. On page 308, for instance, he says, "It was clear to Jay, if not to Franklin, that Vergennes and Reyneval had no comprehension of the true nature of the American Revolution . . . To Jay the evidence of France's motives in backing America had been disclosed." The implication would seem to be that Franklin, after dealing with these gentlemen for six years, had somehow failed to discover their real motives for supporting America. Even a modest estimate of Franklin's judgment of human nature would make this unlikely. The truth is, Jay reacted like a tyro to something Franklin understood before he even arrived in France. A few pages later, describing Jay's supposed hurling of his pipe into Franklin's fireplace, Mr. Morris says, "With Jay's impulsive gesture, 'independence' for which America had fought long and bitterly, suddenly attained a new meaning and dimension." Just what that new meaning and dimension are, Mr. Morris never explains. Again, the implication seems to be that it was something that Jay understood, far more perfectly than Franklin—a curious judgment, when we consider that Franklin was for independence in early 1775, and Jay did not become a reluctant convert until 1776. Jack M. Sosin, perhaps the most authoritative modern historian of the West in the Revolution, writes in *The Revolutionary Frontier:* "Jay's anxieties were not fully justified." He goes on to blame Jay for the loss, at the very least, of the Ontario peninsula to the United States.

153. Smyth, VIII, p. 596. Franklin writes to David Hartley: "I have been a long time afflicted with the gravel and gout, which have much indisposed me for writing. I am even now in pain. . . ."

154. Wharton, VI, p. 30.

155. Smith, I, p. 522.

156. *Adams Papers,* III, p. 38.

157. *Ibid.,* pp. 45, 46.

158. *Ibid.,* p. 82.

159. *Ibid.,* p. 82.

160. Mariboe, p. 554.

161. Hale, II, pp. 208–209.

162. *Adams Papers,* III, p. 77.

163. Morris, p. 418, cites William Franklin to Oswald (c. 1783), Rodney mss, undated, Bundle 13 (copy), William L. Clements Library, University of Michigan.

164. *Adams Papers,* III, p. 83.

165. Smyth, VIII, p. 632n.

166. *Adams Papers,* III, p. 85.

167. Smyth, VIII, pp. 642–643.

168. *Adams Papers,* III, p. 106.

169. Smyth, X, p. 315.

170. Wharton, VI, p. 581.

171. *Ibid.,* p. 670.

172. Smyth, IX, p. 17.

173. *Ibid.,* pp. 91–93, 95.

174. *Ibid.,* pp. 107, 110; 88.

175. *Ibid.,* p. 151.

176. *Ibid.,* p. 172.

177. *Ibid.,* pp. 179–180.

178. Carl Van Doren, *Benjamin Franklin* (New York, 1938), p. 700.

179. Jefferson, *Writings,* XV, p. 176.

180. *Ibid.,* XVIII, pp. 170–172.

181. Smyth, IX, pp. 165–168; Aldridge, *Franklin and His French Contemporaries,* p. 8off.

182. This anecdote was told about Franklin after his return to America. It appears in a collection of miscellaneous newspapers in the files of the American Philosophical Society.

183. Amacher, pp. 133–135.

184. Smyth, III, pp. 434–435.

185. Franklin Papers, mss, F85 x22, APS.

186. Smyth, IX, pp. 252–254.

187. Hale, II, pp. 319–320. For the first time Franklin sounded old. He querulously detailed his minor aches and pains, almost collapsing into self-pity because Temple had abandoned him. The conflicting emotions with which he was trying to cope were also apparent in a line which he obviously added as an afterthought to one of his letters: "Give your father my love." Hale, II, p. 320.

188. Smyth, IX, p. 274; Mariboe, p. 565.

189. Mariboe, pp. 559–562.

190. Aldridge, *French Contemporaries,* p. 202.

191. Smyth, IX, pp. 332–333.

192. Lopez, pp. 120–121, 299–300.

193. Mariboe, p. 559.

194. Smyth, IX, p. 359.

BOOK SEVEN

1. Smyth, IX, pp. 394–395, 405–406.

2. Van Doren, *Writings,* p. 654.

3. Charles F. Jenkins, "Franklin Returns from France," *PAPS,* Vol. 92, No. 6, December, 1948.

4. Smyth, IX, pp. 476, 519.

5. *Ibid.,* p. 472.

6. *Ibid.,* IX, p. 551.

7. *Ibid.,* p. 574.

8. *Ibid.,* pp. 600–601.

9. Clinton Rossiter, *1787: The Grand Convention* (New York, 1966), p. 213.

10. Smyth, IX, pp. 607–609.

11. Van Doren, pp. 754–755.

12. Smyth, IX, pp. 657–658.

13. Van Doren, *Letters,* p. 300.

14. Van Doren, *Writings,* p. 772.

15. *The Writings of George Washington,* ed. John C. Fitzpatrick (Washington, D.C., 1939), XXX, p. 409.

16. Will of William Temple Franklin (copy), Franklin Collection, Yale University Library.

17. Van Doren, *Writings,* p. 688.

18. *Ibid.,* p. 769.

19. *Ibid.,* p. 778.

20. Lopez, pp. 333–334.

21. Smyth, X, pp. 86–91.

22. *Ibid.,* p. 84.

BIBLIOGRAPHY

In addition to the manuscript collections cited in the introduction to my notes, the following works will prove useful for those who wish to make further explorations into the life and times of Benjamin Franklin. They constitute only a small portion of the hundreds of books, monographs and articles consulted in the course of preparing this book. A complete bibliography would run to several dozen pages.

PRIMARY SOURCES

Adams, John. *The Adams Papers: Diary and Autobiography of John Adams,* ed. L. H. Butterfield *et al.* 4 vols. Cambridge, Mass., 1961.

————. *The Works of John Adams,* ed. Charles Francis Adams. 10 vols. Boston, 1850–1856.

————, and Abigail Adams. *Familiar Letters of John Adams and His Wife Abigail Adams, During the Revolution,* ed. Charles Francis Adams. Boston, 1875.

Burke, Edmund. *Speeches and Letters on American Affairs.* London, 1908.

Burnett, Edmund Cody, ed. *Letters of Members of the Continental Congress.* 8 vols. Washington, D.C., 1921–1936.

Conyngham, Gustavus. "Narrative of Gustavus Conyngham, U.S.N., while in Command of the 'Surprise' and 'Revenge,' 1777–1779," *Pennsylvania Magazine of History and Biography,* XXII (1898), pp. 478–488.

Deane, Silas. *The Deane Papers. Collections of the New York Historical Society.* Vols. XIX–XXIII. New York, 1886–1890.

Fisher, Daniel. "Extracts from the Diary of Daniel Fisher, 1755," *Pennsylvania Magazine of History and Biography,* XVII (1893), pp. 263–278.

Force, Peter. *American Archives,* Series 4. 6 vols. Washington, D.C., 1846.

Franklin, Benjamin. *The Autobiography of Benjamin Franklin,* ed. Leonard W. Labaree *et al.* New Haven, 1964.

————. *Benjamin Franklin's Autobiographical Writings,* ed. Carl Van Doren. New York, 1945.

————. *Benjamin Franklin's Experiments: A New Edition of Franklin's Experiments and Observation on Electricity,* ed. I. Bernard Cohen. Cambridge, Mass., 1941.

————. *Benjamin Franklin's Letters to the Press, 1758–1775,* ed. Verner W. Crane. Chapel Hill, N.C., 1950.

————. *The Complete Works of Benjamin Franklin,* ed. John Bigelow. 10 vols. New York, 1887–1889.

Franklin, Benjamin. *Franklin's Wit and Folly: The Bagatelles*, ed. Richard E. Amacher. New Brunswick, N.J., 1953.

——. *The Ingenious Dr. Franklin: Selected Scientific Letters of Benjamin Franklin*, ed. Nathan G. Goodman. Philadelphia, 1956.

——. *Letters to Benjamin Franklin from his Family and Friends*, ed. William Duane. New York, 1859.

——. *Memoirs of the Life and Writings of Benjamin Franklin*, ed. William Temple Franklin. London, 1818.

——. *"My Dear Girl"—The Correspondence of Benjamin Franklin with Polly Stevenson, Georgiana and Catherine Shipley*, ed. James M. Stifler. New York, 1927.

——. *The Papers of Benjamin Franklin*, ed. Leonard W. Labaree *et al.* 14 vols. to date. New Haven, 1959–1969.

——. *Political, Miscellaneous and Philosophical Pieces . . . Written by Benj. Franklin*, ed. Benjamin Vaughan. London, 1779.

——. *The Works of Benjamin Franklin*, ed. Jared Sparks. 10 vols. Rev. ed. Philadelphia, 1840.

——. *The Writings of Benjamin Franklin*, ed. Albert Henry Smyth. 10 vols. New York, 1905–1907.

Franklin, William. *Letters from William Franklin to William Strahan*, ed. Charles H. Hart. Philadelphia, 1911.

Hutchinson, Thomas, and Andrew Oliver. *The Letters of Governor Hutchinson and Lieut. Gov. Oliver . . . And Remarks Thereon . . . Together with the Substance of Mr. Wedderburn's Speech*, ed. Israel Mauduit. London, 1774.

Jefferson, Thomas. *The Writings of Thomas Jefferson*, ed. Andrew A. Lipscomb and Albert Ellery Bergh. Washington, D.C., 1903–1904.

Johnson, Sir William. *Papers of Sir William Johnson*, ed. Division of Archives and History, The University of the State of New York. Albany, N.Y., 1921–1965.

Junius. *The Letters of Junius, &c. Stat Nominis Umbra.* 2 vols. Dublin, 1787.

Letters of Members of the Continental Congress, ed. Edmund C. Burnett. 8 vols. Washington, D.C., 1921–1936.

Madison, James. *Notes of Debates in the Federal Convention of 1787*, ed. Adrian Koch. New York, 1969.

——. *The Papers of James Madison*, ed. William T. Hutchinson and William M. E. Rachal. Chicago, 1962.

New Jersey Archives. First Series. *Documents Relating to the Colonial History of the State of New Jersey.* 42 vols. Newark, N.J., 1880–1949.

New Material for the History of the American Revolution, transl. and ed. John Durand. New York, 1899.

Prologue to Revolution: Sources and Documents on the Stamp Act Crisis, 1764–1766, ed. Edmund S. Morgan. Chapel Hill, N.C., 1959.

Revolutionary Diplomatic Correspondence of the United States, ed. Francis Wharton. 6 vols. Washington, 1889.

Rush, Benjamin. "Excerpts from the Papers of Dr. Benjamin Rush," *Pennsylvania Magazine of History and Biography*, XXIX (1905), pp. 15–30.

Stevens, B. F. *Facsimiles of Manuscripts in European Archives Relating to America, 1773–1783.* 25 vols. London, 1893.

Walpole, Horace. *Journal of the Reign of George the Third, From the Year 1771 to 1783.* 2 vols. London, 1859.

――. *The Letters of Horace Walpole,* ed. Mrs. Paget Toynbee. 16 vols. Oxford, 1903.

――. *The Letters of Horace Walpole,* ed. John Wright. 6 vols. London, 1840.

Washington, George. *The Writings of George Washington,* ed. John C. Fitzpatrick. Washington, D.C., 1939.

Watson, Elkanah. *Men and Times of the Revolution, or Memoirs of Elkanah Watson,* ed. Winslow C. Watson. New York, 1856.

SECONDARY SOURCES

Abernethy, Thomas P. "Commercial Activities of Silas Deane in France," *American Historical Review,* XXXIX (April, 1934).

――. *Western Lands and the American Revolution.* New York, 1937.

Aldridge, Alfred Owen. *Benjamin Franklin, Philosopher and Man.* Philadelphia, 1965.

――. *Franklin and His French Contemporaries.* New York, 1957.

Almon, John. *Biographical, Literary and Political Anecdotes.* 3 vols. London, 1797.

Alvord, Clarence W. *The Mississippi Valley in British Politics.* 2 vols. Cleveland, 1917.

――, and Clarence E. Carter, eds. *The New Regime.* Springfield, Ill., 1916.

Augur, Helen. *The Secret War of Independence.* New York, 1955.

Bache, Richard Meade. "Franklin's Ceremonial Coat," *Pennsylvania Magazine of History and Biography,* XXIII (1899), pp. 444–452.

Becker, Carl L. *Benjamin Franklin, A Biographical Sketch.* Ithaca, N.Y., 1946.

Beer, Sir Gavin de. *Gibbon and His World.* New York, 1968.

Bemis, Samuel Flagg. "British Secret Service and the French-American Alliance," *American Historical Review* (April, 1924), pp. 474–495.

――. *The Diplomacy of the American Revolution.* Bloomington, Ind., 1957.

Bowdoin and Temple Papers. Collections of the Massachusetts Historical Society. Sixth Series, IX. Boston, 1897. Seventh Series, VI. Boston, 1907.

Boyd, Julian P. *Anglo-American Union: Joseph Galloway's Plans to Preserve the British Empire.* Philadelphia, 1941.

――. "Silas Deane: Death by a Kindly Teacher of Treason?" *William and Mary Quarterly,* Third Series, XVI (April–October, 1959), pp. 165–187, 319–342, 515–550.

Bridenbaugh, Carl, and Jessica Bridenbaugh. *Rebels and Gentlemen: Philadelphia in the Age of Franklin.* New York, 1965.

Brown, Wallace. *The Good Americans: The Loyalists in the American Revolution.* New York, 1969.

Burnett, Edmund Cody. *The Continental Congress.* New York, 1941.

Butler, Ruth Lapham. *Dr. Franklin, Postmaster General.* Garden City, New York, 1928.

Carroll, Charles. *Journal of Charles Carroll of Carrollton during His Visit to Canada in 1776,* ed. Brantz Mayer. Baltimore, Md., 1876.

Chinard, Gilbert. "Abbé Lefebvre de la Roche's Recollections of Benjamin Franklin," *Proceedings of the American Philosophical Society,* XLIV, 1950.

Christie, Ian R. *The End of North's Ministry, 1780–82.* London, 1958.

Clark, William Bell. *Ben Franklin's Privateers.* Baton Rouge, La., 1956.

Cochrane, J. A. *Dr. Johnson's Printer: The Life of William Strahan.* London, 1964.

Cohen, I. Bernard. *Benjamin Franklin: His Contribution to the American Tradition.* Indianapolis, 1953.

———. *Franklin and Newton: An Inquiry into Speculative Newtonian Science and Franklin's Work in Electricity as an Example Thereof.* Philadelphia, 1956.

———. "The Two Hundredth Anniversary of Benjamin Franklin's Two Lightning Experiments and the Introduction of the Lightning Rod," *Proceedings of the American Philosophical Society,* XCVI (June 20, 1952), pp. 331–366.

Cone, Carl B. *Torchbearer of Freedom: The Influence of Richard Price on Eighteenth Century Thought.* Lexington, Ky., 1952.

Currey, Cecil B. *Road to Revolution: Benjamin Franklin in England, 1765–1775.* Garden City, N.Y., 1968.

Davidson, Philip. *Propaganda in the American Revolution.* Chapel Hill, N.C., 1941.

Donoughue, Bernard. *British Politics and the American Revolution: The Path to War, 1773–75.* London, 1964.

Duer, William Alexander. *The Life of William Alexander, Earl of Stirling.* New York, 1847.

Einstein, Lewis. *Divided Loyalties: Americans in England during the War of Independence.* Boston, 1933.

Fay, Bernard. *Franklin, the Apostle of Modern Times.* Boston, 1929.

Ferguson, E. James. *The Power of the Purse: A History of American Public Finance, 1776–1790.* Chapel Hill, N.C., 1961.

Fisher, Sidney George. *The True Benjamin Franklin.* Philadelphia, 1899.

Ford, Paul Leicester. *The Many-Sided Franklin.* New York, 1899.

———. "Lord Howe's Commission to Pacify the Colonies," *Atlantic Monthly,* LXXVII (June, 1896), pp. 758–762.

Franklin, Benjamin, and Richard Jackson. *Letters and Papers of Benjamin Franklin and Richard Jackson, 1753–1785,* ed. Carl Van Doren. Philadelphia, 1947.

———, and Jane Mecom. *The Letters of Benjamin Franklin & Jane Mecom,* ed. Carl Van Doren. Princeton, 1950.

Guilday, Peter. *The Life and Times of John Carroll.* Westminster, Md., 1954.

Hale, Edward E., and Edward E. Hale, Jr. *Franklin in France.* 2 vols. Boston, 1888.

Hays, I. Nimis. *Calendar of the Papers of Benjamin Franklin in the Library of the American Philosophical Society.* 5 vols. Philadelphia, 1908.

(Appendix, *Papers of Benjamin Franklin in the Library of the University of Pennsylvania.*)

Henderson, H. James. "Congressional Factionalism and the Attempt to Recall Benjamin Franklin," *William and Mary Quarterly*, XXVII, April, 1970.

Hindle, Brooke. *The Pursuit of Science in Revolutionary America.* Chapel Hill, N.C., 1956.

Kammen, Michael G. *A Rope of Sand: The Colonial Agents, British Politics and the American Revolution.* Ithaca, N.Y., 1968.

Kapitsa, Peter. *Peter Kapitsa on Life and Science,* transl. and ed. Albert Parry. New York, 1968.

Knapp, S. L. "Memoir of Jonathan Loring Austin," *Boston Monthly Magazine,* Vol. 2, No. 2, July, 1826.

Kronenberger, Louis. *Kings and Desperate Men.* New York, 1942.

Kuntzleman, Oliver C. *Joseph Galloway, Loyalist.* Philadelphia, 1941.

Lee, Richard Henry. *Life of Arthur Lee LL.D.* 2 vols. Boston, 1829.

Lewis, George E. *The Indiana Company, 1763–1798.* Glendale, Calif., 1941.

Lopez, Claude-Anne. *Mon Cher Papa: Franklin and the Ladies of Paris.* New Haven, 1966.

Mariboe, William Herbert. "The Life of William Franklin, 1730(1)–1813, 'Pro Rege et Patria.' " Unpublished dissertation. University of Pennsylvania, 1962.

Marshall, Dorothy. *Eighteenth Century England.* New York, 1962.

Mason, William Smith. *Franklin and Galloway: Some Unpublished Letters.* Worcester, Mass., 1925.

Miller, John Chester. *Triumph of Freedom, 1775–1783.* Boston, 1948.

Morgan, Edmund S., and Helen M. Morgan. *The Stamp Act Crisis: Prologue to Revolution.* Revised ed. New York, 1962.

Morison, Samuel Eliot. *John Paul Jones.* Boston, 1959.

Morris, Richard B. *The Peacemakers: The Great Powers and American Independence.* New York, 1965.

Namier, Sir Lewis. *England in the Age of the American Revolution.* London, 1961.

Nolan, J. Bennett. *Benjamin Franklin in Scotland and Ireland: 1759 and 1771.* Philadelphia, 1956.

———. *General Benjamin Franklin: The Military Career of a Philosopher.* Philadelphia, 1956.

"Notes. An Article Found Among the Papers of Roberts Vaux . . ." *Pennsylvania Magazine of History and Biography*, XLVIII (October, 1924), p. 383.

Parton, James. *Life and Times of Benjamin Franklin.* 2 vols. Boston, 1864.

Pepper, William. *The Medical Side of Benjamin Franklin.* Philadelphia, 1911.

Phillips, Hugh. *Mid-Georgian London.* London, 1964.

Quincy, Josiah. *Memoir of the Life of Josiah Quincy, Jun. . . .* Boston, 1825.

"Recommendation by the Congress to Establish Governments in the Several Colonies," *American Archives.* Fourth Series, ed. Peter Force, VI, p. 466. Washington, D.C., 1846.

Rossiter, Clinton. *1787: The Grand Convention.* New York, 1966.

Rowland, Kate Mason. *Life of Charles Carroll of Carrollton with his Correspondence and Public Papers.* 2 vols. New York, 1898.

Schutz, John A. *Thomas Pownall, British Defender of American Liberty.* Glendale, Calif., 1951.

Sellers, Charles Coleman. *Benjamin Franklin in Portraiture.* New Haven, 1962.

Sisk, John P. "Making It in America," *Atlantic Monthly,* Vol. 224, No. 6 (November, 1969), pp. 63–68.

Slick, Sewell Elias. *William Trent and the West.* Harrisburg, Penna., 1947.

Smith, Ellen Hart. *Charles Carroll of Carrollton.* Cambridge, Mass., 1942.

Smith, Page. *John Adams.* 2 vols. Garden City, N.Y. 1962.

Smith, Paul H. *Loyalists and Redcoats: A Study of British Revolutionary Policy.* Chapel Hill, N.C., 1964.

Sosin, Jack M. *Agents and Merchants, British Colonial Policy and the Origins of the American Revolution.* Lincoln, Neb., 1965.

———. *The Revolutionary Frontier, 1763–1783.* New York, 1967.

———. *Whitehall and the Wilderness: The Middle West in British Colonial Policy, 1760–1775.* Lincoln, Neb., 1961.

Stourzh, Gerald. *Benjamin Franklin and American Foreign Policy.* Chicago, 1954.

Temple, John Alexander, and H. M. Temple. *The Temple Memoirs.* London, 1925.

Valentine, Alan. *Lord North.* 2 vols. Norman, Okla., 1967.

Van Alstyne, Richard W. "Great Britain, the War for Independence, and the 'Gathering Storm' in Europe, 1775–1778," *Huntington Library Quarterly, XXVII* (August, 1964).

———. "Thomas Walpole's Letters to the Duke of Grafton on American Affairs, 1776–1778," *Huntington Library Quarterly,* XXX, November, 1966, pp. 17–33.

Van Doren, Carl. *Benjamin Franklin.* New York, 1938.

———. *Jane Mecom, the Favorite Sister of Benjamin Franklin.* New York, 1950.

Volwiler, Albert T. *George Croghan and the Westward Movement, 1741–1782.* Cleveland, 1926.

Wainwright, N. B. *George Croghan, Wilderness Diplomat.* Chapel Hill, 1959.

Watson, J. Steven. *The Reign of George III, 1760–1815.* London, 1960.

Whitehead, William A. *Contributions of the Early History of Perth Amboy and Adjoining Country.* New York, 1856.

Wickwire, Franklin B. *British Subministers and Colonial America, 1763–1783.* Princeton, 1966.

Wright, Louis B. *The Cultural Life of the American Colonies.* New York, 1957.

Zimmerman, John J. "Benjamin Franklin: A Study of Pennsylvania Politics and the Colonial Agency, 1755–1775." Unpublished dissertation. University of Michigan, 1956.

INDEX